ALTOGETHER
US

ALTOGETHER US AUTHORS AND REVIEWERS

FROM TOP LEFT TO BOTTOM RIGHT: Frank Anderson, Mona Barbera, Kim Bolling, Chris and Deena Burris, Jeanne Catanzaro, Sand C. Chang, Candice Christiansen, Marcella Cox, Deborah A. Dana, Daphne Fatter, Fatimah Finney, Daniel Foor, Toni Herbine-Blank, Carmen Jimenez-Pride, Mary Kruger, Kathy Mackechney, Mag Martienz, Susan McConnell, Suzan McVicker, Nancy L. Morgan, Gregg Paisley, Halie A. Parmalee, Mariel Pastor, Pete Patton, Leslie Petruk, Patricia Rich, Jenna Riemersma, Alessio Rizzo, Alexia Rothman, Joan R. Ryan, Gishela Satarino, Richard C. Schwartz, Valerie Simon, Tammy Sollenberger, Julia Sullivan, Martha Sweezy, Cece Sykes, Regina L. Wei

ALTOGETHER US

INTEGRATING THE IFS MODEL WITH KEY MODALITIES, COMMUNITIES, AND TRENDS

JENNA RIEMERSMA
LPC, GENERAL EDITOR

WITH DR. RICHARD SCHWARTZ
AND 30 EXPERT CONTRIBUTORS

PIVOTAL PRESS

Altogether Us:
Integrating the IFS Model with Key Modalities, Communities, and Trends

Copyright © 2023 by Jenna Riemersma

Pivotal Press
Marietta, Georgia
www.pivotalpresspublishing.com

Printed in the United States of America

First Edition, 2023

ISBN (Softcover): 978-1-7349584-2-3
ISBN (eBook): 978-1-7349584-3-0

All rights reserved. Except in the case of brief quotations embodied in critical articles and reviews, no portion of this book may be reproduced, stored in a retrieval system, or transmitted in any form or by any means—electronic, mechanical, photocopy, recording, scanning, or other—without the prior written permission from the author(s) and publisher. None of the material in this book may be reproduced for any commercial promotion, advertising or sale of a product or service.

While the authors have made every effort to provide accurate internet addresses at the time of publication, neither the publisher nor the authors assume any responsibility for errors or for changes that occur after publication. Further, the publisher does not have any control over, and does not assume any responsibility for, author or third-party websites or their content.

Cover design: Yvonne Parks, Pear Creative
Interior design and typeset: Katherine Lloyd, The DESK

To Dick,

In celebration of the 40th anniversary of IFS.

We are forever grateful.

CONTENTS

PREFACE xiii

SECTION ONE
ORIGINS AND ACCESS

1 **OVERVIEW, ORIGINS, AND FUTURE OF THE IFS MODEL** 3
Richard C. Schwartz, PhD and Halie A. Parmalee MSW, LICSW

2 **AN IFS SHORTHAND TOOL** 21
MOVE TOWARD
Jenna Riemersma, LPC

Reviewer: Richard C. Schwartz, PhD

SECTION TWO
MODEL INTEGRATION

3 **IFS AND POLYVAGAL THEORY** 51
HEALING THROUGH COMPASSIONATE CONNECTION
Alexia Rothman, PhD
Reviewers: Richard C. Schwartz, PhD and Deborah A. Dana, LCSW

4 **IFS AND EMDR** 81
TRANSFORMING TRAUMATIC MEMORIES AND PROVIDING RELATIONAL REPAIR WITH SELF
Daphne Fatter, PhD

5 **IFS AND PSYCHODRAMA** 111
TECHNIQUES FOR EXPANDING IFS EXTERNALIZATIONS
Valerie Simon, LCSW, TEP, CET III

6 **IFS AND SANDTRAY** 133
EXTERNALIZING PARTS FOR INSIGHT AND HEALING
Leslie Petruk, LCMHC-S, NCC, BCC

7 **IFS AND PLAY THERAPY** 161
EXTERNALIZING PARTS WITH CHILDREN AND ADOLESCENTS
Carmen Jimenez-Pride, LCSW, RPT-S

SECTION THREE
INTERSECTIONALITY

INTERSECTIONALITY INTRODUCTION 183
WORKING WITH INTERSECTING IDENTITIES
Regina Wei, MA, LMFTA and Sand Chang, PhD

8 **EMBODYING IFS WITH BLACK CLIENTS**............... 185
RECLAIMING A BIRTHRIGHT
Fatimah Finney, LMHC

9 **EMBODYING IFS WITH NATIVE AMERICAN CLIENTS**... 205
COMPOSITE INDIGENOUS VOICES TELL A STORY OF IFS RESONANCE
Julia Sullivan, MBA, Suzan McVicker, PhD, LPC, Gregg Paisley, MBA, and Pete Patton, LCSW

10 **EMBODYING IFS WITH ASIAN AND PACIFIC ISLANDER CLIENTS** 227
CULTURAL, RACIAL, AND INTERGENERATIONAL BURDENS AS WELL AS PROTECTIVE FACTORS
Regina L. Wei, MA, LMFTA

11 **EMBODYING IFS WITH LATINX CLIENTS** 249
CULTURALLY RESPONSIVE PRACTICES IN LATINX MENTAL HEALTH
Gishela Gaby Satarino, MA, LPC-S

12 **EMBODYING IFS WITH SEXUAL ORIENTATION** 269
TRAUMA HEALING AS A PATH TO THE INTEGRATED SELF
Frank Anderson, MD

13 **EMBODYING IFS WITH TRANS AND/OR NONBINARY COMMUNITIES**........................... 289
ALL GENDERS WELCOME
Sand C. Chang, PhD

14 **EMBODYING IFS WITH NEURODIVERGENT CLIENTS**... 315
A NEURO-INCLUSIVE APPROACH FOR THERAPISTS
Candice Christiansen, MEd, CMHC
and Meg Martinez-Dettamanti, MS, CMHC
Reviewers: Kim Bolling, PsyD and Alessio Rizzo, MSC

SECTION FOUR
EMERGING TRENDS

15 **IFS AND PSYCHEDELIC INTEGRATION** 361
ENHANCING SELF-TO-PART HEALING THROUGH THE POWER
OF SACRED PLANT MEDICINES
Nancy L. Morgan, MS, PhD

16 **IFS AND SOMATIC PRACTICES** 391
RECLAIMING OUR BIRTHRIGHT OF EMBODIMENT:
FIVE SOMATIC PRACTICES THAT BRING THE BODY FULLY
TO THE HEALING JOURNEY
Susan McConnell, MAPD, CHT

17 **IFS AND ADDICTION** 419
COMPASSION FOR THE ADDICTIVE PROCESS
Cece Sykes, LCSW and Mary Kruger, MS, LMFT

18 **IFS AND DISORDERED EATING** 449
SELF-LED HEALING FOR A MORE HARMONIOUS RELATIONSHIP
WITH FOOD AND BODY
Marcella Cox, LMFT, CEDS-S

Reviewers: Jeanne Catanzaro, PhD, Susan McConnell, MAPD, CHT, and Mariel Pastor, LMFT

19 **IFS AND GROUPS** 483
THE CREATING HEALING CIRCLES METHOD AND THE POWER OF
SCULPTING IN GROUPS
Chris Burris, MEd, LCMHCS, LMFT

Reviewer: Deena Burris, PhD

SECTION FIVE
RELATIONSHIPS

20 **IFS AND SEXUALITY** 497
SELF-LED SEXUALITY FOR HEALING, PLEASURE, AND
EMPOWERMENT
Patricia Rich, LCSW, CST-S

21 **IFS AND COUPLES** 523
RELEASING SELF-TO-SELF CONNECTION
Mona Barbera, PhD, with contributions by Toni Herbine-Blank, MSN, RN and Martha Sweezy, PhD

22 **IFS AND PARENTING**.................................545
   BECOMING AN IN-SIGHTFUL PARENT
   Leslie Petruk, LCMHC-S, NCC, BCC

23 **IFS AND ADOPTEES** 571
   HEALING PARTS BURDENED BY RELINQUISHMENT TRAUMA
   Kathy Mackechney, LCSW

24 **IFS AND ANCESTRAL LINEAGE HEALING** 595
   RESTORING BELONGING AND RECONNECTION WITH
   ANCESTRAL WISDOM AND COLLECTIVE SELF-ENERGY
   Daphne Fatter, PhD

   Reviewer: Daniel Foor, PhD

25 **IFS AND THE ENNEAGRAM** 625
   CONNECTING TO PARTS USING THE ENNEAGRAM MAP
   Joan R. Ryan, JD and Tammy Sollenberger, MA, LCMHC

ENDNOTES 647

PREFACE

I don't know about you, but I haven't been many places where *all* parts of me were welcome. Most of my life, only the *shiny* parts were invited. Parts that achieved the right things, believed the right things, and looked the right way. Parts that always made the right choices.

I'm not sure where the rest of me was supposed to go, but it was getting pretty crowded in here, trying to keep all the *unshiny* parts on lockdown.

Imagine my surprise when Internal Family Systems (IFS), developed by Dr. Richard Schwartz, handed me the keys to the locks and invited me to become friends with my shiny and unshiny parts alike. The promise of IFS resonated deeply with me:

Who you are is good, and all parts of you are welcome.

What a relief! Right away, exciting new vistas for change and flourishing opened, both personally and professionally.

Along with many others, I owe a huge debt of gratitude to Dr. Schwartz for helping people heal in a way that is empowering, effective, and non-pathologizing.

Altogether Us emerged from my work teaching therapists the integration of IFS with other clinical modalities. But it truly sprang to life when I realized that integration arrives most helpfully in the voices of a collective and began inviting other IFS experts to contribute. Here, you'll meet a group of passionate, highly skilled psychotherapists who are applying the transformative insights of the IFS model with a wide range of clients, communities, and modalities.

- Dr. Schwartz opens the conversation with a history, overview, and future vision of his remarkable model.
- In each of the following chapters, authors explore what the IFS model brings to diverse applications.
- Every chapter concludes with practical takeaways, application-focused appendices, and a "Going Deeper" section to facilitate further exploration.

Intended for both professionals and students, *Altogether Us* aims to expand access to this exciting paradigm in psychotherapy while affirming the vision of Dr. Schwartz to welcome all parts and celebrate diverse expressions of Self-leadership in the world.

As a further expression of gratitude, every book purchased supports the Foundation for Self-Leadership's IFS Leadership Fellows Program (providing IFS training and leadership development to individuals from traditionally marginalized communities).

I'm deeply honored to have had the opportunity to work with and learn from the practitioners who have so generously and impressively contributed. You as a reader are an integral part of this initiative as well, and we thank you.

Warmly,

Jenna Riemersma, LPC (she/her), General Editor
IFS Approved Clinical Consultant, Level 3 Certified IFS Therapist
EMDR, CSAT/CMAT-Supervisor
Writing from the unceded lands of the Cherokee people
July 2023

SECTION ONE
ORIGINS AND ACCESS

OVERVIEW, ORIGINS, AND FUTURE OF THE IFS MODEL

Richard C. Schwartz, PhD
and Halie A. Parmalee MSW, LICSW

At the start of his career 40 years ago, Richard Schwartz had an overriding vision for his professional life. He wanted to affect human self-destruction and suffering on a large scale. He studied, experimented, and found that to be effective he needed to think differently. As we describe below, his clients taught him how to do that and the result is Internal Family Systems (IFS) therapy.

The chapters in this book are a sampling of the future of the Internal Family Systems (IFS) therapy model, which, as we review in this introduction, has garnered interest around the world and is being applied in mental health with a wide variety of populations and a full range of treatment modalities (individual, couple, group, family, and adult and child). In addition to therapists, people from all walks of life, including mental health researchers, lawyers, medical doctors, and educators are leading the way in applying the IFS way of thinking creatively.

We begin this chapter with an overview of IFS treatment, go on to a brief history of the development of IFS, and end with information about current directions.

An Overview of the IFS Model

Internal Family Systems therapy views the mind as a system with natural subdivisions, or sub-personalities, which IFS calls *parts*. IFS posits that these parts all have various vulnerabilities and gifts, exist from birth, and appear along a developmental timeline. Additionally, their intentions are fundamentally positive regardless of their behavior. Because parts live in the psyche, they can travel through time and shift shape at will. Because they live in the body (though they can move outside the body) they can affect the body. And, as you will certainly find if you do some inner exploration, they have feelings, beliefs, opinions, and preferences.

The inner world and its community of parts is dynamic. When one part gets hurt by the implicit or explicit message that they are defective, unacceptable, unworthy, unlovable, or too much or too little, other parts (often barely older) step in to do the protective job of managing that problem. These proactive manager parts keep us organized and functional, generally with inhibition—*do be this, don't be that; do this, don't do that.* When they are afraid, they can become harsh, turning to criticism and shaming. Although their intentions are good, their inhibitory efforts inspire a second group of protectors who are reactive and rebellious. In IFS we call these parts *firefighters* because of their short-term goal of putting out emotional fires *right now*. Like their namesake, reactive protectors can't afford to ponder long-term consequences. To put out the (emotional) fire, they grab the most effective tool at hand for self-soothing or distracting. Think eating disorders and addictive processes with substances, porn, gambling, rage, and so forth (Schwartz & Sweezy, 2020; Sweezy, 2023).

Our most consequential injuries often occur in childhood when we are relatively powerless and our coping options are limited. Proactive young manager parts "solve" the problem of danger by banishing emotional pain and anger to the best of their ability and pushing forward. Reactive firefighter parts then "solve" the problem of too much inhibition, shamefulness, or fear by distracting and self-soothing in various ways that are highly effective in the short run but cause more problems and more managerial inhibition in the long run. Lacking access to internal leadership (the Self), polarized protectors get stuck in their conflicts (*try harder* vs. *give up, comply* vs. *rebel,* and so on). Managers and firefighters are trying to solve the same inner problem in two different ways.

The IFS therapist doesn't take a side in these disagreements. Rather, we appreciate the good intentions of both sides and offer to help with the underlying problem of exiled vulnerability by introducing protectors to an internal resource that can heal old wounds. As Dick discovered, there is an ever-present internal leader that cannot be damaged and is not a part, which we call the Self. We think of the Self as a complementary form of consciousness that is characterized by various centered, relational states. Clients refer to it as their *real* self, which we capitalize to differentiate our meaning from more mundane uses of the word. For ease of remembering and teaching about the Self, Dick chose to focus on eight of its qualities that begin with the letter c: curious, calm, confident, courageous, connected, creative, clear, and compassionate.

The overarching aim of IFS therapy is to help the inner system of parts recognize and rely on the Self's leadership so that exiled parts can release identity burdens and protectors can let go of their jobs. To accomplish this, we negotiate with protective parts to make room for the client's Self in consciousness, after which the client takes the lead to meet, witness, validate, and help vulnerable parts who have been injured and kept out of mind. If an exile is stuck in a traumatic situation in the past, the Self can go into that scene and help it get out.

When the exile is ready, it releases its burdens and leaves the past. The client's Self then checks in with protectors to be sure they've been watching and helps them leave their jobs when they are ready. The more unburdened an internal system, the more room it has for Self-leadership.

The process of unburdening is thus a beneficial cycle. In theory, it is also straightforward and relatively simple. In practice, however, protective parts have many reasons to be wary of outside helpers. They often need to establish a reliable, consistent relationship with the client's Self and the therapist's Self before they feel willing to try something new. While this may sound (and can be!) daunting, it turns out that regardless of the severity or chronicity of trauma in a client's history, they have an undamaged, loving essence within that knows how to heal injured parts and take effective leadership in the inner and outer worlds.

IFS Origins: The Richard Schwartz Story

When I was in college between 1967 and 1971, my father (who was the Head of Medicine at Rush Presbyterian St. Luke's Medical Center in Chicago) got me a summer job as an aide on the Adolescent Psychiatric Unit. I knew little about psychotherapy when I began, but by the second summer, I had opinions about what wasn't working. Patients would improve and go home only to return to the hospital the next summer in terrible distress. As I sat in the day room on weekends during family visits, I watched as parents shamed and demeaned their teenagers and accused them of being a disgrace to their families. But treatment, which was psychoanalytic, did not address or intervene in family dynamics. Patients described their therapists listening, and occasionally ascribing some meaning to their feelings or behaviors, but if the child expressed discomfort or chose not to speak, the whole session might go by in silence. One summer, I grew particularly fond of a delightful 16-year-old girl who was addicted to heroin and confided in me that her father had abused her sexually. During one parental visit her father sat by silently as her mother berated her for harming them and being selfish. She killed herself the next day. When I heard the news, I decided to become a psychotherapist and search for a better way.

As a result, I entered a master's program in 1973. It was not psychoanalytic and covered several therapeutic approaches. I was particularly drawn to Carl Rogers and Fritz Perls. In contrast to the detached stance of analytic therapists, Rogers had a caring, empathic style that made intuitive sense to me. I liked his humanistic, optimistic view that people get hurt throughout their life but are essentially capable and healthy (Rogers, 1954). Perls, on the other hand, was an outrageous, courageous rebel. He struck me as just the right medicine for the mental health establishment. According to Perls, emotions didn't need to be interpreted but expressed and experienced. His "open-chair" technique, in which the client would talk openly to "top dog" and "under dog" parts who sat opposite in an empty chair, was my first exposure to the idea that the mind is made up of different parts and inner conversations (Perls, Hefferline, & Goodman, 1951). I was excited by their styles and ideas, but as I remembered those excruciating experiences in the day room of the inpatient unit, I still felt something was missing.

I was fortunate that the environmental movement, which emphasized interconnections and eco-systemic thinking, was blossoming around this time. Changes in one aspect of a system, it said, would have unforeseen, unintended, often powerful consequences in other aspects of the system. Gregory Bateson's ideas fascinated me, particularly his emphasis on understanding how a person's context affects their behavior and the problems that arise when we judge people without considering their contexts (Bateson, 1979). Non-systemic thinking struck me as a problem for all individually focused therapy models such as analysis, humanism, and Gestalt. None of them gave enough consideration to the influence of family and other social contexts. So, I found Earl Goodman and began to study family therapy, a new discipline at the time, and its systems. My fellow students and I spent many hours watching each from behind a one-way mirror as we saw families under Earl's tutelage. Several seminal family therapy texts that were soon to be published would provide clarity and direction, but lacking these, we based our interventions on vague concepts like homeostasis and scapegoating. The idea was that parents who couldn't manage their own conflicts were making one of their children into the "identified patient" as a distraction. We thought helping the parents focus on their troubled marriage would free the child from being symptomatic.

After a few successes, I believed we had the answer. We were crusaders, I thought, for a revolution in understanding and treating human problems. I pointed families toward the errors of their ways and challenged psychodynamic therapists at conferences. In short, I was obnoxious. Two newly published books (*Families and Family Therapy* by Salvador Minuchin in 1974, and *Change: Principles of Problem Formation and Problem Resolution* by Paul Watzlawick, John H. Weakland & Richard Fisch, also in 1974) answered some plaguing questions and fortified my inflated convictions. Minuchin, for example, claimed to have great success with anorexia, a condition that was very difficult to treat.

Like other family therapists of the time, I saw intrapsychic processes (what was happening inside the client) as irrelevant. Our goal was to produce internal shifts by reorganizing external contexts. Like Minuchin (1974), I believed families needed clear boundaries, including rules about who interacted with whom and how, so that family members were not too close or too distant from each other. Parents needed to be in charge and allied with each other. Every family needed clear leadership to protect children from being parentified (which meant worrying about and trying to protect their parents), inducted into siding with one parent against another, or responsible to save or lead the family, including other siblings. In addition, as I saw it, harmful repetitive patterns and boundary problems developed when family members had extreme negative beliefs about each other. If the therapist could just reframe, as we said, a child's harmful or mysterious behavior and assert that the child intended to protect the family system, other family members would respond more positively to the child.

To assess the family's problem, we tracked their interactions and asked questions aimed at revealing the sequences and patterns of vicious cycles. The symptomatic child was usually inappropriately allied with one parent or had been recruited to protect some other family member, but in some families the opposite was true. Rather than being enmeshed, family members could be cut-off and distant. Similarly, some parents were overbearing while others abdicated their responsibilities entirely. As we saw these behaviors, we were liberal about pointing them out, dispensing our views (which we called *reframes*) regarding the meaning and purpose of the child's behavior, and urging the family to change by following our instructions.

In short, rather than looking for pathology within the psyche, we found it within the family. We knew what the family needed; we were the experts. In this way we were pathology detectives no less than the analytic therapists we disdained who interpreted client behaviors and doled out diagnoses. If a family didn't follow through as we prescribed and didn't change, we called them *resistant* and said the problem was fear. While this diagnose-and-impose attitude worked reasonably well for some families, others were antagonized. Then we tried to manipulate them with what we called *paradoxical injunctions*, which meant telling them to keep doing what they were doing in hopes that they would rebel. In short, we treated families like intimidating adversaries who were so strongly attached to their symptoms that we needed to either impose change on them or jolt them into changing.

I carried this top-down mindset into my first job at the Chicago hospital where I had been an aide years before. I insulted families by insinuating that their suffering was manipulative and alienated them with prescriptions for change. Seeing the poor result, I decided, in 1976, to go back to school and keep learning. This time I studied with Doug Sprenkle, a well-known family therapy teacher and researcher at Purdue University's family therapy doctoral program. Here my biased views about intrapsychic explorations (I thought they were linear rather than systemic) were challenged by the teachings of Murray Bowen, who focused on differentiation (Bowen, 1974) and Virginia Satir, who focused on how people communicated their feelings.

For my doctoral dissertation I decided to test Satir's hypothesis that the individual self-esteem of partners would improve if a couple's ability to communicate improved (Satir, 1964). I found that better communication skills did lead to improved self-esteem, but the correlation did not last at follow-up. Although

I can now say that IFS stands on Satir's shoulders more than any other family therapy pioneer, I was disappointed at the time and moved away from Satir's ideas in favor of the hard-edged, therapist-as-expert mindsets of Minuchin and Haley.

PhD in hand, I began working at the Institute for Juvenile Research (IJR) (basically a state-supported think tank) in Chicago in 1980 as a family therapy trainer and researcher. Much of the early sociological research on juvenile delinquency had emerged from IJR. I taught in a small family therapy training program for troubled kids and families from Chicago's notorious west side, and it was an ideal setting for me to consolidate my ideas. Since our teaching and clinical loads were light, we were able to log many hours watching students and each other work with disadvantaged families from behind one-way mirrors.

During my first year I got interested in how family therapy could benefit individuals with difficult-to-treat medical syndromes, no doubt influenced by my need to convince my skeptical physician father. I was looking for a difficult-to-treat syndrome, and I had a young client who routinely ate huge amounts of food and then vomited it all up minutes later. Her bulimia nervosa, a new diagnosis at the time, fit the bill. In 1983, I conducted a study using a structural/strategic model with the families of bulimic clients with Mary Jo Barrett (Schwartz, Barrett, & Saba, 1985). As recommended by Minuchin, we reorganized the families. This certainly helped the parents, but our bulimic patients kept on bingeing and purging. This was unwelcome news. I was a rising star in the family therapy world and had just co-authored the most widely used family therapy text (Nichols & Schwartz, 1984). I really wanted the study to have positive results. At the same time, I had to admit that family sessions weren't touching something important inside our clients. Out of frustration and curiosity, I finally broke the family therapy taboo about internal inquiry and asked my young clients to describe what happened inside when they were symptomatic. The answers from a client named Quinn (a pseudonym, like all names in this chapter) opened my eyes and planted the seed for IFS.

Quinn, a 23-year-old with a habit of bingeing and vomiting, talked about a war between different parts with distinct voices. She had no control over what they said or did. This grabbed my attention, but I was cautious about its implications. I believed we all had a variety of thoughts and feelings in one mind. To have many inner personalities was to be mentally ill, fractured, damaged, perhaps psychotic. Maybe Quinn was just sicker than I had realized. At the same time, I was identifying with her. I had parts too, and some were just as extreme as hers. This realization scared me. If I were to assert that psychic multiplicity was normal, I could ruin my career.

Quinn described her inner voices getting into loud, contentious arguments before she went on a binge-and-vomit spree. When one voice was critical of everything about her, another blamed either her parents or the bulimia for her problems, a third felt sad and hopeless, and, finally, a fourth took over to binge on comfort foods. Fascinated, I asked other bulimic clients the same questions and heard similar stories. They described feelings, thoughts, and behaviors shifting so abruptly they felt possessed. The evidence for inner multiplicity as the norm became overwhelming. Throughout our days, my clients and I were all moving with fluidity and not much awareness from one personality to the next with different parts taking the leading at different times. Whatever we believed about being a unitary self, our community of parts was conducting business-as-usual inside.

This early cohort of eating disordered clients were the source of the language IFS still uses today: *this part of me is six years old; this part yells at me a lot and calls me names* and so on. We discovered that talking about their parts gave my clients a sense of distance and perspective that allowed for more curiosity and less fear. They were quickly relieved to realize that extreme parts were, after all, a part but not all of who they were. We listened carefully and we learned about the ways of the inner world. What did parts want? How did they relate to each other? Which ones did the clients like and listen to, and which did they hate, fear, or ignore? Their descriptions reminded me of families. Parts were idiosyncratic and distinct. Moreover, they formed alliances and polarized just like families. As the vulnerable, traumatized ones got exiled from consciousness, others managed the client's life, protected from secrets, distracted from stressors, or soothed in moments of pain. They believed the client was young and unlovable, or perhaps, older but incompetent, and in any case, in need of protection.

As I was learning, the past was not irrelevant to the present after all. Although it was still some years before I read Bessel van der Kolk, Judith Herman, and others on the impact of trauma, I was beginning to see that not only was a traumatic past relevant; it was key to healing. But I still had many mistakes to make. The first was assuming that parts were metaphors. If a part showed up like a critical parent, I assumed it was an internalization of the parent. I assumed bingeing parts were really out-of-control impulses. And I thought negative parts were burdensome negative beliefs. I had no idea that healing begins when we view parts as sacred inner beings who are doing their best and deserve our love and affection. As a result, I tried to banish, coerce, or control them.

My next teacher was a client I will call Beth who, despite my best efforts at haranguing the cutting part, would not stop cutting herself. I only gave up on trying to control it and got curious when it really upped the ante and I felt thoroughly defeated. Then the cutting part explained that it didn't want to hurt her or defeat me, but it had a job to do. When Beth was being abused as a child, this part took her out of her body and distracted her from a rageful part. Since it still needed to control the rageful part it continued to cut her. I noticed that the part seemed to be living in the past, back during the time of the abuse, so I asked what it would do if it no longer had to protect her. It said it would prefer to do the opposite of what it was doing and help Beth feel emotions more keenly. To say the least, I was surprised.

I now approached my clients' anorexic, rageful, and suicidal parts with interest and compassion, and I got the same amazing result. Seemingly destructive parts intended to help. They didn't like their extreme roles. If this was true then mental health professionals could stop trying to banish or control impulsive, compulsive parts and instead help them with their fears. As inner families were proving to be much like outer families, I decided to try applying everything I knew from family therapy to psychic parts. My clients and I made some headway with these tactics, but mostly we ran into a lot of hot disputes between parts who thought they were protecting a child and wouldn't give an inch. No single part seemed capable of leading the system of parts and earning everyone's trust. They all seemed to be children who needed relief from too much responsibility.

My third teacher, "Cora," was a young woman plagued by the voice of a pessimist and the voice of a harsh critic. Together they discouraged, shamed, and depressed her whole system. As I listened to Cora's parts arguing over various risks and berating each other, I decided to try something new. I guided Cora to ask her striving critic to step back. Luckily for learning purposes, the part was in a cooperative mood and Cora's attitude shifted immediately. When I asked how she felt toward the pessimist now, she said, in a calm, concerned tone, that she was grateful and ready to help. Her face and posture reflected this new attitude, which seemed compassionate, and from that point on Cora was able to build a connection with her pessimist.

I tried the same "step back" request, which I came to call unblending, with several other clients whose protective parts were equally polarized. I found that we might have to ask two or three voices to step back before the client could shift into being curious and compassionate, but we got there if we were patient. This simple technique has proved crucial to healing. By asking politely, clients could get extreme voices to relax and, if they all relaxed, their competent, compassionate core was immediately available. Wow. I had been looking for an inner leader, and Self was it.

This was an earthquake for me. Experience kept challenging all of my prior assumptions, including the idea that my clients could only develop the emotional resources they needed by investing great effort into internalizing my nurturing presence. Most of my clients had endured deprived, nightmarish childhoods, but they could still access powerful wisdom when their parts stepped back. They could separate from extreme beliefs and feelings and get to a grounded perspective. After watching scores of clients spontaneously embody those eight C qualities of the Self as soon as their parts unblended, I was finally converted to the idea that we are much more than we seem at times, that the Self does not develop over time, that it can't be damaged, and that it is always right there, even if we're only aware of our parts.

When my clients were, what we now call, *in Self*, they didn't just witness their parts passively as they might do when meditating. Instead, they interacted lovingly, creatively, and with compassion, which in turn, transformed their self-image and behavior. The Self's emergent compassion, lucidity, and wisdom gave their parts just what they needed. Witnessing this over and over, I finally stopped giving instructions and instead asked Self open questions like, "What do you want to say to the part now?" Clients would say the perfect words, or they would go to the part and hold it. I knew I couldn't do any better. As a result, my main job became helping clients access and remain in their Self. If they were in Self, I could move out of the way and watch them parent and harmonize their inner families. When this went well, clients felt better by the end of sessions. But there was a big, bad catch. They would often return the next week having had horrible experiences, like spiking high fevers, getting massive migraine headaches, getting into a car accident, and so forth, shortly after leaving my office.

This backlash scared me to the point where I thought about quitting, but Beth's cutting part had said it didn't want to hurt her. I decided I must be scaring my clients' protectors. Sure enough, when I asked each client to focus on the bad experience and listen, they heard furious inner voices lashing out at each other. But as we listened patiently, they calmed down and explained that we had disrupted an intricate defense system by contacting vulnerable parts without their permission. I realized that we were entering a complex ecology and failing to think systemically had been a major blunder. An internal family, like an external one, would of course need us to connect with, reassure, and get permission from skeptical protectors before focusing on vulnerability. I resolved to be humble and respectful and learn the rules of the inner system. With these incremental discoveries, the IFS model slowly came together. Forty years, and many thousands of sessions later, I am glad that roller coaster ride is behind me. Thrilling as it was to make these discoveries, I was often taking risks with my clients and working in the dark.

The Future of IFS

When I realized that I had stumbled on to a fundamentally different, more optimistic view of human nature than the prevailing one, I glimpsed a bigger vision. This way of understanding the mind had the potential to improve all aspects of human relating. With a burden of inadequacy to overcome and much to gain personallly, I decided to devote my life to that vision. It's taken 40 years for that commitment to pay off. IFS is now so popular among therapists that the IFS Institute (IFSI) wait list for trainings is overflowing (a situation IFSI is working hard to remedy). Meanwhile, researchers and pioneers in medicine, science, law, philosophy, and education are embracing IFS, and a wide variety of academic departments in the United States and elsewhere are teaching it. I date this rise in popularity to 2015 when the National Registry for Evidence-based Programs and Practices (NREPP)[1] designated IFS an evidence-based treatment based on the positive outcome of the proof-of-concept study that Nancy Sowell spearheaded and conducted with Nancy Shadick at Brigham and Women's Hospital in Boston (2013).[2] As a result of the NREPP designation, agencies and hospitals began to let therapists use IFS. Since that time other published pilot studies on, respectively, IFS with PTSD (Haddock, et al, 2021) and IFS with depression (2016) have also had positive outcomes. Currently, Zev Schuman-Olivier, Hanna Soumerai, Mary Catherine Ward, Larry Rosenberg, Nancy Sowell, Martha Sweezy, me, and a number of IFS trained clinicians are conducting a larger study using an IFS-based group therapy format to treat PTSD at the Cambridge Health Alliance in Cambridge, Massachusetts.

Many of the clinicians and researchers who are exploring the mental health possibilities of MDMA, psilocybin, and Ketamine are also using IFS as a roadmap. I recently co-led a training on IFS and Ketamine with Phil Wolfson, MD. Ketamine seems to give users quick access to their Self, presumably by calming managers, which in turn speeds the individual's access to exiles who have been hard to reach. Other medicines like MDMA and psilocybin have similar effects, though possibly for different reasons. Several research projects are in the works that will combine these medicines with IFS.

In a (now prolonged) burst of creativity and experimentation, IFS therapists are applying IFS to a variety of presenting problems like obsessive compulsive disorder (OCD), attention deficit disorder (ADD), and major mental illness, as well as to topics related to sexuality, gender, and race. You can listen to interviews that focus on these and other subjects on two IFS-based podcasts, IFS Talks and The One Inside. Book publishing has also flourished. As we write this chapter, over 60 books have been published on various aspects of IFS. Therapists are using IFS in a variety of treatment modalities, including child (Johnson and Schwartz, 2000; Krause, 2013; Mones, 2014; Spiegel, 2017) couple (Herbine-Blank and Sweezy, 2020; Schwartz, 2008); family (Schwartz and Sweezy, 2020), and group therapy (Burris, 2022). Therapists are also combining IFS with various other therapeutic approaches like somatics (McConnell, 2020) and psychopharmacology (Anderson, 2013); and they're applying IFS to a wide variety of problems, including chronic illness (Sowell, 2013; and a work in progress co-authored by Sowell, Sweezy & Schwartz provisionally entitled: *Internal Family Systems Therapy and Physical Illness: Healing Health Problems Related to Stress, Shame, and Trauma* (Anderson, 2021; Anderson, Sweezy & Schwartz, 2019, Anderson and Sweezy, 2017); shame and guilt (Sweezy, 2023); body image, eating issues, and anti-fat bias (Catanzaro, 2023; Catanzaro, 2017; Catanzaro, Doyne, and Thompson, 2018); spirituality (Riemersma, 2020); and addictive processes (Sykes, Sweezy, and Schwartz, 2023; Sykes, 2016).[3] Regarding addictions, I'm a senior fellow at The Meadows treatment center where, thanks to Cece Sykes, therapists have been using IFS for some time.

Culturally, IFS is becoming a meme in the United States. *No Bad Parts* (2021), my most recent book, sold over 100,000 copies in its first year, and is being used worldwide. I've been interviewed on dozens of podcasts, including some hosted by Tim Ferris, Dr. Becky, and Rangan Chatterjee. Dr. Becky, a big fan of IFS, is spreading the word to parents. Authors Lissa Rankin and Gabby Bernstein are bringing IFS to wholistic medicine and spirituality, respectively. I am also excited to report that social activist leaders Ethan Hughes and Karl Steyaert are using IFS to teach front line activists how to be Self-led during protests. Legal mediation expert, David Hoffman, is working to bring IFS to conflict mediation. Parenthetically, I believe IFS can help leaders in all kinds of institutions to become more Self-led. Toward that goal, we recently ran a pilot Level 1 IFS training for executive coaches who work with the CEOs of companies and with political leaders. Based on that experience, IFSI is developing a curriculum to train coaches in IFS.

I am also very pleased to report that we are now a much more diverse community. When I first began teaching IFS, I was working to build interest, and my motto was, of some necessity, *Build it, and they will come*. I did not actively reach out to the global majority or LGBTQIA+ communities. As a result, the IFS interest sphere was majority White, cisgender, and, to some extent, heterosexual until about 10 years ago. That's when my brother Jon, who was our CEO at the time, formed a collaboration with Deran Young, the founder of Black Therapists Rock, to run a series of Level 1 and Level 2 trainings through IFSI. Due to that project, along with a fellowship program sponsored by the non-profit organization the Foundation for Self Leadership, we now have many people of the global majority in the pipeline to become trainers, and Tamala Floyd was accepted this year as our first Black lead trainer. We have also begun to run specialized Level 1 trainings for people with similar interests or identities. For example, this year we will conduct two trainings exclusively for global majority students and one for LGBTQIA+ students, as well as one for those interested in psychedelics.

IFS has also become more diverse globally. During the pandemic, all IFS trainings went online, which had some important benefits. Students loved it, and we began to reach areas of the world that would have been difficult, if not impossible, to reach with in-person trainings. I just completed our first Level 1 training with 33 therapists from Egypt, Lebanon, and Jordan. The week before, I did a two-day workshop for 70 therapists from Russia and Ukraine. We now have on-going trainings throughout Europe and Asia, and we hope to run trainings in Africa and Latin America in the near future. In 2021, the IFS Institute hired a new CEO, Katie Nelson, with a mandate to handle a much-needed expansion of services. She began by expanding and diversifying our administrative staff, which now numbers over 20 and counting. As well as running over 80 training programs per year worldwide, IFSI staff oversee the online circle and continuity programs as well as various workshops and summits.

In this limited space, we can't name the contributions of all the key players or all the exciting new programs, but much of that information is available on the IFSI website (www.ifs-institute.com). As I think about all of this, I feel a combination of pride and overwhelm. Some days I'm reminded of the saying, *When the gods want to punish you, they answer your prayers.* I'll be 73 next month, and I'm working as much as ever. Most of the time I feel blessed to be introducing this potent path to healing to so many levels of our collective system. In truth, IFS is no longer just a model of psychotherapy. For many of us, it is an empowering, harmonizing life practice that helps us shift how we relate to ourselves and each other in much needed ways. In the past, I had to beg therapists to listen to my ideas or come to a training. Clearly, we have come a long way from there. But, to quote Robert Frost (and take the liberty of revising his pronoun to the plural), "the woods are lovely dark and deep, but we have promises to keep and miles to go before we sleep."

KEY TAKEAWAYS

- Dr. Richard Schwartz developed Internal Family Systems therapy because his family therapy training was not effective in treating eating disorders.
- IFS is an optimistic, non-pathologizing approach to mental illness, painful inner conflict, and the aftermath of trauma.
- Psychic multiplicity is normal. All people have psychic parts and a Self.
- Both the Self and parts are fundamentally positive in nature, and the Self is not damaged by experience. Parts get burdened by frightening, shaming experiences and can be stuck at the age when the trauma occurred. Their burdens keep them from understanding their true value.
- Burdens are the negative identity beliefs and extreme, stuck feeling states of injured parts. Protective jobs, which can be lifesaving in any emergency, become burdensome in other circumstances later on. All protective behaviors, however, involve a positive intention.
- The goal of IFS is to restore Self to leadership in the inner system, and release parts from burdensome beliefs and jobs. Healing occurs when the Self is in relationship with parts.
- Although IFS is primarily an approach to therapy, practitioners in many fields, including medicine, law, political activism, and spirituality, are putting the IFS concepts to good use.

AUTHOR BIOS

Richard Schwartz, PhD (he/him) is the creator of Internal Family Systems, a highly effective, evidence-based therapeutic model that de-pathologizes the multi-part personality. His IFS Institute offers training for professionals and the general public. He is currently on the faculty of Harvard Medical School, and has published five books, including *No Bad Parts: Healing Trauma and Restoring Wholeness with the Internal Family Systems Model*. Dick lives with his wife, Jeanne, near Chicago, close to his three daughters and his growing number of grandchildren.

Halie Parmalee, MSW, LICSW (she/her) is an independently licensed, IFS-informed clinical social worker and psychotherapist in private practice specializing in the treatment of anxiety, depression and trauma-related disorders. She provides trauma-informed psychotherapy to children, adolescents and adults in the Boston area and is trained in several trauma-focused modalities including Eye Movement Desensitization and Reprocessing, Trauma-Informed Stabilization Treatment, Trauma-Focused Cognitive Behavioral Therapy, and Child and Family Traumatic Stress Intervention. She has experience working with diverse populations in both inpatient and outpatient clinical settings, most recently working with individuals suffering with co-occurring substance use disorders and serious mental health diagnoses prior to entering private practice. She utilizes a compassionate, strengths-based, integrative approach to psychotherapy rooted in the IFS paradigm. She received a master's in social work from Boston College and is licensed in both Massachusetts and New York.

REFERENCES

Anderson, F. G. (2013). "Who's taking what?" Connecting neuroscience, psychopharmacology and Internal Family Systems for trauma. In M. Sweezy & E. L. Ziskind (Eds.), *Internal family systems therapy: New dimensions* (pp. 107-126). Routledge.

Anderson, F. G. (2021). *Transcending trauma: Healing complex PTSD with Internal Family Systems therapy*. PESI Publishing.

Anderson, F. G., Sweezy, M., & Schwartz, R. C. (2017). *Internal Family Systems skills training manual: Trauma-informed treatment for anxiety, depression, PTSD and substance abuse*. PESI Publishing.

Anderson, F. G., & Sweezy M. (2017). What IFS offers to the treatment of trauma. In M. Sweezy & E. L. Ziskind (Eds.), *Innovations and elaborations in Internal Family Systems therapy* (pp. 133-147). Routledge.

Burris, C. (2022). *Creating healing circles: Using the Internal Family Systems model in facilitating groups.* B.C. Allen Publishing and Tonic Books.

Catanzaro, J. (2023). (Forthcoming with the provisional title: *Self-led eating and well-being: An IFS based approach to healing your relationships with food and your body*). PESI Publishing.

Catanzaro, J., Doyne, E., & Thompson, K. (2018). IFS (Internal Family Systems) and eating disorders: the healing power of self-energy. In A. Seubert, & P. Virdi (Eds.), *Trauma-informed approaches to eating disorders* (pp. 209-220). Springer Publishing Company.

Cykes, C., & Sweezy, M. (2023). *Internal Family Systems therapy for addictions: Trauma-informed, compassion-based interventions for substance use, eating, gambling and more.* PESI Publishing.

Herbine-Blank T., & Sweezy, M. (2021). *Internal Family Systems couple therapy skills manual: Healing relationships with intimacy from the inside out.* PESI Publishing.

Johnson, L. C., & Schwartz, R. C. (2000). Internal Family Systems: Working with children and families. In C. E. Bailey (Ed.), *Children in therapy: Using the family as a resource* (pp. 73-111). W. W. Norton & Co.

Krause, P. (2013). IFS with children and adolescents. In M. Sweezy & E. L. Ziskind (Eds.), *Internal Family Systems therapy: New dimensions* (pp. 35-54). Routledge.

McConnell, S. (2020). *Somatic Internal Family Systems therapy: Awareness, breath, resonance, movement, and touch in practice.* North Atlantic Books.

Mones, A. G. (2014). *Transforming troubled children, teens, and their families: An Internal Family Systems model for healing.* Routledge.

Riemersma, J. (2020). *Altogether you: Experiencing personal and spiritual transformation with Internal Family Systems therapy.* Pivotal Press.

Spiegel, L. (2017). *Internal Family Systems therapy with children.* Routledge.

Schwartz, R. C. (2008). *You are the one you've been waiting for: Bringing courageous love to intimate relationships.* Trailheads Publications, The Center for Self Leadership.

Schwartz, R. C., & Sweezy, M. (2020). *Internal Family Systems therapy* (2nd ed.). Guilford Press.

Schwartz, R. C. (2021). *No bad parts.* Sounds True.

Shadick, N. A., Sowell, N. F., Frits, M. L., Hoffman, S. M., Hartz, S. A., Booth, F. D., Sweezy, M., Rogers, P. R., Dubin, R. L., Atkinson, J. C., Friedman, A. L., Augusto, F., Iannaccone, C. K., Fossel, A. H., Quinn, G., Cui, J., Losina, E., & Schwartz, R. C. (2013). A randomized controlled trial of an Internal Family Systems-based psychotherapeutic intervention on outcomes in rheumatoid arthritis: A proof-of-concept study. *The Journal of Rheumatology*, 40(11), 1831-1841. doi:10.3899/jrheum.121465

Sowell, N. (2013). The Internal Family System and adult health: Changing the course of chronic illness. In M. Sweezy & E. L. Ziskind (Eds.), *Internal Family Systems therapy: New dimensions* (pp. 127-142). Routledge.

Sweezy, M. (2023). Forthcoming with the provisional title: *Shame and guilt in the plural mind*. Guilford Press.

Sykes, C., Sweezy, M., & Schwartz, R. C. (2023). *Treating addictive processes with Internal Family Systems therapy: A compassionate and effective approach for helping people who soothe or distract with substances, food, gambling, pornography, and more*. PESI Publishing.

Sykes C. (2016). An IFS lens on addiction: Compassion for extreme parts. In M. Sweezy & E. L. Ziskind (Eds.), *Innovations and elaborations in Internal Family Systems therapy* (pp. 29-48). Routledge.

GOING DEEPER

1) Websites:
   a. IFS Institute: www.IFS-Institute.com
   b. Foundation for Self Leadership: www.foundationifs.org
2) Books:
   a. Schwartz, R. C., & Sweezy, M. (2020). *Internal Family Systems therapy* (2nd ed.). Guilford Press.
   b. Anderson, F. G., Sweezy, M., & Schwartz, R. C. (2017). *Internal Family Systems skills training manual: Trauma-informed treatment for anxiety, depression, PTSD and substance abuse.* PESI Publishing.
   c. Schwartz, R. C. (2023). *You are the one you've been waiting for: Applying Internal Family Systems to intimate relationships.* Trailheads Publications, The Center for Self Leadership.
   d. Schwartz, R. C. (2001). *Introduction to the Internal Family Systems model.* Trailheads Publications, The Center for Self Leadership.
   e. Goulding, R. A., & Schwartz, R. C. (2002). *The mosaic mind: Empowering the tormented selves of child abuse survivors.* Trailheads Publications, The Center for Self Leadership.
   f. Schwartz, R. C., & Falconer, R. R. (2017). *Many minds, one self: Evidence for a radical shift in paradigm.* Trailheads.
   g. McConnell, S., & Schwartz, R. C. (2020). *Somatic Internal Family Systems therapy: Awareness, breath, resonance, movement, and touch in practice* (1st ed.). North Atlantic Books.
   h. Sykes, C., Sweezy, M., & Schwartz, R. C. (2023). *Treating addictive processes with Internal Family Systems therapy: A compassionate and effective approach for helping people who soothe or distract with substances, food, gambling, pornography, and more.*

You can find the books listed above and many more here: IFS Bibliography and Research: www.ifs-institute.com/resources/research/ifs-bibliography-apa-style

3) IFS Trainings:
   a. IFS Institute Trainings: www.ifs-institute.com/trainings
   b. IFS UK Trainings: www.internalfamilysystemstraining.co.uk/training/ifs-training/
   c. IFS Portugal Trainings: www.internalfamilysystems.pt/
   d. IFS France Trainings: www.ifs-association.com/formations-ifs-internal-family-systems/
   e. IFS Australia Trainings: www.internalfamilysystemstrainingaustralia.com.au/training/

- f. IFS Barcelona Trainings: www.institutoifs.com/formacion-de-profundizacion/
- g. IFS Israel Trainings: www.ifs-israel.org/
- h. IFS South Korea Trainings: www.training.psychologykorea.com/ifs
- i. IFS Russia Trainings: www.ifs-russia.ru/
- j. Life Architect Trainings: www.lifearchitect.com/ifs-bali-retreat/

4) IFS Podcasts:
   - a. IFS Talks: www.podcasts.apple.com/us/podcast/ifs-talks/id1481000501
   - b. The One Inside: www.theoneinside.libsyn.com/

5) Other:
   - a. Online Workshops/Videos:
     - i. IFS Institute: www.ifs-institute.com/resources/videos
     - ii. IFS Online Circle and Continuity Program: www.courses.ifs-institute.com
     - iii. PESI: www.catalog.pesi.com/category/ifsinternal-family-systems

AN IFS SHORTHAND TOOL

MOVE TOWARD

Jenna Riemersma, LPC

Reviewer: Richard C. Schwartz, PhD

Like many people who discover the Internal Family Systems (IFS) model, I can divide my life into two distinctly different periods: before I encountered IFS and after. I first experienced IFS at a workshop where a petite, bubbly therapist was explaining how she had used IFS skills to calmly welcome—and, as a result, disarm—the homicidal part of a client who had shown up to session with a weapon.

This is no ordinary therapist, I thought. *This woman is a ninja.*

IFS is a "constraint release" model, she explained, which means that it believes in the fundamental goodness of all our parts, even the scary ones. It releases unwanted burdens that constrain those positive qualities to reveal the original beauty underneath.

Turns out, there is much in our inner and outer worlds in need of such release. Anxiety, depression, addiction, perfectionism, judgment, violence, hatred, rage—these burdens and more obscure the beauty of who we truly are, divide our communities into "us" vs. "them," and reveal our innermost parts at war.

Much of this suffering is brought about because we instinctively move against[1] the parts of ourselves, and of others, that we don't like. By move against, I mean that we try to force a part of ourselves (or another) stop what it's doing or feeling, which invariably escalates the unwanted feeling or behavior.

When we move against what we dislike, we invariably make our conflict and suffering worse. Warring within and between our parts is creating the very problems it is trying to solve.

We need a new way.

The therapeutic modality of IFS is a new way, although it holds a very ancient truth. IFS offers both the spirit and the means for *moving toward* all parts with transformational compassion and love. At first, this may feel counterintuitive, but what we ultimately find is that it's the only approach powerful enough to transform burdens and darkness, suffering and hate. Spiritual and meditative traditions have spoken this truth through the ages, but it has often felt too idealistic and intangible to apply.

How do I love my enemy? Especially if "my enemy" is within me?

Fortunately, IFS also teaches the *how* of these compassionate truths, so we can actually live them out. And by successfully doing so, the modality has created extraordinary demand. IFS trainings have burgeoning waiting lists. IFS therapists are booked solid. Even for those who can get into a training, it often takes years to gain fluency with the complexities of the model. And many who need relief from symptoms and suffering do not have the free time or disposable income to even contemplate the luxury of personal therapy.

We need more access to this new way.

Many are diligently working to expand access. New IFS trainings and trainers are regularly being introduced.[2] IFS is being offered in groups (Burris, 2022). Traditionally marginalized communities are receiving scholarships and dedicated trainings which, I'm delighted to say, a percent of the profits from this book are dedicated to supporting.[3] Chapter 1 details many new arenas into which IFS is expanding, and books, webinars, retreats, and workshops are regularly appearing to help people connect to the life-changing power of the IFS model.

My hope in this chapter is to join these robust efforts of the collective by offering a simple tool that provides an entry point to the IFS model. I call this tool Move Toward® because the spirit of IFS moves toward *all* our parts with curiosity, compassion, open heartedness, and connection.

I'm grateful that my friend and mentor, Dr. Schwartz, has vetted this shorthand, but of course, it's important to say that Move Toward does not replace IFS training or IFS therapy, nor does it encompass the unburdening (trauma healing) parts of the model. It is simply an IFS-informed tool to support unblending, Self-energy, and Self-to-part relationships, as the following chart describes:

Move Toward is not:	Move Toward is:
The entire IFS model.	A quick IFS tool to help unblend, increase Self-energy, and promote Self-to-part relationships.
A replacement for IFS training.	An introductory tool for those waiting to access an IFS training.
A substitute for IFS therapy.	A tool to check in with parts or manage triggers between sessions. An introductory way to benefit from an IFS intervention for those who don't have access to therapy.
An unburdening intervention.	An unblending intervention.

Think of it as a "quick start guide" to IFS that is simple enough to remember when we are triggered, don't have an IFS therapist handy, and need a little help.

Its goal, like IFS as a whole, is to bring parts into relationship with Self, reestablish our inner secure attachment, and live from who we truly are.

Let's start by understanding the basic terms and spirit of the model.

KEY IFS TERMS

Parts: Subpersonalities that have unique goals, perspectives, values, desires, and emotions. Inner systems have a combination of burdened and unburdened parts which are organized in complex systems of interaction. Parts are present at birth and have a positive intention for the individual.

Protector: A type of burdened part that is organized around preventing exile activation (manager) or soothing exiles after activation (firefighter).

Exiles: Burdened parts that carry painful emotions and beliefs. They are past-oriented[4] and often frozen in time at the moment the painful (burdening) event occurred. Common feelings: shame, fear, powerlessness, hopelessness.

Managers: Pro-active protector parts that are future and goal-oriented[5] and strive to manage our lives to prevent exiles from becoming triggered. Common roles: control, people pleasing, perfectionism, caretaking, judging.

Firefighters: Reactive protector parts that are present-oriented and intent on soothing, numbing, or creating pleasure, rest, or relief.[6] They spring into action after exiles have been triggered to "put out the fire." Common roles: substance abuse, suicidality, self-harm, dissociating, bingeing, porn/affairs.[7]

Self: The undamaged, healing essence at the core of every individual. Self holds the "8 C qualities:" curiosity, calmness, compassion, clarity, courage, creativity, confidence, and connectedness. Self is the compassionate healer and wise leader of the inner system of parts.

Burdens: negative beliefs, feelings, roles, and sensations that parts take on from negative life experiences. Burdens obscure the fundamentally positive nature of exile, manager, and firefighter parts, and parts are not the same thing as the burdens they carry.

Definitions based on the work of Dr. Richard Schwartz and Cece Sykes

Why Moving Against Our Parts Makes Our Suffering Worse

The strategy of moving against is the universal response of our burdened protector parts, and they do their work tirelessly, both inside and outside of us. In our inner world, the primary job of every burdened protector (in either a proactive or reactive way) is to keep our exiles locked in the basement of our souls where they cannot flood but also cannot heal. We hear their mission expressed in phrases like "*conquer* my fear," "*overcome* my anxiety," or "*defeat* my depression."

Some protectors do this politely and others less so. Pro-active protectors (managers) that are burdened with jobs like people pleasing or perfectionism move against exiles in ways that tend to be well received in the world. These protectors make people happy, avoid conflict, and do things really, really, well. It's easy amidst all this nicety to forget that their single-minded focus is to do whatever it takes to prevent our exiles' pain from erupting.

All the reactive protectors (firefighters) that get stuck with jobs like addiction, disordered eating, or suicidal ideation are also moving against our inner exiles that carry burdens like shame, powerlessness, and worthlessness, but they do it in ways that are a lot less welcome in the world. Their move against energy is usually more obvious because they spring into action after the exiles are triggered to get the exiles drunk, starve them, or try to kill them. Our firefighter parts mean well, since they are trying to help extinguish pain, but their energy is much less politely disguised.

Protectors even move against each other. We call this a polarization (such as when a manager that wants sobriety polarizes with a firefighter that wants to act out addictively). We hear the move against sensibility of these protectors expressed in phrases like "*battle* my addiction" or "*conquer* my weight problem."

Our parts do the same thing when threatened by something in the outside world. When a part of another person, group, or culture threatens our exiles, protectors pivot their move against energy to fend off the external threat. Protectors with jobs like judging, spiritualizing, or attacking vigorously oppose the parts of others that they don't like to make them stop their behavior through rejection, shame, judgement, or violence. When that fails, protectors with jobs like rage, dissociation, or control take over to move against the parts of others we don't like to get them to stop their behavior, leave us alone, or do what we want.

We see the painful outcomes of these outer battles play out in daily headlines: war, political animosity, racial hate crimes, mass shootings, bullying, abuse. We "other" the parts of people and groups around us that we view as different or threatening and divide ourselves into "me" versus "you" and "us" versus "them."

We all carry the individual and collective trauma of these painful strategies, and it is creating more pain (exiles) inside us, not less. Moving against makes our suffering worse. But not because the parts that are stuck in these antagonistic roles are bad. They're not. They just have bad roles. We're hurting, and it is human nature to want to avoid pain. Our burdened protector parts move against because their job is to try to help us avoid pain.

Of course, while trying so hard to help us avoid the pain of our exiles, these protector parts wind up making it worse.

Exile part: I'm so fat and ugly. I'm worthless. No one will ever love me.

Manager part: I've got to stop eating all the cookies. Then I'll be skinny, and people will love me. Today I'm eating only kale. Kale for breakfast—check. Kale for lunch—check. Kale for dinn…

Exile part: I've been eating kale for a day, and I'm still fat!

Firefighter part: Forget that! I know what will make things feel a little sweeter. I'm gonna eat all the cookies.

Exile part: Now I'm even fatter! This is hopeless!

So, we get stuck in traumatic, escalating cycles of exiles flooding and protectors fighting, all the while getting further from our desired goals.

The solution is to move toward our parts with curiosity and compassion. Then we can better understand how they become stuck in these awful roles and bring them our support, so they can transform.

Move Toward: Simple but not Easy

Move Toward invites us to adopt IFS's simple, but radically counterintuitive, approach toward the things that trigger us. It invites us to welcome and listen to the parts of ourselves that carry our pain and to offer them support rather than rejection. Sounds easy, but have you ever tried to welcome your panic attack, your depression, or your addiction? If so, then you know that this is a radically challenging thing to do.

The compassionate, non-judgmental approach we're describing here actually is the essence of IFS's Self, and it is synergistic with many spiritual traditions. I explore the spiritual dimension of Self more fully in *Altogether You* (2020), where I echo Dr. Schwartz's observation that what IFS calls our core, undamaged Self is synonymous with what spiritual traditions call the image of God, Buddha nature, Atman, or the divine spirit within us. Meditative and yogic practices refer to it as chi, prana, or flow. It is the essence that embodies and connects us to a greater spiritual energy, higher power, or universe outside of us. For those whose world view does not include a higher power, this essence is simply the highest self. Whatever we might call it, it is the very embodiment of love, and stands in stark contrast to our instinctive, yet unhelpful, move-against responses.

Move Toward	Move Against
Connection	Isolation
We	Us vs. Them/ Me vs. You
Loving	Hostile
Calm	Activated
Curious	Critical

Compassionate	Condemning
Peaceful	Fearful
Open	Closed
Listening	Rejecting
Respectful	Aggressive
Present	Dissociated
Discerning	Judging

Self always moves toward our hurting parts with curiosity and compassion. Self sees the positive intent and positive nature of all our parts, even when they are stuck in feelings or behaviors that are painful and destructive. Self knows that there are no bad parts, only good parts stuck in bad roles (Schwartz, 2021). Through the eyes of Self, all parts of us are truly, deeply "welcome."

It is important to underscore that the principle of moving toward does not mean our burdened parts' behaviors or painful feelings are good or okay. They aren't. Shame, rage, self-harm, aggression, denial, addiction, perfectionism, worthlessness, and blame are painful, negative, harmful feelings and behaviors. And Self knows that truth with clarity. All parts welcome doesn't mean all behaviors are welcome. *Moving toward is simply a more effective and compassionate way to help them change than moving against.*

Distilling Gold

Proficiency in applying the IFS model involves mastering many steps which are taught over the course of three intensive levels of training followed by hours of outside supervision, practice, and the completion of a comprehensive mastery assessment.

My rough approximation of the basic steps of the model looks like this:

1. From therapist's Self-energy, attend to the presenting problem and identify the key parts involved.
2. Assess external constraints and titrate clinical work accordingly.
3. If appropriate, identify target protector part(s), establish client Self-energy, and work with protector(s) using the 6 Fs:
   - Find
   - Focus
   - Feel Toward
   - Flesh Out
   - BeFriend
   - Fear

4. Address protector fears (using direct or indirect access).
5. If appropriate, identify and engage in balanced negotiation with polarized parts (using indirect or direct access).
6. Repeat steps three-five for any additional protectors or polarized parts, as needed.
7. From response to fear question, identify the target exile part and, using "hope merchanting" skills, gain permission from all concerned protectors to work with the exile.
8. Contract with the exile not to flood or immediately unblend exile (if it spontaneously floods when protectors give access).
9. Complete the steps of exile healing (addressing interrupting protectors as needed):
   - Establish/confirm Self-to-part relationship
   - Witness
   - Self-led redo
   - Retrieve
   - Unburden
   - Invite in positive qualities
   - Protector witnessing and protector unburdening/preferred role invitation
   - Self and target parts contract for check-ins
   - Extend appreciation to parts from Self

Of course, this outline covers only the basic steps of the IFS model and does not include many more advanced skills such as working with legacy burdens, unattached burdens, cultural burdens, poly-burdened exiles, multiple exiles with the same burden from differing developmental stages, target switching, protector pile-ons, parts currently in acute trauma, life-threatening protectors, spiritual integration, inviting guides, and collective witnessing.

Gulp.

I promise, it's really like riding a bike. It looks complicated, but once you get the hang of it, it flows. In the meantime, most people newer to the model, both therapists and clients alike, could use a quick-start version of these steps to mine the gold that lies within.

Move Toward offers a quick-start IFS tool expressed in three words: **notice, know,** and **need**. These terms are easy to remember and can be used with any type of part (exiles, managers, firefighters). This aspect alone is quite useful, since the full IFS model works with protectors and exiles differently and requires differentiating the type of part being encountered (a proficiency which takes time to develop).

Move Toward's three steps facilitate the unblending, witnessing, and equipping of parts which is useful in many contexts. These include settling when dysregulated, managing triggers, calming panic attacks, understanding intrusive thoughts, mediating harmful impulses, and checking in with parts between sessions.

> **Unblending:** Part separates its energy from Self (increasing access to Self-energy).
>
> **Witnessing:** Part shares its story and is compassionately heard by Self.
>
> **Equipping:** Part identifies its actual desire/need (e.g., to have its perspective considered in decisions), and Self provides that either internally or externally.

This approach does not attempt to unburden parts, but it does bring them into a deeper connection to loving Self presence (which is intrinsically both informative and healing), while gently providing for the *actual* needs of parts so they are less likely to take over with their harmful strategies or feelings.

Let's look at each of these three steps in more detail.

1. Notice (unblending step)

"What do I **notice** right now in my body, mind or emotions?"

We begin by simply **noticing** (with compassion or curiosity) whatever we are experiencing, without trying to change it or figure it out in any way. We bring our gentle awareness to whatever challenging feeling, thought, or sensation is present and *stay with the noticing until we can notice it with compassion or curiosity*. We do not move beyond noticing until we can notice the part with some degree of openheartedness.

Exile Part: I'm so fat! No one will ever love me (burdened belief).

Firefighter Part: No problem, I'll eat all the cookies, and then you'll feel better (burdened strategy to bring relief to exile pain).

Manager Part: I hate the stupid part that keeps eating all the cookies! It's why we are in this mess in the first place. I wish it would go away (noticing the cookie eating with anger).

Self: I get why a part of me would be angry about the cookie eating. It is making things hard in some ways. I'm grateful for the anger and how it's trying to help me not gain weight and experience all the social judgement that invites. And I'm noticing the cookie eating is also trying to help. I'm feeling curious about how it's doing that (openheartedly noticing all the parts with curiosity and compassion).

If we try to move forward feeling angry, for example, we won't get anywhere because we are trying to have a conversation between two warring parts. It is important to stay with the noticing until we can gain some sense of openheartedness, curiosity, or compassion for the part. That lets us know we are in some amount of Self-energy, which is the position from which we are able to actually help our parts.

This is distinct from typical meditative practices which encourage us to watch the thoughts or feelings float by (attempting to release them through non-attachment). IFS invites us to notice and *connect*, rather than notice and *release*; to welcome and bring into deeper focus the part in question; to enter into an actual compassionate relationship with it from our loving Self presence. As IFS lead trainer Cece Sykes says, we want to "get in relationship (with the part), not get in control (of the part)."[8]

TROUBLESHOOTING

If you've ever tried to compassionately notice your binge eating, terror, social anxiety, intrusive thoughts, or fibromyalgia, you probably know that hating these feelings and behaviors is a lot more instinctive than being curious toward them. Since this step can present many challenges, I include a troubleshooting guide for some of the most common issues:

A. **Multiple Parts:** Sometimes multiple parts clamor for our attention. As we focus inside, we may notice a sad part, an angry part, and a hopeless part present, all needing attention. Or we might become aware of a part that wants to eat all the cookies, a part that wants to dissociate, as well as a part that wants to self-harm. In these situations, we can simply notice and welcome all the parts, invite them to take a moment to communicate collaboratively, and agree amongst themselves which part most needs time with Self right now. The others can arrange for a time in the future when they will get equitable time with Self or in some way have an understanding that they won't be forgotten. Once that feels comfortable for all parts involved, pick back up with **noticing** the target part and continue the process. Be sure to meet with the waiting parts at the time you've agreed to in the future.

"We've agreed Self-Harm can have time with Self right now. Cookie Eater and Dissociate aren't as triggered, so we can wait until tomorrow."

B. **Self-Like Parts:** Self-like parts have qualities similar to Self-energy which makes them a challenge to detect. They want to help, to gain useful information about parts, and to make things better. The difference is that they are working to figure things out, make things happen, or fix and rescue which tells us Self-energy is obscured. Self does not have an agenda to fix or rescue, although Self's desire is for all parts to experience relief and healing. Self does not try to figure things out but rather asks and allows parts to share what they want Self to know. Self does not try to make things happen. When Self-energy is present, healing simply flows. If figure-it-out, rescue, or fix energy show up in the **notice** stage, it can be helpful to ask the iconic IFS phrase, "What are you afraid would happen if you didn't figure out what's going on for this part, rescue this part, etc.?" The answer to this question will reveal the Self-like part's positive intent (what difficulty it is trying to help avoid). We can then affirm its desire to help and let it know that only Self has the ability to understand and heal the target part. If the Self-like part does not feel reassured enough to allow Self to interact with the target part, then the Self-like part becomes the target. If it does settle back and curiosity arises toward the original target part, then pick back up with **noticing** and proceed.

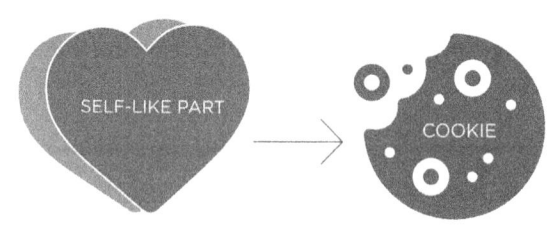

SELF-LIKE PART → COOKIE

"I can fix you!"

C. **Flooding Parts:** Sometimes the part we are noticing takes us over in an overwhelmingly intense way. We become flooded with sadness or shame, for example, or an intense desire to drink or eat all the cookies. This feels terrible, but it is normal and just an indication of how alone and panicked the part feels and how desperately it needs Self's assistance.

If, when you notice the part, it floods in this way, let it know that if it takes you over it will lose access to you (like a cloud covering/obscuring the sun), and you won't be able to help it. Let it know that you don't want it to feel alone with all its pain, so if it pulls its energy back to a lower percentage you'll still get how bad it feels, but it won't lose access to your calm, compassionate, healing presence. You might even offer it (in your mind's eye) a dial so it can try dialing its energy up and down until it finds a workable middle ground. When parts realize this is the best way to receive the support they need, they will typically separate quickly, and the intensity of the feeling will immediately abate. When you regain some degree of calm, compassion, or curiosity toward the part, you can continue with the **notice** step and proceed.

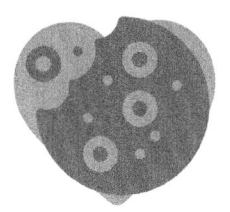

"Eat the cookies!"

"I'm here with you. You're not alone anymore. Tell me what it's like to be you."

Part blended at 90%, almost completely obscuring Self. All that can be felt is the desire to eat the cookies. Cookie part feels completely alone in its quest to self-soothe.

Part unblended to 30%. Self-energy can now be present with it. Desire to eat the cookies is lower and Self's curiosity and compassion are present toward the cookie eating urges. Cookie part feels relieved that Self is there to help soothe more effectively.

D. **Concerned Parts:** It is very common to have parts that don't like what we are feeling and want it to stop. If these arise (for example, we feel hatred rather than compassion toward our cookie eating, or we want our back pain to stop rather than feeling curious toward it), we can listen to and appreciate these parts' concerns until they feel heard and validated.

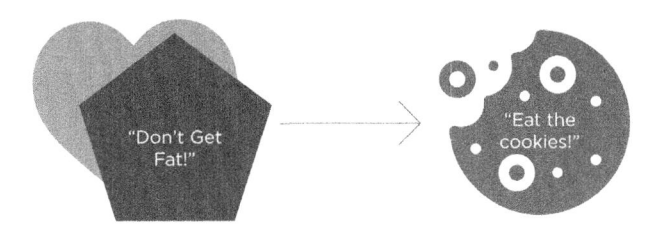

"Don't Get Fat!"

"Eat the cookies!"

"I hate you, stupid cookie eater! Stop it! You're making me fat!"

They may have been taught concern about the target part (if it has been labeled a "character defect" or "sin" for example), and their concerns always make sense (after all, the target part is truly making life difficult). We can reassure them that if they allow Self-energy to be present, it may help the target part not have to feel or do the distressing thing so much.

If the concerned parts don't feel comfortable enough to allow Self to be with the target part at this point, we simply shift our "**noticing**" focus to them instead, and they become the target. But if they are willing to take a seat of honor and allow Self energy to emerge, we will start to become aware of genuine compassion or curiosity toward the original part, and we can return to the **notice** step with the original part and proceed.

Don't Get Fat, in a seat of honor, observing Self and Cookie's conversation.

E. **Frightened Parts:** Sometimes parts of us feel afraid of the part we are trying to notice. This is especially common when the target part has been stuck in a dangerous, overwhelming, or destructive role like suicidal or homicidal ideation, abusive behaviors, rage, addiction, or panic attacks. In this case, let any parts that are afraid know that they don't have to be present for the interaction with the target part—that is Self's job. Let them know that, in your mind's eye, they can go somewhere else that would feel more comfortable, and Self will handle this process. Typically, frightened parts are greatly relieved to learn they have the power to leave and are eager to do so, and the feeling of fear abates quickly. When curiosity or compassion begins to emerge toward the target part, pick back up with **noticing** the original part and continue the process. Make sure you welcome the frightened parts back after Self has spent time with the target part.

"You can go somewhere that feels safe while I help Self-Harm."

F. **Distracting and Numbing Parts:** Many parts are strongly invested in preventing us from noticing what we are feeling, either physically or emotionally. If we have parts that cause us to dissociate (glaze over, leave our bodies, lose time, get lost in our phone or Netflix), distract (start thinking about our to-do list, go blank, not know what we feel physically or emotionally), or get sleepy (start yawning, suddenly feeling exhausted, falling asleep), it is likely that at some point in our lives it was dangerous or unsafe to be in our bodies and aware of our feelings or needs. It's also possible there is fear that the pain we notice will be overwhelming.

DISSOCIATE

COOKIE

We want to welcome, listen to, and validate the reasons they have for not wanting to let us notice what we're feeling. Let them know if they feel safe enough to allow Self to do the noticing (now or in the future), Self might be able to help whatever they're afraid of inside to heal. If they feel reassured and you are suddenly able to notice the original target part, then thank them for their trust and continue the process with that part. If they don't relax (so you still feel distracted or sleepy, for example) then they become the new target part, and you simply change focus to noticing the dissociating part (**notice** the "not feeling" or the "sleepy") and continue from there.

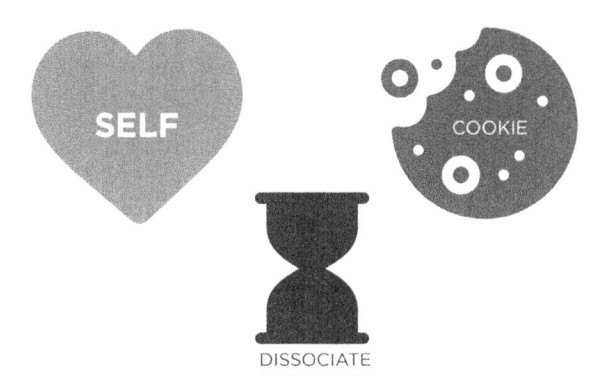

SELF

COOKIE

DISSOCIATE

Dissociate, in a seat of honor where it can observe Self and Cookie's conversation.

A special note: I have found it helpful to invite concerned protectors to "take a seat of honor" in order to watch what is happening between Self and a target part, rather than asking them to "step back." This invites the unblending of the protector energy, but lets the part know it is welcome, and we want it to be an honored witness to the process.

When we can welcome and notice our experience with compassion, we have to some degree unblended and accessed Self-energy. This establishes a secure attachment relationship of the activated parts to the inner loving Self presence, which is intrinsically calming, healing, and reassuring in itself.

2. Know (Witnessing step)

"What do you want me to **know**?"

Once we have established some degree of inner relationship of part to Self (as evidenced by curiosity and/or compassion toward the part), we are ready to get to know it. This is step two of Move Toward: deepening the secure attachment relationship with the part by being a compassionate witness to its story.

Step two involves focusing on the part in whatever way we have awareness of it (an image in our mind's eye, an emotion, thought, or sensation) and asking it, "What do you want me to know about you?" and waiting for the sense of an answer to emerge *from the part itself* (not from us thinking up or trying to figure out the answer). We may get an impression of a word or response or notice memories coming to mind or a shift in sensation. Parts communicate in a variety of equally valid ways.

If we'd like more depth in this step, we can ask whatever "getting to know you" questions seem appropriate, such as:

- What do you want me to know about you?
- When in my life did you first start feeling this way (or doing this thing)?
- What is it like to be you in my system?
- Are you trying to help me in any way?
- Do you have a message for me?
- Do you have any concerns about what might happen if you stopped doing what you do?
- What do you want to be different?

These are the types of questions IFS invites us to use as we get to learn more about parts and develop an understanding of why they become activated and why their feelings/behaviors make sense considering their life experiences. Very often in this step we learn that parts don't like the feelings or behaviors they've been stuck with, but they don't believe any other way is possible.

"What do you want me to know about you? When did you first learn to try to help me in this way?"

"When I was the new kid and getting bullied every day, eating cookies after school made me feel better."

Step two is a deeply healing intervention for the part because it provides a compassionate witness to the part's pain or struggle and to the felt experience that the part is no longer alone or unseen. This step is often the very first time anyone has genuinely cared about the part, been interested in its perspective, offered compassion for it, or provided a sense of companionship and connection. With the growing awareness in our field that trauma isolates and connection heals, the power of this witnessing step cannot be overstated (Anderson, 2021).

3. Need (Equipping step)

"What do you **need** right now to feel less activated/more comforted?"

Once Self has learned as much as the part wants it to know, Self is then able to offer the part comfort and support. We might first begin by inviting the part to, in the mind's eye, turn and really observe the adult Self present with them. Parts are typically stuck at the age in which they become burdened and don't have awareness that time has passed. It can be very reassuring (and often quite surprising!) to the part to tell it how old you are and to update it about your current life circumstances, which are different than the age when it became burdened.

Once the part is fully aware of the adult, loving, healing Self-energy present with it, we can ask the part:

"What do you **need** from me right now to feel a little more comforted and a little less activated?"

As always, we wait for the answer to come from the part rather than trying to figure out what it might need. Only the part itself knows. This question identifies the *actual* need underlying the part's feelings or behavior. We are not asking the part to change in any way, but rather offering comfort and tangible support so that it feels less distressed and more reassured of the capable Self leadership available. This budding trust will set the stage for future unburdening, should the individual wish to engage the full IFS model.

Sometimes in response to the **need** question, we get a sense that the part needs something internally, in our mind's eye, such as a hug from Self, a nap, or a comfort object like a blanket, a stuffed bear, or a cup of tea. Nothing is too odd or unusual a request. As strange as it may sound, when we provide this type of inner, visualized support to our parts (which they typically have never received from a trusted adult), they often feel tremendous relief.

Sometimes we get a sense that the part needs something in our external world. It might need us to use our voice, to set a boundary, to ask for help, or to take its perspective into account in our decision making. In this case we must realistically assess whether we are both willing and able to offer this action. If we are, we set an intention with the part for how and when we will take the requested step.

It is critical that we follow through if we have established an agreement with a part, and then check back with this part to see how it feels after we have taken the agreed step. If we are unable or unwilling for any reason to take the requested action, we can let the part know our concerns and offer a compromise that could meet the part's needs in a different way. Parts whose needs are met in this way are much less likely to become triggered and take over.

Notice, know, and **need** are three simple words, yet offering even just one of these steps to an activated part can be deeply comforting.

Move Toward Helps Our Parts

The goal of Move Toward is to use the wisdom of IFS to help our parts unblend and come into relationship with Self. This is important because Self is the place from which we live our best and most authentic, wise lives. Self deescalates conflicts and increases connection, it calms triggers and minimizes acting out, it regulates mood swings and restores wellbeing, it assesses situations wisely and holds boundaries. Self is the superpower we all are seeking. And it's in all of us. Always.

What does this look like in real life? To flesh it out a bit, let's consider how it might help someone having an urge to eat a whole box of cookies (Not any of us, mind you. But those *other* people who do things like that). A typical response might be to move against the cookie eating part ("I'm such a bad person for wanting to eat this whole box of cookies! What's the matter with me? I'm never going to fit back into my jeans!"). Shame might ensue, and the box of cookies would likely get eaten anyway, followed by more shame. Instead, let's imagine when the urge to eat the cookies emerged, the person took a deep breath, and spent five minutes going through the three steps of Move Toward. Here's what might occur:

Notice:

> I want to eat that whole box of cookies!
> Wait! What were those three words? **Notice, Know, Need.**
> Okay, I'll try it. Let's see—what am I **noticing**?

Well, there's an urgent feeling in my hands, and my thoughts are ruminating about how good the cookies are gonna taste.

I hate this feeling—I'm gonna eat that whole box, and I'll never fit into my jeans!

Well, that's not curious or compassionate…I guess I'll just breathe into this until something shifts…that's better…Now, I feel less hateful toward it and even a little curious about why I want to eat all the cookies.

Know:

> Hi cookie eating part—I feel you in my hands and thoughts.
> What do you want me to **know** about why you just got triggered? (Pausing and waiting for something to come to mind without trying to figure it out or make something happen.)

Hmmm…what's coming to mind is all the stress I've been feeling around this unreasonable deadline at work. I had to work all weekend and didn't get any time to be with friends or to rest. Sheesh—it's been insane!

What are you afraid would happen if you didn't take me over and make me eat cookies? (Again, waiting for something to come up without trying to figure it out.)

I'm getting the sense you're afraid I'd never get any relief or break from work—that you're trying to give me a couple of minutes of pleasure and time for me.

Wow, that makes a lot of sense. Thank you so much for trying to help me have a little relief to balance out the overworking. I'm actually really grateful for that. I've been out of balance for sure.

Need:

I get that you're trying to help me get a break. That makes sense.

What do you **need** from me right now to feel a little less activated, a little more cared for? (Pausing and waiting for something to come up, without trying to figure it out.)

Ah—What's coming up is that you want me to have some breaks from all this work. Of course!

How about if I set my phone timer to go off hourly, and when it goes off, I'll get up and walk around outside for 5 minutes and take several deep breaths. Would that be helpful?

I'm getting a sense that would help a lot, but you still want me to have some pleasure right now because I've been working all day. I get that. But it doesn't seem as urgent now. How about if I eat two cookies right now (instead of the whole box) and take those hourly breaks? Okay—great.

The Move Toward process doesn't have to take a lot of time (probably less time than it would have taken to eat an entire box of cookies), and it can produce quite a bit of insight, as well as much more effective ways to meet the actual needs (which in this case is rest, not cookies) of our parts.

Move Toward: Helping Others' Parts

Move Toward is also helpful when others seek our help. Whether we are in a helping profession, or just in everyday relationships, we all have times when others seek us out for support. Imagine a friend or client confiding their struggle with anxiety in you:

> **Friend/Client:** I've tried everything, but I'm just so anxious all the time! I'm worried about everything. I'm having trouble sleeping, and I even had a panic attack the other day. What should I do?

Notice our instinctive tendency to move against the anxiety and to try to make it stop. Common responses might be: "Try deep breathing." "You should exercise more. I heard that's helpful for anxiety." "Have you thought about medication?" "Why don't you try filling out a thought record and assessing the validity of the anxiety?" "You shouldn't be anxious—there's nothing threatening happening."

We also have ways of spiritually moving against difficult feelings/behaviors, called spiritual bypassing:[9] "Just watch the anxiety like a leaf on the river, and let it float right by and out of consciousness," "Anxiety is a character defect," or "Cast your anxiety on God." There are many ways to use spiritual approaches to try to lock our exile emotions in the basement, so we don't have to feel them.

Notice how move against strategies contain an energy of judgment, can communicate the person is doing something wrong, and encourage the person to disconnect from a part of themselves. They also rely on the listener/helper to have an "answer" or "solution." That's a lot of pressure on both people.

Now let's try it again, but this time imagine offering the support-seeker a Move Toward response:

Friend/Client: I've tried everything but I'm just so anxious all the time! I'm worried about everything. I'm having trouble sleeping, and I even had a panic attack the other day. What should I do?

Notice:

Helper: I'm so sorry. That sounds really hard. When the anxiety comes up, how do you **notice** it?

Seeker: I don't know. It's just like a huge weight on my chest, like I can't breathe.

Helper: Would it be okay to just **notice** the weight on your chest without trying to change it or figure it out in any way? Just be with it with a little compassion or curiosity?

Seeker: Yeah—that's hard to do, but it's settling down a little. I can breathe more deeply.

Know:

Helper: I'm curious why it keeps taking you over. Do you think you could ask the anxiety what it wants you to **know** about it?

Seeker: It's weird, but I'm getting this sense that it feels really young. And I just had a memory pop up from when I was a little kid, and my parents used to leave me at home alone before school when they had to go to work. I felt so scared to be alone at that age. I just made the connection that my spouse leaving on business trips is triggering the anxiety. It reminds me of what it was like when my parents left.

Need:

Helper: Wow. It makes so much sense why that would trigger anxiety. I wonder if there's anything it might **need** from you to feel a little more comforted. Could you ask the anxiety what it needs from you, so it feels taken care of?

Seeker: I'm getting this sense that it just needs to know I'm not alone. It wants me to call a friend in those triggering times right after (s)he leaves for the airport.

What a relief!

Move Toward takes the pressure off the "helper" (fixing, giving advice, figuring out the solution) as well as the "seeker" (disconnecting from a part of themselves, looking for solutions outside their own inner wisdom, forcing themself to do something). And it's easy! We don't have to know a single answer. Just **notice**, **know**, and **need**.

Move Toward offers many relational benefits:

1. It's much easier than having the "answers" to everyone's problems (and persuading them to accept those "answers").
2. We become emotionally safe people because Move Toward holds no judgment, no agenda or pressure, no "right" or "wrong" choices, just curiosity.
3. It avoids the common mistake of aligning with the person's help-seeking part against the part of them that is engaged in the difficult feeling or behavior (which will create resistance to "solutions" that are offered without taking that part's feelings and needs into account).
4. It produces the most helpful insights (because it listens to what the part really feels and needs), beyond what either the helper or seeker could ever know otherwise.

Is this all we need to know if we are professional helpers?

No, of course not.

As therapists, we do need to know how to help the exile parts unburden—either through IFS, EMDR, SE, or other forms of trauma work. And we absolutely want to have all our good clinical and therapeutic skills. All the other modalities we have training in are helpful and good (and integrate quite nicely with IFS, hence this book!). But IFS and Move Toward help us see the beauty in every person and every problem, make symptoms make sense, and show us clearly the path to healing.

Move Toward Does Not Mean Anything Goes

It's important to revisit a point we made earlier: Move Toward does *not* mean anything goes. While it is true that all parts have positive intent, that doesn't mean what they are feeling or doing is okay. Burdened parts' feelings and behaviors are painful and often harmful. Move Toward doesn't mean we let people hurt us or have no boundaries. Just the reverse, actually. Move Toward helps us find our inner strength and set our wisest boundaries when other's parts are harmful.

We have to Move Toward before we can wisely Turn Toward.

Key insight here: We have to Move Toward our own activated parts before we can wisely assess how to Turn Toward other people's hurtful parts.

Darn it all, but we just don't have the power to heal or transform other people's parts. And other people's burdened parts often inflict both small and large harms on our tender souls. Our parts get activated, and often take us over, when we are hurt. In this state we tend to react from our burdened parts. We might get small and not use our voice, get big and attack, try to over-explain to the person why what they did was wrong, throw out threats, run away, fawn and placate, or shut down and dissociate.

It's common to mistakenly believe that some of these burdened parts-led responses are "boundaries" and to get very confused when they "don't work" (i.e., make the other person stop being hurtful or sorry for what they did). The truth is they are all responses *from* our burdened parts. And burdened parts are always trying to help, but eventually they make our pain worse.

To connect to our deep inner Self's wisdom, clarity, and strength, we must first Move Toward our own burdened parts. By **noticing** them (e.g., I'm noticing rage in my chest, and I want to lash out at that person), asking what they want us to **know** (I'm really hurt by what they did) and what they **need** (to speak *for* their hurt, share what the experience was like for them, and calmly leave the conversation if hurtful things continue to happen), they will feel heard and cared for. That allows them to calm down and settle back, permitting Self qualities to spontaneously emerge.

It is from the calm, clear-minded, creative, courageous place of Self that we are wisely able to:

1. Accurately perceive the situation (our parts perceive through distorted filters, Self does not).
2. Discern and select the wisest boundaries, if needed.
3. Follow through with the boundaries (which is critical to their success).

Once we are in Self, we can communicate calmly and clearly (speaking *for* our parts rather than *from* our parts), even with someone who is hurtful, state our boundaries without needing to attack or get small, and courageously follow through with them. Moving toward our own parts gets us to Self. And Self is the place from which we most wisely address our hurts.

This is the space from which we can notice that other people's burdens are not all of who they are. Where we don't confuse people with their parts or confuse parts with their burdens. Where we can remain respectful of others humanness and our deep shared connection while disagreeing strongly. It allows us to protect and advocate without hatred. To oppose with love. To object without vilifying. To advocate for justice and equity with strength and respect for our common humanity. This is the rare and powerful stance that can literally change the world.

Maria and David's Scheduling Conflict: Move Against or Move Toward?

Let's look at the way a typical scheduling conflict might escalate into an all-out parts war when our protector parts take over and do their thing:

Maria: Can you pick the kids up after school next week? I have a project at work that I need to stay late for.

David: Are you kidding me? I picked them up twice last week, and I drop them off every morning! You don't ever think about me and my schedule. You just take advantage of me all the time, and I'm sick of it. What's the matter with you? (Speaking from a defensive part that sees Maria as uncaring and taking advantage)

Maria: Me!? What's the matter with me? I am the one that makes all the lunches and does all the homework time and drives to all the sports events! You can't even help out a little with pickup! You jerk. You are such a chauvinistic jerk! (Speaking from a defensive part that sees David as chauvinistic and uncaring, not helping equally in the relationship)

David: (throwing his phone down) What the hell? (Speaking and acting from an aggressive, physical part that now sees Maria as "the enemy")

Maria: (storming out and slamming the door) You asshole! I should just leave you—I hate you! (Speaking and acting from a threat-making, escaping part that now sees David as "the enemy")

Notice how quickly our conflicts tend to accelerate into damaging, explosive, or alienating encounters when burdened protector parts take us over and start moving against each other. Now let's see how this might have gone if even just one person was able to Move Toward their own parts before Turning Toward the other in a conflict:

Maria: Can you pick the kids up after school next week? I have a project at work that I need to stay late for.

David: Are you kidding me? I picked them up twice last week, and I drop them off every morning! You don't ever think about me and my schedule. You just take advantage of me all the time, and I'm sick of it. What's the matter with you? (Speaking from a defensive part that sees Maria as uncaring and taking advantage.)

Maria: Whoa, time out. I'm feeling triggered. I need a minute—I'll be right back to this conversation when I'm calmer. (Stepping into another room and taking a deep breath while checking in with/moving toward her body and emotions).

Notice:

Okay, what am I **noticing**? Racing heart, tense fists, clenched jaw, anger at David. I understand that. His comment felt mean. It makes sense that a part of me got defensive.

Know:

Okay defensive part, what do you want me to **know** about why you got triggered and took me over just now? Ah—I'm getting the sense you were trying to protect me from feeling attacked and unsupported. That makes sense.

Need:

So, defensive part, what do you **need** from me right now to feel a little less activated and a little more taken care of? I get the sense you **need** me to speak for you and also to make sure the kids have a ride, since this project at work is super important. I can absolutely do that.

Maria: (calmly coming back into the room) Honey, I'd like to come back to that conversation. When I heard you say, "I don't think about you," and "I take advantage of you," I felt attacked and a defensive part of me got triggered. It was trying to protect me from feeling attacked and unsupported. I do need help with carpool next week, but I don't want you to feel taken advantage of. Could we talk about both of our schedules next week? If it's not convenient for you, I can ask a friend. (Speaking for her defensive part from Self and taking action to get that part's needs met more effectively.)

David: (From a dismissive, blaming part) Don't even talk to me right now—I'm so sick of you nagging me all the time! (Pushes Maria backwards as he storms past.)

Maria: (from Self) It is never okay to push me or threaten me, David. Since you've chosen to do that, I will choose to take the kids and stay with my parents this weekend. (Leaving calmly but firmly: stating and following through on a boundary from Self.)

And now let's look at how things might unfold if *both* people were able to Move Toward their own parts before Turning Toward the other:

Maria: Can you pick the kids up after school next week? I have a project at work that I need to stay late for.

David: I know you're just asking for help, but I'm triggered. I need a minute to check in with myself. (Stopping, taking a deep breath, turning attention inside.) Okay, I'm noticing a defensive part of me got triggered when I heard you ask me to help with pick up because I picked them up a couple of times last week, and it is trying to protect me from being unappreciated and taken advantage of.

Maria: Now I'm feeling triggered—give me just a minute to check in with what's going on in me. (Pausing, taking a deep breath, turning attention inside). Hmm—I also have a defensive part that came up when I heard you say the words "unappreciated" and "taken advantage of." It's telling me I do a lot of things like make lunches, drive sports, and do homework time. And I get that. But I can also appreciate how a part of you might feel triggered, since you did help with pickup last week, too. Could we talk about our schedules, and see what would work for us both? If it's not convenient for you, I can ask a friend.

David: A part of me wants to help with pick up because I want to support you, and another part of me wants you to ask a friend because that's the only time I have to go to the gym, which is important to me.

Maria: That makes sense, and I know your workouts are an important part of your routine. If you could help me on Wednesday, I'll ask a friend for the other days.

David: Okay, I'll exercise before work on Wednesday then, if you'll drop the kids off that morning.

Maria: Sounds great—thanks, honey.

David: Sure. Thanks for talking to me about it and caring about my gym time.

Moving toward our own parts is often counterintuitive and difficult but life changing. When we Move Toward our own activated parts by **noticing** how they are showing up, asking what they want us to **know**, and providing what they actually **need**, we connect to our inner Self-energy, create secure inner attachment of our parts to our Self, and discern what is needed in order to wisely Turn Toward the parts of others. As you can see, this doesn't mean conflicts will resolve happily or comfortably, since we can only control one person—ourselves—in any given situation. But this does allow us to maintain Self-energy, to perceive events accurately, and, when needed, to set and follow through on boundaries to keep ourselves safe emotionally, physically, sexually, financially, and spiritually.

Expanding Access to IFS: A Summary

In this chapter, I have introduced an IFS shorthand tool called Move Toward® that captures the spirit of the IFS model: moving toward all parts of ourselves with curiosity and compassion. It is comprised of three simple steps—**notice, know,** and **need**—that allow us to unblend, witness, and equip triggered parts of ourselves (both protectors and exiles), so that we can live in the world with more Self-energy, and then Turn Toward the parts of others with wisdom, clarity, and strength. It is my hope that this simple tool will be a helpful aid to create expanded access to the power and beauty of the IFS model and the Self-led vision for the world that Dr. Richard Schwartz has courageously brought into being.

KEY TAKEAWAYS

- Move Toward® is a shorthand tool for the IFS model.
- Moving against makes our suffering worse.
- The essence of Move Toward® is captured in a three-word mnemonic: **notice, know, need.**
- Move Toward doesn't mean anything goes.
- We have to Move Toward our own parts before we can wisely Turn Toward the parts of others.

AUTHOR BIO

Jenna Riemersma, LPC (she/her) is an Amazon number one best-selling author, speaker, therapist, and consultant. She is the founder and clinical director of the Atlanta Center for Relational Healing and teaching faculty for the International Institute for Trauma and Addiction Professionals. An IFS Level 3 Certified Therapist and IFS Approved Clinical Consultant, Jenna is an enthusiastic "IFS evangelist" committed to spreading the word that all parts are welcome. She lives on the unceded lands of the Cherokee people and is the proud mom of two young adults.

REVIEWER BIO

Richard Schwartz, PhD (he/him) is the creator of Internal Family Systems, a highly effective, evidence-based therapeutic model that de-pathologizes the multi-part personality. His IFS Institute offers training for professionals and the general public. He is currently on the faculty of Harvard Medical School, and he has published five books, including *No Bad Parts: Healing Trauma and Restoring Wholeness with the Internal Family Systems Model*. Dick lives with his wife, Jeanne, near Chicago, close to his three daughters and his growing number of grandchildren.

REFERENCES

Anderson, F. (2021). *Transcending trauma: Healing complex PTSD with Internal Family Systems*. PESI Publishing.

Burris, C. (2022). *Creating healing circles: Using the Internal Family Systems model in facilitating groups* (D. Burris, Ed.). Tonic Books.

Horney, K. (1945). *Our inner conflicts: A constructive theory of neurosis*. W. W. Norton.

Riemersma, J. (2020). *Altogether you: Experiencing personal and spiritual transformation with Internal Family Systems (IFS) therapy*. Pivotal Press.

Schwartz, R. C. (2021). *No bad parts: Healing trauma and restoring wholeness with the Internal Family Systems model*. Sounds True.

GOING DEEPER

From Jenna Riemersma

1) Websites:
   a. www.MoveToward.com
   b. www.JennaRiemersma.com

2) Books:
   a. Riemersma, J. (2020). *Altogether you: Experiencing personal and spiritual transformation with Internal Family Systems (IFS) therapy.* Pivotal Press.

3) Consultation and Supervision:
   a. www.JennaRiemersma.com/consultation

4) Podcasts and Webinars:
   a. Where is God when the World is Falling Apart? Webinar with Dr. Richard Schwartz: www.jennariemersma.com/listentojenna/
   b. The One Inside with Tammy Sollenberger: www.theoneinside.libsyn.com/
      i. IFS and Altogether You with Jenna Riemersma
      ii. IFS and Moving Toward with Jenna Riemersma
      iii. IFS and Altogether Us with Richard Schwartz and Jenna Riemersma
      iv. IFS and **Notice, Know,** and **Need** with Jenna Riemersma
   c. Additional podcasts: www.jennariemersma.com/listentojenna/

5) IFS and Move Toward® Meditations by Jenna:
   a. Insight Timer: www.insighttimer.com/jennariemersma
   b. Sentur app: www.sentur.app/
   c. www.jennariemersma.com/all-courses/

6) Speaking Engagements:
   a. info@jennariemersma.com

From Dr. Richard Schwartz

1) Websites:
   a. IFS Institute: www.IFS-Institute.com
   b. Foundation for Self Leadership: www.foundationifs.org

2) Books:
   www.ifs-institute.com/resources/research/ifs-bibliography-apa-style

APPENDIX A

move toward (with Jenna)

NOTICE

What feeling, urge, or sensation are you **noticing**?
Where is it in your body or mind?
- Racing heart?
- Tight throat?
- Tears in eyes?
- Pit in stomach?
- Headache?
- Is there an image in your mind's eye?
- Are there thoughts or feelings associated with this part?

Let your awareness be with it for several moments.
- Take a moment to honor any negative thoughts or feelings you have about it. They are valid in some regard.
- Continue to do this until you can authentically bring compassion or curiosity to the emotion, urge, or sensation you are focusing on.

KNOW

Ask the feeling, urge, or sensation:
- "What do you want me to **know**?"
- "What caused you to show up just now?"
- "When was the first time you ever felt this way or did this job for me?"
- "Is there anything you're worried would happen if you didn't do this?"

NEED

Ask the feeling, urge, or sensation:
"What do you **need** from me right now to feel a little less activated?"
- To be welcomed and understood?
- To receive a metaphorical hug?
- A specific action?
  - Saying no
  - Setting a boundary
  - Asking for help

For further support: www.ifs-institute.com/practitioners

SECTION TWO
MODEL INTEGRATION

IFS AND POLYVAGAL THEORY

HEALING THROUGH COMPASSIONATE CONNECTION

Alexia Rothman, PhD
Reviewers: Richard C. Schwartz, PhD
and Deborah A. Dana, LCSW

> "The single most important issue for traumatized people
> is to find a sense of safety in their bodies."
> —*Bessel A. van der Kolk*

In his recent book, *The Essence of Healing: A Quest for a MetaModel of the Psychotherapy of Trauma,* Dr. Arthur Mones posits that Internal Family Systems (IFS) is a "MetaModel" of psychotherapy. He explains that as a psychotherapeutic model, IFS views psychiatric symptoms as adaptive reactions, and it contains essential elements that contribute to the effectiveness of psychotherapy across modalities. These elements include appreciating the context in which symptoms developed, lifting the constraints to our essential human nature, focusing on second-order change which involves working with internal and interpersonal contexts to ease symptoms, emphasizing a compassionate and accepting therapeutic relationship, incorporating the experience of the physical body, working with intrapsychic conflict, and reprocessing traumatic memories (Mones, 2022). In my work as an IFS clinical consultant, therapists and practitioners often tell me that IFS seems to work "better" and on a "deeper level" than models they have used before. They report encountering less resistance, working more efficiently with resistance when it does arise, more effectively helping clients change longstanding patterns of thinking, behavior, and reactivity, and effectively assisting clients in healing the wounded and burdened parts of their internal systems, resulting in them moving through the world with greater ease. These therapists also describe feeling less personally drained by the therapeutic work. While, as yet IFS-specific empirical research investigating these claims is limited, the "essential elements" cited by Mones offer some insight into why these phenomena have been so frequently reported by IFS clinicians and practitioners around the globe.

In this chapter, I offer an additional possibility that may underlie the efficacy of IFS. In my opinion, one of the reasons that IFS can be such an effective model of psychotherapy, even for the most traumatized clients, is that in the hands of an attuned, Self-led therapist, the model *can work seamlessly in concert with the nervous system* to promote healing and transformation. This chapter will explore how a basic understanding of Dr. Stephen Porges's Polyvagal Theory (PVT) can offer insight into the apparent efficacy of IFS and can underlie and support IFS work, helping to boost the safety and effectiveness of psychotherapy with even the most traumatized and chronically dysregulated individuals. I also offer several concrete suggestions for ways to integrate these two theories in the service of elevating our IFS practice and more successfully serving our clients.

Basics of Polyvagal Theory

Polyvagal Theory was first introduced to the scientific community in 1994 by its developer, behavioral scientist Dr. Stephen W. Porges. While Dr. Porges was aware that his theory would have applications in multiple medical specialties, including cardiology and neonatology, he never imagined that it would be relevant to the field of psychotherapy. Through the ensuing work of psychotherapist and author, Deborah A. Dana, Polyvagal Theory was brought to the psychotherapy community, and its principles were applied to the treatment of trauma survivors (Dana, 2018; Dana, 2020; Dana, 2021; Porges & Dana, 2018).

Polyvagal Theory offers an understanding of the relationship between our physiological state and our behavior. Specifically, it describes how our autonomic nervous systems evolved to support adaptive responses to various situations, including conditions of safety, danger, and life-threat. The autonomic nervous system (ANS) is a branch of the nervous system that performs multiple vital, homeostatic functions in the human body, such as regulating our breathing, heartrate, and digestive processes. These functions are performed continuously, automatically, and beneath the level of conscious awareness (e.g., we don't have to think about breathing in order to make it happen). Of the many important functions continuously performed by the ANS, perhaps the one of primary interest to psychotherapists is that the ANS constantly scans the environment for signals of safety and danger through a subconscious process called "neuroception." The ANS detects and reacts to cues inside our bodies, in our external environment, and in our interactions with others that suggest that we are either safe or at risk in any given moment.

The ANS contains two branches: the Sympathetic Nervous System (SNS) and the Parasympathetic Nervous System (PNS). The SNS evolved approximately 400 million years ago and is centered in the middle of the spinal cord. It is a system of mobilization that can bring activating energy to our bodies to help us attempt to defend ourselves, or escape, in the face of danger. Within the

PNS, Polyvagal Theory describes two, bidirectional pathways of our 10th cranial nerve, known as the vagus nerve: the dorsal vagal pathway and the ventral vagal pathway.

The vagus consists of a bundle of nerve fibers that travels in two directions and that contains both afferent and efferent pathways. Afferent pathways transmit information from sensory receptors to the central nervous system (i.e., brain and spinal cord), while efferent pathways carry motor information from the central nervous system to various organs. The dorsal vagal pathway travels down from the dorsal motor nucleus in the brainstem to both *regulate* and receive information *from* organs below the diaphragm, including the digestive system. The ventral vagal pathway begins in the nucleus ambiguus in the brainstem and connects with nerves in the neck, throat, face, eyes, and ears to form the Social Engagement System, and it also travels from the brainstem down, to regulate and receive information from organs above the diaphragm, including the heart and lungs. The dorsal vagal pathway evolved first, approximately 500 million years ago, and it helped our reptilian ancestors survive with its ability to cause immobilization, or death-feigning, in the face of life-threatening danger. When not involved in protection, this pathway supports health, growth, and restoration. The ventral vagal pathway, which evolved most recently (approximately 200 million years ago) and is found uniquely in mammals, is a pathway of safety, connection, and well-being. Activity in this pathway downregulates physiological defenses and is associated with an embodied sense of safety, the ability to socially engage and co-regulate with others, and good physical health.

When the ANS is neurocepting cues of safety, and/or *not* picking up cues of danger, the body is in a state of regulation, where the functioning of the SNS and the dorsal vagal pathway of the PNS are overseen and regulated by the activity of the ventral vagal pathway. In this regulated state, a person feels safe and able to connect with others and enjoys the benefits of regulated functioning of their organ systems. However, when the ANS neurocepts cues of danger, it responds in a predictable, hierarchically organized fashion, first described by John Hughlings Jackson (1958, as cited in Porges, 2022) as "dissolution." First, it progresses through a dysregulated state of sympathetically fueled hyperarousal and, ultimately, if the frequency and/or intensity of danger cues is high enough, it proceeds to a dysregulated state of dorsal-associated hypoarousal, where the more recently evolved neural circuits no longer inhibit the activity of the more primitive circuitry. Therapists may be most familiar with these adaptive survival states through their descriptive names of fight, flight, freeze, shutdown, and collapse.

Relevance of Polyvagal Theory to Psychotherapy

In my nearly 25 years as a psychotherapist, I have observed that despite the diversity of content that brings clients to treatment, difficulty regulating their emotional and physiological experience is generally at the heart of their struggles. Clients report being "hijacked" by extreme emotions, experiencing uncomfortable or even intolerable physiological states, and feeling unable to function as desired due to either a lack of sufficient energy or to being flooded with too much energy. These experiences are then commonly associated with thinking or behaving in ways that are distressing and that can result in negative consequences for them or for others in their lives.

Although shifting in and out of regulation is a natural, even frequent, occurrence for all humans, suffering results when we shift into dysregulated states and become "stuck" there, unable to move efficiently back towards regulation (Dana, 2021). This phenomenon of frequently shifting into dysregulation and struggling to return to regulation is often seen in the systems of trauma survivors (van der Kolk, 2014). Dr. Porges and Deb Dana note that traumatic experience can cause a "retuning" of the autonomic nervous system away from patterns of safety and connection and towards patterns of survival and protection (Dana, 2018), such that it is easier for survivors of abuse, neglect, and other types of traumatic experiences to shift into adaptive survival states in the ANS and harder for them to return to a state of embodied safety.

Given the emotional suffering and the impact on physical health, thoughts, and behaviors that existing in a survival state can bring, one of my primary therapeutic goals with any client is to help them progress towards becoming less frequently and severely dysregulated, more easily able to shift back towards regulation when they do become dysregulated, and more firmly anchored in regulation in general, such that a higher level of stimulus is required to dysregulate them in the first place. In IFS terms, I hope that my clients will become able to lead their systems more frequently from Self, have fewer of their parts burdened and/or in extreme roles (and thus less likely to hijack their systems), and find it easier to return to a state of Self-leadership when their parts are inevitably activated in daily life.

IFS and Polyvagal Theory

An understanding of the basic principles of Polyvagal Theory provides helpful guidance in understanding what might be happening for our clients on a biological level in and between sessions. This understanding can inform our approach to IFS treatment, both in sessions and in terms of case conceptualization and treatment planning.

Though continually evolving, our knowledge of the full scope of the association between the impact of trauma on the nervous system and healing through psychotherapy is limited (for more comprehensive descriptions than offered here, see Anderson, 2021; Cozolino, 2017; Ecker, Ticic, & Hulley, 2012; van der Kolk, 2014). Furthermore, specific associations between IFS and the nervous system have yet to be empirically investigated. Nonetheless, as we wait for the research that can further flesh out our understanding of these relationships, observations from thousands of hours of clinical work by IFS therapists and practitioners reveal apparent associations between parts, Self, and the autonomic nervous system.

Parts and the Nervous System

In his book, *No Bad Parts*, Dick Schwartz describes parts as, "sacred, spiritual beings" (p. 17). He has previously referred to them as, "inner people of different ages, temperaments, talents, and desires, who together form an internal family or tribe" (Schwartz, 1995, p. 52). IFS therapists and clients have observed that no matter what they may believe parts to be, parts act and react as whole beings do. Thus, approaching them with the respect, compassion, and collaborative spirit with which we would ideally approach a person in the external world seems to yield the best results.

In my workshops on IFS and Polyvagal Theory, I am frequently asked whether we can conceptualize parts in IFS simply as states of the nervous system, such that the blending of a part would merely signify the body shifting into a different physiological state. I firmly believe that reducing our understanding of parts to "states of the nervous system" would be a step backwards, both in terms of our understanding of parts and in our ability to help our clients. In fact, it appears that one of the reasons that clients in IFS therapy feel so deeply understood, and are able to understand themselves more deeply, is the respectful approach that IFS takes to these parts. We learn to treat parts as whole beings, with their own identities, histories, preferences, characteristics, desires, and even physiological profiles, and we approach them with humble curiosity and a desire to understand them accurately. In turn, parts react to this respectful approach the way a person in the external world would: with relief, softening, openness, and a willingness to share and collaborate.

While parts are not states of the nervous system, they do seem to be very much associated with different autonomic states. Specifically, parts seem to "live in" different autonomic realms, experience various autonomic states, and strategically activate states of the nervous system for protective purposes.

Parts That "Live In" the Adaptive Survival States of the Nervous System

Li is a 43-year-old, single, heterosexual, cisgender male client of Chinese descent. He immigrated to the United States from China at age 21, shortly after both his parents died within a year of each other. He is a financial planner who had experienced great professional success early in his career but has endured many professional downturns over the past two decades, to the point where he struggles to keep a stable job and experiences significant financial hardship.

Li is aware of a part of him that holds tremendous rage and is associated with violent thoughts and impulses in his body. He calls this part "The Beast." Li reports that The Beast is constantly "boiling below the surface." When this part is activated by certain stimuli, including noticing other middle-aged men who appear more professionally successful than he is, Li observes that it influences his thoughts, feelings, and the state of his physiology. He finds himself thinking critically of others and wishing that someone would insult or confront him so that he could have "a legitimate reason to punch them." He also notices increased tension in the muscles of his shoulders, arms, chest, and jaw, and sharper, more shallow breathing. Nonetheless, he remains able to avoid confrontations and violence…most of the time.

Deb Dana, an IFS-trained therapist, has observed that parts can "live in" certain states of the autonomic nervous system, such that they cannot fully take over control of the system unless the autonomic state they live in is active in the body (Henriques & Rothman, 2021, 1:03:09). In other words, while this rageful part of Li is always present in his system, and while it can blend to varying degrees and influence his thoughts, feelings, and physiology, it cannot hijack his system and blend to the point of Li acting on violent impulses unless Li's body has entered a state of sympathetic survival.

The adaptive survival state of "fight or flight" is characterized by significant activity in the sympathetic nervous system without sufficient oversight of the ventral vagal pathway of the parasympathetic nervous system. When Li's SNS becomes highly activated, to the point where it is no longer regulated by sufficient ventral activity, he enters this survival state, which involves recruitment of the Hypothalamic-Pituitary-Adrenal (HPA) axis and the release of cortisol and adrenaline in his body. This survival state is also associated with reduced activity in the prefrontal cortex, which means that Li is far less able to access rational cognitive processes than he typically can, nor can he inhibit impulses as effectively. In this physiological survival state, The Beast can hijack Li's system and control his thoughts, feelings, and behavior to a degree that is not possible when Li has a foothold in ventral regulation.

On several occasions, with The Beast powerfully blended, Li has engaged in violent altercations with other men in public places, destroyed his own personal property at home, and injured himself by punching and banging his head against walls. Following these episodes, Li experiences blending by a strong inner critic, who berates him for his "out-of-control" and "insane" behavior. He then slips into a drained, hopeless state, where he despairs that his life situation will ever improve. In this state of dorsal survival, with the dorsal vagal branch of his PNS highly active without sufficient ventral oversight, a part of Li that is also always present beneath the surface, whom he calls, "The Darkness," can take control of his system. With this part, which lives in the dorsal survival state, powerfully influencing his thoughts, emotions, and physiology, Li feels as though the hopelessness and despair will never end.

Parts That Are Experiencing the Adaptive Survival States of the Nervous System

The young child huddles in the corner of her bedroom closet, her tiny body trembling in terror. The walls and floors of her ancient apartment building vibrate with the shock waves from the exploding bombs in the streets outside. She wants to run to her mother, but she can't move.

Susan McConnell, the developer of Somatic IFS, notes that parts seem to have their own bodies (McConnell, 2020, p. 41). As such, they can themselves experience various states of the nervous system, including becoming stuck in the adaptive survival states of fight, flight, freeze, shutdown, or collapse. The exile described here represents a composite of many exiles that clients from war-torn countries have found and healed over the years. These young children, trapped in traumatic scenes from the past, are holding survival energies in their bodies, sometimes for decades, chronically existing in states that their nervous systems had entered in a natural effort to protect them from unimaginable circumstances. Of course, this situation is not only found in survivors of war, but in the systems of survivors of many types of traumas.

This young exile is stuck in the adaptive survival state commonly called "freeze," which involves significant activation of both the SNS and the dorsal vagal pathway of the PNS. Without sufficient ventral activity overseeing the activity of the other branches, the child is flooded with mobilizing energy and is actively terrified, but she is simultaneously overinhibited by the activity of the dorsal vagus and unable to move. She is thus "frozen," or "scared stiff," like the stereotypical "deer in the headlights."

All types of parts—exiles and protectors—can experience the various autonomic states in their own bodies. When these parts blend with us, we embody the physiological profile of the blended part, as though, temporarily, we are living in the part's body. For example, when a young exile stuck in a terrified, immobilized state is close to the surface, we will feel some of its terror and powerlessness in our own bodies to a greater or lesser degree, depending on how strongly the part is blended with us. We may also notice places in our body where the exile's energy is carried, through somatic symptoms such as tension, pain, dizziness, throat constriction, an inability to breathe deeply and freely, or nausea. While parts can influence our physiology in this way, they also appear capable of *strategically* and *deliberately* altering our physiological state when they feel that doing so would be in our best interests.

Parts That Strategically Activate States of the Nervous System

Marie is a 28-year-old, single, White, heterosexual, cisgender female client. She has a history marked by neglect and abandonment, starting before birth, when one of her mothers left her other mother while Marie was still in the womb.

The mother who raised her was often depressed, disconnected, and neglectful. As an adult, Marie finds that whenever a romantic partner seems to be pulling away from her, she becomes highly anxious. She thinks obsessively about her partner, about why he might be distancing himself from her, and about what she might do to bring him back into connection with her. She frantically attempts various strategies, from compulsively exercising and dieting to alter her appearance, to posting pictures on her social media pages showing her having fun with other men, to texting her partner dozens of times a day. At times, Marie's anxiety is so great that she experiences digestive issues and a complete inability to focus on anything but the latest communication from her partner, compulsively analyzing what it might mean.

Through IFS therapy, Marie is able to connect with the part of her that becomes highly active at the slightest hint of abandonment by a romantic partner. As she gets to know this part, it reveals itself to be a protector. The part tells Marie that it is afraid that if it did not flood her with anxiety and make her obsess over ways to make her partner reconnect with her, she would sink into a "very dark place." Curious, Marie asks the protector if it might allow her to see the part it has been protecting. The protector draws back to reveal a much younger part of Marie, a six-year-old girl, lying on the bed in her childhood bedroom. The young girl lies motionless, her vacant eyes staring at the bedroom wall. Marie feels compassion for the girl and gently approaches her, but the girl gives no indication that she notices Marie. Marie sits on the bed, looking down at the girl with softness in her gaze. She sits this way for five minutes, just sending loving energy to the girl through her eyes and through her gentle tone of voice, as she quietly tells her, "I'm here with you. Take all the time you need." Slowly, the girl begins to show signs of life.

As Marie connects with the exile, she can feel some of the girl's energy in her own body. She notices a sinking sensation around her solar plexus as a lethargy spreads through her limbs. She describes the experience as though her "life force" were draining from her body. She lets the girl know that she can sense what she's feeling, and that she's starting to appreciate the depth of her suffering. The girl communicates without words, allowing Marie to witness her experience somatically. Marie is able to stay present to the physical sensations and also to get a sense of the emotions the girl is feeling without being overwhelmed by them. She now understands, on an experiential level, that the girl is profoundly alone, to the point where she feels she has ceased to exist.

In this example, which is representative of the experiences of many clients who have suffered abuse and neglect in early childhood, we see a protector who is strategically using activation of the sympathetic nervous system to keep the client out of a state of profound dorsal collapse. When Marie senses that a romantic partner might be distancing from her, the protector goes into overdrive, bringing mobilizing energy to Marie's body in an attempt to counteract the pull of the dorsal energy held by the exile that has begun to surface. This protector knows that if Marie is, in fact, abandoned again, she will slip into the state of dorsal collapse she experienced so frequently as a child after efforts to draw her mother into connection failed once again. This protector believes that it's safer for Marie to be in a frantic, active state, doing everything she can to avoid abandonment, rather than lost down the deep, dark well of non-existence.

In this example, a protector strategically activates the SNS to mobilize Marie to prevent impending dorsal collapse. In the systems of trauma survivors, we also frequently encounter the opposite scenario, where protectors strategically activate dorsal-associated numbing, shutdown, or collapse in order to "rescue" clients from overwhelming sympathetic activation. Deb Dana notes that people tend to have an autonomic "home away from home," meaning that there seems to be a preference in each person's nervous system for the autonomic state that their system defaults to when it leaves ventral regulation (Dana, 2021). This default may be related to what the person's system learned was a safer state for them to embody at some point in their past. For some systems, it feels safer to be in a state of sympathetic *hyper*arousal, and for others, it feels safer to be in a state of dorsal *hypo*arousal.

In IFS, when we help clients connect with their protective parts, we find that some of these protectors will admit to strategically activating one survival state of the autonomic nervous system in an effort to shift the client away from the other state, or simply because they feel that one of these states would offer protective advantages in a given situation. It is important to note that for many clients with complex trauma, protectors may not consider being in a state of ventral regulation to be safe and may, therefore, activate one of the survival states, such as making them sympathetically hypervigilant, whenever they begin to embody Self. In these systems, access to Self, or ventral, often must proceed drop by drop, with protectors experimenting with allowing only a drop of access to Self-energy at a time, and then noticing how they feel about the experience. In relationship with the therapist, they can share their fears and concerns about allowing access to Self, as well as what they might need in order to feel able to allow another such experiment. Over time and with accumulated positive experience, it feels safer to allow Self to be embodied, so protectors feel less compelled to block access.

Self and the Nervous System

"Self needs to be embodied for its fullest expression…Self-energy is first and foremost experienced in the body." (McConnell, p. 41)

Polyvagal Theory tells us that the adaptive survival states of the autonomic nervous system are incompatible with experiencing an embodied sense of safety. In other words, when our nervous systems have shifted to an adaptive survival state, whether sympathetic hyperarousal, dorsal hypoarousal, or the combination "freeze" state, we are incapable of feeling safe and of effectively engaging socially with others (Dana, 2020). This suggests that sufficient ventral vagal activity in a given moment may be a necessary, if not sufficient, condition for the embodiment of Self.

When Dick Schwartz was developing the IFS model, he noted that certain qualities were consistently experienced by clients when their parts softened back enough to allow access to Self. These qualities include the "8 Cs" of Self-leadership (i.e., calm, courage, clarity, confidence, curiosity, creativity, connectedness, and compassion). A number of these qualities, such as curiosity, compassion, and connectedness, are also qualities that appear to be emergent properties of ventral vagal activity. In other words, activity in the ventral vagal pathway is associated with the spontaneous emergence of these qualities (Dana, 2018; Porges, 2017).

Several IFS experts, including Cece Sykes and Toni Herbine-Blank, have identified "choice" as another quality associated with Self. They note that when clients are Self-led, rather than hijacked by parts, they are capable of exercising discernment and having choice about how they *respond* to situations and stimuli, rather than simply *reacting* automatically (Herbine-Blank, Kerpelman, & Sweezy, 2016). Similarly, Deb Dana describes the therapeutic goal of helping clients view situations through the lens of discernment, which essentially involves them being able to ask themselves the question, "In this moment, with this person, in this place, surrounded by these things, are you actually in danger, or are you safe?" (Dana, 2020, p. 45) The idea that Self may be associated with ventral activity has numerous implications for IFS therapy, some of which are discussed below.

IFS As a Polyvagal-informed Therapy

Dick Schwartz developed IFS over 40 years ago, largely through listening deeply to his clients and learning from them about how their internal systems were organized and how they operated, as well as how he could be a more effective therapist for them. At the time, Polyvagal Theory was not available to the scientific community, nor were numerous other developments in the field of neuroscience that, in recent years, have provided evidence for a scientific basis for psychotherapy. And yet, the theory and protocol that Dick and his colleagues created decades ago contains multiple elements that allow therapists to work sensitively and in concert with clients' nervous systems to maximize the chances that therapy will be effective.

Active and Passive Pathways of the ANS

For any model of psychotherapy to be effective, clients must be able to actively engage with the therapeutic process. The autonomic nervous system contains both active and passive pathways associated with safety and regulation (Porges, 2017). The passive pathways operate outside of conscious awareness and detect cues of safety and danger through neuroception. The body then reacts to these cues with shifts in autonomic state. If cues of danger are detected, the ANS moves to a more-protected state, and if the neuroception is one of safety, the ANS shifts towards a less-protected state that would allow for deliberate engagement of the ventral vagal safety circuit and, therefore, for social engagement. In a more-protected state, the client's capacity for social engagement is restricted, and the active pathways are not available. What this means for us as IFS therapists is that if our clients' bodies shift into protected states during sessions, the clients do not have access to the critical mass of Self needed to effectively connect and work with their parts in that moment, and they will also find it challenging, if not impossible, to actively engage with whatever techniques or interventions we are attempting to implement with them. It also suggests that if we can help our clients gain a foothold in regulation (i.e., access even a "drop" of Self), the work is likely to proceed more smoothly and effectively. Fortunately, IFS offers numerous ways to facilitate this process that are non-exiling, which means that these methods involve welcoming and connecting with parts, rather than bypassing them, suppressing them, or trying to "manage" them into regulation.

Co-Regulation

The Autonomic Nervous System operates on three basic principles: neuroception, hierarchy, and co-regulation (Dana, 2018). Co-regulation involves us engaging in safe connection with another person, where the regulated presence of that person's nervous system helps draw our own nervous system towards regulation. This process of mutual regulation, in which cues of safety are exchanged between nervous systems and social connectedness results, has been described by Stephen Porges and Deb Dana as a "biological imperative," (Dana, 2018; Porges, 2022) which means that human beings do not survive without it. Those that do survive without consistent experiences of co-regulation often struggle to effectively regulate their autonomic nervous systems.

For us to develop the capacity to regulate our autonomic nervous systems effectively, we require many experiences of safe co-regulation that exercise our neural circuits of connection, including the ventral-associated Social Engagement System. Those of us who were fortunate to be raised by present and attuned caregivers, and thus experienced thousands of instances of effective co-regulation during childhood, tend to have "well-tuned" circuits of connection. This allows us to move back quickly and easily towards regulation when we do become dysregulated in the course of daily life. However, for those of us, including our clients, who did not have adequate opportunities to exercise the neural circuits of connection via safe co-regulation, these circuits may not be very well-tuned, and thus we are likely to experience more frequent and severe dysregulation and struggle to return to regulation. If we learn, early in life, that reaching out for connection is futile or dangerous, then we have no choice but to attempt to self-regulate. The problem with this, however, as Deb Dana notes, is that if we turn to self-regulation before our circuits of connection are sufficiently developed, the result is that we self-regulate for survival and protection, rather than for safety and connection (Dana, 2020).

Trauma experts have emphasized that trauma is not *what happened* to a person, but rather the *impact* of the experience on the body (van der Kolk, 2014). Stephen Porges notes that traumatic experience can impact the nervous system by retuning it away from patterns of safety and connection and towards patterns of survival and protection. This means that after a traumatic experience, individuals may find themselves more likely to experience dysregulation and less able to return efficiently to regulation (Porges, 2022). Thus, even individuals who did receive the co-regulation necessary to foster the development of a flexible and resilient nervous system may experience a *retuning* of their nervous systems as a result of trauma, and thus find themselves less able to effectively self-regulate after the traumatic experience.

One of the primary circuits of connection involved in this process is the vagal brake. The vagal brake is not actually a brake (though it functions much like the handbrake on a bicycle), but rather it's a ventral vagal circuit that connects the medulla in the brainstem to the sinoatrial node of the heart, which is the heart's pacemaker. Electrical and neurochemical activity in this circuit can speed up or slow down our heartbeat. When the vagal brake releases, it allows an increased "dose" of sympathetic energy to be available in our systems, energizing us and mobilizing us for the task we are facing in the moment. However, since this is a ventrally regulated circuit, this does not put us into a survival state. Thus, we can enjoy the benefits of increased energy and mobilization to meet the demands of the situation without the pitfalls of dysregulation. Once the increased energy is no longer needed, the vagal brake re-engages, which slows our heartbeat and our body calms. Those individuals with well-tuned vagal brakes are able to transition flexibly between tasks, ramping up their energy when necessary and returning to a less mobilized and calmer state when extra energy is not needed. In those whose neural circuits of connection are not well-tuned or have been retuned as the result of traumatic experience, the vagal brake may be more likely to release completely as the demands of a situation increase, which results in sympathetic energy flooding the system without ventral regulation and the person entering the state of sympathetic survival.

Given the tremendous benefits to mental and physical health of having a well-tuned autonomic nervous system, it is important that therapy contributes to the retuning of our clients' nervous systems towards safety and connection. Stephen Porges describes Polyvagal-informed therapies as therapies in which the neural circuits of connection are exercised and retuned away from survival and protection and towards safety and connection (Porges, 2021). Although not originally designed with this in mind, IFS is, in fact, a model of therapy that provides repeated opportunities, in every session, to exercise the neural circuits of connection and thus reshape the structure and function of clients' autonomic nervous systems. Although it is beyond the scope of this chapter to describe in detail all the ways that IFS provides this neural exercise, I lay out some of the most important below.

IFS Therapy as Neural Exercise

In any psychotherapy, one of the primary channels through which the neural circuits of connection can be exercised is through the client experiencing safe co-regulation with the therapist. If the therapist can be in a regulated state, even when the client is in a state of dysregulation, the cues of safety that the therapist can convey through their tone of voice, facial expressions, posture, gestures, and even their words can have a regulating impact on the client. Geller and Porges (2014) found that if a therapist can enter sessions in a state of regulation themselves, then their regulated presence helps draw the client's nervous system towards regulation regardless of the therapeutic intervention being implemented. This tells us that the state of our nervous system can impact the state of our client's system, and that our regulated presence can contribute directly to clients' learning, in an experiential manner, to regain a foothold in regulation when they become dysregulated. Even engaging in conversation with us on a regular basis contributes to retuning their nervous systems, given that the vagal brake must release somewhat for the client to have the energy to take a speaking turn in the session and must re-engage to allow them to pause their speaking and listen to us. Given that co-regulation with the therapist is a phenomenon found across psychotherapeutic modalities, what specifically does IFS offer that allows us to take advantage of this particular pathway towards healing for our clients?

The Self-Led Presence of the Therapist

IFS has always placed tremendous emphasis on the Self-led presence of the therapist as a crucial determinant of the success of therapy. In fact, Dick Schwartz says, "I've found that the most important variable in how quickly clients can access their Selves is the degree to which I'm Self-led. When I can be present to my clients from the core of my being…it's as if the resonance of my Self were a tuning fork that awakens their own." (Schwartz, 2004) Dick's observation, emerging from thousands of hours of working with clients, has a scientific basis, as Geller and Porges' study suggests. IFS therapists and practitioners are routinely encouraged, in trainings, consultations, and in their personal therapy, to become aware of the parts of them that get activated with clients, to practice unblending from these parts to access Self-energy, and to befriend and heal these parts, such that they can be available to their clients in an increasingly Self-led way. Polyvagal Theory suggests that this practice is important for two reasons: 1) the regulated presence of the therapist's nervous system draws the client's system into regulation, or in Dick's words, "Self begets Self," and 2) the dysregulated presence of the client or therapist can draw the nervous system of the other into dysregulation. As our clients are frequently dysregulated in sessions, especially in the beginning stages of therapy, or may become dysregulated as they approach parts that are experiencing or using survival states in the body, the ability of the therapist to maintain regulation in their own autonomic nervous system is crucial for the effectiveness of the therapy. As discussed previously, if the passive pathways of the client's nervous system are saying "no," the client will not be able to engage the active pathways.

Internal Co-Regulation

While co-regulation with the therapist is common across psychotherapies, IFS offers another related and extremely powerful way to exercise the neural circuits of connection, one that becomes increasingly available to most clients as therapy proceeds. I have come to call this process, "internal co-regulation." Parts work in IFS can proceed through two modalities, direct access and in-sight. Direct access involves the therapist's Self interacting directly with a blended part of the client, while in-sight involves the Self of the client coming into direct, internal connection with a part of them and forming a Self-to-part relationship.

When clients do in-sight work and are connecting directly with a part of them from Self, they are engaging in internal co-regulation. The target part, who may be experiencing or in other ways associated with dysregulated states of the nervous system, is able to sense the ventrally regulated presence of the client's Self. This draws the part's nervous system towards regulation, much the same way that the regulated presence of a therapist shifts the system of a client towards regulation. This internal co-regulation process can involve the part merely sensing the energy of Self, which in itself can be powerfully regulating, and it can include additional channels of co-regulation, such as the part looking in the client's eyes, hearing their warm tone of voice, or feeling their loving touch.

Through the various practices incorporated into Susan McConnell's somatic approach to IFS, parts can co-regulate with, and be witnessed by, Self on a somatic level. These practices, including somatic awareness, conscious breathing, radical resonance, mindful movement, and attuned touch, allow the client's Self to understand, on an emotional and physical level, what the part is holding and what it has experienced, and allow the part to experience this witnessing and connection. It is important to note that when implemented from Self, the various methods of internal co-regulation included in the IFS model are neither exiling nor bypassing. Though these methods often have the impact of downregulating protective responses in the nervous system of the part, and thus of the client, this comes about naturally through the co-regulation process and the part feeling accompanied and witnessed and understood, not through the client "making the part calm down" or calming the body such that the part, and what it's holding, are no longer accessible. In fact, sometimes "leaning in" to the symptoms of dysregulation by letting the part know that we are noticing and feeling the sensations they are holding in their stomach, or the tension in their muscles, or their inability to take a full breath, or the pressure in their chest, can help the part know they are not alone in their suffering and that someone is finally here to witness and help them release what they have been carrying.

The benefits of internal co-regulation are numerous. One of the primary benefits is that internal co-regulation allows for continuous practice, both in and between sessions, exercising and tuning the neural circuits of connection. Each time we guide a client to connect internally with a part of them, these circuits are being exercised and strengthened. For example, as a client approaches a sympathetically hyperaroused part, such as a highly vigilant protector or a terrified exile, the vagal brake releases somewhat, allowing increased sympathetic energy to flow throughout the body. As the client connects to this part from even a drop of Self-energy, which is accompanied by ventral activation, the vagal brake re-engages and downregulates the sympathetic responses. This releasing and re-engaging process can happen multiple times in an episode of internal co-regulation with a part.

Another significant benefit of internal co-regulation is that it does not depend on the presence of another person and can thus be instantly implemented as needed. While external co-regulation is extremely important and beneficial, the reality for most of us is that we may not always have a safe person to co-regulate with "on call" 24 hours a day. Even for those fortunate to have close relationships with Self-led others, these others have their own systems and schedules and will not always be available when our parts become activated and could benefit from co-regulation. As clients become more capable of connecting with their parts internally, this channel of co-regulation and of exercising and strengthening the neural circuits of connection becomes available to them more often.

Co-Regulation Through Direct Access

As Self-to-part connection requires, by definition, that the client have access to at least a "critical mass" of Self, defined as at least some curiosity toward the part, there are times when clients cannot do in-sight work. For some clients, such as those with dissociative identity disorder (DID), access to Self may not be possible in the beginning stages of therapy. For others whose protectors do grant occasional, or even frequent, access to Self, there may be times when direct access is necessary, such as when a part is intensely activated and refuses to unblend or when the target part does not trust the therapist, trust Self, or believe that Self exists. There are other times when direct access may not technically be "necessary," in the sense that unblending could be achieved in that moment, but where it is preferred and advantageous for at least a few moments if not more, such as when a part feels it would be more thoroughly understood if it could be embodied and speak directly through the client.

The Self-led presence of the therapist is co-regulating whether we are working through direct access or in-sight, but it has a special function in direct access. Specifically, when a client is blended with a part, and thus embodying the part's energy and speaking directly to the therapist from that part, the therapist's ability to hold Self-energy provides co-regulation specifically *for this part*. This is important because for many clients the parts of them that hold or utilize survival energies in the body have not been welcomed, nor been found to be tolerable, by the people in their lives. These parts have been experienced as "too much," as their energy has been activating for parts of others' systems, as well as for other parts of their own systems, and they have, therefore, been interpersonally and intrapersonally rejected and exiled. Therefore, it is possible that these parts have never had the opportunity to experience co-regulation with anyone, even if other parts of the client (e.g., those that are "calmer," or more socially acceptable) have experienced frequent co-regulation. The therapist's ability to unblend from the parts of them that are reactive to the energy of the client's blended part and, therefore, to hold space for that part from Self as the part shows up "in all its glory" can allow this part to finally feel fully and deeply seen, held, and understood. This has the impact of helping the part shift from a dysregulated state to its own regulated state, thus bringing regulation to the body without having exiled the part.

Resistance

Resistance is a commonly observed phenomenon in any form of psychotherapy, including IFS. In various ways, clients indicate that they are uncomfortable with some aspect of the therapeutic process, with the physical environment in which the session is occurring, or with the therapist, and on some level, they push back against the therapeutic agenda. In IFS, we conceptualize resistance as the activity of protective parts whose job is to keep the system safe from perceived threats. Therefore, we understand that if we are seeing resistance in a session, some part or parts of our client are objecting to what is happening in the moment or to what they are afraid might happen if the work proceeds, and they are attempting to protect the client by blocking engagement with the work.

Since our parts live in our bodies, they are intimately tied into our nervous systems, and are thus aware of, and impacted by, the autonomic shifts we experience. From a Polyvagal-informed perspective, therefore, one of the primary reasons we observe resistance in therapy is if protective parts sense that whatever we are doing in the moment, or whatever is beginning to stir within the client, is either dysregulating or has the potential to dysregulate the client's nervous system. One way this phenomenon might unfold in session can be illustrated like this: a) a client and therapist are working with a target part, b) the client begins to sense exile activation under the surface, c) the quality of the energy the exile is carrying is neurocepted by the client's ANS and interpreted as a cue of danger originating within the body, d) the client's nervous system begins to shift towards dysregulation, e) the protector takes some action to derail the work in an attempt to maintain a foothold in regulation.

When this type of pattern occurs, the therapist may notice some of the following common protector strategies: a) the client suddenly "pops out" of internal connection with the target part and begins to narrate, or tell a story, directly to the therapist, b) the client begins thinking about, or analyzing, the situation or the target part, c) the client suddenly experiences numbing throughout their body, d) the client shuts down and becomes non-responsive or starts replying, "I don't know," to every question, e) the client loses concentration. While these are only a few examples of the many strategies protectors can use to interrupt the therapeutic process, the underlying motivation is generally the same: something is happening in the moment in the client's body (or has the potential to happen soon, if the process is allowed to continue) that is uncomfortable and feels unsafe, and the protector aims to counteract or prevent this.

Ironically, the activity of these protectors, who carry the intention of *preventing* dysregulation, often shifts the system *toward* dysregulation, as the client can become either sympathetically hyperaroused or dorsally hypoaroused by the energy and/or strategies of the protectors themselves. At other times, the strategies the protectors use can have a regulating effect on the body, but at the expense of Self-to-part connection with the activated parts. For example, an analytical part can blend and begin intellectually considering and listing the various reasons the exile might be distressed, but as the analytical part has now obscured the client's Self, the exile will not experience a connection with Self nor have the opportunity to be deeply understood in the way it needs to be in that moment.

Appreciating that dysregulation, or the threat of impending dysregulation, is one of the primary motivators for protectors' resisting the therapy process, helps inform our approach to this phenomenon in IFS sessions. In short, if you see resistance, think dysregulation, and take the necessary steps to help re-anchor the client's body in regulation so protectors will sense that it's safe enough to allow the work to proceed.

When protectors have blended to resist or derail the therapeutic work, IFS offers multiple methods to help shift clients' nervous systems back towards regulation, or, in IFS terms, to regain access to at least a critical mass of Self-energy such that both the target part(s) *and* the resisting protectors can experience

Self-to-part connection. One powerful and effective option is to turn toward the protector that is in some way resisting the work and allow it to share its concerns. Often, this involves the use of the "constraint question," "What are you afraid might happen if you didn't make me foggy right now and let me stay connected to this other part?" Many times, the answer to this question points either to an exile (e.g., "You'd be overwhelmed with terror") or to a polarized protector (e.g., "If I don't make you foggy, you're going to start craving alcohol").

We can consider the benefits of listening to and addressing protectors' concerns from both an IFS and a Polyvagal perspective. From an IFS perspective, when we turn toward protectors and listen to and honestly address their concerns about allowing the work to proceed, we are being sensitive and respectful to the inner ecology of the client. Rather than attempting to plow ahead with our therapeutic agenda, we are appreciating that there is an internal culture, and that the citizens of this internal society have preferences, customs, and concerns that deserve consideration. This is a respectful practice, but it also allows the work to be informed by the wisdom held in the client's system that is based on life experience and knowledge of how the client's nervous system and parts tend to react. Welcoming these protectors and their concerns can help inform the direction of the therapy such that, at times, "resistant" protectors can be a therapist's best friend in terms of making the work safer and more effective for a particular client's system.

From a Polyvagal perspective, when we are encountering resistance, it suggests that the client's nervous system may have neurocepted a cue of danger from the external environment (e.g., objects, scents, or sounds inside or outside the therapy room), from us (e.g., something about our energy or behavior, something we said, the intervention we are attempting), or from something inside the client (e.g., a body sensation, the energy of an emerging exile or protector, a thought or memory), and the client's body has started to shift towards dysregulation. As the client shifts to a dysregulated state, they become less able to socially engage, which means they cannot experience Self-to-part connection. By pausing and turning towards these activated protectors with curiosity and openness, and by asking any parts of us with an agenda to soften back such that their energy is not communicated to and, therefore, impacting the client's nervous system, we are implementing an intervention that can bring a sense of safety to the client's body. The message, from an IFS perspective, is, "We're not going to blow past you or make you do anything that doesn't feel okay to you. We're just going to slow down and stay with you for as long as you need us to so that we can understand your concerns."

As the "resistant" protectors are attended to and their concerns addressed, they are often able to soften within moments and allow the work with other parts to proceed. At other times, however, protectors do not feel ready to open space to allow work with other parts to occur, but as the body's defenses are down-regulated, these protectors feel able to relax enough that the client can form a Self-to-part relationship with them, or so that the therapist can form a relationship with them through direct access. In any of these scenarios, the client is experiencing practice shifting from a more dysregulated to a less dysregulated state, and even shifting from dysregulation to regulation. Deb Dana has described the state of the nervous system as "the air all the parts are breathing or the water they're all swimming in" (Henriques & Shull, 2020, 20:57). As the body becomes more regulated, protectors begin to experience an embodied sense of safety, which can either allow them to continue to connect with, and be understood by, the therapist through direct access, or allow for in-sight work, up to and including the deep healing of exiles.

Anchoring in Self

"Trauma victims cannot recover until they become familiar with and befriend the sensations in their bodies." —Bessel A. van der Kolk

An understanding of the basic principles of Polyvagal Theory can offer IFS therapists and practitioners a neurobiological explanation for why certain aspects of the IFS protocol can be vital to the success of the therapeutic process. As such, it can help us appreciate the importance of not bypassing these steps, nor implementing them in a cursory manner (i.e., just moving through them or "checking them off"), and of why we may need to circle back to steps of the process we have already implemented in a particular session.

Once a client has identified a "target part" for a particular session, we begin by having them locate, if possible, the energy of the part in or around their bodies and notice how the part is manifesting. We invite them to notice channels of communication, including body sensations, thoughts, emotions, images, memories, and energies. As the client notices and describes how the part is presenting in that moment, we receive clues regarding the current state of the client's nervous system. We might hear descriptions consistent with sympathetic energy, such as tension, agitation, GI distress, hypervigilance, fear, anger, or a desire to move or escape, or with dorsal energy, such as fogginess, "floatiness," numbing, or lack of energy, motivation, or hope. Whether or not the client can offer verbal descriptions, we can observe signs that suggest sympathetic and/or dorsal activity through the client's nonverbal behaviors (e.g., facial expressions, posture, gestures, vocal prosody). Deb Dana explains that whenever we are interacting with another person, our nervous systems are having a "conversation," with each one influencing the state of the other (Dana, 2021). As we become more attuned to our own autonomic nervous systems we can notice, in our own bodies, the real-time impact of interacting with the client's nervous system, as we may experience a pull towards sympathetic or dorsal states in our own bodies while we are in the client's presence. This is a valuable channel of information for appreciating the current state of a client's system and for identifying trailheads in our own system.

Bessel van der Kolk (2014) cites the importance of trauma survivors befriending the various sensations in their bodies, many of which can be associated with traumatic experience. Polyvagal Theory suggests that it is safe for clients to work with, or "befriend," the various survival states in their nervous system if they have at least an anchor or foothold in ventral regulation (Dana, 2020). But how do we know whether they have that anchor in a given moment?

Perhaps the most valuable question in the IFS protocol involves asking the client how they *feel toward* the target part. From an IFS perspective, the answer to this question lets us know whether the client has access to at least a "critical mass" of Self, defined as feeling at least curiosity towards the target part. If the client does have some access to Self, we can proceed to help them befriend, or form a Self-to-part relationship with, the target part. With this anchor in Self, which involves ventral activity, the client is able to interact safely with parts that are "living in," experiencing, and/or strategically using survival states of the nervous system without being pulled into dysregulation. It thus allows clients to witness even their worst traumatic experiences from a compassionate place that can bring healing to their systems.

Gaining access to Self in a given session is not a one-time event. A client may access Self in one moment, only to approach a part associated with dorsal energy and be pulled towards dorsal survival in the next. They may be experiencing a compassion-filled Self-to-part connection with one protector, only to have another protector become alarmed at the presence of Self-energy in the system and shift them into an agitated, sympathetically charged state. If we stay attuned to the subtle (or not-so-subtle) shifts in our client's physiological state, indicated not only by their nonverbal behaviors but also by what we are hearing them say, which can indicate what their parts are feeling or are concerned about, we know when we need to circle back and help them re-anchor in Self. IFS offers numerous ways to do this re-anchoring, including inviting activated parts to soften back and open space for the client's Self to remain with the target part, contracting with parts not to overwhelm, co-regulating internally with activated parts, addressing parts' fears and concerns through in-sight or direct access, or allowing the client to co-regulate directly with the therapist, using the regulation of the therapist's nervous system to bring some ventral activation to their own. If done in an attuned manner with attention to moment-to-moment shifts in the client's physiological state, IFS therapy can safely provide neural challenge to the client's nervous system, allowing clients to repeatedly exercise the neural circuits of connection and to learn, experientially, how to shift between dysregulated and regulated states in the nervous system.

Expanding Access to Self-energy in the System

Deb Dana discusses the importance of expanding access to ventral energy in the nervous system "from a glimmer to a glow" (Dana, 2020). Similarly, in IFS, we seek to expand access to Self-energy in the system from a drop, which may be all that is permitted by protectors at first, to a wave that flows freely throughout the system and bathes all of the parts. We achieve this expansion of Self-energy in numerous ways, including through the befriending process, where clients extend the curiosity, tenderness, compassion, warmth, or openness they are feeling toward the target part and notice how the part is responding to their presence and energy. As the bidirectional relationship between the part and the Self develops, and the part feels increasingly understood, accompanied, and cared for, the body shifts towards safety and regulation, and protectors feel able to allow more access to Self-energy in the system.

Sometimes, this work flows without the need for therapists to comment on the fact that this access is happening. At other times, however, it is important to bring clients' attention to these moments when even a drop of Self is accessed. This can include sessions with clients whose parts don't believe Self exists, or who don't know what Self-energy feels like in their bodies. For these clients, it can be important for therapists to gently bring the client's attention to the experience as it is happening, to help the client understand, on an experiential as well as a cognitive level, what Self is like and that they are capable of accessing it. Being aware, in the moment, of the embodied experience of Self can also help clients more easily return to this state in the future. In other words, once they know where "home" is, it becomes easier for them to find it again.

Many IFS therapists and practitioners are under the impression that unless they are healing and unburdening exiles in a given session, they are not doing the "healing" work. From a nervous system perspective, this is not true. Polyvagal Theory suggests that any time we are exercising the neural circuits of connection—through internal or external co-regulation, through conversation, through accessing even a drop of Self/ventral energy, and through expanding access to this energy from a glimmer to a glow—we are helping to heal the nervous system, in that we are retuning it towards safety and connection. Communicating this information to the parts of us that are committed to bringing healing to our client's systems, and that may, therefore, have an agenda towards aiming at exile work, can help these parts to relax back. This allows for increased access to Self in the therapist's system, which allows for improved attunement with the client, and allows the work to unfold at the pace that is right for the client's system. This means that the work can unfold at the pace that allows the client to maintain, or more easily regain, a foothold in regulation when their nervous system shifts towards dysregulation and protection. While we always hold the hope that we will be able to facilitate the healing of exiles, as this greatly improves protectors' ability to release themselves from extreme roles, we understand that as long as we are working in concert with the client's nervous system, we are doing healing work no matter what part we are working with.

Conclusion

Polyvagal Theory helps us understand what happens on a biological level when we are autonomically regulated and feeling safe, with the ability to connect to ourselves and others, versus biologically dysregulated and stuck in adaptive survival states, feeling unsafe and self-protective. Decades before Polyvagal Theory was introduced to the scientific community, providing a neuroscientific explanation for some of the observed phenomena in IFS, IFS was already offering a compassionate, non-pathologizing, highly relational approach for helping to shift clients towards safety and connection and away from survival and protection. Through expanding access to Self in the system, healing our traumatized and burdened parts, forming respectful, collaborative relationships with our protectors, and helping protectors release themselves from extreme roles, we reach a new level of internal homeostasis, one grounded in regulation, or Self-leadership. We are then able to carry this way of being out into the world, where our regulated, Self-led presence positively influences the systems of those around us, contributing to the regulation and embodied sense of safety of our partners, friends, children, and even strangers. Deb Dana states, "If we each are a regulated and regulating force in the world, we will change the world one autonomic nervous system at a time" (Dana, 2020, p. 177). IFS offers us a powerful and beautiful way to realize this vision, one which is as healing to us as it is to our clients.

KEY TAKEAWAYS

- The state of the therapist's nervous system impacts the state of the client's nervous system, and vice versa. Working with our parts to allow increased access to Self-energy in the face of client dysregulation can help us embody a regulating presence that will facilitate the therapy process in every moment of our sessions.
- Visiting and befriending the survival states of the nervous system is safe and possible with an anchor in Self/ventral. Attending to the moment-to-moment shifts in client's nervous systems can alert us to when re-anchoring (unblending) is necessary to keep the work safe and/or to improve the chances of success.
- IFS provides numerous opportunities to exercise the neural circuits of connection to retune them towards safety and connection.

- Internal co-regulation, achieved through in-sight work, can provide clients with a method of exercising the neural circuits of connection that is always available to them.
- Direct access can provide co-regulation for a part associated with survival energies that may never have had the opportunity to be received in a co-regulating relationship.
- If you see resistance, think dysregulation and, using non-exiling techniques, help re-anchor the client's nervous system in a state of safety to allow them to engage with the therapy.
- Take advantage of opportunities to expand access to Self, or ventral, from "a glimmer to a glow."
- Any time we help a client access even a drop of Self, or ventral, or help them move from more-dysregulated to less-dysregulated states, we are doing healing work, regardless of the specific part we are working with.
- It is important to remember that we are not aiming to "regulate" parts, as this can contribute to therapists operating from a managerial place, attending vigilantly to the state of the client's nervous system in order to keep it within a narrow "window of tolerance." Through the respectful, compassionate, and collaborative approach IFS offers to working with parts associated with dysregulation in the nervous system, parts will naturally shift towards their own regulated states, thus contributing to regulation throughout the client's body.

AUTHOR BIO

Alexia Rothman, PhD (she/her) is a clinical psychologist in private practice in Atlanta, GA, since 2004. She is a Certified Internal Family Systems therapist, an international speaker and educator on the IFS model, an IFSI Assistant Trainer, and an IFSI-approved professional consultant for clinicians seeking to deepen their knowledge and practice of IFS. She co-hosts the IFS-informed podcast miniseries, *Explorations in Psychotherapy,* and the IFS podcast, *IFS Masters.* Dr. Rothman is a United States Presidential Scholar who graduated *summa cum laude* from Emory University as a Robert W. Woodruff Scholar. She received her PhD in Clinical Psychology from the University of California, Los Angeles (UCLA), where she was an Edwin W. Pauley Fellow and a National Science Foundation Graduate Research Fellow. She has held adjunct faculty positions at Emory University and Agnes Scott College.

REVIEWER BIOS

Richard Schwartz, PhD (he/him) is the creator of Internal Family Systems, a highly effective, evidence-based therapeutic model that de-pathologizes the multipart personality. His IFS Institute offers training for professionals and the general public. He is currently on the faculty of Harvard Medical School, and has published five books, including *No Bad Parts: Healing Trauma and Restoring Wholeness with the Internal Family Systems Model.* Dick lives with his wife, Jeanne, near Chicago, close to his three daughters and his growing number of grandchildren.

Deborah A. Dana, LCSW (she/her) is a clinician, consultant, author, and speaker specializing in complex trauma. Her work is focused on using the lens of Polyvagal Theory to understand and resolve the impact of trauma in our lives. She lectures internationally on the ways Polyvagal Theory informs clinical interactions with trauma survivors, and she works with organizations wanting to bring a polyvagal-informed approach to working with clients. Deb is the developer of the Rhythm of Regulation Clinical Training Series. She is trained in Internal Family Systems and Sensorimotor Psychotherapy and has completed the certificate program in Traumatic Stress Studies at the Trauma Center.

REFERENCES

Anderson, F. G. (2021). *Transcending trauma: Healing complex PTSD with Internal Family Systems therapy.* PESI Publishing.

Cozolino, L. (2017). *The neuroscience of psychotherapy: Healing the social brain* (3rd ed.). W W Norton and Co.

Dana, D. (2021). *Anchored: How to befriend your nervous system using polyvagal theory.* Sounds True.

Dana, D. (2020). *Polyvagal exercises for safety and connection: 50 client-centered practices.* W. W. Norton and Co.

Dana, D. (2018). *The polyvagal theory in therapy: Engaging the rhythm of regulation.* W W Norton and Co.

Ecker, B., Ticic, R., & Hulley, L. (2012). *Unlocking the emotional brain: Eliminating symptoms at their roots using memory reconsolidation.* Routledge.

Geller, S. M., & Porges, S. W. (2014). Therapeutic presence: Neurophysiological mechanisms mediating feeling safe in therapeutic relationships. *Journal of Psychotherapy Integration, 24*(3), 178–192.

Henriques, A., & Rothman, A. (Hosts). (2021, August 5). Reshaping the nervous system and integration with IFS. (No. 8) [Audio podcast episode]. In *Explorations in Psychotherapy.* Portuguese Society for Constructivist

Psychotherapies. www.podcasts.apple.com/us/podcast/reshaping-the-nervous-system-and-integration-with/id1490941234?i=1000531068926.

Henriques, A., & Shull, T. (Hosts.). (2020, July 25). Polyvagal meets IFS: A talk with Deb Dana. (No. 25) [Audio podcast episode]. In *IFS Talks*. Portuguese Society for Constructivist Psychotherapies. www.podcasts.apple.com/pt/podcast/polyvagal-meets-ifs-a-talk-with-deb-dana/id1481000501?i=1000486160028.

Herbine-Blank, T., Kerpelman D., & Sweezy, M. (2016). *Intimacy from the inside out: Courage and compassion in couple therapy.* Routledge.

McConnell, S. (2020). *Somatic Internal Family Systems therapy: Awareness, breath, resonance, movement, and touch in practice.* North Atlantic Books.

Mones, A. G. (2022). *The essence of healing: A quest for a metamodel of the psychotherapy of trauma.* Stoelting.

Porges, S. W. (2022). Polyvagal theory: A science of safety. *Frontiers in Integrative Neuroscience.* 16:871227. www.doi.org/10.3389/fnint.2022.871227

Porges, S. W. (2021). *Clinical applications of polyvagal theory in trauma treatment with Stephen Porges and Deb Dana: Integrating the science of safety, trust, self-regulation and attachment.* PESI. www.catalog.pesi.com/item/clinical-applications-polyvagal-theory-trauma-treatment-stephen-porges-deb-dana-integrating-science-safety-trust-selfregulation-attachment-51529

Porges, S. W. (2017). Vagal pathways: Portals to compassion. In E. M. Seppälä, E. Simon-Thomas, S. L. Brown, M. C. Worline, C. D. Cameron, & J. R. Doty (Eds.), *The Oxford handbook of compassion science* (pp. 189-202). Oxford University Press.

Porges, S. W., & Dana, D. (Eds.). (2018). *Clinical applications of the polyvagal theory: The emergence of polyvagal-informed therapies.* W. W. Norton and Co.

Schwartz, R. C. (2021). *No bad parts: Healing trauma and restoring wholeness with the Internal Family Systems model.* Sounds True.

Schwartz, R. C. (2004). The larger self. *Psychotherapy Networker,* May/June 2004, 36-43.

Schwartz, R. C. (1995). *Internal Family Systems therapy.* Guilford Press.

Schwartz, R. C., & Sweezy, M. (2020). *Internal Family Systems therapy* (2nd ed.). Guilford Press.

Van der Kolk, B. A. (2014). *The body keeps the score: Brain, mind and body in the healing of trauma.* Viking Press.

GOING DEEPER

From Dr. Alexia Rothman

1) Website:
   a. www.dralexiarothman.com

2) Podcasts:
   a. *Explorations in Psychotherapy: An Internal Family Systems Therapy Podcast* Aníbal Henriques and Alexia Rothman, PhD (Hosts) www.podcasts.apple.com/us/podcast/explorations-in-psychotherapy/id1490941234
   b. *IFS Masters: An Internal Family Systems Podcast* Alexia Rothman, PhD and Aníbal Henriques (Hosts) www.podcasts.apple.com/us/podcast/ifs-masters/id1663565953
   c. *IFS Talks: The Therapeutic Dose of Empathy in IFS, with Alexia Rothman* www.podcasts.apple.com/ie/podcast/the-therapeutic-dose-of-empathy-in-ifs-with-alexia-rothman/id1481000501?i=1000510894440

3) Trainings, Retreats and Consultation Groups:
   a. Synchronous and On-Demand: www.dralexiarothman.com

4) Publications:
   a. www.dralexiarothman.com/#optinfooter. A modified version of this chapter will appear in Alexia Rothman's book on IFS and Polyvagal Theory, forthcoming from W. W. Norton and Company, Inc. Please subscribe to Dr. Rothman's website to be notified of the publication date.

From Dr. Richard Schwartz

1) Websites:
   a. IFS Institute: www.IFS-Institute.com
   b. Foundation for Self Leadership: www.foundationifs.org

2) Books:
   a. Schwartz, R. C., & Sweezy, M. (2020). *Internal Family Systems therapy* (2nd ed.). Guilford Press.
   b. Anderson, F. G., Sweezy, M., & Schwartz, R. C. (2017). *Internal Family Systems skills training manual: Trauma-informed treatment for anxiety, depression, PTSD and substance abuse.* PESI Publishing.
   c. Schwartz, R. C. (2008). *You are the one you've been waiting for: Bringing courageous love to intimate relationships.* Trailheads Publications, The Center for Self Leadership.

d. Schwartz, R. C. (2001). *Introduction to the Internal Family Systems model.* Trailheads Publications, The Center for Self Leadership.
   e. Goulding, R. A., & Schwartz, R. C. (2002). *The mosaic mind: Empowering the tormented selves of child abuse survivors.* Trailheads Publications, The Center for Self Leadership.
   f. Schwartz, R. C., & Falconer, R. R. (2017). *Many minds, one self: Evidence for a radical shift in paradigm.* Trailheads.
   g. McConnell, S., & Schwartz, R. C. (2020). *Somatic Internal Family Systems therapy: Awareness, breath, resonance, movement, and touch in practice* (1st ed.). North Atlantic Books.
   h. Sykes, C., Sweezy, M., & Schwartz, R. C. (2023). *Treating addictive processes with Internal Family Systems therapy: A compassionate and effective approach for helping people who soothe or distract with substances, food, gambling, pornography, and more.*

You can find the books listed above and many more here: IFS Bibliography and Research: www.ifs-institute.com/resources/research/ifs-bibliography-apa-style

3) IFS Trainings:
   a. IFS Institute Trainings: www.ifs-institute.com/trainings
   b. IFS UK Trainings: www.internalfamilysystemstraining.co.uk/training/ifs-training/
   c. IFS Portugal Trainings: www.internalfamilysystems.pt/
   d. IFS France Trainings: www.ifs-association.com/formations-ifs-internal-family-systems/
   e. IFS Australia Trainings: www.internalfamilysystemstrainingaustralia.com.au/training/
   f. IFS Barcelona Trainings: www.institutoifs.com/formacion-de-profundizacion/
   g. IFS Israel Trainings: www.ifs-israel.org/
   h. IFS South Korea Trainings: www.training.psychologykorea.com/ifs
   i. IFS Russia Trainings: www.ifs-russia.ru/
   j. Life Architect Trainings: www.lifearchitect.com/ifs-bali-retreat/

4) Other:
   a. Online Workshops/Videos:
      i. IFS Institute: www.ifs-institute.com/resources/videos
      ii. IFS Online Circle and Continuity Program: www.courses.ifs-institute.com
      iii. PESI: www.catalog.pesi.com/category/ifsinternal-family-systems

From Deb Dana

1) Website:
   a. www.rhythmofregulation.com
2) Podcasts:
   a. *Explorations in Psychotherapy: Reshaping the nervous system and integration with IFS* (a conversation with Aníbal Henriques and Alexia Rothman) www.dralexiarothman.com/reshaping-the-nervous-system-and-integration-with-ifs
   b. *IFS Talks: Polyvagal meets IFS: A talk with Deb Dana* (a conversation with Aníbal Henriques and Tisha Shull) www.podcasts.apple.com/pt/podcast/polyvagal-meets-ifs-a-talk-with-deb-dana/id1481000501?i=1000486160028
   c. Additional Podcasts: Conversations with Deb www.rhythmofregulation.com/conversations-with-deb
3) Trainings:
   a. www.rhythmofregulation.com/training
4) Publications:
   a. Dana, D. (2021). *Anchored: How to befriend your nervous system using polyvagal theory.* Sounds True.
   b. Dana, D. (2020). *Polyvagal exercises for safety and connection: 50 client-centered practices.* W. W. Norton and Co.
   c. Dana, D. (2018). *The polyvagal theory in therapy: Engaging the rhythm of regulation.* W. W. Norton and Co.
   d. Porges, S. W., & Dana, D. (Eds.). (2018). *Clinical applications of the polyvagal theory: The emergence of polyvagal-informed therapies.* W. W. Norton and Co.

From Other Sources on Polyvagal Theory

1) Websites:
   a. Dr. Stephen Porges: www.stephenporges.com
   b. Polyvagal Institute: www.polyvagalinstitute.org
   c. Unyte: www.integratedlistening.com/products/ssp-safe-sound-protocol
   d. Kinsey Institute Traumatic Stress Research Consortium (KI-TSRC): www.kinseyinstitute.org/research/traumatic-stress.php

2) Podcasts:
   a. www.polyvagalinstitute.org/pv-podcasts-videos

3) Trainings:
   a. www.polyvagalinstitute.org/courses-1

4) Publications:
   a. Porges, S. W. (2021). *Polyvagal safety: Attachment, communication and self-regulation.* W. W. Norton and Co.
   b. Porges, S. W. (2017). *The pocket guide to the polyvagal theory: The transformative power of feeling safe.* W. W. Norton and Co.
   c. Porges, S. W. (2011). *The polyvagal theory: Neurophysiological foundations of emotions, attachment, communication, and self-regulation.* W. W. Norton and Co.

IFS AND EMDR

TRANSFORMING TRAUMATIC MEMORIES AND PROVIDING RELATIONAL REPAIR WITH SELF

Daphne Fatter, PhD

Eye Movement Desensitization and Reprocessing (EMDR) and Internal Family Systems (IFS) are both robust, evidenced-based models that, when used skillfully together, can provide deep transformation for clients while supporting relational repair between Self and parts. In this chapter, the models' shared principles and differing approaches to healing will be described. This chapter will discuss ways to integrate IFS into the eight phases of the EMDR protocol as well as options to integrate EMDR into the IFS steps. Examples of interventions will be used to demonstrate the various ways to integrate these two models. It is important to note that practitioners should have at least EMDR basic training before using the EMDR protocol, and at least IFS Level 1 training, before using the IFS model to work with exiles.

I want to acknowledge Dr. Kendhal Hart for her contributions as noted throughout this chapter. As clinicians trained in both EMDR and IFS, Dr. Hart and I together bring decades of experience using these modalities to assist clients who are dealing with, for example, complex trauma, combat trauma, sexual trauma, addiction, obsessions, and anxiety.

Model Integration: Shared Trust in Clients' Capacity to Heal

Both EMDR and IFS share an intrinsic trust in the client's organic capacity to heal. EMDR posits that the adaptive information-processing system (AIP) naturally exists in all of us. It is the guiding neurophysiological premise of EMDR.[1] EMDR approaches healing by using BLS to jump start the AIP in the client's brain in order to reprocess traumatic memories. In EMDR, the memory's negative images, cognitions, emotions, and body sensations are integrated with existing adaptive neural memory networks in the brain, so that the traumatic memories are no longer disturbing.[2]

IFS posits that Self-energy (one's compassionate core essence which is undamaged by trauma) naturally exists within us all. The underlying premise in IFS is multiplicity: the psyche is divided into parts, which become burdened, isolated from Self, and stuck in extreme roles, when trauma occurs. IFS helps guide the client to embody their own Self-energy in order to relationally repair with parts, release their burdens, become unstuck from the past, and freely choose their role in the system. When the internal network of parts release the burdens they carry, parts no longer hold the negative images, cognitions, emotions, and body sensations from traumatic memories.[3]

While each model's approach to healing is vastly different, both EMDR and IFS utilize the brain's memory reconsolidation processes to help reorganize the client's system.[4] In EMDR, the traumatic memory is reorganized in the brain such that the client can relate to the memory with flexibility, choice, and a positive and/or more adaptive view.[5] In IFS, the exile(s) and protector(s) connected to the traumatic memory are befriended, witnessed, and unburdened such that the client's system is reorganized so that Self is the leader eliciting choice, flexibility, and the client's innate wisdom.[6]

Selecting Interventions: Integration or Single-Model Approach[7]

Clinicians can choose how much to integrate these two models based on clients' systems, clinical need, and treatment goals. There are some specific situations that clinically warrant using one model over the other (i.e., a "pure" use of the model without integrating the two) as follows:

When to Use "Pure" IFS

Pure IFS may be beneficial in the following scenarios:

- Clients who present with very complex trauma, dissociative parts, heavily burdened protector parts, or heavily burdened exiles that flood in overwhelming ways. Spending as much time as necessary to befriend the client's protective system is critical before the system will allow for exile unburdening and/or before considering EMDR as a treatment option.
- Clients with ambivalence about target processing. This is often evidence of protector activity that IFS techniques (such as the Six Fs or working with polarizations) are ideally suited to address.

When to Use "Pure" EMDR

Pure EMDR may be beneficial in the following scenarios:

- Clients with previous successful EMDR experience.

- Clients who want to focus on single-incident trauma processing with otherwise stable inner systems and no history of complex or developmental trauma.
- Clients who have an adverse or unfavorable response to the concept of parts.
- Acute loss and/or recent traumatic event.

Integrating IFS into the EMDR Eight-Phase Protocol

IFS can enhance each phase of the eight-phase model of EMDR which has been proposed to be particularly effective in treating clients with complex trauma.[8] Integrating IFS provides a consent-based, parts'-honoring relational approach to EMDR while still maintaining fidelity to the EMDR phase protocol. As such, the eight phases of the EMDR protocol will be discussed, applying an IFS lens and IFS interventions to each EMDR Phase.

The following chart illustrates IFS steps that can be integrated into each of the EMDR phases:[9]

EMDR Eight-Phase Protocol	IFS Steps
Phase 1: History taking, treatment planning, & consent for treatment plan	Assessing external constraints, tracking sequences, parts mapping, contracting for treatment plan and experiential IFS.
Phase 2: Preparation & resource development	Using the 6 Fs to befriend managers and firefighters and obtain permission from protective system. Relational repair between Self and protective parts. Befriending Exile.
Phase Three: Assessment	Accessing and activation of Exile.
Phase 4: Desensitization	Witnessing the target exile, do-over, retrieval, unburdening.
Phase 5: Installation	Invitation of positive qualities.
Phase 6: Body scan, future template	Assessing for further unburdening needed to release somatic burdens carried by target exile(s).
Phase 7: Closure	Integration. Appreciation to protectors, invitation to witness unburdened exile, invitation for protector unburdening.
Phase 8: Reevaluation	Checking in with parts.

EMDR Phase One: History Taking and Treatment Planning

While EMDR utilizes a more traditional therapeutic history-taking process, both models initially focus on creating a sense of safety, developing trust and rapport, assessing external constraints (including high-risk behavior), and tracking sequencing. A major conceptual difference between EMDR and IFS is that IFS approaches symptoms through a lens of multiplicity and non-pathology. In integrating IFS into Phase One of EMDR, clinicians can conceptualize the client's clinical presentation as well-intentioned burdened parts trying to help the client in the only ways they know how.

By viewing a client's symptomology through a parts lens, clinicians can approach clients from a Self-led relational stance and provide a treatment plan integrating EMDR and IFS that honors the complexity of the client's system. As such, clinicians can adapt their language in gathering client history by using non-pathologizing parts language, such that any presenting clinical issue is reflected back to the client as a "part" (e.g., "A part of you that feels depressed"; "a part of you that is anxious"). Reflecting parts language back to the client is often met with relief as parts of the client feel seen and heard by the therapist, which builds trust and safety in the therapeutic relationship.

IFS's approach to treatment planning follows the sequence of parts that naturally emerge regarding the presenting clinical issues, befriending protectors and exiles alike. In pure IFS, establishing the therapeutic relationship, assessing external constraints, and assessing high-risk behavior, is done by befriending protectors (both managers and firefighters). There is no formal means for history-taking in pure IFS. After gathering information about the presenting clinical issue, the therapist befriends protectors connected to the presenting clinical issue using the Six Fs which elicits appropriate pacing in the client's system to ultimately obtain protectors permission to work with the exile(s) they are protecting (which then in turn is a potential "target" for Phase Four EMDR processing). As needed, the client's Self can ask the target exile to not overwhelm the system, which further restores trust between parts and Self and creates a sense of safety in the client's system to proceed with witnessing the target exile (which is done through Phase Four in EMDR when integrating these two models).

Identify EMDR Treatment Targets Through Parts Mapping

Therapists can accomplish EMDR phase one goals of history-taking, case conceptualization, and treatment planning, while using the IFS technique of parts-mapping to learn about the client's internal system.[10] Parts-mapping is a visual representation of how parts exist in relation to one another. The parts map continues to grow, change, and develop over time. Therapists can do parts-mapping visually as an actual picture to share with the client or simply as part of clinical notes as therapy progresses. Parts-mapping can also occur as an ongoing homework assignment for clients who might add to their map after each session.[11]

Through parts-mapping, both the therapist and the client can identify sequences of parts' activation in the client's system. This tracking of patterns within the client's system is ideally done in session with therapist and client working together to identify patterns of parts that may be connected, building rapport within the therapeutic relationship, and beginning to contract regarding an overall treatment plan.[12]

From an EMDR lens, parts-mapping allows therapists to track potential EMDR targets by identifying sequences and themes relating to negative cognitions (NCs), emotions, and body sensations for treatment planning purposes. Traditional EMDR uses these NCs and other sensory information to find target memories needing reprocessing in Phases Three and Four.[13]

From an IFS lens, parts-mapping helps both the therapist and client identify protective parts early in therapy. Instead of using the traditional EMDR approach of following the NC to find a target, the therapist can begin contracting with the client to shift to do experiential IFS with the protectors identified in the parts map.

Assessing the Client's Window of Tolerance

An essential concept in EMDR is the "window of tolerance" which describes the nervous system state in which a client has affect tolerance and can function most effectively.[14] IFS evaluates a client's window of tolerance by assessing:

- How much Self-energy can a client access when a part is activated?
- Can a client befriend a part when guided by the therapist (e.g., Is there 'enough' Self-energy for a client to be in Self and access a part at the same time)?
- How easily can the client unblend from an activated part?
- If the client has difficulty unblending, or accessing Self, can the client receive the support of Self-energy from the therapist when needed?
- What parts naturally emerge in between sessions during Phase One? Can the client befriend these parts when the therapist uses the Six Fs?
- How do the client's parts respond to contracting to do EMDR as part of treatment?
- How does the client respond if parts get extremely activated in between sessions?

Answering these questions and/or understanding the landscape of the client's internal system may not be possible until Phase Two when actual befriending of protective parts occurs. It is important to note that parts-mapping often is a bridge to move towards experiential IFS by guiding the client to befriend protector parts identified on the parts map which are connected to the presenting clinical issue.

Contracting with the client and their parts in Phase One includes receiving consent to proceed with the treatment plan and treatment goals. In integrating IFS, this involves asking the client if any parts have fears or concerns about getting to know parts identified in the parts map. This is essentially contracting to shift to experiential IFS to elicit relational connection between the client's Self and parts and befriend protectors to receive their consent.

EMDR Phase Two: Preparation and Relational Connection

In this phase, clinicians are further educating the client about the EMDR process and preparing the client for what to expect in Phases Three and Four.[15] From an EMDR lens, the client learns and practices using resources to support emotion regulation. From an IFS lens, Phase Two is a rich opportunity to elicit relational repair between protector parts and Self, obtaining parts' consent to proceed with EMDR, and beginning to befriend the target exile that will be witnessed and unburdened during Phase Four.

Widening the Window of Tolerance by Unblending from Parts

In Phase One, therapists are assessing a client's window of tolerance to consider the appropriateness of EMDR treatment.[16] In Phase Two, therapists widen the window of tolerance by helping clients unblend from parts and begin Self-to-part relationships using the Six Fs. In IFS language, blending occurs when the client speaks *from* the part instead of *for* the part (i.e., the part takes over the client's system so that accessing Self-energy may be challenging).

When clients are within their window of tolerance, or unblended from parts, they can access Self-energy and readily receive, process, and integrate information even when stressors occur. When clients leave their window of tolerance, from an IFS lens, they are flooded by a part, often a firefighter, which blends with the client in an attempt to decrease an exile's pain from being felt in the system.

As the client increases their access to Self-energy by unblending from parts using the Six Fs (i.e. the IFS intervention to Find, Focus, Flesh Out, Feel towards, Fears, and BeFriend) to befriend activated protector parts, their window of tolerance will naturally widen and parts will blend less frequently because parts will begin to restore their trust in the client's Self. Widening the window (i.e. the client unblending from parts to access Self) translates to more space for safe exposure to material held by burdened exiles.

Using STARR™ Self-Tapping for Attachment Readiness and Repair

Using IFS during Phase Two while guiding the client to unblend and experientially befriend protector parts is the ideal way to ensure client readiness for Phases Three and Four. Using the Six Fs in IFS can lead to the protectors directly giving permission to have Self befriend the exile. Sometimes protectors may initially have difficulty taking in the presence of Self.

I have created STARR™, Self-Tapping for Attachment Readiness and Repair. Using BLS through slow self-tapping initiates an attachment repair process between Self and the IFS target part. In essence, during STARR™, Self is tending to receptivity from the target part by inviting the target part to receive Self presence through slow self-tapping.

Self-tapping is a form of BLS in EMDR known to be cross-culturally well-received,[17] which can be used for resourcing.[18] Self-tapping, traditionally used in Phase Four, is referred to as the Butterfly Hug, during which clients cross their hands with palms facing the chest and interlock the thumbs and then place their open hands on their chest in the shape of a butterfly.[19] STARR™ uses this same form of self-tapping BLS and harnesses it for a natural "call and response" form of communication from Self to the target part. The client uses STARR™ for 20 seconds or less during which both the client and therapist are quiet. Then the client pauses the self-tapping to see how the target part is responding to receiving the slow self-tapping as an initial form of communication from Self.

STARR™ is a multi-sensory option for the target part to initially receive Self-energy from the client. The target part can hear, feel the vibrations, and sense the rhythm of the slow self-tapping. STARR™ integrates the benefits of slow BLS from EMDR and the intention in IFS to retore trust in Self, repairing attachment ruptures between the target part and Self. STARR™ also integrates the shared principle of both EMDR and IFS in that STARR™ trusts the client's ability to know what they need to facilitate healing within their own system. Thus, since the client self-administers the slow BLS, the client decides the pace and weight (i.e., how soft or heavy the tapping is) and the wisdom and sovereignty of the client is respected. STARR™ can be used with protectors and with exiles as follows:

Example of STARR™ with One Protector

Client: "I sense this part in my shoulders, but it doesn't know I'm here."

Therapist: "How do you feel towards it right now?"

Client: "I want to get to know it, and I feel compassion for it, but it just doesn't know I'm here." (The therapist may utilize pure IFS befriending techniques first, and if the part still isn't responding, then can try STARR™).

Therapist: "Okay, let's try using slow tapping to send the part the message you just shared, that you are right here with it, feel compassion towards it, and want to get to know it. Just invite the part to take in the rhythm, the sound, and the vibration of the tapping."

(The client uses STARR™ for 20 seconds or less)

Client: "The part likes the tapping. It's able to feel the tapping, and it's surprised I'm here."

(The therapist can return to befriending by asking the parts its fears using the Six Fs.) Thus, STARR™ can be a means of extending Self-energy to the part in a way that the part can likely receive it.

Example of STARR™ with a Blended Dissociative Firefighter

In IFS, clinical dissociation may be a firefighter part presenting as a "shut down" or "foggy" part.

Client: "I am suddenly feeling foggy."

Therapist: "Okay, let's invite in curiosity about this part. Where are you noticing it in and around your body?"

Client: "I can't tell."

Therapist: "Okay, let's let this foggy part know that you are aware it's here right now. Would that be okay?" (Therapist uses STARR™ and teaches client slow self-tapping)

Client: "Yes." (Client does STARR™ for 20 seconds or less).

Therapist: "What are you experiencing now?"

Client: "The part is still here, but now it's on my right side."

Therapist: "Great, let it know that you are right here with it and are aware it just gave you more space. See how it's responding to you getting that."

(Client does another set of STARR™ for 20 seconds or less.)

Client: "This part really likes to be acknowledged. It's not used to me being here."

Therapist: "And how do you feel towards it right now?" (Therapist can then resume IFS befriending this dissociative firefighter.)

Example of STARR™ using IFS Implicit Direct Access

Sometimes there may be a group of protectors that work together to keep the client blended. That could make it challenging for the client to initially unblend and befriend each one. In IFS, the Self-energy of the therapist may initially be used as Self-energy for both therapist and client. In these clinical situations, the therapist can use direct access (i.e. the therapist speaks directly to the part of the client with client's permission) or implicit direct access (the therapist speaks directly to the client's part without explicitly naming that they are speaking to a part).[20] When a client is blended with a group of protectors, STARR™ can be used to initially invite the blended parts to receive connection from the therapist's Self-energy. In using implicit direct access, initial connection through STARR™ is between the client's parts and the therapist's Self. Then, when more unblending naturally occurs, STARR™ can be used to help parts receive connection and awareness that both the client and the therapist are here with these parts, shifting ultimately to Self-to-part relationship between the client's Self and the target part. For example:

> **Therapist:** "I'm aware that these groups of protector parts are working so hard and seem close to you, am I getting that right?"
>
> **Client:** "Yes, I'm working so hard." (Client speaking from the blended part).
>
> (The therapist can try pure IFS unblending techniques to help these group of parts unblend or use STARR™ to help with unblending.)
>
> **Therapist:** "Can you hear me really acknowledge you and your hard work right now?" (Therapist speaking directly to the hard working part using implicit direct access.)
>
> **Client:** "Yes, I know you are here. It feels good to be acknowledged."
>
> **Therapist:** "Okay, great. Take in this appreciation and acknowledgement from me." (Client uses STARR™ for 20 seconds or less.)
>
> **Therapist:** "What are you experiencing?"
>
> **Client:** "I feel a shift. There are lots of parts working so hard. They can feel the tapping and hear you acknowledge them."
>
> **Therapist:** "Can they hear you sharing that right now?"
>
> **Client:** "No."
>
> **Therapist:** "Okay, let them know that you get that they are noticing me right now as you do the slow tapping." (Client uses STARR™ for 20 seconds or less.)
>
> **Client:** "Yes, they are getting that."
>
> **Therapist:** "Great. Continue the slow tapping, and let's ask them to just receive the tapping knowing that both you and I are here with them." (Client uses STARR™ for 20 seconds or less.)
>
> **Client:** "Yes, they are taking that in and noticing me now."
>
> **Therapist:** "Great. How do you feel towards them right now?"

Client: "So appreciative. They have worked so hard for so long."

Therapist: "Invite them to take your appreciation in as you tap." (Client uses STARR™ for 20 seconds or less). (Since this signifies a shift to a Self-to-part relationship between the client's Self and the target parts, the therapist then can return to IFS for befriending.)

Example of STARR™ in Polarizations

STARR™ can also be used in polarizations, when two or more protector parts are in a power struggle and likely have no awareness of Self. EMDR's "two-handed interweave" can especially be helpful here, using STARR™ to invite in the polarized parts to take in Self-energy.

For example, if pure IFS techniques are not shifting the system, a therapist can use STARR™:

- "Let's try slow tapping, letting these parts know that you are here with both of them right now."
- After a set of STARR™, the therapist can offer: "Invite these two parts to turn towards you, really taking your presence in so they both know you are with them right now."
- After a set of STARR™, assuming the polarized parts took in client's Self presence, then the therapist can proceed with pure IFS in working with polarizations.

Example of STARR™ with the Target Exile

Once protector parts give Self permission to befriend the target exile for EMDR processing, STARR™ can be a helpful option in addition to pure IFS to befriend exiles. STARR™, as a means for exiles to initially receive contact and connection with Self, is particularly helpful when the target exile for EMDR processing is young and/or overwhelmed by its burden, and has difficulty taking in the presence of Self. Particularly for prenatal and preverbal parts, slow tapping can mimic the rhythm of a heartbeat, a familiar anchor and means to help the exile orient themselves relationally, bridging a connection between Self and exile. For example:

Therapist: "Okay, so you can see the baby part, but they don't know you can see them, am I getting that right?"

Client: "Yes."

Therapist: "How do you feel towards them right now?"

Client: "Very loving and tender."

Therapist: "Okay great, let's have you share that with the baby through slow tapping. Would you like to try that?" (Therapist utilizes STARR™)

Client: "Yes!" (Client uses STARR™ for 20 seconds or less).

Therapist: "What are you experiencing now?"

Client: "She is just starting to receive it."

Therapist: "Great. Share the tapping and your love with her."

Client: "She likes that."

It is important to note that STARR™ is for harnessing connection. It is not the same as fast BLS during the trauma processing Phase 4. STARR™ is used to help parts unblend and to help parts receive initial connection with Self. STARR™ is done briefly in session a few sets at a time to facilitate connection, not to make parts "go away." STARR™ enables parts to receptively take in Self presence through the rhythm, the vibration, and the sound of the slow tapping, which can help parts begin to access Self-energy. Once the part can take in the presence of Self-energy, the therapist can resume standard IFS befriending to attend to relational ruptures between the part and Self prior to moving to Phases Three and Four.

Proactively Befriend Protectors

IFS can enhance the EMDR protocol by ensuring that protective parts of the client's system give their full consent to do EMDR and witness exiles in Phase Four.[21] This is one of the key benefits of integrating IFS in EMDR, as receiving consent from the client's protective system minimizes blocking or interruption in Phase Four, as well as adverse reactions after a session.[22] Traditional EMDR protocols are designed to access implicit memory, which often bypasses the protective system.[23] This can lead to what in IFS is called "backlash" in which, after an exile is accessed, activated, and witnessed without consent of the protective system, protector parts blend to protect it in the ways they know how.[24] This typically results in an escalation of mental health symptoms such as suicidality or increased substance use and de-stabilization (due to a hierarchy of firefighter parts becoming activated.[25]

Reconceptualize Blocking Beliefs as Protector Fears[26]

In traditional EMDR, the therapist identifies blocking beliefs during Phase Two. IFS allows clinicians to enhance their conceptual understanding of what is happening when a "blocking belief" or "blocked processing" emerges in session. From an EMDR framework, the term "blocking belief" is a firmly held, distorted belief developed by the client in response to life experiences. From an IFS perspective, blocking beliefs are fears held by well-intentioned protector parts triggered by exile activation. Utilizing the Six Fs of IFS, the therapist can guide the client to befriend the protectors holding "blocking beliefs," ultimately obtaining their permission to proceed with EMDR and befriend and witness the target exile.[27]

Befriend the Target Exile After Overtly Gaining Permission from Protectors

After obtaining consent from the protectors, Self begins to befriend the target exile. When the target exile is ready to be witnessed, after Self has developed a trusting relationship with the exile, the client can proceed to Phase Three.

The client checks in at the beginning of each subsequent session to ensure protectors continue to consent to the client's Self reconnecting with the exile to proceed with processing in Phase Four. The therapist can prompt the client to "take a moment, go inside, and check in with any protective parts that may have concerns about witnessing this experience."[28] The therapist guides the client to befriend any protectors' fears and find out what their concerns are and what they need to move forward, only proceeding when all protector concerns are fully addressed and protectors fully consent.

Honoring The Differing Approaches to Emotion Regulation

Befriending managers and firefighters and asking the target exile not to overwhelm the system is part of contracting and befriending parts to prepare for EMDR. This is the IFS approach to navigating "emotion regulation." It is important to note that emotion regulation, from an IFS perspective, means having all of the protector parts and the exile(s) they are protecting consent to collaborate so the system is not overwhelmed, which happens after trust in Self is restored. This includes asking the target exile to move at a pace in which the connection between Self and exile is not lost, so that the exile can be fully witnessed and can unburden in Phase Four. Befriending the target exile during Phase Two helps prevent exile flooding the system before Self is sufficiently present.

It is important to note that the IFS approach to regulating emotion differs greatly from EMDR. EMDR traditionally uses relaxation, grounding, and containment-oriented techniques to "install" resources for emotion regulation. While these techniques and practices from Phase Two in pure EMDR can access Self-energy in some clients' systems, the process of resource installation may feel forceful to others. For example, installing a sense of quiet, calm, and safety can be perceived as threatening to a protective system which has worked hard to stay busy and distracted, triggering protector parts who may feel bypassed. Integrating IFS in Phases One and Two can help ensure protector parts are not bypassed when the target exile is accessed and witnessed in Phases Three and Four. IFS fosters relational connection, repair, and trusting relationships between protector parts and the client's Self.

Container and Safe Place Shifts to Connection with Self and Retrieval

A container visualization is used during Phase Two in EMDR to help clients hold traumatic content in an imagined container between sessions. EMDR's container visualization originated from the treatment of clients with Dissociative Identity Disorder (DID) to elicit voluntary dissociation of traumatic memories that were not completely processed in therapy.[29] IFS does not ask parts to go into a container. At the end of an incomplete EMDR session (i.e., the target exile in Phase Four is not yet complete in their witnessing and unburdening process), retrieval helps the exile reconnect with Self and choose where they would like to be between sessions. The target exile can leave the traumatic memory they are in at the end of the EMDR session and choose to be with Self any place in the present day that feels safe and restful for the exile. Thus, the continued relationship between Self and the target exile is the relational container that serves as the foundation to return to at the end of the session.

In pure EMDR a "safe place" visualization is also used as a resource at the end of an incomplete EMDR session. Integrating IFS, the exile decides where they would like to be between sessions via retrieval. This can be a real place such as the client's backyard or living room so that the exile can continue to be updated about the client's current life and Self-energy. It can also be imaginal (such as a spa at the top of a mountain protected by trees), and the exile can bring in additional relational resources such as familiar items from the therapist's office, an imaginal pet, or other comforting objects and people. The exile always has access to Self in this safe retrieval space.

A Meeting Place for Protectors[30]

When the client's Self befriends protector parts prior to accessing the target exile, clients can choose a meeting place for protectors to hear each other and connect with Self. Known in IFS as the "conference room" technique, this meeting place is particularly helpful for clients when there are polarized protectors.[31] Therapists can invite clients to choose a location that communicates every protector has an equal seat at the table so that Self, as the leader, can respond to any concerns. Inviting protectors to meet with Self at a conference room table, a round table, or any other meeting place creates neutral territory for protectors. Practicing this regularly creates a familiarity for protector parts and continues to restore trust in Self as the leader of the system.[32] Once the target exile has been befriended by Self, it can be helpful to further check in with the group of protectors that have already given Self permission prior to proceeding to Phase Three.

Example of Getting Protectors' Consent[33]

Therapist: "Take a moment, go inside, and invite all the protective parts that protect this (target) exile to join you at the conference table. Invite these protectors to take in your presence as you sit at the table with them. Invite them to notice that you have connected with this exile and the exile is developing a trusting relationship with Self. Check in with them to see if any protectors want to speak for concerns they might have, knowing that Self will be witnessing this exile's lived experience in the next phase of EMDR therapy."

When IFS is integrated into Phases One and Two, clients benefit from stabilization because parts experience repaired relational ruptures and restored trust between protector parts and Self.

EMDR Phase Three: Assessment and Accessing the Traumatic Memory Network of the Exile

Phase Three activates all aspects of the target traumatic memory network, including the images, related cognitions, emotions, and body sensations. From an IFS lens, this is accessing the traumatic memory network of the exile's lived experiences, including the pain and visceral sensory experience of the burden(s) the target exile is carrying. During Phase Three, the therapist intentionally activates the traumatic memory network of the exile, which intentionally activates the exile's system in order to immediately move to Phase Four, where trauma processing occurs. During Phase Three, the target exile can be at various degrees of blending with the client.

Differing Strategies to Access the Traumatic Memory Network

In pure EMDR, therapists identify potential EMDR targets by identifying negative cognitions, feeling states, and body sensations, and the first, worst, or most recent associated traumatic memory. IFS recognizes this can override and bypass the protective system of the client,[34] which can potentially lead to decompensation in between sessions. As mentioned in Phase Two, an IFS-aligned approach to accessing the traumatic memory network is to befriend the protectors first, getting their consent to befriend the exile(s) they protect, and when the exile is ready, to ask Phase Three questions regarding the exile's worst traumatic memory.

In addition, the therapist can invite protector parts to observe the exile being witnessed during Phase Four trauma processing, which is consistent with recommended protocols for complex trauma.[35] For instance, a therapist can say, "As we prepare to start reprocessing this memory, can you check in with any of your parts that may wish to observe this?"[36]

Modifying Phase Three—Drop the PC and Be Flexible with Getting SUD Rating

In pure EMDR, the client is asked for a positive cognition (PC) (e.g., "What would you like to believe instead of the negative cognition?") and to rate how much they believe the PC as they look at the traumatic scene. From an IFS lens, we can invite curiosity about which part is answering this question (i.e., is the PC coming from the target exile?). In my experience, the part answering this question is likely not the target exile, resulting in disconnection between Self and the target exile. Parts may feel confused and disoriented by this question. Alternatively, when integrating IFS, the therapist does not ask the client to identify or rate the PC, which is consistent with current trends in EMDR that acknowledge that asking the client to switch to verbalizing and ranking takes them out of the traumatic activation.[37] While some target exiles may be able to give an overall SUD (i.e., "How disturbing is this on a scale of 1-10?"), it is important for the therapist to be flexible with the SUD if the exile is unable to articulate it once its ready to share the traumatic memory. From a traditional EMDR lens, the SUDs rating elicits a baseline for tracking progress which helps us ensure goal completion of a target. From an IFS lens, the target exile may not be able to quantify the trauma's impact before it has been witnessed. In addition, in IFS, the therapist and client can both trust the client's system to be able to qualitatively (rather than solely quantitatively) identify progress and shifts in the target exile.

Examples of Options During Phase Three

Dr. Hart proposes that the therapist can say: "Take a moment, go inside, and find the part of you that believes [NC]. Notice how it manifests through emotions, bodily sensations, or thoughts. Hold all those components together and follow my fingers." [BLS]

Or, alternatively,

Dr. Fatter proposes that the therapist can say: "Now that this part (the target exile) is ready to share what it's experienced, what image represents the worst part of the burden it's carrying? What beliefs or burdens (i.e., NC) does the part carry as it shows you this memory? What emotions does that part feel inside with this burden? Where does the part feel that in their body? How much charge is the part feeling right now: big, medium, or small? (i.e., SUDs). Ask the part to be with you as it shares these images, burdens, feelings, and body sensations, and follow my fingers." [BLS]

EMDR Phase Four: Desensitization is Witnessing and Unburdening Exiles

In this section, we will discuss Phase Four and an IFS perspective on why EMDR trauma processing might become stuck. In addition, multiple choices for integrating IFS with interweaves for protector parts and exiles will be provided, along with examples.

During Phase 4, trauma processing occurs. From an EMDR lens, the client is reprocessing traumatic memories using BLS, so that any negative images, cognitions, emotions, and body sensations become integrated with adaptive neural networks, which create more flexible and adaptive thinking, feeling, and behavior. From an IFS lens, the target exile (and associated parts that share the same burden), are being witnessed by Self. The healing steps of IFS including witnessing, do-over, retrieval, and unburdening often occur spontaneously throughout Phase Four of EMDR when using the traditional EMDR protocol or EMDR protocols that allow for unrestricted processing.

As such, during Phase Four, multiple parts can be witnessed, and it is realistic that a different part may speak after each set of BLS. The therapist can trust that the client's system knows what it needs for healing in that EMDR Phase Four processing will elicit whatever specific traumatic memories need to be connected to more adaptive neural networks and whatever sequence of parts need to be witnessed for unburdening and healing.

Once the SUDS (i.e., the level of disturbance of on a scale of 1-10) has decreased as low as it is naturally going to go, the therapist can prompt the client to ask if there is anything else the target part wants to share with the client and then add BLS. The therapist may need to repeat this question multiple times to encourage the part to continue sharing until it experiences complete witnessing.[38]

Choice of EMDR Protocol Determines Range of Accessed Parts

The range of parts that can be accessed during Phase Four will depend on which EMDR protocol is used for Phase Four Processing. For example, if the target exile is focusing on a legacy burden[39]—a burden handed down intergenerationally from family or ancestors—a legacy-attuned protocol can be used in EMDR.[40] From an IFS perspective, parts (both exiles and protectors) carrying burdens handed down by family of origin, parts carrying burdens connected to loyalty to family and family narratives, and parts carrying burdens related to the lived experiences of the client's ancestors are likely to emerge during Phase Four processing.

Stuck or Blocked Processing

Through EMDR Phase Four, the client's system will process as it needs to without therapist involvement. Following EMDR protocol, the clinician only offers an interweave (an intervention to help the client continue trauma processing) when the client gets stuck in traumatic material. From an IFS lens, an interweave can help elicit a Self-to-part connection to enable the client to continue Phase Four trauma processing.

Per EMDR protocol,[41] stuck or blocked processing presents in many ways. Some examples are:[42]

- Reporting "nothing" is coming to them after a set of BLS.
- Looping reporting of information (i.e. responses not changing).

- An inability to integrate healthy and adaptive information despite multiple Phase Four sessions.
- Stuck at the same SUD (i.e., level of disturbance) for an extended period.
- Repeating positive statements without evidence of symptom change.

From an IFS lens when a client is stuck in EMDR, it often means:[43]

- The client lost their Self-to-part relationship.
- There is significant blending with the target part or another part.
- A protective part is uncomfortable with the process and has stepped in.

There are various options for navigating blocked or stuck processing, and the best choice depends on the client's system. The most common interventions are listed here and will be described in more detail with examples.[44]

- Invite in curiosity and explore the block: What part needs attention? Ask the part about its fears or concerns. Unless this protector consents, the therapist does not move forward with BLS or Phase Four.
- Respect that a protector is showing up for a reason. Sometimes, the protector part may need to become the target part. Shift target parts and allow a protector to process briefly.
- Use interweaves for exile(s) including offering do-over, retrieval, and unburdening, or shift to pure IFS to guide the client through the IFS healing steps.
- When the Self-to-part relationship is lost, take the client back to the target memory.
- Use IFS to help the client reconnect with Self and invite Self to provide interweaves.
- Take a SUD (i.e., "On a scale of 1-10, how disturbing it this now?") and identify the part(s) still holding material.
- Reduce the use of cognitive interweaves to avoid inviting cognitive protectors.

Explore the Block and Befriend the Part by Shifting to the Six Fs

When shifting to the Six Fs, EMDR Phase Four processing is paused, and the therapist guides the client to befriend the "blocking" protector. In integrating an IFS lens, the therapist respects that a part is emerging within the client's system for a reason that needs to be tended to, rather than pathologizing the client's process. The therapist invites the client to acknowledge the original target exile to avoid the part feeling abandoned in the middle of Phase Four. The therapist can explain as needed why the focus is switching to address the protector's concerns. Once the fears of the protector are understood by the Self of the client using the Six

Fs, the client asks the protector consent to resume Phase Four processing with the target exile. The therapist then asks the client (in connection with the target exile) to return to the target memory.

In addition, the client can ask the part to step back and give space as needed.[45] This is particularly effective when the therapist and client have shared language to refer to the familiar protector parts related to the target exile.

Examples of asking part to give client space[46]

The therapist might say:

"I am noticing that your thinker part is here again, and I am wondering if you can ask it to give you a little space to continue working with the sad part?" [BLS]

"Notice that distractor part and ask if it can step back and give you a little space to continue doing this work." [BLS]

"Notice that foggy part and ask if it can step back and give you a little space to continue working with this wounded part." [BLS]

In addition, contracting with the target exile to help protectors step back may be needed:

Example of contracting with exile and asking the protector to step back[47]

A "blanking out" or "foggy" part shows up during Phase Four of EMDR, causing the client to lose or be distracted from what they were processing. The therapist might acknowledge the fear of overwhelm, for example, and have the client ask the exile, or target part, to let the information out less intensely. Then, the therapist might ask if this "foggy" part is willing to give some space. "If it thinks you will get overwhelmed again, it can step back in and let us know." The client then is invited to send appreciation and acknowledge protectors when they agree to step back.

If the Protector Doesn't Step Back, Its Burdened Belief Becomes a New Target

Another option involves overt pausing of Phase Four processing, exploring the "blocking belief" held by this part, and then setting it up as its own EMDR target. This option is particularly useful if the protector part does not step back or needs to be further witnessed by Self. Once the client has permission from this part, the fear and burden of this protector part can become the new target for Phase Four EMDR. The therapist will assist the client in identifying a memory related to the burden of this protector part (i.e., the negative cognition that is blocking Phase Four processing). For example, the therapist can ask "When is the first time you remember feeling, thinking, or believing that about yourself?" Then, begin Phase Three with this memory and belief as the target.[48]

Interweaves for Exiles: Retrieval and Do-Over

The retrieval and do-over are transformational IFS steps that can be implemented during Phase Four to help with stuck processing and/or to enhance relational repair between exile(s) and Self. Through these interventions, the therapist invites the client's Self to help free the exile from being stuck in the past, as needed, and offers it an opportunity to have a relational corrective experience. If the part is stuck in the past during processing and not naturally leaving the traumatic scene (i.e., an indicator that the trauma processing is stuck), the therapist can ask: "What does the exile need to happen in the past before it can leave the traumatic scene?"[49]

Sometimes an additional burden is revealed that is preventing the exile from feeling ready to leave the traumatic scene (e.g., a burden of responsibility to a sibling or parent in the scene). When an additional burden is revealed, Phase 4 processing can continue focused on this aspect of the burden.

The do-over, or corrective experience, occurs when the client's Self enters the memory and is with the part in the way it needed a loving and caring adult at the time of trauma. Oftentimes, the client updates the exile with any relevant information about the client's life in the present day. During the do-over, the therapist supports the client in being with the exile from their Self-energy and meets the exile's relational, developmental, and safety needs in the traumatic scene. This "interweave" process can occur with ongoing or intermittent slow BLS administered between parts interweaves and prompts. The therapist can use STARR™ if connection is lost between Self and the target exile. If the target exile knows Self is there, then the therapist can use slow BLS with any form of BLS that client prefers (e.g., with a BLS tapper device, eye movements, or self-tapping) since this is more of a relationally resourcing and reparative experience between Self and exile than reprocessing of material.

Example of Do-Over and Retrieval[50]

Therapist: "Can you ask the part if it feels stuck in the past?"

Client: "Yes, it feels like it is stuck back with my dad, and the part is scared."

Therapist: "Will you ask the part if it is ready to come to the present, or if it needs something to happen before it is ready to do that?" [Slow BLS]

Therapist: "What are you noticing?"

Client: "He says he wants to leave that time and place, but he's worried about leaving his brother behind."

Therapist: "Can you show the part that your brother is an adult and does not need you to care for him in the same way?" [Slow BLS]

OR

"Can you imagine the part bringing your brother with you into the present?" [Slow BLS]

Therapist: "What are you noticing?"

Client: "I showed him where and who my brother is today, and he was surprised to see that."

Therapist: "Notice that." [Slow BLS]

Client: "He feels relieved that my brother is safe."

Therapist: "Can you check in with that part again and see if he is ready to come to the present now, or if he needs anything else to happen before he is ready to do that?" [Slow BLS]

Therapist: "What are you noticing?"

Client: "He wants to leave, but he just feels so much sadness that my dad was never there for us."

Therapist: "Can you see if it feels right for your Self to go into that scene with this part and be there for him in the way he needed someone back then?"

Client: "Yes, I can try that." [Slow BLS]

Therapist: "What are you noticing?"

Client: "My Self put his arms around me and was just there with me. He told me that I am okay and that he's got me now. The part is ready to come up and be with me now."

Therapist: "Can you invite the part to leave that scene with you bringing that part up to be with you in present day?" [Slow BLS]

Therapist: "What are you noticing?"

Client: "I have him here with me. I'm showing him my current life and all the positive things I have going on. All the love and acceptance I have from people around me."

Therapist: "Notice that." [Slow BLS]

Unburdening

Phase Four often naturally facilitates the unburdening process. This interweave also works exceptionally well as an alternative to standard Phase Four processing when the client's SUD gets to a low number after some work in Phase Four. The unburdening interweave process should occur with ongoing or intermittent BLS administered between parts interweaves or prompts, as in the example illustrated below.[51]

Example Outline of the Unburdening Script[52]

- "Can you ask the part where it carries the burden in or around it's body?"
- Can you ask the part, "Are you ready to unload it?"
- If the parts says yes: "Can you ask the part how it wants to unload it?" The therapist may need to make suggestions such as "You can unload it to the light (water, fire, earth, wind)."
- "Can you invite the part to take the burden out of its body in the way that feels right, and let us know when that feels complete?"
- Check in by asking, "Is there more?" until the part acknowledges completion.

Example of Unburdening When SUD is Low[53]

Typically, the client has engaged in several EMDR Phase Four sessions and presents to the session reporting symptom reduction. The therapist prompts the client to rate their SUD, suspecting they are nearing the end of this target. In this example scenario, the client reports their SUD is a two. The therapist walks them through EMDR Phase Three and begins Phase Four. This script outlines how the therapist can walk the client through an unburdening:

Therapist: "Can you take a moment, go inside, and locate where this burden/wound is in or around your body?" [BLS]

Therapist: "What are you noticing?"

Client: "I still feel some of it in the pit of my stomach. It's a lot better than it has been, but every time I think about it, I still feel it there."

Therapist: "Check in with your parts [or body or Self] and see if you're ready to unload it and just notice what comes up." [BLS]

Therapist: "What are you noticing?"

Client: "Yeah, I'm ready to be free of this."

Therapist: "Can you ask in what way you would like to envision unloading this burden? And notice what comes up." [BLS]

Therapist: "What are you noticing?"

Client: "I see myself just grabbing handfuls of it and pushing it out of and away from myself."

Therapist: "Notice that." [BLS]

Therapist: "What are you noticing?"

Client: "I'm handing some of it back to my dad. I'm telling him this isn't mine. This is yours, and I don't want it anymore." [Note: This is the equivalent of a legacy unburdening in IFS]

Therapist: "Notice that." [BLS]

Therapist: "What are you noticing?"

Client: "I feel lighter. This isn't mine. This is his."

Therapist: "Notice that." [BLS]

Returning to Target is Checking in with Parts

In EMDR, Phase Four protocol dictates that the therapist return to the target memory when the client repeats positive statements multiple times, reports no change over two or more sets, or their associations are vague or unassociated with the original target.[54] When the therapist prompts the client to return to the target, the client can access another channel of associated memories intending to work through all of the channels.[55] For example, the therapist asks, "When you think of the original incident or memory, what do you notice?"[56] The therapist remains curious, rather than being too directive, to honor where the client's system will take them next in their process.[57] From an IFS lens, this is allowing various parts to process their unique memory components (i.e., being witnessed and unburdened). It can also assess how much unburdening happened in the preceding BLS sets.[58]

Take a SUD

When taking a SUD, the therapist asks, "How disturbing is the target memory now on a scale of 1-10?"[59] The therapist identifies if there are other channels of association that the client needs to process[60] (i.e., is more witnessing and unburdening needed by the target exile or any other parts in this traumatic memory network?). When the client reports a low SUD, the therapist prompts them, "What keeps it a two and not a one or a zero?"[61] From an IFS lens, this question invites any parts that still have distress around this experience to come up and do some processing. The therapist can also explicitly say, "Could the part of you that feels it is a two say why that is? Would it like an opportunity to process that distress?" Repeating these steps elicits and welcomes all parts to process content related to the target.[62]

EMDR Phase Five: Installation is Inviting in Positive Qualities

Phase Five focuses on integrating positive qualities (i.e., positive cognitions, feelings, and beliefs) after Phase Four is complete.[63] The IFS invitation step can be incorporated by asking the client, "What positive qualities would the target part or group of parts that experienced healing like to take in?" Given that the traditional EMDR protocol for Phase Four attends to multiple parts of the targeted traumatic memory network, realistically several parts processed content during Phase Four. As such, the therapist can prompt the client to "Take a moment, go inside, and get a sense of the parts that experienced healing during the previous phase," then ask what positive qualities the parts would like to take in. This phase strengthens the new positive cognition and supports other parts of the system in integrating new information.[64]

Example of Inviting in Positive Qualities:[65]

Therapist: "Will you call up the qualities you just shared [repeat qualities] and invite these parts to take them all in?" Administer BLS and stop periodically to check in with the client.

The client realistically is in a Self-led empowered state during Phase Five and can communicate to the therapist when they feel their parts have taken in the positive qualities. Subsequently, the therapist can invite the client to return to all the protectors that stepped back and gave permission for Phase Four processing. The client can update the protectors and invite them to witness the parts who just took in positive qualities. The client also sends appreciation overtly to the protectors. For example, the therapist can say, "Can you take a moment to sit with some appreciation or acknowledgment for your inner system that allowed this healing to occur?"[66]

EMDR Phase Six: Body Scan—Checking for Somatic Parts

Body Scan: The body scan invites any parts with remaining bodily sensations related to the target memory into the process.[67] The therapist can follow the same EMDR standard protocol, prompting the client to scan their body from head to toe and share any tightness, tension, or unusual sensations.[68] The body scan provides a final opportunity for any parts to communicate when they may not have words or may express through body sensations.[69] The therapist continues utilizing the standard protocol script, applying BLS each time the client identifies a part with remaining bodily sensations, until there are none or the body sensations are positive or pleasant.

Present Triggers, Future Template, and Completion

After the client reaches resolve with the target memory, the therapist can focus on any present trigger of the target part, either using pure IFS or setting up a new target on present triggers in Phase Three as needed. During this experience, the client has access to more Self-leadership and shifts from the reorganization of their system from previous completion of a target memory. New parts may emerge, or additional layers of burdens elicited by current triggers may be identified and processed, until the new present-day targets are resolved via EMDR.

After activation of targets in the client's current life have resolved, a future template invites the client to experience Self-leadership, agency, and choice over how they want to show up in any anticipated future scenarios. When asking the client to envision a future situation, the therapist uses IFS to help the client imagine a future situation from Self and utilizes slow BLS to enhance positive cognitions/positive qualities that naturally emerge through Self-leadership.[70] If there are parts that have fears or concerns, after receiving consent from the protectors, the therapist returns to fast BLS processing to witness and unburden any parts (protectors or exiles) activated about the future.

EMDR Phase Seven: Closure and Integration

Session Closure: EMDR Phase Seven addresses how to close a therapy session at various points in the EMDR process.[71] When Phase Four is still in-process by the end of the session, the target exile(s) connected to the activated traumatic memory network are in the middle of witnessing and unburdening. As previously mentioned in Phase Two, this is an opportunity at the end of the session for the client to reconnect with exile(s) and retrieve any exile(s) who are in traumatic memories so that the target exile(s) who are present at the end of the session remain connected with Self and land in a safe/resourced place before the session ends.

In addition, the client can set intentions to check in with parts that showed up in the session and appreciate protectors who stepped back and gave consent for Phase Four trauma processing to occur.[72] The therapist may also overtly invite back connection with manager parts to update them to the progress that occurred in session, and to observe the exile(s) who are connected with Self.[73]

Integration—Inviting Protectors to Unburden and Change Roles

Completing Phase Four on a target memory can create significant shifts in the client, and it may take time for the client's system to integrate the changes. Inviting protectors to see the shifts with transformed parts gives protectors an opportunity to be witnessed, unburdened, and to choose a new role in the system. This can be done through pure IFS integration steps or through continued EMDR processing.

Example of Protectors Choosing New Role[74]

Therapist: "What do those parts of you want to do now that they no longer have to obsess and ruminate the way they used to?"

Client: "They want to do all the things in my life that I used to avoid—cleaning my house, staying on top of my to do list, and ensuring that I pay attention to the enjoyable parts of my life. They want to remind me to be grateful for everything I have."

Therapist: "Notice that." [BLS]

Therapist: "What are you noticing?"

Client: "That feels really nice. I look forward to embracing this new way of life. And, that part of me is happy to feel wanted and purposeful."

Therapist: "Notice that." [BLS]

EMDR Phase Eight: Reevaluation

When reevaluating the treatment plan with a client, we can prompt them to check in with their system to see what comes up when checking in with the target exile and/or what specific parts connected to the target memory network may need the client's attention. The therapist again gets permission from protectors to proceed with any additional Phase Four processing needed and/or to proceed with the remaining phases of the EMDR standard protocol.[75]

Integrating EMDR into the IFS Steps

EMDR's BLS and Phases Three through Eight can integrate in a variety of ways with the IFS steps, including helping strengthen Self-to-part relationships and giving exiles choices in how they want to be witnessed.

The various choice points in integrating EMDR into IFS Steps are illustrated in the following chart:

IFS Steps	Options to integrate EMDR
6 Fs: Find, Focus, Flesh out, Feel Toward, Fears of part, BeFriend	STARR™ can be used to unblend, flesh out, and feel towards the part, inviting the target part to receive Self-presence.
Healing Steps: Self-to Part Trusting Relationship	STARR™ while befriending exile (particularly helpful if exile is pre-verbal, very young, carries burdens related to neglect, deprivation and/or attachment wounds).

Witnessing	Choice point to transition to EMDR's Phase Three in EMDR (e.g., asking exile to identify the worst part of memory it wants witnessed), then Phase Four trauma processing, then completing EMDR Phases Four through Eight. Can confirm consent from protectors prior to beginning EMDR Phase Three. The clinician asks for protectors consent each session during Phase Four.
Unburdening	This happens naturally in Phase Four of EMDR (e.g., if started Phase Three and during IFS witnessing stage).
Invitation of Positive Qualities	Can use slow BLS to strengthen a part's embodiment of positive cognitions and positive qualities as determined by the part.
Integration: Inviting protector parts to notice transformation and shift roles in the system.	If needed, protector parts can also be witnessed and unburdened through Phase Three and Four of EMDR, then completing EMDR protocol through Phase Eight (i.e., the protector part becomes the target part for Phase Four processing). Ask protector parts what new roles they want to do for the system after they invite in positive qualities/positive cognitions.
Appreciation	Can use slow BLS to extend positive qualities throughout whole system, inviting all parts to receive Self energy through slow BLS.

As previously mentioned, during the befriending process STARR™ can be used relationally to help parts (protectors and exiles) take in Self presence. Through STARR™, Self is tending to receptivity from the target part (whether it's a protector or an exile). STARR™ is a means to initiate connection, communication, and attachment repair between Self and part. STARR™ can help protector parts and exiles unblend, become more fleshed out, and receive Self-energy. STARR™ helps parts (protectors and exiles) shift into a receptive mode of receiving from Self, which helps them soften and know that they are not alone and serves as a bridge to transition to in-sight IFS (i.e., Self-to-part relationship). When exiles are very young, pre-verbal, have experienced any form of neglect, deprivation, abuse, attachment wounding, or are pre-natal, STARR™ offers a non-threatening, multi-sensory, gentle way for exiles to initially receive Self-energy.

While befriending an exile, switching to EMDR Phase Three and Phase Four can be relieving to exiles, particularly if the target exile is holding burdens and traumatic content that is highly charged (above a 5 on a scale of 1-10, with 10 being overwhelmingly disturbing). In addition, switching to EMDR Phase Three and Four for trauma processing with the target exile can be relieving for clients' systems that carry complex trauma and/or exiles that are highly likely to blend with Self during the witnessing stage of IFS. Prior to switching to Phase Three and Four, consent from the protective system has been obtained, so backlash in the system is less likely, and Phase Two goals have been met.

Giving the client's system a choice in how it wants to be witnessed (i.e., through pure IFS witnessing steps or through switching to EMDR for trauma processing), can feel relieving to exiles and parts that may be concerned and/or overwhelmed by the amount of traumatic content to be witnessed. In addition, EMDR trauma processing can skillfully attend to witnessing multiple exiles, or groups of exiles, that share the same burden.

Once the clinician switches to using Phase Three and Phase Four to do EMDR trauma processing (i.e., witness and unburdening) on traumatic content that is highly charged, the clinician then continues the EMDR protocol (Phases Four-Eight) to maintain fidelity to EMDR's protocol. Given that doing Phase Four traditional protocol will potentially allow access to traumatic content (burdens) from other time periods, thereby activating other exiles, the clinician can determine which EMDR protocol to use given how much access the client has to Self, as well as the agreed upon treatment goals.

Conclusion

As discussed in this chapter, integrating EMDR and IFS can effectively transform traumatic memories, reorganize clients' systems, support relational repair between Self and parts, and ultimately help clients access and receive the enhanced healing benefits of both models.

KEY TAKEAWAYS

- IFS and EMDR both believe that clients naturally have what they need to facilitate healing: AIP in EMDR and Self in IFS. Both models reorganize the client's system using the neurobiological process of memory reconsolidation.
- STARR's™ gentle, multisensory approach supports connection to Self, and is particularly well-suited for parts that easily flood, that are young/preverbal/prenatal, or have experienced deprivation or other attachment trauma.
- Befriending protectors using the Six Fs during Phase Two is critical to gain consent to befriend the target exile before Phase Three. Any "blocking beliefs" that arise are understood to be protector fears that

can be attended to using the Six Fs. This minimizes backlash, blocking, or adverse reactions during or after Phase Four.
- Accessing the traumatic memory network in Phase Three can be done by tracking the negative cognition (EMDR), parts mapping (IFS), and using IFS to secure protector consent to work with exiles in Phases Three and Four.
- Befriend any parts that block processing in Phase Four using the Six Fs, getting their consent to proceed and asking them to step back.
- If Phase Four processing is stuck, use exile-interweaves inviting IFS healing steps of retrieval, do-over, and unburdening along with BLS.
- In pure IFS, switching to Phases Three-Eight gives the target exile and client a choice in how the exile wants to be witnessed. This option is helpful when traumatic content is highly charged and when working with complex trauma.

AUTHOR BIO

Daphne Fatter, PhD (she/her) is an IFS Certified licensed psychologist and an Approved IFS Clinical Consultant. She is also EMDR Certified and an EMDRIA Approved Consultant in Training and has almost 20 years of experience providing EMDR. Dr. Fatter provides innovative webinars and trainings for continuing education, including integrating EMDR and IFS. She provides engaging nuances on trauma treatment to international audiences from her seasoned clinical experience treating PTSD, complex trauma, combat trauma, reproductive trauma, sexual trauma, attachment trauma, loss, and complicated grief.

GOING DEEPER

From Dr. Daphne Fatter on EMDR

1) Website:
   a. www.daphnefatterphd.com

2) Consultation:
   a. www.daphnefatterphd.com/consultation.html
      i. Groups focused on integrating EMDR and IFS.
      ii. IFS Consultation.
      iii. EMDR Consultation as a EMDR Consultant-in-Training.

3) Training:
   a. www.daphnefatterphd.com/ce-trainings--webinars.html
      i. Honoring Clients Where They Are: The Innovative Integration of IFS and EMDR.

From Dr. Daphne Fatter on Other Topics

1) Training: www.daphnefatterphd.com/ce-trainings--webinars.html
   a. Integrating Traumatic Memories: Conceptualization and Clinical Considerations in Evidence-based Approaches to Trauma Processing.
   b. Utilizing Phase-Oriented Treatment and Adjunctive Interventions to Regulate Arousal in Trauma Treatment.
   c. Polyvagal Theory and Evidenced-based Interventions for Arousal Dysregulation in PTSD.
   d. An Introduction to Internal Family Systems Therapy.
   e. Using Internal Family Systems for Therapist Self-Care.
   f. Using Internal Family Systems Therapy in Trauma Treatment.
   g. Internal Family Systems Therapy: Why it Works and How to Know If It's a Good Fit
   h. White Race Socialization and White Therapists: Treatment Considerations Surrounding Racial Traumas among BIPOC clients.
   i. A Self-Inquiry into Race Socialization and Internalized Whiteness for Any Therapist Treating Racial Trauma.
   j. Befriending White Parts that get Activated by Race and Racism: An Affinity Experiential Training for White Therapists.
   k. Trauma-Informed Stabilization Tools.

4) Podcast Interviews:
   a. The One Inside: IFS and Inviting Curiosity with Racist Parts; www.theoneinside.libsyn.com/ifs-and-hope-for-racist-parts-with-daphne-fatter

b. IFS Talks: How Ancestral Medicine Informs IFS Legacy Burdens Work www.podcasts.apple.com/ca/podcast/how-ancestral-medicine-informs-ifs-legacy-burdens-work/id1481000501?i=1000526889560

5) Other:
   a. Anti-racism resources: www.daphnefatterphd.com/anti-racism-resources.html
      i. Anti-racist experiential groups and consultation for White-identified people focused on White race socialization and befriending parts activated by race and racism.

From Other Sources on IFS and EMDR Integration

1) Books:
   a. O'Shea Brown, G. (2020). Internal Family Systems informed eye movement desensitization and reprocessing an integrative technique for treatment of complex posttraumatic stress disorder. *International Body Psychotherapy Journal*, 19 (2), 112-122.
   b. Krauze, P., & Gomez, A. (2013). EMDR therapy and the use of internal family systems strategies with children. In C. Forgash & M. Copeley (Eds.), *Healing the heart of trauma and dissociation with EMDR and ego state therapy* (pp. 295-311). Springer Publishing Company.
   c. Twombly, J., & Schwartz, R. C. (2008). The integration of the Internal Family Systems model and EMDR. In C. Forgash & M. Copeley (Eds.), *Healing the heart of trauma and dissociation with EMDR and ego state therapy* (pp. 295-311). Springer Publishing Company.

From Other Sources on EMDR

1) Books:
   a. Shapiro, F. (2018). *Eye movement desensitization and reprocessing: Basic principles, protocols, and procedures* (3rd ed.). The Guilford Press.

2) EMDR Training:
   a. EMDR International Association Trainings and Therapist Directory: www.emdria.org

5

IFS AND PSYCHODRAMA

TECHNIQUES FOR EXPANDING IFS EXTERNALIZATIONS

Valerie Simon, LCSW, TEP, CET III

On two separate occasions in my career, I had a moment of clarity when I encountered an experiential therapy method for the first time and *knew* I'd eventually be practicing it.

One of those "light bulb" moments occurred at a conference in Washington, DC, where I saw a demonstration of a therapy method many clinicians were talking about. At first, I felt skepticism. The method used descriptors like "firefighters" and "exiles," and from my naive perspective (and a critical part I hadn't yet met), that felt gimmicky. However, when I heard Richard Schwartz, the creator of Internal Family Systems, speak and then share his demonstration video, I was riveted.

In the demo, Richard guided a craggy-faced older gentleman to unblend with various aspects, or *parts,* of his personality. Gently led by Richard, and with his parts' permission, this man eventually moved into a trance-like state, internally connecting with his very young, exiled inner child who was recounting his trauma. As this vulnerable inner child was witnessed with compassion, and eventually unburdened of his pain, the man was able to cry tears he had held inside for decades. At that moment, I knew Schwartz had tapped into something profound, and that IFS was much more than a gimmick.

Many years earlier, at the beginning of my career as a therapist, I'd had a similar "aha" moment. During a personal therapy session, my therapist proposed an experiential exercise. She had me talk to an empty chair that represented someone from my life with whom I was in conflict. As I began to speak, the therapist stood behind me. With my permission, she put her hand on my shoulder and said a few words in the first person, *doubling* what she suspected I was feeling but not expressing. After being told I could correct the double if it were off target, I repeated her very accurate words and found tears welling up immediately—a response that back then didn't come very easily for me. When I was asked to *reverse roles* and found that I could take on the role of the person with whom I was in conflict, I was mesmerized. This was my introduction to psychodrama.

IFS and psychodrama share many threads and synergies in common, yet each method also has unique characteristics. In this chapter, we will explore their intersections and differences, as well as ways to integrate these two innovative therapeutic approaches.

What Is Psychodrama?

As a therapy modality, it comes with a somewhat daunting name. The roots of the word psychodrama are Greek—*psyche* (soul) and *drama* (action)—*the soul in action*. Though often mistakenly associated with the encounter movement of the 1960s, psychodrama actually was created by a Romanian-born, Viennese-educated psychiatrist named Jacob Levy Moreno (known as J. L. or simply Moreno) in the early 20th century. What dominated the world of psychotherapy at that time was Freud's psychoanalysis. In contrast, Moreno recognized that role playing could be therapeutic by increasing spontaneity and creativity for clients. J. L., and later his wife and less-recognized co-creator, Zerka Moreno, were both prolific writers and teachers, and there is far more to the methodology and philosophy of psychodrama than will be covered in this chapter.

J. L. Moreno was privately quoted as saying, "The body remembers what the mind forgets" decades before brain scans existed or Bessel van der Kolk had written his seminal book *The Body Keeps the Score*. He realized that *action* in psychotherapy engaged the body and that through it, healing could occur on a cellular level.

J. L. also was one of the first to recognize the healing power of the group, recognizing that all members, not just the authoritarian White male doctor of his era, had the power to help heal each other. In psychodrama, we typically call our client a *protagonist*, and when facilitating a drama, we are called a *director*. In this chapter, I will use the terms director, therapist, and facilitator interchangeably, as well as client and protagonist.

Classical group psychodrama blends theatre with therapy in what is called *surplus reality*, where we externalize our inner world by enacting scenes with group members whom we request to play roles for us. As a facilitator, I may ask a protagonist to choose someone to play the role of a significant person from their past or present life to enact a scene with them. A group member always has the choice to decline a role if they are not warmed up to play it in the service of the protagonist. I might also ask a protagonist to invite someone to play the role of a *part* of someone—say, a feeling or a critical voice. I might say, for example, "Choose someone to play your fear."

This might feel somewhat familiar to IFS practitioners. In fact, many psychodramatists who are introduced to IFS, myself included, are initially surprised by some of the parallels. One of my first reactions to seeing Richard's IFS demonstration was, "This is kind of like psychodrama inside your mind!" I later learned that Richard had indirectly encountered psychodrama through his training in Gestalt therapy. A little-known fact outside of the psychodrama community is that Fritz Perls, the founder of Gestalt therapy, had trained with J. L. Moreno in the 1950s in New York City (Kellogg, 2004). The "empty chair" exercise appropriated by Gestalt therapy was actually created by the Morenos.

As mentioned, psychodrama was originally conceived to be implemented in groups, but many practitioners have adapted it to work *a deux* between a therapist and client. While with IFS, we usually "go inside," in psychodrama *a deux*, we concretize our inner world and "go outside," externalizing our inner world by role plays using props, empty chairs, artwork, scarfs, pillows, etc. When incorporating IFS theory in individual sessions, we can use psychodramatic techniques to help facilitate the unblending, witnessing, and even unburdening of parts.

Fleshing Out a Part with Psychodrama Techniques

In IFS, an important starting point is to help our clients learn about their parts and discover the ones with which they are blended. When clients connect with their ever-present, but not always accessible Self-energy, their protectors tend to relax, and clients can begin to develop a Self-to-part relationship. Whenever I use these techniques, I ask a client if they have any parts that object to the exercise. If they do, we do not proceed with the exercise until we understand and have addressed all parts' concerns, so that we have full protector permission.

Several psychodramatic techniques can help with the unblending, befriending, and witnessing process:

The Interview. The interview is a psychodrama technique that IFS intuitively uses to befriend parts. In IFS, the therapist can speak directly to a part through an interview approach called Direct Access. This is commonly used when a client is significantly blended with a part, and it allows the Self-energy of the therapist to speak directly to the part as it is embodied by the client. When blended, the client feels as though they *are* the part, and the part will simply speak through the client's mouth in the first person. This allows the therapist to bring Self-energy and compassion to the interview ("When did you first take on this role?" "What are you afraid would happen if you didn't do this job?" "How are you trying to help?") to allow the part to feel honored, understood and appreciated without requiring the client to unblend. This "lending," or modeling, of the therapist's Self-energy toward a part often assists the client in accessing their own Self-energy and, thereby, increases the client's appreciation towards the part.

The Empty Chair. Another psychodramatic technique that can be integrated with IFS is the empty chair technique. This is where a protagonist imagines a part physically in a chair and speaks directly to it. If preferred, the protagonist may select a prop that represents the part to place on the chair. Seeing a part outside of oneself can help with the unblending process as it concretizes the idea that the part is not the whole of a protagonist. Saying whatever a client wants to say to an externalized part can also help the therapist become aware of any other parts that are present. For example, if during an empty chair exercise, a protagonist says they hate the part that is represented in the chair, we would learn that there is an angry or critical polarized part present, and the client is not speaking from Self-energy.

Doubling. When utilizing the empty chair exercise where a client is speaking to an embodied part, the double can help deepen the experience for a protagonist. As described in the introduction, in individual sessions, doubling is when the director stands behind the protagonist and, with permission, briefly says in the first person what they intuitively suspect the protagonist is feeling but not yet articulating. If the double resonates for the protagonist, they repeat it in their own words, but if the double does not feel accurate, the protagonist corrects it. We always remind the protagonist that they have the opportunity to change the double and make it their own.

Doubling can be used either to deepen the emotional experience or when a protagonist is struggling to articulate their emotions with words. If a client chooses a part to speak to and then has trouble starting, after giving some space and asking permission, I might double "there's a part of me that isn't sure what to say to you." Usually after a client repeats or changes the double, they continue with the exercise on their own. A somatic double also can be used to focus on what is happening in the body, something that can lead to further parts exploration.

As the director, I also can offer a double to flesh out other parts I notice are present for a protagonist as they do their work. For example, if a client has decided to speak to an addictive firefighter and is sharing the negative impact it is having on their life, I might double, "There's a part of me that wishes you didn't exist!" or "There's a part of me that is really scared you might take over my life." The client can either repeat or correct the double.

Doubling can be especially helpful when working with a pre-verbal part. For example, if a client is blended with a very young part that throws tantrums, with permission I might double "I am really trying to be seen and heard!" Again, the client can repeat the double in their own words if it feels accurate or correct it if it doesn't. I have seen in many sessions how a well-timed and succinct double can really help a protagonist deepen their connection with a part.

An important distinction when incorporating IFS theory is that I would not double in a way to shift a client directly to their vulnerable exile, as that would bypass protector permission.

Role Reversal. In IFS, once we have a Self-to-part acknowledgement and a client has expressed curiosity about, and some connection to, a part, we begin to witness the part and get to know it more deeply. One psychodramatic technique called role reversal can help with this process. When we externalize a part and begin to dialogue with it using an empty chair, we then can *reverse roles* with it. Reversing roles means that we literally switch physical places with an externalized part in an empty chair and instead of speaking *to* it, we speak *as* it. In IFS lingo, we might say that once we have a Self-to-part relationship, we temporarily blend with a part in role reversal and take on its role. In reversing roles with a part, a client can get to know it better, find out how it is trying to help, learn the history of how it got its role, and develop more compassion for it. This exercise can really enhance the witnessing process. When reversing roles back to Self, a client often has extra insight, clarity, and affection toward a part.

For example, if a client has an addictive firefighter that causes distress, once a Self-to-part connection is established, one can reverse roles with this part and speak as it. The addictive firefighter, speaking through the client's mouth, can then share how it helps and protects, how it got its job, and what its protector fears are. When reversing roles back again, a client usually has increased their understanding and compassion for the part.

The Mirror. The mirror position can be used when a client is trying to establish a Self-to-part relationship and is a unique way to get new perspective when dialoguing with polarized parts. With the mirror, we literally and physically take a step back and out of the system in a way we do not typically do in IFS. With the mirror, a protagonist can observe their parts from a bit of a distance, and even concretize one's own Self-energy. As a director, I would offer that a protagonist enrolls props to stand in for any parts and even a prop to represent the client's Self. Sometimes when a protagonist steps back into the mirror position and sees their own Self-energy represented, they can gain insight into how overactive parts are hindering it. This can increase compassion and understanding for the parts that are working so hard to protect and aid in the unblending process. Literally seeing concretized Self-energy can help us connect with ours, as our overactive, blended parts often forget it exists.

For example, when a client is blended with a polarization between a hard-working manager that wants treatment progress and a binge-eating firefighter that wants to numb pain, we can externalize the inner conflict and have the client step out into the mirror position. After the client speaks to both parts, receives doubling, and even reverses roles with the parts and speaks as them sharing protector fears, we can have the client view, and perhaps interact with, their own concretized Self-energy. Taking a step away, interacting with the two polarized parts, and finally interacting, and possibly reversing roles with, the Self-energy that is always internally present can shift perspective and help the protagonist gain clarity and wisdom. Eventually stepping back into the scene as Self with newly gained perspective and understanding can help parts relax and unblend.

IFS Externalizations and Psychodrama

Unblending is an IFS practice that gently invites parts to separate from Self. In a sense, this creates an "inner externalization." By externalizing parts in the client's inner world as entities separate from Self, we facilitate the development of a healing Self-to-part relationship, which is the first step toward befriending, witnessing, updating, and unburdening parts that are frozen in feelings, beliefs, or sensations of the past.

Psychodrama uses methods of concretizing externalizations by allowing parts to be represented outside of the physical body of the client. This type of externalizing can be manifested with other group members, objects, art, or writing. Clients with numbing, dissociating, or distracting parts seem to respond particularly well to psychodramatic externalizations. Also, when classic IFS Insight and unblending are challenging, externalizing psychodramatic parts exercises can be very helpful.

The following case examples are composites of typical clients with whom I have been privileged to work over many years. All details and identifying information have been changed.

Case Example: Stan and a Family Trauma History

I sometimes run intensives for people with extensive trauma histories where we have several full days to do deep experiential work together. I once ran such an intensive with a young man I'll call Stan, who came from a significant generational trauma history. Stan's parents were childhood survivors of famine and war in Bangladesh and had courageously emigrated to the U.S. without any money or knowledge of English. Understandably, both of Stan's parents had tremendous unprocessed trauma and, therefore, many exiles and extreme parts protecting them. Stan's father had extreme firefighters that medicated either with alcohol or rage. When Stan's father was under the influence, my client, as a child, would both witness and experience physical abuse. Stan had a great deal of anger toward his father, or in IFS terms, he had an angry firefighter that protected his exiled vulnerable inner child. Stan was doing an intensive with me because he was concerned about repeating his family trauma history with his own children.

After Stan mapped out parts he was aware of, he chose a part to "go inside" with and explore. During the exploration of a well-known manager, his thinker, Stan kept opening his eyes, expressed discomfort with the process, and said he had trouble accessing words. I encouraged him to do whatever felt comfortable and reminded his manager with Direct Access that he didn't need to do anything that didn't feel right for him—that he was in charge. After a few attempts, Stan decided it was too difficult for him to start by going inside. I suspected that Stan's blended thinking manager kept him planning, productive, and safe. The territory inside likely was uncharted and frightening, and some other parts we did not know yet were shutting down the process.

A little perplexed, and also knowing I had several full days to work with Stan, I decided to offer him an externalizing exercise using an empty chair. I asked him if there were any parts that did not want him to do this new exercise and, as far as he could tell, there were none. After thus establishing protector permission, I offered that he could put anyone in this chair with whom he felt that he wanted to speak. The choice was his. Stan decided to put his father in the empty chair, and the minute he did, he was able to express himself. He gave voice to an angry firefighter and yelled at his father for his abuse toward the family and was able to physically release some of his rage by throwing a pillow on the ground. I was tracking some of the parts I noticed as they emerged, but I allowed Stan to have a psychodramatic catharsis, blended with his anger.

After the experience of standing up to his father experientially, Stan reported feeling more empowered and connected to his emotions. Once his system was jumpstarted and his angry firefighter expressed itself, we then began to explore it and several other parts. Over a few hours, Stan began to feel more comfortable closing his eyes and directing his attention inside.

Over the course of the intensive, Stan gained valuable compassion for many of his parts and experienced unblending from several, including those whose job was to shut down his system. Stan eventually connected with his vulnerable inner child who had felt fear, sadness, and loneliness as a child. This newfound connection to his exile provided Stan with an opportunity to update this inner child regarding who he is today. By the end of the intensive, Stan was feeling more internally connected to his exiled childhood vulnerability as well as his children's vulnerability. He felt less numb and burdened and was more confident in his role as a father. He also had more clarity about what kinds of boundaries to set with his own father going forward.

Psychodrama Role Theory: Intersections Between Roles and Parts

J. L. Moreno was very interested in the different roles that people play in their lives such as parent, worker, student, lover, dreamer, creator, etc. In simplified terms, psychodramatic role theory is the exploration of different roles that a client has in their life at a given time (Moreno, 1993). Role theory explores how we develop different roles in our lives, typically beginning to explore a new role by imitating others, and eventually expanding to the point where we can uniquely create the role for ourselves. Moreno explored which roles we want to develop in our *role repertoire* and which roles we might feel stuck in with *role fatigue*. We may help a protagonist explore which roles aren't serving them well and explore how to add new roles to their role repertoire. Similarly in IFS, we explore the burdens that our exiles carry and the extreme roles protectors have in our systems. A major aspect of an IFS unburdening process is to help a part free up energy, so it is no longer stuck in the past in a role that no longer serves.

Case Example: Jon's Extreme Firefighter Parts, and Creating a Locogram

Jon is a graduate student with a history of exiles that flood with panic attacks, extreme firefighters that self-medicate with substances and video games, as well as a co-dependent manager part that focuses on others' feelings and needs at the expense of his own. Jon's father struggles with a gambling addiction and the family's finances have been perpetually tenuous because of it, and his mother has a physical impairment that requires medical attention. Their marriage had a great deal of conflict, and as an only child, Jon often tried to intervene. Jon experienced a good deal of relational trauma and neglect when he was young, and he has a skeptical part when it comes to believing he has an inner child. A critical manager thought it was "stupid and unnecessary" to get to know his inner child, even after many months of getting to know its fears and concerns and reassuring this hard-working protector.

During one session where Jon was expressing that he was feeling overwhelmed with responsibility, I offered him a psychodramatic exercise that has IFS underpinnings—the externalization of different roles. Jon created a map on the floor where he wrote on separate pieces of paper (in psychodrama we call this a *locogram*) the different roles he currently had in his life—graduate student, son, worker, romantic partner, caretaker, pet parent, friend, etc. I had Jon walk around his space and stand next to each role and see what it felt like internally as he began to embody it. We then had Jon reverse roles and speak from the role what it felt like to inhabit it.

With protector permission, Jon then moved some of the roles/parts closer to or farther from him depending on his current needs. I had Jon take a step back from this externalization into the mirror position and place a prop representing his Self-Energy in the midst of all of his many roles. After talking to himself from the mirror position, Jon was able to connect with Self-energy and come to the conclusion, with some clarity, that he was focusing too much on his parents' drama and not enough on himself and his schoolwork.

In IFS parlance, Jon connected with his caretaker part. After this moment of clarity, and with some connection to Self-energy, we checked in with Jon's caretaker part to see if it was willing to give some space. With a little negotiating it was, and he chose a prop to represent it from a distance. After Jon returned to his scene from the mirror position, he felt more connection to Self-energy, and his parts gave permission to briefly connect with his young, exiled inner child who held a belief that he was unimportant and needed to take care of others to be loved. Jon had moments of true compassion for this little boy inside. He was not yet ready for an unburdening, but Jon remained in acknowledgement of, and in occasional connection with, his inner child and still refers to him at times. I have continued to act as an IFS "hope merchant" (Schwartz, 2020) to remind Jon that I know we can help heal this little boy who experienced multiple complex traumas as parts in his system learn to trust him.

The Re-Do and Unburdening

A somewhat less emphasized section of the IFS unburdening process is the re-do. When Self receives permission from protectors to enter into relationship with an exile and witnessing of the exile's trauma has occurred, the exile might request a corrective experience. Typically, the Self enters the traumatic memory with the exile and engages with that part in the way it needed a healthy adult to do back then. A re-do might include Self rescuing the exile, setting boundaries with perpetrators, or being with the exile so it is no longer alone in the memory. During IFS Insight, these actions occur internally, in the client's inner experience.

With psychodrama tools, we can externalize this corrective emotional experience. In psychodrama, this re-do scene might be enacted via an empty chair exercise where the adult protagonist can reverse roles with their younger Self and ask them what they would like to have happen. Often this enacted child will request a rescue, a punishment for a perpetrator, or for someone else to be there in the scene with them so they aren't alone. This healing experience, enacted in the client's external world, often spontaneously leads to an emotional catharsis, or unburdening, followed by integration.

For example, I once enacted a scene with a protagonist who had a perpetrator relative who never was held accountable for his traumatizing behavior. In this re-do scene, the protagonist, in role-reversal with her exiled inner child, had the police come and arrest her relative. Once the perpetrator was behind bars, the little girl was able to safely confront this perpetrator and express all of the feelings she had never felt safe to express before. When the protagonist then reversed roles back to her adult connected to Self-energy, there was a very compassionate and healing response to this inner child. With IFS tools, we then can continue the unburdening process.

Unburdening is the step in IFS Insight that follows witnessing and re-do. It involves inviting burdened parts to unload feelings, sensations, and/or beliefs that are carried from past traumatic experiences. Psychodramatic techniques allow the possibility of externalizing the unburdening process through the release or destruction of physical representation of burdens (such as a piece of paper or an object), which can be helpful in concretizing the release of the unburdening work.

Case Example: With a Photo, Suzanne "Burns" a Perpetrator

Before I was conversant in IFS, I had a client I'll call Suzanne in a longer format intensive who had suffered a tremendous amount of physical abuse in her childhood. As an adult, she had protectors who attempted to ensure that she was never vulnerable again. She had parts that took on some of the qualities and energy of her abusers in the process (in IFS lingo, we might call this a "legacy burden"), and she regrettably could lose her temper and abusively yell at her very energetic son. Suzanne had some fears she might become violent with him in the future.

As part of Suzanne's healing journey with me, she wanted to use a photograph of her primary perpetrator in an empty chair exercise and, in something similar to an IFS re-do, she enacted a psychodramatic scene and said everything she wanted to say to this family member that she could not as a child. As often happens with trauma release, she yelled and physically shook as the trauma was released from her body. Then, at Suzanne's suggestion, we took the photo of her perpetrator to a fireplace and burned it. I can't say for sure if the work stuck since this was before I knew about protector permission, but I do know that the externalizing action of burning the photo was very therapeutic for Suzanne. One can only imagine the possibilities with a client who has protector permission and completes an IFS unburdening with a literal experience of releasing her burden to the wind, fire, or any other element! A burial ceremony can occur, a note can be burned and blown away in the wind, or anything else an exile might creatively imagine.

Working with Polarizations

Polarizations occur when two or more parts try to help the system avoid pain in opposing ways. In psychodrama, we might describe this as opposing roles. In a common addiction polarization, we might enact a scene by enrolling people or objects to represent both a manager part that wants to stay sober, and a firefighter part that wants to use drugs again. By externalizing this polarization, a client can speak *to* both parts and, in role reversal, *from* both parts and interact with them. Our polarizations calm down when both sides are heard with compassion, and new options for these parts' interactions become clear. Eventually, exiles driving the polarization can be uncovered, and contracts established to gain permission to unburden the exiles so that the polarized parts might unburden as well. It is especially powerful to externalize and honor the reality that most protectors cannot unburden their roles until the exiles behind them are unburdened.

Case Example: Polarization of Love Addicted and Love Avoidant Parts

Rebecca is a 30-something woman who often comes to session feeling overwhelmed and blended with her parts. She often speaks of many internal polarizations. On one particular day, Rebecca spoke of the part of her that can get very focused on her romantic relationship with a man who is already married, and she can forget about her other responsibilities in life. Rebecca also complained about another part that sometimes wishes she was not in this relationship at all and feels ashamed that she spends so much time thinking about her unavailable partner. This part wants her to focus on her career and "adulting." Rebecca often tries to unblend from her parts more internally, but sometimes more and more parts "pile on," her critical manager emerges, and then another part shuts down her work.

During one session, I offered Rebecca the option to externalize these two parts and suggested that she select a prop to represent each of her self-described "love addict" and "love avoidant" parts. She then spoke to each part, at first from her critical manager, and then when we negotiated for that part to give a little space, from some Self-energy. Once Rebecca was connected to her Self-compassion, she reversed roles with her love addict part who obsesses about her partner. This part was able to explain how she tries to protect Rebecca from abandonment like what she experienced in her early childhood. When Rebecca reversed roles again and re-connected with Self-energy, she was able to have more clarity and compassion for this part that had been trying to protect her since she had the traumatic experience of losing her mother at a young age. I noted an exile that may be unburdened in the future if Rebecca and her parts allowed it.

With permission, Rebecca then explored the other side of her polarization and was able to dialogue with her more hidden love avoidant part who, in role reversal, told her how it was trying to help her work on her demanding career so she could become more independent. This part also was able to share that it feared Rebecca would be swallowed up by any relationship and that she could lose herself in one. When Rebecca better understood this part's intention of keeping her autonomous and less dependent by choosing an unavailable partner, she was able to hold some appreciation for it for the first time. In subsequent sessions, we explored more polarizations with role reversal and slowly there has been more unblending of these parts over time.

IFS and Psychodrama in Groups

Possibilities are endless for how to enact parts in a group using externalizations.

One example is the psychodramatic technique of amplification. Amplification is the slight exaggeration of a part's role to help the protagonist really understand its purpose. For example, in a therapeutic group, I have offered a scene where the protagonist enrolled group members (called *auxiliaries* in psychodrama) to role-play two polarized parts. I had the polarized parts stand back-to-back and the protagonist prompted them each with a "signature" line to represent each of them. They then slowly spun in a circle, staying back-to-back, so one polarized role was facing the protagonist and said its signature line. Then, the next polarized part turned and would face the protagonist and say its signature line. I kept the auxiliary roles rotating around to amplify the polarization and have the protagonist experience the extremity of both sides' rigid positions.

Behind this enacted polarization, I had the protagonist see their vulnerable, young exile, also played by an auxiliary. If the protagonist has never worked with this inner child, I would assume there is no protector permission, and I would not have the protagonist speak to them yet. Having an enactment of an overpowering and blended polarization with a visual to concretize that a young exiled inner child is hiding behind the polarization can be very powerful. I have seen this exercise help shift the protagonist toward more curiosity about the extreme roles of the polarizations, eventually leading to permission to connect with, and heal, an exile.

The Warm-Up

Psychodramatic warm-ups in groups help members connect with each other, and in classical psychodrama, can lead to a protagonist enacting a drama. There are countless examples of warm-ups, but I will offer one here that helps explore Self-energy. As mentioned earlier, a locogram is a warm-up exercise where different criteria are placed on the floor and, in a group, members choose their answers to questions with action. For example, in one of my groups, I wrote each of the eight qualities of Self-energy—curiosity, clarity, compassion, courage, connectedness, creativity, confidence, and calm—on a separate piece of paper and scattered them around the floor. I then asked clients to stand next to a quality of Self that is easiest for them to access and share about their choice with each other. Next, I asked which quality of Self they wish they could access more readily and had group members share with a person close to them, thus facilitating connection between other group members with similar experiences (in psychodramatic terms, their *doubles*). The potential variations of these qualities of Self warm-up are nearly limitless.

Speaking *for* Parts, Not *from* Them

Another powerful IFS tool is the ability to speak *for* a part instead of blending with and speaking *from* a part (Schwartz, 2020). Therapy groups are a marvelous laboratory for group members to practice this de-escalating technique with each other. For example, a conversation might become heated if one group member speaks to another *from* a blended angry part: "You always interrupt me, and I wish you'd shut up already!" It is a very different experience when a group member speaks from Self on *behalf of*, or *for*, a part: "A part of me is feeling frustrated right now since I am having trouble finishing my thought." Group provides the safe container to facilitate this therapeutic communication re-do.

In groups I facilitate, when two group members are having a communication challenge, I sometimes incorporate the IFS technique of speaking for parts with the psychodrama technique of the encounter. J. L. Moreno created the encounter where two people in conflict are invited to sit face to face in the center of the group and talk out their issue (Dayton, 2005). Each participant receives equal amounts of doubling for their inner feelings, meaning if I were to double for one participant I would also double for the other. I have adjusted this psychodramatic technique to invite doubling (with permission) that guides the participants to speak for their parts.

Speaking for Parts Brings Deeper Connection

Let's say that two hypothetical members in a recovery group we will call Lily and Jane were having a challenge around a miscommunication about Lily's alcohol use. Lily was reacting defensively, and Jane was becoming aggressive in her accusation. During an encounter, I might, with permission, offer each a double where I model speaking for the parts I observe. I might stand behind Lily's chair and say, "A part of me is feeling defensive about my drinking." And to Jane, I might double, "A part of me is feeling angry that you are slipping back into heavy alcohol use." As always, after each double, each group member has the option to correct the double or to repeat it in their own words if it resonates. Usually, the encounter continues on with a little further intimacy and then another trigger for one or both participants.

Deepening the encounter with further speaking for any triggered parts and doubling might end up helping both connect with, and speak for, an exile. As stated earlier, I would not double for an exile myself, but I have experienced that when clients themselves connect internally, a powerful interaction can occur. For example, Jane might eventually connect with an exiled inner child that witnessed alcohol abuse and speak for her, "I'm feeling scared and helpless that you are going to die of alcohol abuse like my father did when I was twelve." Or Lily might connect with her young inner child and reveal, "I feel worthless when you don't trust me to drink responsibly. It reminds me of being wrongfully accused by my mother all of the time." It is important to acknowledge exiles when they emerge in an IFS-informed encounter and reassure them that we will return to them in future sessions and, of course, do just that.

Calling on Self-Energy in Groups

One powerful integration of IFS in groups is, as the facilitator, to call on the collective Self-energy of the group as it begins. We can offer a parts meditation where any enervated or triggered parts are welcomed, heard, and invited to wait outside the room for the duration of the enactment to allow the collective Self-energy to hold the participants' work. When auxiliary players are invited to role play for a protagonist during an enactment, we also can ask any triggered parts to wait outside, or be resourced, so no blended parts negatively impact the work of the protagonist. We do remind group members that all parts are welcome, so no one feels they are doing group therapy "wrong" if a part of theirs blends. It is important at the end of the group to check in with any parts that were willing to take a pause, in order to provide closure.

Contributions of the IFS Model

I believe that one of the most important contributions that Richard Schwartz has made to the field through IFS is emphasizing that we *always* ask for protector permission and never proceed without it. This is vital for trauma survivors whose boundaries have been violated in so many horrific ways. We allow the parts to be the boss and set the pace. In psychodrama, it is easy for an eager director (and their parts) to have an agenda and to want a protagonist to go in a certain direction during an enactment. A psychodramatist might do a lovely piece of work with the inner child of a protagonist, only to be informed at the next session that for days after, the protagonist was depressed, drinking more, or otherwise "taken out" by the work. From an IFS perspective, we'd call that backlash, which, while normal, is likely a sign that permission was not granted by the necessary protectors. In IFS, we understand that protector permission for an unburdening might take weeks, months, or even years, rather than "going for broke" to enact a powerful scene in the moment. Schwartz has also provided a step-by-step roadmap to healing in a way that psychodramatists have not. In IFS training, we learn specific steps that must occur before we are able to unburden an exile. There are flow charts in IFS and choice points where a therapist can shift gears when one technique is not achieving a Self-to-part relationship, such as when to use Insight vs. Direct Access, how to address protector fears, and how to work with flooding exiles.

In addition, through IFS, we can instill hope in an otherwise hopeless person by reminding them that innately they have healing Self-energy, and we can extend our Self-energy until a client is ready to connect with theirs. When Self-led ourselves, we can help our clients unblend with their parts and allow them to take the lead; we have no set agenda for them.

Personal Example—A Fledgling Psychodramatist "Fails" At First

We learn psychodrama experientially by participating in training groups and workshops for hundreds of hours, where we have multiple opportunities to be a protagonist, an auxiliary, and a director. Years ago, when I was a fledgling psychodramatist uncovering my own wounds, and without knowledge of IFS, I attended a week-long psychodrama workshop. As a protagonist, I enacted a scene where I interacted with someone from my past who had mistreated me. I couldn't access my anger in the scene, though several group members doubled this emotion for me. At the end of the drama, I felt badly that I hadn't been able to confront this person. The next day I felt very overwhelmed and skipped the training; I felt like I had "failed" as a protagonist. I did end up returning to the workshop the following day, and I shared my experience and felt understood and supported, which was healing for me.

Reflecting on my experience now from an IFS parts perspective, I have some clarity about what happened years ago. The scene where I was to confront the abusive person and have what, in IFS, we call a re-do occurred before my protectors had agreed to it. I was blended with a scared part and my Self-energy was not yet accessible. Workshop members' own activated parts might have had an agenda—possibly a group member's blended caretaker part wanted to help me, or perhaps a member blended with an angry part or picked up some of the anger of an exiled part of me. Whatever the reason, my parts were not ready for me to get angry. I have since worked with, and healed, this exile, but I have never forgotten that visceral lesson about the need for protector permission.

From an IFS perspective, groups offer the potential for powerful collective Self-energy to surround and support the protagonist's work. To ensure this safe container, it is important to begin by intentionally witnessing and unblending any parts which may be activated in group members and the director.

Contributions of Psychodrama

Psychodrama is an action method, and inherent in this approach is body-centered movement. While IFS theory does not discourage a client from moving their body during a session, and even begins by anchoring a part in the body ("Where do you notice this part in or around your body?"), movement per se is not an explicit aspect of the IFS model. Psychodrama, on the other hand, physically embodies roles/parts and clients have a dynamic and physical interaction with them. For many clients, including those who have parts that freeze due to trauma, I find that physical movement and embodiment can be extremely helpful in parts work, as long as there is protector permission.

Modern trauma research has uncovered the negative impact of trauma on both the brain and the soma. Trauma happens *to* our bodies, and it is remembered *in* our bodies. Bessel van der Kolk (2014) discusses how the neurobiological underpinnings of trauma manifest in the body. When we have experienced trauma, both our bodies and specific areas of our brains remember the event, and traumatic memories can be triggered in the present day. When triggers happen, the fight/flight/freeze/fawn response of the amygdala, deep within the brain's limbic system, goes on overdrive, often triggering a physiological response: our heart might start pounding, we might sweat, we might yell easily or burst into tears. Conversely, we might dissociate or "go numb" like Stan, the client I shared earlier. Simultaneously, our prefrontal cortex, the part of the brain where we orient to time and place and utilize logical, sequential thinking, shuts down. We are back at the scene of the crime, so to speak, and it may feel like we are experiencing the day 30 years ago when a traumatic event occurred.

Psychodrama, through its movement and embodiment, greatly facilitates the body's healing from the embedded somatic residue of trauma. Psychodramatic externalizations require moving our bodies, and psychodramatic techniques such as reversing roles and the mirror can keep us embodied and moving in space. Psychodrama can elicit an emotional catharsis through enactments, inviting the expression and discharge of strong emotion or physical action such as shaking, stomping feet, throwing a pillow, or anything else a part might need to release stored traumatic energy.

Modalities to Help Heal the World

Both IFS and psychodrama strive for a global reach. Richard Schwartz has dedicated the last 40 years of his life to developing and sharing IFS with as many people as possible, not only mental health professionals. He generously has said that he believes he co-created his method with his clients who taught him about their parts and Self-energy. The IFS Institute trains therapists as well as non-clinicians, and Richard has worked around the world, sometimes in high conflict regions such as the Middle East. I believe that he looks at IFS as a movement far larger than a mental health modality.

J. L. Moreno had a similar goal for psychodrama. Decades ago, he wrote, *a truly therapeutic procedure cannot have less an objective than the whole of (wo)mankind.* (Moreno, 1993). J. L. did not want psychodrama only to be used in the mental health field. He wanted it to be utilized in schools, business, government, and in families. Moreno wanted heads of state to enact psychodramas to solve conflicts and avoid war. He wanted a child and a parent to reverse roles and stand in each other's shoes. The Morenos believed the method could help heal the world.

Putting It All Together

So, how do we skillfully integrate IFS and psychodrama? Here are a few ideas to use with individuals or groups:

1. When a protagonist is exploring what to work on, we can ask all interested parts to state their preference for the target piece of work and allow Self to moderate a dialogue between the parts to agree on the target for the current session, as well as a timeline for targets that are not given time that day.

2. When utilizing psychodramatic techniques, always ask the protagonist for protector permission before any enactment. Having trained extensively in IFS, I now ask every potential protagonist to "go inside" and see if there

are any parts that have concern with them enacting the scene they have just contracted to do. If there are any parts who chime in, we ask what their concerns are and spend as much time addressing them as needed, until permission is granted. One option to flesh out concerns is to have the protagonist reverse roles with the unwilling part and allow it to speak its concerns. A role-reversal dialogue will either address the concerns or identify a new target scene that does have permission.

3. In a group, ask any potential auxiliary role-players if there are any parts that can't or do not want them to play a role in service of the protagonist. We ask role players to check inside with parts to see if they can show up with Self-energy for the protagonist before accepting a role. It can be quite challenging for a protagonist when a triggered or blended auxiliary is parts-led instead of Self-led.

4. As a director in an individual session or a group, consistently monitor whether there are any of your own parts that are driving your directing. Our most powerful asset as a therapist or group leader is our Self-energy, which, in turn, invites in the Self-energy of our clients, much like a tuning fork. If we are leading out of burdened parts, it will likewise invite the client's burdened parts to take over. Common therapist parts include: the caretaker, the controller, the fixer, and the know-it-all. Check in for any agenda you might have about how you want an externalization scene to go. Work with your parts in your own IFS therapy so they feel comfortable stepping back when you are in a director or therapist role to provide access to your Self-energy.

An Integration Exercise—Going Inside/Going Outside

Here is an exercise you can try at home, and if you are a clinician, you might also try this with a client. In IFS, we often draw "parts maps" or make lists of different parts we are aware of inside of ourselves. If you would like to try mapping yourself, get comfortable in your space and consider putting your phone away. Close your eyes if it feels comfortable, take a few deep breaths, and check in with any physical sensations you might be having. Ask the sensation if it would be willing to communicate with you and tell you about itself. If it is, ask it to share about itself, what part it is, how it helps or protects you, and how it got its job. Let it know it is welcome and that if it wants to share in words, images, or further sensations, it can. If parts mapping is new to you, you might scan your entire body this way and see what parts you meet! The parts that don't like or fear the exercise are welcome too.

For those already familiar with parts work, you may already know several of your parts to add to your map. You can draw them if they communicate with you visually and that feels comfortable for you. Some people might draw a silhouette of their body and write-in or draw different parts that show up in different places in and around the body. Some might prefer to simply make a list. If you have parts that like to organize, you can break them down into your managers and your firefighters if you find that helpful. If this is your first time doing this, take your time, close your eyes, and see who emerges in or around your body. This list or map is not definitive and can always be added to later. There is no wrong way to do this exercise and remember, all parts are welcome!

After creating your map or list, you are invited to choose one part that you feel some curiosity about, perhaps starting with one that does not cause you too much distress or polarization. Make sure no other parts object to you getting to know it a little bit better. Once you've chosen the part and have gotten permission from your other protectors to explore it, you can flesh it out with this psychodramatic IFS externalization exercise:

Place an empty chair in your room. You can choose an object to represent your chosen part and place it on your chair if you'd like. Then begin to speak to this part, saying whatever you'd like to say to it, and ask any questions that you might have. Check in and see how you feel toward this part, and if you are experiencing any of the 8 Cs, know that you are connected to Self-energy. If you feel comfortable, then *reverse roles* and sit in this empty chair, temporarily blending with and speaking as the part. In role reversal, you can answer any of the questions already asked of the part.

If you feel comfortable, you can then reverse roles back and forth more than once and have a dialogue between yourself and your part. If you realize as you speak that you are no longer feeling curious or compassionate toward the part, recognize that you are likely now in another part, one that is possibly polarized with the first part. That is just fine as *all parts are welcome.* If this new part is not already on your parts map, you can add it to your map and explore it another time, or you can add a chair and speak to this new part as well. When you are ready to wrap up, thank this part and any others for showing up and sharing with you.

If that feels a bit uncomfortable for you, you can try the same exercise in written form. Choose a part from your map or list, and then with protector permission, write a letter to this part. You can then reverse roles and write another letter from this part to you and see where it takes you. Whichever path you take, don't forget to show appreciation to the part(s) at the end of the exercise!

Conclusion

Both IFS and psychodrama revolutionized the mental health world in their respective eras, and we owe a great deal of gratitude to Richard Schwartz and J. L. Moreno for expanding the field far beyond traditional talk therapy. Both experiential methods entrust the spontaneous and creative power we have within ourselves to heal, and the synergistic possibilities between IFS and psychodrama—with each modality offering techniques that can enhance the therapeutic power of the other—are as expansive as the Self-energy we each possess inside. I am honored to be on the professional and personal journey of integrating these two remarkable methods.

KEY TAKEAWAYS

- IFS and psychodrama both heal trauma through externalizations. IFS does so internally (through *unblending*) and psychodrama does so externally (through *enactments*).
- Psychodrama techniques that enhance work with parts are the interview, the empty chair, doubling, role reversal, and the mirror.
- Psychodrama techniques can facilitate all stages of the IFS model, including witnessing, re-do, working with polarizations, and unburdening.
- IFS and psychodrama are synergistic in group work, integrating warm-up techniques with qualities of Self, speaking for rather than from parts among group members, and facilitating collective Self-energy.
- IFS brings awareness of protector permission to the forefront, while psychodrama brings the healing power of body movement. Both transcend therapeutic healing and aspire to facilitate healing of global and collective conflicts, traumas, and burdens.

AUTHOR BIO

Valerie Simon, LCSW, TEP, CET III (she/her) has been a psychotherapist, workshop and intensives facilitator, supervisor, and trainer for over 25 years. She is a Certified Level III IFS Therapist, a Trainer, Educator and Practitioner of Psychodrama, and a Certified Level III Experiential Therapist. Valerie is the creator and director of The Inner Stage®, an innovative group practice and training facility in NYC that incorporates cutting-edge experiential therapies. She has run international therapeutic retreats in Italy and Antigua and has trained students at universities.

Most recently, Valerie has developed Play Your Parts[SM], a Self-led synthesis of IFS and psychodrama, and she runs groups and trains mental health practitioners in the hybrid method. For more information on working or training with Valerie or another practitioner at The Inner Stage®, please visit www.theinnerstage.com. Email: valerie@theinnerstage.com.

REFERENCES

Dayton, T. (2005). *The living stage.* Health Communications, Inc.

Kellogg, S. H. (2004). Dialogical encounters: Contemporary perspectives on "chairwork" in psychotherapy. *Psychotherapy: Theory, Research, Practice, Training, 41*(3), 310–320.

Moreno, J. L. (1946). *Psychodrama volume I.* Beacon House, Inc.

Moreno, J. L. (1993). *Who shall survive? Student edition* (based on 2nd ed., 1953). American Society of Group Psychotherapy & Psychodrama.

Schwartz, R. C., & Sweezy, M. (2020). *Internal Family Systems therapy* (2nd ed.). Guildford Press.

van der Kolk, Bessel (2014). *The body keeps the score.* Penguin Books.

GOING DEEPER

From Valerie Simon

1) Website:
   a. www.theinnerstage.com

From Other Sources

1) Websites:
   a. Psychodrama Practitioners and Trainings: www.psychodramacertification.org
   b. IFS Therapists and Trainings: www.ifs-institute.com
2) Books:
   a. Blatner, A. (2000). *Foundations of psychodrama* (4th ed.). Springer Publishing Company. Free link to manuscript: www.blatner.com/adam/books/Foundations of Psychodrama History, Drama, and Practice, Fourth Edition Adam Blatner MD 308p_0826160425_B.pdf
   b. Dayton, T. (2005). *The living stage.* Health Communications, Inc.
   c. Giacomucci, S. (2021). *Social work, sociometry and psychodrama. Experiential approaches for group therapists, community leaders, and social workers.* Springer. Free link to manuscript: www.link.springer.com/content/pdf/10.1007/978-981-33-6342-7.pdf
   d. Holmes, P., Karp, M., & Watson, M. (Eds.). (1994). *Psychodrama since Moreno, innovations in theory and practice.* Routlege.
   e. Moreno, J. L. (1946). *Psychodrama volume I*, Beacon House, Inc.
   f. Nolte, J. (2014). *The philosophy, theory and methods of J. L. Moreno.* Routledge. Free link to manuscript: www.dl.uswr.ac.ir/bitstream/Hannan/139731/1/9780415702874.pdf

IFS AND SANDTRAY

EXTERNALIZING PARTS FOR INSIGHT AND HEALING

Leslie Petruk, LCMHC-S, NCC, BCC

The therapeutic approach of sandtray has been used as both a diagnostic and therapeutic method since its inception nearly a hundred years ago. Currently, sandtray is primarily used, "...as a therapeutic tool of self-expression and healing, as the sandtray allows an opportunity in therapy for a fuller expression of the joining of the mind, body, and imagination together."[1]

The method incorporates the use of a tray that is painted blue to represent water or the sky and is filled halfway with sand.[2] Various miniature toys are placed in boxes that have compartments or on shelves, and the miniatures are separated by categories. *Sandtray* is the term established by Lowenfeld, the originator of the sandtray model, to describe the technique of using miniatures in a shallow box partially filled with sand, and it is free from any theoretical orientation. The term *sandplay* was created by Dora Kalff to distinguish its application within a Jungian framework. She later re-titled her technique as the "World Technique."[3]

Weinrib's definition of sandplay[4] can be considered relevant to both Lowenfeld's sandtray technique or Kalff's sandplay: "A nonverbal, nonrational form of therapy that reaches a profound preverbal level of the psyche. In this psychotherapeutic modality, patients create three-dimensional scenes, pictures, or abstract designs in a tray of specific size, using sand, water, and a large number of miniature realistic figures." (p. 1)

Similar to the way Dick Schwartz developed the IFS model by listening to his clients, Lowenfeld focused on allowing the children to guide her work, so she could observe as a theory emerged from clinical observations rather than attempting to fit children into a mold based on a predetermined theory. She described her approach: "The foundation of the whole concept of the treatment of children was that if given the right tools they would find their way to communication of their interior experience…My approach to the work was that of a clinician, and my aim was to endeavor to devise a method by which direct contact could be made, without interference from the adult, with the mental and emotional life of a child. I set myself as a goal to work out an apparatus which would put into the child's hand a means of directly expressing his ideas and emotions, which would allow a record of his creations and their abstraction for study. I had at that date no theory of the mind and was determined to avoid making or accepting one until I should have achieved objective records from which a theory could be built or checked."[5] A new technique emerged "created by the children themselves," which came to be called "The Lowenfeld World Technique."[6] It was again the children who began to refer to the cabinet containing the miniatures as "The World" and soon thereafter attributed the label "World" to their sandtray creations, hence the title "World Technique."[7]

At the start of a session, Lowenfeld introduced the child to the wet and dry sandtrays and a cabinet containing the miniatures. She then instructed the child to do with them whatever they liked. Older children were given more of an explanation and told that sometimes it is difficult to express things in their head using words and these materials could help them to communicate things in a clear manner. She also informed them they did not have to be "reasonable" and could place objects in the tray upside down or any way they would like. The child was allowed as much time as needed to complete the construction. Lowenfeld recognized the symbolic and projective implications of her method and believed that conversation with the child must occur to avoid misinterpretation by the therapist.[8]

This chapter will review the basic set up to utilize sandtray with clients applying the IFS model. The set up and process is somewhat different for children than adults as will be delineated in the examples provided. As is the case with IFS, the application of sandtray to IFS requires that the therapist meet the client where they are, also taking into consideration their developmental stage. While the scope of this chapter doesn't allow for discussion on play therapy, it should be noted that it is important for the clinician to have training in play therapy and understand a child's developmental stages in order to ethically use sandtray with children.

The Setup

Lowenfeld's sandtray was a wooden tray lined with zinc to make it waterproof. Currently, the "standard" sandtray dimensions are approximately 30 x 20 inches and three inches deep, typically constructed of wood or plastic with the inside painted blue (representing water or the sky). The size is purposeful in that it allows the client and therapist to view the entire scene in a single glance. As sandtray has gained popularity, the size and shape of the trays have varied, and circular, rectangular, and square trays are not uncommon. In their book, *Sandtray Therapy: a practical manual*,[9] Homeyer and Sweeney discuss the various shapes and sizes of sandtrays, the rationale for various shapes, and provide resources for vendors of sandtrays and miniature figures.

Because this chapter is focused specifically on the integration of sandtray and IFS, I will only be discussing the recommended categories of miniatures, and not the broader contents of a playroom. In their manual, Homeyer and Sweeney (2023) provide an extensive list of suggested basic set ideas, resources to find various figures, and a more detailed list for each category of figures (p. 35-41). They also discuss the importance and rationale for organizing miniatures (p. 34-35). Figures should be organized by categories, whether on a shelf or in containers, to provide consistency (particularly for children) and continuity for clients. (It is important to note that toys in a play therapy room and sandtray figures are not randomly chosen.)

Some examples of categories of sandtray figures are listed here:

- **People:** family groups of various ages and cultures, brides, grooms, officiants, celebrants of various religions, occupational figures, figures of people playing a sport or occupied in a hobby, graduates, figures that represent various religious activities (e.g., Bar Mitzvah, first communion), historical figures.
- **Animals:** prehistoric, zoo and wild, farm and domestic, birds, insects, sea life.
- **Buildings:** houses, single family homes, apartment buildings, businesses, churches, temples, mosques, castles, forts, teepees, world trade center twin towers, military tents, barns.
- **Transportation:** various types of old and new cars, trucks, military vehicles, dump trucks, bulldozers, buses, helicopters, airplanes, spaceships, fishing boats, canoes, yachts, rafts, ocean liners, military landing craft, submarines, rowboats.
- **Vegetation:** trees with leaves, trees without leaves, autumn trees, palm trees, pine trees, Christmas trees, plants, bushes, cacti, flowers, hedges.
- **Fences/Gates/Signs:** gates, barricades, various street signs, railroad tracks.
- **Natural Items:** seashells, rocks, sticks, dried flowers, branches, and twigs.
- **Fantasy:** Magical figures such as wizards, witches, and wishing wells and magical creatures such as dragons, unicorns, gargoyle, sphinx, monsters. Folklore figures such as Snow White, Santa Claus, various characters, cartoon and comic book figures, movie characters, ghosts, phantoms, gnomes.
- **Spiritual and Mystical:** figures representing western and eastern religions and other religious groups (e.g., Buddha, Day of the Dead Skeletons), magic or crystal balls, crystals, gold, mirrors, pyramids, other goddesses.

- **Landscaping:** sky, ponds, rainbow, fire, clouds, stars, sun, moon globe.
- **Other Accessories:** bridges and rain.
- **Household Items:** bathtub, furniture, toilet, bed, food, kitchen items.
- **Miscellaneous items:** medical items, wine bottles, beer cans.

Similar to non-directive play therapy, sandtray with children provides unconditional positive regard for clients and meets them where they are. It gives them an opportunity to build a relationship with the therapist, become accustomed to the playroom, and begin to explore the room and toys. In my practice, I have a traditional play therapy room as suggested by Garry Landreth,[10] one of the fathers of non-directive play therapy. I offer two sandtrays in the room, one for dry sand and one for wet sand, along with a wall full of miniatures. My sandtrays are utilized in my work with children, adults, couples, and families. For teenagers, sandtray can be particularly enticing as it doesn't require artistic skill and gives the teen a way to express themselves without necessarily having to talk.

The Integration of Sandtray and IFS

Sandtray as a therapeutic modality lends itself well to integration with IFS. A sandtray provides a literal container in which a client can externalize their inner world of parts. The very act of selecting a figurine to represent a part is an "unblending" experience, as the client is immediately able to adopt Self's perspective and hold an embodied awareness of being separate from the part. This simple act often leads to new perspective and insight about the part and its experience, as well as its relationship with other parts. It allows a client to access their unspoken and unconscious thoughts and feelings and provides a deeply intuitive way of engaging with, befriending, witnessing, retrieving, and unburdening their parts. In contrast to more cognitive interventions which engage the frontal cortex, sandtray and IFS both access the limbic areas of the brain where trauma is encoded, allowing it to be embodied or enacted, processed, and released.

Sandtray and IFS naturally integrate because they hold so many similarities. Both are effective with individuals across the lifespan, as well as with couples and families. Both models trust the client to guide the process and believe that the wisdom for healing resides within the individual, rather than within the therapist. Sandtray and IFS both offer a compassionate and non-pathologizing view of the client's struggles and invite deeper awareness of, and relationship with, the client's inner world. For both, the role of the therapist is to hold a compassionate, curious, non-judgmental space (Self-energy, which requires tracking the therapist's own parts while the client is working). Within the safety of the sandtray container, with the support of the therapist's Self-energy, the client can freely select miniatures to represent their inner parts and explore the relationship of parts in dimensional space. From here, each step of the IFS model can be enacted, with the client naturally adopting the role of Self, holding inner wisdom for what the parts need to embody their healing process.

The Process with Children: A Case Example

As is true with IFS or any other therapeutic model, when doing sandtray with a child or adult, the first step is to develop a trusting therapeutic relationship. It is critical for the therapist to release any agenda for the client as they focus on their work. With children, it is helpful to begin with an introduction to the room, including the sandtrays, usually one wet and one dry, and the intriguing wall of miniatures. The therapist holds space, presence, and unconditional positive regard, allowing the child to naturally begin to explore the miniatures and begin building a scene in the sand. An introduction—such as, "This is my special playroom. In here, you get to decide how you would like to spend your time,"—is an invitational way of introducing the child to the process. Younger children will often take the cue to begin to explore the room and start playing in the sand. Some will start by putting their hands in the sand and feeling the kinesthetics of the sand, moving it around and burying their hands. Others might start by creating an active scene where they drive vehicles around or play out a battle scene. Others will examine the miniatures and meticulously pick the ones they want to use to create a static scene in the tray. How a child approaches the sandtray and their process is typically related to their age and what brought them to therapy. It can also be a reflection of both their internal and external worlds.

For example, an eight-year-old client I will call Timmy (all names and identifying information in this chapter have been altered to protect confidentiality) came to therapy because he had recently been removed from the custody of his mother, who was actively abusing substances and was abusive towards Timmy. His father was the parent who brought him to therapy. In our first session, Timmy stood and stared at me, paralyzed. He appeared fearful to do anything without explicit direction. I reflected what I thought he was feeling internally with mirroring comments such as, "It can feel scary to come to a new place and meet a new person," and "It looks like you aren't sure what you are and aren't allowed to do in here. In here, you get to decide." Timmy just stood and stared at me the entire first session while I continued to reflect on what I suspected he was feeling.

In our second session, he again stared at me with a look of fear. But as I reflected what I sensed he was feeling, I noticed his eyes looking around the room without him moving his head. As I tracked this out loud, I continued to reflect with wonderment: "I wonder if it feels scary for you to decide for yourself what you would like to do. In here, you get to decide." He eventually started to move his head to look around the room, and then Timmy started asking repeatedly, "What should I do?" As I reflected his question, he would take a step closer to me, asking again, "What should I do?" I continued to reflect his fear and uncertainty about deciding for himself what he wanted to do. Each time he took a step forward his voice got louder, again asking me what he should do. I continued to hold curiosity and space for his unknowing, fear, and uncertainty. Eventually, he was right in my face yelling, "Tell me what to do!" I let him know I understood how badly he wanted me to tell him what he should do. I named that he was probably used to being told what to do, but that in our time together, he got to decide. I also reflected that I noticed how his part was getting angrier, louder, and closer to me as he tried to convince me to give him direction. I continued to hold compassion and curiosity, asking Timmy what he would like to do, demonstrating the critical therapeutic belief that he did have agency and deep inner wisdom at his core. He left that session angry.

At the third session, Timmy immediately began walking around the room exploring everything in it, in particular the shelves of miniatures. He picked one up at a time asking, "What is this?" I responded with, "In here, it can be anything you want it to be. What would you like it to be?" He would then put the miniature down and move on to the next one, seemingly anxious about making a decision about what each figure was. After about 30 minutes of this, he asked if he could put a miniature he was holding in the sand. I let him know that it was his choice, that in our time together, he got to decide what he wanted to do. Again I was underscoring, by my non-directive responses, that he was not only allowed to, but indeed capable of, making his own decisions and having his own opinions. Timmy began wordlessly creating an elaborate scene in the sand. I sat with him holding presence and curiosity but not intervening. He became so engrossed in what he was doing that when I gently spoke to let him know we had ten minutes remaining in our time together, he startled. He was so immersed in his internal process and the scene he created in the sandtray representing his inner world that he had been unaware of the time passing.

This continued for several sessions. Timmy would come in and go directly to the shelves to select miniatures with which he would create sandtray scenes. Each scene showed very similar themes of fear and isolation which he was able to enact and express within the safety of the sandtray container. This enactment with miniatures naturally created an unblending experience with his parts, allowing him to adopt the wise Self perspective to witness the parts that were afraid and alone and to offer them Self-led redos and retrieval. After the fifth session, Timmy's father said, "I don't know what you have said to Timmy, but his teachers have started raving about how much better he is doing in school, and he has been much more confident and playful at home with me and my wife. He wouldn't even talk to his stepmother when we first got him, and now, he asks her to play with him."

This case is an example of how sandtray can be a powerful tool of expression and process and does not require the therapist to guide or interpret. Holding space, compassion, and curiosity, while trusting that Timmy knew what his system needed allowed him to work through his emotions without him saying a word at times. After about five months of weekly sandtray sessions, Timmy's parts had gained such a sense of safety and trust that he entered the playroom one day and asked me to pull up a chair and play with him in the sandtray. I followed his lead and had him instruct me what to do. I did nothing without his direction. Just as we wouldn't tell adults what to do in their therapy, the same applies for working with children. He would hand me figures and tell me where to place them in the tray, telling the story as he was building each scene. Gradually, the theme of his sandtray scenes and stories went from stark and fearful (his initial flooded exiles) to aggressive (his protectors) as he illustrated various battle scenes. As Timmy's exiles and protectors all were welcomed to express themselves and be witnessed in the sandtray, Timmy's scenes eventually shifted to a neighborhood scene with a puppy, family, trees, roads with street signs, and cars driving down the streets—an indicator that his parts had experienced transformation and were comfortable allowing Timmy's Self to hold the leadership role in his life. Right around the year-and-a-half mark, Timmy was doing well and ready to end therapy. He was now a playful, confident kiddo exhibiting age-appropriate behaviors. His father reported he was doing well, both at school and at home. The transformation of Timmy's parts, when allowed to express themselves and be witnessed within the safety of the therapeutic sandtray environment, is illustrative of the power of the integration of IFS and sandtray.

It is important to note that IFS-integrated sandtray work can be offered in a directive or non-directive format. For older children, a more directive approach can be helpful. As they "play" in the tray I might offer IFS-informed questions such as "What does that part want us to know about itself?" or "What is that angry one afraid would happen if it wasn't angry?" For younger children, I tend to be mostly non-directive (as I was with Timmy), allowing the child to entirely direct their own process with awareness that the child's Self knows exactly what their inner system needs. Some child clients stand at the sandtray and manipulate the sand, burying their hands and having a wordless kinesthetic experience as they do deep internal work. Other children quietly "play" with their chosen miniatures in the tray, silently enacting what each part intuitively needs. Still others want to narrate, engaging me in the process and even directing me to interact with the miniatures at various times. Regardless of the child's engagement, when we approach sandtray with the fundamental IFS awareness that each child's Self-energy is their most skillful healer, we can offer the child our own Self-energy and connection, curiosity, and compassion as a container while they do their work.

As the sandtray process unfolds, a child's parents will often report behaviors that are reflective of the themes of their trays, demonstrating how parts that are activated and need to be witnessed come into the room in the sandtray setting. For example, if the child's tray illustrated aggressive and angry themes, parents often report that their child was unusually reactive and frustrated that week. When children's trays begin to exhibit themes of nurturing and connection, parents will report the child was very affectionate towards them or their siblings. It is fascinating to me the consistency with which children's scenes exhibit circular patterns when they begin to connect deeply with their own Self-energy. There appears to be a universality of circular energy with Self. I have included visual examples of this.

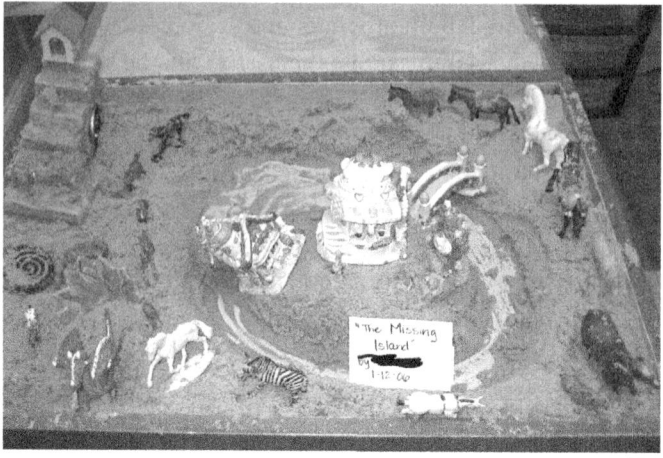

Parents will consistently begin to report that their child is communicating feelings and experiencing fewer meltdowns or challenging behaviors as this access to their own inner Self-energy emerges.

Children who are older and at a different development stage tend to need a prompt or may come into session talking about themselves and/or the problems they are experiencing. It is important to meet the child where they are, build a trusting therapeutic relationship, and integrate the use of the sandtray into the session when it feels natural to do so. Most clients enjoy creating sandtrays, but as with IFS, it is important not to force an agenda onto them, instead offering it as one option out of many ways to help them get to know more about themselves.

The Integration of IFS and Sandtray with Adults

When working with adults, sandtray can be utilized to facilitate the representation of their parts that are related to their presenting problem, helping them to befriend their protectors and clarify the target part(s) they want to explore. A prompt similar to one we use in IFS can assist client's with dropping in: "Check inside and see what part(s) want to be expressed/represented in the sandtray and pick the miniatures that best portray them." For clients who aren't sure what "checking inside" is all about, you can simply ask them to pick some miniatures that represent their thoughts and feelings related to the presenting issue or how they are feeling in the moment. If I notice that a client is stuck contemplating the "right" miniature to select, and a thinking part seems to be directing their process, I will inquire about a "thinking part" to see if it can step aside so they can just notice which parts want to be represented as they scan the figures, without giving it too much thought, to see which one(s) speak to them. For those who aren't familiar with IFS, you can just replace "parts" with "thoughts, feelings, or sensations." Other prompts and specific techniques that can be used will be discussed later in the chapter.

Some clients will come in telling their story and naming a number of their different parts. Reflecting back the parts you hear them name and directing them to choose a miniature to represent each one is a great way to help a client slow down, develop awareness of their parts, and create a "map" of their inner system. As we saw with children, the invitation to choose a figure to represent their thoughts and feelings itself is an unblending technique, allowing the client to gain embodied space from the part that they are interested in getting to know and taking on the Self perspective. In keeping with the guiding principles of the IFS process, always start with the protective system and work "from the outside in" to move eventually toward the more vulnerable exiles. Once a client has mapped, or created a scene with, their protectors, you might direct them to choose a figure that represents the vulnerable part (their exile) that their protectors are working so hard to shield.

Another way to invite clients into the work is to ask them to pick one or more figures that represent the thoughts and feelings they would like to focus on. Figures can represent any presenting problem that a client brings to therapy and allow them to externalize what they are experiencing internally. The "picture" that is created can be seen as a depiction of a client's inner landscape and allows the client to view their parts from a new perspective, often leading to insight. As clients explore this depiction with the therapist, they experience a safe way to get to know and befriend their various parts.

As stated by Homeyer and Sweeney (2023), "Sandtray therapy, similar to art therapy, is an expressive and projective therapy that has the unique and extraordinary quality of being considerably flexible and adaptive. It can integrate a wide variety of theoretical and technical psychotherapeutic approaches. It can be non-directive or directive, completely non-verbal or verbally assisted, and incorporate techniques from a wide spectrum of counseling approaches."

Four Skills Required for a Sandtray Session Utilizing the IFS Protocol

As a guide for clients exploring their inner worlds, the therapist is assisting in the process of developing a healthy inner attachment from Self to their inner "children." This requires that the therapist embody the qualities that cultivate a secure external attachment.

Skill 1: Presence

"While physically preparing the room, therapists should simultaneously prepare themselves. Understanding the person-of-the-sandtray-therapist (POST) includes preparing the Self to provide, facilitate, and join with the client."[11]

Just as in any therapy session, the presence of the therapist is what creates the foundational safety and trust for the client to explore their internal world.

Dora Kalff,[12] a Swiss Jungian analyst who created "sandplay," emphasized the importance of the therapist creating a "free and protected space" to facilitate this process. Therapists must do their own parts work, so they are able to provide this therapeutic holding from an open-hearted, Self-led, and accepting place. The therapist serves as the holder of the therapeutic field, providing an uninhibited presence so they are able to meet the client where they are, allowing a client to do vulnerable and sacred work as they explore their internal world.

Skill 2: Attunement and Reflection

Reflecting is a basic but critical therapeutic skill that communicates deep understanding to a client and helps them to feel seen, heard, and understood (a yearning that we all have as humans). Attunement with the client communicates genuine understanding and activates their ventral vagal social nervous system which in turn facilitates self-regulation, elicits safety, and allows for deeper inner work.

Skill 3: Tracking the Process

As clients are choosing and placing figures, the therapist is tracking the process. Noticing how the client goes about choosing the figures (quickly and instinctually or slowly and methodically), how they approach the creation of the scene that illustrates their parts, how the miniature exemplifies their parts (i.e., what characteristics of the figure portrays the part it represents), and the placement in the tray in relation to other figures are all important pieces of information for the therapist who is tracking the client's sequencing. Did the part choose a figure to represent itself, was it another part, or was their Self-energy guiding the process? This information, tracked and reflected by the attuned therapist, can provide the client with greater insight and a clearer picture of their internal landscape. The representation provides a new perspective as they see an externalized illustration of how their parts interact with one another and learn what they are protecting. For some clients, the awareness of how layered their protective system is provides new appreciation for the role each part plays in their system. As the client illuminates each part and literalizes their inner constellation in the sandtray, a profound deepening occurs. The therapist works with them to recognize the positive intention of their protectors and to appreciate how committed they are and how hard they work in order to facilitate the befriending process. Seeing their parts in 3D is often very powerful and striking for clients and deepens their insight and connection to their inner world.

Skill 4: Curiosity

As the therapist holds a genuine and non-judgmental curiosity towards each of the client's parts, clients feel permission to do the same. This can be particularly effective when judgmental or critical protectors step in. Having the client pick a miniature to represent the critical part and its spatial relationship to the target part allows the client's Self to become curious about why it stepped in, why it does what it does, when it first had to take on the critical job, and what it's afraid would happen if it didn't step in. The therapist's curious and compassionate response to all parts sets the stage for safety for the client to welcome in and get to know their parts.

Steps of the Process

Step 1: Introduction of Sandtray and Prompts

There are various ways in which a sandtray session can be introduced. For younger children a prompt may not even be necessary. As you introduce them to your sandtray room, younger children are typically immediately drawn to the wall of figures or the sandtray—so following their lead and reflecting their behaviors will give them permission to explore and play in the sandtray. For example, a seven-year-old client I'll call Jake entered the room saying, "Wow! Look at all these things!" He immediately walked over to the shelves and began picking figures up and placing them back on the shelf. I simply reflected, "You are amazed to see all these things, and you decided to check them out." My five-year-old client I'll call Jessica entered the room, immediately headed for the dry sandtray, and began to bury her hands in the sand. She spent the entire session manipulating the sand in both the dry and wet sandtrays. I reflected what I thought might be going on inside her at times. For example, "You seem to really like the way the sand feels on your hands." Her resonance indicated the presence of deep (non-verbal) internal work.

With older children and adults, the introduction to sandtray is often related to the therapeutic goal. For the first session, the goal is to get to know a client and begin building a therapeutic relationship. So, you might direct the client to "choose some figures that represent their thoughts and feelings about themselves and their family members and place them in the sandtray." Adult clients typically have specific presenting problems. As you reflect back the parts you hear as they describe their dilemmas, clients expand their awareness and map their inner system in the sandtray.

A client I will call Carol began therapy with the goal of addressing her drinking and depression:

> **Leslie:** (reflecting back what she had stated she wanted to focus on). "So you are wanting to stop drinking and are aware that you have a part that feels the urge to drink in the evening after the kids are in bed. Can you choose a figure to represent the part that creates that urge to drink?" (Client picked a figure of a wine bottle and placed it in the sandtray). "Are there any other thoughts or feelings you experience around the urge to drink in the evening?"

Carol: "I have a voice that tells me I deserve a glass of wine after working and taking care of the kids all day, and I have another part that says, 'Okay, but just one glass.' I always start out that way but end up drinking the whole bottle. I also have a part that is angry at my ex-husband and drinks to keep me from getting angry."

Leslie: "Ah, so there's another part that is angry and is trying to keep you from acting angry. Does it work? And what happens after you drink the whole bottle?"

Carol: "No, I beat myself up and get mad at myself that I've done it AGAIN. I get angry with myself and the kids. I lose my patience with them really easily, and then I feel guilty and horrible, and a part tells me I'm the worst parent in the world."

Leslie: "So, can you pick some figures to represent the voice that tells you that you are deserving of having a glass of wine and then the one who beats you up afterwards?"

Carol: (As she's placing a figure of a young girl and the fierce-looking three-headed dog) "I think it's the kid who never felt like she deserved anything who is trying to tell me I deserve it now, and the part that criticizes me is really angry and attacking."

Leslie: "That makes a lot of sense that a younger part who didn't feel deserving is trying to convince you that you are. The part that beats you up looks really fierce and scary."

Carol: "Yeah, I'm realizing that my little girl is afraid of this one who attacks me so maliciously afterwards."

Leslie: "So, as you look at the figures in the sandtray, what do you notice? Are there any other parts that need or want to be represented?"

Carol: "I have a part that really rationalizes and justifies my drinking and another one that lies about it to my kids. That leads to me feeling really guilty."

Leslie: "So go ahead and add those parts to your scene."

Carol: (Placing a male figure to represent the part that rationalizes, a fairy to represent the one that lies to her kids, and a figure of a girl curled up in a ball to represent her guilt.) "All of these voices swarm around in my head every day, and the one that is critical is the loudest."

Leslie: "It sounds like they are all working really hard to protect you and that you're aware of how the critical voice is the loudest one. Is that right?"

Carol: "Yes, I didn't realize that until just now."

Leslie: "And how are you feeling towards that critical part as you realize how hard it works?"

Carol: "I don't like it—it's really vicious."

Leslie: "Can you ask the part that doesn't like it to step back, so we can learn more about this one that beats you up? Let it know, we aren't going to let it do what it does to you. We're just going to get to know it and learn more about it."

Carol: (Choosing a figure of fire to represent the part that doesn't like it and placing it out to the side.) "This is the part that doesn't like it—I'm going to put it over here."

Leslie: "Great, so it looks like it's willing to step aside while we get to know the critical part that beats you up—is that right?"

Carol: "Yes, but it wants to stand over here so it can see what's happening."

Leslie: "That's great—and let it know if it needs to speak up at any point it is welcome to."

Carol: "Okay, it's good with that."

Leslie: "Now as you put your attention back on the part that beats you up, how are you feeling towards it?"

Carol: "I am wondering about it."

Leslie: "Are you feeling curious towards it or does that feel like another part that might be trying to figure it out?"

Carol: "I am feeling curious. I'm wondering why it becomes so vicious."

Leslie: "So first, can you extend your curiosity and let it know that you really want to learn more about it, and see how it responds to that?"

Carol: "It was way across the room from me and now it is moving closer."

Leslie: "Great. See how close it would like to come."

We continued to have her befriend the part that had taken on the role of drinking and learned that it was doing this job to keep her from feeling the "anguishing feeling of shame and loneliness." This made sense to her as she came to realize that the viciousness of the critical part was equivalent to the shame and loneliness of her vulnerable exile. She chose a figure of a lamb to represent her shame and loneliness and placed it in the corner farthest away from any of her other parts. Then she put a fence around it with the three-headed dog facing outwards to keep anyone from getting to the lamb. Carol became aware that the fence was another protector that shut her down or kept people at a distance to also help protect the lamb (shame and loneliness). She began rearranging the other parts that were in front of the three headed dog naming that there were layers of protectors that were all working to keep her from feeling her shame and loneliness. This visual representation of Carol's system was incredibly powerful for her to see, and she decided that before we went to the lamb all of her protectors needed to be heard.

We spent the next session hearing about the jobs each one of her protectors had taken on, when they had to start these jobs, and anything else they wanted to share about how they were trying to protect her from feeling the loneliness and shame of her vulnerable exile. In the following session, Carol was ready to get to know the exile part that was so lonely and held a lot of shame. We spent two sessions witnessing this little one who was scared and alone, frozen at the age of two, when her brother had been born. The grandmother who took care of her during the day until she went to kindergarten was "mean and scary". Her parents divorced when she was five, and she was convinced it was her fault. We unburdened this little one after it was fully witnessed. In subsequent sessions, we continued to unpack her parts (the angry one and the one who felt like she was a horrible parent), witness their stories, and offer healing to them as well.

Carol continued using sandtray, sometimes working with one scene for several weeks. She directed the process of which parts we worked with and when the protectors were willing to allow her to go to the exile, addressing fears and concerns along the way. After about nine months of working together, Carol came in and announced that she had not had anything to drink for 30 days and that she was ready to attend an AA group. She continued to do IFS and sandtray work with me for another eight months. Last I heard, she was still going to her AA meetings, doing well, and had started dating.

Step 2: Creation/Building of the Sandtray

Noting how children approach the sandtray and their process in the construction of their scene is very useful information. Tracking the process and reflecting to the child begins the process of tracking their parts. For example, "You seem to be really looking closely at all of the different figures and carefully choosing the ones you want to use, or "You knew just which figures you wanted to use to create that scene. It looks like there are two sides, and they are in a big battle. Is that right? I wonder what they are battling over?"

As you reflect the process, you can also get curious about the story that may be playing out in the child's mind. Sometimes I have had a child client respond with "I don't know," when I ask about their sandtray scene, but often (because of the themes of other trays and the information I have about their situation) I can hypothesize what the scene represents and offer that reflection as a possibility to the child. One client of mine whose parents were going through a divorce was a quiet child who had become extremely anxious when his parents separated. His battle scene seemed to be a representation of the inner turmoil he was feeling. He was eventually able to name that he was afraid to talk to either parent about what he did at the other's house, fearing they would get mad at him. We were able to continue to use sandtray to help him work with those parts and others that arose over time. Some weeks he would come in and create active sandtray scenes, while on other weeks he would choose figures and create a stationary scene. Then we would get to know each of his "parts" by getting curious about each miniature that he chose.

Step 3: Externalization and Unblending of Parts

As illustrated in Carol's story, she would choose a figure for each part as it showed up. If a part showed up that was blocking the connection to another part, she would place it in front of the part it was protecting or beside a protector it was working in conjunction with. Whenever we would ask it to unblend, she would move it to the side in the sandtray, so she had the visual of her parts unblending. This is a concrete way to help clients identify, connect with, and unblend from protectors that I have found to be very effective. Of course, there are times that the part that steps in isn't willing or ready to unblend, and in that situation, it becomes the target part. Carol would often then create another scene off to the side of the target part we started with as she represented the new target part and those that were associated with it.

Some children will create a sandtray where they appear totally self-directed, determined, and focused. Others will appear unsure, self-conscious, and anxious. Some are talking and narrating while building the scene, while others do not speak at all, and yet others will intermittently say something. When holding space with anyone who is creating a sandtray, it is important to attune to them and their system, meeting them where they are and reflecting accordingly. The non-judgmental, curious therapist presence is what helps create a container and safe space for internal work, which is often happening even when they aren't saying anything.

Step 4: Processing the Completed Scene

Once a client states they are done with their scene (with children, as with adults we are typically processing as the scene is being created), I will extend curiosity to see what their parts are interested in or willing to share with me. Sometimes, they are not willing to say anything, and that's okay too. I always ask if they would like to give their completed sandtray scene a title or name. This often helps to start the conversation. I write their name, the date, and the title, if they had one, on an index card and place it in the tray. I ask if they would like to take a picture of their scene with my camera, and then ask if it's okay with them for me to take some pictures. I've never had anyone say no. I take pictures from various views and angles.

I may begin the processing of the tray by reflecting things I noticed as they were constructing it, if I didn't do so as they were building it. I will ask them what they noticed as they were creating. For younger children, who won't understand this question, I'll just ask them if they'd like to tell me about their sandtray. I will also ask if there is anything that stands out to them now that they can see it from a different perspective or that they want to share with me about their scene. I may point out something I notice in the scene and "wonder" about it—e.g., "I wonder what this alligator over here is doing and how it's feeling?" or "I wonder what happens next?"—after a child has created an active scene. Providing time and space for children to share about their sandtray, even if it was just an active process of moving the sand around and not a static scene, helps them to feel seen, heard, understood, and valued. Creating this internal connection is part of building a healthy attachment between the client's parts and Self.

Step 5: Session Closure

Providing a 10-minute notice helps to maintain the structure and flow of the process. As mentioned with my client Timmy, I have had child clients who were so focused and involved in what they were doing that when I spoke to give them the 10-minute notice, they would startle. Some children will spend part or all of the session just moving their hands through and around the tray. Clearly, an internal process is happening as they feel the sand and have the kinesthetic experience.

Sometimes children ask if I can leave the scene they created, so it is there for them the following week. I let them know I can't do that because the room gets used by other people, but that I can bring the picture the following week, and it can be used to recreate the scene. Interestingly, I think I have only had one or two clients who actually wanted to see the picture of their sandtray scene in the following session, but I always offer it if that had been the agreement we made. By the next week, they are usually in a different place and want to start where they are in the moment.

Leaving time at the end is important. It is an indicator that you are transitioning to the closing stage of the session and that you are interested in learning about your client, what they created, and their internal world. You can learn a lot about your client through processing their scene with them.

While there has been some writing and research on what completed scenes indicate, it is important to hold those hypotheses lightly. What's important is what it means to the client. While some sandtray therapists don't even process the scene created with their clients, I always hold curiosity about the process, the figures chosen, and the final scene. I open space for clients to share, but if they choose not to, that is okay as well. Taking time upon the completion of the scene to view it and honor the process and creation communicates a valuing of them and their system. In IFS language, these figures likely represent parts within their internal world, and it is imperative that the therapist respects and honors each part that the client has shared of themselves.

What the completed scene could imply has been addressed in the literature. For example, Charlotte Buhler,[13] a researcher on sandtray, developed indicators that identified the need for clinical intervention. The indicators she identified are:

1. Aggressive worlds.
2. Empty worlds (50 figures or less).
3. Distorted worlds (i.e., closed, rigid, and disorganized Worlds).

Dr. Linda Homeyer, committee chair for my thesis,[14] has published a number of books on using sandtray, which I highly recommend.

For my thesis research, I worked with nine to 10-year-olds to see what similarities and differences were exhibited in sandtray scenes of children who were "clinical" versus "non-clinical." The "clinical" participants were children in the custody of the Department of Protective and Regulatory Services and housed at the Buckner Assessment Center in Dallas, TX. It was known that all but one of the children had experienced either physical abuse, sexual abuse, or a combination. For the purpose of my study, the same instructions were given to each participant: "Use these miniatures to build or create a world in the sandtray. You can choose as many or as few as you would like and can have as much time as you want, up to 30 minutes. I will let you know when you have five minutes left, but if you finish before that, let me know that you are done. I will be sitting over here."

Here, I share some of the cases that include the above indicators to illustrate and elucidate how parts are expressed in sandtray:

"Ann," in the non-clinical group, was a 10-year-old Caucasian girl who lived with her biological parents and had two older brothers, ages 13 and 17.
The family income was over $100,000. Her scene portrayed a neighborhood, with a man mowing the lawn and woman gardening. Fences separated the houses on one side. A track in the sand indicated a road on which a police car, an ambulance, and a boy on a motorcycle were traveling. Cats and dogs were also placed throughout. This is an example of a typical neighborhood scene.

"Matthew," also in the non-clinical group, was a nine-year-old Caucasian. He created a small neighborhood scene that included one house and a treehouse. A woman gardener, a man mowing the lawn, and a wishing well were also included. In the lower right-hand corner, Matthew depicted a scene of animals with a bridge that he said was the zoo. This is a typical example which illustrates the differences seen between boys and girls world constructions. His world is less detailed and not as full as those commonly constructed by the girls.

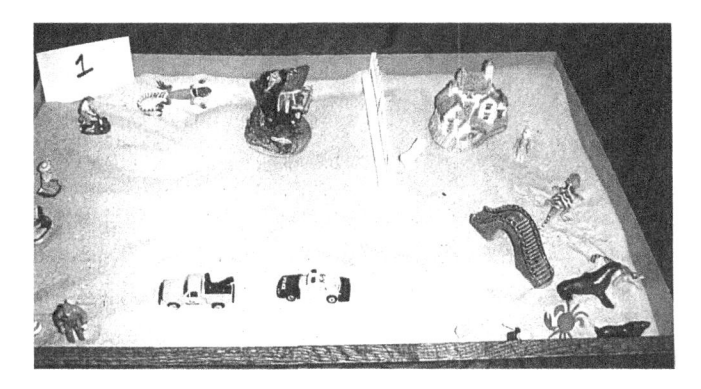

Joe's Aggressive World

"Joe" was at the Center because of physical abuse by his father who had recently been released from jail. His mother was deceased, and his stepmother and sister were out of the country. His scene included seven dinosaurs, three of which were surrounding a helicopter. A fourth appeared to be attacking another helicopter, and the fifth was shown with a lobster in its mouth. He primarily used army men, sea life, and animals (prehistoric and wild). The army men were facing each other in rows as if in battle. A skeleton was laid in the lower left corner. Two snakes were included, with one slithering diagonally through the middle of the tray from the bottom left-hand corner towards the upper right corner of the tray.

A lizard and alligator faced towards the outer edges of the tray. His scene included two monsters, one sitting on a toilet (he laughed as he placed the monster) and the other seeming to be in a posture of attack. The scene of destruction and attack seemed to convey anger about his current situation, feelings of abandonment (the skeleton), and of being trapped (dinosaurs surrounding helicopters).

Frank's "Peaceful" World

"Frank," a 10-year-old African American male, created a typical neighborhood scene in his world. However, in the middle of his scene he arranged a row of people who appeared to be a family sitting in the sand, and then placed a tiger approaching them. When Frank talked about his world, he reported that it was, "…animals that harm people. The animals go out into the jungle, and the elephants and gorillas try to harm people because they're trying to get them and stuff."

He explained, "The reason the police are there is to save people, to protect 'em, and to be happy that this world wasn't so bad. They try to catch criminals that break into people's houses and shoot each other. The rest of the police search for them. The only thing I want in this place is just peace because there's too much gang violence…there's too many kids bringing knives to school and people trying to break in each other's houses that aren't supposed to, and if they had a mother, they wouldn't treat their mother like that. They came in this world for one reason, to have food, shelter, and clothing. Not supposed to go breakin' in each other's houses. If they had an argument, they should of worked it out…they ought to be treated better, so they won't harm anybody."

Frank presented extremely sad, anxious, and inhibited. He spoke very softly, was hesitant to do anything without instruction, and appeared very insecure. His case file revealed that he had been physically and emotionally abused by his mother who had struck him with the wooden handle of a broom and an extension cord. He had also been forced to steal and threatened to be harmed in his sleep. His world picture was seemingly a projection of wish fulfillment as to how he wished his world to be. His story seemed to reveal emotional scars.

Larry's Distorted World

The most chaotic ("distorted," according to Buhler's research) scene was done by "Larry," a nine-year-old American Indian boy who asked the researcher if he was going to be doing a "kids' game." He began the session choosing handfuls of toys at a time and appeared uninvolved. However, as the session progressed, he began creating his scene, appearing very planful and moderately involved (as compared to non-clinical children). He worked at a fast pace, and as he continued, he became less planful and began sporadically placing the miniatures and filling the tray up. He seemed to have a desperate need to fill the tray versus creating a particular scene. His speed came in spurts, working quickly and then slowing down and speeding up again. When given a 10-minute notice, he quickly grabbed as many toys as he could hold and placed them wherever he could find an empty space in the tray. He was unable to tell a story about his scene and became anxious when asked to tell about his world. The center of his scene had two areas enclosed by fences. According to Buhler (1951a), this is a sign of the need for protection.

The case history revealed that Larry had grown up on a reservation in another state, where his mother had abandoned him at the age of one. He was physically abused, neglected, and left unsupervised. He was removed from the reservation by the state because the dad had attempted to shoot him and his siblings. Mom showed up for court and took him and his three siblings to her home in Texas. One of his older brothers was in juvenile jail for raping his mother while she was passed out drunk; his other older brother was in juvenile detention for theft. Within a month of his reunification with his mother, she dropped him off at the center and refused to pick him up. Larry did go back home, but the mother returned him shortly thereafter. He has a juvenile history of stealing and brags that he stole a car with his brother and pulled a fake gun on police. He also experiences enuresis, and during the night he often soaks his bed. Larry's sandtray naturally reflects a chaotic life in both his external and internal world, and provides a window into the stabilization and regulation that could be of support to a young one living in such painful and unpredictable circumstances.

Pam's Empty World

A very sparce scene that included only seven miniatures (a house, two fences, two trees, a mailbox, and a gorilla) was constructed by "Pam," who had been physically abused, neglected, and sexually abused. Her case file indicated that she had 12 siblings. She was placed in foster care by herself, while her siblings had been placed together in groups. She had returned to the center because of "problems" in her foster home, the most noted problem being that she was reportedly urinating on the furniture and all over the house. She constructed her scene in the upper left portion of the tray with only one tree placed in the lower right corner, leaving the remainder of the tray empty. Her empty scene poignantly illustrated her feelings of abandonment and isolation.

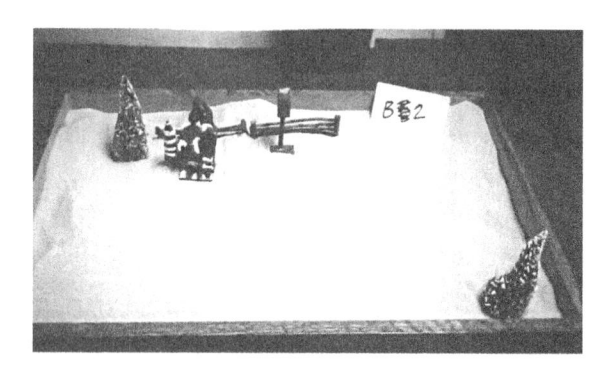

Additional Techniques for Integrating Sandtray and IFS

1. The Genogram

I have always done genograms with parents and/or children in the initial session. I have found it to be an efficient way of gaining relevant family history and information as well as a way to get to know a client. Doing a genogram with sandtray is a particularly powerful way to get to know a client and for them to begin to connect with their internal family of parts. I place a sheet of paper the size of the tray on top of the sand or on a table and draw the circles and squares to represent their family members. I then ask them to pick some figures that represent their thoughts and feelings towards each person in their family, including themselves. Often, the genogram process is a nice springboard to further explore a client's inner world around their significant relationships and experiences.

2. Working with Polarizations

Using sandtray to represent a client's inner polarized (opposing) parts is particularly useful when a client wants to work with their polarized parts as they make an important life decision or when they are feeling an internal tug of war related to something in their lives. Often, when clients are "stuck" in the IFS process, it is because there is a polarized part that hasn't been uncovered. Become curious about this by asking, "Are there any parts that are in disagreement with the point of view of the part we are working with?" Then have the client represent the initial part along with the one that battles with it. This can help you observe and learn what the polarized parts are each protecting which, interestingly, is often the same exile vulnerability. Again, the externalization of and focus on these particular parts can help clients really get acquainted and familiar with their internal world.

3. "Now and Then" Exercise

The "Now and Then" intervention is an exercise I created when working with a client who struggled with the concept of "going inside." She came to session week after week telling stories of how awful things were in her life and how desperately she wanted them to be different, but she had parts that would not allow her to "check inside." As an alternative to "checking inside," I invited her to create two scenes. One in a sandtray that represented her world the way it is today and another in a sandtray that represented what she wanted her world to look like. When she asked, "On the inside or the outside?" I replied, "Whatever one you want to illustrate." She decided to begin with the outside and then do one for her internal world. However, as she created her first world of "now" she ended up doing both. She created a scene representing her current life along with the thoughts and feelings (parts) she was noticing arise as she was talking about it, representing each one with a miniature. She did the same for the "then" tray, which was to create a tray with how she wants things to be and then adding in figures to represent her thoughts and feelings that were arising as she created it. This initial exercise provided a supportive way for the client to turn her attention to her internal world. After the first session, we were able to more deeply get to know each part she had placed in her initial trays. I worked with this client for over a year, and by the time she terminated therapy, she was "going inside" almost every session.

Speaking *for* Parts and the Expression of Self

I am frequently asked by other child therapists how to "teach" IFS to kids. In my experience, kids often intuit the basics of the model. They naturally understand that they have many different parts. The therapist's role is more about helping them attend to their parts that get activated, even when they engage in a behavior that is not helpful, but to understand that behavior is not all of who they are.

The foundational skill of IFS, which is to speak *for* parts rather than *from* them, is very helpful in working with children as well as adults. We illustrate the difference between saying "I yelled," and "A part of me yelled at my friend today because it felt angry with her." Then, "I had another part that felt bad for yelling at her." With sandtray, we can cement the child's natural parts intuition by using miniatures to represent these different parts as a child is telling their story. As with all people, when children feel seen, heard, understood, and valued, they gain access to their Self-energy. As mentioned earlier, my observation has been that children begin to create mandala-type illustrations, or circular depictions in the sandtray, when they are in deeper connection with Self. Self naturally emerges as parts are welcomed and settle back, which brings great access to the calm, curiosity, compassion, and creativity of Self-energy in our work with sand.

Conclusion

This chapter has only scratched the surface of the integration of sandtray and IFS, but I hope it has illustrated the power of using these modalities with your clients. Representing our parts in a concrete way in a sandtray allows us to get to know them and their various dimensions more intimately.

KEY TAKEAWAYS

- IFS lends itself well to the application of sandtray as an effective tool in working with children, teens, adults, couples, and families.
- Sandtray integrates beautifully with IFS to help clients illustrate their internal landscape by using miniatures to represent their parts.
- Similar to IFS, sandtray is a self-directed method that honors the client's system, goes at their pace, and is a collaborative process in which the therapist trusts the client's process to unfold.
- The act of selecting miniature figures to represent parts in a sandtray is an intuitive method of accomplishing what IFS would call unblending.
- The selection and placement of miniatures assists clients in becoming familiar with a variety of aspects of their parts, as well as parts' relationships with each other.
- Self often intuitively emerges in sandtray scenes through the use of circular patterns and illustrations.

AUTHOR BIO

Leslie Petruk, LCMHC-S, NCC, BCC (she/her) is a Licensed Clinical Mental Health Counselor and Supervisor, Board Certified Coach, Certified IFS therapist, and IFS Lead Trainer. She began her work as a counselor in 1996 and, prior to moving to Charlotte in 2001, maintained a private practice in Austin, TX. She is the Director of The Stone Center for Counseling and Leadership where she and her team served children, individuals, and families in Charlotte, NC until 2021 when she transitioned her practice online. Her specialized training in sandtray therapy, play therapy, and marriage and family therapy serve her well as she works with those who are dealing with grief and loss, depression, anxiety, trauma, adjustment, and relational challenges.

GOING DEEPER

From Leslie Petruk

1) Website:
   a. www.thestonecenternc.com
2) Trainings:
   a. Coming in 2024.
3) Publications or Blogs:
   a. Creating A World in the Sand: A Pilot Study of Normative Data For Employing the Sandtray as a Diagnostic Tool With Children (1996). Masters Thesis.

From Other Sources on Sandtray

1) Website:
   a. www.sandtraytherapy.org
2) Books:
   a. Homeyer, L. E. (2010). *Sandtray therapy: a practical manual* (2nd ed.). Routledge.
   b. Homeyer, L., & Sweeney, D. (2016). *Sandtray therapy: a practical manual* (3rd ed.). Routledge.
   c. Homeyer, L.E., & Lyles, J. (2021). *Advanced sandtray therapy: Digging deeper into clinical practice.* Routledge.
   d. Homeyer, L., & Sweeney, D. (2022). *Sandtray therapy: a practical manual* (4th ed.). Routledge.
3) Trainings:
   a. International Association for Sandtray Therapy holds an annual conference and workshops: www.sandtraytherapy.org
4) Podcasts:
   a. sandplay.org, sandplaytrainingworldwide.com www.audible.com/pd/Linda-Homeyer-Marshall-Lyles-Healing-with-Sandtray-Therapy-Part-1 Podcast/B09V3B51J4?action_code=ASSGB149080119000H&share_location=pdp
   b. www.open.spotify.com/episode/4QKCkYpj9CcEMEqg0JkyDi?autoplay=true
   c. www.emdr-podcast.com/sand-tray-therapy-emdr-with-marshall-lyles/
   d. www.synergeticplaytherapy.com/lessons-from-the-playroom-episode-104-integrating-sandtray-attachment-trauma/
5) Supplies:
   a. www.playtherapysupply.com
   b. www.childtherapytoys.com
   c. www.therapistsworkshop.com

APPENDIX A

Exercises to Implement with Sandtray and IFS

Popsicle Sticks

Years ago, I got a box of colored popsicle sticks from the craft store and wrote a feeling word on each one. I included all of the 8 Cs along with every other emotion I could think of. These "feeling sticks" can be used in a variety of creative ways. One of the ways I use them is to shake them up and have a client pick one, place the stick in the sandtray, and create a scene that represents a time they experienced that feeling. This starter can be used with clients who are having a hard time knowing where or how to start.

Painted Rocks

I have several painted rocks that I have created, along with supplies in the room for clients to paint their own rocks, to represent various parts. This is another fun and creative way to help both adult and child clients access their right brain and learn more about their internal system in a non-threatening activity. Adults enjoy this activity just as much as kids. Once the rocks dry, they can be used in the sand to create their scenes and are often incorporated in with various other figures.

Treasure Chest

I often talk with kids about how what we show on the outside (mad, irritated, or even happy) is not always the same as what we are feeling on the inside (scared, sad, or hurt). I ask clients to paint the outside of their wooden treasure chest (another inexpensive item you can get at your local craft store) to represent how they present to the world and the inside of the chest to represent how they are feeling on the inside. They can then create rocks or words on a popsicle stick to place inside of the treasure chest as a container of their parts along with qualities of Self (how they want to feel, how they feel when they are at their best and doing something they love). We might then use those items to create a scene in the sandtray along with their treasure chest. There are many creative ways you can use these items to facilitate the representations and explorations of your clients' parts and what it's like when they are connected with their inner knowing and internal resource of Self.

Online Sandtray

For those who are doing telehealth, an online sandtray is a fun and powerful way to work with clients. You can create any prompt you want to facilitate this process, and through Zoom, you can allow your client to share their screen as they are creating their tray so that you can hold space for the process and then process the product. I have found onlinesandtray.com most user friendly, but there are others web options.

7

IFS AND PLAY THERAPY

EXTERNALIZING PARTS WITH CHILDREN AND ADOLESCENTS

Carmen Jimenez-Pride, LCSW, RPT-S

"To grow up to be healthy, very young children do not need to know how to read, but they do need to know how to play."
—*Fred Rogers*

In 2004, I entered my advanced standing graduate program at the University of South Carolina to become a macro social worker with a career focused on communities and organizations. At the time, I did not intend to do direct client work, but after graduating with my Master of Social Work degree, I began working for child protective services, and my heart became very tender toward little humans.

When I noticed a lack of African American therapists who worked with children, I started to do research on becoming a Licensed Clinical Social Worker focused on direct clinical work with children. I found the Association for Play Therapy, became a member, attended my first play therapy training, and set a goal to become a Registered Play Therapist. A few years later I became fully licensed as a clinical social worker and shortly after became a Registered Play Therapist Supervisor.

In 2018, I was introduced to Internal Family Systems (IFS) and immediately realized the IFS model would blend beautifully with play therapy. I became IFS trained and certified, began integrating IFS in my play therapy practice, and eventually went on to become an IFS Assistant Trainer.

This chapter will focus on the integration of Internal Family Systems and play therapy. As child therapists, we cannot prevent children from experiencing trauma, but we do have the ability to decrease the lifelong impact of that trauma. We can accomplish this by assisting children in developing an understanding that they have an internal system of parts as well as a benevolent core Self that holds the power to empower and heal through the expressive medium of play.

What is Play Therapy?

According to the Association for Play Therapy (APT), play therapy is defined as "the systematic use of a theoretical model to establish an interpersonal process wherein trained Play Therapists use the therapeutic powers of play to help clients prevent or resolve psychosocial difficulties and achieve optimal growth and development" (Association for Play Therapy, 2022). APT gives us a definition that is grounded in theory and evidence-based practice. A more practical way to define play therapy might be "an approach to communicating therapeutically with clients using toys, art materials, games, sandtrays, and other play media, giving clients a safe and nurturing relationship in which they can explore and express feelings, gain insight into their own motivation and into their interaction with others, and learn and practice socially appropriate behaviors." (Kottman & Meany-Walen, 2016) An even more client-centered definition of play therapy might be "a method to use a child's natural language of play to address their emotional wellbeing and decrease the impact of trauma."

As an evidence-based practice, play therapy is thought to be most effective for children under the age of ten. (Senko & Bethany, 2019) But with creativity, play therapy can be used with children of all ages and all developmental stages. It can even be used successfully with adults.

It is important to differentiate between play *in* therapy and *play therapy*. Referring to the APT definition, *play therapy* is systematic and therapeutic, which can turn a traditional game or activity into an interaction with therapeutic benefits. An example of play *in* therapy would be playing a game of UNO™ while having a talk therapy session. That same game of UNO could become a therapeutic intervention as play therapy if when playing a "skip" card, the therapist initiated a discussion of a time when the child felt left out or skipped over, using the card as a springboard to process the child's thoughts and feelings about the event.

Play therapy techniques can be directive or nondirective (also known as child-centered or person-centered). Non-directive play therapy makes no effort to control or change the child and tells us that the child's behavior is at all times caused by the drive for self-realization (Landreth, 2012). When integrating IFS into non-directive play therapy, the therapist is primarily Self-led and connected to the 8 Cs of self-leadership including calmness, curiosity, compassion, confidence, courage, clarity, connectedness, and creativity. The therapist presents with no agenda for the session and allows the child to lead.

Directive play therapy techniques are more planful in the coordination of activities and focus to reach a goal or create space for learning. When integrating IFS into directive play therapy, the therapist may have more managerial energy blended with Self qualities, which allows them to identify and orient toward specific therapeutic goals for the child's sessions.

Both directive and nondirective play therapy can present opportunities for children to express their thoughts and feelings and for the therapist to assist them in moving from hurt to healing.

Play therapy can powerfully facilitate attachment enhancement and repair with both the external and internal systems of the child's world.

Therapeutic Powers of Play

The Therapeutic Powers of Play, which in some way lays the foundation of skillful play therapy, were developed in 1993 by Dr. Charles Schaefer, co-founder of the Association of Play Therapy. Schaefer demonstrated that play initiates, facilitates, and strengthens therapeutic effects, and acts as a mediator that positively influences the desired change in the client (Schaefer & Drewes, 2014). He introduced twenty of what he called "core change agents" across four broad growth categories illustrated in the figure below, and he invited therapists to specifically tailor clinical interventions drawn from one or more of these change agents in order to most effectively reach the child's clinical goals.

Diagram of the Therapeutic Powers of Play
Taken from (Schaefer and Drewes, 2014) and created by Carmen Jimenez-Pride

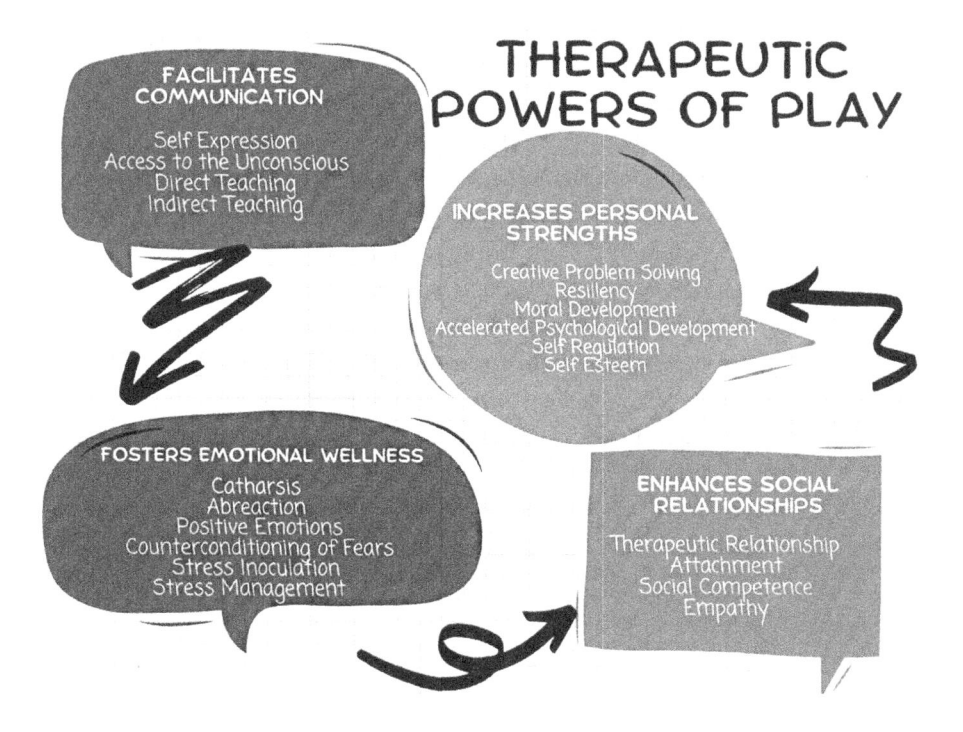

THERAPEUTIC POWERS OF PLAY

FACILITATES COMMUNICATION
Self Expression
Access to the Unconscious
Direct Teaching
Indirect Teaching

INCREASES PERSONAL STRENGTHS
Creative Problem Solving
Resiliency
Moral Development
Accelerated Psychological Development
Self Regulation
Self Esteem

FOSTERS EMOTIONAL WELLNESS
Catharsis
Abreaction
Positive Emotions
Counterconditioning of Fears
Stress Inoculation
Stress Management

ENHANCES SOCIAL RELATIONSHIPS
Therapeutic Relationship
Attachment
Social Competence
Empathy

Facilitates Communication

Self-expression, access to the unconscious, and direct and indirect teaching are the core agents Schaefer identified that promote the larger therapeutic goal of facilitating communication in play therapy. The goal of these agents is to create room for the child to speak their natural language of play and to make learning a fun and creative experience. These agents are specific interventions that invite the child to speak for their parts during play. When working with adolescent and adult clients, these interventions effectively assist clients in connecting with, and embodying, their younger inner child parts. Self-expression can happen when the child is getting to know their internal system, experiencing Self-energy, and externalizing their parts. For example, a child may engage in an expressive arts activity that illustrates an upsetting experience in school. The therapist will then be able to identify which exiles and/or protectors had the experience and how those parts' feelings towards the experience and beliefs may have developed. The therapist can encourage the child to explore self-expression by representing and speaking for all their parts that were engaged in the upsetting situation. Thus, the larger goal of facilitating communication is accomplished both internally (between the child's parts and Self) as well as externally (between the child and the therapist).

Fosters Emotional Wellness

Catharsis, abreaction, positive emotions, counterconditioning fears, stress inoculation, and stress management are the six core agents found under the broad heading of fostering emotional wellness. The goal of these agents is to create better awareness and management of distressing feelings. IFS understands that distressing feelings are often held by vulnerable parts called exiles. In play therapy, exile parts can be externalized as a doll or an object, and the child can be guided to get to know the exile part that carries painful emotions. By developing a Self-to-part relationship in this way, emotional literacy will increase, as will the ability to manage stress and wisely respond to fears. The Self of the child holds all of these skills. Play therapy techniques that invite the child to be curious about their system and increase their understanding of how parts and their beliefs impact their system as a whole, is a powerful way to foster emotional wellness.

Enhances Social Relationships

Therapeutic relationship, attachment, social competence, and empathy are the four core agents that contribute to enhanced social relationships. Therapeutic interventions that utilize these core agents facilitate both internal relationships between parts within the child's system as well as external relationships with peers, parents, and other adults. This is especially important when there have been ruptures within external relationships and limited awareness or trust between parts in the child's inner world. A therapeutic relationship with a clinician who names and believes that the child has a benevolent inner Self that can relate in helpful ways to all the child's parts, is a powerful first step in creating the safety needed to explore and experience these enhanced social relationship skills.

Increases Personal Strengths

Creative problem solving, resiliency, moral development, accelerated psychological development, self-regulation, and self-esteem are the six core agents found under the broad heading of increasing personal strengths. The goal of these agents is to help clients develop skills to successfully navigate both internal and external stressors. With the combination of play and parts work, clients develop resilience by differentiating from their parts that carry challenging feelings and behaviors. They additionally strengthen connection to their inner 8 C Self resources: the clarity and creativity to problem solve effectively, compassion for themselves and others, courage to focus on feared parts or situations, and the naturally occurring positive regard found within the Self. Personal strengths are deepened and expanded through the implementation of these six core agents.

One of the key goals of the powers of play is to enhance the impact of play therapy interventions within the clinical setting. By integrating multiple change agents, interventions are strengthened, which increases opportunities for healing while decreasing the impact of trauma. IFS is ideally suited to enhance these play therapy interventions.

The Intersection of Play and Parts

How do we effectively work with a child who has a hard time expressing their thoughts and feelings and has no awareness of parts or Self?

How might we facilitate healing when a child's exiles have internalized negative beliefs from interactions with their parents, community, and society—beliefs such as "I am bad," or "I'm not enough"?

In my experience, the goal of IFS therapy in these instances is to liberate parts from their extreme roles; restore trust in Self-leadership; achieve balance, harmony, and wholeness; and, bring more Self-energy to internal and external systems. When working with children, the introduction of play to accomplish these goals is critical. Just like adults, children's inner systems exhibit multiplicity (Sweezy & Schwartz, 2020), and children's parts have their own set of beliefs, actions, goals, and feelings. Just like adults, children's parts become burdened through negative experiences with society, community, peers, parents, and family, and may also carry legacy burdens, the intergenerational transmission of constraining negative feelings and beliefs (Sinko, 2017). Yet children may not intuitively understand the concept of Self and parts, and this is where the intersection of IFS and play becomes educational and creative. Play is an essential component of helping children process life experiences, and IFS allows children to engage in play to develop internal awareness and healing.

Age-Appropriate Psychoeducation

(Identifying information for this case study has been changed to protect the identity of the client.)

Eight-year-old Charlotte helped me understand the need for creative psychoeducation about parts when working with children. As we began our first IFS session, I explained, "We are all made up of parts. What parts do you have?" Charlotte responded with an amused face that seemed to say, *My therapist has lost it*. "Can't you see I have hands, feet, legs, arms, and a head?" I was speechless for a few moments, and then we enjoyed a mutual laugh. That moment helped me begin to develop creative, age-appropriate ways to teach children about their parts, to help children understand that their inner experiences, behaviors, and feelings are a reflection of their parts, and that they have a core Self that can connect in empowering and healing ways with any parts that hold distress. This awareness of their inner parts increases children's emotional literacy as well as their sense of resilience.

The graphic below is one such child-friendly tool that I've developed to help children get to know their inner systems.

The Burdened Internal System

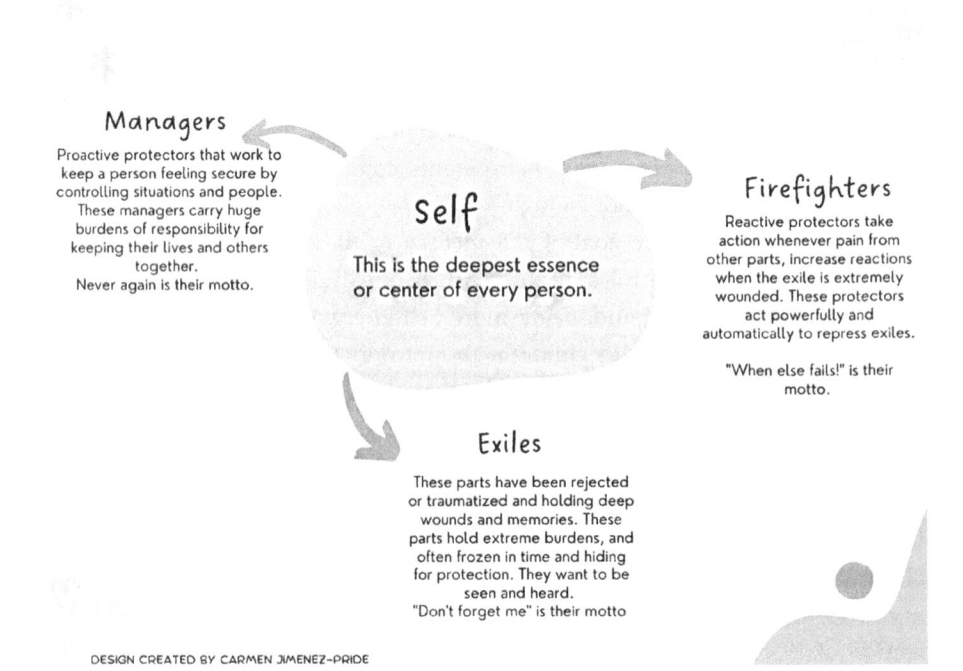

Managers
Proactive protectors that work to keep a person feeling secure by controlling situations and people. These managers carry huge burdens of responsibility for keeping their lives and others together.
Never again is their motto.

Self
This is the deepest essence or center of every person.

Firefighters
Reactive protectors take action whenever pain from other parts, increase reactions when the exile is extremely wounded. These protectors act powerfully and automatically to repress exiles.
"When else fails!" is their motto.

Exiles
These parts have been rejected or traumatized and holding deep wounds and memories. These parts hold extreme burdens, and often frozen in time and hiding for protection. They want to be seen and heard.
"Don't forget me" is their motto

DESIGN CREATED BY CARMEN JIMENEZ-PRIDE

Managers

With this chart as a reference in session, I teach children that their managers are proactive protectors that keep their system going and maintain their daily functioning. I help them see that their environment has played a role in determining how their managers will manage. For example, Charlotte's mother often calls her "Little Angel." It's a term of endearment that lets Charlotte's system know that she is connected to her mother. Not surprisingly, Charlotte will often present in her "Little Angel" part in order to maintain connection with her mother and decrease conflict and the risk of physical, verbal, and emotional abuse. Charlotte's behavior at these times is quiet and helpful. She's being directed from the part that minimizes conflict, but it also keeps Charlotte from expressing her true feelings. With the manager motto of "never again," her Little Angel part is communicating that never again will Charlotte experience the emotional effects of being physically, emotionally, and verbally abused.

Firefighters

Next, we explore firefighter parts that reactively attempt to protect and rescue. Firefighter behaviors may present as challenging behaviors like defiance, physical and verbal aggression, or inattention. I help children understand that firefighters are trying to prevent them from feeling the emotional pain of difficult situations, even though they're often using unhelpful behavior. For example, when Charlotte's parents begin to have physical altercations, she has no control of the situation, and her fears start to increase. She will tend to become dissociative, escaping into her own inner world which feels safer in that moment than her outer world. At school, her firefighters manifest differently. When Charlotte is in math class, and her teacher calls on her when she does not know the answer, she often responds with verbal aggression which is her attempt to soothe her embarrassed exile. I help Charlotte understand that even though her firefighter parts may be behaving in difficult ways, they are trying to help, and when we offer them curiosity and compassion, it may allow us to help them become less reactive or more effective in their approach to soothing pain.

Exiles

"Children are commonly taught to fear and hide emotional pain or terror because adults react to them in the extreme way they react to their own hurt child parts, [that is] with impatience, denial, criticism, revulsion, or distraction." (Sweezy & Schwartz, 2020).

I help children understand that exiles are the parts of them that hold hurt, abandonment, abuse, and emotional pain. In play therapy the term "trauma" is used. Trauma is an emotional response to an event that threatens, causes harm, and increases negative emotions. I often hear "big T" and "little T" traumas referenced. When viewed through an IFS lens, we don't give different weight to various traumas, we simply honor the impact of the burdens, regardless of what type of trauma has created the burdening.

I help children understand that burdens are the beliefs that exiles, and other parts, may carry, but it's not who their parts actually are. A child's part can be burdened by attachment disruptions, trauma, neglect, physical, sexual, and emotional abuse. When children remain in a traumatizing environment, their burdens are often compounded, and they become more entrenched and more difficult to unburden and heal.

I use the colorful illustration below to help children identify burdens their parts carry and to recognize they are not alone—that many children's parts carry these burdens—and that through the power of a relationship of those parts with the child's Self, we can help them unburden and heal.

Common Children's Burdens

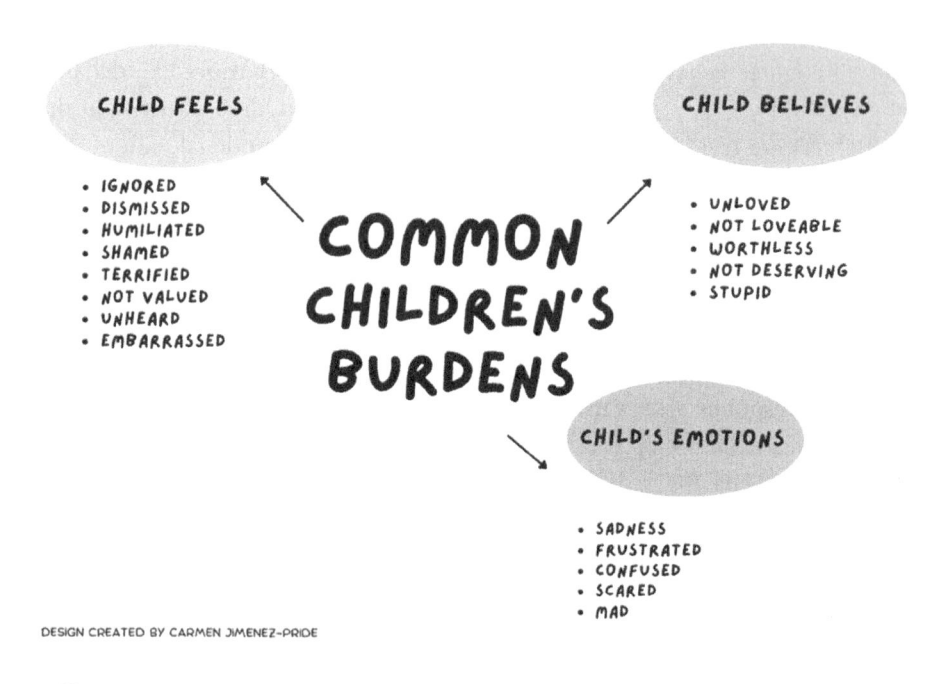

CHILD FEELS
- IGNORED
- DISMISSED
- HUMILIATED
- SHAMED
- TERRIFIED
- NOT VALUED
- UNHEARD
- EMBARRASSED

CHILD BELIEVES
- UNLOVED
- NOT LOVEABLE
- WORTHLESS
- NOT DESERVING
- STUPID

CHILD'S EMOTIONS
- SADNESS
- FRUSTRATED
- CONFUSED
- SCARED
- MAD

DESIGN CREATED BY CARMEN JIMENEZ-PRIDE

Self

"Self makes the best inner leader and will engender balance and harmony inside if parts allow it to lead." (Sweezy & Schwartz, 2020).

As we explore these illustrations and help children identify their parts, I take every opportunity to underscore a key aspect of the child's inner system: Self. I tell them that Self is present from birth, is healthy, wise, and undamaged, and they have the ability to access their own Self-energy. I address this concept with caution, however. When children still live in a traumatizing home, school, or social environment which communicates that they do not have a positive core Self essence, it might even prove dangerous for a child to let down their inner protector energy and open up into the calm, curiosity, compassion, confidence, courage, clarity, connectedness, and creativity qualities of Self-leadership. Unsafe environments are often threatened by displays of Self-energy and meet them with additional abuse. When the child's environment is unsafe, I help them learn that they have a Self, but also how to distinguish when it is safe and not safe to reveal it.

The following visual helps children become familiar with the 8 C qualities of Self so that they are better equipped to access them when needed.

Focus on Feeling® 8 Cs of Self Leadership

QUALITIES OF SELF LEADERSHIP

FOCUS OF FEELINGS®   DESIGN CREATED BY CARMEN JIMENEZ-PRIDE

Calm: *Being centered and grounded, even during stressful circumstances.*

There has been a recent focus in the field on teaching children mindfulness strategies to gain and maintain a sense of calm, yet children's environments are often not calm. Helping children access even a sliver of Self-energy in stressful situations can help their systems regulate in challenging situations. For example, when Charlotte's parents have a verbal or physical altercation, her anxious exile normally starts to flood, which triggers her dissociative firefighter to rush in, causing her to become inattentive to the situation and herself. In the therapy room, we have helped her become aware when the dissociative firefighter blends, causing her to ignore the feelings in her body. We take a few moments to acknowledge how the feelings she experiences show up in her body and help her connect to her embodied Self in the safety of the therapy environment. This allows her to be with the dissociative firefighter and begin to develop a healing Self-to-part relationship with it. I have worked with Charlotte on a breathing technique I call "breathing bigger than the part" where she focuses on how the part shows up in her body and breathes deeply into it. This helps the part "soften back" to a friendly distance (a technique called "unblending" in IFS) so she can get to know the part, rather than being flooded—or overtaken—by it.

Curiosity: *Being genuinely open to learning why parts and people react the way they do.*

Children are natural explorers; they start to seek information at an early age. Babies orient toward the source of sounds, and toddlers constantly ask "why?" Children will explore even when they are directed not to! We can teach children to channel their natural curiosity as an avenue into Self, by having them become curious about their parts' choices, decisions, and behaviors. Charlotte found externalizing parts in a sandtray to be one effective way to separate from her parts and become curious as to their feelings, beliefs, and behaviors.

Sandtray therapy is an expressive and projective mode of psychotherapy involving the unfolding and processing of intra- and inter-personal issues through the use of specific sandtray materials as a nonverbal medium of communication. Sandtray work is led by the client and facilitated by a trained therapist (Homeyer & Sweeney, 2017). Clients select figurines, or other objects, to represent parts, and place them in relationship to one another in a tray filled with sand. A child may bury a part that they feel ashamed of or may place two parts who desire opposite things for the client at opposite ends of the sandtray. A child may select a superhero miniature to identify a part within their system that represents a strong and capable manager, or a small object to represent a part that feels powerless and afraid. The therapist will invite the client to name the miniatures/parts and enact through play the experiences and the beliefs of the identified parts. Parts can be witnessed, retrieved, and reorganized through sandtray play in child-friendly and expressive interactions.

Compassion: *Seeing through parts' behavior to the pain that is driving it. A desire to care for others who are suffering without being overwhelmed by their pain.*

While scrolling through social media, I ran across a video where a father was changing a newborn while his big brother, still a toddler himself, was watching. The newborn was crying, and the big brother started consoling his little brother. "Don't cry, I am right here with you," and "It's almost over. You are not alone." My heart melted. The big brother's compassion recognized the discomfort of his younger brother and responded with care and presence.

In play therapy we can support a child's Self-led compassion for all their parts by helping a child witness their parts' stories with non-judgement. This may be done by allowing a child to select a puppet, toy, or figurine to represent and externalize a part that is active in their inner world. The very act of selecting an external item to represent the part creates an unblending, allowing the child to embody the Self-perspective and get to know the part as a separate entity, to witness its story, to learn where it first began to feel the way it feels, and to develop a compassionate perspective while playing with the representative puppet, toy, or figurine. Just like the big brother, Self will respond with openheartedness and presence to the experiences of all the parts.

Confidence: *Trusting that even if you have made mistakes, you are still good and worthy.*

During Charlotte's session in the playroom, she engaged in sandtray play therapy and accidentally dropped sand on the floor. Charlotte became upset and spoke from an exile, stating "I'm so stupid, I always mess things up."

Me: "It sounds like there is a part of you that feels it always messes things up."

Charlotte: "Sometimes it does mess things up."

Me: "Can you let that part know that it is ok to mess things up in the playroom?"

Charlotte: "Really?"

Me: "Yes, this is where we play, mess things up, learn, and grow."

Charlotte: "It feels better now."

Me: "Just let it know that I still want you and it here in the playroom."

Charlotte: "It feels even better."

Children will gain beliefs about themselves based on their personal experiences and experiences with other people. The most impactful relationships are those the child values, such as with a parent, caregiver, educator, or community member. Children need to feel competent and capable in their situation, and when they experience these feelings, their confidence will increase. When Self welcomes and comforts exiles that feel unworthy or broken, confidence increases both internally and externally.

Courage: *Facing fearful situations, standing up to things that are not right, speaking for your own extreme parts, and apologizing for any negative impact on other people.*

In the playroom, children can face their fears and address fearful situations by externalizing parts, getting to know parts, and having corrective experiences. Children need courage, and with a sense of courage, they feel hopeful. They are willing to take risks and believe they can handle difficult situations externally and internally. Through play, children can practice standing up against things that are not right, like lying, cheating, and bullying.

In the playroom we might enact a fearful experience from school and allow the child to select objects to represent different parts that came up in response. For example, if a child experienced bullying on the playground, they might select objects to represent parts that felt afraid, parts that acted tough, parts that felt embarrassed, parts that dissociated, and parts that wanted to self-harm. By positioning those objects in relation to the child (who would be the embodied representation of Self), we can help the child recognize that each part has a positive intent when activated under stress. The child can then be intentional in making a plan with the inner protective system by inviting in specific protector energy to blend with Self when needed in a future challenging situation. Perhaps the "act tough" protector may be specifically invited to strengthen in these situations and blend with Self when it is unsafe in the external environment to fully embody Self-energy. This could help ensure that exile in distress does not escalate to the point where the self-harm protector needs to jump in. This approach strengthens internal relationships between the child's parts, facilitates more adaptive engagement of the protective system, and reminds all parts that Self is a present and wise internal guide for the collective orchestration of the whole system of parts.

Clarity: *Maintaining a clear and undistorted view of situations and parts, without projections and agenda.*

As we've mentioned, children are natural explorers and seek information about the how and why of situations they experience. When children have the opportunity to increase their emotional literacy, they increase their emotional awareness, and it leads to clarity regarding their parts and how parts show up their lives.

In the bullying example above, we might support the child by facilitating the witnessing of parts and recognizing that parts view the world through the filters of their burdens, which are often distorted. Exiles that believe "I'm bad," for example, may perceive the accidental dropping of a toy as evidence of the child's "badness." By assisting the child in externalizing and witnessing parts that hold these beliefs, they can intuitively connect to the Self-led clarity that an accident is not evidence of "badness" and develop compassion for the part that holds this belief. Each experience of Self-led clarity strengthens the neural pathways of the Self-to-part relationship and the future ability to connect to Self-clarity.

Connectedness: *Feeling a sense of interdependence with the internal system, as well as external people and systems.*

Children are particularly vulnerable to the risk of attachment ruptures, because their connection to their caregivers is a requirement for survival. Like all of us, children also need a sense of belonging in order to thrive. Children who feel safely connected to others are more likely to feel secure in themselves and able to cultivate secure relationships. Connection with children comes naturally until unrepaired ruptures occur. Children who develop exiles that do not feel connected to Self and others often feel isolated, insecure, and lonely, and they are more likely to develop protective parts with burdens that seek attention in unhelpful, reactive ways.

IFS proposes that secure attachment between Self and parts is a deeply protective and reparative resource. Play therapy allows a child to first conceptualize that a fundamentally undamaged and positive Self exists within themselves, then to develop awareness of the normalcy of their various parts, and finally, to begin to cultivate Self-to-part relationships through the experience of enactment and purposeful play. Ultimately, a secure inner attachment facilitates the development of secure outer attachment relationships, as well as the developing ability (as the child grows and gains access to additional external resources) to establish safety when external relationships are unsafe.

Creativity: *Being free to realize creative potential, enjoyment, and exploration.*

Play therapy is an ideal medium through which children can embody creativity through play, while exploring their inner world through direct experiences or through metaphor. Child centered play therapy gives the child the opportunity to explore naturally in the playroom, and the healing steps of IFS are manifest through the child's play activities.

Children can be invited to creatively represent their life experiences through play. They might use placement of dolls in a dollhouse to enact stressful family scenarios and the supportive therapist can provide a compassionate witness to their parts' experiences. A Self-led redo might be enacted, and frightened parts might be allowed to create a playful and safe alternate area to which they can be "retrieved" when frightened. Children whose protectors may be burdened with "freeze" or "dissociative" responses can experience enough safety in the therapy room to unblend and allow the child to connect to this inner healing resource of Self-led creativity through play. The Self quality of creativity is practically limitless in the medium of enactment and play.

The Child's Protective System

Often children are brought to therapy while still residing in risky, dysregulated, or traumatic environments. Remaining in these environments causes (and often requires) the child's protective parts to remain heightened or activated. In contrast, the safety of the playroom becomes a space where the Self of the child has an opportunity to emerge and where parts can relax and be known. In this context, a child's inner system can slowly be mapped, as therapist and child explore feelings, behaviors, and beliefs that arise throughout the child's daily life.

The presence of firefighters may cause children to present "in parts" when they are in environments that cause or threaten emotional harm. With a compassionate understanding of protectors, the therapeutic playroom becomes a positively energized space where all the child's parts are truly welcome, and a critical mass of Self-energy can be present. This allows for the therapeutic relationship to be built externally while Self-to-part relationships are built internally. The Self-led experience will increase the opportunity for unburdening for both protectors and exiles (if external constraints allow), and a restructuring of the child's inner system.

It is always important to remember that, when working with children who continue to remain in harmful environments, asking protectors to "step back" or "give space" is unrealistic and often unsafe. Focus on developing client's Self-to-part relationships and witnessing the parts positive intents. Do not be alarmed in your work with children and adolescents if you don't complete a full IFS process from "find the part" to "integration." Children who have experienced trauma present with strong protectors that are actively working to maintain safety and order within the internal system. It is critical to assess external safety constraints in the child's home, school, and social environment to determine whether unburdening parts is even an appropriate goal. When external circumstances are unsafe, the appropriate therapeutic goal may sometimes be to wisely empower various aspects of the protective system. Unburdening or accessing/witnessing exiles, in particular, may not be warranted until the child is in a more supportive, safe external environment where that more tender work will not provoke external threats of danger. Children are sometimes at greater risk of being physically abused, for example, when they evidence attributes of Self-energy such as courage (speaking up to an abusive parent).

When it is an appropriate therapeutic goal, children are able to witness parts in a creative way and have corrective experiences (do-overs). When allowing the child the freedom to play with the Self-energy of the therapist present, the child can experience spontaneous or directed unburdening, the process in which an exiled part lets go of the painful emotions and beliefs it has been carrying (Sweezy & Schwartz, 2020). Along with the 8 Cs of Self-energy, the 5 Ps (Sweezy & Schwartz, 2020) are also important for the therapeutic process in the playroom: being **Present** with the child during the play and asking therapist parts to step back; **Patience:** being comfortable with the child actively in play when they may be quiet and focused; **Perspective:** recognizing that the child is more than their trauma narrative and dominant parts; **Persistence:** constantly reassuring the child's protective system; and, **Playfulness:** allowing the child's parts to be creative and explore.

During corrective experience play, the child may present as quiet and playing from their parts with limited Self-energy. When the therapeutic relationship increases and the child develops a felt sense of safety, verbal interactions often increase and the therapist will be able to engage with the child's protectors, as demonstrated by the illustration below.

Corrective Experiences with Play

In her play therapy sessions, Charlotte was always drawn to the PlayMobil® area in the playroom. Her first few sessions playing in this area were silent; my response was to hold Self-energy and assure that my caretaker parts remained out of the session while tracking her parts (child-centered play therapy) and reflecting their behaviors. Meanwhile, she created scenes that ranged from the home setting and the school setting to the hospital setting. When I asked if there was anything that she would like to share with me, Charlotte identified her family with people figures. She introduced me to her parents within the home setting, school setting, and hospital setting. Charlotte also represented herself in each setting, at times utilizing metaphors to connect a figure inside to a movie character figure.

While holding Self energy and being present with Charlotte while she played, I made the following statements based on the metaphors she used in her play.

- The little person in the house appears to be fearful and is hiding in the bedroom.
- The little person at school appears to be happy with all her friends.
- The little person in the hospital appears to be scared standing alone.

After multiple sessions with limited verbal communication, Charlotte's play started to shift. She became more expressive and began to give the figures voices. During this time, I observed with Presence and Patience, giving her the space she needed to "witness" her experiences through play. Charlotte began to include me in her play process by asking questions about the scenes she created.

Focus on Parts

Charlotte: "Do you think all houses are not safe for little kids?"

Me: "All houses are different. I wonder what the little girl in the house would say."

Charlotte: "Her name is Charlie."

Me: "Tell Charlie I said hello, and ask her if she would tell us about her house."

Charlotte: "Okay, (silent for a few minutes) she said she does not know if it is safe to talk about her house."

Me: "Can you tell Charlie that she can share what she wants to share, and it is ok to have those feelings."

Charlotte: "Charlie said that sometimes in her house it's not safe because her mom and dad fight a lot."

Me: "Charlie must not feel safe when her mom and dad fight."

Charlotte: "Nope, she does not."

Me: "Can you ask Charlie if there's anything else she wants us to know?"

Charlotte: "Charlie said she is not ready to talk about what happens because she does not know if she can trust us."

Me: "Can you tell her that she does not have to talk about what happens, and she can tell us anything else that she might like."

Charlotte: "Charlie's favorite color is pink."

Me: "Pink is an awesome color."

The remainder of the session focused on getting to know more about "Charlie." When working with Charlotte during this session, she continued to speak for Charlie by sharing information, and I continued to validate what was shared. While reflecting and processing the experience, it appeared that Charlotte was speaking for a part. Although it was not about the safety in the home or experiences with the parents, the information was important to Charlotte to share with me.

While working with Charlotte and her protector, who was not ready to talk about what happened in the house, it was important to facilitate the session with non-directive Self-energy. When working with children during a play therapy session, communication may look different from working with adults. Children's play may be all action and no words, requiring therapists to become comfortable with the silence, and attuned to the deep communication that is happening at the level of play.

The Healing Steps in the Playroom

During play therapy sessions, a lot of time will be spent mapping and assisting the child with gaining the knowledge of their parts by building the Self-to-part relationship through externalizing. This can happen through mapping (drawing parts on paper), sandtray, or free play with dolls and toys. Witnessing the experiences of the parts will naturally take place when the child can engage in non-directive play therapy. It is important to note that retrieval (bringing parts stuck in the past to a safe place) and redo (having Self present in an enactment of a painful event in the way a child needed a safe adult to be) may be a challenge with children that are currently living in the environment that burdened their parts. Although we can retrieve and redo in the therapy room, parts may continue to be at risk for ongoing burdening due to the unsafe external environment.

When working with Charlotte in session, after she witnessed her parts' various experiences, I assisted her with creating a "special place" for the part. This was a mindfulness process that gave Charlotte a place for her parts to go when she starts to think about painful experiences. While in play, I invited Charlotte to move the miniature of Charlie out of the playhouse to another area of the playroom where she felt safer. As mentioned, this can be helpful, in the moment, in the therapy room; however, when the traumatic experiences are ongoing in the child's external environment, parts are not frozen in time and place (they are currently living it), and therefore, retrieval may not be appropriate. The focus instead will be on unburdening the negative beliefs a part holds about itself. Unburdening can be done with external metaphors (e.g. taking a heavy backpack off a doll to represent removing the burden of being perfect in school) allowing the child to have a first-hand experience with the release of burdened beliefs (e.g. "I have to do it perfectly").

While in the session, Charlotte focused on a part that held beliefs of not being good enough. She externalized the part by identifying a miniature and putting the miniature within the sandtray. I told Charlotte that she could add anything into the tray to reflect thoughts and feelings the part may have. Charlotte built a sandtray including miniatures that reflected other beliefs the part held. I then asked her if she was ready to let go of any of the beliefs in the tray. I gave her an invitation to clear the tray in a way that felt right for her. Charlotte buried some of the miniatures in the sand and others she removed. I invited Charlotte to invite positive qualities within her tray to take the place of what she released. Charlotte brought objects into the sandtray that represented positive thoughts and beliefs the part was inviting in to replace its burdens. During Charlotte's next session we took time to check in on the beliefs she unburdened.

> **Me:** "Last session, we pulled out several things from the sandtray. Does it still feel right for them to be out of the tray?"
>
> **Charlotte:** "Yes, I would like to keep all the positive things in the sandtray."

During Charlotte's IFS play therapy sessions she was able to gain knowledge about her internal system, develop Self-to-part relationships, and unburden some of her parts, but she also learned that her parents have parts. She was able to increase her coping skills and begin to interact with her parents' parts without internalizing the negative messaging the actions of their parts sometimes communicated.

As Charlotte experienced, IFS and play therapy are well-suited to create a safe and creative environment for children's parts to heal. The combination of the Therapeutic Powers of Play with the healing steps of the IFS model and the safety of a Self-led therapist are a powerful setting to undergird and support the healing of children's burdened parts.

KEY TAKEAWAYS

- At the beginning of the therapeutic process, it is normal for a child to have little access to Self-energy, and to present with a strong protective system.
- The Therapeutic Powers of Play: 1) facilitate communication, 2) foster emotional wellness, 3) enhance social relationships, and 4) increase personal strengths.
- When working with a child, assessing external constraints is critical to establishing appropriate therapeutic goals. When the child's external environment is unsafe, it may be more appropriate to wisely engage certain protective parts to help support safety, while introducing the concepts of Self and parts. When the external environment is safe enough, witnessing, redos, unburdening and deeper exile work can be facilitated by IFS-informed play therapy techniques.

- Play therapy encourages therapeutic processing in age-appropriate ways, supporting a child's naturally expressive and creative experience.
- The Self-energy of the therapist is a critical part of the therapeutic process, and is embodied by the 5 Ps of Self: Patience, Presence, Persistence, Perspective, and Playfulness.

AUTHOR BIO

Carmen Jimenez-Pride, LCSW, RPT-S (she/her) is the founder and Executive Director of Outspoken Counseling and Consulting. She is a Licensed Clinical Social Worker, Registered Play Therapist Supervisor, and IFS Certified Clinical Consultant. She is also an IFS Assistant Trainer, Certified EMDR Therapist, Registered Yoga Teacher, Registered Children's Yoga Teacher, a Certified Daring Way™ Facilitator, and a Certified LEGO® Serious Play® Facilitator.

Carmen is the developer of Diversity in Play Therapy Inc. and creator/organizer of the Diversity in Play Therapy Summit. She is the 2021 Association for Play Therapy Emerging Leader award winner and President of the South Carolina Association for Play Therapy

Carmen is experienced in clinical treatment of children, adolescents, and adults with culturally diverse backgrounds addressing a wide range of concerns. Carmen's career in the mental health field spans more than 15 years.

REFERENCES

Association for Play Therapy. (2022). *Clarifying the use of play therapy*. Retrieved from Association for Play Therapy: www.a4pt.org/page/ClarifyingUseofPT

Homeyer, L. E., & Sweeney, D. S. (2017). *Sandtray therapy: A practical manual.* Routledge.

Kottman, T., & Meany-Walen, K. (2016). *Partners in play: An Adlerian approach to play therapy* (Vol. 3). American Counseling Association.

Landreth, G. L. (2012). *Play therapy: The art of the relationship.* Routgledge.

Schaefer, C., & Drewes, A. A. (2014). *The therapeutic powers of play: 20 core agents of change.* Wiley.

Senko, K., & Bethany, H. (2019). Play therapy: An illustrative case. *Innovations in Clinical Neuroscience*, 16(5–6), 38–40. https://www.ncbi.nlm.nih.gov/pmc/articles/PMC6659989/

Sinko, A. L. (2017). Legacy burdens. In M. Sweezy & E. L. Zoskind (Eds.), *IFS; Innovations and elaborations in Internal Family Systems therapy* (pp. 164-178). Routledge.

Sweezy, M., & Schwartz, R. C. (2020). *Internal Family Systems therapy.* The Guilford Press.

GOING DEEPER

From Carmen Jimenez-Pride

1) Website:
   a. www.carmenpride.com
2) Books/Workbooks:
   a. Jimenez-Pride, C. (2017). *No, no Elizabeth.* Warren Publishing
   b. Jimenez-Pride, C. (2019). *Elizabeth makes a friend.* Warren Publishing
   c. Jimenez-Pride, C. (2018). *Focus on feelings.* Play Therapy with Carmen Publishing
   d. Jimenez-Pride, C. (2021). *Focus on feelings: Increasing emotional literacy.* Play Therapy with Carmen Publishing
   e. Jimenez-Pride, C. (2021). *Focus on feelings: Positive and negative cognitions.* Play Therapy with Carmen Publishing
   f. Jimenez-Pride, C. (2019). *Amir's brave adventure: Exploring confidence, mindfulness and attachment*
3) Trainings or Workshops:
   a. www.trainwithcarmen.com

From Other Sources

1) Books:
   a. Stone, J. (Ed.). (2021). *Play therapy and telemental health: Foundations, populations, and interventions* (1st ed.). Routledge. www.doi.org/10.4324/9781003166498
   b. Jiminez-Pride, C. (2021). Cultural humility in the telemental health playroom. In J. Stone (Ed.), *Play therapy and telemental health.* Routledge.
   c. Kottman, T., & Meany-Walen, K. (2016). *Partners in play: An Adlerian approach to play therapy* (Vol. 3). American Counseling Association.
2) Trainings or Workshops:
   a. www.a4pt.com
   b. www.ptti.org/training.html
   c. www.learn.synergeticplaytherapy.com
3) Podcasts:
   a. Lessons from the Play Room: www.synergeticplaytherapy.com/lessons-from-the-playroom
   b. Play Therapy Community Podcast: www.playtherapycommunity.com/podcast-2
4) Associations:
   a. Association for Play Therapy: www.a4pt.org
   b. Play Therapy Training Institute: www.ptti.org
   c. Synergetic Play Therapy Institute: www.synergeticplaytherapy.com

SECTION THREE
INTERSECTIONALITY

INTERSECTIONALITY INTRODUCTION
WORKING WITH INTERSECTING IDENTITIES

Regina Wei, MA, LMFTA and Sand Chang, PhD

Intersectionality as social theory seeks to explain the interconnected nature of social categorizations such as race, class, and gender, and show how these identities create multifaceted, overlapping, and interdependent systems of discrimination or disadvantage.[1]

In the following section, the authors explore ways in which the practice of IFS is affected by the complex layers of identity we each embody. They invite you to reflect on the ways in which the identities of practitioner and client impact the therapeutic experience, including a client's overall healing. Further, they propose ways that IFS can be used to challenge systemic oppression where it occurs.

While the chapters here focus on race, gender, sexual identity, and neurodivergence, these identities overlap considerably. For example, we cannot consider the efficacy of IFS for a neurodivergent client without also considering their gender, sexual identity, disabilities, race, and socioeconomic status. Likewise, themes that are evident when working with one racialized group may well apply to other racialized groups or to people of the global, non-Western majority. These groups often contrast with what Tema Okun calls *White supremacy culture*[2] in how they value or express qualities like individualism, productivity and progress, urgency, and perfectionism.[3] This is not to say, of course, that folks who come from non-Western cultural heritages do not embody these qualities, particularly if they grew up in and/or live within Western cultural contexts; the impact of colonialism on non-Western cultures cannot be underestimated. Yet it is not uncommon for people of the global majority to come from cultural frameworks that give greater emphasis to values such as collectivism, group harmony, the importance of parental/family influences and extended kinship networks (which may extend to ancestors), and prioritization of relationships within one's community.

Whether you come to this section as a practitioner, client, or student of IFS, we invite you to consider the following questions:

- Are you aware of how your practice and/or experience as a client is impacted by your multifaceted layers of identity? If so, what does that look like for you?
- If you have experienced oppression and/or marginalization due to your identity, how have your experiences impacted your ability to engage in the therapeutic/healing process when your practitioner or client does not share your marginalized identity/ties? What do your parts need to feel safe within the therapeutic relationship?
- If, on the other hand, your identity is reinforced by the dominant culture (for example, White, heterosexual, cisgender, middle-class, neurotypical, non-disabled), to what extent are you aware of how practitioners or clients with marginalized identities have protector parts that automatically come online in your interactions with them? What parts come online for you when you are in the presence of someone who looks and/or identifies differently from you?
- If you haven't done your own work to dismantle White supremacy or internalized oppression, but that is what your client is trying to do, how productive have you found the relationship to be? Have you been able to take your clients beyond where you are yourself?
- When microaggressions (aka subtle acts of exclusion or SAE) occur, do you know how to work with your parts that hold biases and/or have protective functions that may lead to further subtle acts of exclusion? How can you acknowledge harm done and engage in repair?
- If you make a mistake due to being blended with a part (rather than Self-led), are you able to take responsibility for your parts and their impact on others?
- When you work with clients who experience a kind of marginalization that you do not experience, are you aware that it may take time and earned trust for their protector parts to relax? Have you worked with any parts of you that expect all clients to trust you?

We understand that these are not easy topics to consider, but we ask you to hold these questions in mind while thinking about working with intersectional identities. Some of the chapters primarily address practitioners of the dominant culture; others address practitioners and clients of marginalized identities. Even if you do not have lived experience pertaining to a particular identity or serve clients or IFS learners with that identity, we invite you to read every chapter. The reflections and recommendations presented here can provide a helpful framework for engaging with clients in an open and culturally respectful way and broaden your understanding of how IFS can serve diverse populations.

EMBODYING IFS WITH BLACK CLIENTS

RECLAIMING A BIRTHRIGHT

Fatimah Finney, LMHC

This is some White mess.
I distinctly remember having this thought during the first weekend of my IFS Level 1 training. During a live demonstration of the model between the lead trainer and a participant, I saw every rule I knew about group engagement and how to show up in the world completely disregarded: accusations toward IFS leadership, unfiltered disclosure of family secrets, admission of personal flaws, and expression of any emotion other than cautious cordiality. I was keenly aware that each of these acts crossed lines that would be quite consequential for me in a professional setting. And who but White people get to completely disregard rules of social order without consequence?

I was conflicted. I had just spent a year and a half developing a profound appreciation for this model in my supervision and was eager to get trained in it. Yet, there I was, the only Black woman in the room, faced with an impression that accessing IFS was only possible through privileges that I had not been afforded. I became a therapist with one goal in mind: to be what I couldn't see but what I knew was needed. I spent the first years of my life in Newark, New Jersey within a predominantly Black community. The extent of mental health care that I knew were the inpatient facilities that appeared to be more interested in getting rid of my brother than helping him while he was there. Where were the options of care that didn't shame you for needing help in the first place?

Even after my master's degree, where I learned of a variety of treatment modalities and approaches to healing, I was still in need of a method that didn't start with a stance of, "Here's what's wrong with you, and here's how someone outside yourself can fix it." I craved something that acknowledged that my clients' experiences, and even my own, made sense given what we'd been through. I needed something that addressed not just the individual and the presenting symptoms but also made space for the social context the individual exists in and the larger systems that influence access to healthier, alternative ways of living.

Years later, when I heard my original sentiments echoed in a group of new students, I learned that my initial reaction to the demonstration was not unique to me. I was a teaching assistant for a Level 1 training for Black Therapists Rock, a training that was intentionally curated to center Black therapists learning the IFS model. It was also one of the few times that I've witnessed a demonstration in a training where the client was a Black person. As I heard their questions about the calm, creative, clear qualities of Self-energy and how it applies to their lives, it felt like a full circle moment for me. I was reacquainted with some of my initial skepticism of the relevance of this model to the real problems people in my community face:

- How does one remain calm in the face of police brutality?
- Who has time to be creative and get clarity when they're working multiple jobs and raising three kids on their own?
- Is there a place for righteous anger within a people who have been facing persecution for centuries?

For many that day, the lack of a relationship with Self-energy felt like this healing resource was not of them or for them. In what follows, I offer to you a similar response to what I offered those students and to the part of me that showed up with similar concerns on my first day of training.

One of the prominent privileges that Black people have not had is the privilege of complexity and multidimensionality. The very multiplicity of experience that is a cornerstone of IFS is reflected within the Black experience. Black people exist in a range of colors, ethnic identities, and lived experiences. While there is no singular Black experience, I've found that using IFS with Black clients is inherently a process of reclamation. Establishing a connection with the qualities of Self-energy is not about instilling something new but of uncovering what has always been present and available but blocked by the pervasive efforts of systemic racism. Black clients often come to therapy in need of reclaiming what is already theirs, a birthright of healing. As the therapist or facilitator using IFS, it is essential to understand your role in this dynamic and to be equipped with knowledge and skills to help support what can be a beautiful unfolding.

This chapter is meant to be an aid to help you do just that. To be clear, integrating IFS into practice with Black clients is a topic that could fill a book. What I aim to do in the next few pages is to offer key considerations for the practitioner seeking to deepen their awareness and sharpen their skills in providing culturally affirming IFS therapy to Black clients. I am writing from a North American lens and assuming a Western readership, and yet the overarching principles presented here are widely applicable. To facilitate our discussion, I've organized key points into two categories: Outside of Session and Inside of Session considerations.

Outside of Session
1. Develop Cultural "Self" Awareness.
2. Develop Cultural "Other" Awareness.

Inside of Session
1. Emphasize the 3 Bs: Body, Befriending, and Burdens.
2. Practice Compassionate Accountability.

The goal outside of session is to build intercultural capacity. This involves understanding how your culture has shaped your values and beliefs and influences your therapeutic lens. The goal inside of session is to co-create an environment that intentionally makes space for discussing the impact of racism and other oppressive ideologies, and for the client to reimagine and experience themselves in the fullness of their humanity.

Outside of Session

In my experience as an IFS therapist, I've quickly learned that much of what happens in session is shaped by what is or isn't happening outside of session. From the therapist's perspective, it's clear that if a client doesn't follow through on tasks or techniques between sessions, then the likelihood of their desired changes occurring is notably lowered. Similarly, when a therapist isn't doing their own work outside of session, the quality of the relationship between therapist and client and the treatment provided is likely to suffer. I'm going to focus on key tasks that therapists working with Black clients can prioritize outside of session to enhance the quality of their work inside of session.

Intercultural Competence

Cultural Competence. Cultural Humility. Cultural Curiosity. Phrases like these have been put forth over the years to describe the critical need to cultivate a learner's mind as a therapist. This orientation aligns well with the invitation in the IFS model to lead with curiosity and allow the parts of the client to lead the journey of exploration. Developing intercultural competence is a necessary step to be able to hold space for the parts that show up for Black clients without having the parts of the therapist takeover in irreparably harmful ways.

Mitchell Hammer, the creator of the Intercultural Development Inventory, gives a two-pronged approach to building intercultural competence: increasing cultural self-awareness, and increasing cultural other awareness. Establishing a solid sense of how culture shapes one's own beliefs and behaviors and the beliefs and behaviors of others is the cornerstone of intercultural competence.

Cultural Self-Awareness

Culture is the expected and sometimes unspoken way of being that determines how one engages with oneself and others. It describes how to "do life," and ascribes meaning to beliefs and behaviors that run counter to the cultural norm. Much of what I reference regarding culture will be from the cultural context in which I belong within and of the United States.

Cultural self-awareness refers to knowledge about one's own cultural lens. To clarify, the use of self here is not the "Self" referred to in the IFS model but what is commonly referred to as one's personal knowledge of one's own thoughts, beliefs, and behaviors. Cultivating self-awareness is a process of assessment and investigation of who and how you are as a person first. Your relationship with the values and beliefs of your culture of origin influence how you inhabit your professional role. While there are professional codes of ethics that set standards of practice to which we aspire, we may overlook the gaps between who we aspire (or are mandated) to be and who we actually are. Even when we're aware of the gap between where we are now and where we are headed in building intercultural competence, we may miss how wide the chasm is.

As a therapist, it is essential for you to understand yourself as a cultural being. That is, to learn the different ways that your culture has shaped and is shaping how you view yourself in relation to others. As a therapist working with Black clients, it's imperative that you also understand how your primary cultural lens has shaped your perspectives, assumptions, and evaluations about Black people and how they exist in the world. The extent to which you understand the ways that your culture shapes your beliefs and behaviors plays a critical role in your capacity to engage cross-culturally with greater ease.

According to Zippia, an online career statistics tool, most therapists in the United States identify as White.[1] If you look at the IFS Institute's website, you'll see that most trainers are White. In my Level 1 training and all the trainings I've staffed (not including BTR trainings), the majority of participants and program assistants were also White. With that, I assume that most therapists currently using IFS are White people. And given that most of the authors in this book are also White, I assume that most people reading these pages are as well. This is why I will start with important tips for developing cultural self-awareness for White therapists and practitioners.

Developing cultural self-awareness starts with exploring your culture, and often this involves recognizing that you have one. In my work as a consultant, I've commonly found that people who identify as White initially struggle with the idea of having a culture. A common sentiment I've heard from White people is that culture is something *others* have. It involves eating food, listening to music, or going to shows focused on the ways *others* live, not people who look and live like them. This is the precise effect of the dominant culture in the United States, which leads with White culture being the standard and anything else as different, perhaps even an aberration. Intercultural competence leads with the understanding that everyone has culture, and that differences in culture are to be explored and negotiated rather than trivialized, vilified, or exiled. Without understanding that everyone has a culture, there is less capacity to be accountable for the impact of one's cultural expression.

The dominant cultural expression in the United States centers Whiteness at the expense of non-White people. By Whiteness, I mean cultural norms, beliefs, and behavioral practices associated with White culture and people. The COVID-19 pandemic and the murder of George Floyd created the perfect storm that spotlighted Whiteness in the United States in a way that hadn't been done before, particularly its legacy of brutality and violence against Black people. Instead of being the ideal, Whiteness has been challenged to look at itself and atone for the seeds it has sown and the fruit it continues to bear. The call to "decolonize therapy," a phrase coined by Dr. Jennifer Mullan, was amplified and continues to reverberate throughout the mental health field. According to Dr. Mullan, decolonizing therapy involves "examining and un-learning the effects of colonization, capitalism, and imperialism on our emotional well-being. It's about the returning of practices to their rightful owners. Asking permission. Letting Whiteness dig up their own ancestry, their own relationship with coloniality. With anti-Blackness. With themselves." This implores us to examine how our therapeutic practice has been taught from a lens that privileges Whiteness while pathologizing non-White cultural expressions or styles of engagement. As a White therapist and practitioner, your work outside session is to sit still, dig deep, and take honest inventory of the ways your culture has primed you for inhabiting a racist, dominating, superior disposition toward Black people. Those are a lot of words, yet I wrote each one with intention. How are they landing for you? What's occurring for you in this moment. Take a pause if you need to because there's more.

With reflection and guidance, White people I've worked with were able to recognize patterns of behaviors and beliefs that were indeed their culture, though they had not been associating them as such. If you are noticing that you too have parts that have not considered that you have a culture, Tema Okun's article, *White Supremacy Culture—Still Here* can be a helpful place to start to think more deeply about cultural norms in the United States and the role they've played in your upbringing.

As a White therapist or practitioner, when you look back on the last year, how much time have you invested in understanding yourself as a cultural being and building cultural competence? Where are you now compared to where you were at the start of your career as a therapist? Take time to reflect and answer these questions as you begin this exploration of self-awareness.

1. If you identify as White, how does it feel to be referred to as White? What do you notice now that you've paused to reflect on this aspect of your identity?

2. When did you first become aware of racial differences? What made you aware of them?
3. What's the racial make-up of most of your clients? What role do you play in that being the case?
4. When, if at all, is race explicitly discussed in your sessions?
5. Do you discuss race and racism with clients who share your racial identity? With those who do not? Why or why not?

What do you notice as you read these questions? What parts of you become activated in response to them? Take a moment and make a list of all the parts that have shown up as you've read this chapter, and plan to return to them later. As a consultant, I've had the opportunity to work with White therapists seeking to build their intercultural competence and have listened to, and learned from, a number of their parts. I've commonly heard parts that:

- Avoid speaking about race at all due to fear of saying the wrong thing.
- Feel shame about legacy burdens of racism in their families and themselves.
- Deny any racism or the importance of focusing on it.
- Justify racism and commit to proving why it's Black people's fault.
- Avoid "seeing color" because it causes conflict to do otherwise.

Do you have similar parts? Your parts and their concerns are critical for you to know and tend to as their impact in the therapy room can be profoundly harmful. Sometimes that looks like White therapists trying to convince Black clients that their presenting concerns have nothing to do with racism, White therapists overcompensating and sharing their track record of not being racist, or White therapists looking to their Black clients to validate them to feel less bad about being White.

It is crucial for you to take an honest look at your parts that have absorbed racist beliefs that view Black people as inferior to you and yourself as superior to Black people. Those parts need you to tend to them and unburden them, so you can support your Black clients without the energy of those burdens influencing the quality of care you offer. If you do not, those parts may show up in session with Black clients and create a dynamic that leads clients to caretake or feel pressured to soothe you in a way that is inappropriate and unfair to the client. There is a long history of White people's discomfort leading to the harming of Black people, even to the point of death. As such, Black people may have parts that make sure they are not "too much" or "making White people uncomfortable." Caretaker parts that scan for ways to make sure the therapist is at ease may show up in session with your Black clients. It can look like a client editing what they may truly want to talk about due to not wanting to cause a rift between them and their therapist. It also can look like ending services or no longer making contact after a given session.

"The true focus of revolutionary change is never merely the oppressive situations which we seek to escape, but that piece of the oppressor which is planted deep within each of us." —*Audre Lorde*

If you are a non-Black POC, it is also important for you to explore the ways in which some racist ideas are embedded in your perspectives, consciously or unconsciously, and you may benefit from answering the same questions above. Similarly, if you grew up in a culture that trivializes and distorts the humanity of Black people, your work is to recognize those parts that have beliefs that align with dominant culture views of Black people and ensure that those do not overtly or covertly show up in your treatment of Black clients.

Finally, if you are a Black therapist working with Black clients, it will be important to tune into places where your cultural experiences diverge from those of your clients. While you may share similarities in cultural experiences with your Black clients, it's important not to overemphasize the commonalities at the expense of exploring the differences. Furthermore, it's important to continually assess the ways in which internalization of oppressive norms may be shaping how you engage with, and offer treatment and guidance to, your client. As a Black woman and therapist, I must check parts of myself that have internalized racist messaging that limit my humanity lest I set the same expectations for my Black clients or use interventions that are grounded in stereotypical beliefs.

Cultural Other Awareness

Cultural Other Awareness refers to knowledge about different cultures and ways of being other than your own. This knowledge must include ways of knowing that go beyond what you can read. In addition to books and texts like this one, relational and experiential knowledge is critical. When serving Black clients, it helps to have some foundational understanding of the lived experiences of Black people, both historically and in the present. Knowledge about the external contexts that shape their internal systems is essential. It can be gleaned from the details a client shares as well as information learned outside of session. As an IFS therapist, the goals of developing cultural other awareness should be:

- To recognize that other ways of being are as valid as your own and that the experience of Black people and their cultures are as valid as your own.
- To commit to learning about your clients specifically, and the Black experience generally, both in and out of session.
- To understand Black history and how it can help attune you to parts that hold legacy burdens.

Self-energy is the healing resource in the IFS therapy model. The more access a person has to it, and the more their lives are led by it, and the more equipped they are to navigate the realities of life with ease, openness, and healthy discernment. The eight qualities of Self-energy—compassion, calm, connectedness, creativity, courage, clarity, confidence, curiosity—are gateways that allow a person to deepen their connection to themselves and live with presence and joy.

Unfortunately, for a notable portion of Black people in the United States, access to these qualities has been heavily obstructed. The metaphor of "The Sun and Clouds" is often used to describe Self and parts. If Self is like the sun, then parts and their burdens are like the clouds that can block access to it. Systemic and cultural burdens have ensured that storm after storm after storm were created to make the experience of Self-energy for Black people seemingly intangible and unattainable. The persistence of the White dominant culture to erase the dignity and beauty of a people ignited parts that have led our inner systems for generations as a means for survival. And when a person is constantly on defense and focused on survival, the capacity for their parts to relax back is limited. It's important to have some understanding of the experiences of Black people and the systems that shape them before considering how to apply the IFS model in any useful way for a client,

The Burden of Racism

The truth is that Black people are rich tapestries of experiences, beliefs, dreams, and possibilities. The White dominant culture of the United States has been designed to erase the beautiful complexity of Black people and replace it with one-dimensional, singular descriptors that are often disparaging, stereotypical, and simplistic. If you've read *The New Jim Crow* by Michelle Alexander, *Medical Apartheid* by Harriet Washington, or *The Sum of Us* by Heather McGhee you've learned the persistent and pervasive ways that the justice, medical, and political systems, respectively, have intentionally operated to denigrate and limit the quality of life of Black people. If you haven't read these books, I encourage you to do so. The legacies of antiblackness, racism, sexism, and the relentless systems that bolster their transmission across generations have rendered subpar health, education, financial, and overall quality of life outcomes for Black people. The COVID-19 pandemic has exacerbated the already disheartening conditions in which a sizable portion of Black people, African Americans specifically, exist. A part of me is rolling her eyes at what I am about to type because I am tired of these truths.

"Trauma decontextualized in a people can look like culture."
—Resmaa Menakem

When it comes to mental wellness, only a third of Black people requiring mental health services receive it.[2] This illustrates how, even when Black people name their pain, barriers exist to keep them from getting relief. Some of these barriers are financial, when the cost for care exceeds what a person can afford. (The median income for Black households in 2019 was $44,000. Almost 30 percent of Black households live below the poverty line making less than $25,000 a year.)[3] Some of these barriers have to do with accessibility, where the care requires access to transportation, insurance, or other means to receive help that is out of reach.

Yet, as previously mentioned by Dr. Mullan, even when Black people have both means and access, they still must often navigate a mental health system that pathologizes and minimizes their experiences.

I'm writing this to contextualize what is often decontextualized and deemed "just how those people are." But these outcomes are not just who and how Black people are. They are the conditions orchestrated by the racist beliefs that created the laws and policies that ensure the poor-quality health systems, school districts, and other social determinants that continue to reproduce the low quality of wellness in Black communities.

Even though I cringe in writing this, it's vital to address the burden of racism here. Why? Because the weight of all that a Black person may carry as they work with an IFS practitioner needs to be received and understood from a sociocultural lens. It's imperative that the contributing factors of that weight are examined because Black people have been repeatedly blamed as being solely responsible for their own circumstances.

Of course, there is so much more to the Black experience than burden and oppression. Black people have repeatedly created joy in an existence that wasn't intended to have any. Therefore, as you build awareness of the Black experience, be sure to also listen to and learn about the cultural expressions of resilience: the art, the comedy, the music, and other ways that Black people have established themselves as sources of beauty and inspiration in the world, despite all that was and continues to be kept from them.

Beyond Blackness: Multiplicity of Black Identity

> "To be African American is to be African with no memory and to be American without any privilege." —*James Baldwin*

Black identity is nuanced, and the exploration of it is essential in the therapy space. I write this chapter as an African American, descendent of enslaved Africans brought to the United States. My parents, grandparents, and their grandparents were born and raised in the United States, as were my siblings and I. My identification as "African American" captures my lineage from the African continent and my lived experience of existing in the United States. My experience is distinct from my friends who were born in this country but whose parents immigrated here from other countries like Haiti, Ghana, and Ethiopia. As such, my writing is framed by my cultural lens and will converge and diverge with others who may also identify as Black, but not as African American in the way that I do.

I encourage you to consider the ways intersectionality shows up in your Black clients, and what it is like to exist at those points of intersection. Take note of the differences between Black clients across gender, religion, education, geography, and even family make-up. When working with someone who identifies as Black, get curious about the expression of Blackness that they exist in. Inquire about the depth and texture of their experience, and perhaps, help them separate from the parts of themselves that have internalized the idea that Black people are all the same.

Inside of Session

In the previous section, I highlighted what's important for IFS therapists and practitioners to be tending to, particularly when they aren't with clients. In this section, I will focus on key elements to be aware of while being present with Black clients and engaging them in the IFS model of healing. I begin this section by discussing key areas in the IFS model with specific points for intervention when working with Black clients. I finish with the importance of practicing compassionate accountability in order to successfully navigate the missteps and relational ruptures that can occur on the path toward healing.

The 3 Bs: Body, Befriending, and Burdens

When I'm using the model with clients, I try to remember that at any given time I am doing, or working to have my clients do, three things with their parts: listen to parts, love parts, and liberate parts. With this in mind, there are three aspects of the model that I'll emphasize to create maximum impact when working with Black clients. (If you haven't noticed by now, I enjoy things in groups of three. Add in some alliteration and I am overjoyed.) The three Bs to remember when working with Black clients:

Body
Befriending
Burdens

Intentional focus on listening to the needs of the body, extending love and allowing a great deal of time during the befriending process for parts to fully receive it, and tending to legacy burdens have been essential to deriving the utmost benefit from the model for Black clients I've worked with.

Reclaiming the Body

"Here is what I'd like for you to know: In America, it is traditional to destroy the black body—it is heritage." —*Ta-Nehisi Coates*

The body is the vehicle through which we all experience the world. Black bodies have been heavily pursued, defiled, and disrespected. Our bodies—our skin, our facial features, our hair texture—have been scrutinized, vilified, and used as evidence of supposed inherent inferiority. Oftentimes, Black clients come to therapy with shame and disconnection from their bodies for a variety of reasons. The body has been a recipient of tremendous wounding which is something to acknowledge explicitly in sessions with Black clients. Internalization of these messages can show up in a variety of ways: neglecting their own physical care, engaging their bodies in high-risk behaviors, inability to connect to their bodies when asked to focus on it. In his book *My Grandmother's Hands,* Resmaa Menakem writes, "The body is where we fear, hope, and react; where we constrict and release; and where we reflexively fight, flee or freeze. If we are to upend the status quo of White-body supremacy, we must begin with our bodies." The IFS model has some focus on the body already embedded in it that can be amplified when working with Black clients. From finding the part and seeing if and where it shows up in the body, to eventually releasing burdens that may also involve clearing out a space in the body, there are important ways in which the body can be acknowledged to facilitate deeper healing.

For these reasons and more, it is important for therapists to make space for the body, in any amount, to begin rebuilding the relationship clients have with their bodies from a place of compassion and connectedness. In her book *Somatic IFS*, Susan McConnell discusses the disconnected way that healing is sought and how her approach to therapy was countercultural. She writes, "My approach was not supported by a culture where one looks to a therapist for help with one's feelings and thoughts and then to a bodywork practitioner for problems with the body. This cultural divorce of mind and body with its separate institutional regulatory agencies reinforces the internal splits most of us suffer from." By intentionally including the body, I believe it helps the client to repair some of the impact of the traditional medical model that breaks us into pieces and sends us in different directions to feel whole again. Instead, therapy can be a space where all parts and aspects of a client—spirit, body, and mind—are welcomed. While it is true that everyone's system is different, and some people do not have parts that manifest in their bodies, it is also true that navigating racism provokes an out of body experience. A Black person may be disconnected from their body as a means of surviving within it, which may not reflect their natural way of connecting with their parts. Therefore, even when a therapist is first met with, "I'm not feeling anything in my body," know that this may shift as the client's parts begin to engage with the process and experience Self-energy consistently.

There are two ways that I achieve what I am suggesting here. One is through body-centered meditation that invites clients to notice parts of their bodies.

The intention is to flag how clients' life experiences are being received by their bodies. Susan McConnell describes this as *somatic awareness*, which involves bringing intentional focus to sensations of the body. I've used this at the start of sessions, particularly when it's visually evident, or explicitly named by the client, that a lot has happened since we last met. If you've been in a workshop or training with me and I guided you through a meditation, you've experienced my invitation to focus on your body by starting with your breath. I usually say something like this:

> "Bring your attention to your breath. Notice how much air is coming into your body and how much is flowing out."

> "Feel your rib cage expand as you inhale and feel how it relaxes back toward your spine as you exhale."

> "Feel the gentle swell of your belly as you inhale and feel it's slow retreat toward your spine as you exhale."

> "Find a pace of inhaling and exhaling that feels just right for you in this moment, then bring attention to parts that are present now since tuning into your body."

I also use a form of somatic awareness when a client is finding a target part, to help them deepen into exploration and clarify their experience of the part. Asking specifically how something is experienced in the body can be helpful to bring awareness online about their body and how they inhabit it. What do they notice about the sensation? Does it move or intensify? Is it dull or transient? Does it change as they talk about it with me? What happens as they breathe deeply into it? I'll ask these questions with clients who are developing a relationship with a body they'd otherwise ignore or overlook.

The body always has a story. Black bodies always have stories. Get curious about parts that may not want to focus on the body and their concerns about what might happen if they did. Discerning between a system that doesn't experience parts in an embodied way and parts that are blocking access to the body is critical. Additionally, when any body part is identified with a sensation, be sure to track the experience of that part of the body throughout the work. For example, if a person identifies a sensation in their stomach when they first find the part at the start of the model, I make sure to check back in throughout the befriending, building Self-to-part relationship, and even the healing steps to see how the person is experiencing that body part. It's not uncommon for the body part to experience amplified intensity, a clearing of the sensation entirely, or a completely new sensation. Helping your Black clients track the experience of their bodies feeling different can be a powerful revelation in their work.

Extended Befriending

The heart of the IFS model lies in the quality of the befriending. The befriending process provides dedicated time and attention to parts. It involves hearing and understanding their frame of reference and their life experiences while simultaneously offering all the qualities of Self-energy to these parts. It is for this part of the model with Black clients that I want to offer tips to deepen and strengthen the work. As demonstrated in previous sections, befriending isn't something that Black people typically experience, especially in predominantly White environments. Often, Black people are ignored, overlooked, or targeted in hostile ways. This point in the model is an opportunity to provide a new and corrective experience by supporting the client in offering their parts a radically different reception than what they may be used to. Therefore, when building the Self-to-part relationship, it is essential to not rush the process and to allow the client to spend an extended amount of time with their parts. Check with the target part to see how it's receiving the offer of Self-energy, and whenever there is a positive response, take some time to let the part fully inhabit the experience of compassion, interest, care, or whatever kind of goodness is being sent its way.

Personal and Legacy Burdens

Legacy burdens are burdens that have been transmitted generationally and are detected and released in a different manner than personal burdens. In light of the oppressive ramifications of slavery in the United States, which systemic racism created, skill in detecting and releasing legacy burdens is critically important when serving Black clients. The release of a legacy burden often invites a radical clearing of energy that opens up more space to focus on personal burdens. Once a legacy burden has been detected, a client may invite the part that holds it to assess the portion of the burden that belongs to them (personal burden) versus the portion that belongs to their lineage (legacy burden) and release the legacy burden in a way that clears the burden from the client and their ancestral line. Personal burdens are then unloaded in the typical manner by releasing them in a way that feels right for the client. The resulting freedom from oppressive beliefs, both personal and generational, is the crux of the healing impact of IFS.

Common legacy burdens identified in Black clients I've worked with and other Black people I am connected to include:

- "I need to be strong and not struggle or show vulnerability."
- "I'm on my own. There is no one to save me."
- "I deserve everything that's happened to me."
- "If I was just _____, then I'd be worth it."
- "I need to be strong and hold the family together."
- "Don't be too much."

- "Mistakes equal death."
- "Blackness is bad/inferior/unclean/dirty/sin."
- "Who and how I am is not good/beautiful/acceptable/desirable enough."
- "Keeping White people comfortable ensures my survival."

Helping Black clients increase their awareness of the impact of legacy burdens on their lived experience can be a vital turning point in their healing journey. As previously mentioned, Black people are often perceived as being solely responsible for the conditions in which they find themselves. As such, many may come to therapy with the belief that because they are holding the weight of their lived experiences, they must find a way to deal with all of it. Clinicians who are skilled legacy burden detectors facilitate the release of generational patterns of pain which allows clients' inner systems to become clearer and more spacious.

Compassionate Accountability

If intercultural competence describes the inner orientation and knowledge that one has about self and others, compassionate accountability describes the system of actions that should naturally follow from that competence. When you have awareness of your cultural make-up and the biases that have developed by way of your social location, it becomes more possible to recognize the ways in which the very biases you are working to change can still show up in your sessions with Black clients. Compassionate accountability involves acknowledging and taking responsibility for your impact with humility and grace and offering the same for others.

Whether consciously or unconsciously, there may be perspectives that you hold, or behaviors you engage in, that impact the therapeutic relationship with Black clients due to embedded racist or other dehumanizing assumptions. When this is brought to your attention, responding in a way that allows you to humbly receive feedback and confidently work toward repair is best. Sometimes therapists confuse things like pity, sympathy, fear, and anxiety with being connected to their client's experience. This can lead to Black clients feeling pressure to caretake their White therapist's emotions, which is a cultural legacy burden that reenacts racial trauma. Black people don't need to be saved; they need to be safely centered. To navigate these moments, it is important to cultivate an atmosphere of openness and skill with repairing relational ruptures after they have occurred.

Creating such an atmosphere starts with naming racial differences and discussing race early in the therapeutic relationship. Many people feel quite unskilled when it comes to engaging in dialogue about race and difference. If you do not identify as a person of color, notice what parts of you become activated when you receive this invitation to discuss race with your Black clients. Be sure to check in with parts that may have an agenda to be seen a certain way by your Black clients so that they do not guide your discussion. If you do not, there's the risk of that agenda becoming more important than the needs of your client. Below are a few scripts to help open and move conversations on race forward.

"I'm aware that we have different racial identities. I'd like us to talk about what this difference might be like for you and your parts? Would you be open to that?"

"As you hear from this part, are there any parts that have anything to say about sharing this with someone of a different race than you?"

Questions like these are another way to invite in parts that may be holding back and blocking access to the work due to their focus on the impact of difference that hasn't been named. In my experience, phrases like these, when offered at the right time, have been helpful in creating more trust between my client's system and me as their therapist. I also find it important to acknowledge differences that a client's part names, particularly when I share the identity of the source of their pain. This applies both when there are racial differences and when there are racial similarities. Below is a script of a typical dialogue I have when a client's parts are acknowledging painful experiences with others who share my identity.

"I have gone through a lot of drama, and unfortunately, it's been with other Black women."

"Oh, I see. Well, I am a Black woman being here with you. I'm wondering if that part has any concerns about that?"

Client pauses.

"As you say that, I do notice some thoughts like, 'Well, what is she thinking? I want this to work out and not cause drama with my therapist, but are you like them, too?'"

"Yes, that makes sense to me. I want your part to know that I am not holding any negative judgment about what it's sharing right now. I have parts that resonate with that experience and have been hurt by other Black women. Let your part know that I'd like it to share at any moment it senses anything in me that doesn't feel affirming or simply bothers the part. How's that?"

"Oh, that felt really good, Fatimah. I didn't even know I needed that 'cause I already feel like I trust you. But hearing you say that and acknowledging that, yes, you are a Black woman, and acknowledging my general concern felt really good."

Compassionate accountability starts with attunement and ends with humility. It takes being present with what's present and owning your contribution to the dynamic. It's about being first to model the honesty and transparency that we as therapists can expect from our clients but sometimes fail to reciprocate. It's about setting boundaries while coming up to our line of responsibility and not putting our work onto our clients. And it is always a process that occurs over and over, not a single event.

Conclusion

At its most essential level, the IFS model offers a tool for Black people that is non-pathologizing, affirming, and empowering. The IFS model provides a method of getting reacquainted with the inherent goodness that we all were created with. It's a process of uncovering the hurts, the wounds, and the trauma that has blocked access to love, tenderness, and connection.

For me, becoming a trained IFS therapist clarified my original professional goal. What I didn't see in the field, but what was critically necessary, was transformative Self-leadership. The promise of shifting someone's internal world—unburdening their most shameful and debilitating beliefs and experiences—ignited my passion even further to bring healing, along with a renewed way of existing, to the Black community. After 10 years of serving Black clients in domestic violence shelters, in their homes, in their schools, and in my private practice office, I view this chapter as another expression of my commitment to making sure that Black people are getting the best therapy experience, if and when they choose to opt into it. My hope for therapists is that, after reading this, you are turning the page with some curiosity about who you are and all that you bring with you to your sessions with Black clients, some new ideas and language that you can immediately begin to implement in your sessions, and some awareness of the gaps that still need to be filled that may be beyond the scope of this chapter.

KEY TAKEAWAYS

- Building intercultural competence is essential to the therapeutic process. It involves increasing self-awareness about the impact of your culture on your beliefs about, and behaviors toward, Black people.
- For greater benefit when working with Black clients, emphasize the IFS model's insights on the three Bs: the Body, Befriending, and working through Burdens, particularly legacy burdens.
- Creating a culture of compassionate accountability in your therapeutic relationships allows for ruptures to be repaired with patience and dignity.

AUTHOR BIO

Fatimah Finney, LMHC (she/her) is a skilled licensed mental health counselor and an Assistant Trainer at the Internal Family Systems (IFS) Institute. She currently serves a variety of clients of diverse backgrounds and experiences as an EAP Counselor in addition to her private practice. Fatimah is also a skilled facilitator and DEI practitioner. She uses IFS as a relational framework in her group facilitation and a methodology for understanding the underlying beliefs that motivate behaviors in work settings. She helps individuals and organizations build their capacity and skills in centering diversity, equity, inclusion and social justice. As a Qualified Administrator of the Intercultural Development Inventory (IDI), Fatimah uses this tool to help her clients gain insight into their strengths and growth edges for navigating differences and offer strategies for better cross-cultural interactions.

REFERENCES

Baran, M., & Jana, T. (2020). *Subtle acts of exclusion: How to understand, identify and stop microaggressions.* Berrett-Koehler Publishers.

Hammer, M. (2012). The intercultural development inventory: A new frontier in assessment and development of intercultural competence. In M. Vande Berg, R. M. Paige, & K. H. Lou (Eds.), *Student learning abroad* (Ch. 5, pp. 115-136). Stylus Publishing.

McConnell, S. (2020). *Somatic Internal Family Systems therapy: Awareness, breath, resonance, movement and touch in practice.* North Atlantic Books.

Menakem, R. (2017). *My grandmother's hands: Racialized trauma and the pathway to mending our hearts and bodies.* Central Recovery Press.

Williams, M. T. (2020). *Managing microaggressions: Addressing everyday racism in therapeutic spaces.* Oxford University Press.

GOING DEEPER

From Fatimah Finney

1) Website:
   a. www.healingdifferently.com

2) Books:
   a. Gee, D. H., & Crujido, C. (Eds.). (2022). *Nonwhite and woman: 131 micro essays on being in the world.* Woodhall Press.

3) Workshops (www.healingdifferently.com/offerings):
   a. Microaggressions: Accountability and Relational Repair.
   b. The Trauma of Exclusion: Microaggressions in the Therapeutic Alliance.
   c. Culture, Conflict, and Communication.

4) Podcast Interviews:
   a. IFS Talks—Intercultural Competence: A Conversation with Fatimah Finney: www.podcasts.apple.com/us/podcast/intercultural-competence-and-ifs-a-conversation/id1481000501?i=1000578353095

From Other Sources

1) Books:
   a. Burke, T., & Brown, B. (2021). *You are your best thing: Vulnerability, shame resilience, and the Black experience—An anthology* (1st ed.). Random House.
   b. Coates, T. N. (2015). *Between the world and me.* Text Publishing Company.
   c. Saad, L. (2020). *Me and white supremacy: How to recognize your privilege, combat racism and change the world.* Sourcebooks, Inc.
   d. Menakem, R. (2017). *My grandmother's hands: Racialized trauma and the pathway to mending our hearts and bodies.* Central Recovery Press.
   e. McGhee, H. C. (2021). *The sum of us: What racism costs everyone and how we can prosper together* (1st ed.). One World.
   f. Washington, H. A. (2006). *Medical apartheid: The dark history of medical experimentation on Black Americans from colonial times to the present.* Doubleday.
   g. Alexander, M. (2010). *The new Jim Crow: Mass incarceration in the age of colorblindness.* New Press.
   h. Mullan, J. (2023). *Decolonizing therapy oppression, historical trauma and politicizing your practice.* W. W. Norton and Company.

i. McConnell, S. (2020). *Somatic Internal Family Systems therapy: Awareness, breath, resonance, movement and touch in practice.* North Atlantic Books.
   j. Irving, D. (2014). *Waking up white: and finding myself in the story of race.* Elephant Room Press.
2) Articles:
   a. White Supremacy—Still Here by Tema Okun. www.dismantlingracism.org/uploads/4/3/5/7/43579015/white_supremacy_culture_-_still_here.pdf
3) Courses:
   b. Resmaa Menakem's Somatic Abolitionism: www.resmaa.com/movement

EMBODYING IFS WITH NATIVE AMERICAN CLIENTS

COMPOSITE INDIGENOUS VOICES TELL A STORY OF IFS RESONANCE

Julia Sullivan, MBA, Suzan McVicker, PhD, LPC,
Gregg Paisley, MBA, and Pete Patton, LCSW

Introduction to an Indigenous IFS Storytelling Circle

We invite you to join our storytelling circle. Hear our voices in a composite story as we reflect on how our Indigenous wisdom ways resonate with our IFS practice. Imagine with us the creative transformations that are possible when both Indigenous ways and IFS wisdom are woven together.

If reading our chapter calls out to you, we invite you to be still and listen. Hear the voices of your ancestors, your allies, and the seven generations to come. Allow their words to bubble up from deep within, like a clear spring emerging from the depths of Mother Earth. The voices that have the most to say are often the ones who wait to be the last to speak, and they use the quietest voice. Their words are clear, compelling, and liberating. As you read, if you hear a whisper calling to join us, prepare yourself to consider an invitation that will come.

It is beyond the scope of this chapter to explain the IFS model as it is taught to licensed mental health clinicians. It is also impossible and inappropriate to try to explain Indigenous ways in this chapter. Walking in Indigenous ways and healing with IFS is a lived experience that unfolds over time. Both are nurtured in community, supported by building a trusted relationship with another who abides in the teachings in their spirit, mind, words, and actions. This person comes along side you to support your learning, growth, healing.

Learning IFS is a process like seeds planted in one form deep in the earth, which take in nutrients, burst out of their husk, and boldly make the journey to earth, air, water, sky. Each seed becomes a tender shoot that requires changing levels of care as the shoot becomes strong. The shoot grows roots that run deep to nurture the plant so it can weather the seasons and storms that will come.

Wherever you are when you read this, (seed, tender shoot, or deeply rooted one) our hope is that you will find words that spark your curiosity. As a deeply rooted one, you may discover branches of your mindset that call out for pruning or shaping. We invite you into an adventure of the heart. Most of our reading is done with the "head." Our story is best read from the "heart" or "spirit."

There are times in this composite narrative, beginning with the next section, when we will speak to you as one person. You are welcomed.

Entering a Story of Resonance

Imagine this: You are my friend. You ask me, of Indigenous heritage, to talk to you about my IFS journey. I have not been a huge fan or an eager participant in western mental health services offered to me. Usually all I get is a pathological diagnosis and some psych meds. I participate in my people's sacred traditions and ceremony. They are an essential expression of who I am. They connect me to all of Life, to my ancestors, to my people. I use ceremony to heal and battle what seeks to take me down. I am a warrior, so I stay in the fight. And I enter the fight when others around me call on me.

Then someone I trust told me about IFS. They said IFS was "good medicine," the words we use to describe a healing way that directly or indirectly respects our sacred Indigenous ways. Given my trust in them, I found someone trained in IFS to support me. I had nothing to lose given how angry and hopeless I felt at the time. My most frequent fantasies were about suicide. Most people who knew me had no idea what was really going on inside my head.

After some time had passed in my IFS journey, you noticed a difference in me. You found out I was "seeing someone" to help me. Thick veils I hid behind started to slowly melt away. I started showing up differently to life in powerful ways that you could sense yet could not name. Given our friendship, you asked me to tell you about it.

Rather than give you a clipped answer, I invite you now to join me for some time on the land. I want the vista we take in, the earth that holds us, the plant and animal life that will show up to tell my story as much as my words will. We walk in silence to a sacred spot. While walking I ask my inner system to work well together in the telling of my story. There is so much to share, most of it beyond words. We arrive.

The vista is panoramic. The air dances gently around us. We sit down on the earth. Tree beings surround us. We feel the presence of our ancestors.

Here is my story.

Practicing "Power With" Respect

IFS (Internal Family Systems) is done with us, not to us. When a person practices IFS with us, we both are called to an energetic field that we are accustomed to experiencing only in sacred ceremony with our people, not with outsiders.

A mystery around IFS intrigues us: How did they do that? Going within is not new to us. Connecting with the beings in the inner dimensions is familiar. Yet, when a person practices IFS with us, we are at first surprised. The time dimension becomes elastic. Our inner journey goes both slow and fast at the same time. We go deep in a way that we've never done before. Our permission is sought every step of the way, and still the discoveries shock us. We uncover ancient wounds as if for the first time.

Getting to such a deep healing place has to do with respect. Not the cheap kind. The kind that comes with a price. A practice of "power with" not "power over." A practice of waiting, holding silence, waiting, holding more silence, waiting. Breathing. Breathing some more. Allowing a deep calm to come over us.

We've heard that Self elicits Self, and parts elicit parts. We begin to know what that means when we experience it. Self opens. Parts soften back. Both are right. Both have inner wisdom and know when to step back and when to open. We breathe. We wait. We listen.

Going Within

I listen. Only I can hear what is inside of me. Sometimes I say what I hear. Always I'm told it is not important that I say it out loud. Awareness of the experiences, roles, needs, desires, pain, challenges, influences, and gifts of my own parts is what is important. At first, so many talk at once. Mostly what I've done before is push them away, ignore, or numb myself from their endless barrage.

Sometimes I hear words. Sometimes sounds. It can be a feeling in my body. Or an image that I see. Or remembering scenes from the dream way. I am guided respectfully as I do this inward turn. With respect I allow the wisdom of parts and Self to bubble up from my depths.

Connecting Self with SELF

I seek a connection with the SELF that transcends us all. The SELF is called many things. My favorite name is "GUS" for Great Universal Spirit. The SELF, the Creator, is manifest in all of creation and is the connecting energy in all our relations. It is the SELF that my Self connects with in ways that are undefinable, indescribable. Like love, you know what it is if you've experienced it. Even small beginnings are magnificent. Tiny morsels are potent enough to make me want more. To deepen and enlarge my relationship with my Self to experience SELF more fully, in the dance of giving and receiving.

I am invited to look more deeply into my inner system. It is a universe in there. Beings in motion, spinning, revolving as planets around a sun. Exploding as stars being born or dying. As I peer deeper, I know there are many more universes than the ones I can see now.

Or as I spiral down a level, I begin to experience my inner system like a city. A whopping metropolis. Each city block has a specific purpose to fulfill. A specific life event and its varied impacts to track and avoid, squash, deny, and discipline right out of my inner system…as if that were possible.

At times I get a glimpse, a taste, a sense of a miracle. When Self begins to connect to parts, and those parts begin to trust my Self, wisdom emerges like a gradual awakening from a long, long sleep. Then comes curiosity, and the healing adventure goes deeper.

This is why we wait. We go slow to go fast. We go in Indian time. Sometimes quickly, sometimes slowly. It takes time to behold the inner system, to learn and listen to it. Being willing to speak about it takes more time. It can't be rushed. If I'm rushed, I slow down. Trust is threatened. The pacing comes from within me, not my IFS helper. Power "over" me leads me to shut down. Doing it "to me" pains me. I have learned to retain my sovereignty within. My parts think my inner sovereignty is the only sovereignty I may ever have again, even as my Self knows it never has and never will lose sovereignty. My Self has always been free and powerful, naturally expressing "power with" my parts. My Self supports my parts in not giving their sovereignty to anyone. Even those people I have started to trust. Those I trust don't want to conquer my sovereignty. They cheer me on when my Self liberates my parts.

Witnessing Protectors / Emerging Self

In IFS, I'm assured that "nothing in the IFS space happens without permission." I noticed that when I voiced worry, sadness, guilt, or shame, I felt swirly in my stomach, heaviness in my chest, tightness in my throat, and an ache in my upper spine that radiated into my neck.

I'm asked to put my hands on those parts and send them some compassion. We waited and let the compassion sink in. I was amazed that my parts eased. I felt more spacious inside. Together we pulled in healing energy, and I noticed being my Self in ways that felt both ancient and new. Awkward and yet familiar. Like coming home yet experiencing it for the first time.

At first, I sensed Curiosity, Calm, and Connectedness, which I came to call "the big three." We allowed space for these parts to notice that which is offered from Self. Then when the time was ripe, we whispered a suggestion for my Self to ask my part(s), "How old do you think I am?" In an unhurried tone, another inquiry, "Who do you believe me to be?" Some parts have knowing and respond, "Your Self, your center, your light within." Our two-way conversation between my Self and my part(s) creates wider safety for my whole inner world. Safety within lights the way for honest sharing.

Unburdening As Ceremony

When Self witnesses a wounded part with Compassion, the part begins to express through images, remembered scenes, scents, messages, spirit memory. Burdens are acknowledged until the part feels understood. At the right time, the part meditatively co-creates with my Self a ceremony to release the burdens that have been shared. The pain, shame, rage, grief is offered to earth, air, fire, water, or light—in whatever form the part needs.

IFS people call this ceremonial process an "unburdening." We may release burdened time when sovereignty was ripped from us, the grief we carry over the blood of our children buried in the earth, the rage from the attempts to erase our identity. After we release the burdens, we take in the gifts of our Self and our ancestors. We transform our suffering parts back into their original unburdened inherent nature. We reestablish and enjoy right relationship.

IFS has helped me bring more ceremony to my inner world every day. I bring ceremony into any moment that needs it. As I have gotten to know and then unburden my inner system of parts, my day-to-day reactions to situations have changed.

When we become familiar with the IFS way, our spirits want to share this with others in the medicine way. We also feel a calling to extend this healing to those who came before us. Our IFS helper shows us how to do that.

As you know, my friend, in earth wisdom medicine there are different levels of ceremony. Some are hidden and led only by those ready to hold the sacred teachings found in the deepest waters. The same is true of IFS. Unburdening complex trauma calls for a deep embodiment of Self-energy. Being "trained" in IFS is only the beginning. One can have head knowledge galore and no embodiment. Carefully choose the IFS helper who will walk the healing journey with you. Listen and trust your parts who can sense when someone is patronizing or in conflict with what we know to be true in the medicine. Truth harmonizes with truth. Have no fear to walk away from one person to find another who resonates with the medicine and can open new vistas of healing using IFS.

Listening to Parts

Because of IFS, my parts have come to know I want their input. So now they offer it calmly. They used to have to scream at the top of their lungs for days or years to get my attention. This was the confusion or rage people used to see on my face. My parts are better at taking turns and talk to me at a volume that allows me to listen from the heart. When I hear something that needs release, we do it right then. I find ways to honor the moment and remember to reinforce it later in meditation to affirm the healing. I'm told that this reinforcement or remembering is what builds the new neural pathway in my brain.

Now when I participate in traditional ceremony I experience a deeper harmony as my Spirit, my parts, my body, my Self dance and chant in trance with my ancestors as we honor the intergenerational healing we have experienced.

Exploring the Inner System

Sometimes the inner journey is like this:

I go inside, and I see a Wolf Being with green eyes. Bigger than life. Fierce and wise. Ready to defend and protect me from being violated…again. I love that Wolf. I am glad it is with me. My ancestors are in that Wolf. I know it loves me, and I know it can devour and destroy any perpetrator who comes to call. So many come to call. Many of my other parts get weary of the seemingly endless stream of people and institutions who want what I have and then claim it for their own because they can. Wolf is not tired. Wolf is ready, waiting. Vigilant, brave, wise.

On another day Crustacean appears, hiding under a rock. It likes it under the rock. I like its razor-sharp claws and impenetrable shell. Crustacean is not in there shivering like a coward. It is inside its home. The rock is its friend, its "home sweet home." It wonders about the questions I am asking it that I have never asked before. My curiosity is at first odd, then exhilarating. It wants me to know a lot. It wants me to stop the Self sabotage.

Crustacean sees how quickly I go Chameleon. It used to think it was disgusting. Lately, it admits Chameleon can be absolutely clever. Sometimes being invisible "ain't so bad" Chameleon explains. Chameleon calls it "going stealth." Stealth is such a handy skill to have given many of the places I need to go, who is there, and what I need to do. Most of the time I am stealth. Crustacean and Chameleon have become allies.

Still other times, when I go inside, I see people. Sometimes ancestors, who when we meet, we know. Other times, I see myself at different ages. When I asked one part how old it was, it said "thousands of years old." I already knew I was of the stars. It's good to know my parts know it too.

I also meet very young, tender parts of me. Little One is the part who feels less than, not good enough, overwhelmed, and lost. Little One gets afraid of how angry everyone gets at them for being little. For acting powerless at the worst times. Little One has gotten really good at going deeper into the dark where no one can find them. Where the angry nasty voices can't be heard any more. Little One gets sad from being alone. They wish life was not so hard for them. IFS has helped me find many Little Ones. We retrieve them from the dark places and ask them where they would like to go to be safe. When they are ready, we unburden them too.

Processing Childhood Trauma

Some of this you know, my friend. I tell you my story again to show you a closer look at my IFS healing journey.

My Indigenous biological mother was in her third year of college when she found out she was pregnant with me. Just making it to college was quite a feat for a woman in her day, and even more so for anyone Indigenous. The social system coached her to put me up for adoption with a White family who could give me what she couldn't. She had already internalized the beliefs of her boarding-schooled parents. She believed that sending me to a God-fearing dominant-cultured couple would be better for my future than going back to live with my people where I would know who I was. Rather than support and nurture her, they ripped the small me from her arms. I was adopted by a White couple three days later. They were God-fearing for sure. And since the God of their understanding ruled by fear, they felt completely justified in doing the same to me.

I've had interactions with parts that remember my biological mother saying to me, while I was enwombed, "I'm your biggest fan." Parts of me wanted to hate and blame my birth mother. Others longed for her phantom loving arms. Parts of me wanted to let her off the hook and hate and blame my adopted parents. So many parts. So many polarities. I had no idea I was my own soul's boa constrictor squeezing the very life right out of me.

When I was 39, I moved across the Pacific Ocean to find a place where I felt safe and far away from what remained of my adopted family. I was checking in with my parts about a week after I landed. And…there…I…found…a three-day-old baby, Little One alone in a very dark place.

Little One all alone, heard my Self saying "I have come to take you from this dark place. You don't have to live alone here anymore." Little One was frozen and did not want to move. My Self sat down next to them and waited for Little One to get used to another's companionship. My Self was there unafraid of the dark, and slowly emanated light into the darkness as if for the first time. One day, all the protectors gave me permission to proceed. They accepted the role of observant sentinels who promised to shut it all down if needed. With the protectors' permission, something started to happen.

Car Meets Train Meets Death

My first explicit memory, at the ripe age of 21 months, was a flurry of movement. The family VW Super Beetle was thrown 80 feet when it collided with a Southern Pacific Railroad train engine with my adopted mother driving, and my abuser holding me in the back seat. The next day's front page described the train engineer helplessly seeing a woman staring straight ahead while driving toward the railroad crossing. It was the era before car seats and seatbelts. I became a human projectile. Various Little Ones have played that over and over and over. The replay has happened most days of my life. In Self, several of my Little Ones have shown me various aspects of that day and its aftermath. From floating around in the interior of the VW just before, during, and after being launched, to waking up in the hospital, wrapped in bandages and other hospital apparatus, and weeks later "coming to" all alone.

I wasn't the only one to die in the accident. But I was one of two who died who was revived at the scene. The Little One who carried the memory of waking up in the hospital all alone was found and reinvited back into my heart. A Protector in the form of an angel robed in white, with white wings, smoking a white cigarette was standing outside the heart/room. They waved me in with their cigarette.

Witnessing, Retrieving, and Unburdening

During my IFS session, my Self asked Little One how close they wanted me to be. Sometimes Little One wanted to sit on my lap and be held until they were satisfied. We stayed there together and witnessed some of the bad things that happened to Little One until they were sure I understood. However, Little One wouldn't move until they believed it wouldn't happen again. When I told Little One about the Wolf and the Crustacean Chameleon team, they got interested. "If you hold my hand, with Wolf, Crustacean, and Chameleon by our side, I will slowly start the walk out," said Little One. And so, we walked.

It was quite a long walk with the right amount of time for a slow, spacious, easy conversation. "Where do you want to go?" I asked. We went exactly where Little One wanted to go. We built a special dome over, around, and beneath this place. I told Little One that in the magical alternative IFS universe, anything is possible. It is like a portal into a place where people, time, and materials manifest exactly as we need them. It takes some practice to believe this is true. And once you know it, there's no going back. Creativity becomes a positive reinforcing spiral loop of manifestation.

Tending the Fire

Now I use portals into experiences that I need for healing, learning, or fun. At times I find my parts in a summer or winter camp. Summer camp is a huge homey cave where we can all be closer to the natural windows at the edge, or we can circle around the fire in the center. It is spacious enough for all parts and yet a cool, comfy refuge with a spring in there, too. In winter camp we enjoy the sun through windows of clear ice in our giant snow lodge. Our fire burns there in the center with plenty of soft seating when we gather. In these seasonal homes, the idea of an inner system of parts is a given. I sometimes speak about my parts as inner relatives. When we need to support a healing ceremony for a part, we gather with those who went before, those who are our guides, and those we trust in our day-to-day life.

What we've found after doing IFS for some time is that each person has a unique inner system that is a product of our ancestors' lives, the life we have lived there and then, and here and now. The best and the worst. The ecstasy and the despair. The beautiful and the repulsive. They all weave together in this panoramic living tapestry. The Self deep within is whole, intact, healthy, and strong. Even if some of our parts have done the worst of things, the Self remains unaffected.

Seeing the Self in Me and You

At first, this unassailable Self was hard for many of my parts to believe in. My parts were overwhelmed with shame: swimming in it, drinking it, and rebelling against it. My parts believed I was terminally ill and hopelessly unique. They thought all the rest of humanity might have Selves but not me. If I ever had a Self, they said, it left long ago. These skeptical parts believed my being was unfit for life. As I fully embodied this self-loathing belief, my world got smaller and darker. Ending my life seemed like the most compassionate act to bring relief to my weary system. My parts thought that exiting this life would take away the burden my parts believed they dumped on others just by breathing. Those parts were blind to how they really mattered to others. In their darkness, even the smallest flicker of hope and the tiniest morsel of love made all the difference in the world. Those parts had no idea how magnificent they were and are. They now see in Self, the love for me that remains strong and true.

Connecting and Becoming

This is why we need each other. One person holds up the sacred mirror for another. One person says, "I see the Self in you!" They affirm what they see when our Self shows up in the many ways it does: In the courage it takes to look inside. In the perseverance it takes to wait and wait some more for the parts that are not ready to trust. In the boldness it takes to live life on life's terms, no matter what they are. In the belly laughs that come when we learn how to find humor in the moment.

The Self shows up and finds connection in the most surprising places. Holding the hand of a dying loved one. Having a water fight with a group of children and letting them win. Joining in the belly laughs. Clouds. Sunsets. The stars. Tree beings. Winged ones. Beings of the sea. The earth. The sacred flute. The drum, deep and strong. Tears. Fire. All our relations. When an IFS ally notices your Self, they say, "Your Self is the one who just said, did, or felt that." It is glorious, and at times almost too much for some of our parts to take in.

Still the Self remains. Patient. Strong. Calm. Confident. The Self knows it is alive in and through the SELF. The Self remembers this and that is why it can stay so calm under the most outrageous circumstances. The Self of our whole system sees the Self in our parts and knows how amazing it will be when the part can see it too. It is always worth the wait. Growing like a deeply rooted tree in the soil of our soul, respecting the process moves healing forward.

Accessing Portals

Many years before I knew IFS and knew little about my ancestry, I had the clearest dream that I was a sequoia tree. I was simply living, without much consciousness of being. My roots ran deep in the high meadows of a mountainous region. I remember the presence of other trees near me. The burnished dry grasses were punctuated with the dark greens of us conifers.

In the time it takes for a mountain blue bird to cheer-chirrup its song, I became a bird and soared into the sky. I shot up dizzyingly taller than all the trees around me and waved a little in a breeze. There were no nearby branches where I might steady myself, like holding the hand of a friend. I could see ridge after ridge, way beyond my sight as the dreamer. The air and sights were clear. I heard voices and dogs barking in distant villages. I could immediately focus on a village and know the goings on. My consciousness interfaced with the curve of our Mother Earth. I didn't need to bend around her to instantly be so far away. My perspective was expanded and at the same time couched in my everyday sensory abilities. It was one of those dreams that was so compelling that I went back into it again and again. I am still growing in that soil of my soul and still returning to Sequoia and blue bird awareness.

Living a New Song with Self Leadership

Once we gain easy access with our Self, and our parts unburden and find the Self within each of them, life becomes a whole new song. We are like an orchestra in which each different part seeks to play in harmony with others, the parts within, the beings outside of us. Parts look to the Self as a conductor who encourages all to play and sing from the heart for the sheer magnificence of it. A missed note here and there makes it relatable and human. Perfection is a manufactured structure that may be culturally programmed. Art is manifested with guidance from the spiritual Knowing Ones and unpredictable. Vibrant and alive.

Having an inner system that is Self-led is also like getting on a bus with the Self in the driver's seat. Everyone knows where the bus is going, open to the path unfolding exactly as it will. If the bus breaks down, the parts who know how to fix the bus respond confidently. The others relax knowing that if their skills are needed, they will be asked to activate themselves to benefit the whole. As the bus rolls down the road, every so often the Self does a check in to make sure that the destination is still where everyone wants to go. All voices are heard. Even the quiet, small ones. When needed, a new destination is set, and the trip proceeds with greater satisfaction felt by all. All parts celebrate that all the parts on this bus are one swell, high performing team. They kick back and enjoy the ride!

Weeping For Our Parts

The Self respects all the parts, and respect goes both ways. Sometimes when the best thing to do is weep, the Self invites the other parts who are good at weeping to let go and let it happen. Some things are just too big to face without bathing in some sacred tears first. When the Self starts feeling the chest tighten, it does a quick scan and asks, "Is now the right time and place to do this?" If the answer is yes, then the Self lets go and welcomes the tears. Sometimes years, decades, and millennia of tears come out. One tear can hold a multitude of sorrow, rage, trauma, or pain. Sometimes we weep with and for our ancestors. Our tears water the ground. And the earth is large enough to receive them all. We weep oceans. The oceans know our sorrow and seek to replenish and restore. Our tears ebb and flow like the waves. High tide. Low tide. Small waves and towering ones. Then the seas calm. It looks like the calm sea under a full moon when all is right with the world.

After some good weeping, we are ready to walk back into healing our inner system. Strengthened and restored. We know that if we are not afraid of it, it can't hurt us. We can face the scary parts within with curiosity and compassion. When we come to feel appreciation for our "tor-mentor," we know we have healed and grown. That "tor-mentor" is a person or situation who sometimes painfully shows us the parts that need to heal. "Tor-mentors" are our teachers, whether our parts like it or not. The "shoulds" of life chase us down relentlessly. Our parts are smart and smell a false "should" from miles away. They often use profanity to tell us exactly how they feel about all this false talk that smells of excrement.

Trusting the Wisdom of Parts

When our parts catch us playing burdened games, faking it, trying to deceive, we have learned it is best to pause and think about what the part is saying. If the part sees something we can't see, we let the part know. It is hard to learn while confused. We humbly ask it to explain. Humility includes being teachable. And we have come to recognize the wisdom of our parts. They know where we've been and how we got there. They know what came before us, going back through time, generation upon generation. We stop. We listen. We ask questions from a place of deep curiosity and an open heart. If we get afraid, we ask the part not to overwhelm us. The part will slow down if we need it to. It will be glad that we finally stop to learn. This respect in pacing is often the first proof it sees that there might be hope.

Recognizing Alliances

Sometimes parts find other parts that see the world as they do. These parts form alliances to team up against parts that see the world differently. These polarities can spring up over just about anything. Eat this or don't. Fall in love or play the field. Be bold about who I am or hide. Be a victim or heal. It can get complicated for our systems when the polarity is not an either-or but a multiple-choice option. Coalitions spring up all over the inner landscape. If we are not Self-led, then every coalition can start lobbying to put our distractor parts in the driver's seat to drink, eat, binge watch, or people please.

Our Self clearly explains to all the activated parts how difficult it is to understand anyone with everyone talking/shouting/binging all at once. In this inner cacophony, parts interrupt each other before anyone has had their say. Again, we slow down. Invite everyone to breathe. Thank them all for caring so much. We calmly tell them that we know they have our best interests at heart. We tell them that we want to know the wisdom in each perspective before we make any sudden moves. We ask them to discuss among themselves which part needs our attention. We thank the parts willing to wait their turn. We invite them to listen in and watch the healing work we will do. Sometimes multiple parts who share the same burden are invited to do a collective unburdening if they are ready.

We invite them into an inner circle around a sacred mystical fire. We create ceremony around the listening. Using symbols, plant medicine, or sacred tobacco, we go to a sacred place. As the truth of each part emerges, we find peace. We discern the next right step. We integrate the wisdom of diverse perspectives. We breathe. We thank each part. We ask them all to be ready to return to council as needed. Our parts appreciate that. Our Self likes that too. We offer sacred tobacco into the fire asking the SELF to be with us as we complete the ceremony. We walk away in wholeness and beauty, with a grateful heart. Clear and wise. This whole ceremonial unburdening process happens within the universe of our imagination or with physical objects and people, as location and time allow.

Once my Self and the Self of my plethora of parts were working together, I sent a message requesting guidance from my ancestors. The response came over days and weeks. I was eventually presented with a portal. I wondered what it was.

Finding a Portal

I'd learned by way of received teaching and from experience that parts often present as objects. So, I thought "Hold Self and be present to the qualities that arise." I did this for days and weeks…I noticed that the portal was decorated in a simple but beautiful way. It was gray in color and the frame was at times ornate and at times plain. The surface appeared opaque and kind of a swirly grey.

I noticed a long tube on the ground that appeared to originate from within the portal. It looked like an umbilical cord. I noticed it over several visits and then one time I laid my hand on it…and I was suddenly inside the portal.

I found myself in a crevasse of some type. I foraged around in the opening for a bit and then exited…I arose and flew into the sky. I was over a vast landscape filled as far as the eye could see with green plants and each plant bloomed with white flowers. I held this vision along with my parts for eighteen months. One day while doing a Google search on "medicine plants" or "plant medicine" I came upon a picture of the green plant with white flowers. I had been given a vision of a vast crop of tobacco plants. Tobacco is considered the grandfather of grandfathers of all plant medicine.

Celebrating Self Leadership

Since receiving this vision of Tobacco, I've received much from the portal and am convinced it was a gift from my ancestors. I've received nurturing and a sense of belonging that I've never felt as one who was stolen at birth and adopted at three days old into a "Whites only" culture. Life is good. I have released, and am no longer held captive by, the people whose burdened parts harmed me. I am free and so are they. IFS has helped me recover from the harm done by the parts of others. Sometimes when all I am feeling is betrayal bordering on hate, I imagine an alternative IFS universe in which all of us in Self sit around and laugh about all the madness we created on this earth while we were walking around in these mysterious human bodies.

I know who I am and who my people are. Beauty and wholeness fill my days. I have spoken. I am complete.

Returning to Life

We sit here in stillness, as friends. Taking in the vista. Breathing in the air. Becoming one with the hawk that circles, the raven that calls out. The earth holds us. Letting us take in the words I have spoken and the healing they describe.

I can sense your cautious parts not knowing what to take in or what to say. Coming from my Self I reassure that I offered my journey as one example of what the IFS healing experience can be. Like other healing, it is "sometimes quickly, sometimes slowly."

IFS has taught me how to love my parts, especially the most egregious acting out ones. In loving them, I have come to love my Self.

My friend, you don't have to believe or agree with everything I have said. Imagine these words as a free gift. You can do anything you want with them. Just make sure that all your parts and your Self know that all my parts and my Self loves them deeply.

Now let's walk back home so we can have some more belly laughs and heartily eat our favorite stew I made for us last night!

History of the Indigenous IFS Council

We've been asked to tell the story of how the Indigenous IFS Council was formed. Our story will be of the heart, not the head. We lovingly invite our minds to take a break. Listen and look with your heart. We invite you, in your Self and with your parts, to answer the "why" of our actions.

Our origin story is one of shadow and light. The need was born of intergenerational complex trauma that came from unspeakable atrocities and genocide. Their fruits are despair and all that brings. We won't recite the litany of ills we live with on a day in, day out basis. We are not defined by them and won't be caged with anyone's pity.

However, when a 12-year-old boy shoots himself on the steps of a church after his mother dies from Covid, we are compelled to act. We say to ourselves, and anyone who has the ears to hear, "We have to up our efforts now!" Does this sound "parts-led" instead of "Self-led?" Maybe it is. And it is also an excellent example of one of our favorite IFS slogans: "All Parts Welcome." The sacred practices and traditional healing modalities we already have need to be practiced anew, like our lives depend on it. Because they do. And we want to be open to ideas "new" to us, like IFS. We can explore this new modality and still respect our traditions.

Who We Are

We are Indigenous by blood, some 100%, others not. We have lived in boarding schools. We have lost our knowledge of who we are and found it again. Some had the blessed experience of being raised and rooted in their Indigenous identity and sacred ways. We are BIPOC (a term used in the United States to describe Black, Indigenous, People of Color). We are straight and two-spirited (gay). We were born on reservations. Moved away. Came back. We were born and raised suburban. Our families and communities span a range of what is called socio-economic status. Some live with middle class comforts, others do not. We have clinical degrees and hard-earned letters behind our names to reflect our expertise. We have MBAs. We formed a team who humbled ourselves enough to allow our efforts to be scrutinized and improved by participating in an Action Lab 2022 with the Stanford University "d.school" (Hasso Plattner Institute of Design at Stanford). Council members all agree to participate in monthly 90-minute meetings for one year. Some of us have signed up for a second round of twelve meetings. Some of us work on tribal policy engaging with the federal government. We have a combined sixty plus years in 12-step recovery as alcoholics and addicts. We have experienced life-threatening health challenges. We seek to partner with those who embody Indigenous ways. We have persevered through challenges we choose not to name. Some of us are trained in IFS, others are learning about it through championing our efforts on tribal lands. We have come to love one another in a way that is impossible to describe to others. We all are passionate mental health activists in service to the people.

What We Do

We are simultaneously planting multiple seeds across multiple tribes, using multiple approaches. Our work currently spans the north slope of Alaska, Canada, and the US. Through the miracle and blessing of Zoom, we have a global reach via our 8 C Meetings. We don't have a website (yet), or a social media outreach (yet), or many things we know we need. Major funding would help us stretch our bootstrapped efforts. And our parts also recognize that we don't want to sell our souls to anyone. We know that our ancestors, allies, partners, and our Creator can manifest everything that is needed when the time is right for it to appear.

When, Where, How We Started

Our first meeting was in May of 2021. We generated the 7 Bs (words only) for our first presentation at the 2021 IFS Institute Global Conference. We wanted to introduce ourselves to the IFS community by offering a gift to foster connection. In 2022, we worked with an artist to create the circle symbol and add the bulleted definitions to the word headings we derived in 2021. We shared our deepened understanding at the 2022 IFS Institute Global Conference. In 2022, we also did mental health community outreach on a reservation in "high plains heaven" and elsewhere started a 14-week 12-Step workshop infused with Indigenous values and IFS. We developed a 135-page manual and just received a request for 240 copies by a tribe who are training up leaders in their community to carry the work forward. Since April 2021, we have been hosting a weekly 8 C Meeting that has built a solid community of 20 core members who are geographically dispersed, cross-tribal, not all are Indigenous. We have grown only by word-of-mouth. We are modeling our governance and service structure around the example and success of the 12-step recovery community, modifying it by consensus as needed. Starting one or two additional 8 C Meetings in 2023 is currently under discussion.

Why?

If you don't know why we started, we invite you to spend time on the land. Listen to what she has to teach you. Visit a reservation with no agenda. Seek out an Indigenous person in your community, ask your parts to step back, and build Connection slowly, with no agenda other than your own learning. Continue your own IFS healing so you will be ready to be of service to an Indigenous person who may cross your path. They may be a client if you are an IFS practitioner or therapist. They may be a neighbor who lives near you. Go to a college or university near you and visit the Indigenous Student Center (in Canada they are there by law). Learn the difference between ripping off culture to cheapen it vs humbling yourself before earth wisdom ways and letting them heal you. Most of all, know that we love you.

How the 7 Bs of Indigenous-inspired IFS Came to Be

The 7 Bs were developed by the initial members of the Indigenous IFS Council. We wanted to provide the IFS community with a gift keeping in the spirit of the mnemonic devices we learn about in our IFS training:

- 5 Ps (Presence, Patience, Perspective, Persistence, Playfulness).
- 6 Fs (Find, Focus, Flesh it out, How does the client Feel toward Part, BeFriend, Find out Part's Fears).
- 8 Cs (Clarity, Compassion, Creativity, Calmness, Curiosity, Confidence, Courage, Connectedness).

We noticed there was no list of 7 items. We recognize the importance of 7 in the Indigenous cosmology, so we chose 7 to focus our ideas. We asked ourselves, "What elements of an Indigenous world view allow IFS to resonate with Indigenous people who live connected to the earth?" We discussed. We wrote. We prayed. We found 7 Bs that we all felt worthy of highlighting. We humbly know that these 7 Bs are the results of our discussions and consensus. If others had been on the Indigenous IFS Council, it is possible that some elements and wording may be different. Yet our experience already suggests that the 7 Bs are a helpful addition in helping IFS land well with Indigenous people. When we posted the 8 C wheel (radar chart) and the 7 Bs in our meeting room on the reservation, it was the 7 Bs that drew the most initial inquiry. People looked around, pointed at the 7 Bs, asked us who created that, and when we said, "We did," they took a step closer and found a seat on the couch or chairs we had set up. One person said, "If you made this, then you 'get' us."

IFS practitioners and therapists say that the 7 Bs add a sacred element to the healing work they are doing. With that we are content. The 7 Bs also give proper credit to the Indigenous influences that contributed to the development of the IFS model itself, especially the unburdening process.

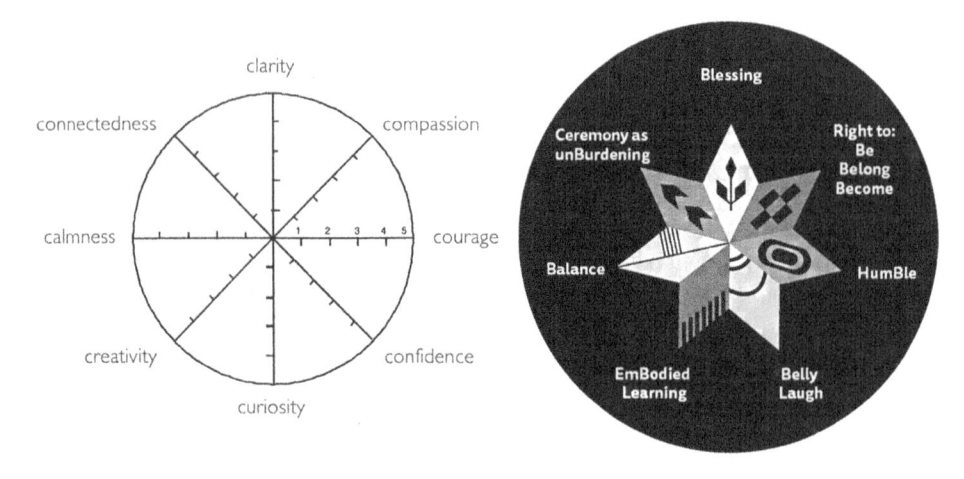

The 7 Bs of Indigenous Inspired IFS

1. **B**lessing
   - To recognize all of life as sacred.
   - To explicitly invite the SELF, the transcendent Creator of all, whose essence is expressed in the human as the Self, into the center of all experiences.
   - To pause and center one's Self as a humble human with parts that are both burdened and magnificent.

2. Right to **B**e, **B**elong, **B**ecome
   - To be accepted exactly for who one is, with no need to be bigger or smaller, better or worse than all your life's experiences have made you to be.
   - To belong to a community who accepts you as you are, hears your voice, sees your natural gifts, and finds ways for you to have purpose and value.
   - To become fully who we are as a Self-led person supported by the empowering, inspiring, challenging, and nurturing community to whom one belongs.

3. Hum**B**le
   - To be "right sized" and teachable, curious about the lessons every part, every person, every experience has to teach us.
   - To be willing to bow down in reverence to SELF as to life, as to a breathtaking manifestation of beauty, a child being born, the moment one falls in love.
   - To be content in or out of the spotlight, as the star of the show, in service to the performers, or in the balcony celebrating others' talents.

4. **B**elly Laugh
   - To laugh heartily in ways that honor the humor life brings and leaves all those who share the moment feeling a greater love and connection with each other.
   - To laugh playfully in a childlike manner embracing outrageous unfettered fun.
   - To laugh from the gut with head thrown back and mouth wide open, bringing a temporary release from all of one's cares and worries.

5. Em**B**odied Learning
   - To learn about one's Self and life in a gradual manner over time from a teacher who knows you well enough to teach at your pace in ways you understand.

- To learn more only when one's walk demonstrates internalization of what has been taught thus far.
- To learn so deeply and practice so much over time that what one knows flows naturally and almost effortlessly from one's being and actions.

6. **B**alance
    - To recognize how a myriad of life's qualities are enhanced when its opposite is attended to, such as inward/outward, positive/negative, rest/work, give/take.
    - To recognize that all parts have a positive intent even when at the surface their behavior appears negative.
    - To recognize the importance of protecting both individuality and community at the same time.

7. Ceremony as Un**B**urdening
    - To recognize the sacredness of the unburdening process by creating markers with ritual and artifacts to symbolize and memorialize what was done.
    - To create sacred space and a protocol that reflects the healing that is being manifested, witnessed by a community who supports.
    - To invite parts to define how they want to invoke earth, air, water, fire, or light as elements that represent the release of burdens that no longer serve us.

Healing and Thriving in Community

The Indigenous IFS Council offers peer-based IFS-inspired programs and services. In one offering, called an "8 C Meeting," participants share their personal IFS story leveraging the format used in many 12-step recovery groups. We share "what it was like" (before IFS), "what happened" (what led to finding IFS), and "what it's like now" (what Self leadership looks and sounds like). We speak for parts from Self and find a unique and priceless community with others doing the same. We use the 8 Cs and 7 Bs as our guides.

We want to honor you for the investment you have made in reading and digesting our words. May your journey of growth and healing with IFS be a blessing to you and others. As you "turn toward" your parts and harvest their wisdom we celebrate the spaciousness you will feel as unburdenings unfold.

KEY TAKEAWAYS

- The Self deep within is whole, intact, healthy, and strong. Even if some of our parts have done the worst of things, the Self remains unaffected.
- Walking in Indigenous ways and healing with IFS is a lived experience that unfolds over time. Both are nurtured in community, supported by building a trusted relationship with another who abides in the teachings in their spirit, mind, words, and actions.
- Learning IFS is a process like seeds planted in one form deep in the earth, who take in nutrients, burst out of their husk, and boldly make the journey to earth, air, water, sky.

AUTHOR BIOS

Julia Sullivan, MBA (she/her) is a social activist who integrates her Latina roots, Indigenous spirituality, and all she gained from being one of the first Latinas to earn an MBA from the Stanford Graduate School of Business. After a 30-year career in executive leadership and organizational development, she now devotes her energy to bringing Self leadership to people using Internal Family Systems (IFS). She co-founded the Indigenous IFS Council to bring an IFS peer-based community model to tribal lands. Currently several pilots are underway as a follow-up to their participation in the Stanford d.school Action Lab 2022. Julia relaxes with frequent walks around a lake with her IFS-trained husband, Chris, basking in the beauty of nature. They often celebrate their twenty plus years of marriage and the fact that their seven grown children from their blended family are all thriving.

Suzan McVicker, PhD, MA, LPC (she/her) works as a Certified IFS Therapist with a passion for sharing IFS in Indian Country. As a Cherokee descendant working with her own parts to unburden from the impacts of colonialism, her experience informs her clinical work. Her knowledge base includes a Native Health program co-taught by the Eastern Band of Cherokee Indians and Western Carolina University, and research with Fielding Graduate University. Currently she weaves education, family knowledge, culture-shifting identity issues, and over 25 years of IFS experience into an exploration of culturally informed work with the Indigenous IFS Council and other Native American circles. She participated in the Stanford University d.school Action Lab to explore peer-to-peer ways to share IFS in Indian country. Suzan loves to swim in outdoor waters, belly laugh with relatives, slowly learn the Cherokee language, and listen to the stories of mountain streams.

Gregg Paisley, MBA (he/him) spent most of his career in the private sector, working as a senior executive in SMB, NASDAQ, and Fortune 500 enterprise software and hardware companies, as well as in professional audio/video/lighting. An enrolled Blackfeet (Amskapi Piikani band), he is one of the few American Indians fortunate enough to have walked that path. Late in life he came to the epiphany that the only possible reason the Creator would shower such undeserved blessings and resources on him is so he could help others find their own blessings. Since retiring from industry in 2003, he has focused on creating jobs, increasing tribal household incomes, and providing social services (especially for underserved tribal children) on a large Montana reservation. Gregg is a member of the Indigenous IFS Council and was on the Stanford d.school team. He is currently piloting a peer-based IFS workshop in Montana.

Pete Patton, LCSW (he/him) is of Inuit descent and was stolen, adopted, and raised in Oregon. Pete earned his Master of Social Work in 1996 from the University of Illinois at Chicago, Jane Addams College of Social Work. Pete interned at the Institute for Juvenile Research, where he attended group supervision with Dick Schwartz. Pete attended the initial Seattle Level 1 and 2 Trainings taught by Dick Schwartz and Michi Rose. For 15 years Pete provided sex offense treatment in the US and Aotearoa/New Zealand. In the last 11 years he has served people suffering from trauma and chronic/persistent pain. Pete lives in Astoria, Oregon on the historical lands of the Clatsop and Chinook Tribes. He works for Clatsop Behavioral Healthcare and is Clinical Lead for the North Coast Pain Clinic. Pete is a member of the Indigenous IFS Council. Pete regularly checks in with his Ancestors and interna-verse of parts.

GOING DEEPER

From the Authors

1) Articles and Written Resources:
   a. McVicker, S. A. (2020). Editorial. *Alcoholism Treatment Quarterly Special Issue on Indian Country.* www.dx.doi.org/10.1080/07347324.2020.1837045
   b. McVicker, S. A., & Pourier, W. "Bim". (2020). Two counselors envision IFS (Internal Family Systems) therapy for addictions treatment in Indian country. *Alcoholism Treatment Quarterly.* www.dx.doi.org/10.1080/07347324.2020.1846479
   c. Sullivan, J. (n.d.). Appendix 19: About Internal Family Systems (IFS). *IAM Inupiaq 12-step IFS Manual.*

2) Podcast:
   a. The One Inside, Episode 116: Be, Belong, Become—How IFS Resonates With the Indigenous Worldview www.tammysollenberger.com/ifs-and-be-belong-become-how-ifs-resonates-with-the-indigenous-worldview-with-suzan-mcvicker-and-julia-sullivan/

3) Video:
   a. Walking Out Ceremony www.communitystories.ca/v2/la-vie-est-une-expedition_life-is-an-expedition/gallery/first-steps-walking-ceremony/

4) IFS "8C" Zoom Meeting:
   a. Email 8Cmeeting@gmail.com for Zoom link

From Other Sources

1) Publications:
   a. Blume, A. W. (2020). *A new psychology based on community, equality, and care of the earth: An Indigenous American perspective.* Praeger.
   b. Morse, G. S., & Lomay, V. T. (2020). *Understanding Indigenous perspectives: Visions, dreams, and hallucinations.* Cognella.

EMBODYING IFS WITH ASIAN AND PACIFIC ISLANDER CLIENTS

CULTURAL, RACIAL, AND INTERGENERATIONAL BURDENS AS WELL AS PROTECTIVE FACTORS

Regina L. Wei, MA, LMFTA

In my experience working with Asian and Pacific Islander (API) clients, and in discussions with numerous IFS colleagues who identify as API or Asian, I find that IFS is a very powerful and effective modality for API clients that leads to deep and profound healing. The IFS model works particularly well within API cultural contexts because of its deeply compassionate, respectful, and Self-led approach that supports healing within the client's cultural context. A Self-led system will always know the culturally appropriate way to connect with, retrieve, and unburden parts. IFS can work its magic with Asian clients as long as practitioners are as Self-led as possible and maintain an attitude of cultural humility and curiosity. Practitioners also need to be aware of and take care of their parts that hold culturally biased preconceptions about how healing "should" take place. Another aspect of IFS that is particularly welcomed by API clients is its non-pathologizing approach that normalizes clients' experiences, particularly of shame, as well as its compassionate approach towards self-soothing behaviors.

My own experience of IFS as both practitioner and client reflects my background as a well-educated, middle-class, second generation Chinese American. My parents, born in China, spent the majority of their childhood and young adulthood in Taiwan before they immigrated to the U.S. in the 1960s. Although I have lived in various Asian countries for a number of years, I am writing primarily from a North American point of view and for a North American audience. I do believe, however, that most of these observations and recommendations are relevant to practitioners and clients outside of North America, and non-American readers can take what follows as a starting point for thinking about how Asian clients can benefit from IFS.

Keep in mind that "Asian" is a political and geographical designation that covers a great deal of heterogeneity. This is due to differences in nationality/country of origin, immigration and/or refugee status, and socioeconomic class and educational level, not to mention age/generation, gender, sexual orientation, (dis)ability, neurodiversity, and more. The term covers people from East Asian, South Asian, Southeast Asian, as well as Pacific Island countries. In fact, there is so much diversity amongst API identities that the categorization is virtually meaningless as a cultural identifier, and any generalizations made about API clients need to be checked against a client's own subjectivity. For example, a young, Southeast Asian, first-generation college-educated client who immigrated to the West before or during their teens (i.e. 1.5 generation) whose family has fled war and violence has a vastly different cultural background and set of experiences from a client who shares a background more similar to my own.

While many API cultures have been affected by the same or similar religious and/or philosophical influences (e.g., Buddhism, Confucianism, Islam, etc.) and while many API countries have experienced significant cultural exchange and flow of people across political borders within Asia, Asians who migrate to the West do so for a variety of reasons, and oftentimes, as a result of political and social upheaval or natural disasters. This means that many API clients carry a significant amount of historical and intergenerational trauma even when they are a generation or more removed from the events themselves.

That said, recurring themes underlie many API clients' search for healing, and what follows are my observations about how these themes play out in clients' lives as well as my recommendations for how IFS practitioners can work more effectively with API clients. As the introduction to the intersectionality section notes, the themes I identify may well resonate with people who come from global majority cultures, but there are specifically API expressions of more global themes. For example, racism as a system of oppression is an integral part of Western society, but racial trauma manifests differently in people depending on their identity. Black American clients and Asian American clients are both subjected to racism on a daily basis, but society does not treat Black folks the same way they treat Asian folks, although both are racialized and othered. I talk more about how racism affects Asian clients below.

Observations and Recommendations

API Identity

The first recommendation for IFS practitioners who work with API clients is that we need to be cognizant of *how our clients identify* as API as well as *what their experiences are like* as API individuals. As mentioned above, a client's ethnicity, their family's country(ies) of origin, how many generations they have lived in the West, immigration or refugee status, socioeconomic class, and educational level all bear on how a client experiences life in their racialized identity in Western society. Generally speaking, the longer a client's family has lived in the West, the more likely they will have assimilated to Western society and norms though the degree to which each family retains the language(s) and traditions of their culture can vary widely.

It is helpful to keep in mind the following data on API origins:

- 71 percent of Asian American adults were born in another country (aka first or 1.5 generation); and,
- the three largest groups by country of origin are Chinese (24 percent), Indian (21 percent), and Filipino (19 percent).[1]

The circumstances around a client's or their family's immigration experience can range from those who enjoyed status and wealth in their home countries to those who arrive in their host country with nothing. Regardless of circumstance, most clients will have significant cultural heritages they draw from that are just as, or more, compelling for them than Western cultural norms. The richness of API clients' cultural identities can be both tremendously positive and—
if their API values are in direct conflict with dominant Western values—a source of tension. How does this tension play out for API clients? Often, they are negotiating and balancing such opposing forces as collectivism vs. individualism; filial piety vs. independence from, and boundary setting with, family members; and interdependence vs. individuation and differentiation.

Finally, in considering how clients experience their API identity, I want to highlight two groups for whom an API identity is more nuanced: multiracial clients and adoptees. Much like clients who are further removed from the generation that immigrated to the West (e.g. third or fourth generation clients), multiracial clients with one API parent and one White parent (or one or two API grandparents) will have both API and White cultural influences as a part of their background, but there may be more tension between these aspects of themselves as they struggle to find a place of belonging. In predominantly White spaces they may feel "not White enough" while in predominantly API spaces they may feel "not Asian enough." Multiracial folks may feel like perpetual outsiders, amplifying the pain of not belonging that many API clients feel. Furthermore, bi-racial Asian-White couples in the West, in navigating the significant cultural differences between them, will cultivate the Asian side of their children's identity to varying degrees, but often the familial culture skews towards the dominant White culture in terms of which language is spoken at home as well as which values are emphasized.[2]

At the time of this writing, more than half of all international adoptees were from Asia, primarily from China and South Korea, and most adoptees were raised by White parents.[3, 4] Similar to multiracial Asian-White clients, adoptees with White adoptive parents may experience a disconnect between how they see themselves and their home culture and how they are treated by a society that racializes them.[5]

Not only might adoptees have parts that seek belonging in spaces that challenge the "authenticity" of their identity, but they may have parts that feel **lost, unsafe, alone** and/or have parts that hold **grief, disconnection, rejection, resentment, anger,** and **confusion** due to their adoption into a non-Asian family whose values and traditions are vastly different from that of their biological family, known or (very likely) unknown. (Throughout the chapter, I will highlight the burdens and jobs that are commonly carried by API clients' parts using **bold** font.) As one colleague observes, adoptees experienced forced assimilation where the loss of connection to their Asian roots was out of their control, giving rise to parts who may feel **helpless** or **powerless**. Meanwhile, many/most adoptees do identify with their adopted family's culture though it does not match their physical features or how they are perceived by others. The dissonance caused by how they feel and see themselves and how others treat them may result in parts that carry burdens of **race dysphoria** or **body dysphoria**. Furthermore, even the most well-intentioned and conscientious White adoptive parents, due to a different lived racial experience, will never fully understand or "get" what it is like for the adoptee to move through the world as someone with Asian features.[6] As a result, adoptees may have parts that **do not feel understood** and/or **do not feel they fully belong anywhere**. For adoptees, IFS exploration and healing can be particularly meaningful as clients connect to parts of themselves that may hold knowledge or wisdom they would not otherwise have access to. For those who are open to such work, IFS can also help connect adoptees with their ancestors through legacy unburdening and even synergistic ancestral healing work, which can be a deeply moving and healing experience.[7]

API Collectivism

The collectivistic nature of API cultures is one of the most important things for IFS practitioners to recognize and acknowledge. While, of course, the degree to which this is relevant depends on a client's age, generation, and immigration experience, I cannot emphasize enough the importance and place that family and community have in the lives of API folks. In conversation after conversation I have had with clients and with colleagues who work with API clients, the theme of allegiance to one's family—to one's parents specifically—as well as a prioritization of familial needs over personal needs came up again and again. This theme is relevant even in the case of non-first generation clients who experience a considerable amount of tension between parts that have internalized the belief that they need to **uphold filial piety** and Western culture-influenced parts that strive for **differentiation** and **individuation** from their families.

In traditional API cultures, children of any age are expected to be respectful towards their parents and elders which means submitting to, serving, and/or taking care of their parents in their old age. When disagreements arise, children are forbidden to talk back or argue with their parents and are expected at the very least to go through the motions of complying. Otherwise, they face censure or even ostracization. In Asian cultures, as with collectivistic cultures in general, one's family or clan provides love, validation, an extended network of connections, resources and support, and it can be incredibly painful to be cast out of the familial fold. Clients who go against their parents often do so at a great internal cost even when they feel it is the right path for them. While many clients willingly obey and serve their parents, other clients might have parts that hold legacy burdens around a sense of **responsibility to their family, guilt, resentment,** and **shame.**

A traditional respect for elders and those in positions of authority may also influence how Asian clients relate to their IFS practitioner. Clients may appear more reticent when talking about themselves or their families, and they may be reluctant to say or do anything that can be perceived as challenging the "authority" of the practitioner. In addition, sometimes clients' communication styles reflect their cultural values of upholding group harmony (although, as with all the observations presented here, the degree to which this is true for any particular client varies greatly). From a Western perspective, clients can appear indirect, less assertive, or self-effacing in sessions. From the Asian perspective, however, respectful silence, subtlety of expression, and non-confrontation are simply considered polite. As one Japanese American colleague observed, in Japanese culture there are oftentimes managers whose jobs are to **pay attention to everybody else** and to **adjust one's own behavior** accordingly. Another way in which this may come into play in sessions is that, as one Chinese American colleague observed, some Asian clients may have **goal-oriented** managers who approach the healing work with an expectation of being directed or told what to do which is, of course, antithetical to how IFS works.

Another important aspect of collectivistic API cultures is the assumption that individuals are extensions of the family and thus are expected to maintain the family's honor or "face." This applies to the line of work or profession they choose, racking up accomplishments that add to the family's prestige or boost the family's status, and not behaving in ways that would sully the family name or make the family lose face. Before discussing how family honor may affect clients' career and professional choices, it is important to note that the Model Minority Myth—the idea that Asians are the most successful minority group in America due to their excellent work ethic and family-centered values—is a narrative of anti-Blackness that was created in the 1960s to pit Asian Americans against other racial groups.[8] While it is true that Asian Americans have the highest median income of all racial groups, it is also true that the greatest income disparity of any racial group is between Asian Americans.[9] This is due to discriminatory immigration laws in the U.S. that historically gave preferential treatment to East Asians who were generally well-educated and/or highly skilled. Since the 2010s, well-educated Indian Americans have become the highest earning Asian American group, and while there is truth to the idea that many Asian Americans are highly successful, it is important to keep in mind that those of Hmong, Burmese, Cambodian, and Laos descent do not enjoy the same level of success and prosperity as other groups.[10] That said, given that almost three quarters of Asian Americans are foreign-born (aka first generation), a desire to succeed materially and professionally in a new country does translate into clients who are highly education and achievement oriented, whether they are doing so to uphold their family's honor, due to parental pressures, or whether they believe in the "American dream" of socioeconomic upward mobility. Sometimes these clients have **goal-oriented** and **achievement-oriented** parts that feel a certain amount of impatience with what can oftentimes be a less-than-linear IFS healing journey.

An example of how these cultural values come into play during sessions involves a therapeutic approach that is quite common in Western psychotherapy: helping clients set healthy boundaries. If a client has strong manager parts who make sure the client is acting respectfully in their role as a child, a suggestion that they set boundaries with their parents or other authority figures may be in direct conflict with what a client feels is right and may result in resistance and/or a strong polarization of managers within the client's system. As I have personally experienced, this kind of tension may come up during the re-do and retrieval process if a non-Asian IFS practitioner, given their own Western socialization, suggests to the client that the Self, as the exile's protector, can set a boundary between an exile and whoever is causing it pain. If the one causing pain is a parent, an elder, or an authority figure, the client may have parts that do not feel comfortable asking them to stand down or stop whatever they are doing because it is considered deeply disrespectful to talk back to or contradict one's elders. In such cases, an approach that is more in alignment with a Self-led experience is for the IFS practitioner to encourage the client's Self to ask the exile what it wants or needs to happen. More often than not what has felt right to my system in the case of familial wounds is that my parts want collective and generational healing: they ask Self to take care of family members so that they are also healed, often with the help of my ancestors.

Case Study

To illustrate how the theme of allegiance to one's parents and family might come up in sessions, I present Amy, a hypothetical composite client drawn from my experiences with API clients.

Amy identifies as second generation Burmese American, straight, cisgender, and non-disabled. Amy is in her mid-30s and works as a doctor at a prestigious medical clinic in a large metropolitan area. She is seeking support for anxiety, depression and burnout; she has never enjoyed her work in the medical field and is considering changing her career to something that allows her to express her passion for creating music. Amy tells me that the thing that worries her the most is telling her parents about her decision as they will surely disapprove; she only studied medicine on her father's insistence. In our sessions, we get to know Amy's parts that hold a great deal of **anticipatory guilt** for letting her family down. There are also **self-critical** parts who berate her for being "selfish" and "ungrateful" given everything her parents have done and sacrificed to enable her to become a doctor. When we explore Amy's system further, we find that the guilt is shielding a part that holds a **fear of rejection** if she deviates from the family script or does something that is not seen as honorable in her parents' eyes. Similarly, we also find that the self-critical part's job is to keep her in line so she won't experience the **pain of being ostracized**, a part that is linked not just to her security but her ability to survive. We discover another part that holds a **legacy burden** in the form of a belief that when a conflict of interests arises, the **family's needs take priority** even if it means that Amy's own wishes or desires are subsumed. The polarization we identify in Amy's system is between parts that feel loyal and indebted to her family and parts that want Amy to explore a career in music. The **anxiety, depression** and **burnout** Amy expressed at the beginning of our sessions are all parts that are trying to manage or have been burdened by the strong polarization between the two camps.

Power Dynamics in API Cultures

While certain power dynamics in API society are not unique to Asian cultures, it is important for IFS practitioners and clients to be mindful of how patriarchy, sexism, and ageism within API contexts affect clients depending on where they fall within the hierarchy. For example, in modern China, Taiwan, Korea, Japan, Vietnam, and Singapore, as well as in other Han Chinese-influenced cultures, the effects of Confucian ideals are still readily identifiable in the ways relationships are structured. In traditional Confucian thought, five relationships govern all human interactions: ruler to subject, father to son, husband to wife, older brother to younger brother, and friend to friend. All but the last describe relationships of unequal power with the first person in the relationship commanding respect or obedience from the second. The gendered nature of the relationships—or the fact that women and nonbinary individuals do not hold any positions of power—reflects China's long history of thousands of years of oppressive treatment of people who are not male.

It is important to note here that most Asian cultures have long and significant traditions of acceptance of transgender individuals. However, as Asian societies currently and historically are heteronormative and social prescriptions are based on a male-female gender binary, I present observations in binary terms to reflect how individuals are viewed or treated in Asian society but am aware of how limiting and oppressive the binary is particularly for nonbinary individuals.

Respect for Parents, Elders, Men, and Authority

While East Asian countries have largely transitioned away from using overt Confucian language, the hierarchies still inform social and familial relationships. There is an enduring respect for elders and for those in positions of authority while men hold the bulk of power in almost all relationships. This is illustrated by how, for example, in Chinese culture older people and people in positions of authority are always addressed by their title and not their first name (which would be considered extremely rude). How one addresses family members depends on their age and relationship to one's parents (e.g., paternal or maternal, younger or older). So, there are four different terms each for "aunt," "uncle," and "cousin," and paternal and maternal grandparents all have different titles. These hierarchical dynamics are true even in countries not directly influenced by Confucianism and are particularly noticeable in the way many API women still struggle for equitable treatment and voice both inside and outside the home regardless of their educational and professional accomplishments. Traditionally, older women and women with children (boys, specifically), have more power than younger and unmarried women.

Preference for boys over girls can be found in the two Asian countries with the largest population. In China, there is a stark gender imbalance where 36 years of the One Child Policy has resulted in one of the most disparate sex ratios in the world: there are 114 boys to 100 girls, and there are now 34.9 million more men than women in China.[11] In India, traditional practices of female infanticide and sex-selective abortions resulted in a skewed sex ratio until only recently.[12] Girls and women lag behind men in areas of literacy, educational attainment, and financial independence. As one colleague of Indian descent put it, boys are treated like kings in India and can do no wrong in the family's eyes, while girls are expected to acquiesce to the wishes of their male family members. Even while contemporary views towards and treatment of women and transfolk are improving in Asia and in the West, I would argue that the effects of thousands of years of gender socialization run deeply in clients' psyches and are still apparent in the burdens that many Asian clients carry.

Effects of Asian Parenting

Another significant power dynamic that is relevant to IFS work with Asian clients concerns the parent-child relationship and how children are generally parented in Asian families. As mentioned above, children are expected to respect and obey their parents. This message is ingrained into children from the crib on, where shame and force are often used to ensure compliance. Children learn early on that it is simply not an option to not obey their parents or elders because if they choose to do so they will certainly face severe consequences. For example, corporal punishment is still commonly used at home and in schools in Asia. At the time of this writing, only Mongolia, Nepal, Japan, and most recently Korea have banned corporal punishment of children, with these changes taking place only within the last few years.[13] A colleague based in Singapore noted that corporal punishment is such an accepted form of discipline that colorful rattan canes used on children are widely sold in markets there.

Even if parents do not use physical discipline, shaming and public humiliation can be powerful motivators to get children to behave or achieve.[14] It is not uncommon for Asian parents to compare their children's achievements unfavorably to other children's achievements as a means of spurring them on towards greater accomplishments. For example, in countries like China and Taiwan, students' exam scores are routinely posted publicly for all to see. Although there has been some pushback from students and parents in recent years, the idea persists that students will be motivated to do better when they see how they rank compared to their peers. Clients who experience typical Asian parenting may have parts that carry burdens of **fear, shame,** and **worthlessness,** as well as harshly **self-critical** parts who try to keep clients in line so they can avoid being shamed or punished.

Finally, Asian parents typically engage in "tough love" and are reluctant to praise children, show them too much affection, or tell them that they love them for fear of spoiling them. Even in families that do not use shame or punishment to enforce the age-old expectation that children obey their parents, this stoic approach can result in burdens of **unlovability, unworthiness, rejection, abandonment,** or beliefs about **not being enough** in clients' systems. Also, as emotional restraint is regarded as a positive quality, children beyond their earliest grade school years are usually taught to not call attention to themselves or disturb others around them through flamboyant emotional displays. As a result, Asian clients may have strong managers that suppress exiles who hold heavy emotional burdens.

Case Study: Linh and Stephen

Linh and Stephen are a straight, cisgender, non-disabled, married couple in their late-thirties, and as with Amy, whom we met earlier, these profiles are hypothetical composites drawn from my practice. Linh identifies as second generation Vietnamese American. Stephen identifies as first generation Taiwanese American as he came to the U.S. in his teens. Together, they have a boy, age six, and a girl, age three. Linh and Stephen are both the first in their family to not only graduate from college but to obtain advanced degrees. When they had children, they decided that since Stephen's job in the tech industry earns enough to support the family, Linh would leave her very successful career in law to stay home with their children. In recent years, however, Linh has started to regret giving up so much of her own life for her family. She wants to go back to work both for the satisfaction of doing something for herself and also for the financial freedom it would give her. But Stephen is urging her to wait until their daughter is old enough to attend kindergarten.

Stephen says that he works very hard to support the family and feels that his efforts are unappreciated when Linh expresses resentment about the amount of time he spends at work or working even when he is home. The couple provides financial support to both Linh and Stephen's parents, but Stephen's widowed mother lives close to them and has significant health issues that require a great deal of his time and attention which, as the eldest son, he feels obligated to provide. Linh does what she can to help Stephen's mom but shares that Stephen's mom has never felt that Linh was good enough for her eldest son and treats her in a dismissive manner. Linh has parts that hold resentment towards Stephen's mother but is afraid to speak up for fear of upsetting Stephen.

In therapy, Linh works with a part that holds **resentment** that is a protector for parts that are **scared to speak up** for herself and her needs because they are afraid of being dismissed, at best, and criticized at worst. The protector also shields parts that hold **deep sadness** that she does a lot of caretaking of everyone around her, but no one cares about, or takes care of, her. The sadness is connected to other parts that feel **lonely** and **abandoned** by Stephen. These parts developed burdens in her childhood when her parents were too busy working to give Linh or her siblings much attention. As we continue to explore Linh's conflicted feelings around returning to work, Linh is surprised to discover that she has a part that feels a **need for Stephen's permission** to pursue her own career. When explored, it turns out that the part carries a **legacy burden** involving a belief that **women should defer to the men** in their family; Linh's own father very much expected that his wife and children obey him without question. Linh also carries **legacy burdens** of wartime trauma that she received from both of her parents who were refugees. These burdens manifest in parts that hold a great deal of **fear** and **anxiety** particularly around financial and material security.

When we explore Stephen's system, we find that he has parts that hold deep feelings of **shame** and **unworthiness**. These parts are related to harshly **self-critical** parts that tell him he is not enough as a husband, son, or provider for his family. Stephen's parts are constantly comparing him to friends and acquaintances who all appear to be hitting material and financial milestones that he and Linh can only dream of. As a result, Stephen has a **workaholic** part that keeps him very busy and always striving to do more or better but that also leaves him without time or energy to be truly present with Linh and the children. This workaholic part also serves to distract from another part that holds **depressive feelings**; Stephen has struggled with depression all his life but always felt too ashamed to seek help. Stephen also has parts that are **polarized** between a deep loyalty to his mother who raised him and his siblings after his father died when he was young and parts that want to be a better and more available husband to Linh; these are connected to parts that feel **guilty** for not doing enough for either his mother or his wife. Stephen also has parts that hold unprocessed **grief** from his father's death as well as feelings of **inadequacy** from his adolescence when he was the only one in his peer group who did not have a father and money was always an issue for them. Like Linh, Stephen has parts that feel **deep anxiety** around financial and material security which feeds the workaholic part.

As the case studies of Amy, Linh, and Stephen illustrate, the above observations about power dynamics within Asian societies provide a general cultural context for practitioners and clients to keep in mind as they engage in IFS healing work. As mentioned, it is important to ascertain the degree to which family values have been influenced by Western values while, of course, taking into consideration a client's own values. However, even clients who are distanced from their Asian roots by two or more generations may carry legacy burdens associated with gender, power, familial loyalty, and the need to achieve at a high level in order to bring honor and not shame to the family.

Asian Clients Living in Racialized Bodies

A sharp increase in hate crimes and violence against Asian Americans in the U.S., particularly since the start of the COVID pandemic, has highlighted the racialized experiences that Asian Americans have endured in the U.S. since the 19th century when they first started immigrating to the U.S.

A Legacy of Injustice and Violence

The Chinese Exclusion Act of 1882, fueled by White xenophobia and racism, is the only U.S. law that targets a specific nationality.[15] Throughout the West, one does not have to dig very deeply into local history and into tax, property and marriage laws in the American West to uncover the numerous examples of anti-Asian sentiment and violence where White folks made it very difficult for Chinese and other Asians to thrive. Vigilantes and Klansmen in California,[16] with support from local governments, targeted Chinese Americans without compunction or consequences, and one of the most horrific lynchings in U.S. history happened to Chinese people in Los Angeles in 1871.[17] Up and down the coast, Chinese immigrants were run out of town, their homes, businesses, schools and places of worship burned, and their livelihoods destroyed.[18] A brutal massacre of at least two dozen Chinese people in Wyoming in 1885 is little known outside of Asian American circles.[19]

While all this may seem like distant history, anti-Asian violence literally hits close to home for me. I grew up in Bellevue, a very prosperous suburb of Seattle, whose population is now 39.3 percent foreign-born and 37.5 percent Asian American[20] largely due to the significant rise in the tech and other industries that have brought in highly skilled and highly educated immigrants from India and other Asian countries.[21] In the late nineteenth century, however, where I grew up had been a sleepy town whose coal mining companies employed Chinese workers. What I did not know, growing up in the 1980s and 90s in the area when the population was overwhelmingly White, was that in 1885 White coal miners terrorized and burned down the residences of Chinese workers who were then forced to live in the forest. The creek they settled along is still known as China Creek, with the waterway's name the only indication that they were ever there.[22]

From violence against Chinese workers in the nineteenth and twentieth centuries to the mass-scale, unconstitutional internment of Japanese Americans during World War II, the U.S. has a long and dishonorable history of anti-Asian violence and injustice.[23] [24]It is hardly surprising, then, that anti-Asian sentiment and anti-Asian hate crimes continue to this day as we can trace a through-line of xenophobia and racism from past to present. Regardless of whether our Asian clients have lived in the country for multiple generations or whether they immigrated within the last couple of decades, Asians in the West live in racialized bodies, a fact that has enormous implications for the healing they seek. Several facets of the racialized experience are specific to Asians: invisibility; being the targets of violence and hate crimes; the demoralizing accumulation of experiences of microaggressions (aka subtle acts of exclusion); dehumanization in the form of being exoticized (for Asians perceived as female) or emasculated (for Asians perceived as male);[25] trauma from Western colonialism in one's home country; and, injuries incurred when people subsume or even reject their Asian identities in order to assimilate into the dominant White culture particularly in areas where there are not significant Asian populations.

Asian Invisibility

Arguably one of the more painful and insidious aspects of the API experience is the feeling, common among Asians, of invisibility. Many factors contribute to feeling invisible, unseen, silenced, and voiceless. On one hand, the age-old respect for authority inhibits many from challenging those in power, while on the other hand people socialized in a collectivistic culture are often reluctant to call attention to themselves or to do anything that would make them stand out from the rest of the group. As L.A.-based psychotherapist Sharon Kwon observes, "our world minimizes us and we minimize ourselves."[26]

Those closer to the immigration experience may not feel that they have a right to speak up as they are just trying to make it in a new country regardless of how long they have been here. Not long ago my father asked me, quizzically, why would I draw attention to myself and look for trouble by speaking up against racial injustice? Maybe it would be better if I put my head down, did my job well, and avoided making waves. "But my job *is* to challenge racism and anti-Blackness in the institution that hired me," I responded. It occurred to me that as someone born, raised and educated in the U.S., I had a certain amount of privilege that my father did not have, as successful as his immigration experience was. Also, while my Chinese heritage is a very important part of my identity, I cannot claim China, Taiwan, or any other country as a homeland, so the need to fight for justice and belonging *here* is something I feel acutely. A certain sense of responsibility toward and the need to truly belong in society is not something that someone like my father feels to the same degree. As an immigrant who came to the States with considerable cultural capital, my father expected to be treated differently—worse, frankly—than White peers and colleagues, so it was neither shocking nor terribly upsetting for him when he experienced racism over the 55 years he has lived in this country. While proud of his American citizenship, my father has a culturally rich non-American identity to fall back on and is a well-respected and active member of the local Chinese community.

Feelings of invisibility are reinforced by the continued perpetuation of the Model Minority Myth that leads so many non-Asian folks to stereotype, pigeonhole, and dismiss Asians as passive, submissive, obedient, and hardworking but lacking the skills for upper leadership. Workplace discrimination, where Asians are rarely promoted beyond middle management, is a well-documented fact.[27] Furthermore, not only do many Asian Americans not feel seen personally and professionally, but they are oftentimes left out in discussions of race that are routinely couched in binary Black/White terms. The many parts that clients may have around feeling invisible may include parts that hold **anger, resentment, guilt** (for taking up space, for being pitted against other races, for proximity to Whiteness), **shame** (for not being a good enough "model minority" or for not suffering "enough" racially), **worthlessness** (not worth being seen or heard), **pressure to conform** to Model Minority Myth stereotypes, and **defiance.**

Overt Acts of Aggression and Subtle Acts of Exclusion (SAE)

The most visible aspect of racialization and probably the most well-known due to increased media attention in recent years are overt instances of anti-Asian violence, from dirty looks, to being spit at, to assaults, to being told to "go back to where you came from." Similar to invisibility, overt violence and discrimination reinforce for many Asians a sense of not belonging, always being the foreigner or outsider, of not being "American enough" but with the added fear of being harmed physically.[28]

More common, and therefore more damaging, than overt acts of violence or hatred, however, are microaggressions or subtle acts of exclusion (SAE)[29] that Asians endure on a regular basis where the repeated, cumulative impact is actually more psychologically stressful. This is because SAE often come from well-intentioned folks who identify as progressive, open-minded, or even allies. How is one to tell a friend or colleague that their comment or joke grates against an old wound?

An example of the toll that microaggressions can have on Asian clients is a recent experience I had in a consultation group led by a very experienced, liberal-identifying White clinician. The topic of racial sensitivity came up when another participant, who was White, asked how they could support White colleagues in working with parts that have formed as a result of racism: parts that hold biases, fear of the other, guilt, shame, defensiveness, anger, etc. When the facilitator responded from a position of authority on racism without inviting BIPOC members' perspectives, I had parts that reacted immediately with a visceral fear to what felt to them like a deeply unsafe situation. I have had numerous experiences throughout my life with White folks in positions of authority who assumed they understood my experience as a racialized person and who did not, because of discomfort or ignorance, ask me about my experience or invite me into conversation. These experiences have galvanized my parts' beliefs that I am **unseen** and **not valued** as an "other" in society.

In this particular situation, it would be helpful to go back forty odd years to see why I have parts that are deeply sensitive to racism and microaggressions. As I have discovered through my own IFS healing journey, my earliest memories of race started when I was three and observed how White folks treated my mother in public. My mother immigrated to the country as an adult, and her English has always been heavily accented. Though my mother was assertive—even forceful—at home, she had parts that were **extremely accommodating, polite,** and **self-deprecating** when she interacted with White people. She also had parts that put on an act of being **charming, "cute,"** and a **little dumb** when she did not immediately understand what people said, which was very confusing to me.

What I saw, as a three-year-old, was that oftentimes White people treated my mother patronizingly, with distaste, or sometimes condescendingly as a curiosity, and I sensed my mother's fear of them. As a child who was in awe of my mother, who seemed all-powerful in my eyes, I had parts that adopted a **visceral fear** of White folks because if she was afraid of them, I should be too. I also had parts that felt fiercely **protective** of her because as I grew older my English was better than hers, and I felt better equipped to navigate American society as someone born and raised here. My own experiences with White folks throughout my childhood only served to reinforce my parts' immediate and deep **mistrust** of White people no matter how nice they seemed or regardless of whether they were actually hostile to me or not. I had only a handful of BIPOC (mostly other Asian American) classmates and no teachers of color until my Mandarin Chinese teacher in high school, and I was constantly stereotyped and treated as an "other" by teachers and peers.

Microaggressions may be completely unintentional and appear minor on the surface, but for Asians and other BIPOC, they evoke years of having lived in a racialized body. In addition to exiles that hold the **deep pain of not belonging** as well as parts that **yearn for validation,** I have many protectors that jump into action whenever a microaggression happens: **people-pleasing, placating, don't-rock-the-boat** parts; a part that is **afraid of upsetting/offending** and a part that **caretakes** White people polarized with a part that **resists** falling into the caretaking role; parts that **want to be seen and heard** polarized with parts that **minimize the hurt** or **do not feel that it is safe** to be vulnerable; an **analytical and rational** part that tries to make sense of what is happening and why; an **activist-educator** part that hopes to help prevent future harm towards BIPOC folks (one that is very active as I write this chapter), as well as parts that hold deep **anger, resentment,** and **sadness.**

For many years, the racialized parts that were most active in me as I moved in predominantly White circles (which was pretty much all the time until I lived in Asia) were parts that helped me survive through **assimilation.** Though I have parts that are **self-critical** and hold some **shame** about that now, other parts adopted the dominant culture's narrative about White superiority and **internalized White supremacy culture.** According to these parts' logic, as long as I could act White enough, I would avoid making White people uncomfortable which would lead to feeling more accepted. This strategy worked for the most part even though it meant downplaying my heritage or even, at moments, **denying my Asianness.** My parts learned, as many BIPOC people's parts do, to **code switch** in conjunction with **hypervigilant** parts who have learned how to immediately ascertain if a person, space, or situation feels safe. I even have a part that makes me suddenly **very sleepy and tired** when I enter predominantly White spaces as well as a *very calm*, **rational, Self-aligned** part that numbs any feelings or emotional reactions in fraught situations.

Asian Clients and Trauma

In addition to racial trauma, Asian clients may come to IFS exploration with traumas that are directly connected to their cultural identity. Most Asian countries have suffered great historical trauma as a result of hundreds of years of Western colonialism in Asia, as well as regional and civil wars, natural and human-created crises and disasters, and Asian—specifically Han Chinese and Japanese—imperialism.

Intergenerational trauma may be behind a range of **legacy burdens** which may include **fears of scarcity,** unresolved **terror** that manifests as constant **anxiety** and **hypervigilance,** a deep **need for control,** seemingly irrational **survival-related** fears around money or food, and deep **grief, sadness,** and **depression** that a client cannot otherwise find an explanation for. Although beyond the scope of this chapter, it is also worth noting that colorism and classism in Asian societies are very relevant to many clients' experiences and can be the source of intergenerational trauma and legacy burdens.

Trauma Around Sexuality

Given the heavily patriarchal and paternalistic nature of most Asian cultures, clients of all genders likely have parts that hold **gender-related trauma** and/or **sexual trauma.** Asian folks socialized as women are expected to take care of everyone else at their own expense, keep the peace and foster group harmony, maintain the family's honor and uphold tradition, and be the primary caregiver for children and aging parents; all this while pursuing their own careers and not falling apart under stress. According to several IFS practitioners I spoke with, this pattern is common even among American-born Asian women. As a result, many women have well-developed manager parts that always **put others'** (e.g. parents, partner, children, friends) **needs first** as well as parts that **feel undeserving** and **stop them from speaking up** for their own needs. It is also very common for women to have parts that are harshly **self-critical** for not doing enough while other parts **self-blame** for not prioritizing themselves or their needs and not keeping promises to themselves. Socialized to always prioritize and acquiesce to male demands, sexual or otherwise, many (straight) Asian women struggle with prioritizing their sexual needs or their right to say no to unwanted sexual advances and encounters inside and outside of committed relationships. Asian women living in Western society must also deal with being objectified and fetishized—or being seen as prudish, frigid, or non-feeling—by members of the dominant culture and by those who have internalized narratives that sexualize Asian women.[30][31]

While one can easily imagine the burdens of **shame, anger, resentment, being silenced or without voice, sadness/grief, fear of abuse/harm,** and **fear of rejection** carried by women and nonbinary individuals in Asian societies, people socialized as male also carry cultural burdens even though they hold the most power as a group. But the power comes at a cost. The male socialization process can be harsh and unforgiving, and enormous pressure is placed on men to conform to narrow gender and familial roles. Men may experience stricter/harsher parenting, peer pressure, and bullying throughout their childhoods to conform to masculine ideals, and they are expected as adults to uphold the family honor through marriage, conduct, and choice of profession. As is the case in most patriarchal contexts, (perceived) weakness or vulnerability are not tolerated in men, and many Asian men carry enormous burdens of **shame, exiled emotions especially around vulnerability,** and **feelings of unworthiness.**

As a result, Asian males may have harshly self-critical managers that **berate** them and make them feel as if they are "never enough," managers that **block access to all emotions and emotional expression,** and firefighters that use **alcohol, pornography, sexual conquests, workaholism, anger/rage, rampant consumerism,** and **disordered eating** to distract them from the trauma of male socialization. Men may have parts that have taken on **burdens of chauvinism** and/or have parts that feel **entitled** to attention and expect to be indulged, catered to, or served while other Asian males have parts that hold **guilt** about their privilege. Finally, Asian males living in Western societies oftentimes feel emasculated by the dominant culture which engenders parts that hold **shame** around their sexual identity as well as feelings of **worthlessness** or even **impotence.**[32]

LGBTQIA+ Asian individuals face multiple layers of oppression due to their intersectional identities. Not only do they carry the same exiles and have the same parts as individuals socialized as female or male, but they have the added stigma and burdens of not conforming to gender-binary and/or heteronormative norms in a collectivistic culture. LGBTQIA+ folks may be pressured by their parents or families to marry someone who is perceived to be the "opposite" gender as well as urged to have children to carry on the family name. At the time of this writing, while a handful of Asian countries allow for same-sex partnerships,[33] the only country to recognize gay marriage is Taiwan, and that, coming in 2019, has been a very recent development.[34] Given the cultural hostility towards non-gender conforming and queer folks in most Asian contexts, LGBTQIA+ individuals likely have parts that carry burdens of **rejection, shame, worthlessness, grief, anger,** and much more. Protector parts may hold **anxiety** and **depression, drive** the system to achieve at high levels, be highly **self-critical** or **self-denigrating,** or engage in **disordered eating.** Common distracting/soothing parts (e.g., firefighters) may include parts that engage in **addictive** behaviors, **dissociation, self-harm, suicidality,** etc. However, it is important to note that Asian LGBTQIA+ clients may also have parts that are enormously **resilient, think creatively outside the box,** and provide the impetus behind **activism.**

Trauma from Western Colonialism

Few Asian countries were spared the effects of Western colonialism and imperialism, and many clients hold intergenerational trauma from the humiliation, losses, and suffering caused by Western subjugation of Asian countries politically, economically, and culturally. Not only were countries torn apart by Western-backed warfare and rapacious exploitation of local resources, including sexual exploitation of women by Western troops,[35] but colonialism in the form of religious, primarily Christian, proselytization actively denigrated and disrupted traditional religions, customs and practices.[36] Clients may have personal or legacy burdens from **wartime trauma** and **refugee trauma,** parts that hold burdens of **shame** from being less "developed" or "weak," **beliefs** that their culture is inferior to Western culture, parts that **idealize Western culture** (similar to parts that seek to assimilate), and fiercely **progress and achievement oriented** parts that are related to parts that **never feel good enough.**

Protective Factors Within Asian Cultures

I have focused on the many burdens and protective parts that Asian clients might discover on an IFS journey, but it is also important to talk about how our clients' cultural heritage can be a source of strength and resilience.

Collectivism

As several colleagues pointed out, collectivism is a double-edged sword that prioritizes a group's well-being over individual interests, *and* it also provides people with a sense of community, a place of belonging, connection, love, and purpose. When people live in extended family structures, there is always someone there—a kind aunt or uncle who looks out for you or cousins to talk to—and those of us who work with trauma know that healing happens through meaningful connection and within community. Furthermore, it can be argued that one reason hard work is a deeply ingrained cultural trait for many Asians is that one is working for the good of the collective, not just for oneself, which gives the work more meaning and import.

Asian Spirituality

While one common stereotype of Asians is that they are all very spiritual, there is some truth to the idea that spirituality and native philosophies are very much a part of many Asian people's cultural values even when they do not identify as religious. Religions, philosophies, and spiritual practices that originated in Asia such as Buddhism, Hinduism, Daoism, Confucianism, Shintoism, ancestor worship, animism, and shamanism, along with religions such as Islam and Christianity can all help provide meaning and a coherent worldview for Asian clients. Traits common in Asian culture—self-examination as a means of self-improvement, a deep connection to Nature, reverence for ancestors, surrender as a decision and choice in the face of insurmountable obstacles, stoicism in the face of difficulty, and a long view of things (e.g., understanding that life is about constant change)—can be sources of spiritual resilience, protection and strength for Asian clients. In addition, as I have experienced personally and witnessed in numerous sessions with clients, an openness to, and connection with, benevolent ancestral guides/spirits can provide clients with profound strength, clarity and guidance; IFS work that incorporates ancestral work can facilitate deep and rapid healing.

As one of the most spiritual forms of healing to emerge from the world of psychotherapy, IFS encompasses many of the qualities that are already an integral part of the Asian psyche. What IFS calls Self is what Asian philosophies already know as the higher self (Hinduism), Buddha nature/mind (Mahayana Buddhism), or the Dao (Chinese Daoism), to give a few examples. Thus, many Asian clients find the modality to be quite intuitive as it already aligns with their understanding of their internal world.

Case Study: Ben

To illustrate how clients can derive strength from, and find resilience within, their Asian identity and heritage, I present Ben who, like Amy, Linh and Stephen, is a hypothetical composite drawn from my practice. Ben is in his early thirties and identifies as second generation Chinese American, transmasculine, queer, and neurodivergent. He was diagnosed with ADHD in college and suspects he may be on the autism spectrum. Ben's cheerful demeanor belies a very troubled childhood where his parents, who did not know about or want to acknowledge Ben's neurodiversity, shamed him for not doing well enough in school. As hard as Ben tried, he could never earn good enough grades and consistently failed courses, much to his parents' chagrin. As the years went by and Ben continued to disappoint his parents, Ben developed exile parts who hold **deep shame** and carry a belief that he is **never good enough.** When Ben came out as trans in college, his father disowned him and threw him out of the house. Fortunately, Ben's maternal grandmother (who is Taiwanese) took him in and let him know that she accepted him as he was. Ben has a special bond with his grandmother who was his primary caregiver in his earliest years when his parents were busy trying to establish themselves in a new country. Also, Ben's mother and Ben's aunt, without his father's knowledge, maintained a relationship with Ben and helped him financially, even offering to pay for therapy.

In spite of the traumatic split from his father, Ben credits his parents with teaching him the value of **hard work and perseverance** and his grandmother for instilling in him a certain **stoicism in the face of hardship** which she attributes to her Buddhist practice. Ben says that had he not learned these traits from his family, he would have taken his own life long ago. Although he does not identify as Buddhist, he thinks about what his grandmother taught him about how one must live a virtuous life to avoid being reborn into a less desirable form; one cannot escape one's destiny through suicide which only generates more and different forms of suffering. More than anything, it is Ben's ties to his loving grandmother and, to a lesser extent, to his anxious but caring mother that keep him going even in spite of the many hardships he faces.

As the case study illustrates, Ben's Asian heritage provides several protective factors even in the face of great challenges that are a result of his gender identity and neurodivergence, not to mention his racialized identity. He benefits from having grown up in a multigenerational Asian household (when his maternal grandparents lived with them) where members of his family looked after him even in spite of the major rift with his father. Ben also draws comfort from his grandmother's stoicism and calm that are a result of her Buddhist spiritual practice and Daoist worldview.

Conclusion

When working with clients who identify as Asian or API, it is essential for us to understand how *our clients identify as API* as well as *what their experiences are like as API individuals.* In this chapter, I present several common themes in Asian clients' healing needs, but these observations should serve only as a starting point for inquiry into your clients' lived experience: what is true of *their* culture, ethnicity, nationality/country of origin, number of generations in the West or outside Asia, socioeconomic class, educational attainment, gender, sexual orientation, disabilities, etc.

In general, working with Asian clients using IFS is no different from working with clients of other racial identities: the protocol and exploration process are the same though specific burdens and ways in which parts express themselves may be culturally specific. Here are some suggestions for non-Asian practitioners working with Asian clients:

Therapist parts:

- Get to know the biases, stereotypes, or preconceived ideas about your client's Asian identity that your parts may hold. Notice parts that feel uncomfortable with not knowing much about another's culture. Be aware of the fine line between expecting clients to educate you about their culture and encouraging them to share their personal experience.
- Be aware of your parts that may react with discomfort, anxiety, recoiling, or dismissiveness when confronted with differences between your cultural background and your clients'.
- Notice parts that have a tendency to pathologize Asian qualities or traits such as reticence, respectful silence, or loyalty to and close ties with parents and family.
- Notice your parts' reactions to Asian clients who have perfectionist parts and "never good enough" parts that drive them towards high academic and professional achievement.
- Welcome in, and work to unburden, your own parts that hold racial trauma whether you have parts that have internalized a belief in White supremacy culture (e.g., a belief that the Western way of doing things is superior or the norm) or hold a marginalized identity.

Recommendations:

- Encourage clients to draw on cultural strengths that may include resilience, familial support, a sense of belonging within their cultural community, ancestral ties or reverence for ancestors, and their spirituality (if applicable).
- Be on the lookout for specifically Asian historical and intergenerational legacy burdens that can be traced back to destructive/harmful events in clients' ancestral homes. Some of these legacy burdens may have been a result of Western colonialism in Asia.
- As with all clients, approach clients with as much Self presence as possible. In particular, curiosity, compassion, patience, playfulness, and connectedness can go a long way in earning a client's system's trust.

KEY TAKEAWAYS

- Most Asian cultures are characterized by a deep-rooted collectivism where families, elders, men, and people in positions of authority are accorded the most respect and privilege.
- Asian clients of all genders very likely have parts that have been burdened by patriarchy, sexism, heteronormativity, classism, and ageism.
- Asian/API folks in the West live in racialized bodies and may experience invisibility, be the targets of hate crimes and racially motivated violence, experience microaggressions or subtle acts of exclusion, and/or be exoticized, objectified as sexual objects or emasculated.
- Clients' systems may carry legacy burdens from intergenerational and historical trauma as well as from the impact of Western colonialism in Asia.
- Clients' Asian heritage can be a protective factor that serves as a resource as well as a source of strength and resilience.

AUTHOR BIO

Regina L. Wei, MA, LMFTA (she/they) is an IFS trained Couples and Family Therapist in Washington state who is pursuing certification in sex therapy. Her work centers on folks who identify as BIPOC and/or LGBTQIA+, and focuses on helping clients heal racial, intergenerational, sexual, and other traumas. Regina has an MA in Couples and Family Therapy and an MA in Modern Chinese Literature and Culture. She has written a novel, set in China, that deals with the themes of trauma, healing, and cross-cultural connections and misses. www.ReginaWei.com

GOING DEEPER

From Regina Wei

Websites:
1) www.ReginaWei.com
   a. IFS and Racial Justice Workshops: www.reginawei.com/ifs-racial-social-justice
   b. Directory of Asian IFS Practitioners: www.reginawei.com/asian-ifs-practitioners

From Other Sources

1) Online Resources:
   a. Hung, N. C. (2016). *Boundaries and belonging: Asian America, psychology, and psychoanalysis* [Doctoral dissertation, City University of New York]. CUNY Academic Works. https://www.academicworks.cuny.edu/gc_etds/1239
   b. Kwon, S. (2021). This is what no one tells you about being Asian in America in 2021. *HuffPost*. Retrieved October 18, 2022, from https://www.huffpost.com/entry/asian-hate-crimes-2021-covid_n_602c00e8c5b6c95056f3dd41
   c. Louie, S. (2014). Asian shame and honor: A cultural conundrum and case study. *Psychology Today*. Retrieved October 18, 2022 from www.psychologytoday.com/sg/blog/minority-report/201406/asian-shame-and-honor

2) Books:
   a. Quek, K. M. T., & Fang, S. R. S. (2017). *Transition and change in collectivist family life*. Springer Berlin Heidelberg.
   c. Quek, K. M. T., & Hseih, A. L. (2017). *Intersectionality in family therapy leadership: Professional power, personal identities*. Springer.
   d. Wang, J. T. (2022). *Permission to come home: Reclaiming mental health as Asian Americans* (1st ed.). Balance.

EMBODYING IFS WITH LATINX CLIENTS

CULTURALLY RESPONSIVE PRACTICES IN LATINX MENTAL HEALTH

Gishela Gaby Satarino, MA, LPC-S

"Caminante, no hay camino. Se hace camino al andar."
"Traveler, there is no path. You make your path as you go along."
—Antonio Machado

I grew up with a mother who read widely, and her love of reading was contagious. Our home library consisted of books written solely in Spanish, and the love of reading I inherited from her eventually led to my professional calling as a therapist. In 1980, we emigrated from San Luis Potosi, Mexico to San Antonio, Texas, and though my mother understood the importance of assimilating into a new country, she was deeply committed to preserving our native tongue and cultural practices. When I was 10, I borrowed a self-help psychology book from the library, titled *Tus Zonas Erróneas / Your Erroneous Zone*, by Wayne Dyer, and I was mesmerized. Although Dr. Dyer's ideas would be foreign for most 10-year-olds, they resonated with me, and I sensed that my soul was home. That day I fell in love with psychology, and my career path and my calling became clear.

I eventually became a Licensed Professional Counselor and now have more than 20 years of clinical experience as a bilingual psychotherapist. I have worked in community mental health and primary care settings providing trauma-informed psychotherapy for at-risk youth, refugees, the homeless, and incarcerated populations, as well as survivors of rape, domestic violence, and torture. My clinical work has always been undergirded by a passion for understanding the ways in which Latinx cultural values impact engagement and treatment outcomes in therapy. Throughout my career, I have worked on outreach efforts aimed at reducing current utilization gaps and bringing the voice of the Latinx experience into mental health. In 2021, my presentation at the IFS global conference, *Culturally Responsive Practices in Latinx Mental Health with Internal Family Systems*, was the first in IFS conference history to be presented in Spanish.

In this chapter, I will make the case for the importance of providing culturally sensitive care to Latinx clients and will present four IFS-informed approaches to providing culturally centered care to Latinx clients who live in the United States:

- Culturally Sensitive Contextual Interview (CSCI).
- Common Polarizations in Latinx Clients.
- Culturally Centered Spiritual Integration.
- Language Switching for Culturally Centered Healing.

Clinicians who are not bilingual or who do not treat the Latinx community may feel inclined to skip this chapter, but I assure you that your clients will to some degree be influenced by, or connected to, the Latinx community, as the numbers make clear.

Latinx in the United States

According to Government Census, "2020 Census Illuminates Racial and Ethnic Composition of the Country," when comparing 2010 and 2020 data, the United States Government Census found that slightly more than half (or 51.1 percent) of the total U.S. population growth between 2010 and 2020 came from the Latinx population. Despite this growth, much remains to be discovered in how therapists respond to contextual and cultural experiences of the Latinx community in mental health.

In The United States, the word Latinx refers to Latinos (males) and Latinas (females) including immigrants or descendants of immigrants from Latin America who are living in the United States. Additionally, the term Afro-Latinx is used to describe descendants of Latin America with African roots. The term "Latinx" has typically been adopted among people who are looking for a more inclusive and gender-free alternative to "Latino" or "Latina." (In Spanish, words are automatically gendered as male or female, leaving no option for those who choose to identify as non-binary.)

In the United States, the terms Latinx and Afro-Latinx have been embraced by a new generation that is prioritizing gender politics. They are bringing a powerful energy, which is creating more in-depth conversations about culture, along with ways of increasing a shared sense of belonging and visibility as a community.

What is Culture?

Kroeber, A.L., and Kluckhohn, C. (1952) provide a comprehensive definition: "Culture consists of patterns, explicit and implicit, of and for behavior acquired and transmitted by symbols, constituting the distinctive achievements of human groups, including their embodiments in artifacts; the essential core of culture consists of traditional (i.e. historically derived and selected) ideas and especially their attached values; culture systems may, on the one hand, be considered as products of action, and on the other as conditioning elements of further action."[1]

Especially with increasing awareness of the importance of a multicultural orientation in psychotherapy, clinicians understand that simply identifying with the client's culture is not the same as being culturally responsive (Cabral & Smith 2011; Swift et al., 2015).[2] Therapists must have additional in-depth learning, training, and conversations around what it means to practice culturally centered psychotherapy with the Latinx community living in the United States. Culture is in the fabric of our souls, which means if we do not fully explore cultural sensitivity, we run the risk of excluding important parts of a client from the therapy room. The question then becomes, "What is culturally centered psychotherapy?"

Culturally Centered Psychotherapy

According to the American Psychological Association, the "culturally centered" approach to counseling and therapy assumes that cultural factors bring a beautiful intersection to the therapeutic process, and that behaviors have no meaning until they are understood in the cultural context in which those behaviors have been learned and are displayed. The goals of culturally centered therapy are a) to establish an accurate awareness of how the therapist is culturally similar and, at the same time, culturally different from the client; b) to gather the relevant facts, information, and meaningful knowledge to comprehend priorities in the client's cultural context; and c), to demonstrate culturally appropriate skills for helping the client change or examine culturally learned behaviors and perspectives."[3]

Additionally, clients' cultural values and our treatment approach need to be congruent. "One of the essentials of the IFS perceptive is that 'systems thinking' encourages us to be ecologically sensitive…Protectors have a right to vet the therapist for competence and safety before letting her enter the inner system. To be worthy of a protector's trust, we must lead from the Self. The onus of proof is on the therapist."[4] This essential perspective of IFS provides an organic anchor for cultural adaptations that fit the needs of an individual client.

One of the ways in which we offer culturally centered care is by making the commitment to engage in an on-going, in-depth conversation regarding our clients' values, traditions, preferred communication styles, generational values, family roles, relational styles, spirituality/religion/faith, hierarchy beliefs, immigration status, integrative stress, social economics, and experiences of discrimination, racism, and confluence of cultures, just to name a few.

In their multicultural guidelines, the American Psychological Association and the American Counseling Association call attention to cultural influences related to marginalized groups. These influences are summarized by Hays (2022)[5] in a framework that begins with the acronym ADDRESSING and highlights:

Age and generational influences,
Developmental or other **D**isability,
Religion and spirituality,
Ethnic and racial identity,
Socioeconomic status,
Sexual Orientation,
Indigenous heritage, and
Gender identity.

Latinx and Afro-Latinx cultures are extremely diverse, and the ADDRESS-ING framework emphasizes this diversity. That is, within Latinx and Afro-Latinx cultures, there are cultural differences related to generational roles and experiences, disability, religion, and so on. It is important that clinicians consider each of the ADDRESSING influences on clients, on themselves, and on the therapeutic process. These influences may present as pride in one's culture, a particular sense of humor, wisdom from cultural experiences, traditional celebrations and rituals, or different ways of honoring deceased relatives and ancestors.

In my experience, the integration of IFS and ADDRESSING improves treatment outcomes for clients with diverse backgrounds. For example, IFS proposes that bringing more Self-energy to our parts can help us connect and increase our compassion across cultures, while ADDRESSING emphasizes understanding the effects of diverse cultural influences on ourselves and our clients' parts. The ADDRESSING framework invites us to hold awareness of our own cultural and social influences, while inviting the client's thoughts, beliefs, feelings, behaviors, and worldview into the therapy room. The integration of IFS and ADDRESSING deepens our understanding of how parts and culture interact.

To illustrate this point, consider the story of Claudia (all names and identifying information in this chapter have been changed):

Claudia is a 48-year-old successful Latinx banker. While living in Mexico, she and her husband divorced, but two years later remarried. During their separation, her husband moved to the US and upon remarrying, she joined him. She presented in therapy struggling with an inner polarization (two parts holding opposite feelings) relating to integrative stress.

Me: It sounds like your transition to the United States has not been easy. Would you like to say more about what it's been like for you?

Claudia: It's been really hard. I'm sad that I can't continue the work I love as a banker because I don't speak English well, but I want to be happy to be here with my husband and figure out how to fit in.

Me: Sounds like one part of you is glad to be here and another part is really sad about what that means for your professional reality. Is that right?

Claudia: Yes, exactly! I told the part of me that missed being a banker that she is dead. I need to stop focusing on it and focus on learning English and being an American.

Claudia did not allow the part grieving her loss of career to enter the counseling room, yet we found that part would show up in outbursts of crying. Our initial sessions were held in English, per her request (which likely came from the part of her that wanted to assimilate). However, after observing that her outbursts of crying were increasing, I became curious about the magnitude of the impact of her ethnic and racial identity experiences ("E" from ADDRESSING) and asked if there was a part of her that might like to have our counseling sessions in Spanish. She agreed and connected with the part of herself that was grieving the loss of her language and culture. This culturally centered intervention allowed her to tenderly welcome that part into session. As we continued to witness the grieving part's burdens related to leaving her country, it was eventually able to feel support and to unburden, and Claudia's crying abated.

In countless examples such as this, I have observed the power of integrating IFS with culturally centered interventions to improve treatment outcomes for Latinx clients living in the United States.

Four IFS-Informed Approaches to Providing Culturally Centered Care

It is clear that cultural sensitivity is a key aspect of any healing initiative. In the following discussion, I offer four IFS-informed culturally informed interventions that allow us to provide culturally centered care for Latinx clients living in the United States.

1. Culturally Sensitive Contextual Interview (CSCI)

The IFS-Informed, Culturally Sensitive Contextual Interview (CSCI) is set of questions that clinicians can ask, both during intake and throughout the duration of client care, that invite dialogue about the degree to which various cultural experiences have impacted the parts of the client. These questions offer a sampling of options from which the clinician can draw throughout the course of treatment to deepen their understanding of the client's cultural context and history.

Latinx clients may believe that all of who they are is not welcome in Western therapy; that they need to "leave some of their parts outside of the therapy room." The CSCI offers all the client's parts an open invitation into the room and space to explore their level of acculturation, immigration history, communication preference, developmental disabilities, acquired disabilities, Indigenous heritage, family values, religious and spiritual practices, and cultural and sociopolitical dimensions, among other important factors.

In the book, *Addressing Cultural Complexities in Counseling and Clinical Practice: An Intersectional Approach,* Hays (2022) offers a guide to the kinds of questions clinicians will want to consider when working cross culturally. These questions are based on the ADDRESSING acronym. Hays's questions include queries regarding clients' identities, strengths, structural barriers, and experiences of racism, ableism, classism, etc. in relation to each of the ADDRESSING influences. Hays' questions lay the philosophical groundwork for the CSCI, which follows (Spanish version in Appendix A):

IFS-INFORMED, CULTURALLY SENSITIVE CONTEXTUAL INTERVIEW (CSCI)

1. What is your understanding of the counseling process?
2. What are your hopes and expectations for our time together?
3. Are there any parts of you that have concerns or fears about coming to therapy? Is it okay for us to check in with those parts and see what they need from me or from us to feel safer and more supported here?
4. What part of you are you most likely to leave out of the therapy room? Is there anything that part would like me or us to know? Is there anything that might help that part feel welcome in our sessions?
5. Are there any parts of you that would like to use your native greetings or farewells in our time together (or in your life in general)? What do those parts envision?
6. What has your experience been seeing therapists, healers, life coaches, spiritual directors, or medical doctors in the past? Is there anything you would like me to know from those experiences that would help make your experience here more successful?
7. Do you have experience seeing Indigenous healers or taking traditional home remedies? What were the outcomes? What was that like for you?
8. What is your language preference in session?
9. Do you speak any other languages? Approximately how old were you when these languages were introduced? When and with whom do you speak these languages?
10. There are people who are ashamed for not speaking Spanish. There are also people who are ashamed for speaking Spanish and feel they may need to hide it. What has language choice been like for you, and does that change in different contexts?
11. Are there ways I can help you feel comfortable communicating in session? Please know whatever way you prefer to communicate is welcome, including the use of proverbs and metaphors.
12. Do you identify with a religious or spiritual tradition? To what degree are faith and/or spiritual practices resources for you?

13. Have you had any challenging or negative experiences with religion? Have any of your beliefs or practices changed over time?
14. Would you like to include spirituality in our sessions? Are there specific practices, such as prayer, that you would like us to use? If you would like to integrate spirituality in session, are there any parts of you that have fears or concerns about that?
15. With whom do you live (e.g., multigenerational family)? What are your roles in the family and community?
16. As you think back on your childhood, which family values were prioritized? How do your current values align with, or differ from, the values with which you were raised?
17. Do you have any beliefs of which your family, friends, religion, and/or community disapprove? If so, what has that been like for you?
18. Were you given any nicknames that your family/friends have used to refer to you? If so, did they feel positive, negative, or neutral?
19. Do you experience any inner conflict surrounding family loyalty issues? Would you like to represent these parts of you with objects in the therapy room and spend some time getting to understand their perspectives?
20. Do you or any of your family members have a disability? If so, how has that affected your life?
21. What is your sexual orientation and relationship history? If applicable: To whom have you come out and what have their reactions been?
22. Does your gender assigned at birth match the gender you identify as now?
23. What are your pronouns?
24. What were the gender roles in your family? How does that affect you now?
25. I would like to learn more about your cultural heritage. How do you identify culturally?
26. Where did you grow up? As a child, did you feel connected with your cultural heritage? How connected to your cultural heritage do you feel now?
27. Have you ever spent time discovering or rediscovering your ancestral history, traditions, art/music, and customs etc.? Which aspect(s) did you connect with, and which did you feel disconnected from?
28. Are there foods, traditions, or spiritual practices from your country of origin that parts of you miss?
29. Are there any political aspects of your experience that are important for you to name?
30. To help me get to know you, what is the racial/ethnic identity in your family of origin? Is that similar or different in your current family?
31. What is your personal or family history of immigration? How long have you/has your family been in the United States? Do you think this topic is related to your current worries?

32. If applicable: Have you heard stories about your ancestors coming to the United States? What messages did you take away from those stories?

33. If applicable: Tell me about the parts of you that wanted to come to the United States. What were the plans, expectations, and goals? How has that compared to your actual experiences?

34. If applicable: Were there any parts of you that didn't want to emigrate? How do those parts of you feel now?

35. What aspect(s) of American culture have been the hardest for you and/or your family?

36. What aspect(s) of American culture have been the most positive for you and/or your family?

37. Is there a part of you that feels pressure to assimilate when you interact with people outside of your culture? Would that part of you like to share what its experience has been like?

38. Would you like to share any experiences you've had of racial discrimination and/or classism?

39. Are there any parts of you that feel unseen or unsafe in the community in which you now live?

40. Is there anything else you'd like me to know about you or your experience that we haven't covered?

It is incumbent on the therapist to approach the CSCI discovery process from a posture of cultural humility. Tervalon and Murray-Garcia define and apply the concept in a way I find helpful: "Cultural humility is an inquisitive, self-reflective, critical, and continuous learning process. Unlike the idea of cultural competence, in cultural humility we never stop learning about our client's cultural and life experiences: it is a dynamic process, shaped by every interaction we have with each person, while keeping our minds and hearts open. Cultural humility is a lifelong process of self-reflection and self-critique whereby the individual not only learns about another's culture, but one starts with an examination of her/his own beliefs and cultural identities." (Tervalon & Murray-Garcia, 1998)[6]

Cultural humility is different from cultural competency. The goal of cultural competency is to learn about another person's culture. By contrast, cultural humility is a posture of deference and openness, being aware of what we don't and can't fully know about a client culture's experience of oppression, violence, colorism, racism, to name a few.

We incorporate culture in our therapeutic interactions when we ask open-ended questions about the cultural background and history of our client and their family and genuinely welcome their perception of their symptoms, viewing the client as the expert of their own life, even if their account may seem unrelated to the presenting problems. When we do, we will learn even more about client's values and how these in turn impact mental health presentations and suggest skillful, culturally centered treatment approaches. Integrating the IFS-informed CSCI into client care helps open the conversation to further exploring a client's external and internal family systems.

2. Common Polarizations in Latinx Clients

The culturally sensitive contextual interview often uncovers polarizations within Latinx individuals living the United States. A polarization is a set of burdened protector parts that are attempting to help the client in two opposing ways. Polarized parts hold negative assumptions about each other, which lead each part to become more extreme in trying to gain control over the other. Protective polarizations are omnipresent and present clues to the existence of exiles.

Polarizations are common in all people, but perhaps even more so in those who hold identities rooted in two different cultures. This cultural "split" invites parts to form in opposition to each other (e.g., one part wanting to acculturate and another part wanting to speak Spanish, such as we saw with Claudia). Thus, when providing culturally centered care to Latinx clients living in the United States, it is important to listen for common polarizations and welcome both sides into the room to be witnessed, particularly the "sides" of a polarization that may not naturally feel welcome in the dominant culture.

The following composite client case descriptions illustrate options for working with polarizations typical in Latinx clients living in the United States.

Maria is a 52-year-old woman who moved to the United States from Mexico in order to provide a better educational future for her two children. She sought counseling to address her anxiety. Maria had one part that felt grateful to be living in the US and able to provide education for her children, but she also had another part that felt guilty for those family members who were left behind. Because Maria's culture valued gratitude and viewed speaking about other emotions as disrespectful, she initially attempted to conceal the part of her that felt guilty, choosing instead to speak from the part that felt gratitude. As I welcomed and normalized both sides of her polarized parts, Maria was able to bring some Self-energy to the guilty part as well as the grateful part. I assured Maria she didn't have to speak any of the part's feelings out loud, as long as the part that felt guilty could be witnessed by her inner Self. With this culturally centered IFS intervention, Maria was able to get to know the guilty part, while honoring her cultural norms of not speaking negative emotions out loud, learn of this part's love and concern for her family members in Mexico, and bring it some comfort and support, resulting in a reduction in her anxiety.

Luis is a 16-year-old male who moved to the US from Honduras. Luis presented in therapy with inner conflict surrounding parts polarized by the use of language. He had one part that wanted to continue speaking Spanish to preserve his native tongue and connection to his culture, and he had another part that wanted to speak English in order to feel more included, empowered, and protected. It was helpful to Luis when we identified this inner struggle as coming from parts of him that wanted to help him in opposing ways, but not as all of who he was. He was able to begin to access Self qualities of curiosity and compassion for these parts, witness their stories and desires, and build an agreement with them that he (Self) would consult them both before entering new environments, so they could determine as a team whether it was safe to speak Spanish or whether English would feel wiser to his system in that context. Luis was grateful for this new flexibility, and his inner struggles around language decreased.

Valeria moved to the US at the age of 14. She was raised in a multigenerational Latinx household and experienced internal conflict due to parts polarized around generational cultural values. One part of Valeria wanted to honor, identify with, and preserve generational beliefs (in this case, that the family is of higher priority than the individual), while another part was pushing her to adopt new dominant social and cultural practices in the US. I asked Valeria to invite each of those parts to speak with her in turn and share what they were afraid would happen if they didn't hold these positions. When the exiles (vulnerable parts) driving the protective parts behaviors were identified and unburdened, the polarized parts were able to soften their stances and develop a more harmonious partnership, allowing her to prioritize time with her family while choosing to join a club at school that didn't conflict with family responsibilities.

In working with polarizations, it benefits parts who are in conflict to take turns sharing with Self and each other what their concerns are and how they are working to protect the client. A technique I find helpful to facilitate this work is called the *conference table*, developed by Michi Rose.[7] In this IFS intervention, polarized parts are invited to sit down on opposite sides of an internally visualized table with the client's Self. This allows the Self to mediate, witness, and ultimately bring harmony to previously oppositional parts. In the client's mind's eye, Self can also set the table in any way that feels culturally affirming, perhaps with traditional Latin foods or décor, while the parts converse. By offering the incorporation of culturally familiar items into the internal space of parts, we create safety for parts to orient in an inner space that feels welcoming.

3. Culturally Centered Spiritual Integration

Every client is unique, and every client's expression of their culture and spirituality is also unique. However, many Latinx clients do hold some form of cultural affiliation with Christianity. This does not mean that all Latinx identify as Christians, but according to the Pew Research Center, more than three in five Latinos identify as Catholic and one in five identify as Protestant, meaning 81 percent identify with some form of Christianity.[8] (It is important to note that religious affiliation does vary with immigration generations, with more recent immigrants identifying more strongly with Catholicism). It has been my experience that many Christian-identifying Latinx clients want to incorporate culturally and spiritually sensitive IFS integration into their clinical work. When this is the case, it offers unique therapeutic possibilities for inviting access Self and enhancing the parts work process. Christian-identified clients often resonate with the conceptualization of Self as the Divine, the Holy Spirit, or the Image of God (Riemersma, 2020). For clients who indicate a desire to integrate their Christian spirituality into IFS work, we can offer this option as a way of accelerating access to Self-energy.

Important Considerations in Spiritual Integration

Do not offer spiritual integration without all parts' consent. Consent for spiritual integration is a critical first step. Through an IFS lens, we understand that many different parts of a client may have many different experiences with spirituality, religion, or the concept of the divine. Some may be positive, while others may hold spiritual trauma. Therefore, in order to provide ethically-sound spiritual integration, we must first explore the experience of spirituality with all parts to determine if we do, in fact, have internal consent from all the parts to provide this type of integration. IFS author and therapist Jenna Riemersma notes, "This is a key piece of how IFS helps us offer truly culturally competent care, by honoring all parts of the client's spiritual experience, not just their primary religious identification" (personal communication, 2022).

Be attentive to spiritualizing managers. Spiritual activity can emerge from the core Self, as well as from managerial protectors who use spiritual language or behavior to "be pleasing to God." (Riemersma, 2020) If the spiritual energy feels like it has an agenda, it will be important to first unblend from the spiritual manager that is attempting to direct the integration process, learn what it is afraid would happen if it allowed Self to be the connection to the Divine, and then address its concerns. Many protector parts are unaware of the existence of Self or do not trust it to be "good enough for God," so an updating process may be necessary before proceeding with spiritual integration.

When internal consent has been granted and the client's Self is in leadership in the process, the following approaches can provide culturally centered spiritual integration for Latinx clients.

Inviting a Divine presence as a guide. Clients can be invited to pray, or "invite in," a Divine presence as they understand it (God, Jesus, Holy Spirit, Mary, Guardian Angels, Saints, etc.) to guide and support their IFS session. This might happen at the beginning of a session or during a significant piece of work that needs additional support. By inviting spiritual support in this way, the client often feels a deeper connection to the vibrant quality of Self energy, both the Self within and the greater Self/Divine outside of themselves. Offering such an option to clients who identify as Christian can be beneficial, especially if the client has difficulty creating a Self-to-part relationship.

To illustrate this point, consider Rosa, a 42-year-old female Latinx Christian client. She was born in Central America and immigrated to the United States with her husband and children when she was 25. Rosa was seeking counseling to address her anxiety. During our work together, Rosa and I explored her request to integrate her Christian faith into our work. We invited and addressed concerns that a few of her parts had about the process and, eventually, gained internal consent from parts who collectively wanted to invite Jesus in at any point in the session when it would feel supportive.

Later, as she was finding, focusing on, and befriending the part of her that held her anxiety, a blocking protector emerged that held fear that the anxious part would take over and flood Rosa's system. It blended with, and blocked, her Self-energy out of concern that being with the anxious part would trigger a panic attack.

Rosa heard the blocking part's concern, validated that it made sense, then asked if the blocking part would feel more comfortable if Jesus were present with the anxious part. The blocking firefighter was greatly relieved, believing Rosa's system would not become overwhelmed if Jesus were present. Rosa paused and invited all the parts to join her in welcoming Jesus to join them. Then she got an image of Jesus coming to the anxious part with an energy of love. Rosa's exhausted anxious part spontaneously turned into a young child who fell asleep in Jesus' arms, welcoming the respite and comfort. With the presence of Jesus as support, Rosa's anxious part received the rest, witnessing, and unburdening that it so deeply needed. Rather than unburdening to air, water, fire, or earth, the part wanted to unburden its anxiety into Jesus' hands.

Inviting spiritual gifts as positive qualities. After unburdening in an IFS session, parts are invited to bring in essential, positive qualities that they may need going forward. This process further reinforces the part's healing. Christian Latinx clients may identify more closely with the "gifts (or fruits) of the Holy Spirit" as being the essential positive qualities necessary to move toward wholeness. In Rosa's case, in the presence of Jesus, the part that had unburdened the anxiety chose to invite in the spiritual fruits of peace and love. It experienced Jesus bringing those qualities into its body which felt deeply healing and connective for the part. It also felt a restored secure attachment to the Divine through this interaction.

Utilizing culturally and spiritually centered symbols in retrieval. Retrieval is the step in the IFS process where a part that has been stuck in the past gains access to Self and is retrieved into a more comfortable location. Comforting surroundings are an important part of this step and offer the opportunity for parts to utilize cultural/spiritual rituals, or other symbolic objects, to create a space that feels optimally safe and secure. It is important to remember that the part being worked with is the one that should identify any ceremony or symbol that it would like to be present. When offered spiritually centered retrieval, Rosa's part that had held anxiety asked for a lighted votive candle as a symbolic object to honor the unburdening, as well as for a rosary that she could pray as a sign of gratitude and remembrance.

Praying for parts during check in. An underemphasized, but important, aspect of IFS therapy is the check in process that happens between the client's Self and parts between sessions. For Latinx clients integrating spirituality into their work, Self-energy can be accessed by inviting the divine (in whatever form feels right to the client's system) to join the check in. Client's Self can also pray for each of the parts that have been worked with (a practice known as intercessory prayer), perhaps inviting God or Jesus or Mary to be with the part during the check in and bring comfort to it. The practice of praying for parts between sessions often creates a more connected relationship between the Self and parts and between the whole inner system and the divine.

4. Language Switching for Culturally Centered Healing

Santiago-Rivera and Altarriba (2002) note, "Though little is known regarding the encoding and storage of emotion words (e.g., love, hate, fear) in bilingual memory, and theoretical explanations are lacking, researchers have identified differential patterns of usage as a function of language dominance or proficiency that have direct implications for therapy." Various researchers have suggested that when people learn emotion words in their first language, they register more deeply than their second language counterparts. For example, "Emotion words in the first language have been experienced in many more contexts and have been applied in varying ways. The contexts in which they appear help to create multiple traces in memory for these words and strengthen their semantic representation. In contrast, emotion words learned in a second language are often not as deeply coded."[9]

As we have seen, Latinx clients often have parts with differing preferences for language, and it is an empowering intervention to welcome each part to speak in the language with which it feels most comfortable. This is possible even if the therapist is not bilingual, requiring the therapist to gently check in, "Does that part feel like you really get what it's saying?" and "Is there anything more it wants to share with you?" While the client may need to briefly translate the part's comments in order for the therapist to follow, this culturally centered approach allows parts to express themselves more fully which can in turn lead to more congruent trauma unburdening. Particularly when trauma has been encoded in the client's neural networks in a native language (the trauma happened in a Spanish-speaking context, for example), it has been my experience that the IFS witnessing and unburdening steps are most effective when they occur in the language in which the trauma was encoded.

The following example illustrates this point. Gabriela is a 40-year-old female whose early childhood trauma was coded in Spanish (at that time her only language). She was born in the United States to Mexican immigrant parents who only spoke Spanish. During one of her sessions, a four-year-old exile was discovered, and even though there was a strong energetic Self-to-part relationship, she was unable to communicate with the exile. I suggested language switching to Spanish, and immediately the exile began to speak. The exile had not been able to understand Self speaking in English because the four-year-old part had not learned English. Language switching allowed Gabriela to access memories coded in her native language, and allowed the exile to be witnessed and unburdened.

The beauty and uniqueness of IFS is that the majority of the healing work happens between the client's Self and parts, which have the ability to language switch even if the therapist is not multilingual.

Language switching may serve many clinically significant functions in a client's internal system. Researchers have shown that switching is deliberate, predictable, and very often influenced by the context and the situation in which it occurs (Perez-Foster, 1998).[10] A culturally centered therapist, therefore, will be attentive to times that parts use language switching in support of their roles. A protector, for example, may switch to the less dominant language when describing a challenging memory in order to prevent the exile it involves from becoming triggered. There are a myriad of situations in which language switching is a useful tool and trailhead in Latinx clients' parts work, and we must always allow the client to be the expert on their internal and external systems. As Richard C. Schwartz often teaches, our most effective intervention is to "Just ask the part."

A Welcoming and Culturally Sensitive Context

This chapter has discussed the importance of culturally centered therapeutic approaches when working with Latinx clients living in the United States. IFS welcomes parts that have experiences with immigration and acculturative stress, racism, language switching, and generational value conflicts to name a few. With the awareness that it is incumbent on the therapist to provide this context for the therapeutic work, I've offered four options for IFS-informed interventions: the Culturally Sensitive Contextual Interview (CSCI), Recognizing Common Polarizations in Latinx Clients, Culturally Centered Spiritual Integration, and Language Switching for Culturally Centered Healing. It is my hope that these tools will create a more welcoming and culturally sensitive context in which Latinx clients in the US can receive care and inspire both multilingual and non-multilingual therapists in providing culturally affirming support to their Latinx clients.

KEY TAKEAWAYS

- In light of the fact that Latinos represent the largest contributors to recent US population growth, culturally centered care for Latinx clients living in the US is a high mental health priority.
- Latinx clients often face multiple stressors, including immigration and acculturation, conflicting cultural values and traditions, pressures for language fluency and switching, social economics, and experiences of discrimination, racism, and marginalization.
- The IFS-Informed, Culturally Sensitive Contextual Interview (CSCI) is set of questions that clinicians can ask, both during intake and throughout the duration of client care, that invite dialogue about the degree to which various cultural experiences have impacted the parts of the client.
- It is important to be attentive to common parts polarizations in Latinx clients.
- Culturally centered spiritual integration can enhance Latinx mental health outcomes and IFS therapeutic interventions.
- Language switching can present opportunities to understand parts protective strategies as well as to facilitate effective trauma healing via original encoded language.

AUTHOR BIO

Gishela (Gaby) Satarino, MA, LPC-S (she/her/ella) is a Licensed Professional Counselor Supervisor and Certified IFS Therapist. She has over 20 years of clinical experience working in community mental health and primary care settings providing trauma-informed psychotherapy for at-risk youth, refugees, the homeless, and incarcerated populations, as well as survivors of rape, domestic violence, and torture. Gaby's clinical work is undergirded by a passion for understanding the ways in which Latinx cultural values impact engagement and treatment outcomes in mental health, and it has focused on community outreach work aimed at reducing utilization gaps among Latinx communities. She sees clients and trains clinicians through her private practice in Dallas, Texas.

GOING DEEPER

From Gishela (Gaby) Satarino

1) Website:
   a. www.gabysatarinocounseling.com

2) Workshops:
   a. "Ni de aquí, ni de allá" / Neither from here nor from there. Looking at a cultural framework for Latinx immigrants living in the United States. www.gabysatarinocounseling.com/ifsworkshoplatine
   b. Culturally Responsive Practices in Latinx Mental Health with the Internal Family Systems Model. www.gabysatarinocounseling.com/ifs-workshop

3) Podcasts:
   a. Sollenberger, T. (2022-2023). *The One Inside: An Internal Family Systems podcast.* IFS and Culturally Responsive Practices in Latinx Mental Health with Gaby Satarino. www.audacy.com/podcast/the-one-inside-an-internal-family-systems-ifs-podcast-82d08/episodes/ifs-and-culturally-responsive-practices-in-latinx-mental-health-with-gaby-satarino-1db7f

From Other Sources

Pamala Hays

1) Website:
   a. www.drpamelahays.com

2) Books:
   a. Hays, P.A. (2022). *Addressing cultural complexities in practice: Assessment, diagnosis, and therapy* (4th ed.). American Psychological Association.

Patricia Arredondo

1) Website:
   a. www.arredondoadvisorygroup.com

2) Books:
   a. Gallardo-Cooper, M., Arredondo, P., & Delgado-Romero, E. A. (2014). *Culturally responsive counseling with Latinos.* Wiley.
   b. Arredondo, P. (2018). *Latinx immigrants: Transcending acculturation and xenophonia* (1st ed.). Springer.

APPENDIX A

Entrevista Culturalmente Sensible Informada de IFS
(Culturally Sensitive Contextual Interview (CSCI)—Spanish Version)

1. ¿Cuál es tu comprensión del proceso de consejería? O ¿Qué piensas del proceso de consejería?
2. ¿Cuáles son tus esperanzas y expectativas del tratamiento?
3. ¿Hay alguna partes de ti que tenga preocupaciones o temores acerca la terapia? ¿Está bien para ti que nos comuniquemos con esas partes y veamos qué necesitan de mí o de nosotros para se sientan más seguras y apoyadas aquí?
4. ¿Qué parte de ti es más probable que dejes fuera de la sala de terapia? ¿Hay algo que a esa parte le gustaría que supiéramos? ¿Hay algo que pueda ayudar a que esa parte se sienta bienvenida a nuestras sesiones?
5. ¿Hay partes de ti a las que les gustaría participar en alguna de tus formas habituales de saludo y despedida? ¿Qué visualizan esas partes?
6. ¿Cuál ha sido tu experiencia viendo terapeutas, curanderos, life coach, directores espirituales o médicos? ¿Hay algo que te gustaría que supiera de esas experiencias que ayudaría a que tu experiencia aquí sea más exitosa?
7. ¿Has acudido a curanderos o tomado remedios caseros? ¿Cuáles fueron los resultados y qué significa para ti?
8. ¿Cuál es tu idioma o idiomas preferidos para la sesión?
9. ¿Hablas otro idioma? ¿Aproximadamente cuántos años tenías cuando aprendiste esos idiomas? ¿Cuándo y principalmente con quién hablas esos idiomas?
10. Hay gente que se avergüenza de no hablar español. También hay personas que se avergüenzan de hablar español y sienten que deben ocultarlo. ¿Cómo ha sido la elección del idioma para ti? ¿Cambia en diferentes contextos?
11. ¿Hay alguna manera en que puedo ayudarte a que te sientas cómodo comunicándote en la sesión? En nuestras sesiones, debes saber que cualquier forma de comunicarte o describir las cosas es bienvenida, incluido el uso de dichos refranes y metáforas.
12. ¿Te identificas con una tradición religiosa o espiritual? ¿Hasta qué punto la fe y/o las prácticas espirituales son un recurso de vida para ti?
13. ¿Has tenido alguna experiencia difícil o negativa con la religión? ¿Alguna de tus creencias o prácticas ha cambiado con el tiempo?
14. ¿Te gustaría incluir tu espiritualidad en nuestras sesiones? ¿Hay prácticas específicas, como la oración, que te gustaría que usemos? Si deseas

integrar la espiritualidad en la sesión, ¿hay alguna parte de ti que tenga temores o preocupaciones al respecto?
15. ¿Quién vive contigo (por ejemplo: una familia multigeneracional)? ¿Cuál es tu función(es) en la familia y la comunidad?
16. Al recordar tu infancia, ¿qué valores familiares se priorizaron? ¿Cómo se alinean o difieren tus valores actuales con los valores de tu infancia?
17. ¿Tienes ciertas creencias que tu familia, amigos, religión y/o comunidad desaprueban? ¿Cómo ha sido eso para ti?
18. ¿Tu familia o amigos te pusieron algún apodo para describirte? Si es así, ¿los sentiste positivos, negativos o neutrales?
19. Hay alguna parte en ti que tenga sentimientos, creencias o experimente conflictos internos relacionados con problemas de lealtad familiar? ¿Te gustaría representar estas partes tuyas con objetos que se encuentren alrededor de la sala de terapia y dedicar algún tiempo a comprender sus perspectivas?
20. ¿Tú o alguno de tus familiares tiene una discapacidad? ¿Cómo ha afectado eso a tu vida?
21. ¿Cuál es tu orientación sexual? ¿Cuál es tu historial de relaciones? ¿A quién le has dicho y cuáles han sido las reacciones de las personas?
22. ¿El género que se te asignó al nacer es el mismo que el género con el que te identificas ahora?
23. ¿Cuáles son tus pronombres?
24. ¿Cuáles eran los roles de género en tu familia? ¿Cómo te afecta eso ahora?
25. Me gustaría conocer más sobre tu herencia cultural: ¿Cómo te identificas culturalmente?
26. ¿Dónde creciste? De niño o niña ¿te sentiste conectado con tu herencia cultural? Ahora ¿qué tan conectado te sientes con tu herencia cultural?
27. ¿Alguna vez has pasado tiempo descubriendo o redescubriendo la historia de tus antepasados, tradiciones, arte/música, costumbres, etc.? ¿Con qué aspecto(s) te conectaste y con cuál te sentiste desconectado?
28. ¿Hay alimentos, tradiciones o prácticas espirituales que extrañan algunas partes de ti?
29. ¿Hay algún aspecto político de tu experiencia que sea importante mencionar?
30. Para ayudarme a conocerte mejor, ¿cuál es la identidad racial/étnica en tu familia de origen? ¿Es similar o diferente a la de tu familia actual?
31. ¿Cuál es tu historia personal o familiar de inmigración? ¿Cuánto tiempo ha estado tu familia (o tú) en los Estados Unidos? ¿Sientes que este tema está relacionado con tus preocupaciones actuales?
32. Si corresponde: ¿Has oído historias sobre la llegada de tus antepasados a los Estados Unidos? ¿Cómo crees que te ha impactado esto?

33. Si corresponde: Cuéntame acerca de tus partes que querían venir a los Estados Unidos. ¿Cuáles eran los planes, expectativas y metas? ¿Cómo ha resultado eso?
34. Si corresponde: ¿Había partes de ti que no querían emigrar? ¿Cómo sientes eso ahora?
35. ¿Qué aspecto(s) de la cultura americana han sido los más difíciles para ti? ¿Qué ha sido lo más difícil para tu familia?
36. ¿Qué aspecto(s) de tu experiencia estadounidense han sido los más positivos? ¿Cuáles han sido las experiencias más positivas para tu familia?
37. ¿Hay alguna parte de ti siente presión para integrarse cuando interactúas con personas fuera de tu cultura? ¿Le gustaría a esa parte compartir cómo ha sido su experiencia?
38. ¿Te gustaría compartir alguna experiencia que hayas tenido sobre discriminación racial y/o clasismo?
39. ¿Hay alguna parte de ti que se siente invisible o insegura en la comunidad en la que vives ahora?
40. ¿Hay algo más que le gustaría que supiera sobre tu experiencia que no te haya preguntado?

EMBODYING IFS WITH SEXUAL ORIENTATION

TRAUMA HEALING AS A PATH TO THE INTEGRATED SELF

Frank Anderson, MD

It took a long time for me to sort through what it meant for me to be gay in the world. My internal system needed to process my childhood trauma history before I was able to consider navigating issues surrounding sexual orientation. As a young adult, I married a woman in an attempt to conform to heteronormative standards and—for a while—benefited from all the privileges that came with presenting as a married, White, heterosexual, male. It wasn't until I was 32, and a well-established psychiatrist, that I finally embraced my gay identity and came out publicly. There were benefits and downsides to coming out later in life. I had the advantage of a broad lens through which I defined myself in the world, but I was also "developmentally delayed" because I didn't experience the normal stages of coming out during my adolescence and young adulthood. As I've aged, sexual orientation has become more central to who I am as a person, and, because of significant cultural shifts that occurred in my lifetime, it is easier now to integrate my sexual orientation with my sense of self, my professional life, my family of origin, and within culture and society.

In this chapter, I will draw on personal and professional experiences that have informed my understanding of what it means to be in the LGBTQIA+ community today. I will also demonstrate how the IFS model can support LGBTQIA+ individuals coming to terms with their orientation, exploring the coming out process, and navigating the challenging dynamics of identifying as a sexual minority in a heteronormative culture. Along the way, I will touch on generational differences, the impact of changing technology, law, science, and clinical frameworks, and of course, the pervasive influence of trauma. I write primarily from a Western cultural framework, but the IFS concepts I will present, and their application to the issue of sexual orientation, are applicable cross-culturally.

Mind the Gap

It has been my observation that cultural shifts relating to sexual orientation have created a generation gap in Western culture. There is, for example, an "old orthodoxy" for those who are over 40 and didn't grow up in the social media era.[1] Of course, every individual is unique, and this generalization is admittedly somewhat arbitrary, but it is important for clinicians to be mindful of the impact generational norms have had on the developmental process for many sexual minorities. With that caveat, I suggest that:

Those Over 40:

Perceive a greater distinction between gay men and lesbians.
Are less comfortable with bisexuality and gender fluidity.
Were deeply affected by the AIDS crisis.
Are less familiar with transgender individuals.

Those Under 40:

Face fewer obstacles integrating sexual orientation into social and professional identity.
Grew up with (relatively) less hatred and discrimination.
Still struggle to embrace transgender rights.
Aren't as aware of the impact of HIV on the LGBTQIA+ community.

Those over 40 grew up in a pre-*Will and Grace* and *The Ellen Show* era. There was a separatist mentality between lesbians and gay men. The AIDS epidemic had a devastating impact on the "over 40" gay male cohort, decimating large segments of the population, and creating an undercurrent of fear, confusion, and isolation. There were few role models remaining to demonstrate how to come out or live as a gay man in society. Prejudice and hatred were more culturally sanctioned, underscored by such graphic atrocities as the 1998 beating and murder of Matthew Wayne Shepard, a gay American student at the University of Wyoming.

In the intervening years, there have been significant cultural shifts away from pathologizing sexual minorities. Although discrimination certainly still exists, the younger generation is generally more attenuated to inclusion, diversity, and acceptance. Many in the "under 40" cohort may not even know who Matthew Shepard was. As a general rule, there is more familiarity and comfort with individuals who identify as trans and non-binary in culture today. The natural plurality of sexual orientation and gender identity is more integrated into society, and many even find a sense of pride, community, and belonging in their identification as gender fluid or gay.

Access and the Law

The explosion of the internet and social media have had a profound impact on access to information about sexual and relational norms and connection with other like-minded LGBTGIA+ individuals. This instantaneous and pervasive availability of information, sexual content, and sexual connection, in my estimation, has both positive and negative aspects. Sexual minorities are no longer going through self-discovery in isolation. They have a way to normalize and validate their sexual development and coming out experiences, and they have easier opportunities for advocacy. There are role models, peers, and a sense of community via social media, online forums, and film.

That being said, dating and hook-up apps such as Grindr and Scruff make access to anonymous, instant sexual contact with strangers available to anyone at any time. This has had a significant impact on the gay community and has introduced new dynamics for LGBTQIA+ individuals, both single and coupled. These online sources of instantaneous sexual connection have impacted the desire for intimacy and fueled the demise of previously vital gay-centric bars and organizations, changing the structure and shape of LGBTQIA+ social networks.

Undoubtedly, the landmark Supreme Court ruling in June 2015[2] (which held that the Fourteenth Amendment guarantees the right for same-sex couples to marry as one of the liberties protected by the United States Constitution) changed the legal and political landscape for the LGBTQIA+ community. Protection of this basic human right to be treated equally, and to exercise autonomy in the choosing of a marriage partner, was a critical step in the case for LGBTQIA+ equality.

My own coming out process occurred before this Supreme Court ruling, and I can describe my experience as unsettling. As a (perceived) straight, cisgender, White male, I held the absolute highest privilege in our culture and society. I instantly was marginalized and lost much of the privilege I had previously held when I came out. I hadn't changed; I was still the same person. But the way society viewed me, and the legal rights I held before and after coming out were vastly different. As the political landscape continues to change, we need to be mindful of the profound impact these changes have on all aspects of LGBTQIA+ individuals' lives.

Sexual Orientation, "Disorder," and Trauma

Those of us who are old enough to remember the Stonewall Uprising on June 28, 1969[3] (which catalyzed the gay rights movement in the United States and globally), may also be aware that up until 1973, the American Psychiatric Association considered homosexuality a "disorder" that was listed in the DSM[4] (Diagnostic and Statistical Manual of Mental Disorders). Thereafter, it was removed, but the terms *ego syntonic* and *ego dystonic* were used to indicate sexuality that was consistent with or inconsistent with one's fundamental beliefs and personality. By the time the DSM-V[5] was published in 2013, the distinctions, along with their implied or stated pathologies, were dropped entirely.

For a young man or woman whose orientation and sexuality were different from the norm at this time, it was nearly impossible to feel healthy, confident, and secure within oneself when culture, society, and the medical community saw you as "disordered," pathological, a person who was "wrong" and needed to be "fixed." While the medical and therapeutic world has shifted, this perception still exists today in certain communities.

The *nature versus nurture* question regarding the origins of sexual orientation has long bedeviled social discourse, yet emerging research has positively influenced the trend away from labeling orientation as pathology. In the largest study of its kind, an international team of researchers led by Harvard and MIT geneticist, Benjamin Neale, recently analyzed data on sexual experiences and DNA from nearly half a million participants and found that genetic factors account for about 32 percent of same-sex sexual behavior.[6] Another study led by Brendan Zietsch of the University of Queensland, Australia asked 477,000 participants whether they'd had sex with someone of the same gender and if they identified as gay or straight.[7] They found five single points in the genome that seemed common among those who had same-sex experiences. These markers explained less than one percent of the differences in sexual activity among participants in the study. When researchers looked at overall genetic similarity, it accounted for eight to 25 percent of the behavior. The authors concluded that genetic similarities cannot definitively show whether a given individual is gay.

At a simplified level, this means that same-sex sexual behavior does seem to have a genetic component, however, non-genetic factors exert a significant influence on sexual behavior as well. The scientific picture continues to present a complex understanding of the underpinnings of sexual orientation and invites us to explore more dimensional understandings of sexuality than a purely binary approach suggests.

I will say from *experience* that my orientation feels much more innate to me as a person than a factor of past events or of my environment. What I believe about *environment*, however, is that it is entirely possible that, for an LGBTQIA+ individual growing up in an unaccepting community, the likelihood of becoming a target for traumas such as violence, abuse, and bullying certainly increases. There is a complex interplay at work between genetics, environment, trauma, and other factors that render the conversation around orientation much more sophisticated and intricate than a simple either-or perspective might suggest.

As we broaden the dialogue around sexual orientation, it is important to first become familiar with basic terms and definitions. While there is some fluidity with definitions and how people in the LGBQTIA+ communities choose to apply them, there are a few key terms with which to be familiar.

KEY TERMS

Agender. Denoting, or relating to, a person who does not identify as having a particular gender. That is, without gender.

Ally. A straight, or heterosexual, ally is a heterosexual and cisgender person who supports equal civil rights, gender equality, and LGBTQIA+ social movements, challenging homophobia, biphobia, and transphobia.

Asexual. A lack of sexual attraction. Asexual people may experience romantic attraction, but they do not feel the urge to act on those feelings sexually. Asexuality is considered a sexual orientation.

Bisexual. Sexually attracted to both men and women (one view), attracted to two or more genders (another view).

Cisgender. (sometimes cissexual, often abbreviated as 'cis') People whose gender identity matches their sex assigned at birth. For example, someone who identifies as a woman and was assigned female at birth is a cisgender woman.

Gay. Sexual or romantic attraction to people of one's same gender. Often used to refer to men.

Genderqueer. A person whose gender identity cannot be categorized as solely male or female, similar to non-binary.

Intersexed. A person born with reproductive or sexual anatomy that is not typically female or male. For example, a person might be born with female genitalia but have mostly male-typical internal anatomy.

Lesbian. A woman who is sexually attracted to other women; a gay woman.

LGBTQIA+. Acronym used to signify Lesbian, Gay, Bisexual, Transgender, Queer, Intersex, and Asexual people collectively. The inclusive '+' symbol holds space for expanding and new understandings around gender and sexual identity.

Non-binary. People who don't exclusively identify as either a man or a woman (also: genderfluid).

Pansexual. 'Pan,' meaning 'all,' denotes a person who is attracted to people of all genders.

Queer. To exist in a way that may not align with heterosexual or homosexual norms. Although it's typically used to describe a person's sexual orientation, it can also be used to express a nonbinary gender identity.

Transgender. Individuals whose sense of personal identity and gender does not correspond with their birth sex.

With this brief foundation, we can now turn our attention to the use of the IFS model with clients navigating issues relating to sexual orientation.

IFS and Sexual Orientation

In IFS we hold the belief that everyone is born with subpersonalities, or parts, as well as Self-energy. IFS believes that parts are forced to take on extreme roles when faced with overwhelming life circumstances. Parts that take on the role of protection, come in two forms, extreme or reactive (firefighters) and proactive (managers). Parts can also carry wounds or pain from trauma. We call these wounded parts exiles. When working with protective parts, the goal in IFS is to learn about their job and their fear, and to get their permission to access and heal the exiles they are trying to protect. As exiles are healed, protectors can move into more preferred roles, and Self can be restored to its rightful place as the leader of the internal system.[8]

Sexual Orientation: Part or Self?

In conceptualizing sexual orientation through an IFS lens, people often ask, "Is sexual orientation a part?" or "Is it an added dimension of Self?" In my experience with clients—and speaking for myself personally—sexual orientation is not a part, but rather it is a dimension of Self. It is a natural and healthy aspect of who we are, not a part of us, or a burden to be lifted from a part. Sexual orientation is deeply connected to the experience of Self, and one of the most rewarding aspects of my job is to observe the emergence of Self-energy in clients when they connect to their truth regarding their orientation.

Sexual orientation does, of course, have an embodied quality; however, it has been my experience that in the spiritual realm, orientation and gender fall away. This has been my observation regardless of sexuality or gender: straight, gay, bi, pan, male, female, trans, neutral, or fluid. I have found that the spiritual realm is a place of love, connection, and unity; a state in which all are connected and distinctions such as these no longer remain. Of course, everyone's experience of the spiritual is unique, and this is a new area of inquiry. I invite you to explore how it feels for you and for your clients.

Therapists' Parts

When providing care to LGBTQIA+ clients, it is critical that therapists work with their own parts relating to their sexuality and sexual history. Therapist parts that hold unresolved shame or confusion around sexuality tend to blend and obscure therapists' Self-energy when working with clients around sexual issues. Self-energy is the therapist's greatest asset in working with all clients, but particularly so when creating safety and spaciousness for LGBTQIA+ individuals. Straight individuals don't necessarily need to work on their sexuality in the same way that gay people do because they live in a world where their sexuality is normalized and integrated into mainstream society. Straight therapists must, therefore, be intentional in working with their own parts and develop comfort with discussing a variety of aspects of sexuality, sexual orientation, and sexual practices that are outside their personal experiences.

Therapists need to continually seek education when working with the LGBTQIA+ community. It is important, for example, to understand the difference between being "gay-friendly" and "gay-affirming" and to have some familiarity with terms associated with the gay culture and practices such as those we've discussed here. The LGBTQIA+ community is broad and encompasses a wide range of people, ideals, views, and experiences. Of course, therapists don't need to have the exact same lived experience as their clients in order to provide ethical clinical care (and it is always appropriate to be honest and offer Self-led curiosity when we are unfamiliar with something), but it is incumbent on the clinician to educate themselves, and to not impose the burden of education on their clients.

Because our culture is heteronormative, we all carry some degree of homophobia. This is true whether we are gay or straight. It's important to acknowledge this openly and directly with our clients to create the honesty and safety for them to struggle with their own. As a gay male therapist, when I'm working with someone dealing with orientation—say, a female who's coming out as a lesbian or a male teen who is coming out as gay—I will say something like, "Even though I'm gay, I, like everyone in our culture, have a level of internalized homophobia because of the messages and beliefs I subliminally took in from the world I grew up in. There may still be places in me that I may not be aware of that hold sensitivity around sexual orientation. If you ever sense any of these, please let me know."

Clinicians of all sexual orientations can provide skillful clinical care to members of the LGBTQIA+ community if they are curious, willing to educate themselves and to hold empathy (the capacity to resonate with another's feelings) and compassion (the desire to help them).[10] The human capacity to empathize allows us to connect with what it feels like to be excluded, what it feels like to be marginalized, and what it feels like to be shamed or criticized. These are universal experiences which suggest we all have the capacity to have empathy for our clients whose lives have been deeply shaped by trauma around their sexual orientation. We also have the capacity to hold a caring and compassionate stance for the experiences they have gone through.

THERAPIST AND AUTHOR, JOE KORT, PHD, PROPOSES QUESTIONS FOR THERAPISTS TO ASK THEMSELVES WHEN WORKING WITH LGBTQIA+ CLIENTS:[9]

- Do you disclose your sexual orientation when asked?
- Do you acknowledge your own implicit homophobia or heterosexism?
- Do you try to adopt a "blank screen" as a therapeutic style? (Understanding that non-disclosure creates a differential in therapy.)
- Do you use correct terminology?
- Do you offer resources other than you?
- Do you have LGBTQIA+ literature in your waiting room?
- Do you use heterosexist and heteronormative paperwork in your practice?
- Do you know the stages of coming out as gay or transgender?
- What age do you think is 'acceptable' to come out or transition?
- Do you believe your client was gay at birth?
- Do you believe that gay or trans couples should be able to get married and/or have children?

Mapping Parts

A first step when working with clients who are exploring sexual orientation is to understand their inner landscape. Generally, I like to begin by mapping out the parts of my client that are connected to each system (a system being a collection of protective parts along with the wounded part(s) they protect). When working with someone who is examining their sexual orientation, I'm particularly, but not exclusively, curious about the parts of them that are connected to sexuality, their gendered parts, the parts that are related to culture and society, as well as the parts associated with their family of origin. Most people struggling with sexual orientation will have burdened parts related to culture and society, as well as their family of origin. Systemic heteronormative beliefs transmitted by society, ethnic backgrounds, and religious institutions are often internalized in ways that burden LGBTQIA+ systems. This layer needs to be acknowledged and healed for an individual to have an unburdened relationship with their sexual orientation.

Wound

The collection of parts related to sexual orientation can be intricate and complex. For example, an individual might have several parts associated with sexuality (i.e., the part that is attracted to men, the part believes that's wrong, the part that feels it's betraying God, and the part that is fearful of telling their parents). The same is true for parts connected to gender, society, and family legacy. Therefore, I tend to create more detailed parts maps within each category, as illustrated below.[11] Protective parts connected to sexuality, gender, society, and family may share similar wounds, or they can be independent of each other. It's important to map out each system and determine the relationship between them. For example:

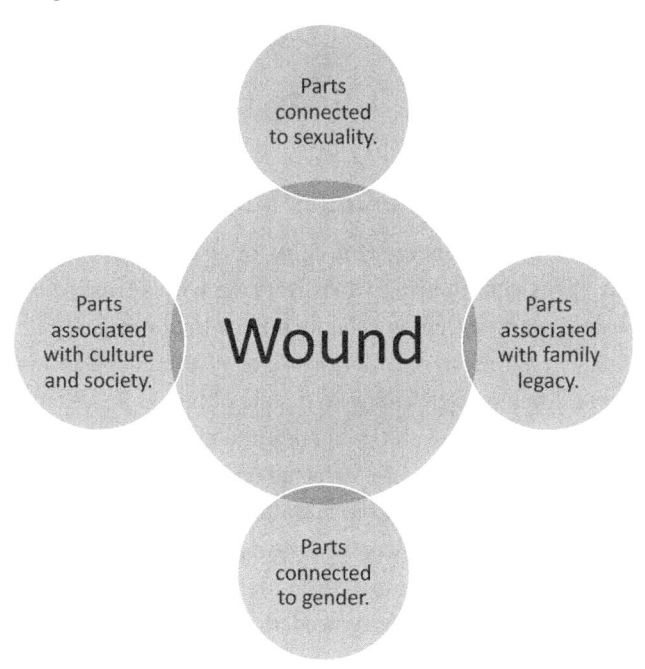

Diagram: A central circle labeled "Wound" surrounded by four circles: "Parts connected to sexuality." (top), "Parts associated with family legacy." (right), "Parts connected to gender." (bottom), and "Parts associated with culture and society." (left).

Parts Connected to Sexuality

This can quickly become complicated when dealing with multiple parts within an individual's numerous internal systems. To add to the complexity, it's also common for parts to conflict with each other. This conflict (called a "polarization") might occur between parts within the same system (e.g., two opposing parts from family legacy) or they can be from different systems (e.g., one part from gender, in conflict with another part connected to sexuality). Thus, mapping can be helpful for therapists and clients alike. By externalizing and concretizing the various parts and their relationships with one another, mapping helps parts unblend (creating separation between parts and the Self), reduces overwhelming emotion in the system, helps create more clarity in treatment planning, and streamlines the process of gaining permission from protectors to access the wounded part(s) that need to be healed.

Parts Connected to Sexuality:

Extreme Parts:
- A part that has anonymous sex.
- A part that excessively masturbates.

Preventative Parts:
- A part that hides its desire to be liked.
- A part that says what other people want to hear.

Wounds:
- A part that feels unwanted.

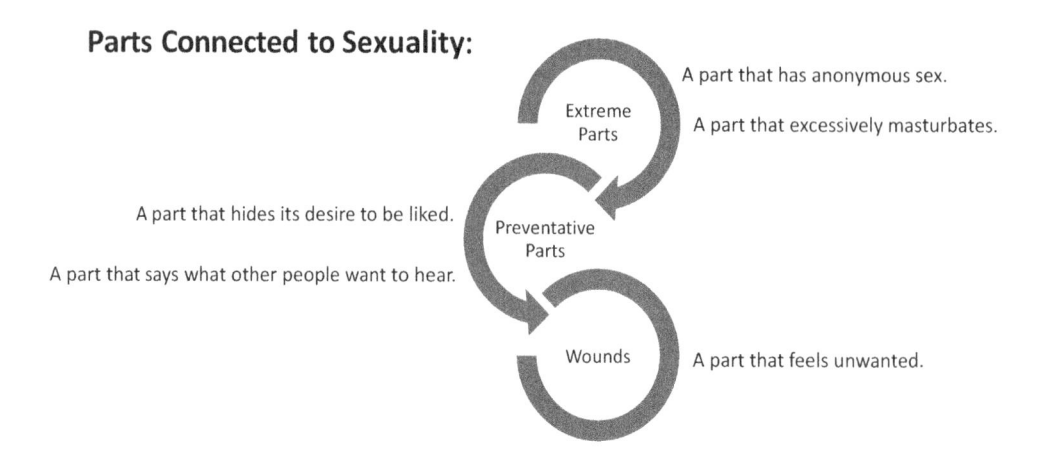

Self-Energy and Self-Adjacent Parts

As therapists, our own Self-energy (the calm, open-hearted, compassionate presence within us all) is vital to bring when working with sexual orientation. Self is also the state we hope to invite our clients into as they navigate the complex and challenging issues relating to orientation. As I've referenced in my book, *Transcending Trauma*, I believe Self-energy is a state of being. It lives in the mind and utilizes integrated neural networks in the brain to express itself. The Self connects to our internal energy, as well as the external energy in our environment. I experience the Self as a maximally integrative state in which all is connected and flows together in unison. It inherently has the knowledge and capacity to heal. Again, I do believe that sexual orientation is a component of Self-energy.

LGBTQIA+ individuals may have needed to develop parts that make connection with Self challenging. When a child grows up in an environment that is different from, or not supportive of, their natural feelings and desires, it is common for messages to be internalized such as "I am different," and "There must be something wrong with me." These are the burdened beliefs of exile parts. In order to survive, fit in the world, and prevent the activation of these exiles, protector parts take on jobs such as disconnecting from feelings, detaching from intuition, and severing the connection from the authentic Self. For those in the LGBTQIA+ community, there's much rejection and disavowing of the Self in order to survive. This disconnection tends to begin at an early age and continue for many years for those whose sexual orientation is different from the cultural norm. One way of surviving is to develop Self-adjacent parts (what some refer to as Self-like parts): parts whose job it is to mimic the qualities of Self to keep life running smoothly but who are not actually the Self. Skillful therapists will honor these Self-adjacent parts in clients and the critical role they have played in creating safety and maneuvering in an unwelcoming world. These resilient and resourceful parts are often *the unsung heroes* in the client's system and need to be appreciated and honored by therapist and client alike.

Sequence of Healing

Order is important in the healing process, particularly when there are complexities such as internal and external wounds; cultural, familial, and religious burdens; and relational repair with Self to be considered. The beauty of IFS is that it invites the client's Self to direct the order of healing that is right for their unique inner and outer system and avoids the imposing of therapist-led preferences on the process.

It can be helpful to map the order of healing to orient to the therapeutic process. With each client, I cluster the pieces of work, and invite the client's system to direct us. I might say, "So we've got your history of disconnection with your dad, the fact that your mom was depressed, being bullied at school, and you coming out and telling your friends and family. Let's go inside and see if your system can tell us what feels right to tackle first; what order of healing feels best for you?" By honoring parts and inviting the client's Self to choose the order of healing, we ensure the greatest chance of successful release of parts' wounds and the opportunity to experience sexual truth in connection to the authentic Self.

There is no right or wrong way to approach this order. Some clients will need to address issues relating to sexual orientation before moving on to past trauma. Others will choose the reverse (which I find is most common). Still others may toggle between the two, titrating the work as their system allows. A client might embrace their gay identity one day and reject it the next. It is important for therapists to trust the pace of the client's system and avoid pushing or resisting the coming out process. Each client's system knows its own unique "right" pacing and order.

Healing the Self-to-Part Relationship

As LGBTQIA+ individuals come to terms with their sexual orientation, there is often a need to repair the internal connection between the Self and parts. This relationship may have been severed in a variety of ways. It may have been unsafe for the individual to exhibit Self qualities such as confidence or authenticity—these qualities may have been viewed as threatening to the external world and punished or met with abuse. The construction of Self-adjacent parts is often a matter of survival from even the youngest age. Parts may hold anger, resentment and hurt from the felt experience of being abandoned by the Self and left alone to survive in a world that wasn't safe or welcoming. The trauma of being a sexual minority often leads to the burdening of exile parts which in turn leads to the development of protector parts, all of which obscure access to Self. For these and many other reasons, the Self and parts of LGBTQIA+ individuals often have experienced a great deal of separation. Thus, relational repair between Self and parts is a necessary first step before other healing work can be done.

There are a wide variety of parts that may need repair with Self. Parts that carry wounds may hold self-loathing, shame, a sense of unlovability, and powerlessness. Parts that protect may become burdened with extreme roles such as rage, self-harm, hyper-sexuality, withdrawal, disconnection, or sexual numbing. Systems often possess both sympathetically activated and parasympathetically blunted protective parts, which at times can rapidly switch from one extreme state to another. These seemingly self-sabotaging, potentially dangerous extremes are common, but it's important to compassionately remember that they ultimately serve a function of protection.

During the AIDS epidemic, I served as medical director of an HIV day treatment program, and several of the clients I worked with were consumed with self-hatred and self-loathing for having contracted HIV. Many engaged in unsafe sexual practices, and several felt unworthy of receiving love in a healthy, safe manner. Clients often believed that this was who they were, and what they deserved. I now hold compassion for the range of parts that were present in their system, protectors and exiles alike, that were doing their very best to survive in a hostile world with little or no access to Self-energy. Unblending from these tenacious parts can be challenging, so engaging in direct access (when the therapist's Self talks directly to the part) is a vital step in helping parts to separate. This paves the way for Self to gain permission from protective parts to access the vulnerable exiles they are working so hard to protect.

Identifying Wounded Parts

Multiple wounded parts can present in each person's system. However, shame and emotional wounds related to sexual orientation are ubiquitous in the lives of LGBTQIA+ individuals, and the internal exile dialogue can be excruciating: *I'm totally unacceptable. I'm disgusting. I'm completely unlovable.* The repetitive experience of exiling circumstances in LGBTQIA+ individuals' lives is a visceral reality that it is critical for the therapist to acknowledge and respect.

In addition to deeply embedded shame, there is often a profound sense of neglect for those wounded parts who have been isolated from the nuclear family, the local community, and mainstream society. Parts not only feel betrayed by the Self for being left behind, they also often feel abandoned by well-intended parents or primary caregivers. Neglected parts wonder, *Why didn't anybody see me? Why wouldn't anyone help me? Didn't anybody know what was going on?* Too often, no one was tracking or tending to them. No one was there for them. No one understood. And this betrayal happened over and over again leading to distorted beliefs such as: *I really must be horrible if my own parents, my family, my teachers, and friends don't notice or care about me.*

To date, I have never worked with an LGBTQIA+ person, who *doesn't* hold some amount of shame and neglect attached to their sexual orientation or gender. When mapping out a shame cycle with a client, first look at what the culture, society, and family of origin have said to them—the externalized shamer. Also look at the parts that internalized that energy and used the shame in the service of protection—the internal shamer. *You idiot, if you act different, people will like you.* Last there is the part that holds the shame itself—the exiled part. *I am bad., I am wrong., It must be my fault.*

The various parts that protect the shame wound (i.e., the critic, the sexual acting out, the suicidal impulses and actions, the numbing and the dissociation) also hold shame about their own behavior. There is complexity to effecting change within the system when there are so many layers of shame; external, internal, and held within the exile. Neglect wounds hold a similarly complex set of parts.

Past Trauma

To heal the inner system of parts, first, we identify the array of parts that are linked to orientation (i.e., sexuality, culture and society, family legacy, and gender), next we recognize the collection of parts that are related to relational or attachment trauma, usually originating from the past. It's important to remember that each system can have an internal and external landscape of parts connected to it. As you can see, this quickly becomes intricate and complicated, so clarity is key here.

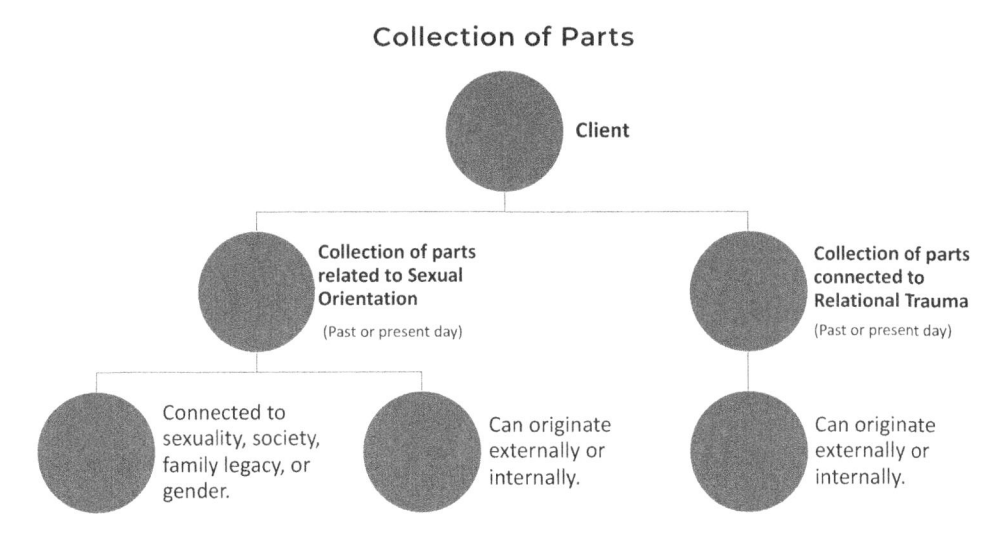

Collection of Parts

Client

Collection of parts related to Sexual Orientation
(Past or present day)

Collection of parts connected to Relational Trauma
(Past or present day)

Connected to sexuality, society, family legacy, or gender.

Can originate externally or internally.

Can originate externally or internally.

Coming Out

While keeping in mind all the complexity mentioned above, a vital component of offering skillful care around issues of sexual orientation is also developing familiarity with the stages of the coming out process.

It's important to be aware that, even for the younger generation, coming out is not an easy process. Even with today's more progressive and accepting cultural norms, depression, anxiety, suicidality, and self-harm within the gay community are alarmingly high. According to the Trevor Projects National Survey on

LGBTQIA+ Youth Mental Health in 2020, 75 percent of youth reported experiencing symptoms of anxiety, while 62 percent reported symptoms of major depression. 42 percent had suicidal ideation, and 12 percent attempted suicide within the year (the rate being 20 percent for trans and nonbinary youth). 72 percent experienced discrimination due to their sexual orientation or gender identity. Youth who had access to a supportive, affirming space reported lower rates of suicide attempts (8 percent vs. 20 percent).[12] That is why it is important to understand and bring genuine support and sensitivity to the coming out process, while holding an awareness of the potential difference between the inner and outer worlds.

When working with clients navigating their own sexual orientation, it is important to assess the safety and support of the external environment—the culture in which the person lives—while also being mindful to assess their internal landscape. Sometimes the external environment appears to be affirming and safe, but the person still internalizes the unspoken and subliminal toxic and harmful beliefs held by the environment, and of course, the reverse can also be true. Even in affirming and welcoming communities, the internal experience of a person's parts can still be heavily burdened as a result of multiple factors such as cultural beliefs, family legacy burdens, and complex trauma from the past. A person may have a loving, supportive family and still have parts that feel "wrong and broken."

These inner burdens happen in ways that are often unconscious. Well-intended parents are often unaware of their own internalized homophobia and stereotypic gender role biases. They may say things like, "Boys shouldn't wear pink," "Girls are gentle and kind," or "Boys don't play with dolls." As a child, I remember hearing a derogatory joke associated with gay men having sex, and when I was told what it meant, it was accompanied by a look and feeling of horror and disgust. This had a profound impact on me: *That's gross. I never want to be a part of that. People who do that are hated and made fun of.*

My children were raised by two dads, but growing up they didn't see their experience represented when they turned on the TV to watch Mickey Mouse, or Bob the Builder, or Caillou, for example. In most shows, everybody had a mommy and a daddy. The boys were tough and strong, and the girls were sweet and had tea parties. It was confusing for them, even though it wasn't explicitly stated. What becomes internalized often is unacknowledged. This is how internalized homophobia and shame becomes ubiquitous.

Stages of Coming Out

A current understanding of the coming out process is informed by an identity model developed by Vivienne Cass, as Australian clinical psychologist, and sex therapist.[13] Her model was one of the first to treat LGBTQIA+ people as normal in a heterosexist society instead of treating homosexuality and bisexuality themselves as problematic. She describes six stages of LGBTQIA+ identity development:

Stage 1. *Identity confusion.*
Stage 2. *Identity comparison.*
Stage 3. *Identity tolerance.*
Stage 4. *Identity acceptance.*
Stage 5. *Identity pride.*
Stage 6. *Identity synthesis.*

These stages are not necessarily linear or sequential. Some people go from stage one to stage four and then back to stage two, for example. Coming out is less of an event and more of a process which usually takes years. It's important for therapists to be aware of this timeframe because most individuals who come out have no idea how long it will take (as a result of never previously having gone through the stages).

I find it helpful with clients who are coming out to identify their parts related to each stage. Each of these stages of identity development can have *different parts* and *different wounds* associated with them, while at other times there is overlap. Stages one through three are connected to parts that are usually internal, and can be unrecognized for years, while stages four through six are connected to parts that are external (that interact in the world). For example, when shame is present—and it almost always is—stage three (identity tolerance) tends to be connected to the internal experience of shame, "I believe I'm gay," while stage four (identity acceptance) is related to external shame, and statements such as, "If I tell my parents I'm gay, they'll hate me and probably disown me."

Identity Confusion

Therapists will often meet clients in stage one, identity *confusion*, when they are developing awareness and asking whether they might be gay or lesbian. This process may be subconscious early on, only to slowly move into conscious awareness toward the end of stage one. The question of orientation itself is often terrifying and there can be a range of parts (e.g., denial, fear, hopelessness, uncertainty, hopefulness) associated with this stage. Particularly as young people progress through adolescence and become cognizant that their sexual desires differ from the norm, many polarized parts emerge internally to navigate this challenging inner emerging awareness.

Identity Comparison

In the *comparison* stage, individuals are looking to family, friends, and society for helpful points of reference. Often these comparisons cast an unfavorable light on the individual making them. Parts that come up in this stage include exiles that feel less-than, or different, as well as protective parts that begin masking. I remember looking at my uncles and my older male cousins and comparing myself to them. I would try to mimic their behaviors and mannerisms. Internally I'd ask, *Am I acting like them? Do I talk like they do?* These questions haunted me when I was just five and six years old. I was already in identity comparison because as far as I could tell, I did not act, talk, or feel like them—but I had no idea why at the time.

Identity Tolerance

It's one thing to be confused about who you are. It's another thing to compare yourself to who you think you should be. And it's yet another thing to begin to *tolerate* the differences and the discord that comes along with them. Parts that emerge in this stage often include shame, self-hatred, and self-harm, even for younger individuals who live in a more accepting environment. This stage is enormously difficult and requires great courage for anyone in the coming out process. Mapping the parts associated with this stage can be enormously helpful because unburdening wounded parts here will prevent clients from getting stuck, depressed, and suicidal while moving forward in their coming out process.

Identity Acceptance

At some point—which can take years or decades—a person's awareness of themselves shifts. There is an inner sense of congruence: *This is who I am. This is who I'm attracted to. And I'm okay with that.* This stage ushers in what Kort calls the "gay adolescence" because internal acceptance precipitates an external seeking of *belonging*.[14] In this developmental stage it is normal for different personas to be explored. Am I a jock? Am I a partier? Am I butch or femme? Do I belong in the leather community or prefer to dress in drag? This trying on of identities is an important part of gay identity and coming out, which is not a one-time event, but a process that often takes years, as individuals explore different aspects of themselves, find community, and experience belonging that they may never have experienced before. Common parts that arise in this stage relate to wounds of isolation and neglect from the past, as well as parts associated with the coming out process.

Identity Pride

Pride is a stage that brings enormous relief: *I feel good about who I am, and I'm happy to be a part of this community.* People sometimes remain here, in the belonging group for many years, and never branch out or move on. Sometimes this is due to reluctance to work through unresolved trauma from their past. "It feels so good to finally belong, I never want to leave this space and don't want to address the times in my life when I felt alone, isolated, and misunderstood." This is a time when LGBTQIA+ individuals tend to live, work, and play in same-identity spaces and soak in the safety and sense of belonging that accompany them.

Different protective parts can emerge in this stage, around the unfamiliarity of feeling happy or self-assured. "Is it really okay to feel good? Am I going to get attacked if I'm happy?"

This is often the stage where the intersection of past and present occurs. I personally struggled with embracing identity pride for many years because I'd experienced trauma as a result of simply being who I was. It felt dangerous to feel good and happy about being me, and my protective parts were organized around creating safety by keeping the real me hidden. For me, this stage involved a gradual transition into comfort, self-assurance, and self-confidence in my own identity, in my own skin.

Identity Synthesis

The sixth and final stage is *identity synthesis*, a time of settling and integration. Pride is internalized, shame and trauma have been released, and group identity has been resolved. In this stage the person feels good about themselves and comfortable holding a place in the world. In synthesis, people leave the safety of their orientation-defined community and become individuals in the larger world. When I first came out and went to Provincetown (a gay community in Massachusetts), people in the community warned me with a wink and a smile, "Come, have some fun, but don't get stuck here." I took their advice. I went to Provincetown, bought a house, and lived there for six years, Thursdays through Sundays. Then, I sold my house, had kids, and moved to the suburbs.

By then I could honestly say, *I'm okay with who I am, and I don't need a group to feel secure about myself. I love being a part of my community, but I'm also an individual who has a job and friends in the larger world.* After the several years it took me to fully come out. I no longer felt that there was something wrong with me. I felt comfortable with my sexuality and believed I deserved to be happy and hold a place in this world, just like everyone else.

Stage six often brings up parts dealing with loss and meaning. Again, it's a stage that requires looking at the past and letting go of what no longer serves. It may involve feeling the pain of what was, mourning the loss of what could have been, and comfortably settling into what is. At the intersection of identity synthesis is self-forgiveness and the forgiveness of others. This brings about true peace and happiness moving forward.

The stages of coming out activate a range of different parts, different subsystems of protectors and wounds, and different clinical goals and outcomes. IFS informs our work with each client's own unique inner and outer system by trusting their own inner Self-led wisdom, allowing their system to dictate the order and pacing of the work, and welcoming every part and honoring the wound it has carried, or the job it has had to take on, in order to ensure survival. As we help clients repair the relationship between their Self and parts, so parts release their burdens, clients come to a place of secure identity and an integrated sense of self that allows them to embody a full state of sexual and emotional wellness, with the ability to thrive in the world.

Conclusion

In summary, it is my belief that navigating issues of sexuality and sexual orientation for LGBTQIA+ clients is traumatic. Even for well-adjusted people in healthy and supportive external environments, holding and processing the shame that is inherently embedded in the coming out experience, takes time. Burdens need to be healed and released for the person to be authentically who they are. For those who identify as LGBTQIA+, the trauma of coming out is often proceeded by a lifetime of complex relational and societal trauma. For them, the process of coming to terms with their sexual orientation and healing their trauma presents unique challenges that deserve to be honored and processed in a safe, informed, and permission-granting context. When therapists tend to their own parts and show up with love, compassion, genuine curiosity, and Self energy, the chance of success increases exponentially.

KEY TAKEAWAYS

- It is important to become familiar with LGBTQIA+ terminology.
- Sexual orientation is an aspect of Self, not a part or a burden.
- Therapists have an ethical imperative to work with their own internalized homophobic parts and educate themselves about issues relating to sexual orientation.
- Mapping parts, and systems of parts, relating to sexual orientation provides a helpful guide for inner work.
- The client's inner system, not the therapist, directs the sequence of healing.
- Repair is often needed between Self and parts.
- The 6 stages of coming out are: identity confusion, comparison, tolerance, acceptance, pride, and synthesis.

AUTHOR BIO

Frank Anderson, MD (he/him) completed his residency and was a clinical instructor in psychiatry at Harvard Medical School. He is both a psychiatrist and psychotherapist. He specializes in the treatment of trauma and dissociation, and he is passionate about teaching brain-based psychotherapy and integrating current neuroscience knowledge with the IFS model of therapy.

Dr. Anderson is a Lead Trainer at the IFS Institute with Dr. Richard Schwartz and maintains a long affiliation with, and trains for, Bessel van der Kolk's Trauma Center. He serves as an advisor to the International Association of Trauma Professionals (IATP) and was the former chair and director of the Foundation for Self Leadership.

His most recent book, entitled *Transcending Trauma: Healing Complex PTSD with Internal Family Systems*, was released on May 19, 2021, and his forthcoming book, *To Be Loved: A Memoir of Truth, Triumph and Transformation*, will be released May 7, 2024. He maintains a private practice in Harvard, MA.

GOING DEEPER

From Dr. Frank Anderson

1) Website:
   a. www.FrankAndersonMD.com
2) Books:
   a. Anderson, F. G. (2021). *Transcending trauma: Healing complex PTSD with Internal Family Systems therapy.* PESI Publishing and Media
   b. Anderson, F. G., Sweezy, M., & Schwartz, R. C. (2017). *Internal Family Systems skills training manual: Trauma-informed treatment for anxiety, depression, PTSD & substance abuse.* PESI Publishing & Media.
3) Podcast Interviews:
   a. www.frankandersonmd.com/podcasts
4) Trainings and Consultations:
   a. www.frankandersonmd.com/courses/ifs-trauma-consultation-group

EMBODYING IFS WITH TRANS AND/OR NONBINARY COMMUNITIES

ALL GENDERS WELCOME

Sand C. Chang, PhD

The material in this chapter is a culmination of over 20 years of clinical experience providing trauma-informed care to trans and/or nonbinary clients. I am a Chinese American queer, trans, nonbinary, genderfluid person living on occupied Kumeyaay land, also known as San Diego, CA. I am upper middle class, non-disabled, non-religious, spiritual, sober, and living in an average sized body. I do not speak for all trans and/or nonbinary people, and I am aware that my lens is very much situated in the global North. I write from both personal and professional experience, and I am passing down information that I have learned from generations of trancestors and trans liberation movement workers.

In my early IFS training, I did not receive information on how the model could be best applied to trans and/or nonbinary communities. I am sad to say that there is much work to be done to make IFS more accessible to people of all genders. What I have shared about applications of IFS is based on my experience as a client and as a therapist to trans and/or nonbinary clients. I would like to acknowledge and express gratitude for the other IFS therapists who I have collaborated with in teaching IFS to trans and queer communities: Nic Wildes, Sundaura Lithman, Griffen Jeffries, Lance Hicks, Kai Thigpen, and Lisa Gallegos. I share these learnings with the hopes that trans and/or nonbinary communities might be able to access IFS as a vehicle for healing and liberation within the context of a safe and affirming therapeutic relationship.

Trans and/or nonbinary communities are diverse and varied; therefore, as with any particular cultural or demographic group, it is difficult to write a chapter that can be universally applied. In fact, this is one of the biggest challenges in gender affirming health care and mental health treatment: holding awareness of the larger systemic issues that affect trans and/or nonbinary communities while also centering the needs of each individual and their specific circumstances, backgrounds, and experiences.

You may be wondering who is included when I use the term trans and/or nonbinary in this chapter. The short answer is: Anyone who considers themself to be trans and/or nonbinary. The longer answer is: Trans and/or nonbinary people who have a felt sense of gender that does not fully align with societal expectations based on sex assigned at birth. I use "and/or" here intentionally to communicate that some, but not all, trans people are nonbinary. And some, but not all, nonbinary people are trans. When I use the term trans and/or nonbinary, I am including:

- Anyone who self-identifies as trans and/or nonbinary, regardless of how others/society may perceive them.
- People who use any number of terms (sometimes more than one) to describe their gender, including trans man, trans woman, trans masculine, trans feminine, nonbinary, genderqueer, gender neutral, agender, gender fluid, gender nonconforming, and more.
- People who are seeking gender-affirming medical interventions to change their bodies or appearance, as well as people who do not desire or cannot access these medical services.
- People who have genders that fit into a binary gender system, as well as people who either do not relate to this binary, relate to both sides of the binary, or fluidly move between them.
- People who face interpersonal and institutional barriers due to western, colonialist, binary, cis-centric views of gender.[1]

Like everyone else, trans people have life experiences that are shaped by other aspects of social and cultural identity; for example, race, ethnicity, religion, socioeconomic class, ability, neurotype, body size, and more. It is important to keep intersectionality in mind, which includes not just a person's intersections of identities, but also the systems of power and oppression that accompany these identities. Many trans people, due to systemic discrimination, have experienced barriers to accessing material resources, including those that may support a person's transition or what they need to be perceived accurately by others.[2]

Awareness of trans people has increased significantly over the past decade, however, there is a great deal of misinformation and very limited representations of the diversity of trans and/or nonbinary communities in the media. In my experience, most health care professionals are not trained to consider gender beyond the binaries of male/female, man/woman, or masculine/feminine. In addition, many people mistakenly conflate gender identity with sexual orientation (sometimes because the acronym LGBTQIA+ suggests that this is one community rather than many subcommunities). But again, in my experience, the needs of trans and/or nonbinary people and clients, particularly when it comes to the practice of IFS therapy, are distinctly different from the needs of people who are gay, lesbian, bisexual, or queer in terms of sexual orientation, attraction, and relationship.

This chapter provides foundational information about trans and/or nonbinary communities and how to apply Internal Family Systems (IFS) therapy in a way that is culturally responsive and inclusive to clients who belong to these communities. My hope is that the information provided in this chapter can benefit IFS practitioners of all genders, including trans and cis practitioners, who work with trans clients. This chapter may also aid readers working with clients who are cis but who have been harmed by the imposition of the binary gender system.

Unlearning to Learn

One of the biggest challenges to learning how to be an ally to trans and/or nonbinary people and provide affirming care is that we all come with a lifetime of baggage around gender! There's so much stuff crammed into that baggage that sometimes it can feel like there's no room for anything new, anything different from what we've carried around our whole lives. In order to learn how to truly live and embody gender liberation, we have to unpack and examine the things that we forgot we were even carrying, things that we just thought were part of us or part of normal, everyday existence. Most of us have parts that hold assumptions about what it means to be a man or a woman, how people in these categories are supposed to act, dress, talk, or interact with others, and so on. As is often the case with socialized norms, our parts can take on these beliefs so strongly that we aren't even aware of them. Living within a sexist and patriarchal society, most of us, even people who carry relative privilege within this system, have parts that carry burdens with respect to gender. In other words, none of us approach working with gender with a blank slate. In order to learn how to work respectfully and effectively with trans people, we have to be willing to *unlearn* everything we have taken for granted as the truth about gender and gendered bodies.

Unlearn *everything?* At this point your protectors may want to jump in with questions or even active resistance against the thought. What I want to let them know is that there is no right or wrong way to be in your body or gender, but unlearning what has been assumed can make space for greater choice. Sometimes it's helpful to hold things up to the light so that you can see if they're still worth holding onto or if it's time to let them go.

The following meditation is provided to help you connect with the parts of you that have been affected by gender training and socialization.

IFS MEDITATION ON GENDERED EXPERIENCES

Start by getting into a comfortable position. Take some time to arrive here at this very moment, wherever you are. Sit up tall, feel your feet on the floor or wherever they are, and feel the support of the chair or seat underneath you.

Become aware of your breathing and gradually deepen your breath. Breathing in, breathing out…slowly breathing in, holding for a moment, and then exhaling slowly. Try to have your inhalations be the same length as your exhalations. You can count to five while you inhale, and count to five as you exhale. Keep doing this for a few rounds of breath.

Now turn your attention to what feelings and thoughts are present with you in this moment, acknowledging that there may be many, and some of them may even seem contradictory. Maybe there's a part of you that's tired. Maybe a part of you that is excited or nervous. Maybe a part that is scared. Notice if there's a part of you that is judging or going into protective mode. Notice the parts of you that are resisting this exercise. Just notice whatever comes up. You can even thank those parts of you for working so hard to protect and guide you. There is room for all of these parts of you, all the feelings that are present in this moment.

Now take a moment to acknowledge the part of you that is aware of your own experience of being gendered in the world, whether you wanted it or not. If there is pain, or confusion, or discomfort of any kind, just notice that. If there is an absence of feeling, just notice that. See if you can get curious. I invite you to allow yourself to notice all the ways in which your own gendered experiences are present today in your learning. If that's difficult, that's okay too. Just notice that. If you can, bring compassion to those parts of you.

If there is a part of you that is concerned about image, or about appearing smart or like a "good therapist" or "good trans ally" or is afraid of making mistakes, perhaps you can offer some compassion to that part as well. Maybe you can let that part of you know that it can rest, that it doesn't have to work so hard, or that it can pull back so that you can feel more connected and grounded. I invite you to bring the qualities of curiosity and compassion to the different parts of you that might have feelings about gender, whether it be your own gender or other people's genders.

Keep breathing as you notice what is coming up for you.

Now take your time to slowly read through the following series of statements. For each one, just notice the feelings and reactions that come up. Try your best to just allow yourself to feel whatever you feel, without judging or needing to fix or change anything. Pause if needed to take time to acknowledge and witness the parts that are responding. Notice if the following statements are true for you:

1. You have ever worn makeup, shaved your legs or underarms, or worn nylons.
2. You were ever told not to cry.
3. You have ever worried you were not tough enough.
4. You've ever been asked if you were a boy or a girl.
5. You ever changed your diet or exercised to change your body size, shape, or weight or to appear more masculine or feminine.
6. You have ever been called a wimp, queer, or sissy.
7. You have ever been told to act like a man or you told someone else to act like a man.
8. You ever felt limited in what careers were open to you based on your gender.
9. You've ever been so afraid to use a gender-segregated public restroom that you ended up in pain, or with an infection.
10. You have ever been forced to fight, or were in a fight, because you felt you had to prove yourself.
11. You were ever told not to do something because it wasn't ladylike, or you told someone else not to do something because it wasn't ladylike.
12. You've ever not known what to check in the "gender" box on a job application.
13. You've ever felt happy when someone referred to you with a different gender pronoun than the one associated with your sex assigned at birth.
14. You ever limited your activity or changed your plans to go somewhere out of fear for your physical safety.
15. You've ever had security called on you because someone thought you were in the wrong bathroom.
16. You've ever not worn something you liked because you were worried it would look too feminine or too masculine.
17. You know or know of someone who is trans and/or nonbinary.
18. Someone close to you is trans and/or nonbinary.
19. You have ever felt shame in using the wrong name or pronoun for a trans and/or nonbinary person.
20. You have ever felt defensive after using the wrong name or pronoun for a trans and/or nonbinary person.

These statements may have brought up different feelings, different parts of you. Let these reactions be sources of information for you about where to offer some attention or care, or where you may want to commit to learning more. No matter what has come up for you, see if you can just let it know that it belongs…see if you can send some compassion. We have all been affected by gender training, and we have all participated in it. Keep in mind that while few of us were willing participants in systems of gender-based oppression, we are all accountable for the parts of us that continue to engage with them or even parts of us that benefit from them.

In this last moment, I want you to set an intention, knowing that it's okay to not be in that intention perfectly, but that that's what it is…just an intention.

Take three more deep breaths, and when you are ready, continue reading. You may also choose to take a break and resume later. You may want to jot down some notes about what came up for you or what you want to return to. Do whatever feels like the most caring thing for you and your parts. Send appreciation to whatever parts allowed themselves to be known or seen by you. Thank yourself for taking the time to reflect.

Foundations of Gender Affirming Care

In this section, you will learn about best practices for using affirming language with trans and/or nonbinary people. You will be introduced to some key concepts and terms. You will then learn skills for respectful interactions as well as tips on how to repair after making a mistake. While you are reading along, try to maintain an awareness of your parts and your own gendered experiences in the world.

1. Using Respectful, Affirming Language

Language matters. When it comes to describing aspects of social or cultural identity, the words we use have the power to affirm or deny a person's truth about who they are. Whether intentional, as in the case of blatant hate speech or name-calling, or unintentional, as in the case of microaggressions, words can influence a person's sense of safety or wellbeing. Many people are still unfamiliar with or confused by trans and/or nonbinary people, identities, and experiences. As a result, trans and/or nonbinary people are subject to harmful or inaccurate speech quite frequently in their everyday lives.

Language is ever evolving, and when it comes to the terminology used to refer to gender or other aspects of trans and/or nonbinary experience, considering context is essential. There is no universal language to refer to trans and/or nonbinary people because there is no universal, monolithic trans community. The language that is considered affirming to some may not be to others. Language can vary greatly based on age, cohort/generation, demographic or cultural background, and geographic location. Much of the commonly accepted or widely used language with respect to trans experiences and identities is situated in the global North. Considering the wide variations in language and communication, we as IFS practitioners should strive to center the self-determination of each individual, as well as follow that person's lead.

The following terms, concepts, and recommendations reflect current practices in using affirming language. *Note: The more commonly used terms are included for the purposes of this book, but many more terms can be used to describe gender identity.*

2. Applying Key Terms and Concepts

Anti-trans bias or transphobia: Fear, mistrust, hatred, or disbelief of trans and/or nonbinary people. This may be expressed in negative attitudes/beliefs or exclusionary behaviors.

Ciscentrism: A system of oppression that privileges the experiences and rights of cisgender people and pathologizes, erases, or others the experiences of trans and/or nonbinary people.

Cisgender: Adjective to describe people whose sex assigned at birth and gender identity are aligned. A person who is assigned male at birth and who considers himself a man would typically be considered a cisgender man. A person who is assigned female at birth and who considers herself a woman would typically be considered a cisgender woman.

Gender binary (or binary gender system): A system based on White, Western, colonialist ideals, that categorizes people into two mutually exclusive categories of male/man/masculine and female/woman/feminine.

Gender dysphoria. An experience of distress that some, but not all, trans and/or nonbinary people report in relation to their sex assigned at birth or how they are (mis)perceived by others. It is also a mental health diagnosis that is used to justify the medical necessity for gender-affirming medical care. Gender dysphoria may be general or more specific to one body part (e.g., breasts, genitals). Not all trans and/or nonbinary people have gender dysphoria.

Gender expansive: This term is sometimes used to describe a community of people whose genders are not cisgender; it is often used to describe youth. This is more often used to describe a community ("gender expansive youth") than an individual label or gender identity.

Gender expression: This refers to how a person expresses their gender outwardly. This may include clothing, hairstyle, mannerisms, and more.

Gender identity: This refers to who a person knows themself to be in terms of gender. This may or may not be visible or apparent to outside observers. Some examples of gender identities include man, woman, nonbinary, genderqueer, agender, gender neutral, and more. It is not necessary to know or memorize exact definitions of each gender identity; the most important thing is to believe someone and mirror back the language that people use to refer to themselves.

Nonbinary: Adjective to describe a person whose gender does not fully align with binary gender categories (male versus female, man versus woman, masculine versus feminine). There are many different kinds of gender identities that are considered part of the nonbinary category. Some nonbinary people consider themselves to be both, neither, or fluidly moving between binary gender identities of man and woman.

Self-identification or self-determination: The idea that not all aspects of a person's identity can be determined objectively or perceived accurately by others. Therefore, it is necessary to rely on each individual's inherent sense of their own identity and the language (e.g., name, pronouns) the individual designates to describe who they are with respect to gender or any other cultural identity (e.g., sexual orientation, race).

Sex assigned (or predicted) at birth: This refers to the sex that is assigned or predicted, typically by a medical provider, and is indicated on a person's birth certificate, typically M or F.

Trans (or transgender): Adjective used to describe a person whose gender is not fully aligned with the gender associated with sex assigned at birth. Some people simply consider themselves trans, while others refer to themselves as trans men, transgender men, trans women, or transgender women.

Transition. A process, not an event, that some, not all, trans and/or nonbinary people choose in order to feel more at home in their bodies and/or the world. Transition may include social transition (e.g., changes in gender expression, gender role, name, pronoun, and gender marker) and medical transition (e.g., hormone therapy, surgeries). Not all trans and/or nonbinary people desire medical transition, and many who do cannot afford to do so.

Trans man, transgender man, on the trans masculine spectrum: A trans or transgender man, or someone on the trans masculine spectrum, is someone whose identity is as a man regardless of being assigned female at birth. Trans men should be referred to the way other (cisgender) men are referred to (typically with he/him/his pronouns) unless otherwise indicated.

Trans woman, transgender woman, on the trans feminine spectrum: A trans or transgender woman, or someone on the trans feminine spectrum, is someone whose identity is as a woman regardless of being assigned male at birth. Trans women should be referred to the way other (cisgender) women are referred to (typically with she/her/hers pronouns) unless otherwise indicated.

Two-Spirit (sometimes denoted as 2S): This is a term used in some Indigenous cultures to describe people who may have a gender that does not fit into the binary gender system. Oftentimes, Two-Spirit people may have traits or gender expressions of more than one gender. This term should only be used by and for people who are Indigenous.

The following terms should be avoided, as they are not, or are no longer considered, affirming or inclusive:

Biological male or male-bodied, biological female or female-bodied: These terms rely on physiological or genital determination instead of self-determination to indicate a person's gender. Saying someone has a male or female body does not give adequate or accurate information about that person's gender, body, or medical needs.

"Both" men and women: This terminology is binary and exclusive. A more inclusive alternative is "people of all genders."

Cisgendered or transgendered: There should be no "ed" on the end of these words.

Opposite sex: This concept is outdated and inaccurate. Men and women are not opposites; they are different from each other under a diverse range of genders. A more inclusive alternative is "someone of a different gender."

"Preferred" (name or pronouns): Names and pronouns are typically not a preference. Simply refer to them as a person's pronouns.

Sex change: There is no such thing as a sex change; there are many different medical interventions that a person can choose in order to feel more affirmed in their gender and/or bodies. ***Transgenders:*** Trans and transgender are adjectives, not nouns. It is disrespectful to refer to people in this way.

Transgenders: Trans and transgender are adjectives, not nouns. It is disrespectful to refer to people in this way.

Transvestite: This is typically a derogatory term that is based in a Western, pathologizing psychiatric model and is not used by people in trans and/or nonbinary communities.

Transsexual: This term is outdated, but there are still people who use this term to refer to themselves. Therefore, avoid using this term to refer to individuals or groups of people unless you know that the person/group uses this term.

3. Respecting Self-Determination

It's important to use the most affirming terms to refer to someone. These are the terms that the person has designated for themself and that are in line with their sense of who they are. The correct name to use for someone is the name that the person designates or chooses for themself, regardless of legal name.

Pronouns are units of speech that are used when speaking about someone in third person. In English, we typically use the gendered pronoun sets or series of he/him/his and she/her/hers. It is important to use the correct pronoun when referring to someone; failing to do so, whether intentional or unintentional, can be hurtful. The correct pronouns to use to refer to someone are the pronouns that the person designates or chooses for themself, regardless of their name, gender identity, or gender expression. Examples of pronouns: she/her/hers, he/him/his, xe/xem/xyr, they/them/their, ze/hir/hirs, ey/em/eirs (among others). Some people use more than one set of pronouns, such as he/him/his and they/them/their. When this is the case, you may want to challenge yourself to alternate in using both sets of pronouns. If you tend to default to the pronouns that are more familiar or easier for you to use, challenge yourself to practice using the less comfortable or familiar set of pronouns.

A special note about gender neutral pronouns: In the English language, there is no widely used gender neutral pronoun. Therefore, it can take extra intention and practice to use more unfamiliar pronouns with more ease. The singular form of the pronouns they/them/their has been used in literature dating back to as early as the fourteenth century, including by respected authors such as Chaucer, Shakespeare, and Austen (Young, 2019). If you have a part that can get really stuck on grammar, this is a place where it may need some updating so that it understands that the singular use of they/them/their is grammatically acceptable. We want to center respect for others' self-determination while working with the parts of us that want to refute, argue, or are scared of change.

Maintaining Openness with Transgender and/or Nonbinary People Seeking Therapy

Trans and/or nonbinary people seek therapy, counseling, or coaching for a wide variety of reasons. Some want to work on concerns pertaining to gender, while others are simply looking for a practitioner that they do not need spend time (and money) educating about gender or trans and/or nonbinary experiences. Therapists and practitioners commonly make the mistake of over fixating on a client's trans experience, even becoming deskilled in providing care that they are skilled and competent to offer to cisgender clients. For example, some practitioners assume that every trans person who appears in their office is interested in talking about gender or sharing their gender history when in fact clients may have concerns that are unrelated to gender. Practitioners may have parts that tend to generalize, especially if exposure to and experience working with trans and/or nonbinary clients is limited. Keep in mind that working with one trans and/or nonbinary client does not automatically grant expertise in working with all other potential clients who are trans and/or nonbinary.

When in doubt, return to the eight Cs of Self-leadership: Calm, Clarity, Confidence, Courage, Curiosity, Creativity, Connection, and Compassion. My colleague, Nic Wildes, and I often include a ninth "C"—Community/Collectivism—which we define as the capacity to be mindful and caring of those around us, maintaining awareness of how one's liberation is inherently connected to the liberation of others, including people who experience marginalizations that are different from our own. This additional "C" can be the cornerstone for IFS to foster collective liberation.

Recognize Therapist Parts

Most therapists and practitioners did not receive formal training in working with trans and/or nonbinary communities. A growth mindset and stance of humility (which are related to Curiosity, one of the 8 Cs) will go a long way in working with trans and/or nonbinary clients. Here are some special considerations for cisgender and trans and/or nonbinary practitioners.

If you are cisgender, it's important to keep in mind the long history of harm that trans and/or nonbinary communities have experienced at the hands of cisgender mental health providers. A history of formal gatekeeping dates back to the 1950s in the U.S. (Chang, Singh, & Dickey, 2018; Denny, 2002). Even if you have the best of intentions and consider yourself an ally, clients may not feel safe immediately with you. Take time to build rapport, to name and own your own cisgender identity and privilege, and to be ready to be part of a repair process even if you, personally, did not engage in the harm. If there are things that are confusing or that you don't understand regarding trans and/or nonbinary people and their experiences, take time to educate yourself. Seek consultation, read, watch films, listen to podcasts. There are lots of resources out there! Taking an active stance in learning more will prevent you from relying on your clients to educate you (which is a common experience that clients have when working with cisgender therapists).

If you are a trans and/or nonbinary practitioner, you will want to be aware of your own parts and your own experiences that may or may not be similar to those of your clients. Many trans and/or nonbinary practitioners share that they have parts that identify with our clients' experiences, and if they have not done work with their own parts this could be a barrier to being able to help a client in their growth and healing with respect to that particular part or concern. A very common concern is being part of a gatekeeping establishment; sometimes this can result in a part that denies the fact that as practitioners we often do hold gatekeeping power that we cannot deny. We may have to work with the parts of us that do not want to be part of harmful establishments or be seen as the enemy to our own communities (especially in the case of writing letters for gender-affirming medical interventions). We may have fears of harming our clients in the ways that we have been harmed, which can lead to necessary thoughtfulness but could possibly lead to blending with parts that want to be liked or who do not want to upset the client in any way.

Because most of us were socialized in a transphobic world, we are all susceptible to anti-trans bias or binary bias (even trans and/or nonbinary people!). Here are some common misconceptions and microaggressions to be aware of and what these parts might sound like, as well as what it might look and sound like for a response to be more affirming (and perhaps unburdened):

Common reactions to trans clients (from burdened parts)	Gender-affirming responses
A part that conflates gender identity and sexual orientation, assuming that all trans and/or nonbinary people are gay or that they transition in order to be heterosexual (remember, there are gay trans men and lesbian trans women).	Awareness that gender identity and sexual orientation are separate constructs that may be more or less related depending on the individual; awareness that trans and/or nonbinary people have a wide range of sexual orientations.
A part that gets very uncomfortable when a client does not conform to gender roles or stereotypes. "I can't believe he was wearing a dress."	Being comfortable with people of all genders wearing whatever they want to wear.
A part that feels compelled to know what a person's gender is or what their assigned sex was, typically within a binary framework. "Is the person a man or a woman?"	Feeling comfortable not knowing what someone's gender or assigned sex is/was.
A part that assumes that every presenting concern must be related to gender or trans and/or nonbinary identity.	Understanding that trans and/or nonbinary clients come into therapy for concerns unrelated to gender, just like cisgender people do.
A part that feels helpless or entitled, leading to demands on the client to provide education. "I don't know anything about that; please educate me. Please tell me when I make a mistake."	Feeling a sense of agency and empowerment in doing one's own research or reading to learn about trans communities and experiences. Taking responsibility rather than having an expectation for trans clients to educate their providers.
A part that firmly believes that a binary gender system is an absolute truth or the normal, healthy, or right way to express gender.	Understanding of and comfort with a system of gender that is broad and goes beyond a binary system; an understanding of trans and/or nonbinary identities as normal parts of human diversity; humility regarding other people's genders and how they are expressed.

A part that wants to avoid gender or deny the importance of it: "I don't see gender."	A balanced and nuanced understanding of the role and importance of gender; knowing that gender is significant in many ways and cannot be erased while also knowing that it does not define a person; an awareness of the larger social systems that create real differences in how people navigate and experience the world.
A part that pathologizes trans and/or nonbinary identities or treats them as synonymous with having gender dysphoria.	Understanding that some, not all, trans and/or nonbinary people have gender dysphoria; understanding that trans and/or nonbinary people are not defined by a psychiatric diagnosis.
A part that thinks all trans and/or nonbinary people are sick or mentally ill. May be quick to pathologize a trans and/or nonbinary person or their parts as defensive, guarded, non-compliant, or even personality disordered.	An understanding that systemic barriers increase the risk for mental health problems; an awareness that being trans and/or nonbinary does not mean someone has mental health problems.
A part that believes that if a trans and/or nonbinary person only gets the right therapy or works through their trauma, they will not have to be trans and/or nonbinary or transition. This is extremely dangerous as this part may engage in practices akin to conversion therapies, which are ineffective, harmful, and unethical.	Understanding that trans people and non-trans people may have trauma, and medically necessary treatment should not be withheld from anyone based on gender; awareness that trans people should not be held to a higher standard of mental health than non-trans or cisgender people.
A part that is fascinated and may ask intrusive questions about people's gender histories, bodies, medical histories, surgical histories, or sexual practices.	Maintaining appropriate boundaries and only asking questions that are clinically relevant; being mindful that curiosity is not the same as clinical rationale.

A part that engages in body appraisal by making comments (positive or negative) about a trans and/or non-binary person's appearance, whether they successfully pass, etc. "You look so good I never would have known you were trans!"	Maintaining appropriate boundaries and refraining from commenting on others' appearances without consent.
A part that believes that the external perceiver, particularly health care professionals are the "experts" who can determine whether someone is "really" trans or ready to transition. May be overly protective to the point of being paternalistic or gatekeeping.	Trusting that trans people are the experts on who they are; respecting self-identification, self-determination, and bodily autonomy. Using harm reduction models when put in position of gatekeeping (e.g., writing letters).
A part that tries really hard to be a good ally, sometimes to the point of centering oneself instead of the other person. May want to be liked or seek approval.	Centering those most marginalized and de-centering one's image; knowing that true allyship is about action and may not always garner recognition.
A part that collapses into grief or rage when hearing injustice.	Taking care of one's own parts so that one's reaction does not overshadow the client's needs or feelings.
A part that over fixates on individual change and may minimize protector fears or concerns about external barriers.	Understanding of how crucial it is to be aware of external or environmental barriers and their impact on trans people; validating clients' experiences.
A part that assumes shared experience because of proximity (e.g., being gay or lesbian, having a trans partner, or even being trans oneself).	Refraining from making assumptions; knowing about common/general themes related to trans experience but centering the lived experience of each individual.
A part that envies a client who feels more free in their gender or who may have access to certain privileges that the provider does not have.	Welcoming a diversity of experiences without feeling threatened.
A part that feels nervous to work with a client because of dual relationships or small community concerns.	Maintaining appropriate boundaries; knowing when there is nuance and dual relationships are unavoidable; seeking consultation as appropriate.

Here's a question worth considering, regardless of your gender: *Would I be comfortable seeing a trans and/or nonbinary therapist for my own medical or mental health care?* Ask yourself this question and notice how your parts respond. Your own reactions or thoughts (and possibly the biases they reflect) can be the rubric that helps you identify which of your parts need to be tended to in order to effectively work with trans and/or nonbinary communities. If you would not feel comfortable seeing a trans and/or nonbinary practitioner yourself, that is a sign that you may need to take time to learn more and work with your parts before taking on a trans and/or nonbinary client.

Accountability and Repair

Mistakes happen, and ideally, they lead to learning, growth, and repair. This is how true allyship develops: not by being perfect, but by applying lessons learned and changing behavior. For IFS practitioners, this also includes working with our own parts that may either carry bias, perfectionism, or have a hard time with owning and apologizing for mistakes.

I cannot emphasize this next point enough: When our behavior harms people, it is often because we are blended with a burdened part. *While harmful behavior may be due to a part, we cannot bypass accountability by simply blaming it on that part. We must own that we are each responsible for our parts and their impact on others, no matter how good our intentions are.*

When mistakes happen, these are common burdened parts that tend to show up:

- A part that makes excuses or wants to explain/justify why the mistake happened.
- A part that believes that it's not capable of change (e.g., "I'm too old for this.").
- A part that gets defensive.
- A part that denies the impact of the harm (e.g., "Why is this such a big deal?").
- A part that wants to prove allyship through proximity (e.g., "I have a trans sibling.").
- A part that wants to blame the other person (e.g., "Why is this person getting so upset?").
- A part that apologizes profusely or wants assurance or forgiveness.
- A part that spirals into shame or self-flagellation.
- A part that has a hard time not being right or being an expert.
- A part that wants to point the finger at the other person being blended or not being Self-led. Keep in mind that it's not always safe for protectors to unblend after being harmed.

- A part that wants to center intention over impact.
- A part that goes into victim mode (e.g., "This is just as hard for me.").

The best thing we can do after making a mistake is to pause or slow down. This is the perfect time to do a "U-turn/you-turn" (Schwartz & Sweezy, 2019). This will make it more possible to ground or return to Self-leadership and to spend time with the parts that need attention from us. Ideally, this will prevent further harm from occurring. So much of the time, the initial harm is exponentially exacerbated by a lack of accountability or genuine efforts to repair and restore trust.

So, what do we do when the external world calls for a timely response, yet our parts are not ready? The good news is that we have choices, and we can speak for our parts. We can say, "I get that I harmed you with my mistake, and I am committed to spending time with my parts so that I can do better," or "I have parts that are having strong reactions, and I am committed to returning to this conversation when I know I will not cause more harm and when I am more capable of repair."

When we are ready, we can offer the opportunity to repair, keeping in mind that the other person may or may not be ready or available for that. Keep in mind that being misgendered is typically very distressing (even if there are protector parts that do not allow the hurt to be witnessed by others). The following list provides some guidelines for effective, accountable, Self-led repair after you have participated in a gender-related harm or microaggression.

Components of Self-led Repair:

1. Connect to Self-energy as much as possible, especially to the qualities of Compassion, Calm, Courage, Curiosity, and Connection.
2. Show appreciation: "Thank you for telling me. I know that this is emotional labor."
3. Acknowledge and own the mistake: "I misgendered you by using the wrong pronouns."
4. Apologize: "I am really sorry."
5. Commit to behavioral change: "I am committed to changing my behavior so that I do not cause further harm."
6. Be open to listening and learning: "I am open to hearing anything that you need to say."
7. Follow up by doing whatever is necessary on your end to prevent the mistake from happening again (read, educate yourself, seek support from others).

Gender Inclusive IFS

Being able to apply IFS in an affirming way with trans and/or nonbinary clients involves a), acquiring the essential awareness, knowledge, and skills to provide affirming care and avoid common harms; and b) learning specific ways that the IFS model can be adapted to address the specific needs of these communities. We can start with looking at how to think about gender and parts.

At the 2018 IFS conference, my colleague Nic Wildes presented a workshop entitled, "Is gender a part?" In our collaborations and co-teaching, we have led conversations to help people examine this question and related ones. The short answer is: "No. Gender is not a part." It's not a part any more than race is a part or having a certain eye color is a part. We can have parts that have reactions to these aspects of who we are or who have had experiences, both positive and negative, related to these aspects of who we are. But no, gender does not stand alone as a part. In fact, it's likely that many of our parts have reactions to being gendered in the world.

Let's look at a related question: "Do parts have a gender?" The answer to this is: "Yes, sometimes, often, but not always." There is no one way to have a gender, or to be a woman, or to be a trans man, or to be a nonbinary person. So, there isn't any one way for a part to express having a gender (or lack thereof). Cisgender people often have parts that have genders or gender expressions that are different from who they are in their lives; however, having parts with different genders does not make a person trans and/or nonbinary and certainly does not equal lived experience as trans and/or nonbinary in the world.

Most people have experienced some kind of pain or trauma related to gender, and it's important to remember that these are often legacy or cultural burdens. A trans and/or nonbinary client may have a trailhead that seems specific to present challenges, but often there are deeper familial or cultural factors that are relevant. Therapists who are struggling to provide affirming care to trans and/or nonbinary clients are likely to have parts that carry legacy or cultural burdens with respect to their own gendered experiences. For example, a cis woman who has experienced a great deal of sexism or misogyny may struggle to see that she has gender-based (cis) privilege. It is important for cis practitioners to do their own healing work around gender, as neglecting to do so can lead to invalidating or other forms of harm toward trans and/or nonbinary clients.

Key Tips and Considerations

Here are some key tips for applying IFS in a way that is affirming and inclusive of people of all genders, including trans and/or nonbinary people. These tips can be applied toward working with cisgender people, since many cisgender people have parts that are a different gender from what they are in their everyday lives.

1. Do not assume the gender or pronouns of a part. If you find yourself automatically gendering a part (in your head or in your speech), pause and check in with the parts of you that you may be blended with. Ask these parts if they would be willing to give you space so that you can be open to however this part is showing up.
2. Refrain from using any gendered pronouns for parts. You may use "it" to refer to the part unless/until the client uses a pronoun (e.g., she, he, they) for the part. Example: "How are you feeling towards this part?... Let it know that you really get what it's sharing with you."
3. You can ask the client what a part's pronouns are, but it's not really necessary. It's better to just wait and follow the client's lead.
4. When a client identifies a young part, do not assume the gender of that part. Do not refer to it as a "little boy" or "little girl." Not all parts are the same gender as the client. Alternatives you can use include, "the part" or "the little one" or "this younger part."
5. Do not assume that all parts have a gender (or are even human-like).
6. Do not assume that all parts have a static, binary gender (male/man or female/woman). Some may be nonbinary, fluid, agender, etc. Some parts may show up one way during one session and a different way during a different session.
7. If you have a part that is curious about your client's gender or gender history, pause to check in with your parts. Only ask about gender if it is relevant to what the client is sharing.
8. Refrain from assuming or making comments about shared experience based on gender, such as "We women…" Not all people of the same or similar gender have the same experience.
9. If you know that using the correct pronouns or truly seeing a client in their authentic gender will be challenging for you, consider referring the client to another practitioner. Keep in mind that a client's parts will not allow the work to move forward if there are concerns about, or experiences of, being misgendered.
10. Do not use IFS with the goal or expectation of helping someone to not be trans. This is a form of conversion therapy, which is harmful, ineffective, and unethical (Coleman et al., 2011).
11. Keeping in mind that there is an overlap between neurodivergence and trans experience, be mindful of ways of communicating that reinforce neurotypical norms (Gratton, 2019).
12. Keeping in mind that some (not all) trans and/or nonbinary people experience gender dysphoria or have experienced physical trauma, conversations that reference the body can be activating. When asking about the way that a part shows up somatically, it is best to ask for consent. This

conversation can be had before starting Insight work or as you are orienting someone to how you work as an IFS practitioner. Example: "In my work I tend to ask about how parts show up in the body as physical sensations. How do you feel about that?" "Please let me know at any point if you do not want me to ask questions about your somatic experience or body sensations." (Some clients may feel comfortable with somatic work on some days but not others, so ongoing consent may be necessary.)

Understanding Reactions to Transphobia: A Case Example

Encounters with transphobia and discrimination are all too common for trans and/or nonbinary people. Every client, depending on their individual histories and circumstances, will have a different way of responding and coping. This may be different on different days or vary based on context. Here are some common parts to be aware of that might show up for clients who are being impacted by systemic and interpersonal anti-trans bias, microaggressions, and discrimination:

- "Don't speak up" or "stay quiet" part.
- "Don't be a doormat" or "speak up" part.
- Hypervigilance or scanning part.
- Wanting to hide or not be seen part.
- Fear of coming out or disclosing part.
- Fear of rejection part.
- Educator/teacher part.
- Sad/hurt part.
- Impostor part (one that doesn't feel seen or validated as legitimate).
- Tired/exhausted part.
- Advocate or activist part.
- A part that overcompensates for anticipated negative judgment and overcompensates by being virtuous, good, nice, overachieving, smart, etc.
- Angry part.
- Dissociative part.
- Firefighter parts who pick up more extreme behaviors: addictions, disordered eating, self-harm.

To illustrate, let's look at an example using the tool of externalizing parts. (This is a composite client, not a real client, and any similarities to actual people you know or are aware of are purely coincidental and perhaps reflections of common experiences that trans and/or nonbinary people experience.) Charley (they/them) is a multiracial nonbinary trans masculine person who frequently gets mispronounced and misgendered because others perceive them as being a woman or feminine. They bring this up in therapy often and struggle with not knowing how to respond. For Charley, not having one consistent way of responding is a source of stress and even brings up a part that judges them and accuses them of being an impostor. In this particular session, Charley's therapist, Dr. Jovi (they/them), invites Charley to map out the different parts and their roles. Charley describes these parts as being similar to different animals. Dr. Jovi guides Charley using Insight.

The following is a transcript (or trans-cript, if you will) of part of the session:

Dr. Jovi: We've been talking about what happens for you when people misgender you, and you've talked about a lot of parts that have reaction.

Charley: Yeah, for sure. There's so many! It feels like a zoo!

Dr. Jovi: Wow, a zoo? Tell me a little more about what parts show up and how you experience them.

Charley: I actually visualize these parts as different kinds of animals. There's a part that looks like a dragon and just feels rage. It wants to scream and breathe fire at people. It's fed up because I've told my co-workers a gazillion times. And my pronouns are even on display with my name during video meetings! This part feels really intense. But then immediately, another part jumps in. This one is like a professor that wants to educate, stay calm, cool, and collected, be a "good trans" and just be very helpful and understanding. It looks like a peacock. Professor Peacock at your service! Very accommodating.

Dr. Jovi: So, this dragon part really feels rage and wants to scream at people, but then Professor Peacock comes in to educate.

Charley: There's another part that is just so annoyed at the ways that I take care of cisgender people when they are the ones that are harming me! This part wants me to have a backbone and stand up for myself. This one is like a dog—like a grumpy looking pug that's just rolling its eyes.

Dr. Jovi: So, the pug is feeling grumpy at how Professor Peacock tries to educate cis people.

Charley: Yeah, and then there's another part…the one that gets really quiet. It's like a lamb. It doesn't want me to say anything or draw any more attention to me.

Dr. Jovi: Aah, the silence of the lamb!

Charley: Yeah! [laughs] And then there's a bear just floating through space going into dissociation. It cannot bear to stay present. And then, on top of all of this, there's a part that just feels like an impostor. It looks like a raccoon with a mask. It doesn't like that the way I respond is inconsistent. Like I don't know which part of me is going to come out.

Dr. Jovi: Wow, it sounds like you are aware of so many different parts. Which is great because we have the opportunity to work with them and for you to build a relationship with them. Is there one of those parts that you'd like to get to know better today? Or that you are feeling the strongest?

Charley: Today, definitely the dragon. I'm just feeling so pissed off. Over it! It wants to flip a table!

Dr. Jovi: Okay, great, sounds like you want to spend time getting to know this dragon part. Before we do that, check to see if there are any other parts that have concerns about you getting to know this part.

Charley: They seem to be on board. They are worried about what will happen if the dragon runs the show.

Dr. Jovi: Does that make sense to you, that these parts might feel concerned about that?

Charley: Yes, for sure.

Dr. Jovi: Perhaps thank them for sharing their concern. And then see if they might be willing to step to the side to give you enough space to have a conversation with the dragon part.

Charley: Yes, they are okay with that. They appreciate being acknowledged.

Dr. Jovi: Okay, so now take a moment to just connect to that dragon part. How are you experiencing it?

Charley: It's red. It's really angry. It's breathing out fire. I feel this pressure in my chest. I can feel that this part wants me to do something.

Dr. Jovi: So, just notice the way this part is getting your attention. Is this part aware of you?

Charley: Yeah, it really wants my attention. It appreciates that we are taking time to be with it.

Dr. Jovi: And how are you feeling towards this part, Charley?

Charley: I feel pretty open, actually. I do want to better understand what happens when this part jumps in.

Dr. Jovi: Let the part know that you are interested in getting to know it better and see how it responds.

Charley: It's open to that.

Dr. Jovi: Start by just asking the part to tell you a little bit about its role, how it's trying to help you.

Charley: This part…is sick and tired of people getting it wrong, and it's saying that it's not even the initial misgendering. It's the way people respond without any accountability, just getting defensive. It's saying that it wants to protect me from getting hurt again and again.

Dr. Jovi: Does that make sense to you, what the part is sharing?

Charley: Yes, it does. I can really feel how much this part wants to fiercely protect me. With all the fire. Like, "Don't come near me."

Dr. Jovi: Wow, yeah, that does sound like a fierce protector! Ask the part how it feels about its role. Does it like its job? Anything it doesn't like so much?

Charley: It feels powerful. It feels proud of being able to protect me. And it feels kind of…exhausted! Like it is on guard all the time. It doesn't really love being in this role all the time, but it feels like it has to be in order to protect me.

Dr. Jovi: Ask the part what it's worried would happen if it didn't do its job. What is it worried would happen to you?

Charley: It's saying that if doesn't do its job then I'll be hurt, that I would have to feel the hurt underneath.

Dr. Jovi: Does this make sense, what this part is saying about wanting to protect you from the hurt? I'm wondering if there's another part that's feeling the hurt, and this part is trying to protect it or protect you from having to feel it?

Charley: Yes. Exactly. I can feel that. And the part is kind of nodding, letting me know that it doesn't want me to get overwhelmed by these feelings, by the part that's feeling these feelings.

Dr. Jovi: Does that make sense to you?

Charley: Yeah.

Dr. Jovi: Let the part know that you get it, that it totally makes sense.

Charley: Yeah, now I can see that the dragon is kind of softening, getting a little smaller, and I can see this other part. Looks like a younger version of me.

Dr. Jovi: What are you noticing about this younger version of you? And is it aware of you?

Charley: Well, I notice this part looks really sad, actually. Yeah, he sees that I'm here.

Dr. Jovi: And how are you feeling towards him?

Charley: I feel a lot of care for him. And compassion.

Dr. Jovi: Take a moment to just send him some of that care and compassion. And then just notice how he responds.

Charley: He's taking it in…he likes being in connection with me. We are now just sitting next to each other on a bench, side by side, kind of touching arms.

Dr. Jovi: That sounds very sweet, like the two of you are really getting to be with each other.

In this session, Charley spontaneously visualized and related to their parts as different animals. This is a method of externalizing. There are other more concrete ways that externalization can be used or invited, such as using stuffed animals or puppets or sandtray figures. This can be used with both Insight (therapist facilitates connection between client's Self and parts) and/or Direct Access (therapist interacts directly with client's parts), depending on whether there is a critical mass of Self-energy. Charley first named the different parts (that happened to show up as animals) that have responses when they get misgendered. Then Dr. Jovi and Charley contracted to work with the angry dragon part. Charley was able to connect with the part and help it to feel safe and understood enough to unblend, thereby making visible an exile that is feeling hurt. Finally, Charley was able to start building a Self-to-part relationship with the hurt exile. This was a great start to Charley being able to move through the healing steps to help the younger exile part to unburden. Notice that throughout the session, Dr. Jovi did not use any pronouns to refer to any of Charley's parts. It wasn't until Charley used the pronouns "he" and "him" for their younger part that Dr. Jovi reflected these pronouns back to Charley in the session. This is an example of following a client's lead and not assuming the gender or pronouns of any part.

Creating Inclusive IFS Learning Communities

In an ideal world, people of every cultural background or identity would be able to access IFS. Unfortunately, practitioners with marginalized or minoritized identities do not always find IFS learning communities to be accessible. Many trans and/or nonbinary therapists experience being "the only one" in IFS trainings. There is a great need for affinity spaces where there is more relative safety and less of a chance of experiencing systemic harm (such as being misgendered in training spaces). In 2022, Nic Wildes and I offered foundational courses on IFS for queer and/or trans therapists. We aimed to create safer spaces for queer and/or trans therapist and practitioner communities, as well as increased access for queer and/or trans clients seeking an IFS therapist. I hope that there will be more affinity trainings available in the future. In the meantime, we encourage cisgender IFS practitioners in training to consider how they talk about gender, and to maintain awareness of their cis privilege in relation to trans practitioners in training.

KEY TAKEAWAYS

By now you have learned essential terms, concepts, and skills so that you are better equipped to work with trans and/or nonbinary clients. Let's review some key tips and recommendations:

1. Be willing to unlearn what you have assumed to be true about gender, including beliefs about trans and/or nonbinary people.
2. Engage in your own healing work with parts that are carrying burdens related to gender.
3. Always center self-determination by using affirming and respectful language (name, pronouns, terms to describe gender).
4. Challenge assumptions about the gender binary and people with binary identities as the norm.
5. Maintain awareness of the diversity of trans and/or nonbinary people with respect to other cultural/intersectional identities as well as presenting concerns that are unrelated to gender.
6. When speaking about parts, follow the client's lead. Refrain from using pronouns or gendered terms to refer to a part until or unless the client does.
7. Strive to be humble and accountable after making a mistake; engage in Self-led repair.
8. When in IFS training spaces, be aware of your own gender-based privilege and maintain awareness that not everyone is cisgender, or a man or woman, etc.
9. When in doubt, pause and reconnect with Self-energy.

Thank you for taking the time to read this chapter and to invest in making "all parts welcome" a reality for trans and/or nonbinary clients seeking IFS therapy.

AUTHOR BIO

Sand C. Chang, PhD (they/them) is a Chinese American nonbinary psychologist, educator, and DEI consultant who works at the intersection of somatics, trans health, eating disorders, trauma recovery, and body liberation. They are certified in IFS, EMDR, and Body Trust. Sand co-authored *A Clinician's Guide to Gender-Affirming Care* (New Harbinger, 2018) and served as a section editor and author for *Trans Bodies, Trans Selves*. They also co-authored the APA *Guidelines for Psychological Practice with Transgender and Gender Nonconforming People* (2015) and are a past Chair of the APA Committee on Sexual Orientation and Gender Diversity. Sand has taught courses on Internal Family Systems for queer and trans therapists. They are passionate about training practitioners to apply IFS in a way to make all parts truly welcome. Outside of work, Sand is a dancer, pun-off competitor, and smoosh-faced dog enthusiast. They live on Kumeyaay land also known as San Diego, California.

REFERENCES

Chang, S. C., Singh, A. A., & Dickey, l. m. (2018). *A clinician's guide to gender-affirming care: Working with transgender and gender nonconforming clients.* New Harbinger Publications.

Coleman, E., Bockting, W., Botzer, M., Cohen-Kettenis, P., DeCuypere, G., Feldman, J., . . . Zucker, K. (2011). Standards of care for the health of transsexual, transgender, and gender nonconforming people, seventh version. *International Journal of Transgenderism, 13,* 165–232. www.doi:10.1080/15532739.2011.700873

Denny, D. (2002). The politics of diagnosis and a diagnosis of politics: How the university-affiliated gender clinics failed to meet the needs of transsexual people. *Transgender Tapestry, 98,* 17–27.

Gratton, F. V. (2019). *Supporting transgender autistic youth and adults: A guide for professionals and families.* Jessica Kingsley Publishers.

James, S. E., Herman, J. L., Rankin, S., Keisling, M., Mottet, L., & Anafi, M. (2016). The report of the 2015 U.S. Transgender survey. *National Center for Transgender Equality*. Retrieved from: www.ustranssurvey.org/

Schwartz, R. C., & Sweezy, M. (2019). *Internal Family Systems therapy.* Guilford Publications.

Young, E. (2019). *They/them/their.* Jessica Kingsley Publishers.

GOING DEEPER

From Dr. Sand C. Chang

1) Websites:
   a. www.sandchang.com
   b. Psychotherapy: www.sandchang.com/psychotherapy
   c. Clinical Consultation: www.sandchang.com/contact
   d. Training: www.sandchang.com/training-overview
   e. DEI services: www.sandchang.com/dei-consulting

2) Books:
   a. Chang, S. C., & Singh, A. A. (2018). *A clinician's guide to gender-affirming care: Working with transgender and gender nonconforming clients.* New Harbinger Publications.
   b. American Psychological Association. (2015). Guidelines for psychological practice with transgender and gender nonconforming people. *American Psychologist, 70*(9), 832-864.
   c. Singh, A. A., & Dickey, L. M. (Eds.). (2017). *Affirmative counseling and psychological practice with transgender and gender nonconforming clients* (pp. xv-274). American Psychological Association.
   d. Chang, S. C., Singh, A. A., & Dickey, L. M. (2018). *A clinician's guide to gender-affirming care: Working with transgender and gender nonconforming clients.* New Harbinger Publications.

From Other Sources

1) Books:
   a. Tannehill, B. (2018). *Everything you ever wanted to know about trans (but were afraid to ask).* Jessica Kingsley Publishers.
   b. Johnston, A. (2023). *Am I trans enough? How to overcome your doubts and find your authentic self.* Jessica Kingsley Publishers.
   c. Sharman, Z. (2021). *The care we dream of: Liberatory and transformative approaches to LGBTQ+ health.* Arsenal Pulp Press.

EMBODYING IFS WITH NEURODIVERGENT CLIENTS

A NEURO-INCLUSIVE APPROACH FOR THERAPISTS

Candice Christiansen, MEd, CMHC
and Meg Martinez-Dettamanti, MS, CMHC

Reviewers: Kim Bolling, PsyD and Alessio Rizzo, MSC

"All parts of you are welcome," Dick Schwartz said softly. He certainly sounded sincere, yet we looked at each other skeptically. *Does he really mean that?* we wondered.

It was 2018, and Dick was giving a keynote presentation at an addictions conference that we attended together. His comment caught us both off-guard. In all our years as licensed clinicians, we had not deeply considered the concept of multiplicity. We had both been taught, and therefore assumed, that multiplicity meant a person had "Dissociative Identity Disorder." Candice found herself wondering, *If this is true about having parts, how can it be possible that all parts of me are really welcome?*

Candice is a late diagnosed Autistic woman who spent over 40 years living amongst a Neuro-majority (e.g., Neurotypicals) where many aspects of her have *not* been welcomed or accepted. Parts of her had become quite skilled over the years at hiding her Autistic traits to protect her from being rejected. Dick's comment was a surprising, yet gentle, invitation to welcome the parts of her that had been burdened by the assumptions, biases, and stereotypes she had experienced for being Autistic.

Candice and Meg are the closest of friends, actually more like sisters, who have worked together for nearly a decade. Meg was one of the few people whom Candice initially trusted to share about her diagnosis as an Autistic woman. Through their relationship, Meg has become a strong ally and advocate for Candice and other Neurodifferent individuals both personally and professionally.

During the break, we decided to approach Dick to ask him to elaborate on his comment, "All parts are welcome." Candice felt her heart pounding out of her chest as we approached him; her fear of rejection was potent. However, as we spoke to him, she quickly noticed a calm wash over her. He had a reassuring presence as he signed the books we purchased, "May the Self be with you."

Who is this guy? we mused as we walked away. *Some kind of yogi?* His calm, kind, and non-judgmental presence resembled that of a yogi, not the founder of a therapy model. At that moment we both expressed an excitement to learn more about Internal Family Systems (IFS).

Soon after the conference, we decided to sign up for IFS Level 1 training, as well as every IFS webinar, workshop, and consultation group we could find. We were both disappointed to learn that many IFS therapists we encountered knew little about Neurodifferences and many made harmful assumptions about Autism in particular. Still, we decided to continue learning and figured we would at some point create a Neuro-Inclusive Approach to IFS. Candice also recognized that she needed to find an IFS therapist to explore her parts that had become activated during a recent IFS workshop.

At first, Candice felt reassured by how soft spoken, calm, and patient her therapist was towards her. After a couple months of doing telehealth, she decided to tell her therapist about her Autism diagnosis. By then, Candice trusted that her therapist wouldn't judge her. Candice was shocked by her IFS therapist's response.

"I don't think you are Autistic," her therapist said. "I think you have trauma."

While it was true that many of Candice's parts carried burdens from trauma as a result of childhood abuse and the Neuromajority's treatment of her, Candice knew her Autism was not misdiagnosed trauma, or a "part" according to the IFS model. She knew her Autism was part of her "hardware," her neurobiological and genetic makeup.

Candice stared at the screen in disbelief, thinking, *Wait, what? Why is she dismissing my Autism?*

Her therapist continued, "If you are Autistic, then you are the highest functioning Autistic woman I have ever met. I know because I used to evaluate school-age Autistic boys."

Candice glared at her onscreen therapist as a fierce protector said sharply, "I *am* Autistic. If you spent more than an hour with me once every few weeks, you'd see." Another part of Candice wanted to crawl into a hole and disappear. She felt shame welling up. Here was yet another therapist who was supposed to be safe and accepting, using a model known for its compassion, but instead she felt judged and dismissed. Parts of her began to feel skeptical towards IFS. *If this model teaches therapists to welcome and accept all parts of their clients,* she thought, *then why isn't my Autism also accepted, including the parts of me that are continually traumatized by an oppressive Neuro-majority?*

As much as Candice wanted to disappear in that moment, parts of her felt incredibly angry. Although she had become accustomed to these kinds of microaggressions, she felt furious that it was happening again, and in the safety of a therapeutic relationship, no less.

When Candice shared what had happened, Meg felt the urgent flood of frustrated parts within her. She suggested that Candice find a new therapist, but it was during the pandemic and waitlists for mental health professionals were incredibly long. Candice really needed support, so she decided to continue working with the same therapist; however, fierce protectors remained present to ensure she didn't bring up being Autistic again. This was incredibly painful since Candice had exhausted parts who had been skillfully masking her Autism for decades and longed for a safe place to relax. Candice also considered being Autistic an important part of her identity, and yet she didn't feel like she could share this with her own therapist because of implicit bias.

We feel it is important to share Candice's story to shed light on the need for a Neuro-Inclusive Approach to IFS for clinicians and helping professionals working with Neurodivergent individuals. With this in mind, we address our goals for this chapter in two parts: 1) increasing awareness and sensitivity around Neurodifferences by highlighting the origin of the Neurodiversity Movement; and 2) providing education about how IFS can assist with healing and empowering therapist parts and Neurodifferent client's internal systems by introducing a Neuro-Inclusive Approach to IFS.

We encourage you to review the list of key terms related to Neurodifferences in Appendix A that we have compiled in order to better understand the terms used in this chapter.

Part 1: Increasing Awareness and Sensitivity around Neurodivergence

It is common for therapists to conflate the term Neurodiversity with Autism, and more recently, Attention Deficit Hyperactivity (ADH). (*In this chapter, we have "ditched the Ds." We chose to do this to demonstrate how we speak to our clients. When we refer to Attention Deficit Hyperactivity and/or Attention Deficit and Autism, we do not include the word "disorder" intentionally because these are not disorders, they are neurological differences.*) Yet, according to the actual meaning of this word, coined by Judy Singer in the late 1990s, *everyone* has a Neurodiverse brain. Variation in Neurology is natural; there isn't one brain that is more normal or abnormal than another (Meadows, 2021). However, because of confusion surrounding the term, we believe it is pertinent to include a brief history of how the Neurodiversity Movement began, including what motivated Judy Singer to coin the term in the first place. Our hope in doing so is to shed light on how we can create more acceptance and inclusion around the Neurodiversity paradigm.

In the 1990s, Autistic people who didn't fit neatly into the predominant medical boxes of physical, intellectual, and psychiatric disability were labeled "mentally ill." These individuals were *not* mentally ill, but hard-wired neurologically to view, understand, process, and behave in the world differently. While the popular approach to treatment at the time was psychodynamic with the goal of addressing past trauma, it proved incomplete, since what was going on inside these individuals was *not* trauma based, but rather the result of a natural *neurological* variation in their brain. At the time Singer referred to this neurological difference as "high functioning Autistic" or Asperger Syndrome (Singer, 2017).

As part of her honors thesis in sociology, Singer was intent on developing a new social paradigm for understanding Autism. Her diversity perspective conceptualized Autism as a social model of disability which describes disability as *the incompatibility between the physical, cognitive, or emotional characteristics of a given individual and the characteristics of their social context* (Singer, 2017). Therefore, a person may be "disabled" not because of an impairment but by the failure of their environment to accommodate their specific needs.

For example, an Autistic adult may thrive in a structured, sensory-friendly environment where their schedule is consistent, and where they have explicit expectations surrounding their job description. However, if they are employed at a chaotic workplace with a constantly changing schedule and have a vague job description in an environment that is overstimulating, they may struggle to complete their job duties. As a result, they may be labeled as deficient. However, their challenges are not because they are Autistic; rather, they are in an environment that does not accommodate their specific learning and support needs.

To describe this more explicitly using IFS language, we often use the analogy of one's "hardware" vs. "software" and "software viruses." Your brain, autonomic nervous system, body, and other innate aspects of your intersectionality (i.e., race, sexual orientation, etc.) make up your biological "hardware" and, therefore, are distinct from *parts* or "software," in your internal system. How your parts are burdened by the impact of an unwelcoming society and the protective strategies that they learn or create to cope in a burdened environment relate to the "software" or "software viruses" present in the system. The "hardware" is not a disease, mental illness, or a result of trauma, nor is it meant to be "cured" by therapeutic intervention. It is the "software" (e.g., parts) and more accurately, the "software viruses" (e.g., burdens) that create discomfort in both the internal systems and external lives of Neurodifferent clients.

Although Singer focused specifically on Autism at the time of her thesis, she acknowledged that the scope of those who were neurologically diverse was much broader. She also knew that the term "neurologically diverse" was too lengthy and found herself saying "Neurodiversity Movement." (Singer, 2017, page 19).

Since Singer's original thesis, the Neurodiversity Movement has evolved and includes several different types of Neurodifferences: Autism, Sensory Processing Issues, Tourette's, Ehlers Danlos Syndrome, Dyslexia, Dyspraxia, Dyscalculia,

Dysgraphia, Meares-Irlen Syndrome, Hyperlexia, Downs Syndrome, Synesthesia, Schizophrenia, Obsessive Compulsion, Bipolar, and Attention Deficit Hyperactivity (ADH).

While the Neurodiversity Movement currently advocates for the inclusion of all of these types of Neurodifferences, significant attention in recent years has been given to Autism and ADH. Neuro-minorities who are Autistic and/or ADH have increasingly joined together on social media to share their unique voices in order to dispel the harmful myths that persist. For many Autistic and ADH individuals, self-identification signifies validation of one's inner knowing, and a sense of inclusion and belonging within their Neurodivergent communities. This is especially true since relying on the medical model for a "formal" diagnosis continues to influence the deficit perspective in which Neurological conditions are viewed and discussed (Chapple et al., 2021). This includes a reductionist view of Autism and ADH that overemphasizes environmental trauma as the cause of distress and challenges associated with these diagnoses.

In the last decade, there have been significant advances in understanding the genetic basis for Autism (Reilly et al., 2017). Research continues to reaffirm that Autism is a highly heritable, polygenic condition that is strongly linked to genetic factors that involve the development and function of the nervous system, mitochondrial function, the immune system, and epigenetic regulations (Reilly et al., 2017). Likewise, research on ADH confirms that there is at least some neurobiological component to this diagnosis even if the environment exacerbates symptomatology (Hayman & Fernandez, 2018).

Although there has been an increased awareness of Neurodiversity both scientifically and socially, Neurodifferent individuals continue to experience harmful biases and microaggressions in school, work, and community settings by mental health and medical professionals and within their own social groups and families (Mel, 2021). Microaggressions are statements or actions that involve indirect, subtle, or unintentional discrimination against members of a marginalized group (Williams et al., 2021).

Candice felt the impact of a significant microaggression at the time of writing this chapter. She attended a conference on trauma and addiction and the keynote speaker, a distinguished medical professional in the field of trauma therapy, told the audience about a protocol he created that was able to "cure" his patients of Autism.

Candice was horrified by what he said. This was a well-known medical expert asserting that Autism is similar to a disease in need of a cure! He completely disregarded the wealth of research that describes the complex and heterogeneous array of developmental, genomic, neurobiological, and cognitive differences within Autistic individuals (Baron-Cohen & Lombardo, 2017). His comments also resembled the damaging assertions of treatment approaches like conversion therapy for individuals who are LGBTQIA+.

Given that even medical and psychological experts continue to spread harmful myths and make micromicroaggressions, many undiagnosed and late diagnosed Neurodifferent adults, similar to Candice, develop resourceful protector parts that learn to hide or mask their traits in order to fit in with the Neuro-majority. These parts may present as more sociable, make eye contact, act like they understand what they are reading or hearing, and appear able to tolerate environments that actually create intense anxiety and discomfort. The very important role of masking parts is to keep the individual safe from further marginalization, microaggressions, humiliation, rejection, and in some cases, danger. The burdens an exile often carries underneath these protectors might include feeling weird, broken, not good enough, rejected, unlovable, or like damaged goods to name a few.

In his book, *Unmasking Autism* (2022), Autistic social psychologist, Devan Price, likens Autistic masking to "… a state of exclusion forced onto us from the outside. A closeted gay person doesn't just decide one day to be closeted—they're essentially born into the closet, because heterosexuality is normative and being gay is treated as a[n]…aberration" (p. 8).

Similarly, many Neurodifferent individuals have masking protectors adept at protecting against real or perceived rejection. This is often the result of a brain-based trait ("hardware") called Rejection Sensitive Dysphoria (RSD). Although RSD is not considered part of a formal ADH diagnosis in the United States, it is one of the most common brain-based symptoms of ADH not caused by trauma, though it often feels extremely painful and traumatic. RSD feels like extreme, disruptive, emotional dysregulation, and pain triggered by the perception that one has been rejected or criticized (even if it is constructive criticism). Someone who experiences RSD feels a sense of falling short or failing to meet internal or external standards or expectations (Dodson 2022).

RSD often activates hard working and loyal protectors who may mask to be accepted; however, they may also reject others before they are rejected, enter situations ready to fight/defend their position, experience emotional outbursts, withdraw from social situations, ruminate and perseverate on rejection, or even become suicidal. Many Neurodifferent individuals have managers and firefighters that also protect against real or perceived rejection through internal shaming, attempting to control outcomes, and even succumbing to addictive processes to escape or numb.

Psychiatrist William W. Dodson, MD, estimates that by age 12, children with ADH "hardware" receive 20,000 more negative messages from their parents, teachers, and other adults than their non-ADH friends and siblings (Dodson, 2016). It is evident that our ADH clients with RSD have fierce protectors who have learned their important roles from external environments wrought with implicit bias, microaggressions, and in some cases, explicit verbal and emotional abuse.

As we consider how to change this dynamic and advocate for clients with all types of "hardware," it is vital that we acknowledge that Neurodifferences are just one aspect of a person's identity and lived experience. Gender, age, sexual identity, race, ethnicity, socioeconomic status, physical abilities, and learning differences also deserve consideration.

In Part 2 of this chapter, we will introduce our Neuro-Inclusive Approach to IFS that assists with healing and empowering Neurodifferent clients' internal systems while also helping to heal and empower therapists' parts in a way that accepts and celebrates all types of Neurodifferences.

Part 2: A Neuro-Inclusive IFS Approach: How IFS can Assist with Healing and Empowering both Therapists' Parts and Neurodifferent Clients' Systems

In the past few years, we have recognized the need for an affirming approach to healing that honors the multi-dimensionality of every human being no matter what their Neurotype. The IFS model does a beautiful job of acknowledging that "all parts are welcome," and in this section, we hope to build on that strength by offering a Neuro-Inclusive Approach to IFS that includes affirming clients' Neurological differences.

Similar to what Autistic individuals experienced in the 1990s, when Neurodifferent individuals enter a therapeutic setting, their "hardware" is often labeled as the "presenting problem" to be corrected, or it is conflated with trauma. We have found that by discerning between our clients' neurological differences and their protector parts, the gentle and validating process of IFS can be utilized to heal exiled parts. These parts are often burdened by both personal experiences and the social and cultural burdens we've presented in this chapter. By validating and supporting our clients' Neurodifferences ("hardware") while honoring their fierce and hard-working protectors ("software"), our clients are able to move toward their exiled parts.

A Neuro-Inclusive Approach to IFS offers four goals for therapists who work with Neurodifferent individuals by inviting therapists to: 1) Use curiosity with Neurodifferent clients around their sensory, learning, and internal system needs; 2) Access Self-energy to navigate a client's need for safety if microaggressions occur; 3) Explore therapist's individual, legacy, and cultural burdens related to implicit bias, judgment, and stereotypes against Neurodifferent individuals; 4) Creatively implement IFS mapping exercises with Neurodifferent clients to flesh out Neurodifferent traits vs. client parts.

Goal 1: Use curiosity with Neurodifferent clients around their sensory, learning, and internal system needs.

We have noticed that sensory sensitivities ("hardware") related to our clients' environments can activate protectors to shut down their system in order to ensure parts aren't flooded. Likewise, sensory sensitivities can also cause parts to feel agitated, irritable, annoyed, uncomfortable, angry, and to struggle to focus, for similar reasons. It is important to be curious with these protectors and explore what they need from your Neurodifferent client in order to feel safe enough to soften back. For example, protectors may need some time at the beginning and throughout the therapy session to address actual sensory issues (lights, sounds, smells, tastes, internal and external sensations) that may be impacting protectors.

Providing support for any sensory needs including encouraging self-stimulating behavior, or "stimming," often helps protectors feel safe and assists our Neurodifferent clients in managing Autonomic Nervous System dysregulation. Sensory soothing behavior also helps our Neurodifferent clients focus, concentrate, experience calm, and remain present during the session. We often suggest various options to help clients sensorially soothe during our sessions. Examples include dimming the lights, averting or closing eyes, rocking back and forth, bouncing, fidgeting, wiggling, getting up and standing, walking, stretching, and using a weighted or soft blanket.

Similarly, at times our ADH clients will experience distraction during the session. "Distraction" is considered an ADH trait ("hardware"), so a client who is distracted by "bright shiny lights" or noises in the hallway of your office will experience being distracted quite differently from a part that is trying to "take the client out" in an attempt to protect them from vulnerable parts who feel activated. When this happens, we are curious and encourage our client to take a moment and ask if it is a part who is distracting them or if it is a trait related to their ADH brain.

Similarly, one aspect of IFS that immediately resonated with us is the importance of mirroring clients' words and language when describing their internal system. This therapeutic detail seems foundational in aligning the therapist with the client and their parts. From a Neuro-Inclusive perspective, mirroring the clients use of words and language when talking about their "hardware" and intersectionality can enhance safety and trust within the therapeutic relationship.

For example, some of our Neurodifferent clients use identity-first language when speaking, such as "I am a non-binary, Autistic, queer human" or "I am a cisgender, ADH male." These clients have shared that identity-first language feels empowering to many parts of them, especially since most have experienced dismissal of their multiple identities. Yet other Neurodifferent clients use person-first language when speaking, such as "I have OCD" or "I have Dyslexia."

By mirroring language chosen by our Neurodifferent clients, we strengthen the therapeutic relationship by aligning with our client's chosen identification. For many of our Neurodifferent clients, this allows them to have a corrective experience in therapy where their parts feel safe, validated, and accepted. It has also been helpful to invite our clients to share how parts of them feel about different labels or identifiers, including identity-first and person-first language.

Speaking of language, functioning labels have been identified within the Neurodiversity Movement as harmful towards Neurodifferent individuals. Examples of functioning labels include using descriptors that refer to a Neurodifferent person's level of functioning, such as "low functioning," "high functioning," "under-functioning," or "over-functioning." These labels segregate Neurodifferent people into preconceived categories of the Neuro-majority's view of what is normal vs. abnormal. They also limit Neurodifferent individuals' ability to receive accurate support services, particularly if they are categorized as "high functioning."

With that said, some Neurodifferent clients' parts will describe their Neurodifference using functioning labels. For example, both of us have heard our Neurodifferent clients describe their diagnosis in ways that sound like, "I have a mild case of ADH," or "I have high functioning Autism." Embodying curiosity with our clients as they explore what these labels mean to various parts within them creates a safe and trusting alliance between us and our client's parts, especially those parts who may feel distrusting of the therapeutic process.

We have also found it helpful to ask our Neurodifferent clients how they learn information, particularly as it relates to exploring parts. As we introduce IFS in therapy, we often ask our clients if they learn by listening, through imagining parts, seeing parts using visual aids, and/or through connecting to their body via touch. We often say, "I want to ensure that you feel safe and supported in all ways during our sessions. One aspect of using a Neuro-Inclusive Approach to IFS therapy includes mapping parts as well as your Neurodifferent traits. There are various ways to do this." We then provide examples of various ways to map parts such as visually imagining the parts, using visual arts or music to depict them, matching them to pictures or objects, using figurines, or through their bodily sensations. Candice often shows her Neurodifferent clients pictures she has drawn and figurines that represent her Neurodifferent traits as well as her parts. Encouraging our Neurodifferent clients to map their Neurodifferent traits as well as their parts, in whatever way feels natural to them, supports their specific learning style and enhances safety and trust in the therapeutic relationship. Mapping techniques and exercises will be explored in the fourth goal of this chapter.

As helping professionals, we can support our Neurodifferent clients no matter what diagnostic labels they choose to use or not use. We can respect their voices, choices, and experiences by mirroring Neuro-affirming words and language that resonates with and validates all parts of them. While embodying Self-energy, we can explore any accommodations they and their parts need during sessions to feel comfortable. Viewing Neurodifferent individuals as human beings with various support needs, while embracing all parts of them, aligns with a Neuro-Inclusive Approach to IFS therapy that all humans and parts are welcome.

Goal 2: Access Self-energy to navigate a client's need for safety if microaggressions occur.

During our combined 25 years' experience as practicing clinicians, we have heard many well-meaning mental health and medical professionals use microaggressions against their Neurodifferent clients.

Not so long ago, Meg had an experience when she attempted to weave in Neuro-Inclusive language during a session, and it soon became clear that the impact did not match the intention. A Neurodifferent client was sharing about their relationship and asked her for advice. As they shared, Meg noticed the individual was perseverating on one specific aspect of the relationship. Before fully thinking, she found herself saying to the client, "Let's be honest, there is Neuro-difference playing a role here." The client sunk back in their chair and appeared deflated. Meg immediately knew that the opposite of validation had just occurred.

When microaggressions like this occur in a therapeutic relationship, the harm that is caused can be long-lasting. This is especially true if the therapist becomes hostile or defensive about their microaggression if or when it is brought to their attention. If invalidated, many clients feel hurt, confused, angry, distrusting, and betrayed by both the helping professional and the therapeutic process (Williams et al., 2021). Often it is parts, who are wounded by microaggressions, and their fierce protectors that are seeking therapeutic support in the first place, hoping to be seen, heard, known, and understood.

Therefore, creating a safe and inviting space at the beginning of therapy to discuss how to navigate microaggressions is essential to building safety and trust in the therapeutic relationship. This can be achieved by the therapist embodying their own Self-energy including a non-assumptive presence of open-mindedness, compassion, and curiosity towards the client and their own internal process.

To proactively set the stage, an example of what we often say to our Neurodifferent clients is something like, "I recognize that during our time together, I may have burdened parts that use microaggressions against you. If this happens, I want to do whatever is necessary to make amends with you and your parts." We also realize that some of our Neurodifferent clients may need an explanation of what microaggressions are since, as we have shared, many Neurodifferent individuals have protector parts that have been combatting damaging myths, stereotypes, prejudice, and blatant microaggressions for most of their lives. They may be so skilled at doing this that they may not even recognize these harmful messages when they occur.

We also empower our Neurodifferent clients by saying, "Ask your protector part what I can do to help you feel safer if parts of me commit a microaggression against you?" At times, if we commit a microaggression, we will say, "In order to help you feel safer, I am committed to working with my part(s) that hold(s) this legacy burden and ensuring they are not present for our sessions." We reassure our Neurodifferent clients that we are committed to their safety and well-being as part of our therapeutic relationship.

Going forward, when we have made a microaggression against a Neurodifferent client, we acknowledge the microaggression and make a repair, from a place of empathy and compassion. From this Self-led place, we acknowledge and apologize for the part(s) of us that made the microaggression against our Neurodifferent client (Anderson, 2021). This is important in all therapeutic relationships.

Returning to Meg's story, as she watched her deflated client retreat into themselves, she felt the pang of guilt and responsibility for committing a microaggression. This was brought to her attention by her gracious therapist's parts. Deep within, she felt the pain of being shamed, something other parts of her were familiar with. She accessed this feeling to empathize with her client. She then leaned forward and said, "I'm so sorry. I just used a microaggression against you when I said that." Her client looked up at her and said, "Is that why I felt ashamed when you said, 'Let's be honest'?" Meg nodded and used this opportunity to own her legacy burdens surrounding Neurodifference and commit to working with her parts so her client felt safe during their sessions. During this healing moment, Meg invited her client to let her know in the future when they noticed parts of her that caused them any sort of pain or discomfort.

Admittedly, moments like this can be uncomfortable for our therapist's parts who were trained after all to be the "expert" in the room. Yet part of embodying Self-energy is to humanize ourselves and our parts with our clients. As Dr. Frank G. Anderson (2021) explains,

> "With compassion, our parts are not activated and we are not blended. Rather, we remain in a calm state, connected with the client's presence and capable of identifying their pain without getting overwhelmed… being present with our clients requires a delicate balance of being empathically resonant (being with our own parts)…as well as having a compassionate…perspective" (p. 38).

As therapists, when we are too blended with our parts, we often cause more harm than good when addressing microaggressions. The third goal of a Neuro-Inclusive Approach to IFS focuses on working with therapist's parts. For now, it is important to know what *not* to say when addressing microaggressions. Avoid responding from defensive parts that may sound like, "I didn't say that," or using a defensive tone to explain, "That was not my intention," without acknowledging their impact. This type of response diminishes your Neurodifferent client's experience and reinforces their lack of trust in you and the therapeutic process. It can also reinforce burdened parts who have internalized microaggressions and justify the strategies of manager parts to make the client behave in a way the Neuro-majority expects (e.g., masking).

Goal 3: Explore therapist's individual, legacy, and cultural burdens related to implicit bias, judgment, and stereotypes against Neurodifferent individuals.

Many times, therapists do not recognize if or when they commit a microaggression against Neurodifferent clients. As we have discussed, these types of biases, judgments, and stereotypes tend to be unconscious, subtle, and exist not only in individuals but in larger systems and institutions (Williams et al., 2021). Correspondingly, microaggressions are often individual and legacy burdens that our parts carry, transmitted from a person's family of origin, community institutions, and culture. In many helping professions, myths about Neurodifferences are prevalent, leading therapists and medical professionals to be taught what Neurodivergence looks like and what it doesn't look like.

When therapists enter the field, they are often burdened with preconceived ideas about Neurodifferences that undoubtedly perpetuate implicit biases and judgments. We have encountered many therapists with protector parts that wield rigid beliefs, like those described in Part 1. This often leads them to believe that naming or addressing Neurodifference is completely outside of their scope of competence. In fact, we often observe that some types of Neurodifferences, like Autism, are not even on the radar of many clinicians. Unfortunately, some clinicians inaccurately diagnose Autistic individuals with similar symptomatic presentations that they feel more knowledgeable about or are more comfortable with, such as Narcissistic Personality Disorder, Borderline Personality Disorder, or Antisocial Personality Disorder. By consciously or unconsciously dismissing Neurodifferences, therapists' burdened parts can unintentionally traumatize or retraumatize Neurodifferent clients and perpetuate the burdens of their internal systems. This is especially true if Neurodifferent clients are saddled with inaccurate and often negatively connotated labels. Therefore, an essential aspect of working with Neurodifferent individuals is to identify, befriend, and heal your parts that carry individual, legacy, institutional, and cultural burdens around Neurodifference.

We have developed a Neuro-Inclusive Inquiry using IFS, located in the Appendix along with a short list of common clinical myths of Autism and ADH, to inform and guide therapists and other helping professionals when practicing such a courageous self-exploration. Through this type of internal work, therapists can embody Self-energy and help unburden their parts that might unintentionally bring microaggressions into the therapeutic relationship.

Goal 4: Creatively implement IFS mapping exercises with Neurodifferent clients to flesh out Neurodifferent traits vs. client parts.

Similar to Candice's experience with her own therapist, we have noticed an overgeneralization of all types of Neurodifferences being misdiagnosed solely as trauma. Consequently, as discussed in Part 1, well-meaning therapists may mistake traits of Neurodifference as trauma symptoms or burdened parts. When using IFS, one way to help therapists distinguish between traits of Neurodifference ("hardware") and a client's burdened parts ("software" and "software viruses") is to creatively implement visual IFS mapping exercises.

Traditional IFS mapping encourages clients to connect with a part by going inward and noticing thoughts, feelings, impulses, and sensations then drawing a visual representation of it on a piece of paper (Schwartz, 2021). By doing this, parts can become externalized and unblended, which often allows for other parts to come forward and be identified and witnessed. However, some Neurodifferent clients may not be able to visualize their parts due to aphantasia (the inability to visualize), or they may have difficulties with interoception (feeling sensations in their body), or alexithymia (difficulty identifying and describing emotions) (Aphantasia Network, 2022). Additionally, many Neurodifferent clients naturally name aspects of their "hardware" or traits of Neurodifference when mapping their inner worlds.

We have witnessed the benefits of offering a variety of options for mapping. Below is a selective list of techniques and strategies that we have used with the various Neurodifferent learning styles we have supported (e.g., visual, auditory, and/or kinesthetic learners).

Neurodifferent Learning Style	Mapping Technique or Strategy
Visual *(imaginative or artistic)*	Encourage clients to draw, paint, sculpt, etc. to distinguish between their parts and ND traits.*
Visual *(concrete)*	Premade visual aids such as nesting dolls, finger puppets, play therapy figurines, parts cards, genograms, or even photographs can be helpful. Example: A creative client once used a video game to create electronic human versions of their parts distinct from their ND traits.*
Auditory	Encourage clients to explore sound, silence, and music as a way to name and distinguish their ND traits from their parts. Example: Some clients with "auditory stims" may use a specific sound to regulate their nervous system and choose songs or music to represent their parts.
Kinesthetic *(preference for tactile stimming or need for movement to learn)*	Suggest that clients move around the room or demonstrate their parts and ND traits with body postures or facial expressions. Examples: A client who was a drummer demonstrated an angry part through drumming on his thighs while another client sat on their hands to represent a "masking" manager part. One client shared, "My ADH brain feels like a laser when I'm focused on my interests and a flood light when I'm in crowded spaces; my manager parts try to control the laser and a part shames me when the flood light turns on"

*Visual examples of client artwork and concrete mapping are provided in the Appendix.

As you support your Neurodifferent client with mapping their internal systems and Neurodifferent traits, you will notice that almost always, they identify parts, primarily protectors, that have learned to cope with being perpetually stigmatized by the Neuro-majority. For example, manager parts that have learned to protect a client by "masking" traits of Neurodifference may have internalized cultural burdens which perpetuate microaggressions within a client's internal system. As a result, these protectors may be extremely critical of the client for having perceived "deficiencies" related to their Neurodifference. When these parts are forward, the client may behave in ways that are viewed as socially appropriate and acceptable by the Neuro-majority, even though their rigid role exhausts their internal and physiological systems. "Masking" parts are often related to other parts within a subsystem, including parts that are burdened by suicidal ideation, fear of failure, chronic shame, loneliness, isolation, severe anxiety, and depression (Pearson & Rose, 2021).

Masking is a common protective strategy within a Neurodifferent client's internal system. When "masking" parts are present, the client will often resemble a chameleon, changing how they look and act to fit in with each new situation. "Masking" parts work incredibly hard to ensure that the exiles burdened by not feeling good enough, not fitting in, feeling socially inept, or feeling deficient and defective are hidden deep inside where no one can harm them. When "masking" parts are active or in charge in a Neurodifferent client's internal system, it can impact their ability to receive accurate and necessary support or services. This is especially true if they have been labeled as "high functioning," a label that may actually be the agenda of the "masking" part.

Likewise, if the therapist's parts of the clinician have an agenda, Neurodifferent clients' "masking" parts will often resist unblending because they can sense the agenda of the parts that are forward in their therapist. In response, other parts within the "masking" subsystem may come forward, including parts who carry burdens of perfectionism, do-it-right, people pleasing, and being compliant. Therefore, helping professionals who embody Self-energy such as unconditional acceptance, curiosity, calmness, compassion, non-judgment, and patience during IFS can create a sense of safety and trust in their therapeutic relationship for Neurodifferent clients to get to know their protectors on a deeper level.

Referring back to Goal 1, when a therapist is curious about their client's sensory and environmental needs, this curiosity can invite "masking" protectors to relax and allow the clients' nervous system to regulate. Over time, this demonstrates that the client's individual traits of Neurodifference are welcome in the relationship. We once witnessed a client's "masking" subsystem enter the therapy room and sit upright and stiffly, despite the comfortable chair provided. By being curious about how the client felt at that moment, we learned that a protective part felt like it was in the "principal's office." When we invited the part to see how our therapy room was designed to be Neuro-Inclusive, this well-meaning protector was able to relax via the client attending to their sensory needs; they took off their shoes, curled up under a weighted blanket, and played with a fidget spinner.

As this part relaxed, it was able to unblend enough for the client to get to know it, as we began the IFS protocol. Some protector parts may not unblend so quickly, and it may take more time and sessions for protective parts to get a sense of safety from the therapist before relaxing or softening. To support this, we often demonstrate our own sensory needs during sessions by using stim toys or naming when we need to break eye contact. In our experience, when our Neurodifferent clients see our traits of Neurodifferences expressed, their whole system feels validated and reassured, including their "masking" protectors. (See details about common protectors and subsystems in our Neurodifferent clients in the two-page overview located in the Appendix.)

Being creative during the mapping and befriending process allows our Neurodifferent clients to experience a Neuro-Inclusive IFS Approach where their natural learning styles are supported, their sensory profiles are tended to, and parts have an opportunity to experience the necessary safety and trust to unblend. Additionally, having the support of a compassionate, accepting, patient, and curious therapist is the crucial first step in freeing parts of their extreme roles, reestablishing trust via embodying Self-energy, and creating increased harmony and balance within a Neurodifferent clients' internal system (Pastor & Gauvain, 2021).

The promise of the journey to wholeness through IFS begins with honoring all parts and all people. IFS therapists who embody a Neuro-Inclusive Approach honor their clients Neurodifferences and other identities, as well as all their parts. In this way, IFS therapists become hope merchants for their clients' parts as they move toward the healing of traumatic experiences with medical and psychological professionals. Likewise, adopting a Neuro-Inclusive Approach to IFS invites healing within the therapist's internal system as they courageously explore their own individual and legacy burdens. It is through this Neuro-Inclusive Approach to IFS that we affirm that everyone is welcome, including every type of Neurodifference, gender identity, sexual identity, age, ability, race, religion, class, language, and cultural identity.

KEY TAKEAWAYS

- Our brain, autonomic nervous system, body, and other innate aspects of our intersectionality (i.e., race, sexual identity, etc.) make up our biological "hardware" and, therefore, are distinct from our *parts*. It is important for IFS therapists to honor this distinction when working with Neurodifferent individuals.

- When supporting Neurodifferent individuals, be curious about their sensory, learning, and internal system support needs at the beginning of the therapeutic relationship. Humanizing their support needs and making adjustments or accommodations in sessions allows Neurodifferent clients to create trust in the therapeutic alliance.
- It is important that IFS therapists acknowledge that microaggressions can exist in the therapeutic setting, commit to identifying the parts that commit microaggressions, and are willing to courageously explore our own individual, legacy, and cultural burdens related to implicit bias, judgment, and stereotypes against those who are Neurodifferent.
- When using IFS with Neurodifferent clients, creatively implement mapping exercises to assist in the naming and noticing of Neurodifferent traits as "hardware" and distinct from the client parts and overall internal family system. This process validates the clients innate Neurodifference as an important aspect of who they are and not as something that needs to be judged, changed, or cured.

AUTHOR BIOS

Candice Christiansen, MEd, CSAT-S, CMAT-S, Certified EMDR, IFS (she/her) is the Founder and Clinical Director of Namasté Center for Healing, a holistic healing center in Utah. Candice identifies as an adult diagnosed Autistic female who has provided therapy to both Neurodifferent individuals and mixed Neurotype couples for close to 20 years. Her expertise is using a Neuro-Inclusive Approach to IFS with Neurodifferent adults and mixed Neurotype couples who are healing from intimate betrayal and a variety of sex, relationship, and intimacy issues. Candice is the host of *Fabulously Candice: The Sexiest Podcast about Neurodivergence.*

Meg Martinez-Dettamanti, MS, CSAT, CMAT, EMDR-Trained, IFS (she/her) is the Chief Program Officer at Namaste Center for Healing in Millcreek, Utah. Meg has worked closely with Candice for nearly a decade and their relationship has grown into a close friendship. Meg has a Neurodifferent family and has been an advocate for Neurodifferent individuals, as well as other marginalized populations, throughout her career as a helping professional working with children, teens, adults, couples, and families. She is committed to helping Candice develop therapeutic resources for Neurodifferent individuals globally.

REVIEWER BIOS

Kim Bolling, PsyD (she/her) is a Licensed Psychologist in private practice in Nashua, NH, working with couples and individuals. Kim is a Senior Staff Member for the powerful couple modality Intimacy from the Inside Out® (IFIO), which is based on the Internal Family Systems (IFS) model. Kim is a Certified IFS Therapist and Clinical Consultant for IFS. She has a special interest in Neurodiversity, and combines her training as a Neurodiverse couples counselor with IFS and IFIO to bring an insight-oriented approach to working with Neurodiverse couples. Kim has presented her work at the Annual IFS Conference and has been a featured guest on the Neurodiverse Love podcast and presenter and facilitator for several conferences for Neurodiverse couples.

Alessio Rizzo, MSC (he/they) is a Level 3 certified IFS psychotherapist, and a gestalt psychotherapist for individuals and groups living in London (UK). He specializes in gender, sexuality and Neurodiversity. He is also a clinical consultant, a psychotherapy trainer, and a writer. Alessio worked as a psychotherapy trainer for one of the leading training institutes in the UK and delivered a workshop on IFS and OCD with IFS Spain. His IFS articles have been published in the IFS Foundation's journal "Parts and Self," and he regularly publishes on his free IFS blog, which attracts thousands of monthly readers. Alessio has been delivering introductory IFS workshops in Italian in the past year and is working towards bringing IFS therapy to Italy in Italian, his mother tongue.

REFERENCES

Adan, A., Fortunato, P., & McAllaster, G. (2021). Defining and celebrating neurodiversity. *Rowan University DEI Blog*. Retrieved April 12, 2022, from https://sites.rowan.edu/diversity-equity-inclusion/blog/2021/09/defining-celebrating-neurodiversity.html

Aphantasia Network. (2022). *What is Aphantasia*. Retrieved May 23, 2022, from www.aphantasia.com/what-is-aphantasia/

Anderson, F. G. (2021). *Transcending trauma: Healing complex PTSD with Internal Family Systems therapy*. PESI Publishing.

Barber, S., Gronholm, P. C., Ahuja, S., Rüsch, N., & Thornicroft, G. (2019). Microaggressions towards people affected by mental health problems: A scoping review. *Epidemiology and Psychiatric Sciences, 29*, e82. www.doi.org/10.1017/S2045796019000763

Baron-Cohen, S., & Lombardo, M. V. (2017). Autism and talent: The cognitive and neural basis of systemizing. *Dialogues in Clinical Neuroscience, 19*(4), 345–353. www.doi.org/10.31887/DCNS.2017.19.4/sbaroncohen

Chapple, M., et al. (2021). Overcoming the double empathy problem within pairs of autistic and non-autistic adults through the contemplation of serious literature. *Frontiers in Psychology,* 12, 708375. www.doi.org/10.3389/fpsyg.2021.708375)

Catthoor, K., et al. (2015). Psychiatric stigma in treatment-seeking adults with personality problems: Evidence from a sample of 214 patients. *Frontiers in Psychiatry,* 6, 101. www.doi.org/10.3389/fpsyt.2015.00101

Csecs, J., Iodice, V., Rae, C. L., Brooke, A., Simmons, R., Quadt, L., Savage, G. K., Dowell, N. G., Prowse, F., Themelis, K., Mathias, C. J., Critchley, H. D., & Eccles, J. A. (2022). Joint hypermobility links neurodivergence to dysautonomia and pain. *Frontiers in Psychiatry,* 12, 786916. www.doi.org/10.3389/fpsyt.2021.786916

Dana, D. (2020). *Polyvagal exercises for safety and connection: 50 client-centered practices.* W. W. Norton and Company.

den Houting J. (2019). Neurodiversity: An insider's perspective. *Autism: The International Journal of Research and Practice,* 23(2), 271–273. www.doi.org/10.1177/1362361318820762

Dodson, W. W. (2020). New insights into rejection sensitive dysphoria. *Additude.* www.additudemag.com/rejection-sensitive-dysphoria-adhd-emotional-dysregulation/

Dodson, W. W. (2016). Emotion regulation and rejection sensitivity. *Attention.* www.chadd.org/wp-content/uploads/2016/10/ATTN_10_16_Emotional Regulation.pdf

Eckstein, S. (2018). *Inner Active Cards.*

Fagrell Trygg, N., Gustafsson, P. E., & Månsdotter, A. (2019). Languishing in the crossroad? A scoping review of intersectional inequalities in mental health. *Int J Equity Health* 18, 115. www.doi.org/10.1186/s12939-019-102-4

Goldstein, T. (2020, June 16). *Neuro cloud and neurodistinct, neurodiversity refined.* Retrieved May 15, 2022, from www.timgoldstein.com/blog/neurodiversityrefined

Hayman, V., & Fernandez, T. V. (2018). Genetic insights into ADHD biology. *Frontiers in Psychiatry,* 9. https://doi.org/10.3389/fpsyt.2018.00251.

Henderson, D. (2021, January 15). PDA: Not what you think it is! *Dr. Donna Henderson.* Retrieved May 21, 2021, from www.drdonnahenderson.com/post/grow-your-blog-community

Jones, D. R. & Mandell, D. S. (2020). To address racial disparities in autism research, we must think globally, act locally. *Autism.* 24(7):1587-1589. doi:10.1177/1362361320948313

Kapp, S. K., Steward, R., Crane, L., Elliott, D., Elphick, C., Pellicano, E., & Russell, G. (2019). 'People should be allowed to do what they like': Autistic adults' views and experiences of stimming. *Autism: the International Journal of Research and Practice,* 23(7), 1782–1792. www.doi.org/10.1177/1362361319829628

Meadows, J. (2021, August 12). *You're using the word 'neurodiversity' wrong.* Retrieved February 12, 2021, from www.jessemeadows.medium.com/youre-using-the-word-neurodiversity-wrong-e579ffa816a8

Mel Planet Neurodivergent Admin. (2021, May 12). *Identifying and overcoming microaggression directed toward individuals with developmental conditions.* Retrieved May 14, 2021, from www.planetneurodivergent.com/identifying-and-overcoming-microaggression-directed-toward-individuals-with-developmental-conditions/

Mel Planet Neurodivergent Admin. (2021, May 5). *Um…can you stop yelling? Neurodivergent sensitivity symptoms.* Retrieved May 21, 2021, from www.planetneurodivergent.com/um-can-you-stop-yelling-neurodivergent-sensitivity-symptoms/

Mendes, E. A., & Maroney, M. R. (2019). *Gender identity, sexuality and autism: Voices from across the spectrum.* Jessica Kingsley Publishing.

Neurodiversity & neurodivergent: What do they mean and how do they impact me as a PGR? (2021). *UofG PGR Blog.* Retrieved May 13, 2022, from https://uofgpgrblog.com/pgrblog/2021/3/24/neurodiversity.

Pastor, M., & Gauvain, J. (2021). *Internal Family Systems institute: Level 1 training manual.* IFS Institute, Inc.

Pearson, A., & Rose, K. (2020). A conceptual analysis of autistic masking: Understanding the narrative of stigma and the illusion of choice. *Autism in Adulthood.* Volume 3, Number 1, 2021 ©Mary Ann Liebert, Inc. DOI: 10.1089/aut.2020.004352

Reilly, J., Gallagher, L., Chen, J. L. et al. (2017). Bio-collections in autism research. *Molecular Autism* 8, 34. www.doi.org/10.1186/s13229-017-0154-8

Riemersma, J. (2020). *Altogether you: Experiencing personal and spiritual transformation with Internal Family Systems therapy.* Pivotal Press.

Riemersma, J. (n.d.) *Move Toward with Jenna: Guided worksheet for Moving Toward™ difficult feelings and urges* [handout].

Schwartz, R. C. (2021). *No bad parts: Healing trauma and restoring wholeness with The Internal Family Systems model.* Sounds True.

Silvertant, M. (2021, September 7). *What we experience is not who we are.* Retrieved May 22, 2022 from www.embrace-autism.com/what-we-experience-is-not-who-we-are/

Singer, J. (2017). *Neurodiversity: The birth of an idea.* Singer.

Siyayoganathan, S. (2022). *The reality of masking: Understanding the neurodivergent perspective.* Retrieved May 5, 2022, from www.lunariasolutions.com/blog-post/the-reality-of-masking-understanding-the-neurodivergent-perspective/

Stenning, J., & Rosqvist, R. B. (2021). Neurodiversity studies: mapping out possibilities of a new critical paradigm. *Disability and Society,* 36:9, 1532-1537, DOI: 10.1080/09687599.2021.1919503

Thye, M. D., Bednarz, H. M., Herringshaw, A. J., Sartin, E. B., & Kana, R. K. (2018). The impact of atypical sensory processing on social impairments in autism spectrum disorder. *Developmental Cognitive Neuroscience,* 29, 151–167. www.doi.org/10.1016/j.dcn.2017.04.010

Tobik, A. (2021, August 5). *Quotes about autism.* Retrieved May 21, 2021 from www.autismparentingmagazine.com/quotes-about-autism/

Williams, T. D., Shamp, L. M., & Harris, K. J. (2021). Microaggressions in psychotherapy. *Psychotherapy Bulletin. Society for the Advancement of Psychotherapy.* Retrieved April 30, 2022 from www.societyforpsychotherapy.org/microaggressions-in-psychotherapy/

GOING DEEPER

Candice is the founder and clinic director of the globally known outpatient healing center, Namaste Center for Healing (NCH). Meg is the Chief Program Officer at NCH. Together they implement their Neuro-Inclusive Approach to healing with IFS as a major tenant when supporting individuals, couples, families, and small groups. Namaste Center for Healing's website is www.NamasteAdvice.com. Both authors are consultants for the International Institute of Trauma and Addiction Professionals (IITAP) and often facilitate Neuro-Inclusive and IFS-informed webinars and workshops through this institution.

From Candice Christiansen

1) Websites:
   a. www.namasteadvice.com
   Namaste Center for Healing is an outpatient treatment center in Millcreek, Utah that specializes in our Neuro-Inclusive approach to therapy and offers therapeutic services, coaching, and holistic practices such as reiki, sound bowl healing, yoga therapy, Ketamine Assisted Therapy (KAT), and medication management. Offerings include:
      i. Therapeutic services: www.namasteadvice.com/neuroinclusivetherapy
      ii. Coaching: www.namasteadvice.com/mindful-sessions
      iii. Holistic Offerings
      iv. Classes for Neurodifferent individuals and their families
      v. Customized Intensives: www.namasteadvice.com/intensives
   b. www.CandiceChristiansen.com

2) Podcast:
   a. Fabulously Candice: The Sexiest Podcast about Neurodivergence www. autismandintimacypodcast.com

From Reviewers

1) Websites:
   a. www.kimbolling.com
   b. www.therapywithalessio.com

From Other Sources

1) Autism-specific Websites:
   a. www.Embrace-Autism.com
   b. www.socialautie.blogspot.com
   c. www.PlanetNeurodivergent.com

d. www.Neuroclastic.com
   e. www.Neuroqueer.com

2) ADD/ADH Websites:
   a. www.Additudemag.com
   b. @HowtoADHD YouTube channel
   c. Adhdgirls.co.uk

3) Annual Neurodiversity Week Celebration:
   a. www.Neurodiversityweek.com

APPENDIX A

Key Terms Around Neuro-Inclusivity

Autism: A lifelong Neurological variation of genetic origin. A naturally occurring expression of human Neurodiversity that is present in any race, gender, sexual orientation, or cognitive ability.

Neurodiversity: The diversity of human brains and minds; the infinite variation in Neurocognitive functioning within our species (Walker, 2022).

Neurodiverse: a group of people whose members vary Neurocognitively from each other. For example, a classroom of Neurotypical students and Neurodifferent students is a Neurodiverse classroom (Walker, 2022).

Neurodiversity Movement: a social justice movement that seeks civil rights, respect, equality, and full social inclusion for the Neurodifferent individual. This movement began with the Autism Rights Movement; however, these movements are not one and the same. The Neurodiversity Movement seeks to be inclusive of all Neuro-minorities, not just Autistic individuals (Walker, 2022).

Neurodiversity Paradigm: a perspective of Neurodiversity that includes the following fundamental principles:1) Neurodiversity is a natural and valuable form of human diversity; 2) having one "normal" or "healthy" type of brain or one "right" style of Neurocognitive functioning, is a culturally constructed fiction, no more valid than the idea that there is one "normal" or "right" ethnicity, gender, or culture; 3) the social dynamics that manifest in regard to Neurodiversity are similar to the social dynamics that manifest in regard to other forms of human diversity (e.g., diversity of ethnicity, gender, or culture) (Walker, 2022).

Neurodivergence: the state of being Neurodifferent. Some types of Neurodivergence are genetic and innate while other types of Neurodivergence are produced by brain-altering environmental experiences. (Walker, 2022). Genetic and innate types of Neurodivergence were discussed in this chapter.

Neurodivergent (abbreviation, ND): Coined by Kassiane Asasumasu, refers to having a brain that functions in ways that diverge significantly from the dominant societal standards of "normal." For instance, having developmental, intellectual, psychiatric, or learning disabilities (Adan et al., 2021). This term is often interchangeable with the term Neurodifferent.

Neurodistinct: Coined by Tim Goldstein, creator of The Neuro Cloud™. This refers to humans whose thinking is distinct from Neurotypical individuals (Goldstein, 2020). This term is often interchangeable with the term Neurodivergent and Neurodifferent.

Neuro-inclusive: The act of valuing Neurologically different perspectives.

Neurotypical (Abbreviation, NT): Neurocognitive functioning that is considered to be within the societal standards of "normal." It is defined as the opposite of Neurodivergent, not synonymous with non-Autistic (Walker, 2022). Although it is not a considered a derogatory word, many Neurodifferent individuals do not like this word due to its "othering" connotations.

Neuro-majority: Another word used to describe the dominant Neurological type, Neurotypical (NT).

Neuro-minority: a group of people who share a similar form of Neurodivergence that is largely innate and that the Neuro-majority views in a discriminatory or oppressive way (Walker, 2022).

Microaggressions: Coined by Columbia professor, Derald Wing Sue, who describes intentional or unintentional behaviors, insults, and indignities which demean, shame, marginalize, or outright intimidate individual groups of people. These can be subtle, automatic, and unconscious (Mel, 2021).

Masking: Sometimes called "social camouflaging," this term describes artificial performance of social behaviors that are seen as more socially acceptable in a Neurotypical society (Siyayoganathan, 2022).

Common Clinical Myths about Autism and ADH

Common Clinical Myth: Autistic individuals are not good communicators and don't have empathy.

Truth: Many Autistic individuals communicate via writing, music, hand gestures, and facial expressions, as well as verbally. Many demonstrate emotional and somatic empathy.

Common Clinical Myth: ADH individuals can't focus and engage in experiential therapies or groups.

Truth: ADH individuals often hyper-focus on things they are interested in. Many do very well with experiential therapy and are creative thinkers.

Common Clinical Myth: An individual is not Autistic if they are able to make eye contact.

Truth: Many Autistic individuals have learned to make eye contact as part of masking, even if it is uncomfortable.

Common Clinical Myth: Autism and ADH are just an excuse for bad behavior.

Truth: Autism and ADH are brain differences. They are not an excuse.

Common Clinical Myth: Autism and ADH are caused by trauma or too many stimuli.

Truth: Both are Neurological conditions whose traits may be exacerbated by external stimuli. Many Neurodifferent individuals have experienced trauma in their lives.

A Neuro-Inclusive Inquiry for IFS Therapists Working with Neurodifferent Clients

Find a quiet space free from distractions. With your eyes closed or taking a soft gaze, begin going inward by connecting with your body. Bring your attention to your breath in this moment. Notice the sensations of breathing without any judgment or trying to change the rhythm or pace.

Then, if it feels right, draw in a deeper inhale through your nose and allow yourself to exhale just a bit longer. As you engage in slower, deeper breaths, you will enhance your present awareness in this moment. Allow yourself to stay with your breath for 3-5 inhales and exhales. At this point, be curious if you feel connected to the qualities of Self-energy such as calm, curiosity, open-mindedness, and compassion.

When you feel present and embodied, ask inside about a Neurodifferent client with whom parts of you have struggled, felt challenged around, or with whom your parts have judged. As you bring awareness to this client, notice, and name any thoughts, feelings, sensations, or urges that arise inside of you. Notice where you feel them in or around your body.

Acknowledge any thoughts or feelings that arise that feel challenging or judgmental. You may place your hand on that area of your body and quietly say, "I can feel you here. I am here with you." Pause and see what you notice inside. Remain present to whatever arises, free from any agenda. As you connect with your body in this tender way, you may notice thoughts, feelings, sensations, or urges become quieter and begin to soften or you might notice that the parts you are connecting with have messages or requests to share with you.

Continue to listen and acknowledge inside. Notice if you feel a genuine sense of compassion or curiosity. Pay attention to any insights you have during this inquiry.

Pause this exercise and write about what you noticed before continuing.

Following the Trailhead—Identifying the Burden

As you listen inside, move toward the parts that hold fears, stories, or emotional reactions toward Neurodifferences or Neurodifferent individuals. From the space of curiosity and compassion that you have accessed, begin to focus on this part or parts without any agenda. Notice how close or far they feel. How many parts are present and connected to these emotions and beliefs? If there is more than one, ask if they can come sit around you in a circle at about the distance of friends having coffee. Ask which part needs your attention first. Reassure all parts that they will get time with you. Let them know that you are hoping to get to know them all better.

With your attention focused on one part (target part). Notice if you get a sense of the part; do you see an image or sense an energetic presence? Does the presence of this part feel familiar? As you are curious about this part? Notice how you are feeling toward it. If you notice any feelings of concern, fear, or judgment, gently acknowledge these other parts that are near, reassuring them that they do not need to change how they are feeling. Gently ask them to soften back into the circle or give you space in another way as you continue to get to know the target part. You may need to spend some time with the concerned parts before returning to the target part. Allow all concerns to be validated.

If you feel Self-energy toward the target part, express your curiosity by asking this part what it needs you to know about its feelings toward Neurodivergence or your Neurodifferent client. Reassure it that you respect it and want to take it seriously. Listen to any fears or concerns. Notice if this part is coming from a place of protection (i.e. has a job… to judge, criticize, or avoid). If so, listen with compassion and ask if the part is willing to show you who it is protecting. If there are any fears about this, listen and acknowledge them respectfully.

As you learn more about this part and its burden of protection, take the time to befriend it until it feels ready to show you who it is protecting. Notice that some protector parts may not be protecting a specific exile in your system, but they themselves may be burdened by legacy burdens from families, institutions, and larger communities. If this is the case, listen to the part as it shares where it learned its fear or concern regarding Neurodivergence or Neurodifferent individuals. Ask the protector part if it is open to new data from you. If it is, you can share what you have learned in this chapter. Ask the part if it would be willing to observe with you, even through your own eyes, as you invite Self-energy into your sessions with all clients and lead from this space. Some protector parts might be relieved and not want to be present with your clients anymore. Others may want to show up with you in a different way. Be curious about this. Return to the other parts gathered around the circle and complete this same process with them. If you are time-limited, commit to your parts when you are able to return and hear from them or address their concerns.

If you find there is a vulnerable exile that is being protected by the inherent biases toward Neurodifference or Neurodifferent individuals, it is important that you get permission from all protectors to move toward this part. Identify this as a trailhead to address in your own therapy.

Negotiating with Parts before Sessions

After you have identified protectors and/or exiles connected to fears, judgments, or concerns, it is important to maintain relationships with these parts. Include them in whatever IFS practice you have. Before sessions with clients, specifically, your Neurodifferent clients, take a moment to go inward and compassionately request that all parts soften back so that you can bring Self-led energy into the session. The following is an example of how to make this request.

Before your session, take a moment to go inward, first by bringing your attention to your breath. Notice any parts that are forward and gently acknowledge them by placing your hand where you feel them in your body or by energetically turning toward them. Let them know that you are preparing to go into a session with a client and ask if they would like to go somewhere that feels safer, more comfortable, or even more fun while you work. Allow them to do so with your help if needed. If parts want to be present while you work, request that they soften back and observe giving you space for Self-leadership. It can be helpful to create a way to communicate with the parts that want to stay, such as placing your hand on your body where they are or noticing their energy outside of your body. Deep, regulating breaths can also reassure some parts.

If you are working with specific parts with fears, concerns, or judgments about Neurodivergence in your own therapy, gently request that they find somewhere safe and comfortable while you are in sessions with your clients. Reassure them of when you will attend to them inside, whether in your next therapy session or at another time. Always, thank them for their trust.

Steps for Creative Mapping with Neurodifferent Individuals

The following steps can be followed loosely to help your clients be curious about their inner worlds and map their parts and Neurodifferent traits. Refer to the table in "Goal 4" for details about tools and strategies for mapping.

1. **Setting the Stage.** It is common for many clients to need a concrete description of what "mapping" is. As IFS is introduced and woven into the therapeutic process, we have found it beneficial to set the stage for mapping clients' parts and their Neurodifferent traits. This is done by explaining the intention of the mapping exercise and providing examples of the various ways to map our internal systems such as visually imagining the parts, using visual art or music to depict parts, matching parts to pictures or objects, using figurines, or through various bodily sensations. Candice often shows her Neurodifferent clients pictures she has drawn and figurines she uses as examples of mapping Neurodifferent traits as well as parts. Additionally, we have found Sharon Ekstein's Inner Active Cards (2018) to be particularly helpful with our Neurodifferent clients.

   This sounds like, "I want to ensure you feel safe and supported in all ways during our sessions. One aspect of using a Neuro-Inclusive Approach to IFS therapy includes mapping parts as well as your Neurodifferent traits. There are various ways to do this…"

2. **Meeting the "Key Players."** With whatever medium or tool your Neurodifferent client chooses to map their inner world, you will notice that oftentimes, the "key players" in their internal family system emerge first. We allow our Neurodifferent clients to begin without any agenda, giving them space to meet these parts and traits that are present.
   a. This sounds like, "As you connect to the parts and traits that are present with you now, view the parts cards (or begin to draw, write, etc.) without any set expectations. Allow yourself to connect with authentic curiosity to what you are seeing, hearing, sensing, or feeling."

   If you are using cards, figurines, or other objects, you can also encourage the client to arrange the objects in a way that feels genuine to their current experience. In whatever way they are mapping, when the client appears to be finished, we invite them to share their experience. This often leads to them sharing their stories.
   b. This sounds like, "Typically when our clients map their parts, it tells their story. If it feels right to share with me, I would love to learn about your parts and the Neurodifferent traits that you identified." As they share, you might add, "Is there any meaning around how you have chosen to arrange them?"

3. **Who is Doing the Mapping?** At this stage, most clients will have several cards, figures, or drawings that they have created, and often, they can articulate these parts and traits in relation to themselves in the present moment. At this time, we often check for the presence of Self-energy and are also curious if we sense a manager who is doing the mapping exercise or if there is a specific hardware trait that is being engaged during the exercise.
   a. This sounds like, "As you look at your parts and traits, how are you feeling toward them? Are there any that you don't care for? What do you need me to know about them?" If clients are visual and imaginative, you can ask, "How are you experiencing your parts? Do you see them through your own eyes?" If they are auditory learners, you may ask, "Do you hear them?" and so on.

   This will often give you information about whether or not there is Self-leadership or if a part is facilitating the mapping exercise. If there are other feelings, thoughts, and urges, that do not align with compassionate curiosity (or another aspect of Self), respectfully acknowledge the part and gently ask if it is willing to pick a card, figure, or be depicted artistically.
   b. This sounds like, "Thank you so much for all your help with this exercise, we would like to get to know you better as well. Are you willing to pick a card/figure for yourself? If not, are you willing to observe while (client's name) completes the exercise with me?"

4. **Checking for "Hardware."** By this point, there may be Neurodifferent traits that have already been identified and named. Still, it is important to explicitly be curious if there are traits being depicted as parts, and vice versa. This is where your experience of learning about Neurodifference will be paramount. We often default to the IFS go-to of "Just ask…"

   This sounds like, "I notice that you named a 'distracted part.' Ask, is this experience of distraction your brain, or "hardware", responding to an external cue, or is this a part protecting you by distracting you when you feel pain?"

5. **Circling Back Around.** After fleshing out parts that are "key players," including those that may be doing the exercise for the client, and naming their Neurodifferent traits as their "hardware," it is important to circle back and ask the clients to view the cards, figures, objects, or their own piece of art again to see if anyone is missing.

   This sounds like, "As you look at your cards or art, how are you feeling toward it? (check for the presence of Self) Are there any parts that are missing? Does it feel like any of your Neurodifferent traits have not been represented?"

6. **Noticing the "Quiet Ones."** When you circle back around, it is common to find many parts that are quieter, have less "airtime" in the system, or that have been exiled or pushed away by the key players but come forward to be seen, heard, known and understood. During the mapping process, it can be hugely beneficial to spend some time welcoming these parts and hearing anything they might initially need to share.

   This sounds like, "I noticed that you pulled several other cards (or drew, etc. several other parts). Are these parts quieter in your system? Have they been exiled or pushed aside by others? We want to welcome them and acknowledge that they often don't get a chance to speak or share. We hope to get to know them better in therapy. Can you let them know this? Is there anything they need you to know today?"

7. **Wrapping up the Mapping.** Mapping will likely take several sessions, and it is something that can be revisited throughout the therapeutic process. It is important toyou're your Neurodifferent clients know that you are moving on to getting to know protector parts using the IFS protocol. Many Neurodifferent clients need us to explain the IFS protocol in a concrete way.

   This sounds like, "Now that we have mapped several of your parts and Neurodifferences, we are going to begin to get to know them better.

Below are some examples of how we have mapped parts visually, namely using Sharon Eskstien's Inner Active Parts Cards. (Eckstein, 2018).

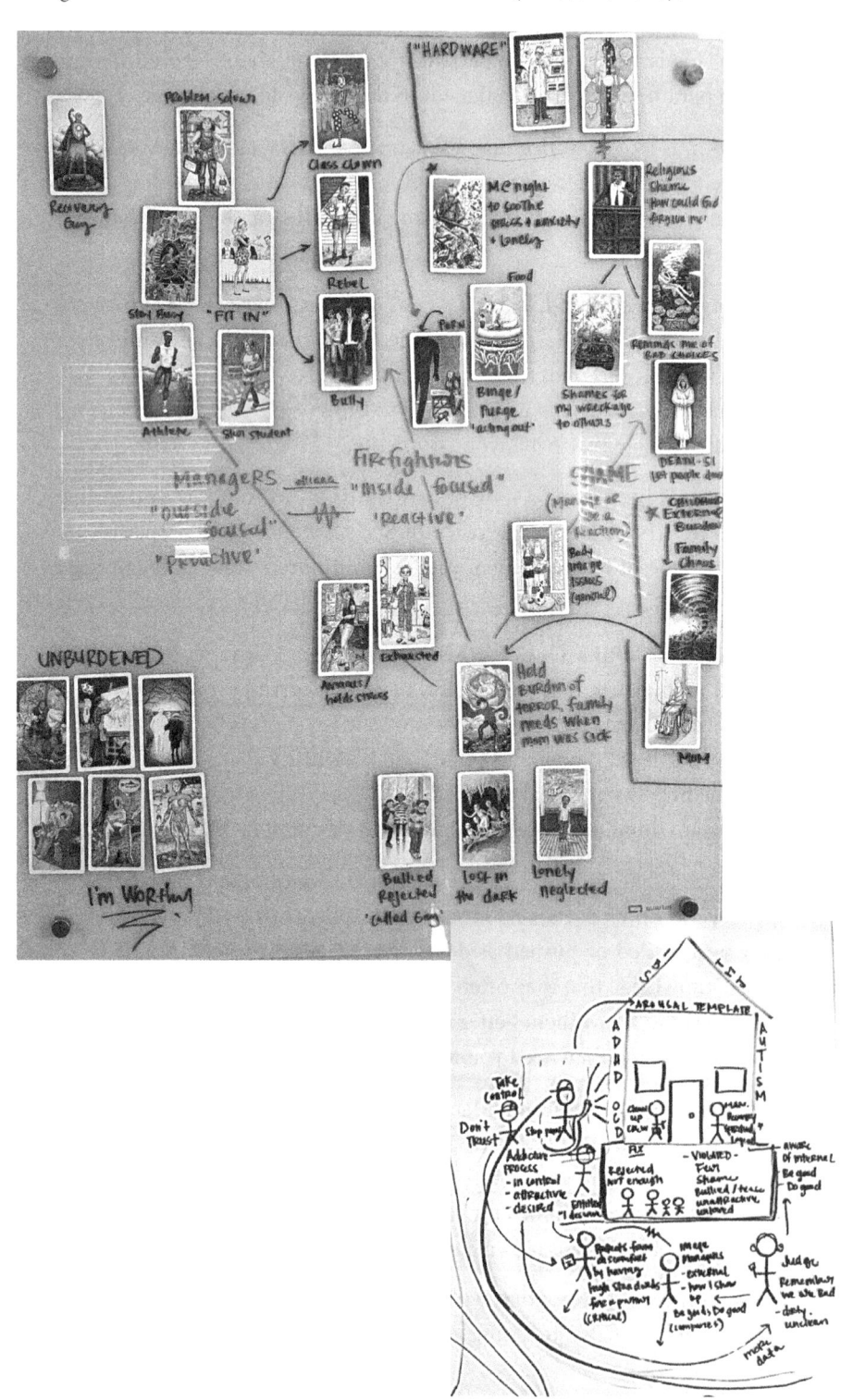

Common Protectors and Parts Constellations in Neurodifferent Clients

These lists and the accompanying visual were created based on our experience and what we commonly observe in our Neurodifferent clients. You may notice that the ways parts protect and how they are burdened are similar if not exactly the same as other "Neurotypical" individuals. However, we also know that internal family systems are unique, and many different parts may show up in relation to Neurodifferent traits. These lists and examples are by no means exhaustive.

Common Neurodifferent Traits ("Hardware") that May Impact Internal Family Systems

- Rejection sensitivity or Rejection Sensitivity Dsyphoria.
- Sensory sensitivity—overstimulation and/or under-stimulation.
- Autonomic Nervous System Meltdowns.
- Autonomic Nervous System Shutdowns.
- Emotional empathy—feeling deeply and intensely, often physically, with others, sometimes without being able to express verbally.
- Alexithymia—difficulty identifying and describing emotions. Neurodifferent individuals often feel emotions very strongly, even if they can't identify or describe them.
- "Rigid" thinking—stems from a dysregulated autonomic nervous system.
- Concrete thinking—needing things to be spelled out articulately and clearly.
- Hyper-focus—can be related to a special interest or a concern or worry; can sometimes feel like "looping."
- Anxiety—often related to the uncertainty and unknowns in a Neurodifferent person's environment.
- Distraction—due to a Neurodifferent brain wired for novelty.

Common Protector Parts in Manager-Roles ("Software")

- Social Masking Parts—very skilled at blending in, like a chameleon, to fit into social situations. Often want to be seen as "fitting in" or "high functioning."
- Insecure or Judging Parts—remind clients of their weaknesses or what other people have told them are "deficiencies," specifically related to their ND.
- People Pleasing Parts—often want to be seen as "fitting in" or "high functioning."

- Prover Parts—hard-working manager parts that often want to be seen as "high functioning" and often carry burdens of perfectionism.
- Perfectionist Parts—attempt to control outcomes and appear "perfect" in any given situation; often want to be seen as "high functioning."
- Comparing Parts—compare to others and can even use internal shaming in an attempt to motivate; often want to be seen as "high functioning."
- Ruminating Parts—Anxiously ruminate or review social interactions with others in an effort to remind the client "what not to do."
- Compliant Parts—insistent about following rules and being seen as "good" or "moral."
- Loyal Parts—fiercely loyal externally to individuals whom they feel emotional empathy for, even if the person is unsafe, abusive, or not reciprocal in the relationship.
- Advocate Parts—Advocate externally for things that feel unfair or unjust; often very proactive and engage in online/offline groups (i.e., on social media).
- Entertaining or "Funny" Parts—use humor and wit to "fit in" or create space between the client and others to prevent harm or overwhelm.

Common Protector Parts in Firefighter Roles ("Software")

- Depressed Parts—aid in withdrawing and/or numbing behaviors or feelings of apathy and disconnection to protect from the pain of rejection.
- Dissociating Parts—similar but can be more intensive than Depressed Parts in how they shut out the outside world or takes a client "out" of reality.
- Angry or "Emotional Outburst" Parts—may come across as irritable, short, defiant, and argumentative.
- Distracting Parts—distract the client from feeling emotionally or physiologically overwhelmed; may use stimming behaviors to do this.
- Sleepy Parts—similar to dissociating parts in the desire to "shut out" the world by putting the client to sleep.
- Raging or Angry Parts—reactive parts with anger via verbal or physical outbursts.
- Defender Parts—bully or reject others before they are rejected or in the name of another person, often because they feel so deeply. May appear defensive and argumentative.
- Justice Parts—respond, in some cases resentfully, to real or perceived injustice. May be more "reactive" than the Advocate Parts who engage in proactive strategies.

- Lone Wolf Parts—withdraw socially and appear to embrace isolation and solitude to protect from judgment, often despite the desire for connection or validation.
- Parts that Engage in Addictive Processes—engage in coping tools that "stop the pain" and, in some cases, meet unmet needs of the person. Can develop into addictive processes (substances, sex, screens, gambling, food, etc.).
- Suicidal Parts—aware of the option for death to find relief from pain.

Common Burdens of Exiled Parts ("Software Virus")

- Burden of Shame—holds shame, often from social judgment, bullying, or criticism of the client's Neurodifferences.
- Burden of Anxiety—namely, fear of failure, judgment, or being seen as inadequate or inferior.
- Burden of Emotional Overwhelm—exiled parts may feel emotional empathy and be overwhelmed with the physical and emotional sensation.
- Burden of Defectiveness—the belief that the client is unworthy, unlovable, or not good enough.
- Burden of Fear of Failure—burdened by the specific fear of not succeeding in a given situation and being judged as less than.
- Burden of Loneliness—holds the burden of loneliness, isolation, and feelings of disconnection. Often holds the belief of being an outcast.
- Burden of Fear of Dangerous People—namely the fear of being unsafe due to bullying, exploitation, judgment, and microaggressions.
- Burden of Fear of Being Ostracized—namely the fear of being rejected, deprived of relationships, or being "kicked out of the tribe."

As you are supporting your client in mapping their Neurodifferent internal family systems, it's important to remember that while some parts appear to be experts in their protective role, some are more versatile and move between roles or jobs. Additionally, some do their role in a more proactive, managerial way in one instance and show up in a more reactive, "firefighting" way in another.

Additionally, it is important to note that sometimes protectors are responding to "hardware" or Autonomic Nervous System responses (i.e., environmental overstimulation or under-stimulation) and not necessarily an exile's trigger or trauma danger cue. This means that there may not be a trailhead to traditional unburdening protocols but a check-in with protector parts to see if the ways they are protecting (strategies) are healthy and in balance with the system as a whole (i.e. masturbation, substance use, dissociation, or suicidality).

APPENDIX B

Neuro-Affirming Autism Screening Tool
Developed by Aly Dearborn, LMFT and Candice Christiansen, LCMHC

This neuro-affirming autism screening tool is designed to assist clinicians in the exploration of autistic traits using best practice recommendations for languaging and presenting autism as a neuro-type, not as a disorder.

Screening questions are based on a combination of the author's lived autistic and professional experience, as well as a synthesis of primary findings in clinical autism research conducted from 2014-2023 centering female autistic voices.

In efforts to present a solidly neuro-affirming screening tool, we have chosen not to include existing (pathologizing) descriptors of autism as presented in the DSM-V. Instead, we encourage the exploration of *"Autistic Ways of Being,"* which normalizes autistic preferences for communication, particular passions, sensory needs, and other aspects of the autistic experience.

For more guidance on the neuro-affirmative approach to adult autism assessment using a social disability model, we highly recommend *The Adult Autism Assessment Handbook: A Neurodiversity Affirming Approach,* by Davida Hartman, Tara O'Donnell-Killen, Jessica K.Doyle, et al, (2023).

Neuro-affirmative View of Autism (Based on DSM-V Criteria)

Adult clients who respond affirmatively to all 3 of criterion A - A1, A2, & A3 **and** *at least 2 of 4 of criterion B - B1, B2, B3, &/or B4, would benefit from further exploration of autistic identity. Keep in mind that these criteria must be met across the lifespan.*

A. Differences in social communication and interaction with others. Must be manifest by all 3 of the following (A1, A2, and A3):

A1. Differences in social communication with others, including tendencies to "talk passionately about special interests," "go off on tangents," or to prefer avoiding "small talk."

A2. Differences in the experience of non-spoken communication, including tendencies to "avert eye contact when speaking" or engage in "stimming" while talking, and how facial expressions, body language, and gestures are used in conjunction with spoken communication.

A3. Differences in experiences of developing, maintaining, and understanding friendships and relationships with others.

Neuro-Affirming Autism Screening Tool

B. Preferences for particular calming and/or energizing and balancing movements or activities, particular tasks, special interests and/or sensory experiences. <u>Must be manifest by at least 2 of the following (B1, B2, B3, and/or B4):</u>

B1. Preferences for particular or repeated motor movements, use of objects, or vocalizations that might be balancing or regulating such as "stimming" or repeating particular words or phrases.

B2. Preferences for particular routines, schedules, or ways of doing things to enhance sense of comfort and security. Preferences for advanced notice of potential changes or transitions in order to be more prepared, and desires for sameness, such as taking the same route, or eating the same foods everyday.

B3. Particular interests or passions for specific topics or activities and a capacity for prolonged and intensive focus on these interests.

B4. Differences in ways of identifying and experiencing the senses. Includes all 8 sensory systems (sight, taste, touch, hearing, smell, interoception, proprioception, and vestibular); high sensitivity, low sensitivity, unique fascination with, and/or unique experiences of the senses.

C. *Traits must be present since early childhood (but may not fully manifest <u>until demands exceed capacities for masking</u>)*

The following pages offer screening questions for further exploration of the above diagnostic criteria. A longer version with additional screening questions is available upon request.

© May 26, 2023. Aly Dearborn, LMFT and Candice Christiansen, LCMHC. All Rights Reserved. Do Not Copy.

Neuro-Affirming Autism Screening Tool

Exploration of (A1): *Differences in social communication with others, including tendencies to "talk passionately about special interests," "go off on tangents," or to prefer avoiding "small talk."*	*Autistic ways of communicating & interacting with others* - Do they often worry whether they are talking "too much" or "not enough" in social situations? - Do they often wonder "what's the right way to act?" and make significant efforts to observe or find out "the rules" prior to engagement in a new situation? - Is it easier for them to talk at length about certain topics than others? Lose track of whether others are still listening if sharing about an interest area? - Can they get easily bored or agitated when listening to others talk about things that are outside of their area of interest? Do they find "small talk" exhausting, pointless, or difficult? - Do they often ruminate about past social interactions, replay conversations, or mentally prepare for future conversations by practicing what they are going to say? - Do they prefer activity-based social events over less structured events, like parties?
Exploration of (A2): *Differences in the experience of non-spoken communication, including tendencies to "avert eye contact when speaking," engage in "stimming" while talking, and how facial expressions, body language, and gestures are used in conjunction with spoken communication.*	*Autistic experiences of non-spoken, non-verbal communication* - What is their felt experience with giving or receiving direct eye contact? - Do they shift their gaze when speaking or when listening? Do they describe eye contact as "intense," "uncomfortable" or "distracting?" - Do they find other forms of communication easier than speaking? - Do they prefer catching up with friends via text or email communication to phone calls? Prefer to use emojis, gifs, or memes to communicate rather than words?

© May 26, 2023. Aly Dearborn, LMFT and Candice Christiansen, LCMHC. All Rights Reserved. Do Not Copy.

Neuro-Affirming Autism Screening Tool

	- Do they find it easier to communicate and/or listen in 1:1 interactions than in groups?
Exploration of (A3): *Differences in experiences of developing, maintaining, and understanding friendships and relationships with others.*	*Autistic experiences of developing, maintaining, and understanding friendships and relationships* - Have they been bullied or deliberately excluded by others? - Have they often felt "different," "like I don't belong" or "not normal?" Feel alone even with others? - Do their friends tend to be older than them in which they take a "mentee" type role or much younger than them in which they take a "mentor" type role? - Do relationships feel like "hard work?" Do they feel like managing multiple relationships is "exhausting?" - Do they struggle to understand how someone else thinks or feels about them unless it is obviously displayed or stated? - Do they feel highly sensitive to the energy or emotions of others?
Exploration of (B1): *Preferences for particular or repeated motor movements, use of objects, or vocalizations that might be balancing or regulating such as "stimming" or repeating particular words or phrases.*	*Autistic preferences for particular or repeated motor movements, use of objects or vocalizations that might be regulating* - Do they ever notice certain parts of their body moving in rhythmic or repetitive ways? - Does engaging in repetitive, rhythmic movements occur in a variety of states, including *contentment, boredom, or overwhelm?*

© May 26, 2023. Aly Dearborn, LMFT and Candice Christiansen, LCMHC. All Rights Reserved. Do Not Copy.

Neuro-Affirming Autism Screening Tool

	- Do they hum, make certain noises or vocalizations, count numbers, or say certain words or phrases when content, bored, or to soothe? - Do they have any unique flexibility of the joints?
Exploration of (B2): Preferences for particular routines, schedules, or ways of doing things to enhance sense of comfort and security. Preferences for advanced notice of potential changes or transitions in order to be more prepared, and desires for sameness, such as taking the same route, or eating the same foods everyday.	*Autistic preferences for routines and sameness; particular ways of managing change & transitions* - What are their experiences with big transitions, like relocating, relationship ending, job loss, etc.? What about small transitions, like shifting from one task to another? - Do they have particular habits, patterns, schedules, or daily routines that are hard to change? What happens if a daily routine is disrupted? - Do they tend to "get stuck on details" via ruminative thinking about past, current, or future events? - How do they react to unexpected events, like cancellation of plans or unpredictable behavior in others?
Exploration of (B3): Particular interests or passions for specific topics or activities and a capacity for prolonged and intensive focus on these interests.	*Autistic special interests or passions for particular topics or activities* - Are there certain subjects, topics or hobbies they get very excited about and can engage in deeply or talk about for long periods of time? Conversely, is it difficult to engage in or discuss non-interest-area topics? - Do they have a lifelong tendency to dive "all-in" to certain areas of interest or get hyper-focused or "obsessed" with a specific person, topic, or activity for a period of time, avidly pursuing additional information and gaining expert-level knowledge in particular topics?

© May 26, 2023. Aly Dearborn, LMFT and Candice Christiansen, LCMHC. All Rights Reserved. Do Not Copy.

Neuro-Affirming Autism Screening Tool

	- Do they have a particular fondness or empathy for animals, the climate, and/or other vulnerable populations? - Do they engage in various forms of activism or get extremely passionate about particular socio-political issues? - Is their thinking about social issues black & white? Is it difficult for them to maintain relationships with others who don't share their views?
Exploration of (B4): *Differences in ways of identifying and experiencing the senses. Includes all 8 sensory systems (sight, taste, touch, hearing, smell, interoception, proprioception, and vestibular); high sensitivity, low sensitivity, unique fascination with, and/or unique experiences of the senses.*	*Autistic ways of sensing and experiencing the senses* - Do they have high sensitivity or intense reactions to certain sounds, smells, images, textures, or tastes that are perceived as negative? - Do they have intense reactions to sensory inputs that they perceive as positive and pleasurable? - Are they a selective eater, with particular types of foods that they eat or don't eat? Were they told they were a "picky eater" growing up? - Do they have a tendency to notice or get irritated by seams or tags in clothing? - Do they have intense (positive or negative) reactions to certain types of touch or physical contact?

To review, (adult) clients who respond affirmatively for all 3 of criterion A - *A1, A2, & A3* **and** at least 2 of 4 of criterion B - *B1, B2, B3, &/or B4,* **and** traits have been present across the lifespan would benefit from further exploration of autistic identity.

The following are additional screening tools that have been clinically validated with female samples though they do not (yet) reflect recommendations from the autistic community for incorporating a neuro-affirmative approach.

- ***Camouflaging Autistic Traits Questionnaire (CAT-Q)***
  https://link.springer.com/article/10.1007/s10803-018-3792-6

© May 26, 2023. Aly Dearborn, LMFT and Candice Christiansen, LCMHC. All Rights Reserved. Do Not Copy.

Neuro-Affirming Autism Screening Tool

- *Girls Questionnaire - Autism Spectrum (GQ-ASC)*
  https://www.liebertpub.com/doi/10.1089/aut.2019.0054

Thank you for your interest in learning more about neuro-affirming approaches to autism assessment. We hope our screening tool is useful. We are available for additional consultation or training on the integration of this material into your practice.

For contact information:
Aly Dearborn: www.alydmft.com & Candice Christiansen: www.namasteadvice.com

© May 26, 2023. Aly Dearborn, LMFT and Candice Christiansen, LCMHC. All Rights Reserved. Do Not Copy.

Neuro-Affirming Autism Screening Tool

[Addendum]

Though not part of the formal DSM-V criteria for diagnosis, the following domains of experience are commonly reported by (female) autistics across the clinical literature and are included below for further exploration:

Multiple experiences of victimization, across the lifespan	- Do they have a chronic history of being bullied, excluded by peers or colleagues? Experiences of sexual harassment, sexual assault, or other forms of intimate partner abuse, including financial exploitation? - What has been their experience with asking for or receiving support for any of these issues?
Masking & Camouflaging *may not be a conscious behavior	- Do they put a lot of effort into learning to understand or mirror other people and why they act or do what they do? (e.g. "give the right amount of eye contact," "don't talk too much about interests, hide stimming? - Put a lot of effort into people- pleasing, dressing like others, trying to "fit in," etc.? Do they easily pick up on "catch phrases, accents, or mannerisms of others?" - Do they use alcohol, cannabis, or other substances to help them feel more at ease in social situations or interpersonal interactions?
Alexithymia	- Is it easy to identify their feelings? - How do they experience the feelings of others? - Do they feel emotions really strongly to the point of overwhelm but struggle to verbalize them? Or explain them to others?
Hyper-Empathy *Strong sense of social justice, loyalty, and honesty*	- Do they identify as a Highly Sensitive Person? - Have strong intuitive capacities? (even if they have been told their intuition is wrong via gaslighting?) - Experience strong affective, somatic, or responsive empathy for others ? - Are they "generous to a fault?" Do they care deeply & intensely about others? The underdog? Animals? - Would they be described by others as "sensitive, caring, and honest?" Do they value fairness, honesty, loyalty, and integrity? Do they struggle to lie or experience distress about telling minor "untruths" (e.g., calling in sick to work; etc.)?

© May 26, 2023. Aly Dearborn, LMFT and Candice Christiansen, LCMHC. All Rights Reserved. Do Not Copy.

Neuro-Affirming Autism Screening Tool

"Spiky" Profile	- What are their experiences with navigating the various domains of life, including school, work, relationships, and home life? Are there areas of significantly high achievement, contrasted with areas of more difficulty? - In their academic history, were there large discrepancies in comprehension of different subjects? - Labeled as being a "Black and White" thinker? Or Creative, "out of the box," "original thinker?"
Executive Functioning and Attention Differences	- Have they been screened for or diagnosed with ADHD? - What systems have they developed in order to be more effective in executive functioning tasks, like planning, organization, or managing time? - What is their experience with initiating, switching, or stopping tasks? - Do they report a need to write things down to help them remember verbal instructions? Do they have preferences for visual aids or tech support to remember appointments, etc.? - Have they had experiences of "flow state" and/or hyperfocus when engaging in areas of interest in which other external stimuli or interoceptive cues fade from awareness (e.g., unaware of hunger, thirst, physical posture)
Rejection Sensitivity Dysphoria	*Real or perceived experiences of social rejection experienced as extraordinarily painful and intolerable, with acute physical and emotional pain and significant nervous system dysregulation akin to death-like experiences.* - Have rejection experiences been a trigger for suicidal ideation or self harming behavior like hitting themselves, head-banging, or cutting? - Do they over apologize for perceived mistakes, saying "I'm sorry" all of the time? - Do they have a long history of being "people pleasing" and/or "conflict avoidant?"
Energy Management Differences & Fluctuating Needs	- Have they had periods of intense work followed by periods of extreme exhaustion and burnout? - Do they often need long periods of rest after being "out in the world?" *Support needs may vary widely depending on the nature of the demands ;sensory issues, time of day; or other factors*
Common Physical Health &/or Other Medical Conditions	- Were they premature? - Any personal or family history of epilepsy or other neurological disorders? - Chronic Gastrointestinal issues, like Irritable Bowel? - Chronic sleep difficulties? - Ehlers-Danlos syndrome? Hyper-mobility?
Gender Dysphoria	- Have they had a period of gender questioning? - Do they currently identify as gender fluid, non-binary, or trans?

© May 26, 2023. Aly Dearborn, LMFT and Candice Christiansen, LCMHC. All Rights Reserved. Do Not Copy.

Neuro-Affirming Autism Screening Tool

Proposognosia *"Face Blindness"*	- Do they have difficulty putting faces to names? - Do they have a hard time recognizing someone when they see them out of context, like running into a colleague at the grocery store?
Emotional Regulation Challenges	- Do they struggle with emotional regulation and/or have a tendency to become easily dysregulated into an anxious or shut down state? - Do they have a history of "tantrums" (e.g., "autistic meltdowns") as a child? - Do they have a history of suicidal ideation or self-harm in periods of intense emotional distress?
Disordered Eating	- Do they have periods of time in which they experience no appetite or "disgust" for certain foods? Or times in which they have more difficulty eating or "forgetting to eat," resulting in unintended weight loss? - Do they have a history of diagnosis with avoidant-restrictive food intake disorder (ARFID), anorexia nervosa, or another eating disorder? - Is it difficult to "feel full" or know when they are hungry? - Are there periods of time in which they experience intense hyperfocus on a perceived body imperfection or body dysmorphia?

Thank you for your interest in learning more about neuro-affirming approaches to autism assessment.

We hope our screening tool is useful and we are available for additional consultation or training on the integration of this material into your practice.

© May 26, 2023. Aly Dearborn, LMFT and Candice Christiansen, LCMHC. All Rights Reserved. Do Not Copy.

EXPLORING A NEURO-DIFFERENT INTERNAL FAMILY SYSTEM

A Neuro-Inclusive Approach to IFS

NAMASTÉ CENTER FOR HEALING

Common Neurodifferent Traits "Hardware"
- Hyper-Focus
- Emotional Empathy
- Rejection Sensitivity Dysphoria
- Alexithymia
- Sensory Sensitivity

Common Protectors "Software"

Our protective parts show up for many different reasons. Often they arrive to protect exiled parts from the outside world or to protect the outside world from the burdens of exiled parts.

In a neurodifferent system, sometimes protector parts respond directly to "hardware" and not necessarily an exile's trauma trigger.

Examples of protectors in manager-roles include: Masking, Judging, Critic, Pleasing, Proving, Comparing, Analyzer, Logical, Ruminating, Compliant, and Entertaining.

Examples of protectors in firefighter-roles include: Dissociating, Distracting, Sleepy, Raging, Defending, Isolating, Engaging in Addictive Processes, and Suicidal.

Common Exile Burdens "Software Viruses"

When someone's neurodifferent traits are judged, shamed, or oppressed, exiled parts are burdened.

Examples include: Burdens of shame, anxiety, defectiveness, lonliness, and fear of judgment and unsafety.

©2023. Namasté Center For Healing. All Rights Reserved.

SECTION FOUR
EMERGING TRENDS

IFS AND PSYCHEDELIC INTEGRATION

ENHANCING SELF-TO-PART HEALING THROUGH THE POWER OF SACRED PLANT MEDICINES

Nancy L. Morgan, MS, PhD

> "To fathom Hell or soar angelic/
> Just take a pinch of psychedelic."
> —*Humphry Osmond*

The summer of 1975 held the promise of a new era. The Vietnam War had officially ended, my home state of Colorado was in full-scale preparations for its upcoming centennial birthday, and the country was preparing for its bicentennial. I had just turned 17 and in two months would begin my senior year of high school. Celebration was in the air.

Throughout high school I had been curious about psychedelics and had heard stories of positive and mystical experiences from many of my friends. In mid-July my friends and I were enroute to a day of music at Colorado's Red Rocks Amphitheatre. It seemed the perfect opportunity to accept an invitation to try the "magic mushrooms" brought for the occasion. The driver and front-seat passenger agreed to wait until we reached the venue, but my friend and I decided to take ours on the drive.

Within a half-hour of ingesting, a grin spread over my face. I remember experiencing an effervescent tingling sensation in my body and a feeling that all was well with the world. As I stared out the window at the majesty of the Rocky Mountains on my left, the only word I could form was, "Beautiful." But that didn't express even a tenth of what I was truly feeling.

When the car pulled over for a break, I took the opportunity to walk in the adjacent forested area. Glancing down I became mesmerized by the busy activity of ants moving bits of sand up and down their mound. Looking up I was entirely taken in by the towering spruce, pines, and fir swaying rhythmically in the breeze. The thought of simply staying in that spot seemed so much more appealing than sitting on a cement bench amidst a throng of concertgoers. But the choice was not mine to make, so I returned to the car and off we went.

After that carefree summer, my attention shifted to whether and where I would be going to college. There were times I experimented a bit more with psychedelics, but once I completed my undergraduate degree my focus turned toward graduate school and figuring out what I was going to do with my life. In 2000, I received my doctorate in clinical psychology and began working with adults, specializing in trauma and attachment. I could never have imagined that four decades later my path would lead me back to psychedelics and that I would be reunited with psilocybin cubensis, "magic mushrooms" once again, this time in a therapeutic setting.

In December of 2019 I received my certification as a Psychedelic-Assisted Therapist and Researcher (CPTR) through the California Institute of Integral Studies' (CIIS) pioneering training program, and with that became the second certified IFS therapist to graduate from the program (having received my certification as an IFS therapist in 2018).

CIIS had begun preparing psychedelic researchers and therapists in 2016 in anticipation of the need for highly qualified professionals in the field of psychedelic research and therapy. Graduates have gone on to help design and facilitate critical psychedelic studies and to integrate psychedelic therapy into current medical, psychiatric, and spiritual practices. Graduates are now mentoring, supervising, consulting, and training therapists and researchers in the therapeutic uses of psychedelics.

Following my CPTR certification, I updated my website and listed IFS-informed preparation for, and integration of, psychedelic experiences among my services, and within a matter of weeks requests to provide training, supervision, consultation, and therapy began appearing in my email, as did invitations to present on psychedelic therapy for psychological associations in the United States and abroad. This immediate response to my listing surprised me and revealed how much the world had changed over the past 50 years.

Throughout this chapter I refer to those utilizing psychedelics as *clients*, given the clinical therapeutic focus of my work. To those who sit in support of those clients I use the term *guide*, though many long-time guides believe that rather than guiding their clients they are in fact "sitting in service to and behind the medicine."

The Psychedelic Renaissance

The word *renaissance* combines "back" or "again" with "birth" (naissance, from the Latin *nasci*, "to be born"). Why the renaissance of psychedelics after 50 years of harsh federal and state laws imposing severe penalties for use and possession?

Most would say it is primarily due to the tireless efforts of Rick Doblin, founder of the Multidisciplinary Association for Psychedelic Studies established in 1986, research pioneers such as Roland Griffiths, William "Bill" Richards, and the team at Johns Hopkins University, Charles Grob at UCLA, and many others whose research revitalized the interest in psychedelic research, medicine, therapy, and healing. This tidal shift was further enhanced by the publication of Michael Pollan's *How to Change Your Mind*, which became a *New York Times* No. 1 best seller in 2018.

Just how common are psychedelics today? A 2013 article examined the estimated lifetime use of psychedelics based on 2010 data gathered by the National Survey on Drug Use and Health (NSDUH). The data, collected before the current boom in psychedelic research, revealed there were over 30 million psychedelic users in the United States.[1] This number does not include the use of psychedelics in research settings or in the sanctioned religious ceremonies utilizing peyote and ayahuasca.

For this discussion, I focus primarily on the psychedelics that have taken center stage over the past twenty years in the emergent field of psychedelic sciences. However, positive findings reported from research on psychedelics not covered in this chapter such as 5-MeO-DMT (5-methoxy-N,N-dimethyltryptamine) will likely lead to additional studies and renewed consideration regarding future use in clinical settings.

What Psychedelic Research Shows

Johns Hopkins University, NYU, UCLA, Harvard, Yale, UCSF, and the University of Wisconsin are among the many US universities that have been, and continue to, contribute data to the growing field of psychedelic research.

Research is sprouting up in the US heartland as well thanks to the work of IFS-trained palliative care doctor and researcher, Lou Lukas, MD, the founder of Heartland Palliadelic in Omaha, Nebraska. Dr. Lukas's research focuses on easing the end-of-life distress of those diagnosed with pancreatic cancer, which is expected to become the second leading cause of cancer-related deaths in the U.S. by the year 2030.

According to the site psychedelicinvest.com, 309 universities worldwide are engaged in 628 clinical trials involving psychedelics with many more research proposals waiting for approval by the Food and Drug Administration (FDA). Psychedelics have been shown to support clients' restored feelings of connection, clarity, and perspective, and reduction or elimination of existential anxiety, PTSD symptoms, depression, and anxiety.

Over the course of my CPTR training, I had the very good fortune of learning from many of the luminaries in psychedelic research. The host of stellar instructors included Janice Phelps, founder of the training program; Bill Richards, his son Brian Richards, and Mary Cosimano from Johns Hopkins; Charles Grob from

UCLA; Tony Bossis and Jeffrey Guss from NYU; Nicholas Cozzi from the University of Wisconsin; Michael and Annie Mithoefer of the MAPS MDMA research trials; Usona co-founder Malynn Utzinger; along with other notables including David Presti, PhD, professor of neurobiology at UC Berkeley; David E. Nichols, Adjunct Professor of Chemical Biology and Medicinal Chemistry at UNC, Chapel Hill; and Maria Mangini, Natalie Metz, Bob Jesse, Diane Haug, and Patricia James.

In one of his lectures, Dr. Guss, a psychoanalytically trained psychiatrist, identified that integration is the least well-defined aspect of psychedelic therapy and varies from therapist to therapist. He also found that the frame through which therapists have been approaching research participants and understanding the clinical process was inconsistent.

Research protocols have varied relative to the number of hours subjects receive therapy prior to, and following, their psychedelic sessions, and there has been no clear sense of which therapeutic modality to employ.

These issues led Dr. Guss to seek out a highly defined therapy for psychedelic research and for treating patients clinically. Guss and his research team sought to delineate an explicit and replicable, evidence-based model that intentionally built upon both the neurobiological actions of the medication and the phenomenology of the drug experience. They surveyed Interpersonal Therapy, Logo Therapy, Mindfulness-Based Cognitive Therapy, and Acceptance and Commitment Therapy (ACT).

In 2019, Guss, et al. published an article identifying ACT as the model that best provided their team with the ability to manualize a therapy protocol for use in their clinical trial of psilocybin-assisted therapy which they were undertaking for major depressive disorder.

When I learned that IFS had not been considered among the evidence-based therapies, I decided to write my final paper on utilizing IFS for the integration of psychedelic experiences. There had been many times over the course of my CPTR training that IFS could have been introduced, but it was only over the week of instruction offered by the Mithoefers, both IFS trained, that the model was given recognition. I felt its time had come.

I published my paper in hopes of reaching a wider audience to whom I could introduce the model, especially researchers and therapists who were neither trained in, nor familiar with, IFS. Though now in its 40th year, IFS did not gain widespread attention until it was designated an evidence-based therapy in 2014. Since that time the demand for IFS trainings, therapists, practitioners, and resources has grown exponentially and, as a result, the model is now receiving considerably more attention in emerging psychedelic training programs.

> "Just because the light is green doesn't mean you shouldn't look both ways before stepping into the street."—*Garth Stein*

Before anyone considers working with psychedelics in any capacity, it is wise to pause and remember that we can easily be led by parts whose desperation to reduce our suffering is so great that they unwittingly lead us into making unhealthy, unboundaried, and unsafe decisions. Harm can and has been done by unskilled researchers, therapists, and guides during and following psychedelic experiences.

In addition to many mystical and insightful psychedelic experiences, there are also those that have taken clients spiraling down harrowing corridors and into deeply disorienting realms. To ensure we return from a psychedelic experience to a life that supports integration of those experiences, we need to inform ourselves, consider our physical and emotional health, our level of interpersonal supports, and whether there are external constraints to address.

One truly can "fathom hell or soar angelic" as was noted by British psychiatrist Humphrey Osmond, an early pioneer in psychedelic research who introduced the term psychedelic at the New York Academy of Sciences meeting in 1957. Osmond derived the term from the Greek words *psyche* (for mind or soul) and *deloun* (for show), and in a letter to author Aldous Huxley penned the now famous quote, "To fathom Hell or soar angelic/Just take a pinch of psychedelic."

Due to the political climate of the 1960s through the 1990s, only the risk factors associated with psychedelics made the news, despite the early promise of research conducted in both Canada and the United States. Consequentially, in 1970 the Drug Enforcement Agency classified psychedelics as Schedule I substances. This brought an immediate halt to all research and drove the use of psychedelics underground where they have remained ever since. Schedule I is the most restrictively regulated drug schedule under the United States Controlled Substances Act of 1970.

Legalization & Psychoactive Substances

Research outcomes have begun to appear on the benefits of the San Pedro Cactus, a sacred cactus native to the Andean mountains of Peru, Bolivia, and Ecuador also known as wachuma, and on the iboga bush of Africa. Iboga is a perennial rainforest shrub native to Gabon, the Democratic Republic of Congo, and the Republic of Congo.

In 1991, the National Institute on Drug Abuse (NIDA) funded research into ibogaine. The studies in rodents found that ibogaine reduced how much heroin, morphine, cocaine and alcohol the animals consumed. This work primed the FDA to greenlight a clinical trial of ibogaine in humans for cocaine dependence, but the study was stalled in the early stages due to a lack of funding and contractual disputes. NIDA abandoned its interest in ibogaine, citing safety as one concern.

Given the current paucity of research data in the United States on San Pedro Cactus and Iboga, their potential benefits have not been included in this chapter.

The psychedelic substances that are covered in this chapter are those that have garnered sanctioned approval for use in the United States, albeit with conditions attached.

Ayahuasca

Despite being classified as Schedule I substances not all psychedelics have remained illegal in the United States. Ayahuasca, for example, a South American psychoactive brew that has been in use as a ceremonial sacrament among the Indigenous peoples of the Amazon basin for over 1000 years, gained U.S. protection under the Religious Freedom Restoration Act of 1993 (RFRA).

The RFRA protects two churches based in Brazil that are gaining widespread popularity in the United States, the Santo Daime and the União do Vegetal (UDV) church. Both churches use ayahuasca as part of their religious practices and earned the right to do so through two separate legal actions that found in both cases the government cannot interfere with religious conduct unless it can demonstrate to a court that it has a "compelling interest" in doing so. If it is unable to do so, RFRA requires the government to allow church members to practice their religion.

Santo Daime is an amalgamation of different faiths. Its sermons feature elements of Catholicism, African rituals, and Indigenous traditions. Daime translates to "Holy Give Me" in Portuguese and is another name for ayahuasca, the brew made from the leaves of the Psychotria viridis shrub along with the stalks of the Banisteriopsis caapi vine. The União do Vegetal ("the union of the plants") church ceremonies are identified as esotericism with a doctrine combining Christianity with reincarnation and the progress of the individual soul to increasingly higher spiritual levels.

Peyote

Under a federal law approved by Congress in 1994, members of the Native American Church are authorized to possess and use peyote, the psychedelic cactus found on limestone soils of the Chihuahuan desert of southern Texas and northern Mexico. For 10,000 years, Indigenous peoples of the Americas utilized and preserved peyote from South Texas, across the Rio Grande, to the Wirikuta desert in the state of San Luis Potosi, Mexico. For tribes North of the Rio Grande, peyote use came more recently and is held as a sacred medicine utilized to support healing resulting from ongoing colonial trauma as well as to maintain Indigenous identity, religious practice, and cultural sovereignty.

Ketamine

Ketamine is a legal FDA-approved medicine with psychoactive properties and is increasingly being prescribed for those diagnosed with depression. At high doses, ketamine occasions psychedelic experiences that are shorter in duration than psilocybin or Ayahuasca. Psychedelic in-office sessions and at-home ketamine use is increasing and is receiving favorable reviews from those for whom it has been prescribed. I currently work with several clients who use low-dose ketamine weekly following an at-home protocol I developed with a client in 2018.

Clients take prescribed ketamine in the form of rapid-dissolving tablets in the comfort of their own homes with at least one adult family member, a "sober sitter," at home with them. The low dosage induces a gentle reflective state and subsequent therapy sessions optimize the integration of the material that surfaced.

Though I can speak to the positive use of ketamine in at-home settings, I cannot speak to whether there are benefits rendered in other settings where neither preparation, therapeutic support, nor integration of ketamine experiences are present. There is a growing concern in the psychedelic community regarding the number of ketamine infusion clinics opening throughout the United States that appear to be motivated by the promise of profit over client welfare. It is up to each of us to make our own determination and decide for ourselves whether we are looking for quick fixes or long-term healing, and to recognize whether we are parts-led or Self-led in our pursuits.

In summary, despite overwhelming positive research outcomes, other than the sanctioned use of psychedelics as a religious sacrament and FDA-approved research, the U.S. Drug Enforcement Agency's listing of psychedelics as Schedule I drugs remains in place and until rescheduled will continue to deem psychedelics as having "no accepted medical use and a high potential for abuse."

Shifting Public Opinion, Growing Demand

June 17, 2021, marked 50 years since President Nixon declared drugs "public enemy number one." This proclamation waged a full-out offensive that poured hundreds of billions of dollars into law enforcement which led to the incarceration of millions, disproportionate numbers of whom have been Black, Latinx, and Indigenous people.

Today, the majority of American voters believe the policy has mainly increased drug-related harms and contributed to overcrowding the nation's jails and prisons. A 2021 poll reported by the ACLU found that public opinion has shifted substantially.

- 65 percent of voters supported ending the war on drugs.
- 66 percent of voters supported eliminating criminal penalties for drug possession and reinvesting drug enforcement resources into treatment and addiction services.
- 63 percent say drug use should be addressed as a public health issue, while only 33 percent say it should be addressed as a criminal justice issue.

The shift in public opinion was most evident when in 2020, the State of Oregon decriminalized drugs and legalized the use of psilocybin by licensed psilocybin-assisted therapists and facilitators. Colorado became the second state in the nation to follow Oregon's lead and in the midterm elections of November of 2022, voted to decriminalize drugs and legalize psilocybin. Colorado state authorities will regulate healing centers and licensed practitioners will provide the psilocybin to participants. An advisory board will solicit community input and prepare recommendations for the state health authority. The first healing centers are expected to open in 2024.

The passing of the ballot initiative allows those 21 and older to grow, possess and share psychedelic substances but not sell them for personal use. It also allows people who have been convicted of offenses involving these substances to have their criminal records sealed.

In addition, a growing number of cities across the United States including Santa Cruz and Oakland, California; Denver, Colorado; Somerville, Cambridge, and Northampton, Massachusetts; Seattle, Washington; Detroit, Michigan; and Washington, DC have also decriminalized many if not all psychedelics.

Prospective clients are coming from all social classes and sectors. Clergy members, police officers, physicians, teachers, academics, wealthy young Silicon Valley executives, veterans of the past three wars, and more, all hoping to experience relief from their single-incident or life-long challenges resulting from early life traumas.

Among the reasons for the increasing number of clients turning to psychedelics include a desire to find alternatives to the psychiatric drugs they have been prescribed for decades, many of which have deleterious side effects. In addition, many cannot afford therapy or have themselves been wounded by the mental health system, so they are not interested in services that could again expose them to further rejection, shame, or humiliation.

Guides are often unprepared for how intensive working with certain clients can be and several guides with whom I spoke reported an increasing number of clients who carry diagnoses that have disqualified them from participation in research studies seeking psychedelic experiences and supports. Their desperation for healing is palpable.

The Imminent Need for Psychedelic Support Services

With word spreading about the benefits of psychedelics, 3,4-Methylenedioxy-methamphetamine (MDMA) and psilocybin have been deemed "breakthrough therapies" by the Food and Drug Administration and are heading towards national approval for use under strictly regulated conditions by 2023.

Rick Doblin said in a 2021 interview that, if approved by the FDA, treating the anticipated one million people in the first ten years of MDMA-assisted therapy alone would require more than 35,000 trained therapists. Approval for legal psilocybin therapies could spark the need for an additional 15,000 psychedelic-trained therapists in the following year.

While state and national regulators determine protocols, a wide range of training programs are emerging. But future requirements for legal psychedelic therapy are uncertain, which makes selecting the best training or certification program especially difficult. Programs for training therapists for psychedelic-assisted therapies are varied with some prioritizing techniques, while others focus on how to work with new compounds. Some of the programs focus primarily on research, while others focus more exclusively on psychedelics themselves.

Given that the demand for psychedelic-assisted therapists will far exceed the supply based on current projections, the time is now to identify ideal psychotherapeutic models for working with psychedelics and offering programs that can provide training and certification in those models.

There are currently over 10,000 people worldwide on the waiting list for the IFS Level 1 trainings, so many of the individuals already working with psychedelics have been unable to gain access to what IFS has to offer. In response, I began offering trainings introducing the IFS model to psychedelic researchers, therapists, and guides in 2019 as a space holder until the IFS Institute could offer a Level 1 training specifically for those currently working with psychedelics.

In the process of screening prospective participants for my workshops, I've seen that almost all applicants had been preparing, sitting for, and integrating clients' underground psychedelic experiences for decades. Eighty percent identified their primary goal for wanting IFS training was to learn how the model could support their clients' integration practices as well as their own.

Commencing in September of 2022 the Internal Family Systems Institute initiated IFS Level 1 trainings nationally and internationally specifically designed for those already working with psychedelics. Unlike other IFS Level 1 trainings, these trainings were by invitation only to ensure that MAPS-trained therapists as well as researchers, guides, and others working with psychedelics have the opportunity to be trained in the IFS model.

Completion of Level 1 training is a prerequisite for the Level 2 and Level 3 trainings, which offer specialization in several different areas including working with couples, trauma and neuroscience, addictions, and more. It also qualifies participants to pursue certification as IFS therapists and practitioners should they choose to follow that path.

Current Practices of Integration

Before we look at what the IFS model can bring to the integration process, we should acknowledge that current integration practices in the U.S. unfortunately do not adequately account for the integration of psychedelic experiences found in collectivistic communities in Peru, Brazil, Africa, and Mexico. These countries have a rich cultural heritage replete with practices and ceremonies that support the use of psychedelics, primarily ayahuasca, psilocybin, and ibogaine.

In the U.S., our culture still ascribes to the rugged individualist ideal. This cultural norm does not provide a natural container for the integration of psychedelic experiences. In fact, it provides the opposite, and people who travel abroad to participate in psychedelic ceremonies often return to find themselves in need of support in order to process their experiences. Many are reaching out to therapists to help integrate the material that surfaced in their experiences. However, because so few therapists are trained to work with psychedelics, and so few therapeutic models offer the integration supports needed, many clients are left to their own devices.

In 2019, I invited over 50 primarily U.S.-based guides to share their feelings and thoughts about integration. The majority of these guides have accumulated hundreds of hours preparing, sitting for, and supporting their clients' integration processes.

> "Integration is the most essential part of doing medicine work. It knits the awareness that has come through, sometimes beyond the narrative way that we encounter the world."

> "Integration is the processing and assimilation of new awarenesses and insights as well as repatterning old ways of being into new, healthier ways of being in the world; aligning thought and action to manifest a desired outcome that, previous to the experience, was not being created in one's life."

> "Integration, especially if you have had an experience that has been really dismantling to the ego, challenges the ways that you have structured your life. That can be very frightening and disorienting, so the integration also serves to create a way to creatively and usefully be with that other awareness, braiding the worlds of that very liminal numinous space into the mundane space of our everyday life."

> "Integration is where clients get to bring the fruit of their journey's harvest into the salad of life and create a living, breathing practice that will ultimately change their life and get them on the path to healing themselves and their relationships and learning acceptance of what is and love of the divine in all of its ordinary and non-ordinary magic."

Mona Tara, a senior member of the Santo Daime church in Ashland, Oregon and a graduate of the CPTR training program, offered her views regarding the integration of the church's ayahuasca ceremonies, called "Works."

"The longer one does this, the more one realizes the importance of integration. One of my first ayahuasca ceremonies involved a death experience and hell realms, and there was no one to help me understand any part of it. I ended up finding a book by Alberto Villoldo that helped a lot—leading me to work with him. But for many, many years, integration was just not a real part of the experience. One was left trying to process alone. Journaling was the thing for many years, but I believe our Daime community would be much bigger had we understood the need for new people to have some form of integration afterwards. Following the CIIS CPTR program this past year, I finally came to understand more fully, not only the importance, but also ways to accomplish integration. We are working on it."

Dick Schwartz views integration as the harmonious, collaborative, and loving operation of human systems at any level. He notes that the German derivation of the word heal means to "make whole," and that integration is central to making people, or systems of people, harmoniously whole. He cautioned, however:

"Without proper guidance, psychedelic experiences can create the opposite of integration—polarization, exiling, and psychosis-like disintegration of psychological systems. To prevent such experiences and to promote integration, guides need an ecologically sensitive map of intra-psychic territory that can anticipate and calm fearful and backlash reactions to the massive shifts in that territory that psychedelic experiences can create."[2]

Alison Walmsley, a subject in the MAPS Phase II MDMA study, shared that while everyone is talking about integration, she fears it is becoming a buzzword at risk of losing its meaning.

Dick and Alison are not alone in their concerns. Similar concerns were voiced by the guides I interviewed:

"I think as the psychedelic movement is becoming more medicalized, it's replicating all those old medical structures which actually don't really encourage the participation of the patient in their healing, and that would extend to the clinics that may have a very small nod toward integration and then kind of drop the person after a short period of time. There is concern about the whole thing, the whole animal of psychedelic work, which is the integration."

"Integration is mixing things together to improve a situation. For me, it's about mixing a new experience into my psychology. It takes time for my mind and body to process the experience which settles over time.

My initial reaction is not what lasts. What lasts is what integrates and becomes part of my psychology. I know it when I'm suddenly making new and improved choices."

"While it is deeply concerning to hear when integration is not at all a part of this work, I find my role is to do my best to trust in the experiences of others and, in this very situation, share, with as many people as possible who have any kind of influence in this world, the benefits of integration."

"Without integration, a person lacking in support, spiritual practice, and a healthy routine, etc., may end up psychologically fragmented, potentially resulting in more chaos or upset than they were experiencing previously."

"Guides who do not wield the tools of integration as aptly as they do the tools of ceremony guidance, or ceremony preparation, have the potential to do a disservice to their clients. The clients of such guides can lose the true focus of this work and may even end up using the medicine, journey after journey after journey, to allow their egos to keep their patterns intact without making the often-painful changes required. Journeys then stand to become nothing more than experiences and lore instead of agents of true change and might actually support the client's existing pattern structures."

"People seem to be showing up with more significant medical, psychological, and spiritual maladies. Addiction, pain, anxiety, depression, and grief are becoming more and more a part of the human condition in our culture, and the complexity of those coming for healing must be met with competence. Which means integration."

"Without integration of the work done, it simply becomes a memory, and old patterns and ways of being are easy to fall back into, if they stopped at all. There is also greater risk involved in what someone may experience after a psychedelic experience if they do not have the tools and foundational practices to ground and center themselves, especially if the work stirred stuff up."

One of the remarkable research findings well known in underground circles for many years has been the spontaneous emergence of parts during psychedelic experiences. Because psychedelics provide clients with an enhanced view of their lives, they frequently witness themselves from a Self-state that enables them to compassionately view how they have exiled parts of themselves in an attempt to evade the pain and emotions connected to those exiled parts.

How IFS Can Support the Work of Researchers, Therapists, and Guides

IFS is unique among therapies in that it holds that the Self is the client's healer. Through understanding the dynamics of the internal system, clients can learn to be their own "parts detector" and learn the ways to unblend so they can access their Self-energy.

The Adverse Childhood Experiences scale is beginning to be considered by guides seeking to gain a greater sense of how significantly early life trauma may have impacted their clients' lives. Several guides I spoke with are now incorporating the ACE scale into their intake process and referring clients with high ACE scores to more experienced guides or to therapists specializing in trauma for the purpose of extended preparation sessions. As a result, many IFS therapists and practitioners are now receiving those referrals.

I have worked with several clients with early life trauma who as adults were diagnosed with inflammatory illnesses. As we gained permission from protective parts to go to the exiled parts they protected, it was not uncommon for these clients to initially experience painful flareups. I recall one client asking, "Do you think my pain is connected to my exiled part?"

When I have invited exiled parts to pull back some of their energy, clients have reported feeling their pain subside. Physical ailments, and in particular inflammatory diseases that involve ongoing inflammation where the body does not return to its original healthy state, are due to a range of factors that can cause inflammation overload. Lifestyle habits, such as smoking and diet, genetics, and pollutants in the environment are linked to autoimmune diseases, where the body's immune system turns on itself, also lead to chronic inflammation. Psychedelics have the capacity to shine the light on these ailments by drawing the client's attention to the places where pain is held. If the client is guided to go toward the source of the pain and offered the supports to do so safely, long-held tears are often released, and a new sense of relief is experienced.

In the mid 1800s physician Henry Maudsley noted, "The sorrow that has no vent in tears may make other organs weep." IFS therapists and practitioners are aware that the body holds the pain when tears have not been able to be released at the time the pain was suffered. For that reason, we begin facilitating the healing process by inviting clients to turn a soft focus inside their bodies as we ask from where, in or around the body, a part is signaling. Protectors often signal from the head, jaw, neck, shoulders, back, chest, and solar plexus. Exiled parts often signal from the heart.

I think of the example of an engine warning light. When it comes on in my car, I know to bring it to the dealership. I would never attempt to cover up my dash so I would not have to look at the light, yet that is what I have done with the countless signals my body has sent. I know I am not alone. Psychedelics have a way of bringing us back to what needed to be witnessed and processed, that for years had been suppressed.

I utilized psilocybin a few years ago in the office of a very experienced guide. Memories of witnessing my brother's beatings at the hands of my stepfather came flooding back, and I began crying. The tears didn't stop for more than two hours, and by the end of the session I had filled two waste baskets with tissues. These were not new memories, but what was new was the realization that, though I had shared these stories with friends and processed them in therapy, I had not released the tears I had been unable to cry when the abuse was taking place. I was simply too paralyzed with fear.

Since that session, I was able to connect with parts still trapped in the past that carried tremendous grief, fear, rage, hopelessness, and despair. They had been there waiting to be seen. Supporting their unburdening relieved them of the enormous weight they had been carrying for decades.

Michael Mithoefer has shared that during the early phases of the MAPS MDMA trials, he noted that 70 percent of research subjects had spontaneously begun speaking from Self, expressing compassion for their parts for the first time in their lives.

The book "Acid Test" tells the story of Nick Blackstone, an Iraqi war veteran who took part in the MAPS MDMA trials. He came to understand that he had imprisoned a part of himself that scared other parts because they saw what this part had been capable of doing in Iraq. When Nick opened the prison door, he embraced the part and apologized. The part was grateful and shared that it didn't want to carry so much fear and rage and had felt terrible about what it had done.

When asked what IFS represents to him, an IT specialist who guides shared:

"IFS is a prism which allows guides to empower their clients to auto shift into their higher selves and create bonds and relationships with parts that the parts never had in the way they needed when they were young."

He went on to say:

"Without IFS, guides run the risk of remaining at the center of the therapeutic process alongside the client, instead of slowly fading like the Cheshire cat into the background. This self-empowerment is the ultimate goal of the guide—to help the adulting client come to a relationship, learn to hold and love all of their parts, and graduate from the guide's care."

A retired surgeon who guides shared:

"To date, IFS, for me, seems most compatible in looking at and processing the psychedelic experience...because it is so relatable and provides an easy and understandable format."

Another guide offered:

"I might rephrase the question to ask if a psychedelic substance can be utilized to support the integrations of IFS therapy. In either case, my answer is yes! It's powerful work. That said, I am not a therapist. The credibility of my answer resides in my facilitated psychedelic experiences. The job of the facilitator was to allow me to have my experience without interference. Since I have learned more about IFS and parts work, I understand that what I craved during my journeys were the questions of a skilled practitioner taking me deeper into the trauma, revealing what I was not able to access on my own. The potential for healing is great."

Whether a psychedelic experience comes by way of research, a church ceremony, individual work with a guide, or an individual experience without a guide—which, though not ideal, is a common practice—the longer and higher quality the integration, the better the outcome. Therapists and practitioners who are knowledgeable about psychedelics can be invaluable following a psychedelic experience.

An elder leader of Ayahuasca ceremonies always begins with the admonition, "The medicine will give you what you need, not what you want." Integration of lovely experiences is important, but especially important is the integration of challenging experiences, for in those lie the greatest potential for moving through places where clients have been stuck.

Integration is one of the healing steps in the Internal Family Systems (IFS) therapeutic model. It is that stage toward the end of the healing process when the protective parts that had stepped back are invited to return so they can experience the previously exiled part unburdened and reunited with the client's Self. This can be emotional for protective parts. They are typically relieved to realize that the part they protected is no longer trapped in the past, which frees them up to consider how they might want to use their energy in a new way. But sometimes these protectors don't know what else they can do because protecting was all they had ever done. This is where the therapist or practitioner can ask the protectors if there is something else that they would like to do, something they might not have ever considered possible.

I worked with a woman in her mid-twenties who had a very critical protector. She described this protector as a Marine with a buzz cut, broad shoulders, and a stern bearing who was unrelenting in his criticism of her. When the exiled part it protected was healed and this protector was asked what it would like to do instead of being so critical, the client said she felt an immediate softening. A smile crossed her face, and she said, "He wants to be a cheerleader."

How IFS Supports Clients' Psychedelic Experiences

The IFS model offers a way for clients to review, rather than relive, their traumas. In witnessing the pain, they gain a greater understanding of its impact on their lives. Psychedelics offer the same vantage point.

Integration is critical to the health of our bodies, minds, and spirit. If we move on too quickly from our experience, without time to sit quietly so the process can become part of us, we can feel scattered, confused and ungrounded and become susceptible to questioning the relevance of what happened. When we allow the experience time to settle, it becomes part of us and supports our healing.

Patrycja Radecka, an IFS-trained psychologist, and her partner Coen de Koning, an IFS practitioner who holds a degree in physics, offer IFS-informed psilocybin truffle sessions in the Netherlands. They share a passion for self-development and personal growth, and not just with the help of psychedelics. On their website www.therapeuticsittingservice.com, they share that some of their most profound experiences have come from facing, and staying with, their own pain with the loving support of another.

In late 2021, Patrycja, Coen, and I wrote an article titled, "Internal Family Systems: A Therapeutic Model for Each Stage of the Psychedelic Experience," published in the Journal of Psychedelic Psychiatry. In the article, Patrycja and Coen shared their views on integration and offered their therapeutic supports that include IFS therapy, art therapy, psychodrama, vocalization and movement, and meditation. They also invite clients to express their experience in ways that can help them become aware of what was really going on in the experience. These methods can help uncover the meaning just beyond the direct experience. The integration work then relates those experiences to clients' daily lives.

Coen said that the integration process can become quite intuitive when approached from the IFS perspective that we are a multiplicity and contain many parts, some of which are carrying burdens that can be revealed and released prior to, during, and following the psychedelic experience. When Self-to-part relationships are harmonized, we lead from Self rather than from burdened parts—an ideal therapeutic goal with or without the use of psychedelics.

"You are not a drop in the ocean. You are the entire ocean, in a drop."
—*Rumi*

IFS-Informed Integration

IFS-informed integration begins with IFS-informed preparation. Preparation for a psychedelic experience sets the tone for the research, therapy, ceremony, or guided session. It orients an individual to the world they are about to enter.

IFS-informed preparation includes questions regarding clients' parts' hopes, fears, and concerns in addition to traditional questions regarding physical and mental health histories. Agreements are made relative to what both the guide and the client affirm they will abide by to ensure a safe, supportive, and healing space throughout the entirety of the medicine experience.

It is very common for clients to have polarized parts. One part may be very eager for the healing it hopes will be possible, but another part may be terrified. If the terrified part's fears and concerns are not considered it is possible that the entire experience could be blunted or even blocked. It can also result in backlash during and after the psychedelic session.

The thought of the client being out of control or saying or experiencing the very things protectors have worked so hard to keep exiled are common protector fears, so it is essential to consider their fears and take the time necessary in preparation to ensure all parts' fears, concerns, and needs are recognized. Use of the IFS 6 Fs will be very beneficial at this point. Identifying the fearful part, finding out where it is located in or around the client's body, focusing on how that part is experienced by the client (tightness, pain, numbing, etc.), asking the client how they feel toward the part, befriending and fleshing out what the part wants the client to know, and learning what the part fears will go far to build a stronger relationship between the client and their parts.

Parts' fears are often allayed when guides provide more information, offer to titrate dosages, and assure parts that they will be included in the integration sessions following the psychedelic session.

Once protectors start to feel they can "step back" it allows for tremendous access to the client's Self. It is not uncommon for spontaneous Self-to-parts work to occur without prompting once a Self-to-part relationship is formed. Healing begins with deep, open-hearted, loving connections with our protectors which then enables our exiled parts to come forward to be held in the healing balm of Self-energy.

If a part remains fearful, that is a red flag to not go forward with the session and to instead continue to offer extended preparation sessions. Creating an aftercare plan that includes checking in with parts also affirms that the client is not going to abandon them.

Psychedelics are not for everyone. Careful attention needs to be paid to clients who are routinely dysregulated, without emotional support, or living with external constraints that threaten their wellbeing or safety.

A final word on preparation. It is important to remind clients that no significant life decisions should be made for at least a month after the psychedelic session regardless of the clarity of the messages received in the session. This is to ensure against later backlash and unforeseen consequences that could negatively impact not only the client but others in their lives as well.

The influence of early psychotherapies striving for ego dissolution and catharsis made their way into underground guiding practices and have been utilized by many guides over the last four decades. Though guides intended to do no harm, there was still harm done, especially to those clients who had experienced early life traumas and suffered deep attachment wounds—i.e., clients who as children felt neither seen, heard, nor loved.

The issue of what is best for clients is contested by guides. Some believe that playing chaos music, for example, is an essential part of a psychedelic experience and are, therefore, resistant to moving away from what they perceive as necessary in a client's psychedelic experience. Clearly there is a power differential in psychedelic sessions, and anything that impacts a client's sense of safety warrants reconsideration.

IFS does not ascribe to the belief that "ego death" or "ego dissolution" are necessary for a client to heal, nor is it necessary to push a client into uncomfortable states, so pursuing these outcomes would not be a part of an IFS-informed psychedelic session. Quite to the contrary, in fact.

The majority of experienced guides I interviewed do not believe they know what is best for clients, although I have encountered a number who do. Beware the guide who believes it is their calling to be their client's healer. Such beliefs do not reflect the Self-energy that Dick Schwartz referenced when he shared his thoughts on how IFS can inform the training of guides:

> "The guide must know how to maintain Self-energy, holding qualities like calm, compassion, confidence, clarity and connectedness and keep the space around the journeyer safe from psychic entities that can enter when they are out of their bodies. Guides must also be able to help journeyers approach the parts of them that spontaneously arise with curiosity and compassion, which means they need an understanding that all parts are valuable regardless of how extremely they present."[3]

There is a difference between parts-led guiding and Self-led guiding, just like there is between parts-led and Self-led therapy sessions. Therapists are more likely to negatively impact their clients if they are not aware they are leading from parts. The challenge with being blended is that we don't typically know when we are. This is an area of training that IFS Level 1 provides that no other therapy can offer because no other therapy recognizes that we are both parts and Self and that harmonization of the Self-to-part relationship provides the ideal container for healing.

If I am blended with a part, I am far more likely to be impacted by what a client brings up in therapy because my own system will be activated. The same is true, but magnified, in guiding because, unlike a 50-minute therapy session, psychedelic experiences last for hours. Whether we are a therapist or a guide, we need to check in with ourselves to see if we have an agenda. Are we, for example, interrogating or imposing ourselves rather than sitting with clients in calm, curious, connected, and compassionate Self-energy?

Many clients have said that though their psychedelic experiences were agonizing, something of value was gained from them. This can be true for clients with parts whose strength is mining value from difficult situations and who may also have more resources, and external supports. They can learn and grow from myriad challenges. Yet many clients are not that resilient, lacking resources and external supports. So, what might motivate one client could very well debilitate another. This is the reason therapists tailor therapy sessions to meet their clients' needs rather than injecting their own beliefs about what is right for the client into the therapy sessions.

I have been referred clients who have utilized psychedelics and whose guides felt entirely overwhelmed and in need of therapeutic support themselves to integrate what came up for them during the psychedelic session. Some clients clearly were not ready for psychedelic sessions and their protective systems fought against the influence of the psychedelic for the duration of the session, which created an intense and unpleasurable experience.

In the early days this would have been called a "bad trip," which was assumed to occur by chance. Now we can consider that the agony might have been attributed to polarized parts in the client's system, and that working with those parts during preparation sessions might have made the difference in whether a client's experience was akin to a hell realm or soaring with angels.

If the former occurs and clients enter those hell realms, there is the risk of the client becoming rageful, physical, overcome by paranoia, and desperate to escape. Such instances put both the clients and their guides at risk. Therefore, every effort to ensure the psychedelic experience is held in a safe container increases the likelihood that the client will benefit from the experience.

One way to do this is to ensure integration sessions help clients consider how they experienced their psychedelic sessions and what the sessions offered that they can now consider as they return to their lives. Inquiring into whether clients feel they received valuable information can also explore how their parts experienced the session.

Parts use our bodies in many ways and communicate with us through bodily sensations, thoughts, emotions, aches, pains, tightness, etc. So, when we inquire into how clients experienced their psychedelic session, we listen for who it is that is responding and stay curious about what that part and other parts are feeling and why.

We can explore how the client's experience related to their intention for the session. An exploration of parts' hopes, fears, and concerns sheds light on how parts in a client's system relate to one another.

If the client doesn't feel the psychedelic experience met expectations, it can be tempting for them to consider a different psychedelic or going to a different guide. Exploring these impulses will support gaining a deeper understanding of the tension and how parts are working to try to alleviate it.

Since intentions are often set by parts, inviting clients to listen to what a part was hoping for, had its intention been realized, can offer a great deal of information about parts' needs. These needs can be explored in subsequent IFS integration sessions and/or in therapy sessions.

Psychedelic sessions can include experiences in the physical, spiritual, emotional, and relational realms, so identifying the realms in which parts presented themselves provides a trailhead for further exploration. Parts can be very creative and will use any means available in an effort to do their jobs or express their emotions.

Practices that support IFS-informed integration are enhanced when we can access the natural world. Walks in nature or engaging in dance, yoga, or other expressive arts such as drawing or working with clay can deepen the integration of clients' experiences because they reconnect clients with their embodied parts.

Years ago, I heard a Tara Brach talk that began with the story of a man returning from work and stopping at his table to put his keys down and go through the mail. His little daughter excitedly came up to him and tugged on his pant leg. He continued looking through the mail. She tugged some more. After another minute of tugging, he finally looked at her and said, "What are you doing down there?" She looked up and said, "I live down here."

Our parts live in our bodies and benefit immensely when we put down the mail and turn a soft focus inside. They have often waited for our attention for decades. Because so much gets opened up in a psychedelic session, and because the sessions run for so long, opportunities abound to connect with our parts during, and following, a psychedelic session.

Many parts make connections with clients during the psychedelic experience that they had not been able to make previously, so it is not surprising that those parts may want to seek out additional psychedelic experiences at the earliest opportunity. This, however, does not allow integration to be fully processed and can inhibit the effects of future psychedelic sessions.

One woman who had gone into her second psilocybin session felt no effects at all though she had taken the highest dose allowed by the guide, a dose that would clearly occasion a psychedelic experience. When the guide inquired into what had happened in a previous psilocybin session with another guide, the client reported she had taken a lower dosage but felt the full effects including profound insights. The insights included the message that she needed to slow down. Had she slowed down? No.

She had continued working at the same fevered pitch and had taken no time to integrate any of the material that was offered during her first session. The adage, "Psychedelics give us what we need, not what we want," comes to mind. In this case, the fact that the mushrooms had no effect could be as important a message to heed as had there been a psychedelic experience. I can hear my mother's voice in my ear saying, "No desert until you finish your dinner."

It can be especially meaningful for clients to share whether they experienced Self-energy during their psychedelic experiences and if they did, how they experienced it. Sometimes clients have deep and meaningful connections with what was previously beyond their knowing and can only describe it as indescribable. But inviting them to reconnect with those feelings and share what it was like to exist beyond the constructs and contexts of everyday life provides a perspective many clients have never had and feel deeply grateful for acquiring. A list of IFS-informed questions to be used during integration sessions has been added to the end of this chapter.

Stages of Integration

Integration of a psychedelic experience begins within the first hours following the psychedelic experience with the client sharing and processing their experience with the guide. The client will still be feeling some of the waning effects of the psychedelic but will be able to sit up, eat some food, and reflect on their experience.

It can be very beneficial for guides to write down as much as they can when clients speak during their psychedelic experiences. It is not uncommon for clients to remain entirely silent during their experiences but then, once the effects wane, become very talkative. The more the guide can get down the better, as this will become the material that will be revisited during the integration sessions with the client.

Within one to 10 days following the experience, the guide should reconnect with their client via phone, videoconference, or in person to support the integration process. An example of IFS-Informed Integration questions is included in Appendix C. These integration questions are designed to help clients make meaning out of the material that surfaced and to facilitate the incorporation of that material into their lives.

It is ideal if guides follow up with at least a second integration session a week following the first integration session, or at the latest a month from the date of the psychedelic experience, to further support the integration of material.

Psilocybin   *Placebo*

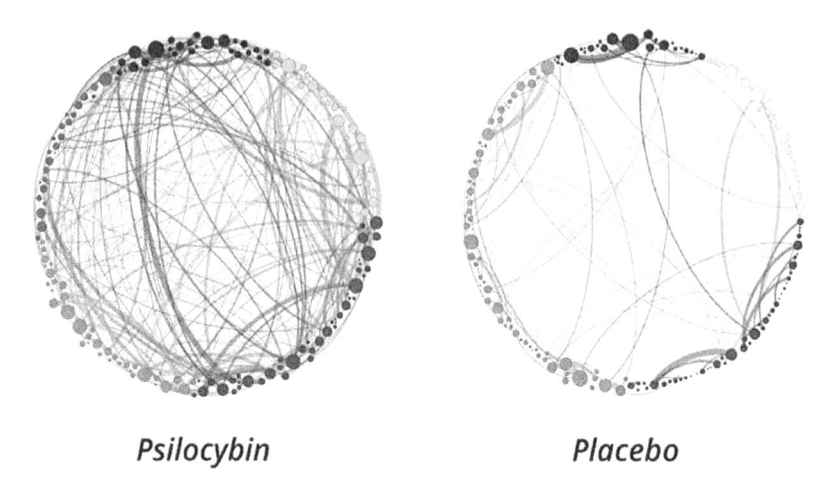

Source: The Royal Society, Nature Reviews Neuroscience 10, 186–198

The image on the left reflects neural activity during a psilocybin session and reveals the significant increase in connections between regions of the brain that do not usually communicate with each other. The image on the right reflects the brain's activity once the filtering processes resume and limit the connectivity.

Integration takes place in the filtered state featured on the right. Therefore, the sooner the integration can happen following a psychedelic session the better. Once the daily habits of life return it will be harder to access the material that was revealed.

Conclusion

"Tell me, what is it you plan to do with your one wild and precious life?"
—Mary Oliver

Perhaps the greatest gift a guide can give a client is to lead from Self. To do this, guides need to do their own personal work with their parts. This is an ongoing process of staying connected with our internal system, learning about our protectors' hopes, fears, and concerns, and unburdening our exiled parts. When we stay attuned to our inner family of parts, it creates the space that enables us to be more deeply connected with others.

This process of liberating our parts from their extreme roles, restoring our parts' trust in the Self and reharmonizing our systems, enables and empowers us to then engage in Self-led research, therapy, and guiding. Integrating the psychedelic experience is essential to the achievement of clients' personal goals and growth. The intention to process the information gained during psychedelic experiences through the non-pathologizing, systems-oriented lens of the Internal Family Systems theoretical framework helps clients understand how best to turn internal messages into real world change.

A guide recently introduced to IFS told me:

"I am finding IFS to be incredibly compatible to this work. I find this work has the ability to bring our awareness to parts we may not have otherwise been able to access under "normal" circumstances. Using the model of IFS to continue to work with and heal those parts during and after an experience, I feel, has the potential to accelerate the process, as well as provide a framework from which someone can work effectively and safely on their own or with a therapist."

This chapter is dedicated to all who have come before and contributed so much to healing themselves and to guiding the healing of others. May all psychedelic experiences be well-prepared, held, and integrated.

KEY TAKEAWAYS

- Psychedelics are not what does the healing, Self does the healing. Psychedelics open the pathways to Self.
- IFS-informed integration begins with thoughtful and thorough IFS-informed preparation sessions.
- IFS-informed integration is the ongoing process of reviewing the material that arose during the psychedelic session and facilitating its incorporation into clients' lives.
- Healing through community supports enhances the integration process. IFS supports include the IFS and Psychedelics Facebook page, the IFS Online Circle, IFS podcasts such as The One Inside and IFS Talks, and IFS resources such as the books and recordings available through the IFS bookstore.

AUTHOR BIO

Nancy L. Morgan, MS, PhD (she/her) is a Level 3 trained, Certified IFS Therapist, an Approved IFS Clinical Consultant, and an Assistant Trainer with the IFS Institute. She is a California-licensed clinical psychologist and a Licensed Professional Counselor in Oregon and Colorado. Nancy leads Introduction to IFS workshops for psychedelic researchers, therapists, and guides, and Introduction to Psychedelics workshops for IFS-trained therapists and practitioners. In 2023, Nancy received her certification as a Psilocbyin-Assisted Facilitator through InnerTrek, Oregon's first licensed Psilocybin-Assisted Facilitator training program. You can learn more about Nancy at www.theguideinside.com.

GOING DEEPER

From Dr. Nancy L. Morgan

1) Website:
   a. www.theguideinside.com

From Other Sources

1) Websites:
   a. www.chacruna.net/integration-psychedelics-spirituality/ps://psychedelicstoday.teachable.com/p/psychedelic-integration-self-care
   b. www.psychedelicintegrationcoach.com
   c. www.medicinalmindfulness.org/psychedelic-integration-circle-boulder
   d. www.youtube.com/watch?v=E-5eFeICIf4
   e. www.integration.maps.org
   f. www.erievision.org/integration-3
   g. www.doubleblindmag.com

2) Books:
   a. Westrum, R., & Dufrechou, J. (2019). *The psychedelics integration handbook.* Self-published.
   b. Buller, K. et al. (2019). *Integration workbook: Planting seeds for growth and change.* CreateSpace Independent Publishing Platform

Psychedelic-Assisted Psychotherapy Training Programs and Resources

Certificate Programs

Internal Family Systems Institute—Level 1 trainings with an emphasis on psychedelic medicines. www.ifs-institute.com/trainings

California Institute of Integral Studies—Psychedelic-Assisted Therapies and Research Certificate (CPTR) One year. Application is open to professionals licensed in their fields. www.ciis.edu/research-centers/center-for-psychedelic-therapies-and-research/about-the-certificate-in-psychedelic-assisted-therapies-and-research

Fluence—Psychedelic Integration Therapy Certificate (PIT) 120 hours. Application is open to licensed therapists. www.fluencetraining.com/programs/certificate-programs

InnerTrek—Oregon's first psilocybin-assisted therapy training program whose mission it is to spark healing and wholeness through the state's newly legal psilocybin therapy and wellness framework. www.innertrek.org

Integrative Psychiatry Institute—Psychedelic-Assisted Therapy Provider (PATP) Certificate one year. Application is open to licensed therapists, physicians, nurses, or other mental healthcare professionals. www.psychiatryinstitute.com/ipi-year-long-psychedelic-assisted-therapy-training

Naropa University—Psychedelic-Assisted Therapies Certificate. 10 months. Application is open to all. www.naropa.edu/academics/extended-campus/psychedelic-assisted-therapies-certificate

Oregon Health Authority—Oregon Psilocybin—Training Programs with Approved Curriculum. www.psilocybin.oregon.gov/training-approved

Synthesis—Psychedelic Practitioner Certificate 18 months. Application is open to health, wellness, and other personal mental health professionals. www.synthesisinstitute.com/psychedelic-practitioner-training

Additional Psychedelic Training Resources

Multidisciplinary Association for Psychedelic Studies—MDMA Therapy Training. 100 hrs. www.maps.org/2021/10/29/information-for-people-seeking-training-in-psychedelic-assisted-therapy Note: This training is IFS-lite informed (Michael and Annie Mithoefer's segment).

Healing Realms—Ketamine-Assisted Psychotherapy (KAP) training. Four months. www.healingrealmscenter.com/ Note: This training is IFS-informed.

Psychedelics Today—Vital: Immersive, Inclusive, and Personal Psychedelic Training for Professionals. One year. Note: This training features Dick Schwartz as one of the trainers. www.psychedelicstoday.com/2022/01/27/introducing-vital-psychedelic-training-for-professionals

APPENDIX A

Preparing IFS-Informed Guides

1) **Know your system and actively work to unburden your own burdened parts.**

   Having your own IFS therapist or practitioner to work with, particularly after difficult psychedelic sessions that may activate your parts, is highly valuable.

   Being part of a community of guides is essential and supports our ongoing learning, sharing, and growth. If the community is IFS-informed it also enables us to share a common language and perspective.

2) **Bring non-directive, calm, curious, courageous, connected, compassionate Self-energy to the client's experience.**

   Clients benefit from being able to co-regulate to our Self-energy in the early and later stages of a psychedelic experience. Once deep in the experience the client may enter a non-ordinary state of formlessness or feel unified with all.

3) **Prepare client's fearful parts and create a plan for how those parts can be cared for so clients can approach, rather than flee from, frightening stimuli.**

   This step is an essential element in the preparation stage.

4) **Inquire about bodily sensations and the parts connected to them that emerged before, during, and after the psychedelic experience.**

   Somatic experiencing of pain can arise during a psychedelic experience. This is a time when gentle, calm, and confident direction can be offered to go "in and through" allowing the process to unfold rather than trying to avoid it.

5) **Invite all parts to process their hopes, intentions, and felt sense of the session.**

   See Appendix C for IFS-informed questions that can be used during integration sessions.

APPENDIX B

IFS-Informed Preparation

Intention (Set from Client's Self)

What do you wish to gain from this experience?

Parts' Consent

People often refer to feeling that a part of them feels one way while another part feels another way. This is a good thing and reflects the multiplicity of our minds. Our bodies and brains are always interacting and communicating with us, but we often do not slow down enough to listen. I invite you to turn a soft focus inside and notice what your internal system is communicating to you.

A. Can you speak for the part of you that brought you here today?
   1. If that part of you gets what it wants, what does it hope will be different?

B. Do any parts of you have concerns or fears about this work? (e.g., "A part of me is hopeful and another part is nervous.")

   1. **Find**—Where do you find this part in/around your body? (e.g., is there tightness anywhere?)
   2. **Focus**—How do you experience it? (How is it for you to feel these feelings?)
   3. **Feel toward?** How do you *feel toward* this part of you? (Are feelings of compassion, curiosity, openness, etc., present or are other feelings present such as fear or concern?) If any of the 8 Cs of Self are present continue, but if they are not, then work with whichever other parts are present.
   4. **Be Friend**—What would this part like you to know about it?
   5. **Flesh out**—What does this part of you want you to know about how it is feeling about your journeying? (Just ask and listen, try not to think of an answer).
   6. **Fears**—What are the parts' fears and concerns?

Optional—Adverse Childhood Experiences Score

Link to free test:
www.npr.org/sections/health-shots/2015/03/02/387007941/take-the-ace-quiz-and-learn-what-it-does-and-doesnt-mean

Notes for Oneself as the Guide

1. What part(s) in my system want to guide this client?
   a. Why?
   b. What are my fears or concerns if I choose to say no to the client's request that I guide them?
2. What part(s) of me may not want to work with this client?
   a. Why not?
   b. What are the fears or concerns of my parts(s) regarding working with this client?
3. Is there anything else that might affect my ability to guide this person from Self?

APPENDIX C

IFS-Informed Integration

Questions to invite clients to consider as they integrate their psychedelic experiences:

- Did you receive any valuable information during your experience? If yes, how has having this information been for you?

- Did anything happen during the medicine session that did not feel right to you? If yes, would you be open to sharing what you experienced and how that experience impacted you?

- How did your experience relate to your intention(s)?
    Parts' hopes?
    Parts' fears or concerns?

- What do you understand about your intention?
    Did any part or parts get what they had been hoping for?

- Was there a door that opened for you?
    How are your parts responding?

- On what level(s) do you feel this experience took place? Physical, spiritual, emotional, relational?

- Are there any practices you imagine engaging in daily/weekly to deepen the integration of your experience? When you do so, how are your parts responding? How are you responding to your parts?

- If your parts had the opportunity to experience another psychedelic session, would they want one?
    Which parts are replying?
    What are they wanting you to know?
    Do they feel fully seen by you?
    How do you feel toward them?

- Did you have an experience of Self-energy during your psychedelic experience? If so, how did you experience it?

- If you were to begin working with one of the parts that may have surfaced during the psychedelic session, which part would you like to begin working with?

IFS AND SOMATIC PRACTICES

RECLAIMING OUR BIRTHRIGHT OF EMBODIMENT: FIVE SOMATIC PRACTICES THAT BRING THE BODY FULLY TO THE HEALING JOURNEY

Susan McConnell, MAPD, CHT

The Five Practices of Somatic IFS

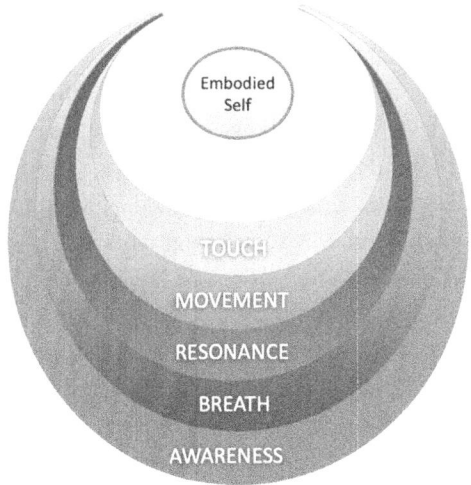

- Embodied Self
- TOUCH
- MOVEMENT
- RESONANCE
- BREATH
- AWARENESS

© Susan McConnell 2016

In the early days of IFS, a training session would not be complete until we sang "It's in Every One of Us" by David Pomerantz, often accompanied by a video that showed faces of people from all over the planet. The "it," of course, is Self, and the song tells us we can find this Self in everyone "by and by" by opening our hearts and our eyes. There is a second verse that most of us could not sing because we were moved to tears. This verse admits we are not as awake as we can be, having bought the ticket yet watching only half of the show.

It was at least ten years before I was ready to take on the challenge of this second verse as an IFS trainer. Which parts of us as therapists are not fully awake?

What is the rest of the "show" we may be missing? Prior to being a Senior IFS trainer, I had been steeped in many somatic practices. I had been a bodyworker, and I was a teacher of Hakomi, a body-centered, mindfulness-based psychotherapy. I, along with other Hakomi therapists, influenced the developing IFS model to include the body to some degree. This verse called me to include the body even more so we can watch the whole show—the 80 percent or more of our communication that is nonverbal and often below our consciousness. It called me to restore our embodiment so we can be as awake as we can be.

I began in earnest to incorporate the somatic practices of awareness, breath, resonance, movement, and touch with the IFS Model. The first words of my book *Somatic Internal Family Systems Therapy* are, "Including the body story along with the verbal story in therapy illuminates and awakens what has been obscured in darkness."[1] By bringing the body fully into every step of the IFS Model, the practices of Somatic IFS awaken us from our disembodied slumber so we don't miss the nonverbal part of the show. The centrality of the body in healing trauma and every clinical issue has been well-researched and documented. Since the publication of this book, Somatic IFS continues to evolve, to deepen, and to expand, influenced by the readers and the participants in my workshops and trainings. It is becoming clear that our bodies hold burdens from transgenerational traumas as well as systemic forces of oppression and inequity. Somatic IFS addresses disembodiment at every level of our systems, from the subcellular to the planetary.

For this chapter, I will primarily focus on the internal and interpersonal levels, with the understanding that individual disembodiment has its roots in collective trauma which results in social fragmentation, polarization, genocide, and other forms of violence to the earth and living beings. Workers' bodies are exploited for profit; bodies are colonized by religion. The burdens are embedded in our bodies as well as our institutional structures. Our birthright of embodiment—the felt experience of our connectedness and our interconnectedness—is exiled, and the effects of this disconnection trickle through every cell and at every stratum of our society.

Bodies that are valued are able-bodied, White, thin, and cisgendered. What is not valued—trans bodies, Black and Brown bodies, female bodies, disabled bodies—gets exiled. Yet what is exiled is not gone. It waits in our bodies and in the collective body. The somatic practices, combined with the IFS Model, help to restore our birthright. We invite the body out of exile from our individual and societal wounds and restore and cultivate our body's awareness, sensitivities, and responsivity. We reclaim that psychology is physiology. We reclaim our connectedness with our inner bodymind world and with all living beings. Becoming fully embodied is a revolutionary act. It releases the creativity, resilience, coherence, and agency to heal the collective body and to restore the wholeness of the fabric of our society.

Recently a former student described Somatic IFS as "the deeper, wider river flowing below the river of IFS." This river has been fed by recent scientific research and ancient healing and spiritual traditions. It flows with wisdom from Hakomi psychotherapy and other body-centered psychotherapies, various forms of bodywork, Zen Buddhism, and many movement practices. Many IFS therapists have travelled with me on that river in order to restore their connectedness with their inner bodymind world and with all living beings. Now as Somatic IFS Therapists, they have contributed to the depth and span of this river with their commitment to attend to the somatic aspects of their own and their clients' inner world. Their questions, comments, and shared experiences have broadened and deepened my understanding of the potential of Somatic IFS for individual and collective healing. Woven throughout this chapter are comments from participants in my Somatic IFS trainings who share their experiences with integrating these practices with the IFS Model, both personally and with their clients. Their quotes are shown in *italics*, with some specific information edited out to protect confidentiality.

The Somatic IFS Therapist uses the practices of awareness, breath, resonance, movement, and touch with themselves in the therapist role and with their clients to free the inherent Embodied Self-energy. To free the body from its largely exiled state requires that we know our bodies as soma—our subjective experience—rather than as *corpus*—an object to be fixed, measured, used, and improved upon. We work with our disconnected bodies as carefully as with any exile. We recognize and welcome parts that have learned to fear a return to embodiment of our internal systems.

These five practices are interdependent and mostly sequential, and they serve the expression and transformation of our parts' right-brain, primarily implicit communication. The foundational practice is Somatic Awareness, which includes *interoception*, the internal awareness of sensations, and *exteroception*, awareness of sensory information arising from outside the body. Awareness of the body naturally leads to Conscious Breathing, where we may discover protector parts restricting our breathing to manage our feelings, or exiles expressing their fear or unworthiness through habitual breathing habits. With Radical Resonance the Embodied Self reverberates with parts' earliest attachment wounds recorded subcortically. Their wounds are transmitted as vibrational frequencies to our resonant brains and bodies to rewire the burdened habitual relational patterns. The practice of Mindful Movement explores the eloquent dance of spontaneous movements and gestures that reveal the parts' body stories frozen in the tissues to restore the flow of energy and information as it sequences through the body. All of these sequential and interdependent practices support the practice of Attuned Touch, the "crowning jewel," which includes imaginary touch, client's touch, and touch from the therapist. These practices, together with the IFS Model, lead to the state of Embodied Self. As Dick Schwartz has written in the forward to my book, when Self-energy is fully embodied, "it is like the parent has returned home and the children can relax and be children."[2]

I invite you to journey on this river to explore for yourself how somatic practices can bring an additional dimension to the powerful and empowering IFS model, resulting in a cognitive, emotional, spiritual, and physiological process that lives and breathes. Each of these practices is a natural bodymind response to life. Any one of them is a doorway into meeting and getting to know a part, to seeing the interconnection of parts, to healing them so that a new wholeness is attained—a new integrated level of health and wellbeing. Perhaps as we reclaim our birthright of embodiment, we will become a tipping point of transformation for societal systems formed during four hundred years when mind has dominated the body and has truncated our capacities for wholeness.

> "The Church says: The body is a sin.
> Science says: The body is a machine.
> Advertising says: The body is a business.
> The body says: I am a fiesta."
> *Eduardo Galeano, from* "Window on the Body."[3]

Somatic Awareness

You can see from the Somatic IFS logo that Somatic Awareness is at the base, supporting and holding the other practices. The adjective "somatic" emphasizes that we turn inward to experience a subjective, rather than an objective, sense of our bodies. Many of our parts are busy objectifying our bodies, often because others, and our culture, have first regarded our bodies as objects. Our image managers work full time on various aspects of our appearance. Our caretaking, critical, controlling, analyzing, overworking, and pleasing managers also drive our bodies. Our firefighters find many creative ways to use and abuse the body to get their jobs done. These objectifying parts tragically cause damage, even death, to our bodies and to others' bodies. Our culture supports and rewards this objectifying view. It takes a strong intention, along with permission from our protectors, to turn our eyes inward towards our internal landscape. Without a strong connection to the inner world of our body, our sense of ourselves is determined by outside forces of the dominant cultural norms.

Awareness is central to any healing process. With an open, accepting attention to the moment-by-moment unfolding of our internal experience, we notice sensations and lack of sensations. This often reveals a part with a story that perhaps can be told in no other way. As the story is witnessed and the burdens are released, awareness *of* our body amplifies the awareness *in* our body. We are *being* a body rather than *having* a body. From *Somatic Internal Family Systems Therapy*

p. 64: "Our clients may have a coherent verbal narrative of their personal histories that they explicitly remember, but what of their histories before they had language? What of the events of their lives that have been exiled, suppressed, and erased from their conscious memories? These stories are waiting to be told through sensations and movement impulses. The thwarted experiences, overwhelming traumas, or faulty attachments that bring our client to seek therapy are revealed before that client even opens their mouth to speak."

One exercise I have assigned to the participants in my Somatic IFS Trainings is to notice a body sensation and to stay with it for fifteen minutes. They quickly discover their distracting protectors. They find narrative parts, analyzing parts, and critical parts that fear the sensation means there is something wrong with them. They find parts that fear the sensations will get too intense, parts that have learned to ignore unpleasant sensations, and parts that believe this kind of attention is a self-indulgent waste of time. Most recognize performing parts that fear they won't do this exercise right. Being experienced IFS therapists, they skillfully befriend these protectors who then allow them to bring focused Self-energy to the original body sensation. The jaw tightness, heaviness in the stomach, and jitteriness in the legs, all disperse, resolve, and become soft, calm, tingling, or light, followed by a heightened awareness, all from the intention of staying present with the body sensation.

> *It started as a small painful part but lessened in intensity and spread as it dispersed. Now it feels quite good, 'seen' and warm.*

The students understand that if they have parts that fear body awareness, they can expect their clients' protectors to be fiercely devoted to keeping the door to the body locked tight. Befriending their own protectors builds their compassion for their clients' protectors. They know their client's parts may have needed to dissociate from the physical aspect of their trauma. They invite the client to find parts that, like their own, fear or resist going inside to notice body sensations.

The students use interoception to find parts and to check for their degree of Embodied Self. They also invite the client's internal awareness, and the therapist might find body sensations that mirror a client's bodily experience that is not yet in the client's awareness.

> *When he was noticing the sensation…I both felt the heaviness and I also felt this stuck energy around it in my body and especially in my arms. I let him know what I noticed inside and asked if he felt anything like that too. He checked and did notice the energy as well. He had not been aware of it before.*

The Somatic IFS therapist uses exteroception—the client's awareness of the external world—to establish safety for clients with a history of trauma. They consider proximity, turning off the video camera, altering the room lighting and sounds, and inviting the client to bring in comforting objects. They understand their clients are also using their own exteroceptive abilities to track the therapist for signs of safety.

The therapist takes note of the client's posture, gestures, facial expressions, and overall energy. Their clients' bodies are telling the stories of their traumas and their faulty attachments that have been suppressed or erased from their conscious memories. The Somatic IFS therapist integrates that nonverbal information with the client's verbal communication. They might begin by inviting the client to find a place in their body that feels "safe enough" to focus on and to notice what safety and stability feel like in the body. Does connecting with the sensations of their feet on the floor bring a sense of safety? What sensation tells them that? As the protectors that use the body to do their jobs, or that try to avoid the body altogether, begin to trust Self-energy, how is this Self-energy evident in the body? Which qualities show up, and how and where?

Inviting the sensations, welcoming them, and deepening the sensory experience facilitates the six Fs of the IFS process. A body sensation often leads to a part. The sensation may be the only way the part can be found and known. The body may be the only channel left to the part to be found, befriended, and its story witnessed. When the associated emotions, thoughts, and memories of the story become overwhelming, shifting to the body sensation alone brings regulation.

"Body time" is much slower than our usual ordinary state of consciousness. We engage the right brain structures. The therapist invokes this slower pace with their body, their breath, and their words—pace, tone, the prosody of the voice. A student of the Somatic IFS training told me this practice helps slow down and quiet thinking parts with narratives or storytelling tendencies. Another reports, "As I slow down, I have a sense of 'being with' rather than 'doing to.'" Some students have discovered Somatic Awareness to be particularly useful with addictions and eating disorders. Their clients notice that smoking, drinking, using drugs, and eating harmful food actually don't feel good. These substances, believed to be soothing by protectors, are not doing the job. One student spoke of a client who used a pornography addiction to manage his grief about the ending of a long-term relationship. She helped him find the grief in his heart and stay with it. The pain of the vulnerable parts can be extreme. She speaks of another client who is *no longer numbing her feelings with drugs, [so] feelings like anxiety are experienced now very strongly, and the somatic awareness supports the client to be able to be with it.*

When the protectors trust they won't be blamed or shamed, they are more willing to let go of their failed strategies. They collaborate on the search for what will be truly soothing to the parts they are trying to take care of—the vulnerable ones holding most of the pain. When the body stories are told and witnessed, the pain held in the body's tissues and organs is released and we can more fully inhabit our bodies. Our inherent capacity for awareness and feeling bodily pleasure is restored.

As one student put it: *Awareness alone is transformative. Combined with IFS, it is life changing.*

Conscious Breathing

Awareness of our body naturally brings an awareness that we are breathing, and we use that focused awareness to bring a deep consciousness to this largely unconscious behavior. Luckily for us and other aerobic creatures, breathing is a largely unconscious, involuntary act. If we had to intentionally activate our respiratory muscles to breathe about a thousand times every hour, we either would not get much else done or we wouldn't live very long. Also, luckily for us as healers, we can bring consciousness to parts that have been outside of our awareness and voluntarily make changes to influence our internal states. As Sufi mystic and poet, Rumi, has written, "There is one way of breathing that is full of shame and constriction. Then there is another way: a breath of love that takes you all the way to infinity." The practice of conscious breathing addresses both of these ways of breathing.

The process of breathing parallels the process of healing from Self-energy. As structures in our brain stem automatically detect the need for oxygen, they send nerve impulses to the diaphragm, resulting in a drawing in of air through the nasal passages. Our soft palate, our respiratory diaphragm, and our pelvic diaphragm make room to receive the life-giving energies. This air is diverted into increasingly smaller structures, eventually reaching the tiny sacs that diffuse oxygen molecules into our blood cells, bringing in the crucial oxygen with every breath. Similarly, our many burdened parts are in our bodies awaiting the Self-energy which arrives on the stream of our awareness, bringing spaciousness, presence, aliveness and nourishment to each needy part. With sufficient Self-energy, the part's burdens, like the built-up carbon dioxide, can be effortlessly released, taking us, if not "all the way to infinity," closer to emotional, physical, and spiritual health.

This practice of simply being conscious of our breathing is surprisingly powerful, and just as surprisingly challenging. Awareness of our habitual breathing patterns may reveal the parts that use our respiratory structures to do their jobs and to tell their stories. We find manager parts that contain and suppress emotions. We find vulnerable parts that believe they don't deserve to fully receive the outside world. From *Somatic Internal Family Therapy* p. 98: "As a bridge between the unconscious and the conscious, attending to the breath is a valuable tool in psychotherapy. When we bring consciousness to our largely unconscious breathing patterns, we bring awareness to parts that have been lying outside of our conscious awareness. Rapid breathing may point us to a fearful, activated part, while shallow breathing may be associated with dissociation or depression. Differences between the inhale and exhale may relate to existential beliefs, birth trauma, or protective parts trying to control emotions. Sometimes the simple act of bringing conscious awareness to the breath brings a change. A deep, slow breath can be the bridge taking us from anxiety to excited anticipation."

My manuscript deadline for my book on Somatic IFS was March 2020, just as the world was becoming aware of a new, spikey molecule that was spreading exponentially on the breath of infected people. We have come to regard breathing, talking, and singing as a health hazard. Mask wearing has affected our breathing. The heat, humidity, decreased O_2 and increased CO_2 cause even people with healthy lungs to work harder to breathe, sometimes leading to fatigue, anxiety, and claustrophobia. Conscious breathing reveals how this COVID-19 virus has affected our bodymind systems.

I begin every Somatic IFS training session with a meditation. Focusing on the breath, we turn inward. We bring an open curiosity to our habitual breathing patterns—to the pace, rhythm, depth, the difference between inhale and exhale, what is moving in the body, and any restrictions to that movement. We find a part. We breathe into it. The inbreath brings a gentle "hello, I notice you. I'm here." We breathe out any distractions so we can stay present to the part.

> *I notice that my body is absolutely still in a frozen way. I…take a deep breath in…to give me a bit of space. [I find] a part…who holds herself in, makes herself small and breathes shallow so nobody will see her…she told me that shallow breathing helps so people don't notice her because she is afraid.*

We breathe with the part. The part feels rocked in the rhythm of our breath, in the constancy of our attention to it. We breathe Self-energy to where it lives in our tissues, our organs, or our bones, letting the part know we are here. We invite it to let us know it more deeply, to understand its experience, its beliefs, behaviors, and the emotional and physical pain it carries. We pause at the end of the exhale. In that pause, new neural synapses can form.

> *After noticing my breath for a few minutes, I start to feel the relaxation spreading. Spaciousness starts to fill my body. Years of practicing unblending using my breath pays off.*

The practice of conscious breathing also includes specific practices from ancient healing wisdom as well as recent scientifically based instructions, such as Pranayana Yoga and Polyvagal Theory. Yogic breathing practices are effective in assisting with emotional regulation and accessing Embodied Self-energy. Yogis teach us that *prana* can travel on the breath up the spine to any part of the body, bringing Self-energy to befriend and witness parts. From Polyvagal Theory we learn that sympathetic activation of the Autonomic Nervous System shows up as rapid breath in the upper lobes of the lung, while slower, shallow breath indicates the parasympathetic dorsal vagal state. We can regulate and shape our nervous systems through intentionally slower breaths, longer exhales and resistance breathing for sympathetic activation, and use rapid, "sipping breaths" to shift from the collapsed, frozen, dorsal vagal state. With the state of social engagement restored, Self-energy is available to witness and "re-story" the trauma. That is effective in assisting with emotional regulation and accessing Embodied Self-energy.

> *I take a deep inhale, expanding my upper chest. My posture shifts, my chest moves up and my shoulders move back and down. I feel the coolness of the air moving into my mouth and down my trachea. The deeper my inhale, the longer my exhale. I notice how I enjoy focusing on my breath.*

This practice bridges our inner and outer worlds, and concepts of matter and energy. The energetic field that extends beyond our skin boundaries is created by the movement of our subatomic particles. We breathe in oxygen from the surrounding space, and we also breathe in energy from the Field of Self to bring into coherence our own biofields, integrating our physical, mental, emotional and spiritual aspects. We can imagine breathing, not from our nostrils, but breathing in from the top of our heads and out through our pelvic floor. We imagine a point about two feet above our heads and breathe in the energy from that point. We might experience this energy as white light, a warmth, or as a tingling, or we might just imagine it flowing down into our core. We breathe out through our pelvic floor and let go of any energies we no longer need. This practice establishes our vertical alignment. Our head returns to its place of ease at the top of the spine. Breath flows easily into an open chest, supported by the entire torso. Self-energy flows along our core. This practice often is an opening to communicating with our Guides.

> *I focus again on my breath—the slow inhale and exhale. With the inhale I feel my diaphragm lower, my stomach expand, my chest rise, and my shoulders and my back body open as the air around me enters my lungs. I feel my shoulders relax with each breath. I imagine the breath coming from the earth, moving up my body and out the top of my head. I stay with this breath for a while, breathing in from the earth and out from my head. This helps clear the heaviness in my head. The vertical connection between earth and sky grounds me in my Self. It brings calm and connection and makes space for my Self-Energy to flow. My parts are still there but they have softened in the presence of Self.*

The Somatic IFS Therapist, connecting with the energies from above and below, uses conscious breathing to invite their clients to turn their attention inward. Finding a part, breath helps them to focus on it.

In my practice, I first encourage my clients to stay with their breath without trying to change anything and to notice how they are breathing. My experience is that gentle encouragement rather than a directive is more welcomed by a client as I am not "trying" to get them to a certain place.

A pregnant client thought her restricted breath was caused by her belly pressing up against her diaphragm. As she explored her breathing, however, she found an exile afraid of giving birth. As this part felt seen and heard, her breathing flowed easily.

Breathing into the part helps the client stay with the part and deepen into it. The client feels more spaciousness and sends their Self-energy to the part inhabiting the body. The client breathes with their part.

An orthodox young mother who had early trauma and has issues of addiction and anxiety and attachment...is able to use her breath as a way of shifting tightness in her chest and expand shallow breathing that often occurs. Initially she was able to feel these bodily shifts. In more recent sessions, she can feel her soul (neshama) in a freer sense of energy as it talks to parts that are anxious and tight.

If the part blends, the client attunes to the rhythm of their breathing and breathes in space between themselves and the part. The client's part releases its burdens on the outbreath, and on the inbreath brings in restored qualities. The breath assists in integration and completion at the end of the session. Throughout the session the therapist tracks the client's breathing and may comment on a change in their habitual breathing pattern. They might synchronize their breath with the client's to foster a deeper connection.

Our breath is fundamental to our speech, and our speech is fundamental to our lives and healing. Our parts' voices may have been exiled, silenced, and shamed, their truths and their stories remaining buried in our tissues. The voice quality—the volume, tone, intonation, pitch and pace—is shaped by the parts. The therapist's voice is essential in the therapeutic relationship. As they connect with the earth, intentionally lower their pitch and slow the pace to "body time." Self-energy is transmitted on the resonant sound waves in person and online to their clients.

To help clients restore embodied speech we may begin with a breath into where the truth resides in the body, letting out a sigh, the first whisper riding on the exhale of the truth waiting to be born. Eventually, with invitation and encouragement, the exiled vocal expression and the truth of the parts' stories can be restored.

Through our breath we come to know the universal dance of our essential unity and interdependence. Linking us with all living beings on the planet, and bridging earth and sky, the unconscious and the conscious, the interpersonal and the intrapersonal, the material with the ethereal, our breath is always available to us to return us to our bodies and the present moment, again and again. Our breath helps us to cross the bridge from activation to relaxation, from blended parts to Self-energy.

We gather all the wisdom from conscious breathing as we enter the realm of relationships. Our interacting interpersonal systems offer more complexity and more opportunity. The relational dance can be risky and delicate; the relational waters can be choppy, winding, and sometimes stagnant. Yet our vertical alignment has been established by the energetic current from the earth and the sky flowing through our bodies. We are grounded. Our bones support an upright posture. Our breath flows easily, feeding our hearts and brains with oxygen and prana. Our organs and our parts enjoy the spaciousness. Our verticality creates a lightning rod and a buttress as we explore the richness of this horizontal field of relationship.

Radical Resonance

The term "resonance" refers to the interaction of vibrating systems and has been traditionally associated with fields of acoustics, physics, chemistry, and electronics. Scientists have been able to measure the vibratory frequency of the earth and living beings, including all the structures of the human body. Somatic IFS assumes parts and Self have vibratory frequencies that influence each other and interact at the intrapsychic, interpsychic, and larger systems levels, transcending space and time. Much of this energy exchange is below our level of awareness, but our resonant capacity, obscured by parts, can be restored.

The adjective "radical" comes from the Latin *radicalis*, meaning "having roots." The practice of resonance is rooted in science, including the explosion of discoveries in neuroscience and spirituality. The psychobiological roots of relational trauma run deep, either becoming entangled or cut off, disconnected, and isolated. The therapist must be willing to meet the client at this radical, deeply rooted place of wounding, as I describe on p. 131 of my book (ibid.) "The implicit stories of the parts' neuronally based and embodied relational patterns floating in the intersubjective, often turbulent waters of the therapeutic relationship compel a response that may require therapists to descend into the mysteries of their own bodymind. The clarity of Self-energy prevents floundering in an empathic puddle of emotions. Rather than being an observer or even an experienced guide, the therapist reverberates with the tremors of abuse, neglect, betrayal, and abandonment."

This practice of radical resonance assists us in navigating the emotional waters of the relational realms. Parts that arise in relationship carry energy and information as burdens from their attachment experiences that are transmitted as vibrational frequencies internally and externally. Our bodies, especially our right brain structures, our hearts, and our guts, provide the vehicle for the psychobiological attunement of Self-energy necessary to rewire our burdened, habitual relationship patterns. The Somatic IFS Therapist relies on the earlier practices to support their resonant capacity.

> *As the therapist, I can use interoception with the IFS Model in order to be mindful of what is happening in my own gut and heart. It helps me be more grounded, centered and confident. It helps me to be a better therapist.*

Just as an instrument sounding a perfect pitch can bring a slightly off-key instrument into coherence, Embodied Self-energy can resonate with the parts' frequency, bringing it into coherence. We transmit our inner coherent state of Embodied Self-energy and it brings coherence to our relationships and to larger systems. It has the power to restore coherence to the institutional structures that perpetuate collective traumas.

When in Embodied Self-energy, the therapist's resonant body reverberates with the somatic soundtrack of their clients' early relational traumas. With this co-regulation, the client's Self eventually emerges as the primary secure attachment figure. The dynamic interplay co-created within this relational field exponentially increases the coherence.

In my Somatic IFS trainings, I ask students to notice what happens in their bodies as they remember a challenging relational situation or moment, and to explore what can restore a feeling of a safe, loving connection in their body.

> *In the challenging situation, my body recoiled. I was shocked and felt as though I had been slapped by her unexpected reaction and words. I pulled away, inward towards myself. The openness in my heart area closed. There was a tightness in my chest. My shoulders tensed. My jaw clenched. My breath was more shallow, rapid…To regain my heart connection I took some breath in through my nose and out through my mouth. This was not enough. I yawned, which relaxed my jaw and released more tension. I shrugged my shoulders and let them relax. I then remembered to find my feet on the floor to ground myself and to sense the energy flowing from above me. This helped, but each time I recall the event, I have to begin again.*

Many students reported that the challenges they encounter in their therapeutic relationships are outgrowths of their early attachment experiences.

> *I took time after our practice group to sit with this feeling of being "disconnected" in session. I used Somatic Awareness to deepen into the emotions and sensations associated with being "disconnected." After a short period, I began to feel the disconnection as the "fearlessness" of that little 4-year-old me who learned to disconnect from his fear so he could perform his job as*

mom's protector. That four-year-old boy had grown up into a therapist who could disconnect but still be the highly effective robot who could perform his job as a therapist.

I've been sitting with this four-year-old me throughout the entire training. Somatic awareness, breath, and conscious touch have all helped me reconnect with him. As the connection has deepened, I've witnessed some of his pain and felt him move through my body—primarily between my stomach and behind my forehead. I currently feel a lot of curiosity and compassion for him, but I've also felt the impact that he's had on all of my relationships—both in my personal life and as a professional. I can feel the Self to part relationship deepening.

Somatic IFS Therapists understand that successful therapeutic outcomes depend mostly on the quality of the therapeutic relationship, and that relationship depends on the therapist's ability to be in Embodied Self-energy.

What I realize now is that what I believed to be my Self-energy is clearly more of a self-like part that jumps in when my system is dysregulated. This part helps me do my job but does not allow for resonance because it is too concerned with thinking about what could ease my client's discomfort.

Restoring the resonant quality of our bodies requires that we are aware of and heal our parts that carry burdens from our early attachment experiences. These attachment burdens manifest in various ways, including physically, as tension, feeling ungrounded and disconnected from our bodies or parts of our bodies, and constricted breathing. They show up as emotional symptoms of flatness, numbness, insecurity, dissociation, over-identification, and anxiety. The associated behaviors could involve avoidance, difficulty with boundaries (too rigid or loose), disconnection, over-identification, defensiveness, and self-blame.

My personal early attachment wounds, which I experienced as disorganized attachment and feeling like I was neglected, led to a very unhealthy relationship with my body and food over the years. Noticing avoidance of working with clients with similar issues. Somatic IFS practices can be helpful for me in these situations by connecting to my breath and help me notice the tension that I am holding in my body when my firefighters arise...I will breathe in gently, connect to my heart space...I will put a hand on my chest and say "I've got you" to remind my parts that I am here to support them.

In our trainings we experiment with resonating from different places of our body. We resonate from our hearts, our right brains, and our guts. We find burdened parts that have blocked our capacity to resonate.

I learned not to show myself. I learned to detach or disconnect and stay silent…I also have parts that judge my abilities and I find them in my neck, as though someone were grabbing me by the back of the neck and telling me I had done something wrong. My throat at times constricts, preventing me from speaking my truth. My heart hardens with the belief that I am not enough and never will be. My belly can be filled with worry and anxiety that I will do something wrong and someone will be harmed because I haven't done enough.

Based on an understanding acquired from a study of embryological developmental organization, we also experiment with resonating from our front, middle, and back bodies.

Connecting from the back body and the knowledge that my body has an innate wisdom at a cellular level to take in what it needs and keep out what does not serve has helped immensely.

Feeling into my back body helps me access my boundaries and creates a protective shell for my vulnerable parts. In the days that follow I continue to focus on observing and listening from front, middle, and back body. I choose where to focus depending on the context, who I am with, and how activated my system feels.

I have also made a breakthrough through becoming aware of where these parts live in my body—the withdrawing protector in my back body, the pleasing ones in my front body, and the yearning exile has also been in my front body. By shifting where I listen from to my middle body, I have found myself more able to hold Self-energy.

As we restore our inherent resonant capacity, there is potential for our relationships to radically alter. Our conditioned concepts of "therapist and client" and "self and other" begin to dissolve. Our relationships transcend the interpersonal, intrapersonal, and transpersonal. Our experience of Self-energy expands to include the Field of Self where we may experience spiritual Guides. The hope is that we can live more harmoniously with other humans and with all living beings on the planet.

Mindful Movement

We first move in the womb and don't stop moving until we die. Our motor skills develop throughout our life span. At every age, our emotions, intentions, beliefs, needs, and desires are expressed through movement. The experiences throughout our lives, including the painful ones, affect our motor development. Our movement and lack of movement are testaments to these stories. The practice of mindful movement can restore the flow.

If we experienced parents with anxious or controlling manager parts or unpredictable behavior, some movements, like reaching out or pushing away, may have been experienced as dangerous. Early trauma may have trapped our developing bodies in an exhausting cycle of overactivation and immobilization. Their interrupted movement stories are evident in frozen postures and faces, repetitive gestures, disturbances in gait, and stiffness. Both movement and lack of movement are manifestations of the client's inner world.

Any interference or interruption in our motor development affects our lifelong movement patterns as well as our perceptual, cognitive, and social development. Mindfulness is brought to a stroke of the face, a hand to the heart, a shrug, or a hunch of the shoulders with the intention to find, focus, and flesh out the parts and to allow the untold story to unfold. These habitual movements of posture, gait, and gestures are a somatic record of parts' burdened beliefs, emotions, and thoughts. Students of Somatic IFS begin with mindfulness of their own habitual movements.

> *A habitual movement I make is shrugging my shoulders and letting out a big sigh. As I repeat this movement, I get very sad and a little bit hopeless. This part feels like it has the weight of the world on its shoulders and is not seen or heard by other people. It shows me that it's not sure what to do, so it is frozen in my shoulder. I have met this part before, but this is new information for me regarding this part.*

> *What is hidden in the motion of gritting my teeth? Sitting with this, I became aware of at least two parts…One part is a protector. The gritting teeth turned into more of an open growl. My arms and hands came up into a "pounce-ready" stance. "Give her the space to be who she is, express who she is." The other part sharing the gritting teeth is the frightened exile who is afraid to open her mouth….She learned it was not safe to be expressive.*

Bringing mindful exploration of movements may lead to protector parts or protectors polarized with exiles. Firefighters may use nervous jiggling, extreme sports, sexual acting out, and, at the most extreme end, suicide and homicide to distract from the exiles' stories or to attempt to soothe or discharge pent-up energy. Managers may commandeer fitness exercises and block movement impulses from the vulnerable parts to kick, run, bite, suck, or even to express joy, curiosity, and sexual energies. We watch for signs that the movement story is blocked. We listen to the movement story being told along with the verbal story as the client's hand curls into a fist or touches their heart. Inviting a mindful awareness and perhaps a slow repetition or exaggeration of the movement may reveal a part and the interrelationships between parts and assist in the flow of the healing process.

Some movement therapies, such as Body-Mind Centering, consider five movements—yielding, pushing, reaching, grasping, and pulling—to be the foundation of both physical and psychological development. These movements begin in utero. As the embryo floats in the amniotic waters playing with these movements, it is preparing for its emergence onto solid land. Exploring these five movements through our heads, tails, and four limbs allows us to directly enter the preverbal matrix of our parts' experience. The client's earliest attachment wounds can be healed through imaginary movement and actual movement by revisiting these stages of motor development through these movements.

The stories of interrupted motor development from conception through childhood are waiting in our tissues for someone to listen. Movement may be the only channel for them to be heard. They wait for us to invite mindfulness to their present movements to reveal the burdens from their early attempts to reach out, to cling, or to push away. The blocked or failed movements want the opportunity to move and to sequence through the body to completion.

From p. 205 *Somatic Internal Family Systems:* "We bring mindful awareness to the movements of yield, push, reach, grasp, and pull. As we yield, we feel the floor support us, even rise up to meet our body. As we yield even more, as our tension melts away and our body surrenders into this support below, from deep within our body eventually arises a delicious impulse to move, to feel our power, to push against, to push away. That movement leads to others. We may roll on the floor to allow every part of our body to also know the floor. Our limbs may want to rise up, to reach into space. Movement, large and small, fast and slow, free and choreographed, is a natural way for living beings to express their truest natures and their relationship to the grand wider world."

A student shares a session that involves these practices:

> *One of my habitual movements is that I hold a clenched fist. When I focused on this there were two parts that emerged. One wanting, reaching for and grasping at life —food, relationships, opportunity. The other part is a protector not allowing the reaching for motion. It holds me back, clenching my fist in anticipation of the hurt that will inevitably come. It's a bracing against allowing my young part to want or need. This seems like the push pull "tug of war" that was described in the book with the client Lori.*

The example named about the client Lori is from my book (page 201). This chapter includes case examples of applying the five movements with early developmental trauma, relational ruptures, eating disorders, chronic physical symptoms, and grief and loss.

Motor development may also be blocked later in childhood as a result of trauma. The following are two similar examples from Somatic IFS Therapists who use Mindful Movement with clients whose childhood sexual abuse thwarted their ability to push away, to stop, to say "no."

> When working with a client who had experienced childhood abuse, as the young one was telling her story, the client kept putting her hand up, as if to ward off. It was a half-hearted movement, but there. As we explored and exaggerated this movement the client moved from warding off, to firmly holding her hand up in a STOP sign. She said NO! With encouragement, she repeated the movement and the yell again and again until she broke down into tears. We moved from there into an unburdening.

> Last week I had a session with a client who had been sexually abused as a young child and in the Re-do we used movement to embody the missing experience of saying no, with her arm outstretched and the flat of the hand pointing outward saying no, she stretched her arm several times out and repeated the no. When she asked the young part of her what qualities it would like to invite, it was playfulness and the wish for dancing. I then encouraged her to allow that to happen in the session, and she started dancing.

The practice of Mindful Movement, through reenacting the early movement patterns, can uncover and free the impulses to move that have been blocked or distorted. The memories and emotions may be released, and the part's story witnessed. The parts' burdens—acquired, inherited, or energetically transmitted intergenerationally—can be cleared. By incrementally moving through the developmental stages to access and witness implicitly held memories, we correct disturbances in the developing bodymind, and reconnect us with our embryological wisdom and creativity. Self-led movements are restored and expressed in powerful, graceful, integrated movement.

Attuned Touch

This practice involves three situations where touch may be used with the IFS Model—imaginary touch, the client's Self-touch, and touch between the therapist and the client. This last situation requires sufficient Self-energy in both client and therapist to ensure this touch is safe, ethical, and effective. The Somatic IFS logo, with Attuned Touch at the apex, supported and embraced by the first four practices, illustrates the dependency of this practice on awareness, breath, resonance, and movement.

> Awareness is key, both in my own body and in asking the client to be tracking for any changes in need/consent to the touch. Breath has been helpful to notice for tracking for the attunement of the touch, and to deepen the attuned touch with synchronized breath. Resonance is everything when touching, the nonverbal pathway of feeling and listening beneath the somatic and verbal expression. Movement is a helpful evolution from being

touched and Self-touch, as a soothing motion, completion, or integrative movement.

Appearing as the smallest of the shapes in the logo reflects that touch, especially therapist-to-client touch, is typically used less than the underlying practices in a Somatic IFS session. Attuned touch by the therapist is the most controversial of the five Somatic IFS practices. In an attempt to protect patients and clients from touch abuse, many regulatory agencies have forbidden the use of touch in psychotherapy. Several students shared their experiences with agencies, with cultural populations, and from their training that limits their use of touch.

My training greatly affects my use of touch with clients, as I was trained to completely avoid all touch with clients. In fact, when I have offered touch to clients, that trained part of me has felt uncertain if I was doing something wrong.

In my non-private work, the agencies I worked with significantly limited or forbade touch. Even as I offered movement therapy or yoga groups, my touch was significantly limited, if at all…My physical/no touch boundaries were important not only for our safety, but also to help preserve the therapeutic container of our relationship and relationship to the different programs I served.

I carry varying credentials which have acclimated and attuned me to the healing use of touch. However, as discussed, the population I work with requires a specific cultural sensitivity, which I have, given my upbringing in that community. Thus, my cultural upbringings conferred upon me the sensitivity to not use touch, despite my appreciation for its potential as a healing agent.

I am a naturally touch-oriented person, who has spent the majority of my career resisting my parts instincts to touch clients.

Although well-intentioned, proscribing healing touch entirely because of fear-based, misinformed, and cultural protective parts can leave clients deprived of the touch that could heal their touch wounds. And sadly, the policies have not protected clients from abuse of touch from therapists. Several students have shared they know of clients who have been sexually abused by their therapists.

I know SO SO SO many people that have had sex with their counselor or therapist.

Research has shown it is therapists' burdens around touch that are the risk for touch abuses. These parts need healing, not to be shamed, frightened, and controlled by risk management approaches, ethical review boards, and insurance companies. The best insurance against touch violations is for us practitioners to resolve our own wounds of touch neglect or abuse. This work is essential for therapists practicing attuned touch. The therapist's awareness and healing of their own history of touch neglect or abuse has been shown to be the most reliable way to protect clients from touch abuse.

Participants in trainings explore their touch histories and the influence of their particular cultural norms regarding touch to find parts carrying burdens from harmful and deficient touch. Most all of us hold these wounds, and these burdens will interfere with our Embodied Self-led touch. Somatic IFS Training participants share their touch histories:

> *Soothing and nurturing were seen as unneeded indulgences. This intensified my need for touch, so I have been getting that need filled second hand. As a result, I do have parts that can override and go in for a hug for me—not based on what the client needs.*

> *Culturally I feel I wasn't brought up with touch, and I didn't touch my kids much after they were babies…I have a diagnosis of sensory processing disorder, making me sensitive.*

> *I know I also have my own touch-deprived part that lives in my mid-back, and who, as a single person, rarely gets touched, because it is an area of my body that I can't reach on my own for Self-touch. I became very aware of this part during the pandemic. Before then, I was always able to ask a friend for a hug, and that part would get touched periodically. This part has informed me of how important therapist attuned touch could be for many individuals.*

> *I tend to distance myself a lot from people since the pandemic and am not someone who naturally touches before this in an everyday situation. If face-to-face, I may need to work on a lot of my own parts to be genuinely congruent in this and for it not to feel awkward…And I would be very challenged touching anyone these days.*

Attuned touch considers the hierarchical aspect of therapy, and the touch history, culture, gender, race, ethnicity, and religion of both therapist and client. Physical touch is a powerful communicator, conveying many messages, psychological and cultural. The message sent through touch may be distorted by the receiver's parts.

> *[I ask myself] what part of my system is initiating the touch; Do they have protectors or exiles that would be bypassed and not consenting of touch? Does my intuition sense that it could be helpful in the moment? Is there potential harm? Could this help access Self, soothing, compassion, ventral*

vagal activation, and co-regulation? Could this help them ground?

I generally am more careful with touching people from a different cultural, ethnic or racial background than me. Before touching these clients, I take more care in talking about their experiences with touch, and the cultural understandings or norms that have shaped their experience of touch.

I rarely touch cis-male clients. I have a part that worries about the touch being misunderstood or sexualized. This part is smart. It knows from experience that many adult cis-men aren't touched by people who aren't also sexual partners, and that this sometimes leads their parts to confuse all touch as sexual. I also know that my part amplifies the risk of this because of some of my own experiences with cis-men.

The client's history of sexual trauma requires particular sensitivity and may be contraindicated with some trauma survivors until their system has stabilized, allowing for Self-led consent.

I have been more hesitant offering touch to clients with a sexual trauma history, and while it hasn't been a total no-go zone, I have generally avoided it. The training is helping me to see that it need not be eliminated as an option out-of-hand, but with care and skill in identifying and working with the sometimes polarized needs of various parts, with consent from all parts, and the presence of Self-energy, it can be an extremely important part of healing for these clients holding touch trauma.

When these factors are considered, and the client's parts are all agreeing to the touch, it is crucial that the touch is from Embodied Self. Touch tacitly conveys the therapist's inner state in the relationship, even more than facial expression or tone of voice. The client attaches meanings to the touch that are rarely spoken, even if the client is conscious of them. The therapist engaging in touch stays attuned to the moment-by-moment response to the touch.

Given all these sensitivities to be considered, why even include touch in the practices of Somatic IFS?

It turns out that years of research, as well as anecdotal evidence, show that attuned touch is actually the jewel on the crown of Somatic IFS. It is a vital component for healing a wide range of clinical issues. Countless research studies have pointed to the healing potential of touch for traumatized clients and indicate that the physiological and emotional damage from trauma can be reversed through touch. The taboo against touching reflects and exacerbates disconnection and dissociation from the body. In some cases, withholding touch as a therapeutic intervention with clients who missed out on necessary touch may further the wound of touch neglect.

Many of our clients have not had enough of the right kind, and have had too much of the wrong kind, of touch. As a result, their psychological and physiological burdens adversely affect their lives today. Some have parts that crave touch and seek inappropriate touch. Some are terrified of physical contact. Some have trouble setting touch boundaries, having difficulty distinguishing between safe and unsafe touch. Some sexualize all touch.

The practice of attuned touch harnesses the healing potential of this intervention while avoiding the harm. It addresses the symptoms of trauma—emotional dysregulation, touch aversion, distorted body image, anxiety, depression, self-esteem, and trust—and restores a sense of their own power or agency, especially in setting limits and asking for what they need. The client, in charge of the kind of touch and the amount of touch, has a reparative experience. The client's parts can let go of past meanings and associations of touch violations and replace them with associations of comfort, connection, and pleasure.

Attuned touch addresses the burdens of relational trauma that may begin in the womb. Touch is our first language, and it is the primary means of connection in the womb and early infancy. The bonding established by warm, sensual contact, communicating security and belonging, is more crucial for healthy development than is food. When the young being's tactile experiences do not establish this secure connection, attuned touch carries the implicit message of safety and connection, of comfort and pleasure from the Embodied Self to the young parts. Touch can be the most potent form of implicit communication when words alone don't "touch" the young parts. All of our lives, touch is a building block of secure attachment.

> *I find touch especially helpful for issues of early attachment wounds and pre-verbal traumas, and those, when ready, with touch/sexual abuse violations. I have also found it to be essential at times with clients with parts with dissociation.*

> *I have found it particularly helpful for individuals with early attachment deficits, anxiety, loneliness, loss and grief, and physical pain or illness, and in couples work, for attunement, bonding and repair of relational ruptures. I am now aware of its benefit for touch abuse (it makes so much sense!) and can imagine how helpful it would be for people with body dysmorphia. I can see that it could be potentially helpful with PTSD, depression and really any concern.*

> *I am using client's Self-touch more frequently and more intentionally than I did before this Somatic IFS journey. I used to use it mainly for containment and comforting parts flooded with emotion or to assist parts in a dissociative state to ground.*

I have worked with one young orthodox woman who experienced childhood trauma and was having trouble connecting sexually with her husband. We used movement and touch for her own exploration and comfort level, and she eventually transferred this into the intimacy with her husband.

Recently I had a session with a lot of attuned Self-touch of my client that was very beneficial. It is a client with long term porn and masturbation addiction. In the session he touched the arm with which he usually masturbates and was able to release some of the tension that the arm and fist was holding…the arm revealed the reason for the tension: the masturbation addiction…Because there is a lot of shame, and thanks to the focus on the somatic, the body told the story and the client was listening with compassion, and also, he was able to comfort the arm with his other arm, so the Self-touch was more than words would had been able to give. It was a very healing experience for the client. After the session, the tension in his chest and arm was much less, and he was very grateful. I told him that it was a Somatic IFS Session, and that I was able to do that because of my current Somatic IFS Training.

Whether the touch is imagined in the client's inner scenario, is from the client, or is from the therapist, attuned touch offers an additional and often more effective nonverbal route for a Self-to-part relationship as it is supported by the other Somatic IFS practices and assists with every step of the IFS Model.

Elaine's Story:
How Somatic Practices Free Up Embodied Self-energy

I considered concluding with a discussion of Embodied Self-energy, but instead I will share a recent Somatic IFS session that illustrates using these five somatic practices with the IFS process to unburden and free up Embodied Self-energy. My client's name and identifying information have been changed.

Elaine has a strong faith, a loving family, and a successful, satisfying career. She is intelligent, creative, kind, and courageous. She is now married to a loving, supportive woman. She has worked with me in the past to heal the effects of childhood trauma from a life-threatening, chronic childhood illness that spanned her entire childhood. Although only one organ was diseased, the medication and the effects of the disease affected many other organs and systems in her body. She spent much of her childhood alone in the hospital. When her disease was in remittance, she was able to go to school, but she was taunted and rejected by her classmates because of her symptoms. Meanwhile, her family and her conservative Christian community fervently prayed for her healing.

Elaine's internal and external systems had grown accustomed to a series of remissions followed by a crushing disappointment when her symptoms inevitably returned. When in early adolescence the disease was finally cured, there was no celebration of her final healing. We could say that her body was cured but she was not healed. The burdens the parts carried as a result of this trauma remained.

Her protectors had even more work to do when, also in early adolescence, Elaine began to notice her attraction to girls. The message from her church was that this attraction was "sinful, impure, degrading, shameful, unnatural, indecent and perverted."[4] With this additional layer of fear and shame about her body, she put her emerging sexual energies on lockdown.

By the time Elaine, now in her fifties, started therapy with me, firefighter parts were using self-harm behaviors and various substances—food, alcohol, smoking—to drown her emotions and to try to soothe her pain and shame, causing many other serious health problems. Elaine and I recognized how strong and effective her protectors had to be, and we understood the accumulated fears they carried even as we also realized how much they were hurting her body. As we gained their trust, they backed off on most of their more extreme behaviors, and we got to know the ones they were protecting that carried burdens of hopelessness, shame, fear, and hatred of her body.

In a recent session, we again addressed these protectors that have been turning to substances and turning away from her body. She hears them say, "You are wrong, bad, broken. We hate this body. You will never get better." Listening to these words, Elaine feels a sensation in her upper arms, a place that carries scarring from the bloating of her illness. She tells me she has covered her upper arms all of her life because of her shame. She hears the words, "this [scarring] proves you will never get better. You will always be wrong, bad, and broken." Her breathing brings enough spaciousness to separate from these persistent beliefs, and she feels compassion towards this part. Elaine breathes compassion from her heart to her arms. Her arms ask to be touched. Holding her upper arms with both hands, Elaine and the part revisit the many physically, emotionally, and spiritually painful experiences as tears stream down her face. She tells me she feels weighed down by shame and hopelessness.

I notice her breath becoming shallow and rapid. I bring her awareness to this and suggest we breathe together. Several deep, slow breaths help Elaine's system regulate. Elaine returns to holding and stroking her arms and listening to the part's pain. She decides to bring her hands down from her upper arms in order to breathe more fully. She breathes into her heart, opening her chest, and sending this breath to her upper arms. She recalls a hymn about the breath of God healing the spirit and quietly listens to it as a smile plays on her lips.

I suggest that it is possible for us to help her change the part's message of shame and hopelessness connected with the scarring. Elaine's part is interested. Elaine tells her part the scars are proof that she survived the illness. She tells her part that most of her body as a child had been fine, healthy, and strong. As the part lets go of the negative beliefs forced on her from the painful experiences of her childhood, tears run down Elaine's face. She tells me these tears are not of sadness but of relief. She lets go of her arms and wipes her tears. A smile comes to her face. She is smiling at the little girl. She breathes with her. She says she feels the breath of God fill her body and the little girl's body. Her smile widens, and she sits more upright. She lets me know she sees the little girl playing and dancing all around. She sees how strong, clever, playful, and witty this little one is.

This session with Elaine involves all of the somatic practices in combination with the IFS process to free up her Embodied Self-energy. Elaine still struggles at times with sustaining a loving, kind relationship with her body. The trauma from the illness that threatened her life for her entire childhood left physical, emotional, and spiritual scars. She has come to recognize the physical signs in her body that let her know when she is in Self. Most of the qualities used to describe Self-energy are found in the body. When she feels disconnected from her body and her community, she knows she is in the grip of a part and is likely to engage in harmful and impulsive behaviors. These parts are more accessible and more readily trust her Self. Embodiment, like Self-energy, is a lifetime enterprise. Like for many of us, Elaine's Self-energy emerges as an embodied experience of her spirituality. "It turns out this divinity that we call Self in IFS is a powerful, healing presence. Each Somatic IFS practice serves to restore and support our inheritance of being fully embodied and fully our authentic, essential Selves. We look without. We breathe in bits of each other with every breath we take. We touch our hands and our molecules intermingle. We realize we are much more alike in body and mind than we are different. We are all made up of earth, air, fire, and water and we all depend on these elements. We sense the web of connection that includes ourselves and every being." (Ibid, p. 284)

Embodiment, like Self-energy, is on a continuum, with dissociation at one end and full embodiment on the other. Becoming embodied is not the end point of our existence but rather the beginning of awakening to spiritual wisdom.

KEY TAKEAWAYS

- The Somatic IFS practices facilitate every step of the IFS process with individual, transgenerational, and societal transformation.
- Protectors that fear opening to body awareness deserve our respect and appreciation for their resourceful survival strategies.
- Self-energy is fully potentiated when embodied.
- Parts' stories may be stored in implicit memory, recorded subcortically, and expressed nonverbally.
- Transcending the false dichotomy of mind-body dualism leads to Spirit.

AUTHOR BIO

Susan McConnell, MAPD, CHT (she/her) is the author of *Somatic Internal Family Systems Therapy: Awareness, Breath, Movement and Touch in Practice*, published in 2020 by North Atlantic Books. She is the creator of Somatic IFS, a culmination of her training and experience with various somatic, spiritual, and psychotherapeutic modalities and blending these modalities with the traditional tools of the Internal Family Systems framework. Embodying the internal family—the subpersonalities as well as the essential core Self—brings compassionate witnessing to the implicit body stories of individual hurts and societal burdens. Susan offers Somatic IFS retreats, workshops, and trainings in Somatic IFS to participants throughout the world. As a senior trainer for the IFS Institute since 1997, Susan has taught therapists, developed curriculum, and mentored other trainers. She has over forty years of experience teaching and leading groups throughout the world.

GOING DEEPER

From Susan McConnell

1) Website: www.embodiedself.net
   a. Information about online and in-person Somatic IFS retreats, workshops, and trainings.
   b. Somatic IFS Practitioners Directory.
   c. Newsletter signup to receive information about upcoming programming.

2) Books:
   a. McConnell, S. (2020). *Somatic Internal Family Systems therapy: Awareness, breath, resonance, movement, and touch in practice.* North Atlantic Books.

3) Podcast Interviews:

   IFS Talks:
   a. www.internalfamilysystems.pt/multimedia/webinars/somatic-ifs-susan-mcconnell-new-book
   b. www.internalfamilysystems.pt/multimedia/webinars/embodying-ifs-susan-mcconnell

   The One Inside:
   a. www.theoneinside.libsyn.com/somatic-ifs-with-susan-mcconnell
   b. www.theoneinside.libsyn.com/ifs-and-a-somatic-ifs-meditation-with-susan-mcconnell

4) Workshops and Videos:
   a. Life Architect: four-hour video introduction to Somatic IFS with didactics, meditation, and practice instructions: www.lifearchitect.com/somatic-ifs/
   b. Embody Lab: Two two-hour videos: www.theembodylab.com/integrative-somatic-trauma-therapy-certificate. (Part of the 2022 Integrative Somatic Trauma Therapy Certificate Program).
   c. IFS Continuity Program. "An Introduction to Somatic IFS; An Embodied Approach to Healing Trauma." An archive of the course is available for purchase at the IFS-I catalogue and for new members who join the Continuity Program it is available at a discounted rate: www.courses.ifs-institute.com (9 1/2 hrs.).

From Other Sources

1) Books/Workbooks:
   a. Sweezey, M., & Ziskand, E. et al. (2013). *Internal Family Systems therapy: New dimensions.* Routledge.
   b. Eigen, C. (Ed.). (2014). *Inner dialogue in daily life: Contemporary approaches to personal and professional development in psychotherapy.* Jessica Kingsley Publisher.
   c. Siegel, D. J. (2018). *Aware: The science and practice of presence.* Random House.
   d. Siegel, D. J. (2012). *The developing mind: How relationships and the brain interact to shape who we are* (2nd ed.). Guilford.
   e. van der Kolk, B. (2014). *The body keeps the score: Brain, mind and body in the healing of trauma.* Viking.
   f. Dana, D. (2018). *The polyvagal theory in therapy: Engaging the rhythm of regulation.* Norton.
   g. Schore, A. (2019). *Right brain psychotherapy.* Norton.
   h. Bainbridge Cohen, B. (1993). *Sensing, feeling, and action: The experiential anatomy of body-mind centering.* Contact Editions.
   i. Bainbridge Cohen, B. (2018). *Basic neurocellular patterns exploring developmental movement.* Burchfield Rose Publishers.
   j. Hartley, L. (1995). *Wisdom of the body moving.* North Atlantic Books.
   k. Mardou, S. (2022). *Somatic IFS: A self practice.* Amazon.com Kindle Edition.
   l. Aposhyan, S. (2004). *Body-mind psychotherapy: Principles, techniques, and practical applications.* Norton.
   m. Aposhyan, S. (2021). *Heart open, body awake: Four steps to embodied spirituality.* Shambhala Publications.
   n. Pert, C. (1997). *Molecules of emotion: The science behind mind-body medicine.* Touchstone.
   o. Menakem, R. (2017). *My grandmother's hands: Racialized trauma and the pathway to mending our hearts and bodies.* Central Recovery Press.
   p. Montagu, A. (1971). *The human significance of the skin.* Harper and Row.
   q. Rothschild, B. (2000). *The body remembers: The psychophysiology of trauma and trauma treatment.* Norton.
   r. Levine, P. (1997). *Waking the tiger: Healing trauma.* North Atlantic Books.
   s. Levine, P. (2010). *In an unspoken voice: How the body releases trauma and restores goodness.* North Atlantic Books.

IFS AND ADDICTION

COMPASSION FOR
THE ADDICTIVE PROCESS

Cece Sykes, LCSW
and Mary Kruger, MS, LMFT

In this chapter we offer a paradigm shift for the treatment of clients struggling with addictive activity. In many current approaches, clients with "addictive" struggles are viewed differently from clients with "emotional" struggles and are often referred to programs that pathologize parts that are acting out addictively and that focus primarily on symptom control. We view treatment differently.

Through the compassionate lens of IFS, we understand addiction to be a systemic process, we recognize the positive intention behind compulsive activity, and we address the underlying pain that drives it. We believe that this non-shaming approach ultimately creates a more stable and enduring healing. Our hope is that this IFS approach will help bridge the unnecessary divide between psychotherapy and conventional addiction treatment. We welcome you on this journey!

During the COVID-19 pandemic, clinicians had a front row seat while isolation, loss, and other pressures exposed a universal need to soothe and escape. Thousands of witty memes—wine, pizza, chocolate—flooded social media, normalizing and even celebrating our desire for substance-fueled relief. For some, the need opened the door for a frank dialogue about alcohol, gaming, food, or other compulsive issues. For many, the struggle with substances and escapist practices was nothing new. Yet we find that therapists often do not routinely ask their clients about drinking patterns or drug use, nor invite in-depth discussion about latent preoccupations with eating, spending, or sex. It is a puzzling omission—therapists who deftly handle complex trauma issues often report feeling out of their depth around potential addiction issues.

Our view is that this clinical disinclination is rooted in broader cultural assumptions about addiction and how to treat it. For decades, people who struggled with compulsive behavior have been viewed negatively, criminalized, or labeled "addicts." Despite many efforts toward change, this stigma continues to be embedded in our culture. Prior to the founding of Alcoholics Anonymous, problematic alcohol and drug use, and other compulsive behaviors such as gambling, were viewed as a moral failing. Later, the medical profession focused on a biological perspective, creating a disease model which attempted to neutralize characterological issues. Unfortunately, the medical lens simply shifted the view of the sufferer as genetically flawed, leading to an even more limiting and hopeless perspective. In an attempt to reduce stigma, diagnostic changes in the DSM V relabeled "addiction" as "substance use disorder," which was an improvement, but it still failed to address catalytic underlying trauma and other causes of addictive behaviors. The field is rife with treatment philosophies that focus on a singular aspect of addiction (biological, behavioral, criminal, psychological, or spiritual), all of which tend to miss the systemic nature and complexity of the addictive process. In each of these approaches, people with addictive behaviors (labeled extreme firefighters in IFS) are viewed with fear or judgment and pinned with a badge of shame. Treatment approaches centered upon control and elimination of a person's addictive parts overlook underlying emotional issues, effectively demonizing behaviors and blaming the clients they are attempting to help.

A critical moment presents itself in therapy when clients gather the courage to disclose compulsive behaviors. Already harshly judging themselves, they are making a vulnerable, risky admission that's often not attempted until they are overwhelmed and desperate. Yet needed help is not easy to access. Many therapists without addiction-specific expertise refer these cases out to addiction specialists, treatment centers, or 12-step programs. On the surface, this is a supportive strategy. Therapists want clients to receive appropriate support, and these types of referrals should enable the client to get expert help. Particularly when the client is in a life-threatening situation, stabilizing treatment is indeed the best course.

However, this approach also creates challenges. Often, specialists are not available, the client doesn't have access to, or insurance for, residential centers, and local community programs have lengthy waiting lists. At this early stage, many clients are also often too scared and uncertain to join a group requiring a pledge of sobriety. Thus, the client is not welcome to stay in therapy, yet unable to take a next step. The revelation of addictive issues has merely kicked the clinical can down the road leaving the client with nowhere to turn. The implicit message to the client—"Get over your addictive problem somewhere else, and then you can come back and have therapy about your addictive problem."—can be both confusing and humiliating. Further, it can impair trust in future clinical interventions. We believe clinicians and clients deserve better options.

We take the position that addictive issues are common clinical issues, and that the IFS model is tailor-made to address them. In this chapter, we present case examples that demonstrate new conceptualizations and compassionate, effective interventions. We explore how to work with client issues when engaging with 12-step programs, and we highlight the role of therapists, who are understandably daunted both by traditional views of addiction and by the complexity of higher-risk behaviors.

In the first section, Cece describes consultation with an IFS therapist who reached out when a new client reported substance use issues. She shares interventions for the therapist, client, (and ultimately her partner) as they eventually come to embrace IFS's non-judgmental, systemic approach. In the following section, Mary offers case vignettes exemplifying the shift in systemic thinking that comes from IFS inner work. She also shares case illustrations about connecting clients to 12-step programs and other important ancillary support.

All client and consultee names in this chapter have been changed to protect confidentiality.

The Paradigm Shift:
Cece's Case with Roberta and her clients, Jessica and Harvey

Roberta contacted me (Cece) for IFS consultation. She had recently completed my workshop on addictive processes which seemed perfectly timed for her newest client, Jessica. An employed, White, female in her thirties, Jessica was struggling with chronic drinking and various types of drug use. She and her husband, Harvey, had recently begun traditional couples therapy, however after Jessica's substance use was identified, they had been told to find an addictions specialist to work with instead. Jessica agreed with her husband that she was 'getting worse,' and contacted Roberta, who had been recommended to them.

1. Creating Hope: A Non-Judgmental Clinical Relationship

In the first session, Roberta explained that she did not consider herself an addictions counselor, but she utilized a model called Internal Family Systems (IFS) that takes a more compassion-based approach to treating substance use. Jessica was interested, so Roberta continued. She clarified that the IFS model views problematic substance use as parts of a person that persistently engage in harmful, but well-intentioned, attempts to soothe underlying pain. Roberta explained that this approach steers clear of simply labeling someone an "addict" coping with "addictions." Instead, Roberta and Jessica would work collaboratively to treat all aspects of Jessica's functioning, enabling them to fully understand and address her *addictive processes*. Roberta noted that in other parts of Jessica's life, such as work, for instance, she could function well; her parts engaged in addictive behaviors don't constitute Jessica's entire identity. Roberta affirmed her full support of Jessica's goals to change her alcohol and drug use, noting that "when we understand the role of the parts that use substances," we inevitably find reasons underlying their compulsive tactics and discover "they are motivated by *good* intentions, even if the behavior they are engaged in is creating harm."

2. Offering Compassion and Hope

In her welcoming and honest introduction of herself and the IFS model, Roberta set the stage for transparency and hope about working with Jessica on her addictive behaviors. This normalizing, non-judgmental, and collaborative connection sets the stage for change and genuine teamwork. Roberta learned later about the relief Jessica's system felt in this new clinical context. Previously, Jessica had undergone a short-lived treatment experience where she was told that she had become "an addict" and could learn methods to cope and be sober, but her addictions were a permanent condition that she would be saddled with for the rest of her life. For Jessica, this interpretation of her struggles felt like a bleak, hopeless verdict that compounded the despair of her exiled parts already burdened by feelings of shame, failure, and hopelessness.

When we locate the client on a universal human continuum, recognizing that many people use various practices and substances to seek comfort and relief from pain, we normalize strategies of parts that are using, while also appreciating that their current strategies are no longer working. IFS therapists understand that addictive parts have a job to do—they are trying to soothe or escape the emotional wounds that exiled parts are carrying. In other words, they have a significant role in the inner system as a protector of last resort. With an IFS lens, we can honor firefighter parts' capacity to temporarily soothe and relieve underlying shame while acknowledging they are unintentionally creating chaos and danger along the way.

It may not be immediately clear to a new client that these chaotic parts deserve positive regard for their attempts to help. However, reframing their role places "acting out" activities in a new light and invites the client to risk a more honest reporting of their compulsive patterns. We offer a person-first perspective that widens the clinical lens to include every part of the client's system. The invitation from the therapist to work together assumes that the client has inherently positive resources and capabilities. In IFS terminology, they have a Self. All Jessica knew was that maybe now there was a plan, and she felt hope.

IFS sees the inner world systemically, dividing the psyche into three distinct, inter-related categories: managers, firefighters, and exiles. Each of the three teams is made up of numerous parts allied by similar roles, intentions, and strategies for maintaining a functioning, dynamic, inner community. I view addiction as "a systemic process characterized by an unremitting, cyclical inner power struggle between two protective teams, each driven to use opposite methods to maintain the system and prevent a flood of exiled emotional pain." (Sykes, 2016). The manager team seeks stability and control and, in an addictive system, develops a ruthless internal campaign to constrain extreme firefighters through censure and hostility. The firefighters, who are committed to relieving pain and worthlessness, respond to manager control by doubling down their pursuit of relief by any means possible, no matter the cost or the chaos. As long as an escape from pain is needed, they will provide one. These two protective teams are continually reactivated by exiles, the third group of parts, and the exiles' desperation for connection and release from trauma, loneliness, worthlessness, and attachment wounds. The term *addictive processes* expands the lens of both client and therapist and more accurately reflects the developmental and cyclical progression steered by *all three categories* of parts to become entrenched and extreme. This wider lens loops in each aspect (part) of the client's inner world to become a potential part of the solution rather than remaining an unacknowledged part of the problem.

Roberta reported that in the next few meetings, Jessica began admitting that she was drinking vodka before therapy, and also needed a drink before meeting with the relationship counselor, and definitely before phone calls with her mother because "with alcohol it is easier to relax and to open up and talk." Jessica said she had a long history of using alcohol, cocaine, and other "party" drugs. After her miserable experience in rehab, she had been sober for a few weeks, but her using rapidly escalated, becoming worse than prior to treatment. What prompted her increased using made sense to Jessica later in therapy (shamed firefighters and hopeless exiles), but at the time, Jessica felt labeled, judged, and fearful about her capacity to get better. Believing that she'd gone to treatment and only gotten worse exacerbated her shame and hopelessness.

Regarding her childhood, Jessica identified her father as an alcoholic who died when she was four. This left her alone with her mother who became chronically ill and depressed. Jessica then took on the responsibilities of her mother's caretaking. She reported feeling terribly guilty that "to this day" she cannot seem to do a better job of "helping her mother."

Roberta appreciated Jessica's openness and felt they were off to a fine start. However, Jessica's truthful reports about drinking before sessions activated her own anxious parts and Roberta felt uncertain about handling this issue and worried it could harm therapy. In IFS we say all parts are welcome, but should those firefighters really be allowed to attend the session? As Roberta put it, she "felt good quoting the basic theory (of IFS) but living up to it was another story."

3. Collaboration: Avoiding Therapist-Client Power Struggles

Jessica's honesty about drinking before sessions seemed both admirable and confusing to Roberta. Jessica said she knew she "should be sober" for therapy, but felt substances were her only path to "opening up," which she wanted to do. This juncture can create a dilemma for both client and therapist. On the one hand, it seems like therapy is more limited while the client is taking substances. On the other, using substances is the reality—the here and now in Jessica's life. And isn't she in therapy because she depends on substances?

Traditionally, therapists are advised not to meet with clients if they have been using substances, and, like most clinicians, Roberta was influenced by that overriding directive.

But let's view this dilemma in a larger context. Therapists don't turn away depressed clients when they are especially sluggish and apathetic, nor send home an anxious client overcome with frenzied, racing thoughts. Similarly, clients who arrive for therapy gripped by obsessive eating fears or listless and disoriented after hours viewing porn are considered viable for a session. Yet these common clinical conditions create significant limits upon the client's capacity to express thoughts, identify feelings, focus internally, and maintain a coherent narrative. While of course it is a matter of degree, we invite you to consider: Is it truly necessary, especially at the outset, to uniquely ban clients who are using substances from attending their therapy simply because they are not at their best? In all cases, is not each client overrun by protective parts that are simply doing the thing they do?

Certainly, facing the uncertainties of a client with substance issues brings special challenges. Sometimes Jessica cancelled because she drank too much, and at other times—although not always—was too altered to do inside focusing. Roberta could feel her managers activated and occasionally found it hard to stay compassionate. At our next consult she asked for direction. Should she tell Jessica firmly not to drink before therapy or cancel sessions for drinking and ask Jessica to report any substances use to her?

I appreciated Roberta's struggle and normalized her managers' fears and expectations. It is hard work for our therapist parts! Yet this is exactly when it is most important for therapists to resist letting managers take over the connections. In order to avoid getting mired in a manager-firefighter stand-off with Jessica, we helped Roberta's managers to step back. I emphasized that Jessica is taking risks when she is truthful about her drinking and her inability to "go inside." Jessica is not placating or pretending with Roberta; she is being authentic, as hard as that might be for the therapist.

When a therapist leads with directive managers, it derails collaboration and often will further activate a client's defensive parts: *You're making such a big deal about this, I barely had one drink! I'm not high. I'm just tired tonight! It's not my fault; I was doing fine all day until sh*t happened, and I had to take something!* Therapist-manager to client-firefighter exchanges create an external polarity that frustrates both parties and circumvents clinical work. Meanwhile, behind the scenes, the client's ever-sensitive exiles are listening to the therapist, too, and drawing their own conclusions: *Roberta is mad. She doesn't like me anymore! What is wrong with me? Nothing ever works—why should I keep trying?*

Externalized polarities with the therapist ultimately re-burden already ashamed exiles and shift the focus from the real issue: the client's *internal* polarities. As tempting as it is to focus on rules, Roberta can remind her parts that

Jessica has her own managers who already tell her to be sober for sessions. Keeping the focus on Jessica's inner polarization, rather than the external dynamic with the therapist, moves the work forward and eliminates Roberta's managers from the unenviable "voice of reason" role.

In future sessions, Roberta invited Jessica to explore these issues openly. This reassured Jessica that her therapist could see how hard she was working. Roberta asked her to choose a time of day when it might be easier to be sober (Jessica chose morning). Roberta also clarified that when she asked about using, it was not to be controlling—it would simply help them both be on the same page. Now the work could return to helping Jessica focus on her inner system and her core polarizations between her parts needing to drink/use drugs and her parts wanting to "do the right thing." Roberta helped Jessica use a visualization called the Conference Table Exercise (Appendix C) that invites each team of parts to take a position with Jessica at the head: managers who want sobriety, control, and normalcy on one side, and firefighters using substances and trying to soothe anxiety and loneliness on the other.

Unblending and Working with Addictive Polarizations

Roberta was able to help Jessica use the visualization and assure her two protector teams that she needs them both: she needs parts that keep her on track and doing the right thing, and she needs parts that help her feel better when she is hurting and overwhelmed. When the system is burdened, the behaviors of both protector roles are extreme. Managers are too harsh or too people-pleasing; firefighters are too avoidant and too soothing. Helping Jessica to unblend from her protector teams is a key early intervention, often setting up the first experience they will have of being listened to with curiosity and compassion (from Self.) Rather than focus on symptomatic behavior, we identify the team's *roles in the system that try to meet underlying needs.* This is not as difficult as it sounds. Jessica protectors are simply extreme versions of normal human drives rooted in a very common struggle: we all search for balance between parts of us accomplishing and striving on the one hand and parts seeking pleasure, relaxation, and rest on the other.

When we welcome both sides at the same time, the client can unblend and, finally, separate from the battle, which allows the client to feel clearer and more empowered. For Jessica, and most clients in early stages of their work, there will be a team of parts who want to stop or limit using, and a team of parts committed to numbing or soothing, who do not feel ready to stop. When the therapist's Self and client's Self accept the client's system as it currently exists, the protectors feel heard for their positive intentions and the exiles notice the safe environment and outside support and start to feel hope.

Later in the work, Jessica was able to expand her inner focus to include over-responsible managers that worry about her mother, anxious parts that worry about everything, firefighter parts that are angry when Harvey blames her for their problems, and escapist parts that try to avoid accountability with Harvey. As protectors feel more Self-energy in the system, the client is freed up to notice and make short, direct contact with exiles. Jessica eventually found exiled parts who felt insufficient and alone, parts that had felt overwhelmed and ashamed, and "not enough" exiles that fear she does not do enough for her mother.

Help for Therapist Parts: Treating a System, not a Symptom

As the work continued, Roberta and I continued to meet periodically. Roberta found that unblending from her managers was a full-time job, although it became somewhat easier over time. She reported: "…slowly my manager parts softened and started to trust the unknown, realizing it never is, or was, my responsibility (or even in my power) to control Jessica. The main lesson for me was to learn to remain available and openhearted toward all of Jessica's parts, without any expectations regarding her use of alcohol and drugs."

Roberta continued to focus Jessica on connecting with her whole system and noticing the connections between those parts using substances and other stressed parts. She recognized how her firefighter's use of alcohol and cocaine was useful at helping to soothe the obsessive thinking of managers as well as to medicate the shame of exiles. While the therapist and client accept the valuable intentions of these escapist soothers, we also guide the client to see their inner cycle: firefighter's short-term relief is followed by harsh manager backlash, activating more shame for exiles and long-term consequences. We help clients unblend and build ongoing trust with both protector teams and ultimately come into relationship with the underlying exiled burdens the system is trying to avoid.

An essential way to deepen that trust of the using protectors is to offer new options. What if we help the critical managers unblend? And if we can safely relieve the suffering exiles holding shame and pain, would that help the using parts to ease up? Acknowledging that firefighters turn to substances *for a reason* relieves shaming, is illuminating, and opens up Self-led compassion. This awareness softens inner manager critics, too, which relieves exiles and firefighters both. This new inner work, however, does not automatically translate to less using. Though Jessica experienced many new inner connections and insights, recently her using seemed worse and Jessica cancelled a few times.

Therapy Is not Linear: Back to Polarities

Roberta contacted me to report that she was anxious because Jessica seemed worse and was "unstable." Supportive of her fears, I validated the impact of having a client who is ramping up their substance use. I assured Roberta that erratic stops and starts are common, and healing addictive systems is seldom orderly.

The urge of the therapist's manager parts at this juncture is to work harder, which is understandable. However, when we can resist our urge to control, and refocus on guiding the client back to her own inner polarity, we are actually returning the power to her system. Jessica's managers are already on record that they want her to have a stable life. Her firefighters, like all firefighters, don't obey a therapist's orders anyway, or at least not for more than a short while. If Roberta can stay clear and help Jessica unblend from her addictive polarity again and connect to her firefighters from Self, her inner system will have the chance to rebalance.

When Jessica brought curiosity to her escalating firefighters, they showed her the hurt exile that activated them again: things were very stressful in her relationship at home, she said. Would it be possible for her husband Harvey to attend their sessions, too?

Including the External System

Roberta invited Jessica to discuss this possibility, and Jessica laid out the issues she was feeling with Harvey. She told Roberta that she wanted her husband to learn how they could work on her issues *together*. She felt her relationship with Harvey was related to her addictive processes, and she often felt misunderstood and viewed as "the problem." This was impacting her closeness and trust with Harvey, while activating core exiles.

Jessica and Harvey soon met for the first time with Roberta. Trained in IFIO, an IFS model for couples therapy, Roberta used similar interventions to her individual work, including finding parts, inner focusing, and tracking the systems. With Roberta's guidance the couple started tracking which protector parts were triggering one another, such as when Jessica used substances and Harvey reacted with judgmental and controlling parts. Harvey was intrigued and agreed to meet individually with Roberta so he could get to know his parts better.

Roberta checked in for consultation about the couple's work. I explained how the same polarization Roberta was working on with Jessica would apply to Jessica's partner as well. It is extremely common, almost universal, that a person struggling with heavy using practices has partners, friends, colleagues, or drug counselors who, either directly or unconsciously, want to take over the manager functions and tell them what to do. After all, the client's well-intentioned firefighters have significant consequences that negatively impact both the client and those in relationships with the client. Of course Harvey felt anxious, judgmental, and controlling! I explained that if Jessica helped Harvey track his polarized parts and unblend from controlling managers, he would have more Self-energy available for both his own hurting parts and for the relationship. This would allow Jessica to reattach to her own inner critical managers, who basically want what Harvey's managers want, too.

We also discussed how Harvey's caretaking parts were sometimes accommodating and fearful, putting Jessica's needs too much ahead of his own. If he could focus and pay attention to them, he could find his exiles and learn how to care more effectively for his own needs. As long as one partner has parts that try to control or placate, firefighters in the other partner will react. I emphasized that the more Harvey stayed out of Jessica's inner system, the more he could help. If he worked with his managers trying to control her, it freed both Jessica and Harvey to "stay inside their own triangle." Ultimately this allowed them each to connect to exiles behind their protectors. This didn't imply that Jessica's firefighter's behaviors were okay or didn't impact Harvey. It simply freed Harvey's inner system to focus on more effective ways to meet his own needs (including boundaries, if necessary) and eliminated external clashes that distracted Jessica from dealing with her own inner conflicts.

At this point, Roberta began weekly sessions with Harvey and bi-weekly couple sessions. She felt Harvey was open and motivated to learn about his own parts.

The challenge for Harvey was unblending from his caretaker parts, no matter what mood Jessica was in, and to connect to his exile that was afraid of losing Jessica. Harvey became less polarized and was able to see the negative impact of his controlling and caretaking, which he had not realized. Initially, the focus was solely on Jessica. Now that Harvey was exploring his own parts, Jessica said it felt more equal and mutual—they both had work to do! Roberta noticed that Jessica was now much more motivated to continue her own therapy, and from then on, she hardly ever canceled a session.

The couples' work continued, and Roberta learned how to map the two systems using a triangle graph—Jessica's system and Harvey's system—and track their parts with them.

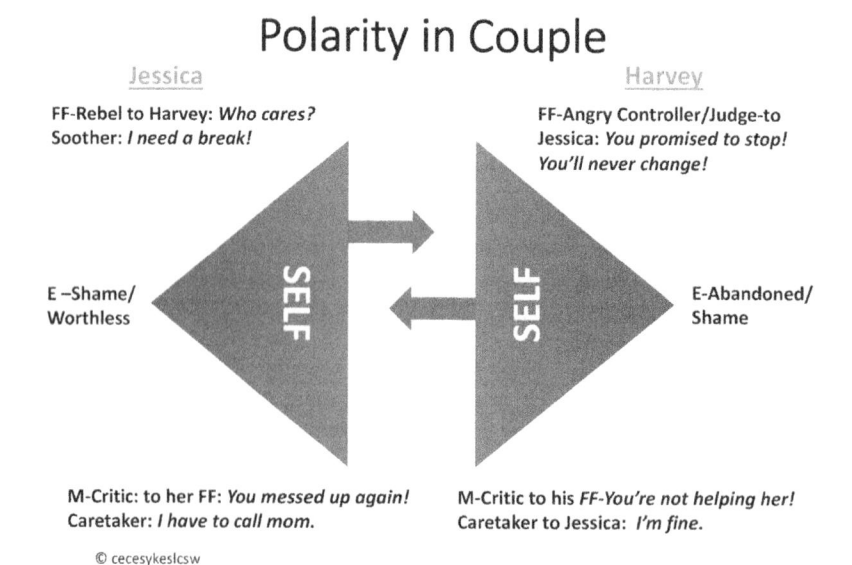

Polarity in Couple

Jessica
FF-Rebel to Harvey: *Who cares?*
Soother: *I need a break!*

E –Shame/Worthless

SELF

M-Critic: to her FF: *You messed up again!*
Caretaker: *I have to call mom.*

Harvey
FF-Angry Controller/Judge-to Jessica: *You promised to stop! You'll never change!*

E-Abandoned/Shame

SELF

M-Critic to his *FF-You're not helping her!*
Caretaker to Jessica: *I'm fine.*

© cecesykeslcsw

She explained that growth meant focusing less on their partner's parts, and more on their own. By tracking their relationship patterns, Jessica and Harvey became aware that they both had the same wish for connection, but that their protectors inadvertently prevented it. Harvey worked on recognizing and unblending from his manager agenda, reminding his parts that when his managers tried to rescue or control Jessica's using, her firefighters rebelled, and her own managers, who also wanted stability, tended to go offline. This also reduced the shame Jessica's exiles felt and supported Jessica's focus on her firefighter parts. Jessica's commitment to her firefighter work was reassuring to Harvey and freed him to focus on more effective ways to care for his parts that felt hurt and fearful. Their relationship improved, yet Jessica continued to use occasionally, and at times, her substance use again became a central focus.

Self-Leadership: Progress, not Perfection

When Jessica's firefighters escalated their using, Harvey's parts became reactivated and both lost access to their Self-energy, a common pattern for couples. When the individual who uses has intensified using, it understandably can trigger fearful or hopeless exiles in their partner. Roberta reported the clients' relationship was reverting to Jessica's using and defensive parts clashing with Harvey's fearful and judgmental parts, eliciting some hopelessness for both. In consultation, Roberta and I discussed how to acknowledge Harvey's understandable frustration and fear while helping both to see that Jessica's managers shared some of the same fears. I normalized how discouraging and worrisome it feels when firefighter activity seems intractable, modeling the same supportive empathy that she could offer to Harvey and Jessica. Roberta could see the relationship and communication improving in many ways, and I advised her to underscore the many positive choices each partner had been making in their relationship and overall functioning, too.

In conventional treatment settings, the primary focus is on the client achieving complete abstinence, while other improvements are often minimized or ignored. In contrast, this IFS approach views change as developmental, occurring over time, and helps clients appreciate each incremental success. We normalize the uneven process and understand that firefighters might make changes but still not feel entirely able to relinquish their posts (fully trust the process). Improvement is assumed to be incremental when treating anxiety or depression, and we believe treatment of compulsive or addictive behavior is often incremental as well. A Self-led view of clinical progress tracks and validates clients when they are able to make new decisions to shift their behavior as well as tracks and explores the parts that continue to believe their burdened behavior is necessary. "Relapses" or re-intensifed using are not viewed as "bad" or "a failure," but simply a real-time indicator that exiles have been re-activated and protectors are back in action, at least for now. While the negative impact is not minimized, helping clients reconnect to their activated parts will reveal "trailheads," including hurt exiles that need more attention and care.

Jessica and Harvey continued their individual work. Harvey identified his parts that came up if Jessica spent a night using, and was learning how to unblend and "speak for" his sadness, fear, and anger. Connecting to and understanding his own needs gave him new clarity and empowered him to stay within his own system or "triangle." From this more Self-led place, Harvey was also able to be more curious and open to Jessica's process and learn how wounded exiles activated her firefighter's using. Jessica, in turn, worked to unblend from her defensive protectors that focus on blaming or avoiding Harvey. She was able to reassure Harvey of her commitment to finding inner balance, to changing her using patterns, and to their relationship. He could see that she was equally concerned about her firefighter's using and still diligently working to heal her system. When a couple's protectors are Self-led, love and care is communicated along with speaking for fear, anger, and stress. This allows the painful, polarized patterns of blaming critic versus rebellious defender (which deeply reinjure both sets of young exiles) to be replaced with clarity and connection. Roberta and I discussed how to support more healthy connection by tracking their *positive* interactions (detecting for Self) and highlighting when Jessica and Harvey tried a new behavior, even if wasn't perfect.

A central aspect of therapy with addictive processes involves detecting parts-led behaviors that have often become extreme, and building new, trusting connections between Self and these parts. We interrupt negative sequences and validate positive ones, both in the individual and within a couple. In addition to tracking parts-led activity and what goes wrong, it is important for the therapist to recognize new choices and Self-led decisions, even if these are not directly related to substance issues. Emphasis on healthy boundary setting, finding a voice (speaking from Self), and identifying underlying (exiled) needs is core to all effective treatment. When we are working on healing a burdened addictive system, "any little change" (Szalavitz, 2016) is valuable, institutes new choices, and moves the work forward.

The Opposite of Addiction Is Connection, Inner and Outer

Jessica and Harvey continued individual and couple sessions. In one couple session, Jessica reported she had been drinking vodka and snorting cocaine. Roberta began by helping Harvey unblend and bring Self-energy to his parts that were concerned and upset. Then Roberta and Jessica worked to connect Jessica's firefighters with her Self-energy to learn what had activated them and how they were trying to help relieve her exiles' pain.

All parts of Jessica's and Harvey's systems were watching this process intently. When she unblended, Jessica could bring compassion to her cocaine-using firefighter's desperate attempt to relieve the pain of a recently triggered exile carrying shame. Jessica's managers then could soften their harsh criticism of the use. This acceptance helped the using firefighters feel understood and strengthened Jessica's connection to them, which generated even more compassion in her system. Hearing this exchange, Harvey's managers also softened toward Jessica's firefighters, and his acceptance helped Jessica feel embraced and understood, rather than judged. When Jessica's cocaine-using part trusted the validation of its positive intent, it relaxed and agreed not to buy more cocaine. Jessica's parts had vowed to quit cocaine before, but this time the Self-led inner connections persisted, and her firefighter didn't feel the same overwhelming drive. Jessica was able to convey that same trust and connection with her drinking part as well, and sometime later Jessica stopped drinking alcohol. She and her firefighters could see that the old intention of using substances to "make it easier to connect" was no longer needed. She felt more open and safe when she spoke to Harvey. Jessica was connecting from Self—far more satisfying!

Jessica and Harvey's improved relationship was healing to both of their systems. For Jessica it was especially healing for her exiles who had felt judged and shamed, and she continued to report feeling more relaxed and open to Harvey. Harvey's exiles, in turn, felt less fearful of potential chaos or losing the relationship. Their painful manager-to-firefighter power struggle truly had shifted. Jessica and Harvey reported a new feeling of mutuality "between two equal humans."

As of this writing, Jessica has been free of any use of alcohol and drugs for many months. She and Harvey continue to do individual and couple work and enjoy their relationship. Jessica and her mother have a healthier connection, and Jessica feels empowered to speak honestly with her family and take care of her own needs. Jessica described the turnaround as "the beginning of the next chapter of the journey. When I was sober, Roberta and I started doing even more work, because we started working you-with-me, rather than you-working-with-a-drunken-me." Jessica opened up to her friends and colleagues about her journey, sharing her huge appreciation of this approach and of IFS. She wrote a blog for her company outlining her process—from using substances to healing and connection. Recently, she invited Roberta to give an IFS workshop to her colleagues.

Creating Third Order Change:
Mary's Stories of Kyle, Carl, Chloe, Tina, and Richard

I (Mary) deeply resonate with Cece's description of IFS's Self-led, nonjudgmental approach to befriending using parts and working with the entire addictive system. In contrast to traditional symptom-focused, shaming approaches that tend to escalate firefighter behavior and resistance, I have found this collaborative IFS approach creates the opportunity for third order change, which is essential in healing the complex inner and outer systems involved in addictive processes.

Third Order Change

Our starting point for clients is that IFS therapy offers a major conceptual shift in how we view the addictive system. Researchers and family therapists Paul Watzlawick, John H. Weakland, and Richard Fisch first posited a new view regarding problem development and change in their 1974 book, *Change: Principles of Problem Formation and Problem Resolution*. From their work, family therapy adopted the concept of First Order Change and Second Order Change. First Order Change refers to a behavioral change and focuses specifically on a symptom/behavior. Second Order Change refers to a change in which external influences and interactions are adopted, which supports the importance of family therapy when working with clients. We view IFS as a postmodern therapy that considers the influence of the client's inner world as a third system that helps develop and maintain problematic behavior, hence a Third Order Change (Kruger, 2015). As such, it dramatically amplifies the impact of the work.

In the following case, I discuss the fictional example of Kyle to illustrate how each approach changes the focus.

Scenario One—*first order change*—represents a more traditional approach of working with addictive clients. Within first-order change, Kyle might enter treatment for an alcohol/substance abuse problem with an individual therapist who uses a linear approach to problem solving. The main focus is the behavior and how to eradicate it. The advantage to this approach is that it gives Kyle an opportunity to be heard and to be witnessed, to build a relationship with a therapist, and to have a system of support and caring. Difficulties can arise when there is no focus on intimate people in the client's life. Kyle had a partner with highly critical protectors that attacked his using behavior, activating Kyle's own inner critic and feeding his shame. In addition, the therapy did not acknowledge the voice or power of Kyle's using parts, which missed the opportunity to invite those parts into the therapy. In first-order change approaches, therapists may be pulled to lead with their own unexamined parts that polarize and mis-attune with a client's system. All these unaddressed issues could leave Kyle unable to stop using or lead to relapse.

In **Scenario Two**—*second order change*—the external system and Kyle's relationships are included in the scope of treatment. Kyle is introduced to the idea of family therapy and group/12-step work in conjunction with individual work. In addition to focusing on Kyle's alcohol/substance use, this approach allows Kyle to see the impact of external interactions, relationships, cultural norms, and external constraints/stressors on maintaining the addictive cycle. This approach increases Kyle's possibility of a lasting recovery as it acknowledges that there is a systemic aspect to the addictive cycle. However, as Kyle's inner system is not acknowledged, Kyle, and others involved in second-order change approaches, may not be able to maintain change, since the wounded parts in their inner system which are underlying the behaviors have not been acknowledged.

In **Scenario Three**—*third order change*—Kyle's healing is grounded in the IFS approach, which included his inner work and a multi-systemic view. Kyle engages in individual, family, group, and 12-step work with an eye toward what is happening in Kyle's inner system, as well as his outer system. In this approach, Kyle develops relationships with all his parts, depolarizing inner conflicts and increasing access to Self-energy (which for many of our clients becomes a spiritual connection). IFS also attends to family legacy and cultural burdens related to Kyle's alcohol/substance use. In addition, IFS allows us to gain the trust of the protective system and help Kyle gain permission to unburden the exiled parts which keep the protective firefighters and managers active. The ability to unburden the exiles holding legacy, cultural, and personal burdens, such as shame and worthlessness, is key in maintaining recovery. In the prior two scenarios, Kyle's trauma wounds were not healed, and this left Kyle vulnerable to relapse. By unburdening the traumatized exiles that drive firefighter behavior, IFS reduces the risk of relapse and improves chances for a positive recovery. In this way of working, and in order to increase effectiveness, it is paramount that the therapist acknowledges their parts in the process as well. IFS therapy represents a third order change and a paradigm shift in working with clients like Kyle.

IFS and 12-Step Programs: Client Examples

One of the most active debates between the addictions and psychotherapy fields is whether there is value and relevance to 12-step groups such as Alcoholics Anonymous, Narcotics Anonymous, Sex and Love Addicts Anonymous, Overeaters Anonymous, and Al-Anon. Our view is that, for many clients, 12-step groups continue to be valuable components of the recovery process and are a complement to IFS Therapy. We recognize that not all clients will find support in a 12-step program—they are not for everyone. Yet we find that more clients may look into 12-step support if their treating therapist is informed about how it works. Carl Jung, in the Big Book of Alcoholics Anonymous, recognized that his therapeutic skills alone were not enough to help his clients suffering from an advanced case of alcoholism to maintain sobriety. He named "vital spiritual phenomena" which result in "huge emotional displacements and rearrangements" and result in "a completely new set of conceptions and motives" as offering the best possibility for recovery. Both IFS therapy and 12-step programs offer this possibility and work beautifully to enhance each other.

I will share some ways in which IFS therapy and 12-step groups can work together, starting with my own personal experience.

My reaction to the suggestion of attending an Al-Anon/ACOA meeting many years ago was that it was a cult. Many of my parts didn't trust the idea, but IFS therapy wasn't available then to explore those parts concerns, resulting in it taking two years for me to gather the courage to attend, despite other parts of me having curiosity and the possibility of hope. I hold this experience in mind when beginning work with new clients who may or may not have had prior experience with 12-step groups.

Collaboration and Trust First

Once a trusting relationship has been established with my client, I may broach the topic of attending a 12-step group, in addition to the work we are doing together. Rather than expressing the idea as a mandate coming from a managerial part of myself, I hold it lightly, with curiosity regarding my client's reaction, what parts are activated, and how this can become a trailhead in our work together. When my client, Carl, entered treatment, he had already had some 12-step experience with SAA. I asked him what was activated for him as he considered reentering the program. He indicated that he did not like thinking of himself as having a "disease." Rather than my manager part debating that with him, I became more curious and asked how that terminology landed with him. He revealed a sense of shame and feeling flawed (the underlying exiles). We took some time to acknowledge those parts of him and to hear a bit more. I presented the idea that one could frame the word *disease* as a state of systemic imbalance rather than a genetic defect. His acting out behavior was actually the burdened behavior of a part, not who he truly was. We also explored where else and when he felt shame and a sense of being defective and offered those parts the hope and possibility of healing. I checked to see how that landed with him, asking him to check inside. He experienced relief and a sense of calming which enabled him to access 12-step support which became one of the cornerstones of his recovery journey. This client wasn't "resistant" to treatment, but rather had parts that had valid concerns and fears. Working from the IFS therapy perspective helped to uncover, validate, and offer other viewpoints to his parts.

I like to keep in mind that clients who are exploring the impact of the addictive process/addictive behaviors are on what both Joseph Campbell and Patrick Carnes have referred to as a "Hero's Journey" requiring an intense amount of courage and perseverance. In our role as therapist, it is important to recognize this and offer hope for change and support for the journey. I congratulate my clients for the courage to enter both the therapy room and 12-step meetings, or other supportive programs, offering that they are "walking the ancient path of the hero," who will discover the parts that are keeping them stuck and the unseen inner strengths that will aid their transformation. In IFS therapy, we view this as the therapist being a "hope merchant."

Addressing Protector Fears with Compassion

Many clients also have parts that fear that they cannot be honest with their therapist or their 12-step group about their addictive behaviors for fear of rejection, judgment, or criticism, and that they must be abstinent and symptom free. This is another trailhead inviting exploration. When my client, Chloe, first entered treatment with me, she experienced a very negative reaction and punitive response from her opioid treatment program when she revealed that her eating disorder had escalated when her opioid use had remitted. In our IFS work together, we welcomed the voice of "ED" (Chloe's eating disorder part wanted to be called ED) and the opioid user into the room. It proved to be a great relief for ED and the opioid user to be welcome and not judged or punished, which these parts voiced in session. Both were willing to consider other options as a team, and to allow access to the exiles they were protecting, which had been leading to chronic relapses. The internal and external manager concerns around perfection in recovery, and the underlying low self-worth and shame of exiles, often cause firefighters to remain underground. Besides addressing this in the therapeutic context, I also remind clients that the same applies to 12-step meetings, that it is "progress, not perfection." While there are coins offered for periods of abstinence, there need only be a curiosity (or "desire to stop the addictive behavior," as named in the 12-step literature), not a mandate to stop. Both IFS therapy and 12-step groups recognize that the road to recovery is not smooth and linear. Other supports and options need to be in place before the addictive behavior (firefighter) can let go.

The First Step of the 12 Steps is: "We admitted we were powerless over alcohol (or another firefighter)—that our lives had become unmanageable." This is often one of the most difficult aspects of the program for our clients and their parts to comprehend. IFS therapy can help the client find an interpretation that fits for both this step and other components of the various 12-step programs. Loss of control is a real fear of protectors—both managers and firefighters—whose job is to suppress/repress/prevent more vulnerable parts (or each other) from taking over the system. Protective parts can react to this step as an attempt to get rid of them and to open up the client for more hurt and victimization.

When asked what their fears were, Chloe's ED and opioid user parts both voiced this concern in session. I framed for Chloe and her parts that this was a step of empowerment. With their agreement, we explored how that could be a possible outcome. We began by exploring and mapping Chloe's own addictive process, which helped her and her parts to see that she was stuck in a process that was having negative consequences for her system. The parts of her that were planning and monitoring her food intake were constantly being foiled by ED—her bulimic part. When ED was activated and having difficulty soothing and controlling Chloe's exiles, the Opioid User would jump in to try to help (the two parts actually working as a team). At this point, Chloe's Big Critic would become extremely loud, which would then result in feeding her shame-filled exile and even more escalation of ED and Opioid User. Chloe and her parts were able to see how the escalation of this process had led her to develop severe medical complications which required hospitalization and almost resulted in death. Her protectors were all in agreement that death was not the goal. They had all been working valiantly to protect Chloe's exiled part that was burdened with shame and self-loathing. Upon this discovery, they could admit that they were exhausted and powerless to help in the way that they hoped. With reassurance that they could still have a place within Chloe, ED and Opioid User became willing to explore other roles and ways to be there for Chloe. And the Planner and Big Critic were able to relax and have a more balanced role in Chloe's system. When all of Chloe's parts came to this collective awareness of "powerlessness," it actually offered the opportunity to open to Chloe's Self, and the Self of others in her group, which brought empowerment and manageability to Chloe and her parts. NA and group work have become important components of Chloe's recovery.

Opening to Self-Energy

Another area clients may struggle with in 12-step programs is the idea of a Higher Power, and/or letting go to a Higher Power. Although a number of the early founders of AA were influenced by Christian beliefs, some held other faiths, and some were atheists or agnostics. Hence, they were aware that the concept of a Christian God wasn't applicable or appropriate to everyone that might "enter the room." The concepts of "a power greater than ourselves" and "as we understood" presented in the Second and Third Steps fit beautifully with the spiritual aspect of IFS therapy. In both IFS therapy and 12-step work, people are invited into their own personal spiritual evolution, as it works for them, without influence or interpretation from others, including their therapist, sponsor, or an influencer. Our clients can come from a variety of religious or spiritual backgrounds, or none at all, any of which could be experienced as supportive or the source of wounding. Our clients may also have parts that are untrusting of others, and certainly of a God. After experiencing terrible loss, sadness, loneliness, and possibly severe trauma, they may have parts that feel abandoned by everyone *including* a Higher Power.

When Tina entered the therapy room for the first time, she presented as someone who felt hopeless and abandoned, was addicted to prescription drugs, and struggled with an entrenched eating disorder. Cycling in and out of treatment programs and various therapists' offices, her issues had only become more extreme. Tina and her siblings had grown up with a father who had been a combat medic with untreated, severe PTSD. Her mother, who tried to keep the family together and functioning, was prone to periods of depression. The household was marked by periods of extreme violence perpetuated by her father, who also engaged in alcohol abuse and numerous affairs. With no place to turn and no way of escape, Tina's parts turned to bulimia by age 11, using food, purging, and exercise as a way of self-soothing and escape. By high school, Tina had developed additional protector parts that were abusing alcohol and drugs regularly. Although she was extremely bright, her addictive behaviors began to interfere with her functioning and school performance, making it impossible for her to pursue her own career and dream to attend West Point. Her life cycled out of control, and she was relegated to low paying jobs with little opportunity and endured several bad relationships. When we first met, her mother who was her sole source of nurturance and stability, had succumbed to a long and painful death.

In one session, Tina reported to me that she didn't believe in a God, or any spiritual path or Being, because she felt that no Higher Being would allow such suffering. This became both a trailhead and a cornerstone of our work together. Rather than suggesting a 12-step meeting, offering "proof," or reading inspirational quotes, I asked any parts of me that wanted to influence Tina to step back and let me be present with her. From a place of compassion and curiosity, I asked her to tell me how she had come to feel abandoned. This revelation was actually a trailhead to the burdens that Tina's exiles were holding—fear, loneliness, shame and self-loathing. I also asked Tina how the bulimia and prescription use helped her. Her parts revealed that they brought her a routine and rules to follow, as well as a sense of calm, safety, and companionship; and that they were Tina's Higher Power. As we worked slowly over time, gaining trust from her protectors, Tina's Self-energy began to emerge, and her addictive behaviors began to remit. She began to attend group therapy and also 12-step meetings. Once her parts had gained enough trust in her Self, she was able to go deeper into unburdening her exiles. Four years into treatment, Tina emerged as the most spiritually-connected member of our group. Tina left therapy after five-and-a-half years to pursue a spiritual path that she defined and that resonated with her system. Her parts were no longer using prescriptions or engaging in disordered eating. She had reconnected and made amends with her father, who eventually sought treatment at the VA. She successfully navigated the loss of her life partner, and she adopted a young teenager who had also experienced a difficult life.

Self-led Moral Inventory and Unburdening "Character Defects"

The language of Steps Four and Six are additional areas that commonly trigger clients' parts. Step Four states, "Made a searching and fearless moral inventory of ourselves," and Step Six states, "Were entirely ready to have God remove these defects of character." When spoken from a manager part, these statements will often kick off an inner rebellion and trigger shame. However, from a more Self-led stance, the inventory can feel freeing. Character defects are recognized as the burdens the parts are carrying, not core personality traits.

The question I ask to help clients identify their parts is: "What comes up for you when you hear the Step Four terminology?" Invariably, Big Critic, Judgment, and Shame parts come up. I also ask, "What if you were to take a compassionate look at these parts from your Self, knowing that you don't have any bad parts, only good parts stuck in bad roles?" From the IFS perspective, I use the first question to discover what parts are triggered and need attention. From the second question, I invite Self-energy to offer hope and options to parts. I also ask, "What comes up for you when you hear "defects of character?" Like many, my client, Sadie, had an exile that believed she was broken when she first entered NA. I asked her, "What if we were to view the term 'defects' as burdens rather than a judgment on you or your parts? And what if 'God removing defects of character' was actually Self lovingly building new relationships with parts, ultimately relieving their painful burdens?" This resonated for Sadie, enabling her to go deeper into her IFS work, where she unburdened her little girl who held the family's "brokenness," and to deepen her work in NA. Often the key to helping client's parts feel openness toward 12-step language and activity is to translate, or reframe it, into terms the client is comfortable with and make sense based on their life experiences.

Avoiding the Polarization Trap

My former client, Richard, whose drinking firefighter chronically relapsed with alcohol, came in one day to tell me he had decided to sponsor himself because he wanted to do things differently. Rather than polarize with his parts, I became curious and explored those parts who had formed that decision. A part of him had made this decision because he was trying to escape his Inner Critic, and the judgment and shame that emerged in the sponsoring relationship. While he was out on his own, without his sponsor or AA group, we continued to work together with those parts. We also discovered that the Drinker was connected with this dynamic and was escalating while he was on his own, and that a scared young exile boy was needing attention. I was careful not to align with being in or out of the AA program, whether he should drink or not drink, or work with his little boy without permission from his protectors. I simply helped him welcome all his parts and repair their attachment to Self. Working with his parts in this way enabled his inner system to become more connected and accepted, which allowed him to return to a recovery community where he felt safe and could live without drinking. By then, all of his parts engaging in the addictive process were in agreement.

A Collaborative Path:
Healing Addictive Processes Is a Systemic Process

In our view the IFS model offers a major paradigm shift for treating clients with addictive processes. With the compassionate IFS lens, therapists can avoid common clinical power struggles, effectively destigmatize addictive behaviors, and address underlying trauma and attachment wounds. We hope the case examples presented here demonstrate the benefits of both the client and the therapist working actively on their inner systems every step of the way. In each scenario, we are striving to create a collaborative context and help expand the clinical lens beyond firefighter activity to include all the parts embroiled in the conflicts that shape any addictive system.

Around the question of 12-step work and sponsorship, we avoid taking the conventional "manager position" of hastily directing clients to attend or risk failing. Instead, we focus first on establishing a trusting, curious, and open-hearted context and invite clients to share their treatment experiences with us. Given the omnipresence of 12-step programming in addiction treatment, we find that most of our clients, as well as many therapists we encounter, have acquired very definite impressions of 12-step programs and of how treatment for any addictive behavior should look. Inviting our clients—and therapists seeking consultation—to share their prior exposure to 12-step meetings and to previous treatment programs is an important early intervention. This space for inquiry can help identify judgments, fears, shame, and other beliefs their parts have been holding. Often clients (and clinicians) are also struggling with significant grief and prior wounding from their experiences with treatment (or lack of treatment) for their parents, siblings, partners, or other loved ones. Working with all the parts clustered around this history will help them identify burdens, be open to new possibilities, and build a shared understanding with their therapist.

Our goal is for the client to make a Self-led decision about whether 12-step meetings, or more intensive treatment, are right for them at this time and what other options to pursue. Clients healing from addictive behaviors typically benefit from finding various kinds of support and resourcing in addition to psychotherapy. It may be 12-step work, couples or family therapy, a new writing class, or joining a sports team or meditation group. We don't set the agenda; we accept there is not one path or one right way to healing. In our experience, when therapists ensure that managers are out of the way, clients prove they have enormously creative resources for meeting their needs and finding solutions to their struggles.

From the systemic viewpoint, "disease" actually represents an imbalance in the system (person). As a systemic therapy, IFS can effectively address all the interactive aspects (parts) of the system that are impacting addictive behavior. In this approach we seek to discover how and why those imbalances occur and to restore harmony and equilibrium to the system. We don't need to label or interpret a client's addictive behaviors; instead, we work collaboratively to uncover and explore the parts of them that are activating the process. We recognize the uniqueness of each individual's story, and by healing their underlying exiles, they can build inner compassion and define their own journey.

Our view is that the therapist's system impacts the client's system in every interaction. We actively work with our parts holding bias or fears, adding our Self-energy rather than more control or more shame to the relationship. We accept the client as they show up today, in the here and now, understanding that change takes time and pain underlies the need for any firefighter behavior. We hope the nonjudgmental clarity and commitment of this approach offers a path forward for therapists and will help address and relieve the stigma and confusion that surrounds so much well-intentioned work on addictive processes.

KEY TAKEAWAYS

- Create a non-judgmental context for collaboration with the client dealing with addictive behaviors. Hold compassion for addictive parts and offer hope for real transformation.
- Normalize the desire for pleasure or escape as part of the human condition, not unique to someone struggling with addictive behaviors. Reframe "addict" to "person with parts using behaviors or substances to try to relieve exile pain."
- Identify the addictive system and positive intent of the parts that are acting out. Treat the system, not the symptom. Include the client's external system.
- Invite the client and all their parts to define the vision for change rather than assuming a singular goal of abstinence.
- Build Self-to-protector connections and learn the positive intention of both teams of protectors (managers and firefighters). Help clients track the parts involved in their using cycles.
- With the *client*: Build healthy, supportive connections to protectors and gain their trust for witnessing and unburdening exiles that trigger polarized protectors. For the *therapist*: Bring Self-energy to therapist parts that feel anxious or polarized with the client's system. Avoid therapist-manager to client-firefighter power struggles.
- Introduce Self to relieve the addictive manager-firefighter polarization.
- In engaging with the 12 Steps: Establish collaboration and trust first. Address protector fears compassionately. Remain open to Self-energy.
- From the 12-step traditions, consider: Progress not perfection: change is often incremental. The opposite of addiction is inner and outer connection.

AUTHOR BIOS

Cece Sykes, LCSW (she/her) is a consultant and Senior Trainer with the Internal Family Systems Institute where she specializes in trauma and addiction and educates therapists around the world on how to apply the IFS therapy model to addictive processes. Additionally, Sykes is exploring how psychotherapy affects the therapist's life. She lectures, consults, and leads workshops on these and related topics, and has a private practice in Chicago. She has co-authored a number of articles on treating the impact of sexual trauma in families and authored the chapter "An IFS Lens on Addiction: Compassion for Extreme Parts" in the 2017 book, *Innovations and Elaborations in Internal Family Systems Therapy*.

Mary Kruger, MS, LMFT (she/her) is an AAMFT supervisor and an IFS Lead Trainer. She is the founder of Rimmon Pond Counseling, an IFS-based private practice located in New Haven, Connecticut, and has specialized in addictions, eating disorders, and trauma for more than 25 years. Mary has developed a variety of creative ways to work with parts and access Self-energy in individual, relational, and group contexts. She enjoys sharing her experience in teaching and consulting on a national level. Mary is noted for her humor, creativity, passion, and love of dancing and people. She also offers private therapy, consultations, and workshops.

GOING DEEPER

From Cece Sykes

1) Website:
   a. www.cecesykeslcsw.com

2) Publications:
   a. Sykes, C. C., Sweezy. M., & Schwartz, R. C. (2023) *Internal Family Systems therapy for addiction: Trauma-informed compassion-based interventions for substance use, food, gambling and more*. PESI Publications.
   b. Sykes, C. C. (2017). An IFS lens on addiction; Compassion for extreme parts. In M. Sweezy & E. L. Ziskind (Eds.), *Innovations and elaborations*. Routledge.
   c. Sykes, C. C. (2001). Why I love my firefighters. *Self to Self IFSA Journal*, 5(6).

3) Trainings:
   a. IFS Level 2: A Compassionate Approach to Addictive Processes: IFS, Addictions and Eating Disorders. www.ifs-institute.com/trainings/level-2
   b. IFS Level 3: www.ifs-institute.com/trainings/level-3

4) Seminars and Webinars:
   a. IFS Continuity Program: IFS and the Voices of Addiction; 4-module Seminar: Cece Sykes LCSW, ACSW, Mary Kruger, MS LCPC Richard Schwartz, PhD. www.courses.ifs-institute.com/item/internal-family-systems-ifs-voices-addiction-47446
   b. Life Architect: Compassion for Addictive Process; 3-Module Seminar www.lifearchitect.com/compassion-for-addictive-process/
   c. PESI Webinar: Internal Family Systems: A Compassionate Approach to Trauma and Addictive Processes; Anderson, Frank MD; Sykes, Cece LCSW; Schwartz, Richard PhD. www.courses.ifs-institute.com/item/internal-family-systems-ifs-compassionate-approach-trauma-addictive-processes-72167

5) Podcasts:
   a. Positive Sobriety: Explaining IFS with Cece Sykes; Episode 50 www.podcasts.apple.com/ie/podcast/episode-50-explaining-internal-family-systems-cece/id1434354560?i=1000462158013
   b. Love, Pleasure and Joy; Cate McKenzie: www.catemackenzie.com/cece-sykes-on-compassion-for-addictive-processes/

c. IFS Talks; Anibal Henriques and Tisha Shull: www.podcasts.apple.com/gb/podcast/ifs-talks/id1481000501
      i. IFS and Extreme Parts 9-19-2019
      ii. Compassion for Addictive Processes 8-24-2020
      iii. Therapist Role: Heart Lessons of the Journey 10-2-2202
      iv. Therapeutic Relationship and Addictive Process: Help for Managers! 1-29-2022.
      v. Masters Series with Toni Herbine- Blank; March 2023
   d. Truth, Love and Beauty; Sara Avant Stover: Compassion for Addictive Process: April 2023 www.podbay.fm/p/she-talks/e/1614502802
   e. The Weekend University; Niall McKeever: IFS Approach to Addictive Processes; April, 2023 www.podcasts.apple.com/eg/podcast/the-weekend-university/id1233173966 and www.youtube.com/channel/UCfTRIfHYqucAxDx99rQig/videos?view=0&sort=p
   f. Amy Crawford; Turning In: "IFS and Addictive Processes" Interview with Cece Sykes, May 2023. www.turninginpod.buzzsprout.com/share

From Mary Kruger

1) Website:
   a. www.mpkruger.com

2) Trainings and Webinars:
   a. IFS Level 2: A Compassionate Approach to Addictive Processes: IFS, Addictions and Eating Disorders. www.ifs-institute.com/trainings/level-2
   b. IFS Continuity Program: Internal Family Systems and The Voices of Addiction—Cece Sykes, LCSW, ACSW; Mary Kruger, MS, LMFT; Dr. Richard Schwartz, PhD. www.courses.ifs-institute.com/item/internal-family-systems-ifs-voices-addiction-47446
   c. Life Architect: Working with Highly Conflictual Couples from the IFS Perspective. www.lifearchitect.com/working-with-highly-conflictual-couples/
   d. Mountainside Treatment Center YouTube Webinars: www.youtube.com/c/MountainsideTreatmentCenter

3) Podcasts:
   a. IFS Talks; Anibal Henriques and Tisha Shull: Addiction and Eating Disorders with Mary Kruger: www.internalfamilysystems.pt/multimedia/webinars/addictions-and-eating-disorders-mary-kruger
   b. A Recovery Journey: A talk with Mary Kruger: www.podcasts.apple.com/us/podcast/a-recovery-journey-a-talk-with-mary-kruger/id1481000501?i=1000487083491

  c. The One Inside; Tammy Sollenberger: IFS and Shame and Addiction with Mary Kruger: www.tammysollenberger.com/ifs-and-shame-and-addiction-with-mary-kruger/

  d. Truth, Love and Beauty; Sara Avant Stover: Mary Kruger on Befriending our Eating Disorders and Addictions with IFS Therapy: www.podbay.fm/p/she-talks/e/1614502802

From Other Resources

1) Publications:
   a. Lewis, M. (2015). *The biology of desire: Why addiction is not a disease.* Public Affairs Books.
   b. Szalavitz, M. (2016). *Unbroken brain, A revolutionary new way of understanding addiction.* Picador, Macmillan Publishing.
   c. Hart, C. L. (2021). *Drug use for grown-ups: Chasing liberty in the land of fear.* Penguin Books.

APPENDIX A

Useful Questions for Working with Addictive Systems
(Mary Kruger, 2015)

1. What brought you here today? How are other parts of you responding to the idea of being here?
2. Does any part of you have concerns about being here? About working together? Ask these parts what they need from you or from me to feel safe or to feel heard.
3. What does the part of you that uses say about being here? Your last treatment? 12 Steps? Group therapy?
4. What are you concerned would happen if you couldn't drink, drug, purge, etc.? (Have the client ask the part, if able to differentiate from the part.)
5. Can you tell me what your using experience is like? How it happens? (This is a good way to track and map parts, help clients unblend, and uncover polarizations.)
6. What are you concerned would happen if we dealt with your more vulnerable parts? (Have the client ask the firefighter part, if able to differentiate from the part)
7. Ask the eating part (or other firefighter) how it's responding to our work with shame, worthlessness, etc.?
8. Ask the drug using part (or other firefighter) how effective it is in achieving its intention? Would it be interested in a more effective way?
9. How has the part that uses porn (or other firefighter) responded to our work? And between sessions?
10. If your firefighters/parts that use were to stop, how would the people around you respond? Who would notice? What would that be like for you?

APPENDIX B

Triangle Exercise
for Mapping for a Polarized System

Once you identify a client's addictive polarity, map it onto a triangle, which will show the client how their exiles and protectors interact. To begin, invite the client to draw an inverted triangle.

Label managers at the top left point and firefighters at the top right point. Place the exile (or exiles) at the bottom point.

Then invite the client to turn their attention inside and notice their stabilizing manager parts trying to maintain the system and anxious/critical managers trying to control firefighter activity. List these parts at the manager point of the triangle.

Next, have them once again turn their attention inside and notice their all their firefighters. Include any firefighters using compulsive practices and any using substances or food. List these parts at the firefighter point of the triangle.

Finally, invite them to notice any exiles, i.e., shame or worthlessness, that come up during the exercise and to list these parts at the bottom of the triangle.

(Instead of writing down their parts, the client may prefer to draw their parts or choose figures to represent their parts using sandtray toys, IFS-inspired cards, magazine cutouts, and so on.)

Once the client finishes listing all of their parts, ask them to jot down the intentions and fears of both protective teams and of the exile. The client may wish to draw solid lines between parts who are particularly allied and broken lines to show which parts are most in conflict. When the triangle drawing is complete, here are some questions you may want to ask the client:

1. What do you observe now that you have some space from the polarity?
2. How do you feel toward these two teams now?
3. Which part-to-part relationships stand out?
4. Which parts are most polarized?
5. How do you feel toward your exile(s)?
6. Have you met all of these parts before?
7. Which part (or polarity) wants your attention first?
8. What does this part (choose one specific part to focus on) want from you?
9. When this process is complete, thank the parts who showed up and save the triangle for future sessions. If the client wants, they can take it home and keep adding parts or details about the motives of the parts they know to date.

Copyright © 2023, Sykes, Sweezy & Schwartz, IFS Therapy for Addictions: Trauma-Informed Compassion-Based Interventions for Substance Use, Eating, Gambling and More. Reprinted with permission. All rights reserved.

APPENDIX C

The Conference Table Exercise:[1]
Overview of the System
Reprinted with permission of PESI Publishing

The conference table is a user-friendly exercise in which the client's Self welcomes their risk-taking firefighter team, their controlling manager team, and their exiles to sit together at a table. This can become a recurring intervention that the client can evoke at home as well.

When clients struggle with addictive processes, their two protector teams can't trust each other; there is not enough Self-energy and space to work with one protector without the polarized part interrupting.

In this visualization we guide the client to unblend them at the same time. The techniques described here facilitate simultaneous unblending of the two protective teams, inviting a third space for exiles. From Self, at the head of the table, the client has a vision of the system.

1. First, ask the client to sit at the head of a big conference table.[2] Next, invite the protective teams to sit on opposite sides of the table. Invite all the managers to take one side. When that feels complete, invite all the firefighters to occupy the other side of the table.
2. Exiles are invited to take a seat across from the client's Self, at the foot of the table. Once everyone is arranged, be sure that the client's Self is present at the head of the table. If not, the client can ask the part who is sitting in for them to join its team and to let the Self sit down.
3. Next, guide the client to validate both the firefighter and manager teams for their positive intentions, and assert that each of them is needed. They may want to get rid of each other, but the Self intends to keep everyone on board. Invite them to shift their gaze away from the others, look to the Self, and consider the possibility that they no longer have to challenge or fix each other because the Self will help the exiles they protect and set them free.
4. Then ask who needs attention first. When a target part (or team) volunteers, ask the client how they feel toward this part (or team). If they say something negative, help the reactive part unblend. You might need to facilitate some shuttle diplomacy (moving between protector teams) to illustrate that the Self can handle both teams. Then listen to the target part (or team), validate its good intentions, explore the pros and cons of what it does, and ask if it is ready to try something new. Then do the same with the other side.

5. Finally, ask if it would be good for everyone if the Self could help the exiles that these two teams protect. When they agree, ask the client what they notice in their body now. If protectors are unblending, they will name a sense of space or calm or something along those lines. If exiles activate, invite them to sit with the Self. Reassure everyone that the Self is committed to the whole system and that no one is alone.

Copyright © 2023, Sykes, Sweezy & Schwartz, IFS Therapy for Addictions: Trauma-Informed Compassion-Based Interventions for Substance Use, Eating, Gambling and More. Reprinted with permission. All rights reserved.

IFS AND DISORDERED EATING

SELF-LED HEALING FOR A MORE HARMONIOUS RELATIONSHIP WITH FOOD AND BODY

Marcella Cox, LMFT, CEDS-S

Reviewers: Jeanne Catanzaro, PhD,
Susan McConnell, MAPD, CHT, and Mariel Pastor, LMFT

> "…and i said to my body. softly. 'i want to be your friend.'
> it took a long breath. and replied, 'i have been waiting
> my whole life for this.'"—*Nayyirah Waheed*

Internal Family Systems (IFS) originated from Dr. Richard Schwartz's work with clients seeking treatment for eating disorders. After failed attempts to control and defeat the parts of clients that were engaged in harmful eating patterns, Dick became curious about these parts and was surprised to learn that, in spite of their negative effects, each had a positive intention for the client. Not only were the parts well-intentioned and serving a protective function, but they felt trapped in their roles and would prefer to be doing something else, if the pain they were concerned about could be healed. Intrigued, Dick went on to discover that within every individual lay an undamaged Self with the power to heal these burdened parts and offer wise and effective leadership to their internal world.

This was a paradigm-shifting breakthrough. No longer did clinicians need to battle with the stubbornly entrenched eating behaviors of their clients. Not only was battle unnecessary, it was also wildly unhelpful. Dick discovered that a far more effective way to transform damaging patterns was to become curious about them and provide compassionate assistance to the parts engaging in them, so they would no longer feel compelled to remain in painful roles. Out of an initial "failure," the IFS model was born.

I am honored to serve in the same area of clinical work that originated this model that has proved transformational in my own life, and I invite you to join me in an exploration of the ways in which the compassionate IFS approach can provide effective, non-pathologizing care to others who are suffering.

I write from the vantage of years of professional experience in various eating disorder treatment settings (most recently outpatient), and personally through the lens of my own healing. I have training in Internal Family Systems (IFS), Somatic IFS, Mindful Self-Compassion, Brené Brown's The Daring Way™, and Body Trust®. As a White, cisgender, heterosexual, educated, middle-class, middle-aged, straight-sized woman, I acknowledge the many privileges and identities that I hold, and I am continually learning the ways in which cultural, legacy, and personal burdens relating to food and bodies influence disordered eating and body shame. My desire is for all people to experience the freedom of a Self-led relationship with eating and their own bodies. Further, I hold hope for all bodies to experience liberation from social and political systems of oppression that designate certain bodies as more worthy, healthy, and desirable than others, so that all people might feel safe and worthy in their own lived, embodied, experience.

In this chapter, I will discuss the prevalence of disordered eating, the causative impact of cultural burdens of oppression and body-objectification, as well as legacy and personal burdens (which cause individuals to develop parts that disconnect from needs, desires, bodies, and Self) contributing to disordered eating patterns. I will compare traditional approaches to healing with the IFS approach to healing burdens and restoring embodiment for more presence, safety, and comfort in one's body. I write from an admittedly Western perspective and outpatient lens, and while cultural application may vary between regions, the IFS principles I describe are applicable in various treatment settings, as well as cross-culturally. My hope is that you will leave this chapter sharing my enthusiasm to support all people in reclaiming their birthright of embodiment and Self-led relationships with eating and movement.

Laying the Groundwork

In order to grasp the complexity of the construct of disordered eating, it is important to explore the prevalence of eating disorders, common terms and definitions, and also the causative factors in the environment and culture that set the stage for disordered eating to flourish.

Prevalence and Access to Care

Eating disorders and disordered eating are significant, lethal, and widely misunderstood issues in the United States. According to research, nine percent of the U.S. population, or approximately 20 million American women and 10 million American men, will have an eating disorder in their lifetime.[1] Eating disorders, as defined by the DSM, have the second-highest mortality rate of all mental health disorders, second only to opioid addiction.[2]

This complex mental health condition impacts individuals of all ages, genders, sexual orientations, races, ethnicities, and socioeconomic classes, however disparities in access to treatment are clear. Despite similar prevalence rates of disordered eating, people of color are half as likely to be diagnosed or receive treatment as White-bodied individuals.[3] Rates of diagnosed eating disorders are higher among LGBTQIA+ identified individuals, with transgender people experiencing significantly higher rates than cisgender individuals.[4] Men have a higher prevalence of disordered eating than many would suspect,[5] and the rates for older females have increased,[6] as our cultural expectations of aging have shifted. Underdiagnoses among certain demographics, lack of support and access to care, stigma, and stereotypes around disordered eating often serve as barriers to treatment.

The Importance of Screening

In light of this prevalence, screening becomes an essential tool. It has been my professional experience that the thriving weight loss industry and diet and wellness cultural messages related to food, our bodies, and our appearance, fuel many people's disordered relationship with food and their bodies. Author and scholar, Nina Piran, highlights how hyper-idealized body images promoted by the media and our society make clear that certain bodies hold power, favor, and privilege (thin, White, able, young, cisgender, heterosexual), while others are marginalized and experience cultural oppression (full-bodied, non-White, older, disabled, LGBTQIA+). Conflicting messages about food internalized from our culture ("Indulge in this yummy thing! But don't get fat!") intertwine with intergenerational and personal burdens to lay a complex groundwork for disordered relationships with food and bodies.

Cultural messages that conflate unrealistic ideas of weight with worth communicate that all but those few who fit the narrow definition of "desirable" are "worthless." To survive this traumatic objectification, many begin to manipulate food and exercise, which often results in parts turning to disordered eating patterns. These burdened behaviors separate us from our authentic selves and disrupt our natural ability to listen to and trust our bodies and have an intuitive relationship with food and movement. In light of the widespread impact of these factors, it is critically important that helping professionals screen for eating and exercise patterns, even for clients who are not presenting for treatment specifically related to food or body image.

Effective screening and treatment for disordered eating is complicated by the fact that external appearance and superficial weight-based markers are not a clear indicator of disordered eating or eating disorders.[7] The tendency of people, including health professionals, to correlate eating disorders and disordered eating with body size and weight means many people go undiagnosed and untreated, while others are subject to pathologizing labels such as "obese," and "overweight" (referring to the Body Mass Index [BMI] scale that measures a person's weight relative to their height but fails to account for age, sex, muscle, or fat mass and should not be used to assess for disordered eating). The BMI has been used to objectify and oppress bodies, creating cultural burdens, some of which are covered in this chapter. For this reason, I will not be using the words "obesity," and "overweight." To inform our discussion, it may prove helpful to review some basic IFS[8] and disordered eating terms and definitions.

Self: The undamaged core of every individual that contains the "8 C" qualities: calm, courageous, compassionate, connected, curious, creative, confident, and clear-minded. Self is the ideal leader of recovery, as well as an individual's entire inner system, and holds the power to heal all parts.

Parts: Unique subpersonalities that have their own sensations, feelings, perspectives, beliefs, and goals. Parts can be unburdened (existing in their naturally positive state) or burdened.

Exiles: Vulnerable, often young, burdened parts that hold our core trauma messages and feelings. The pain of the exiles drives the behavior of managers and firefighters, thus, healing the exiles is key to healing the system of disordered eating. Some exile beliefs that fuel disordered eating patterns include "I'm unlovable," "Something's wrong with me," "I don't matter," "My body is disgusting," and "I'm worthless."

Managers: Parts that have taken on burdened roles trying to proactively prevent the pain of the exiles from becoming triggered. Typical manager behaviors in disordered eating include restricting, over-exercising, and obsessing about and trying to control one's weight. Manager and firefighter energy is typically balanced, such that typical manager-led approaches to changing behavior only fuel firefighter backlash.

Firefighters: Parts that have taken on burdened roles trying to reactively extinguish the pain of exiles after they've become triggered. Typical firefighter behaviors in disordered eating include bingeing, purging, and compulsive exercising without concern for consequences. Parts that carry disordered eating behaviors may shift from proactive approaches (managers) to reactive approaches (firefighters) in their attempts to manage internal and external triggers.

Burden: The impact of trauma that is carried by parts, which distorts their original positive essence. Parts are not the same as their burdens, and, in fact, are often quite the opposite. Self can heal burdens through a process called "unburdening" and restore parts to their original positive essence.

Polarization: Burdened parts that operate in opposition to each other. Common polarizations in disordered eating include manager-firefighter (restrict, binge), firefighter-firefighter (binge, purge), exile-manager (shame, obsess), etc. For example, restricting managers attempting to achieve an idealized body weight trigger exile feelings of deprivation, which in turn activate bingeing firefighters attempting to soothe the sense of deprivation. Polarizations are often, though not always, balanced in strength.

Disordered Eating: This exists along a spectrum and describes burdened interactions with food that may or may not meet criteria for a specific DSM eating disorder. Subclinical disordered eating patterns involve interactions with food that undermine an individual's quality of life, including yo-yo dieting, cycles of restrictive and binge eating, rigid food rituals, and loss of control associated with eating and exercise. These patterns often trigger the very exile feelings (e.g., guilt, shame) that they are attempting to control or soothe.

Eating Disorder: A type of disordered eating such as Anorexia Nervosa, Bulimia Nervosa, Binge Eating Disorder, and Other Specified Feeding and Eating Disorders (OSFED) that meet DSM diagnostic criteria based on the level of obsession about food and one's body, and the negative impact of those thoughts and behaviors on one's physical, psychological, and social functioning.[9] Eating disorders are a subset of disordered eating, but not all disordered eating patterns meet the criteria for a diagnosable eating disorder per the DSM.

Restricting: The behavior of burdened protectors that limits food intake, often in an attempt to achieve an idealized body weight, shape, or size. Restricting certain foods may also be an attempt to achieve "optimal health" and may lead to an obsession with healthy eating or Orthorexia Nervosa (not yet a diagnosis in the DSM). Restricting managers are often polarized with bingeing firefighters (who binge with food, substances, work, spending money, etc.), both of which tend to be dissociative and, thus, distance individuals from a mindful experience of body sensations.

Binge Eating: The behavior of burdened, chaotic, reactive protectors that may involve consuming large quantities of food in one sitting and/or eating in response to emotional triggers. Bingeing parts typically hold intent to soothe, comfort, distract, dissociate, reward, celebrate, or rebel against rigidity or control. It is important to note that binge eating may also be a response to primal hunger caused by food deprivation, which intensifies hunger cues and thoughts about food because the body is starving. Binge eating in this context may not involve burdened parts at all but may simply be the result of a biological survival reflex. When working to unburden a bingeing part, we can invite the client to ask the part what percentage of the bingeing is a biological response to primal hunger and what percentage is driven by a burden. The biological response to primal hunger, of course, cannot and should not be "unburdened," but the burdened percentage of the behavior can in this way be accurately identified and released.

Compensatory Behaviors: The behaviors of burdened protectors that include exercise, purging, fasting, and the use of laxatives and weight loss teas, and other measures, to avoid weight gain, or to alleviate guilt or shame after eating. Proactive mangers may use these strategies to ensure the body stays at a particular weight or size, while reactive firefighters may use compensatory behaviors to "fix" what they perceive as an imperfect body or to relieve increased anxiety and shame after experiencing a perceived loss of control with food.

Environmental Factors

Before we can effectively address an individual's disordered relationships with food and body, we must first explore the societal and institutional systems that oppress and marginalize certain bodies, while objectifying and idealizing others, and lay the groundwork for disordered eating and body shame to flourish.

Award-winning author, researcher, and teacher, Niva Piran, invites us to take a comprehensive view of the causative cultural factors contributing to disordered relationships with food and bodies, providing research that highlights social forces girls and young women experience that work toward disembodiment. In her book, *Journeys of Embodiment at the Intersection of Body and Culture: Developmental Theory of Embodiment* (Piran, 2017), Piran examines the impact of oppression of specific bodies based on social caste (class, race, gender, ability, immigration status, health, and sexual orientation). She argues that individual's embodied journeys are directly related to their social location, with those inhabiting less empowered status (bodies of color, women, etc.) experiencing greater social oppression and resultant disruption to the experience of freedom to be fully embodied. Piran's research shows that disrupted embodiment is associated with a range of behavioral issues, such as:

- Disordered eating and eating disorders.
- Consumption of substances aimed at weight control (e.g., smoking, diet pills, amphetamines, cocaine).
- Self-harm and neglect.
- Sexual activities with no desire or protection.
- Avoiding public exposure without body alterations to meet required "beauty ideals."

Piran's research rings true as we observe in the statistics above that American women are twice as likely to be diagnosed with an eating disorder as American men and rates among LGBTQIA+ folk are markedly higher than cisgender heterosexual individuals. Thus, bodies that have historically been unsafe to inhabit, or that culture has deemed "less worthy," are at elevated risk of objectifying their own body and attempting to conform to idealized body images promoted by culture and to develop ways of coping that remove them from their bodies, leading to disembodiment.

Cultural Oppression: Diet and Wellness Culture

"When people say they want to lose weight, they often mean, 'I want to be respected. I want to be loved. I want to be seen. I want liberation from fear and self-loathing.' Weight-loss culture will never give us those things because it is founded on fear/hate-based systems like sexism, racism, classism and ableism."—*Virgie Tovar,* You Have the Right to Remain Fat

American diet and wellness culture[10] equates a person's weight with their worth, suggest that rest is lazy and that one's body shape or size is earned by willpower. Lucrative weight loss industries normalize disordered eating, profit from comparison and insecurity, and marginalize larger bodies.[11] These powerful forces create what IFS calls cultural legacy burdens (burdens transmitted generationally through culture) that infect clients and clinicians alike: toxic energy or beliefs about food, body size, or weight that are absorbed from environmental influences including government, institutions, communities, schools, religious organizations, and families.

The nearly $160 billion annual weight loss industry in the U.S.[12] profits from the promotion of one rigid diet after the next: from fasting, detoxing, and juice cleanses to elimination-based approaches (no-carbs/fats/sugars/etc.). Apps, smart watches, and fitness trackers gobble up biometric data and track everything from calories consumed to units of exercise expended, serving up a continual database of measurements relaying "success" or "failure," "worthiness" or "worthlessness."

The pervasive cultural belief that body size and one's health is directly correlated with willpower and personal choices about diet and exercise, fails to acknowledge broader systemic factors such as the role of genetics, as well as social determinants of health such as access to fresh fruits and vegetables, lean protein, and safe neighborhoods to engage in physical activity, not to mention trauma, oppression, environmental inequalities, and disparities in our healthcare system.[13]

Cultural burdens involve layers of implicit bias and affect the treatment different bodies receive within our cultural institutions. Systemic racism, patriarchy, sexism, materialism, sizeism, healthism, heterosexism, and homo- and transphobia disempower and discriminate against bodies of color, larger bodies, female bodies, and trans bodies. In stark contrast stands the quiet truth that every human body, regardless of health or size, is worthy of respect, compassion, and sound medical care.

Award-winning author and researcher, Sabrina Strings, traces the racist roots of fatphobia in her book, *Fearing the Black Body: The Racial Origins of Fat Phobia* (Strings, 2019). She notes "My research shows that anti-fat attitudes originated not with medical findings, but with the Enlightenment-era belief that overfeeding and fatness were evidence of 'savagery' and racial inferiority, and have roots in racism and anti-blackness."[14]

"You are not afraid of being fat. You are afraid of being treated like a fat person."
—Virgie Tovar, author and anti-weight-based discrimination activist

Weight bias leads to weight stigma, which can be overt, like fat shaming and bullying in schools and social media, or more covert, like public spaces not accommodating larger bodies. Bullying and weight stigma are often internalized by self-critical or self-objectifying parts and continue to harm an impacted individual long after a specific incident of stigmatization.

Weight bias is often perpetuated under the guise of concern for one's health. Much like weight stigma, "healthism" (a moral imperative to be healthy) is prevalent in our society and can also lead to disordered eating and negative body image.

"Equally damaging is our insistence that all bodies should be healthy. Health is not a state we owe the world. We are not less valuable, worthy, or lovable because we are not healthy. Lastly, there is no standard of health that is achievable for all bodies."
—Sonya Renee Taylor, The Body Is Not an Apology: The Power of Radical Self-Love

Diet Culture Burdens Become Personal Burdens

"When we live our lives in this perpetual state of body monitoring, we are living passively, being judged and consumed by ourselves and others—not as self-actualized humans actively making choices."
—Lexie and Lindsay Kite, More than a Body

Americans' internalization of toxic cultural messages about bodies and beauty standards leads us to battle with our own individual bodies. Culture objectifies (views bodies as separate from spirits, personalities, emotional and relational beings, and souls) an idealized body shape, which leads to individually burdening interactions even in the most innocuous exchanges: "You look great. Have you lost weight?" or "They've really let themselves go." Objectification values appearance over the fullness of our humanity and leads to the internalization of individual burdens of shame, self-loathing, body dissatisfaction, self-objectification, and self-hatred (exiles). Burdened manager jobs develop in response, to control, monitor, restrict, or surgically alter, which can lead burdened firefighter parts to reactively binge, purge, or engage in other compensatory behaviors. Parts understandably become burdened with jobs that ignore the nutritional, rest, or movement needs of the body and override hunger, injury, or pain to conform to this acculturated ideal.

Another example is weight discrimination in the medical field.[15] People in larger bodies may avoid necessary medical care for fear of being weighed and told to lose weight. This weight stigma leads to internalization of shame, anxiety, depression, and stress which are catalytic in disordered eating patterns, such as binge eating for relief.

It is important to note that there are some medical conditions that require clients to manage their intake of certain foods. Even for individuals who do not have burdened parts around food and body, this can trigger a felt sense of deprivation and set off polarizations of parts that restrict and parts that binge. Regardless, the IFS approach to these types of medical conditions helps parts establish a nurturing relationship with Self, and it supports Self-led food choices that will be least likely to provoke or create a burdened systemic response internally.

Intergenerational and Traumatic Legacy Burdens

Families often actively embrace diet and wellness cultural burdens and pass them on to their offspring. For example, a mother with body image burdens may body-shame her daughter and pressure the daughter to diet with her. IFS refers to these as legacy burdens—that is, burdens that are passed down through family lineage.

Intergenerational trauma can also be a source of legacy burdens that influence disordered eating and body shame. Legacy burdens due to colonization, slavery, wars, religion, natural disasters, and famines can lead to a disrupted relationship with one's body and affect the ability to feel safe living within a certain body type that has been devalued, enslaved, or starved. Living as a refugee, becoming orphaned, or experiencing the traumatic or premature death of a loved one, are among the traumatic experiences whose epigenetic impact can be passed from one generation to the next. Food scarcity and deprivation resulting from war, land displacement, famine, or natural disaster are also traumas that cause intense psychological distress, affect one's relationship with food, and can be transmuted through legacy burdens to future generations.

Other traumatic experiences, attachment wounds, losses, relational boundary violations, divorce, domestic violence, abuse, neglect, and parental loss can lead to feelings of abandonment, betrayal, fear, anger, grief, and shame, and they can create additional burdens that become exiled in ways that often impact the relationship between food and body. Sexual assault and victimization of all genders (a violent consequence of patriarchy and objectification of bodies) often distances clients from their own bodies and may leave them feeling like their body is a weapon that was used against them. For women, menses, pregnancy, miscarriage, and menopause and, for both men and women, illness (including chronic conditions), may change their bodies in ways they aren't prepared for. These are just a sampling of transgenerational legacy burdens and personal burdens that impact the relationship between body and food, which ultimately limit access to Self-energy in the body and the ability to feel a true sense of safety in one's own skin.

So, as you can see, the symptom of disordered eating is often undergirded with complex cultural burdens, legacy burdens, familial burdens, and interpersonal burdens. There is profound complexity to the formation of disordered eating symptoms, and therefore, there is multidimensionality necessitated in treatment.

Traditional Treatment Approaches

Traditional treatment approaches tend to focus on eliminating the symptoms of disordered eating without considering the system of parts behind them and the motivations that drive them. Schwartz describes a popular treatment motto from his pre-IFS days in eating disorder treatment: "Defeat ED!" "ED" stood for eating disorder,[16] and the personified battlefront imagery used with this treatment approach fairly accurately represented the hostile lens through which disordered eating behaviors were viewed.

These more traditional approaches are still widely used and often feel coercive to clients, attempting to force acquiescence through threats of higher levels of care for non-compliance, directive eating plans, or restrictions on exercise without understanding the protectors engaged in the behaviors or healing the exiles that are driving them. While the urgency to stop disordered eating patterns is certainly understandable due to the severity of their associated risk, these power-over approaches stand in stark contrast to the compassionate and collaborative IFS framework and are marked by high rates of relapse and mortality.[17]

New Perspectives: A Non-Diet, Weight-Inclusive Approach

When transitioning out of traditional treatment approaches for eating and body issues, an important first step is to take a non-diet, weight-inclusive (meaning bodies of all shapes and sizes are welcome and not asked to change) approach for ALL bodies. Weight-normative care is rooted in our diet culture and relies on weight and weight loss as indicators of health and well-being. Weight loss is rarely sustained and leads to weight cycling. Research has found that those who lose and gain weight repeatedly have a higher risk of mortality than people who maintain a stable weight.[18]

A weight-inclusive approach is an alternative that emphasizes non-weight-based markers of health and well-being where treatment interventions aren't centered on body weight. Clients may gain weight during the recovery process, particularly if they are weight suppressed or malnourished. This approach also helps clients understand the impact of internalized messages that they're responsible for their weight and their worth is tied to it. It welcomes the parts of our clients that might be grieving the loss of their thin privilege or those that are angry that trying to change their body didn't work or that this is their body, even though they don't want it to be their body.

Healing Through Restored Embodiment

With the foundation of a weight-inclusive approach, we can begin to turn our attention to the gift of embodiment. Restoring embodiment is the foundation of my approach to help my clients heal their relationship with food and their bodies. Embodiment is the subjective experience of being in a body rather than the objective experience of evaluating what our bodies look like, which leads to body image struggles. The body gives us all sorts of emotional and physical signals for our survival. Our culture encourages us to suppress these signals in deference to the mind. Since trauma and its burdens disrupt embodiment and cultural legacies encourage us to objectify and disconnect from our bodies, it makes sense that healing happens through reconnecting to the body.

The key is connection. Just as connection is the foundation of relationships, connection is the foundation of embodiment. Through embodied connection, we can transcend the reality that bodies are not perfect, and they deserve respect and care. We can have compassion for parts wanting us to lose weight to feel safe and acceptable, to change for other people's validation, or to make them more comfortable. Being embodied means we can attune to the subjective experience of how it feels to live inside our bodies and identify with our experience. Through embodiment, we experience the truth that our bodies belong just as they are and are a part of the diverse way human beings are in our world.

> "But experiencing and valuing yourself as a whole, embodied human means making sure you aren't prioritizing validation from others above your own well-being, health, and happiness, and not prioritizing an external perspective of who you are."
> —*Lexie and Lindsay Kite,* More Than a Body

Our body is our first language. Before we have words, we express our needs and feelings through our bodies based on what sensations we experience, whether it be hunger, fullness, fatigue, discomfort, amusement, or happiness. The body has inherent wisdom to find sources of nourishment to sustain life when there is deprivation, to find safety when there has been trauma, and to find safe connection when there have been violations. When nourishment, safety, and connection aren't available, our parts help our bodies by dissociating or becoming psychologically over-ruled.

Relational wounds are also embodied, and if not healed, are the somatic foundation of our future relational lives (e.g., a "pit in our stomach" when someone doesn't show up or a clenched jaw when in an unsafe relationship). For most of us, becoming more embodied takes intention and practice to notice and attune with Self-led care to whatever sensations we are experiencing, whether they be warmth, calmness, and ease or tension, achiness, and fatigue. Relational wounds are healed in relational attachment, and IFS is a remarkable approach that allows us to support secure relational attachment between a client's parts and Self internally. This is profoundly healing for the parts who carry food and body burdens, and it is the foundation for Self-led, restored embodiment.

IFS and Compassionate, Collaborative Treatment

IFS understands disordered eating to reflect a complex interplay of neurobiological factors, epigenetic influences, cultural and societal messages, and personal burdens, which is why IFS draws collaboratively on support from a multidisciplinary treatment team (medical, nutritional, psychiatric, therapeutic) to provide the highest ethical standard of care with the most robust possible treatment outcomes. The IFS-informed clinician respects the complex and interrelated dynamics at play in the development and treatment of disordered eating.

IFS, however, brings a unique lens to this multifaceted treatment approach. In contrast to traditional treatment approaches, IFS views the symptoms of disordered eating as reflective of well-intentioned protective parts that are trying to help solve a problem or ensure survival but have become stuck in unhelpful strategies for doing so. IFS does not attempt to control, force, judge, or struggle with parts engaged in disordered eating patterns, but rather it comes into relationship with these parts and offers them more effective (Self-led) ways to heal exile pain and achieve their fundamentally positive goals. IFS understands disordered eating patterns to be the result of escalating interactions between an inner system of parts, and not the malicious behavior of a "bad" part that needs to be eliminated or defeated.

Exiles that are burdened with painful feelings and beliefs (such as shame, worthlessness, powerlessness) from negative life events bring an underlying energy to the inner systemic "family" of parts. Manager parts (in proactive attempts to prevent exile pain from becoming triggered) run the individual's daily life with rigid strategies such as restricting, controlling, and over-exercising. When they fail, and exile feelings such as shame or fear flood, firefighter parts (with reactive strategies such as bingeing or purging) take over in a desperate attempt to soothe or silence exile pain. Thus, external behaviors are understood to be a reflection of well-meaning parts which have become stuck in rigid and conflicting roles that escalate in a choreographed systemic pattern.

A typical client with exiles that feel "unlovable" and "alone" may have a strong inner critic manager that internally shames the client's body in a misguided attempt to force the client to lose weight and thus become "lovable." This critical part may provoke another inner manager that restricts food all day at work in an attempt to silence the withering barrage of criticism. After restricting all day at work, the client goes home to an empty house with feelings of deprivation which trigger the "alone" and "unlovable" exiles. That provokes a firefighter part which steps in and binge eats at night in a misguided attempt to soothe the exiles.

As with all burdened protectors, their well-intentioned behavior evokes the very thing they are trying to avoid, thus escalating the patterns of reactive cycling.

IFS suggests that the most effective way to help their behavior transform is to help the individual's Self establish a compassionate relationship with each part and heal the pain it is holding or attempting to protect, thereby allowing the entire systemic interaction to unburden. By thus unburdening parts into their preferred, positive roles within the individual's system, the client is freed to establish a Self-led pattern of eating. Self does not hold shame or idealized body image and is thus able to respond to the actual nutritional and other needs of the body. As such, Self-led eating is not a diet or a way of "healing to lose weight." Self-led eating, free of protector's burdened and extreme behavior, flows from easeful embodiment and comfort in whatever body size results from a deep listening to the needs of the internal system.

This process is complex and happens slowly over time, unfolding within the context of a trusting therapeutic relationship and skillful therapeutic contracts that honor and gain permission from all parts. Because eating and body image issues don't transform overnight, it's important to let clients' parts know that recovery takes time and is a non-linear process that often happens in subtle shifts. By providing this type of up-front psychoeducation to all the inner parts, IFS clinicians can head off frustration, shame, and hopelessness that can emerge when clients' manager parts set expectations of firefighter change happening quickly. It is also important to let clients' parts know that building relationships between Self and parts doesn't always result in an immediate reduction in behaviors, but rather, it is an approach to systemic healing which takes into account the (usually opposing) goals of every part in the system and is marked by compromise rather than by the "victory" of one side over another.

Therapeutic Alliance: All Parts Welcome

IFS is deeply client-centered and directed, and in IFS therapy, all parts of the client are truly welcome. IFS clinicians build a therapeutic alliance with all parts of the client and avoid viewing the client as a singular, monolithic entity with behaviors that just need to be forced to "stop." A critical part of creating safety in the therapeutic context is to avoid aligning with any one part (such as the part that wants the bingeing or the restricting to stop) against other parts, and, thereby, becoming sucked into the polarized patterns that actually brought the client into therapy in the first place.

Treatment goals, then, are set by a collaborative and evolving negotiation between the client's opposing parts. By inviting the client's Self to guide all the inner parts as a collaborative and respectful "treatment team," IFS stands in stark contrast to approaches in which the therapist is the "expert" and clients are encouraged to distrust their parts' perspectives and to view their body and habits through eyes outside of themselves.

It can be difficult not to get pulled into aligning against a part when a client is sharing disturbing behavior—actively restricting, binge eating, purging, or over-exercising. Clinician's Self-energy is what is needed most to respond with compassion and care such as, "It sounds like it was a tough day for you, and I'm here to help you hold it. As you share with me what is happening inside of you, can we bring somatic awareness in this moment? Can we stay with that and trust that it will lead to what needs attention in the session today?"

Therapist Parts and Self

IFS understands that the therapist's inner system impacts the therapeutic experience as much or more than the client's inner system, and the therapists' greatest healing attribute is a critical mass of their own Self-energy. This is true, regardless of what model of therapy we are practicing. As co-regulating individuals who powerfully utilize interpersonal mirror neurons, we understand that the Self of one person invites forward the Self of another. Another way to say that is that in the absence of judgement or agenda, all parts can relax back, and Self can emerge. Similarly, the presence of activated parts in one individual invites the activation of parts in another. Any judgement, agenda, or control (energy carried by parts) naturally and unconsciously brings up parts in another person (such as resistance, compliance, dissociation, etc.).

Self evokes Self and parts evoke parts. Self is a flowing state of connected curiosity toward all client parts, even those engaged in harmful behaviors. While Self does desire the client's well-being and understands that the behavior burdened parts engage in is harmful, it has no energy of coercion, persuasion, or forcing. It is respectful, honoring, and invitational. It invites client self-determination. Self-energy is the single most powerful force for healing that we possess and is the ultimate source of healing of eating disordered parts within all of our clients. It's important to note that, while Self is deeply compassionate for the suffering that burdened behaviors inflict, Self does not believe that the behaviors or feelings parts are burdened with are good or okay. Instead, Self understands the most effective way to transform them is through compassionate relationship.

In contrast to the power of Self-energy, most therapists have many different "therapist parts." These are parts that often draw us into helping professions: parts that are good at figuring things out, that want to fix, that want to "do it right," and sometimes that want to control. These parts can be very helpful in life, and they often serve us well in accomplishing things, helping others, and knowing the right answers. In fact, most of us have spent years in graduate level training programs learning how to strengthen these parts of ourselves. We are usually so identified with these parts that we think they are who we are. We think they are Self. And indeed, these parts often look like Self on the surface. They are well-intentioned, caring, and want to be helpful. However, therapist parts will come with an agenda (getting the client to stop ____ behavior, gain weight, etc.), judgement ("____ behavior is bad" "____ behavior is good"), and the belief that a certain outcome is needed or reflects our skill as a therapist.

Therapist parts often hold activation about the client's struggles and may become aligned or polarized with clients' parts, trying to "get a client to" do something. This results in increased "resistance" by the clients' parts that feel their agenda is threatened. That's why doing our own personal work is the most important thing we can do to advance our skills as an IFS helper. Until all our own parts, especially these so-called "Self-like parts," come into a trusting, healing relationship with our own Self-energy, we will not be able to bring the most important therapeutic quality to our clinical work: our Self.

In addition to being a client with our own IFS therapist, it can be helpful to have some real-time strategies for detecting Self-energy when we are working with clients' extreme parts. Some "parts-detecting" questions we can ask ourselves are:

1) How open is my heart toward my client?
2) How calm or spacious do I feel in my body (skull, brain, jaw, spine, etc.)?
3) How do I feel *toward* my client/my client's disordered eating/my client's progress/etc.?

If our heart isn't open, we don't feel calm or spaciousness internally, and we don't notice some of the "8 C" qualities of Self-energy, we may be blended with a part. This becomes a "trailhead" for our own compassionate personal work. It can be challenging work to divest ourselves of cultural burdens that come with society's diet and wellness culture, our clinical training, legacy burdens that we carry from family, or personal burdens from our own parts that may have engaged in the same (or opposite) behaviors as the client.

Common therapist parts that can arise during disordered eating work are:

- Parts that feel powerlessness (over client choices).
- Parts that don't trust that clients actually have an inherent ability to heal (Self).
- Parts that feel fear (of disordered eating risks).
- Rescuing or advice-giving parts.
- Weight or appearance-biased parts.
- Controlling or persuading parts.
- Caretaking parts.

When we as therapists do our own work, the bind our clients are in becomes clearer—those protectors trying to control weight or appearance may help us feel that we belong (even if it's based on fitting in), get validation from others (even if it is superficial), and protect us from experiencing weight stigma, but the toll on our mental, physical, emotional, and spiritual lives is high and limits the ability to show up fully and authentically as ourselves.

Triage, Multidisciplinary Support, and Crisis Management

When we learn that clients are engaged in disordered eating patterns, it is an important first step to recommend they see their doctor to rule out medical issues due to nutritional deficiencies or malnourishment, and possibly seek the support of an IFS-informed, anti-diet dietitian. Disordered eating behaviors can impact a client's sleep, physical well-being, memory, attention, motivation, and concentration, and they can affect their ability to make use of therapy and access to Self-energy. Due to the physical and psychological effects, treatment of disordered eating usually involves a multidisciplinary team approach, collaborating with doctors, dietitians, and psychiatrists. It can admittedly be difficult to find an IFS-informed multi-disciplinary team, but it is my hope that as the model grows, this will become a much more widespread reality for both clients as well as treatment teams.

Unfortunately, disordered eating sometimes escalates to the point of crisis. "All parts welcome" sounds well and good when the behaviors parts are engaged in are non-lethal, but what about parts whose behaviors are threatening the client's life? Restricting and purging parts can be particularly adept at depriving the brain of the nutrients that it needs to think clearly and make Self-led decisions. These parts are typically the ones that present for the highest levels of care, and they are the ones that lead to precariously elevated mortality rates among eating disorders. What then?

Just as with other life-threatening parts' behaviors such as suicidality and homicidality, risk-mediation is key. These are specialized instances in which an IFS lens would still welcome and honor all parts of the client and get to know their positive intent but might be forced, as a result of the seriousness of the client's state, to intervene in ways that parts may not prefer in order to save the client's life. A hypothetical example follows:

> **Therapist:** Good morning, Amy. Your doctor sent me your labs and vitals, and your weight is dropping again. We discussed at the beginning of working together, that I'd let you know if I am concerned about your health and safety and feel we might need to look into getting you extra support. Based on the results from your recent doctor's visit, I am worried. I'm wondering if we might be able to invite in the part of you that is continuing to restrict food and see what it wants us to know about why it is restricting to this extent?
>
> **Amy:** Okay, sure. It's definitely here and on high alert.

Therapist: Wonderful. See if you can send it some appreciation for how hard it's working and how vigilantly it is standing guard to try and protect you. Let it know it is a really valued member of the team here.

Amy: Yes, it's appreciating my attention and acknowledgement, and it's proud of my weight loss.

Therapist: I'm glad it's aware of your attention. Can you let it know what I shared about your weight getting to the point of being a concern for your health and safety, and see if it's aware that things are that serious?

Amy: No, it didn't realize that, but it is terrified of me gaining the weight back and then being out of control. It believes if I take one bite, I'll go crazy, eat everything, and be a fat, unlovable slob.

Therapist: Let it know that worry makes sense, especially since your body has been deprived of food and could end up binge eating due to primal hunger. Let that part know that we really respect how seriously it takes the importance of making sure you're lovable, and we also don't want it to have to navigate a potential war with binge eating.

Amy: It appreciates that. It relaxed a little and sat down. It's pretty exhausted.

Therapist: Let it know that we don't want to dishonor its desire to help you in this way, and we also need to make sure you stay alive so that there can be a "you" to love. I'm wondering if it would be open to talking about some possible options for how we could do both?

Amy: It says, "no way." It doesn't trust treatment recommendations because it's been forced to eat before by providers, and that's been a disaster.

Therapist: I totally get that, and I'm so sorry it's felt forced in the past. Can you let that part know that I really don't want to force it to do anything. I know it is having you restrict for a good reason, and I don't want it to have to work so hard that you wind up in the hospital again or are forced to go into treatment. I remember how distressing that was in the past for you and for this part. I'm sure we can help, and I'd much rather that we work with it directly if it will let us.

Amy: It feels panicky about that, but it also sees your point. It wants to know what you have in mind.

Therapist: I'd like to see if it knows what it needs to do to keep you safe and out of the hospital or a higher level of care.

Amy: It says I would need to eat enough to stop the weight loss.

Therapist: Can you check with the part that is restricting to see if it would be willing to do that? I know neither of us wants you to be hospitalized. And if it's willing to eat enough, we will continue our work allowing your Self to befriend and heal the part it's protecting that feels unlovable, so that it won't have to keep doing this exhausting job. Would it be open to that?

While we don't want to get into polarization with our client's parts by trying to control them or force them to do anything, there are certainly times when we are ethically mandated to do what is necessary to save a client's life. Even in these instances, we do so in a way that invites all parts into the dialogue and gives the part engaged in the life-threatening behavior every possible alternative option. When we treat these parts with respect and show how we can help them get to their goals (in this case, healing the pain of the exile that feels unlovable) more effectively, we have the best possibility of helping them to mediate their behavior and cooperate with the healing process.

Working with Protectors

One of the brilliant contributions of the IFS model is the awareness that we must always work with protective parts first and gain permission from them before we attempt to work with parts that hold vulnerability (exiles). This is the key to preventing flare-ups from protective parts whose job it is to keep vulnerable parts hidden. So, while we know that it is the pain of the exiles that drives the disordered eating behavior (and, therefore, ultimately holds the key to long term healing), we always start our work with the protectors.

While beyond the scope of this chapter, it is important to note that protectors have complex relationships with one another that do not exclusively involve food. Other common paired polarizations are with food and sex, substances, work, and spending. For example, parts may overeat while shutting down sexually, and then switch to restricting food while acting out sexually. Managers and firefighters can also act in tandem ("fused") such as when overworking parts and restricting parts are in charge during the day and then may be supplanted by drinking parts and sexual acting out parts that try to bring relief at night.

In whatever manner they present themselves, protector work always comes first in IFS. We work with protectors using the "6 Fs" of IFS that can be found in the *Internal Family Systems Skills Training Manual* (Anderson, Sweezy, and Schwartz, 2017):

Find: Where do you find this part of you in or around your body?
Focus: Turn your attention inside and gently focus on this part.
Flesh Out: How do you experience it? What do you notice about this part?

Feel Toward: How do you feel toward this part of you? (Self-detecting question. Only continue if the client feels an "8 C" quality toward the part.)

BeFriend: Ask the part what it wants you to know about itself, and how it is trying to help you.

Fear: Ask the part what it is afraid would happen if it didn't take you over and make you do this? (Exile-revealing question. The answer describes the exile part it is trying to protect.)

It is the protectors (both managers and firefighters) that engage in disordered eating behaviors, trying to help individuals cope with past trauma or navigate cultural bias and harm. Since food is one of the few self-soothing strategies accessible to even young children, individuals experiencing trauma often learn early how to regulate overwhelm in their nervous system by restricting, bingeing, or purging. When we develop a Self-to-part relationship with these well-meaning protective parts, we learn more about how they took on their jobs and how they are trying to help. Some of the positively intentioned, protective functions of disordered eating behaviors include:

- Soothing, comfort, nurturance.
- Distraction, numbing, sedation.
- Getting attention, serving as a cry for help.
- Expressing anger or rebellion.
- Discharging tension.
- Providing structure, predictability, identity.
- Serving as punishment of oneself or body.
- Manipulating the body to be smaller or larger to provide protection/safety.
- Avoidance of intimacy.

These behaviors provide only a temporary fix, offering only the illusion of control and/or safety, and often have long-term negative consequences. Protective parts attempting to cope by managing food and eating, are often stuck in the past, at the time they became burdened, and are not aware of any other ways of coping or of the presence of Self which can provide more effective leadership of the inner system.

Common Polarizations

Disordered eating protectors are almost universally polarized. Some common polarizations include:

- Parts that want to lose weight vs. parts that want to have a more peaceful relationship with the body and food.
- Parts that want to comply with therapy (or please the therapist) vs. parts that want to rebel and do what they want.

- Parts that want to recover and heal vs. parts that don't want to change.
- Parts that long for care vs. parts that believe they deserve to be punished.
- Parts that feel superior vs. parts that feel inferior.
- Parts that obsess about the body vs. parts that avoid or neglect the body.
- Parts that eat in a rigid and controlled way vs. parts that eat in a chaotic, out-of-control way.
- Parts that want to care for the body vs. parts that neglect or abuse the body.
- Parts that want to experience more embodiment vs. parts that fear the pain involved in embodiment (from abuse, neglect, etc.)
- Parts that want to hope that therapy will bring healing and inner peace vs. parts that don't trust therapy and don't believe the therapist can handle the pain that will emerge.

When negotiating with these protectors, we honor both sides of every polarization. Only when the host of protectors feel trusting enough of Self and have given permission for Self to connect with the vulnerable parts, do we move forward with the deeper "trauma work," unburdening the exiles that fuel the disordered eating behaviors.

Working with Exiles

I believe all human beings have a birthright of embodiment, to feel at home and comfortably exist in our sensory bodies just as they are and to be in connection with ourselves and one another. When negative life circumstances occur, our exiles become burdened with painful feelings and beliefs that, when triggered, block our birthright of connection to Self and others. Exiles are created when natural phases of development are interrupted or with devaluing experiences, trauma, and attachment wounds. Exile burdens such as shame, fear, and powerlessness feel overwhelming when they become triggered. To avoid inner overwhelm and external shaming, clients "exile" these inner wounded parts and are left feeling fragmented as a result. Whatever the source of those burdens, the trauma remains within the tissues, autonomic nervous systems, and endocrine systems of our clients' bodies.[19]

With an eye to reestablishing a secure inner attachment to Self, we approach the healing work with exiles in whatever modality in which we have training and competency. Those who have completed, at minimum, level 1 IFS training can use the IFS steps of connecting to Self, witnessing, retrieving, unburdening, bringing in positive qualities, and having unburdened exiles witnessed by protectors. Others of us might use EMDR, SE, psychodrama, sandtray, brainspotting, or other trauma healing methods. However we are trained to do the deeper healing work, we can call upon the principles of IFS to help update the protective system when the exiles have been healed. We can also offer protectors the option of releasing their burdensome jobs and being restored to their original positive roles, if sufficient healing has occurred for the exiles they protect.

IFS also helps us understand that all parts need ongoing connection with Self-energy to remain in an unburdened state. Healing is not a destination, rather it is a relationship that develops with Self over time as all parts' secure inner attachment. One reason why shifts in behavior take time to manifest is because relationships and trust take time to grow. As IFS therapists, we are not delivering an outcome, but we are establishing inner relationships that will continue to flourish and deepen over time.

Somatic IFS—Coming Home to the Body

As we've seen, IFS gives us the framework for treating a whole person, not just the parts that engage in disordered eating. Disembodiment is at the core of disordered eating and body shame. A somatic approach to IFS helps clients return to an embodied connection with any parts who have absorbed negativity about the body and food, be they protectors or exiles. Somatic IFS,[20] developed by IFS Lead Trainer, Susan McConnell, provides additional tools to bring clients back home to their body—to work with the managers and firefighters using the body to protect and the exiles using the body to tell their stories. Somatic IFS integrates the IFS model of therapy with five body-based practices: Somatic Awareness, Conscious Breathing, Radical Resonance, Mindful Movement, and Attuned Touch, to embody Self-energy and work with protective, burdened parts and polarizations held in the body. These somatic practices can be used to enhance or deepen any of the steps in the IFS model. Somatic IFS leads us closer to Self-energy.

Self-energy is about embodied awareness. When we embody Self-energy, we can have Self-leadership and trust our ability to guide our clients to embody Self-energy to work with all their parts, including those that protect by restricting, controlling, bingeing, purging, and over exercising. We can recognize that a client's belief that their body is intolerable is coming from a part that we can help them get to know without judgment or an agenda. We can guide our clients to listen with compassion to their parts as they are and unburden the beliefs and shame about and the trauma held in their bodies as we work toward dismantling the toxic diet and wellness culture that harms us all.

Self-led practices of awareness, breath, resonance, movement, and touch reconnect Self with protectors, exiles, and polarizations held in the body. We begin working with the parts that may fear embodiment by making space for these protectors. There may be many parts that fear embodiment because then they will feel all the pain that they have been avoiding. However, when clients can embody more Self-energy, they have more space to be present and compassionate towards their pain.

We might encourage them to take one step after another with just enough light to see the next step, which can take a lot of courage. We help clients become curious about what parts are afraid would happen if we did pay attention to the client's body, for example. For those that don't feel it is safe, we can get curious about how to make it safe and find out how they learned that it's not safe. When a part can open a bit more, and there is more capacity to return to embodiment (that is, the felt sense of being in one's sensory body), our clients are more present with themselves and the process.

Somatic IFS helps us slow the process of healing to sync with body time. As therapists, it is important to slow down to become aware of what is happening in our clients' bodies. Bodies move much slower than minds, which can jump quickly from one topic to the next. There is an art to being open-hearted with our clients and in the timing of inviting clients to turn their attention inward toward their parts. So much has been exiled that the body carries and the mind has tried to erase. When we witness the body—the somatic story—we more deeply witness the exiles whose stories are not always made available verbally or in conscious memory. We attend to ways in which the body moves, facial expressions, tone of voice, discrete shifts. By so doing, we bring tender attention to even the most vulnerable parts of our clients.

Clients may have difficulty with embodiment, and their parts may also distract, dissociate, and use their nervous system to take them out of their bodies. With Somatic IFS, we may use Somatic Awareness to just be curious about the felt sense of distraction, dissociation, or what is happening with their nervous system. We might use Conscious Breathing to stay with one sensation by simply sending a breath to it and letting it know we are with it, whether it be an impulse to run, reach out, push away, avoid, or sink into a pit of shame. Radical Resonance will give clinicians information about their client's systems by bringing up similar sensations in their own. These practices help slow the process down, so we can stay with the protector as it reveals why it is doing what it is doing and what it might be afraid of it wasn't able to run, reach out, push away, avoid, or sink into a pit of shame. Mindful Movement might invite the part to engage in the body action that was not able to be completed in the past or restore flow of movement that was blocked by protectors. Attuned Touch, by the client to themselves (or occasionally with consent and safety, by the therapist to the client), may tangibly communicate the felt safety of coming home to the body to complete the embodiment process. Attuned touch sensorily communicates to parts that they are not alone, there is someone there offering comfort and support. Somatic IFS helps heal the powerlessness, loss of control, and disconnection of exiles from Self by offering empowerment based on the trust of inner wisdom, being present for life, and finding spiritual purpose.

I have created a composite client (a mixture of a variety of clients) in the example below, to show what IFS and Somatic IFS work looks like in an actual session.

Stella's Healing Journey

Stella is a 32-year-old, White, cisgender, able-bodied, female who presented in treatment to address a restrictive eating disorder and patterns of compulsive exercise. Stella's compulsive exercise started after receiving praise for her athletic skill from a middle school track coach, and it heightened when she discovered running as a way to connect with her emotionally unavailable, critical, father. A part of her learned she could gain connection with her dad if she would run and run "perfectly," and she could gain a sense of worth and significance when she excelled in athletic endeavors. Her father praised her for her running abilities, and part of her feared if she ever stopped running that she would lose her father's attention and love.

Stella's father's own restrictive eating, overworking, and overexercising parts, as well as his critical comments about her weight, fueled a part of her that learned to restrict food to try to keep her body at an "ideal" size to attempt to gain his approval and connection. These parts of Stella softened back when she was in a supportive environment, like graduate school, and parts of her also emerged that truly longed to have a harmonious relationship with food and her body.

Stella's treatment included regular work with me, as well as a recovery coach, dietitian, medical doctor, and psychiatrist. During our work together she began a dating relationship, got married, experienced infertility, left a job, and finished graduate school. With each of these stressful life transitions, her restrictive parts would activate, in an attempt to help her control what felt overwhelming. Over time, however, Stella made significant progress toward Self-led eating and movement as she helped these parts establish a healing relationship with her core Self.

Over the holidays, however, Stella's father made a comment implying that she was "letting herself go" by not watching what she ate. He expressed concern that she was becoming "depressed" because she wasn't exercising the way she used to and was gaining weight. In my office, Stella shared that she started exercising twice daily and began restricting again after hearing this hurtful remark.

Marcella: "As you share your father's comment, what do you notice happening inside of you?"
(Somatic IFS—Somatic Awareness: bringing attention to the body)

Stella: "I'm noticing a lot of tension, and also fear about losing dad's love."
(Finding the parts)

Marcella: "If it feels okay, let's stay with that tension. How do you experience it in your body?"

(Focusing on the protector)

Stella: "It's a tightness in my jaw."

Marcella: "What do you notice about the tightness?"

(Fleshing out the part: slowing the process down and exploring the sensations in the body.)

Stella: "It feels constrained. Like it can't move. It isn't going to let me open my mouth to put any more food into my body.

Marcella: "How do you feel toward it as it's showing you how constrained it feels?"

(Feel toward)

Stella: "I feel so compassionate toward it. I'm sorry that it feels like it can't move."

(Compassion, an 8 C quality, indicates presence of Self and safety to continue)

Marcella: "Can you send that constrained feeling a breath of awareness to let it know that you are with it and feel compassion toward it?"

(Somatic IFS—Conscious Breathing for unblending and connection)

Stella: (exhaling): It appreciates that and is relaxing.

Marcella: Can you ask what it's afraid would happen if it did relax your jaw and let you eat?

(Identifying the protector's fear to discover its positive intent and the exile it's protecting)

Stella: "It says it's afraid my dad wouldn't love me."

(Revealing that the exile is a part that feels unloved)

Marcella: "Let it know that fear makes so much sense. Ask it if we could help the part of you that holds that fear of dad not loving you, so it wouldn't have to lock your jaw down like this. Would it be interested in that?"

("Hope Merchanting"—offering a better way to get to the protector's goal of helping the exile)

Stella: "Oh yeah—it's exhausted and keeping me from eating is an impossible job. But it doesn't believe we can actually help."

(Receiving permission to go to the exile)

Marcella: "Of course not—it's probably never met your Self who is able to help. Ask if it would be open to showing you the vulnerable part of you that it is protecting so we can help."

Stella: "I'm getting an image of a little girl. It's me when I was little, and she's showing me memories of my father fat-shaming my brother and poking him in the stomach. It's just awful."

    (Connecting to and beginning to witness the exile)

Marcella: "How is she experiencing the awful?"

Stella: "It is like a punch to her gut. It literally hurts in my gut."

Marcella: "As you feel that sensation, is there any sound or movement you want to make?"

    (Somatic IFS—Mindful Movement to discharge the unresolved experience)

Stella: "I want to push him away from my brother and say, 'Stop it!'"

Marcella: "Great—do that if you'd like."

Stella: (pushing the air forcefully away from her) "Stop it!"

    (Engaging and completing the behavior that wasn't safe to enact when she was young)

Marcella: "See if there is more that she needs to move or if she would like you to know more."

    (BeFriending and witnessing the exile)

Stella: "Yes, she is showing me that my brother had a learning disability and so most of the attention went to him. She felt bad for him, but there was also no space for her struggles."

Marcella: "What happens when she senses that you are getting what it was like for her?"

Stella: "She's crying now. She was always told that she was too sensitive and had to hold back her feelings otherwise she would be criticized."

Marcella: Let her know her tears are welcome, and there is nothing wrong with her sensitivity. Can you notice what she needs from you now?

Stella: "Yes, I'm stroking her hair and telling her that her sensitivity is one of her many gifts." (Stella is stroking her own hair)

    (Self-led do-over of the original traumatic experience)

Marcella: "What happens when she feels your hand stroking her hair and hears your validating words?"

    (Somatic IFS—Attuned Touch creating connection and comfort through self-touch)

Stella: "She just collapsed on her bed with me next to her."

Marcella: "Is it okay with you to just let her collapse?"

Stella: Yes. She's just breathing, and I'm stroking her hair. (Stella lays down on the couch and strokes her own hair. A minute or two passes). She just shared with me that there is no one there to help her."

Marcella: "Let her know that you hear that. Can she feel you with her?"
   (Radical Resonance and building Self-to-part relationship with further witnessing)

Stella: "Yes, she can feel me, and she is calmer."

Marcella: "How is that for her to feel you with her?"

Stella: "She likes it, and she is telling me that she hates how mean her father can be."

Marcella: "Is there more she needs you to know about that?"

Stella: "No. She knows I know. But she also really loves her father."

Marcella: "Does that make sense to you?"

Stella: "Yes, her father also has some good qualities."

Marcella: "Ask her if she would like to hold onto the love she has for her father while releasing the negative beliefs about herself that she took on as a result of her interactions with him."
   (Unburdening invitation)

Stella: "Yes, she wants to do that by opening the door to the cage that has been keeping her trapped and small. She's smiling and standing up now and taking up space!"
   (Unburdening)

Marcella: "That's wonderful to see! Ask her how she feels."

Stella: "She says she feel liberated, like she can take up space and move."
   (Spontaneous taking on of positive qualities: taking up space and movement)

Marcella: "I'm so glad! Ask her if she's happy here or if there's somewhere more comfortable that she'd like to go with you."

Stella: "She wants to come to the beach with me and play in the ocean."

Marcella: "Perfect—go ahead and bring her to the beach and let her do that."
   (Retrieval)

Marcella: "Can we check in with the part that was holding tension in your jaw from earlier and see how it is doing?"

(Inviting protectors to witness the healed exile)

Stella: "That part is so relieved to see her out of the cage. It's wanted her to be free."

Marcella: "I'm so glad that part feels relieved. Ask it if, now that she's doing better, it would like to release the heavy job it's had of keeping you from eating, and do something that it would like better?"

(Invitation to protector to unburden)

Stella: "Yeah, it would rather help me savor the flavors of foods and really be present to the pleasure of eating again."

Marcella: "Great, let it release whatever it wants to from your jaw, and fully embody the savoring of the pleasure in whatever way feels right to it."

Stella: "It's pulling black rope out of my jaw and burning it up in a fire, and now it feels relaxed and free."

(Protector unburdening restricting job and embodying savoring)

Marcella: "That's wonderful. Let it know it never has to go back to the restricting again."

Although this dialogue represents a hypothetical, composite of client experiences, we might work next with a compensatory overexercising part until it is unburdened as well. There also might be more witnessing and unburdening from the part that was restricting. And as we conclude each session, I would encourage the client to check in every day with all three of these parts to make sure they are feeling secure in their newfound relationship with Self and their newly unburdened states. This connection resets the neural pathways and helps the parts to settle securely into their new roles in the inner system.

Concluding Thoughts

In this chapter we have explored the vast underpinnings of social, cultural, familial, and personal burdens that set the stage for disordered eating, as well as traditional approaches to treatment. In contrast, we've discussed the compassionate, inner relational attachment approach of IFS and Somatic IFS that allow for a Self-led healing and restoration of the gift of embodiment. It is a privilege and a joy to watch clients unburden internalized shame in IFS therapy, reclaim their playfulness, worthiness, and joy, and step into the fullness of who they are with confidence and connection. I wish you this privilege as well.

KEY TAKEAWAYS

- Trauma—be it burdens from our diet and wellness culture, social violence, personal trauma, or intergenerational trauma—creates burdens that separate us from our bodies. A non-diet, weight-inclusive approach for treating disordered eating prevents further harm and stigmatization.
- "Body image" is narrowly focused on how we are seen from outside. When we ask about body image, we are directing an individual to move dissociatively outside of their body and objectify themselves by looking at themselves through the eyes of a critical, judging other.
- Embodiment guides us to the subjective experience of how it feels to live inside our bodies and to identify with our experience. Embodied IFS heals trauma, restores Self-leadership to the inner system of parts, and invites authenticity.
- Somatic IFS brings body-centered practices to heal the somatic experiences at the core of most eating and body issues, thereby increasing embodiment.
- Healing parts burdened around food and body opens the door to Self-led eating. Unburdened parts receive and respond appropriately to signals from the body, feel freedom to be fully in the body, and know the body is worthy of belonging and respect just as it is.

AUTHOR BIO

Marcella Cox, LMFT (she/her) specializes in treating disordered eating, body shame and trauma. She is the Founder of Kindful Body, a collaboration of experienced disordered eating professionals who provide online therapy and nutrition counseling throughout California. She cofounded the IFS Telehealth Collective, a multi-state mental health group practice dedicated to providing high-quality Internal Family Systems Therapy online with lead IFS trainers, Mariel Pastor, LMFT and Paul Ginter, EdD. Marcella is a Certified IFS Therapist and Approved IFS Consultant, Certified Eating Disorder Specialist, Supervisor, and Certified Body Trust Provider. She provides supervision, clinical consultation, and professional workshops for therapists and healing professionals.

REVIEWER BIOS

Jeanne Catanzaro, PhD (she/her) is a clinical psychologist who has specialized in treating eating disorders and trauma for the past 25 years. An Approved IFS Clinical Consultant, she has written two chapters on using IFS to treat eating disorders, one in *Innovations and Elaborations in Internal Family Systems Therapy* (2017) and another in *Trauma-Informed Approaches to Eating Disorders* (2019). For the past ten years she's been focused on healing eating issues across the spectrum. Her book, tentatively titled *Unburdened Eating: An IFS approach to Healing Your Relationships with Food and Your Body*, focuses on healing the cultural legacy burdens that keep people from having Self-led relationships with their bodies.

Susan McConnell, MAPD, CHT (she/her) is the author of *Somatic Internal Family Systems Therapy: Awareness, Breath, Movement and Touch in Practice*, published in 2020 by North Atlantic Books. She is the creator of Somatic IFS, a culmination of her training and experience with various somatic, spiritual, and psychotherapeutic modalities and blending these modalities with the traditional tools of the Internal Family Systems framework. Embodying the internal family—the subpersonalities, as well as the essential core Self—brings compassionate witnessing to the implicit body stories of individual hurts and societal burdens. Susan offers Somatic IFS retreats, workshops, and trainings in Somatic IFS to participants throughout the world. As a Senior Trainer for the IFS Institute since 1997, Susan has taught therapists, developed curriculum, and mentored other trainers. She has over forty years of experience teaching and leading groups throughout the world.

Mariel Pastor, LMFT (she/her) is a licensed marriage and family therapist, supervisor, and international Lead Trainer for Internal Family Systems. Trained in IFS since 1998, she developed the Unburdened System mandala and workshops, and is the principal author of the IFS Level 1 Training Manual. She is a Co-Founder and Clinical Director of the IFS Telehealth Collective—a multi-state psychotherapy practice of licensed and pre-licensed therapists dedicated to IFS. Pastor's roots in Integral Theory inform her integration of somatic therapies, social justice, and spirituality within the IFS framework. Her previous career in entertainment and love of working with artists inspired Character Mapping—an innovative coaching and Master Class program helping actors, writers, and directors build compelling backstories with processes for their artistic health. At the heart of Character Mapping is the System of Selves—Pastor's unique application of parts work, IFS, and personality typing systems. More information is available at Character-Mapping.com.

GOING DEEPER

From Marcella Cox

1) Websites:
   a. IFS Telehealth Collective—www.ifstherapyonline.com. A virtual group practice of skilled clinicians trained in IFS for clients in California, New York, Florida, Massachusetts, Oregon, and Michigan.
   b. Kindful Body—www.kindfulbody.com. An IFS informed group practice providing online therapy and nutrition counseling for disordered eating in California.
   c. Marcella Cox—www.marcellacox.com. Information about IFS and Somatic IFS consultation, supervision towards becoming a Certified Eating Disorder Specialist (CEDS), online workshops, and retreats.

From Jeanne Catanzaro

1) Books:
   a. Catanzaro, J., (anticipated release 2023). *Unburdened eating: An IFS approach to healing your relationships with food and your body.* Pesi Publishing and Media.
   b. Catanzaro, J., Doyne, E., & Thompson, K., (2019). IFS (Internal Family Systems) and eating disorders: The healing power of self-energy. In Seubert, A. J., & Virdi, P. (2018), *Trauma-informed approaches to eating disorders.* Springer Publishing Company.
   c. Catanzaro, J., (2017). In Sweezy, M., & Ziskind, E. L. (Eds.). (2016), *Innovations and elaborations in Internal Family Systems therapy.* Routledge.

2) Podcast Interviews:
   a. IFS Talks—Healing our Relationships with Food and Body with Jeanne Catanzaro. www.internalfamilysystems.pt/multimedia/webinars/healing-our-relationships-food-and-body-jeanne-catanzaro
   b. IFS Talks—Self-led Eating During Stressful Times with Jeanne Catanzaro. www.internalfamilysystems.pt/multimedia/webinars/self-led-eating-during-stressful-times-jeanne-catanzaro

From Susan McConnell

1) Website:
   a. www.embodiedself.net

2) Books:
   a. McConnell, S. (2020). *Somatic Internal Family Systems therapy: Awareness, breath, resonance, movement, and touch in practice.* North Atlantic Books.

3) Trainings and Workshops:
   a. Life Architect: four-hour video introduction to Somatic IFS with didactics, meditation, and practice instructions: www.lifearchitect.com/somatic-ifs/
   b. Embody Lab: Two, two-hour videos: www.theembodylab.com/integrative-somatic-trauma-therapy-certificate. (Part of the 2022 Integrative Somatic Trauma Therapy Certificate Program).
   c. IFS Continuity Program. "An Introduction to Somatic IFS; An Embodied Approach to Healing Trauma." An archive of the course is available for purchase at the IFS-I catalogue and for new members who join the Continuity Program it is available at a discounted rate: www.courses.ifs-institute.com/

4) Podcast Interviews:
   a. IFS Talks: www. internalfamilysystems.pt/multimedia/webinars/somatic-ifs-susan-mcconnell-new-book, and www.internalfamilysystems.pt/multimedia/webinars/embodying-ifs-susan-mcconnell
   b. The One Inside: www.theoneinside.libsyn.com/somatic-ifs-with-susan-mcconnell, and theoneinside.libsyn.com/ifs-and-a-somatic-ifs-meditation-with-susan-mcconnell

From Mariel Pastor

1) Website:
   a. www.MarielPastor.com. Information about IFS consultation and retreats, and access to the Unburdened Internal System Mandala available in five languages.
   b. www.Character-Mapping.com. Online programming and consultation for actors, writers, and directors to help them build character backstory and artistic health.
   c. www.ifstherapyonline.com. A virtual group practice of skilled clinicians trained in IFS for clients in New York, California, Florida, Massachusetts, Oregon, and Michigan.

2) Books:
   a. Pastor, M. & Gauvain, J. (2020). *Internal Family Systems level 1 training manual.* IFS Institute.

3) Workshops and Trainings:
   a. Celebrating the Unburdened System Retreat, March 24-27, 2025. Bevaix, Switzerland. Contact: secretariat@ifs-association-suisse.org
   b. IFS Level 1 Training, Portland, OR. Hybrid on-site and virtual. November 2023—March 2024. www.ifs-institute.com/trainings
   c. IFS Level 2 Training, Bristol, UK. On-site. November 23-27, 2023. www.ifs-institute.com/trainings
   d. IFS Level 1 Training, Copenhagen DN. On-site. March and June 2024. www.ifs-institute.com/training
   e. IFS Institute Continuity Program. "Trailheads to Transformation: Harvesting Resources from the Unburdened System." A continuing education resource for graduates of IFS Online Circle or Level 1 training. An archive of the course is available for purchase at the IFS-I catalog and for new members who join the Continuity Program it is available at a discounted rate. www.courses.ifs-institute.com/item/trailheads-transformation-harvesting-resources-unburdened-system-79521
   f. Character Mapping Online Masterclasses. www.character-mapping.com

4) Podcast Interviews:
   a. IFS Masters, April 22, 2023: Growing within a Self-led IFS Practice with Mariel Pastor & Paul Ginter. www.podcasts.apple.com/pt/podcast/ifs-masters/id1663565953?i=1000610192200
   b. IFS Talks, May 14, 2022: Befriending Self-like Parts with Mariel Pastor. www.internalfamilysystems.pt/multimedia/webinars/befriending-self-parts-mariel-pastor
   c. IFS Talks, January 16, 2022: Common Pitfalls in IFS Language with Mariel Pastor. www.internalfamilysystems.pt/multimedia/webinars/common-pitfalls-ifs-language-mariel-pastor
   d. IFS Talks, February 19, 2020: Celebrating the Unburdened System with Mariel Pastor. www.internalfamilysystems.pt/multimedia webinars/celebrating-unburdened-system-mariel-pastor

Additional Resources

1) Websites:
   a. The Center for Body Trust—www.centerforbodytrust.com
   b. Virgie Tovar—www.virgietovar.com

c. Nalgona Positivity Pride—www.nalgonapositivitypride.com
   d. Sand Chang, PhD—www.sandchang.com
   e. Association of Size Diversity and Health—www.sizediversityandhealth.org
2) Books:
   a. Catanzaro, J. (anticipated release 2023). *Unburdened eating: An IFS approach to healing your relationships with food and your body.* Pesi Publishing and Media.
   b. Gaudiani, J. (2018). *Sick enough: A guide to the medical complications of eating disorders.* Routledge.
   c. Gordon, A. (2021). *What we don't talk about when we talk about fat.* Beacon Press.
   d. Harrison, C. (2019). *Anti-diet: Reclaim your time, money, well-being, and happiness through intuitive eating.* Little Brown Spark.
   e. Kinavey, H., & Sturtevant, D. (2022). *Reclaiming body trust: A path to healing and liberation.* TarcherPerigee.
   f. Kite, L., & Kite, L. (2021). *More than a body: Your body is an instrument, not an ornament.* Harvest.
   g. McConnell, S. (2020). *Somatic Internal Family Systems therapy: Awareness, breath, resonance, movement, and touch in practice.* North Atlantic Books.
   h. Piran, N. (2017). *Journeys of embodiment at the intersection of body and culture: The developmental theory of embodiment* (1st ed.). Academic Press.
   i. Strings, S. (2019). *Fearing the Black body: The racial origins of fat phobia.* NYU Press.
   j. Taylor, S. R. (2018). *The body is not an apology: The power of radical self love.* Berrett-Koehler Publishers.
   k. Tovar, V. (2018). *You have the right to remain fat.* Feminist Press.
3) Articles:
   a. Siber, K. (2022, November 10). You don't look anorexic. *The New York Times.* www.nytimes.com/2022/10/18/magazine/anorexia-obesity-eating-disorder.html
4) Podcast Interviews:
   a. Food Psych Podcast, Christy Harrison, MPH, RD, CDN. www.christyharrison.com/foodpsych/
   b. Maintenance Phase Podcast, Aubrey Gordon and Michael Hobbs. www.podcasts.apple.com/us/podcast/maintenance-phase/id1535408667

IFS AND GROUPS

THE CREATING HEALING CIRCLES METHOD AND THE POWER OF SCULPTING IN GROUPS

Chris Burris, MEd, LCMHCS, LMFT

Reviewer: Deena Burris, PhD

The purpose of group work is to help people feel a greater sense of belonging and to counteract the traumatic isolation, disconnect, and societal individualism that has and still is causing so much suffering in the world. From an early age, I longed for a community in which I felt a sense of belonging and shared purpose. My early childhood experiences in my school, community, and family became an unpredictable mix of experiences that often felt isolating, confusing, and emotionally dangerous. When I looked back on my childhood, I realized these could have been my only experiences were it not for my involvement in several structured groups. For example, church youth groups in my teens and early twenties and rites of passage groups in my late twenties and thirties provided an environment that valued connection, support, celebration, and an intention to see each other authentically. These experiences gave me the opportunity to see the contrast between the often isolating and emotionally dangerous environments of my early years versus the environments with others where there was more intentionality.

When I began training with the IFS community in my mid-thirties, I again experienced that sense of belonging and purpose with my IFS colleagues. As I moved into larger trainer roles and eventually became an IFS Senior Lead Trainer, I became more intrigued with how the structure, purpose, safety, and experiential component of these groups became such a powerful healing environment for the alienation people were feeling. I began noticing how these intentional IFS training groups gave participants a different type of structural environment, one which came from the facilitator's intentionality and attention to the group field. The building of an intentional container space was the work of the trainer and their staff. The culmination of these structured and contained spaces, comprised of group experiences and purpose, helped to build a sense of community. These experiences often contrasted with the individualized Western culture in which many of us live.

Although this sense of belonging in the IFS training process was the experience of many participants, it was not the experience of all. Some participants continued to feel unseen, unsafe, and/or disconnected from others. Because this internalized, felt sense of community was so transformative in my own life, I felt drawn to explore how group experiences could be transformative for some and not for others. This led to my work on the topic of groups, particularly IFS in groups, and how I both operate in and facilitate groups. I continued to ask myself why this sense of belonging that people were experiencing and expressing was frequently absent in the individual lives of participants, and I worked to explore, evaluate, and express what I have come to refer to as the Creating Healing Circles Method.

Why Do IFS in Groups

When I began as an IFS Lead Trainer and felt anxiety or apprehension starting a new training, I would check-in with my parts with the following statement, "People are _____". Based on what I heard back from my parts, I could discern which parts were most active in anticipation of the upcoming training and were needing support. For example, I discovered parts that carried anxiety about what might happen, such as participant judgement or ridicule. After I presented at trainings, I would often have different parts that replayed my teaching presentation verbatim, evaluating harshly for accuracy and perfection. Often, I heard that people were dangerous, judgmental, rejecting, and unsafe. This gave me many trailheads from which to work with my parts. It was the combination of working with my parts *and* experiencing this intentional group environment that supported my internal transformation in these areas.

I began to realize that in individual sessions with my clients, the predominant question of "I am _____" is explored. If my clients' lived experience was that "People are _____" (ex. dangerous, unsafe, unpredictable, etc.), I would encourage them to seek out organized communities where they could further explore the topics we were discussing in individual therapy. Those organized gatherings, however, were often not structured or intentional enough to further support my clients' healing. These experiences with my individual clients, combined with my experiences with IFS training groups, reinforced my understanding that many people need to first have a therapeutic group experience before they can generate community belonging for themselves outside of a therapeutic space. The common principle of not asking clients to do something outside of therapy that they have not first done in a therapeutic setting applies to communal and group belonging as well.

Often when people experience social anxiety, they make the internal statement, "If I can only do/be _____ (e.g., interesting, witty, pretty, smart, etc.) enough, I will fit in and belong." This question, "People are _____" seldom gets asked. If these beliefs about people are not settled in a person's internal system, then, under stress, the tendency of protective parts is to generalize these fears and anxieties. These generalizations about people often cast doubt about the person's ability to feel a sense of belonging in community.

MEASURING YOUR "PEOPLE ARE…" RESPONSE

Let's explore this simple statement, "People are _____." Complete the following statement and notice the felt sense in your body as you fill in the blank.

"People are _____."

- First, what sensations do you notice in your body when you complete that statement for yourself?
    - Do you notice…constriction, avoidance, withdrawal, activation, pressure, tension, etc.? or
    - Do you notice…calm, spaciousness, expansiveness, tenderness, warmth, openness, etc.?
- Second, what feelings go with those sensations?
    - Do you feel…fear, anger, hopelessness, resentment, resignation, etc.? or
    - Do you feel….compassion, love, gratitude, etc.?
- Finally, based on your sensations and feelings, identify three descriptive words to complete the sentence, "People are _____."

This exercise serves as a starting place to begin noticing and tracking how these feelings and parts shape our perception and decisions. For example, if you go to a social engagement and note sensations of tension in your chest and throat and feelings of fear or resignation, this indicates that parts are protectively engaged toward a strategy for safety. In the IFS model, this insight is referred to as a *trailhead* and could be brought to therapeutic group setting where it could be explored more thoroughly.

The Creating Healing Circles Method

Using the Internal Family Systems model as the foundation, a system for working in groups has evolved in my practice over the years. One of the visions I bring to the group work process is a deeper understanding of what is possible for both the individual and communities, through an enhanced felt sense of community and what process best supports those outcomes. The method that has evolved in my work with groups, and which I discuss in more depth in my book *Creating Healing Circles: Using the Internal Family Systems Model in Facilitating Groups,* involves the following three specific principles:

- Highlighting Experiential Group Work
- Developing the Self of the Facilitator
- Understanding Group Development and Process

Importance of Experiential Group Work

The Creating Healing Circles Method focuses on experiential group work. Talking *about* parts (as often found with process-type groups) is different than *doing* experiential parts work. While sharing and noticing parts that arise in a group is a natural occurrence, an experiential group goes deeper into transforming both the participant's internal system and connecting to a larger felt sense of community. A group based on this type of Healing Circle is designed to help participants specifically identify their parts, set intentions toward Self-leadership, learn unblending skills, and work experientially using the IFS tools of direct access, sculpting, psychodrama, and insight work.

Self of the Facilitator

There is a long-held understanding that you cannot take others where you have not gone yourself. Self-leadership is developed through an internal process of befriending and unburdening parts that carry maladaptive ways of protecting and carrying burdens from trauma or neglect. In a group setting, participants are often highly aware of the hidden agendas, the unhealed parts, and the unconscious dynamics of the facilitator.[1]

The Self of the facilitator does not just refer to how one feels toward their own parts or feels toward other people. This reference to the Self of the facilitator refers to the ability of the facilitator to hold Self-energy when in a dynamic, interpersonal interchange with others. Often, a facilitator may see themselves as being in Self-energy but may feel challenged when participants' parts arise and/or become polarized either internally or with others. When developing Self-leadership as an IFS facilitator, especially in a Healing Circles group setting, it is highly recommended that facilitators continue to work experientially with their own system and track their own parts' dynamics, particularly in interpersonal relationships.

In addition to being competent in the IFS model and having the ability to hold Self-leadership in a group setting, a group facilitator should also develop group facilitator skills. I dedicate entire chapters to the Self of the Facilitator as well as Essential Group Leader Skills in my book *Creating Healing Circles*. For the purpose of this chapter, I will briefly highlight the following list of the group leadership skills essential in the Creating Healing Circles Method.

ESSENTIAL GROUP LEADER SKILLS[2]

1. Obtaining Permission for Pausing and Interrupting
2. Supporting Intention Setting
3. Creating Workable Contracts
4. Assisting with Parts Detection
5. Modeling and Promoting Speaking for Parts
6. Facilitating Unblending
7. Using Reflective Listening and Facilitating U-turns
8. Tracking Individual and Group Sequencing
9. Supporting Self-Led Feedback and Accountability
10. Working with Participant Projection and Transference

Group Development and Process

The group field refers to the felt, energetic state of the group as a whole. As a facilitator, being aware of the dynamic nature of the group field plays a major role in how a group is designed and what type of therapeutic interventions are chosen. As noted by the research of psychologist, Bruce Tuckman, all groups go through different stages of development—forming, storming, norming, and performing. The ability of facilitators to read the state of the group and assist with successful transitions from one stage to the next is an important component of creating environments for healing.

Sculpting:
An Important Tool in Creating Healing Circles

In my years of doing group work, I have come to appreciate the immense healing potential of sculpting exercises. In an IFS sculpting, one participant externalizes a representation of their own parts by asking other participants to role-play an embodiment of those parts. Sculpting is a process by which these parts can be externalized as a living and moving organism. While a mini-sculpting can be used to highlight or identify one or two parts in a dyad or small group setting, a full sculpting involves multiple parts of a participant's system, with several members enrolled as parts. In a full sculpting, the participant can experience and visually observe an overview of their internal system and explore their more complicated and often obscure internal patterns. A participant can get a full picture of how their parts are in a protective stance against real or perceived external threats.

While mini-sculptings are possible in an online group setting, I have found that the healing nature of full sculptings is best realized in an in-person setting due to the length, complexity, and potential for overwhelm that can best be supported while in the physical presence of others. It is also important to note that when group members are enrolled as a part, they are simply mirroring back how the participant instructs them to represent the part. Additional interpretation or expressions by the role-playing group member creates confusion and is not a component of an IFS sculpting process. It is very important in this process to let the part describe itself and to have the group member participating in the sculpting role play to accurately mirror back the description of the part without adding to, embellishing, or interpreting what they believe the part is feeling or experiencing. A sculpt allows the process to unfold at the participant's pace and while supporting their Self-to-part relationships in accordance with the IFS model.

The Power of Sculpting in Group Work: A Case Illustration

The Creating Healing Circles Method for using the IFS model in a group setting works with intention. Participants experientially work to create a clear intention for their therapeutic experience. They begin by identifying where they currently locate themselves emotionally, behaviorally, and systemically in their life and imagine future growth areas. The following case study illustrates a participant's work during a Creating Healing Circles in-person training and how sculpting played a role in that process.[3] Sculptings are often a long and complex process involving multiple parts and multiple dynamics. The case study presented here focuses on one specific dynamic involving two specific parts. It is *not* a "how to" guide in the sculpting process. This sculpt is outlined in phases to help illustrate the progression and unfolding of the sculpting process and the powerful healing potential of a sculpting exercise in an in-person setting.

Phase One: Check-in

During introduction and check-in in the large group, participants were asked to experientially identify where they were emotionally, systemically, and behaviorally in that moment. What parts were predominantly leading their system? What were they currently carrying coming into the group? Where did they find themselves on their growth path? One of the group participants, Jill (all names and identifying information have been changed), presented that she was feeling very isolated, emotionally distant, and having a difficult time feeling emotionally engaged in her work. She also had a sense of despondency and hopelessness.

Phase Two: Mapping Exercise

In the first IFS mapping exercise, the group was asked to locate themselves and their intention, blocks, external resources, and essential qualities. On her map, Jill illustrated a considerable amount of hopelessness and feelings of overwhelm. She was particularly hopeless about raising children during a time of climate change and unrest in the world. Jill, who had spent most of her life being an advocate and activist for many causes, described herself as feeling burned-out, hopeless, and disengaged. These emotions and parts were blocking her from being able to energetically feel inspired and motivated toward her intention. On her map, Jill indicated that her intention was to feel free of anger, worry, sorrow, and obligation and to have internal and external space where her spirit could run free.

Phase Three: Externalizing and Sculpting Parts

To begin Jill's sculpt, the map that she created earlier was displayed on the wall and these illustrated parts on her map became the starting place for the sculpting.[4] Jill read her intention and listened to it being read back to her. Her intention stated, "I am free of anger, worry, sorrow, and obligation. I have internal and external space where my spirit can run free." She checked inside to make sure the words and phrases resonated with what she was wanting to create and began noticing what parts presented inside. The map also supported Jill's exploration of parts in relation to her intention.

As she began, Jill described historical and legacy burdens as a backdrop to the overwhelm and hopelessness she was currently feeling. Through this process, she identified several parts and asked group members to role-play these parts. The sculpting process with two of Jill's parts is described below. These two parts have been highlighted here to demonstrate the complexity of both the dynamics between the parts and the multilayered nature *within* the individual parts.

> *Overwhelmed, young, vulnerable part:* She identified a young part that felt weighed-down living under the weight of the historical and legacy trauma from her family lineage. This young part was illustrated in the sculpting as feeling alone, disconnected, and unaware of anyone available for support.
>
> *Critical part:* Jill sculpted a part that was critical of the vulnerability expressed by the young part due to various privileges from her family and socio-economic status. She described being considerably blended with this part and having a difficult time being compassionate toward the younger exile.

Once these two parts were externalized and mirrored back to her by two of the group participants, the sculpt slowed down to give Jill time to sit experientially with the parts she had sculpted. Jill became aware of the immense heaviness, hopelessness, and shame that she carried in her body. As the sculpt continued with the support of the group, she was able to become curious with what she carried in her body.

Through this process, Jill was able to unblend from the overwhelmed, young, vulnerable part and became more curious about the critical part's protective function. As she came into relationship with the critical part, she heard directly from the part how it was carrying trauma from a rise in White nationalism in the United States which was combined with her own family legacy trauma. She was able to see these layers of historical, cultural, and legacy burdens which created the feeling of hopelessness and resignation.

Also alive in the critical part was the drive to create a better world for her children. (Note: This is an example of how parts are layered and are more than the burdens and difficult roles they carry.) The witnessing of both the burdened and inspirational nature of the critical part supported that part coming back into relationship with Jill's Self. It was able to release both its constrained role and the physiological burden it was carrying from those overlapping events. The critical part became aware of how it could support Jill in less harsh ways and contribute to creating possibilities of a better future for her children. The person role-playing the critical part then physically stepped back to mirror a more relaxed and supportive posture as Jill continued the sculpting process.

In releasing the legacy burden, Jill was then able to access greater capacity for her own Self-energy and come into a Self-to-part relationship with the overwhelmed, young, vulnerable part which she had identified earlier in the process. In having a group member role-play the young, vulnerable part, Jill was able to experience having that part be seen by her more adult Self, helping to foster internal repair and attachment. The young part went from feeling collapsed and despondent to feeling more enlivened and available for additional healing and attachment repair in Jill's internal system. The sculpting process allowed Jill to have greater access to this young, vulnerable part, supporting greater possibilities for unburdening in Jill's individual therapy work after she returned home.

After completing the sculpt, Jill reported feeling more spacious, open, and inspired toward living with more freedom, spontaneity, and social engagement. To further support this transformation after she returned home, Jill reported spending more time in nature with her significant other where she could foster a greater sense of spaciousness and freedom. In a follow-up conversation, Jill reported a greater curiosity and imagination in ways to use sculpting in her professional practice and ways to use the Healing Circles method, especially around the topics of grief.

IFS group work provides vast opportunities for deep, experiential exploration of our internal systems. It is important to remember that parts and systems change with direct engagement with Self-energy. It is the presence of this Self-energy that helps transform old survival patterns and supports the release of burdens when the parts are seen and valued. While being in a group that processes *about* parts and their roles can be helpful in gaining insight and feeling supported by the group, processing alone does not lend itself to deeper healing work. It is the experiential component of the IFS model that supports the Self-to-part relationship that naturally evokes the innate healing potential embedded in each person. In a group environment where people are lending additional Self-energy to the healing process, more in-depth healing through experiential exercises such sculpting assists in the potential for deeper transformation. When this type of deeper experiential work is done in groups, it helps to create an internalized sense of community which can then be expressed out into the larger community, with the intention of restoring our connection to each other and the natural world.

KEY TAKEAWAYS

- **The Power of IFS in a Group Setting:** Using IFS in a group setting can help people feel a greater sense of belonging and counteract the traumatic isolation, disconnect, and societal individualism that has and still is causing so much suffering in the world.
- **Measuring Your "People Are _____" Response:** Exploring the sensation and feelings associated with asking and answering this question can provide trailheads from which to work with our parts.
- Many people need to first have a therapeutic group experience before they can generate community belonging for themselves outside of a therapeutic space.
- **The Creating Healing Circles Method:** Using the IFS model as a foundation, the Creating Healing Circles Method focuses on three main principles in the group work process:
    - The importance of group work as an experiential process.
    - The importance of the continued development the Self of the facilitator.
    - The importance of understanding group development and adapting the group process to meet the stages of the group.
- **The Power of Sculpting:** The experiential component of a full, in-person IFS sculpting exercise offers immense healing potential where a participant can experience and visually observe an overview of their internal system and explore their more complicated and often obscure internal patterns.

AUTHOR BIO

Chris Burris, MEd, LCMHCS, LMFT (he/him) is a Senior Lead Trainer for the Internal Family Systems Institute where he provides Level I, II, and III trainings in the IFS model. He has been an IFS Therapist since 1999 and a practicing psychotherapist since 1987. Chris is trained as a Marriage and Family Therapist and uses a mind-body approach to psychotherapy. He has worked extensively with children, adolescents, couples, individuals, and organizations. In addition, he has facilitated groups on topics such as men's issues, sacred activism, rites of passage, couples, healthy relationships, performance enhancement, and bullying. Since 1990, he has been an active participant with men's groups and rites of passage programs. He also facilitates consultation and supervision groups for trained therapists. In addition to being a psychotherapist, Chris has trained in many nature-based models with Animus Valley institute, School of Lost Borders, The Foundation for Shamanic Studies, and The Center for Conscious Eldering. He currently lives in Asheville, NC with his wife, Deena, and their daughters where they enjoy being active in the beautiful Blue Ridge Mountains.

REVIEWER BIO

Deena Burris, PhD (she/her) is a tenured Associate Professor in the Department of Business at the University of North Carolina Asheville where she teaches courses in global business and global finance. Her PhD is in the field of International Development. Prior to joining the faculty at UNC Asheville, she was a tenured faculty at Guilford College in Greensboro, NC. Her academic research and publications are in the field of development finance. Prior to academia, she worked in the field of international banking. In her journey of personal growth, Deena has been a passionate student and practitioner of meditation and spiritual discovery. In combining her academic and research skills, her experiences and knowledge in international and cultural systems, and her understanding of spiritual and emotional growth, she brings a depth of perspective to the topics of human and societal growth. Deena has enjoyed merging these multiple perspectives and collaborating on writing projects with her husband, Chris Burris. She lives in Asheville, NC with her husband and daughters.

GOING DEEPER

From Chris Burris

1) Website: Burris Counseling
   a. www.burriscounseling.com

2) Books:
   a. Burris, C. (2022). *Creating healing circles: Using the Internal Family Systems model in facilitating groups,* (D. Burris, Ed.). Tonic Books.

3) Trainings and Workshops:
   a. www.burriscounseling.com/workshops-trainings/

4) Podcast Interviews:
   a. www.burriscounseling.com/podcasts-featuring-chris/

SECTION FIVE
RELATIONSHIPS

IFS AND SEXUALITY

SELF-LED SEXUALITY FOR HEALING, PLEASURE, AND EMPOWERMENT

Patricia Rich, LCSW, CST-S

The terrain of our sexuality is broad and extends far beyond our actual sexual experiences. It includes how we feel in our own skin, connect with ourselves and others, move energy through our bodies, and move our bodies through the world. Our sexuality informs how we identify ourselves and build our families, and how we express our passion, eroticism, and power. It is in the realm of sexuality that our physical body and its reproductive capacities meet the imprint of society and the stories of our lives, shaping the beliefs and roles we take on. From an IFS perspective—and not surprisingly—a host of parts have jobs in relation to our sexuality. They perform essential functions like managing what we let in and what we let out, preventing unwanted consequences and maximizing our chances for survival including the propagation of the species.

Sexuality offers the potential for some of life's greatest pleasures but can also bring some of the deepest forms of pain and shame. Most of us carry at least a few sexual burdens, biases and blind spots acquired through personal experience, as well as family and cultural legacies. As therapists, we can be challenged addressing client sexual issues and remaining Self-led. And in our personal lives, we can similarly struggle to access Self in the realm of sexuality and may face the same dilemmas as many of our clients.

You are not alone if you have not brought the same level of insight to sexuality as you have brought to other dimensions of life. Most therapy programs barely address this vital area, and even skilled practitioners of holistic approaches like IFS are often silent about this topic. Therefore, you may never have considered the many benefits of befriending sexuality personally and professionally. You may not have considered how parts can use the resource of sexuality to do their jobs or the ways that sexual burdens can accrue throughout a person's life. You may not have explored the power of Self-Energy as not only a healer of sex parts, but a life force energy with qualities of sensuality and sexuality of its own. And you may not have had the guidance and support needed to venture further into the murky terrain of your own sexual system, bringing compassion and light to the parts that may be hidden there.

I have been exploring ways that IFS can illuminate the understanding and experience of sexuality for many years now and am excited about this powerful integration. But before going further, I would like to acknowledge a few things.

First, the topic of sexuality is vast. In this chapter we will only begin to explore the possibilities IFS brings to its exploration. Second, the topic of sexuality can trigger lots of parts. I invite you to notice what arises for you as you read this chapter which may take the form of thoughts, memories, body sensations, impulses or something else. You may wish to write these down so you can come back to them later or to take a break to be with them as they arise, remembering that there are no bad parts and that any part may hold an important aspect of your sexual story.

Third, there is great variety in the ways that people and parts experience and express their sexuality including the absence of sexual feelings and behavior. In the confines of this chapter, I am not nearly able to represent all of these and regret that some of your parts may not feel adequately reflected. Fourth, sexuality can be used abusively, and many people and parts carry wounds from having been harmed in this way. Those with significant sexual trauma may benefit from approaching this topic slowly and with support.

Fifth, I bring a perspective shaped through my own identities as a middle aged, middle-class, White, educated, United States born and bred, cisgender woman. While I relate with people who hold identities very different than my own, I do not regard myself as an expert on anyone else's lived sexual experience and invite you to adapt or discard anything you find here that is not a fit for you. Lastly, all client examples included here are created by me, inspired by my work with many people but use fictitious names.

Now I would like to share a bit more about my own personal and professional journey toward Self-Led Sexuality.

"I need help!"—A Personal Story

In a typical week as a sex therapist, I receive calls from people distressed by a wide range of sexual challenges. Their concerns may focus on what their genitals are or are not doing or what their partner's genitals are or are not doing. They may not know what or whom they desire sexually, or struggle with not behaving in ways that align with their values. They may not feel sexual desire but want to, or a partner wants them to. They may be curious about what more is possible for themselves or their relationships but not know where to start. Or they may carry challenging personal histories that constrain access to more ease and comfort in their sexual lives.

I see people in their twenties through their eighties, single, coupled, polyamorous, conservative, kinky, and of diverse sexual orientations and genders.

While the details of each person's situation vary, common themes often emerge. People have typically struggled for many years with their sexual issue before seeking help, and then when they do, they have difficulty finding doctors and therapists who can truly hear and help them at the deepest levels. Beneath the presenting issue are often feelings of shame, loneliness, fear, and despair. And they face confounding puzzles: How can all these disparate thoughts, feelings, and body sensations be here at the same time? How can I make sense of this and overcome the pain? And is there possibly a pathway toward pleasure for someone like me?

I also hear from therapists who seek consultation because they would like to feel more clear, calm, and confident addressing sexuality with their clients. They recognize gaps in their training and want to know that they are practicing ethically and are up to date with the many changes in how people identify themselves and express their sexuality. They may have encountered an unfamiliar sexual symptom or scenario or recognized that a client's sexual material triggered them in ways that limit the amount of presence and compassion they bring to their work. They may struggle with issues similar to those of their clients and seek help for themselves. I also hear from sex therapists who are at ease with the subject matter but seek a new lens through which to approach the sexual dilemmas of their clients, one that offers the potential for personal transformation as well as symptom reduction.

I know how that latter group feels, for even after many years of training as a clinical social worker and sex therapist, I too was seeking something more when I had the good fortune of a colleague introducing me to the IFS model in 2012. I began learning IFS to help my clients overcome "sexual dysfunction" but quickly recognized that IFS offered something more. I found in IFS a respectful and empowering pathway toward deep intimacy with oneself and others, a way to live authentically that often led to symptom reduction but did not depend on it in order for people to feel a greater sense of self-acceptance, ease, and satisfaction. IFS offered a way for people to navigate complex inner and outer sexual landscapes in a mindful way and to find and actually heal sexual wounds. And over time I came to see that IFS can open the way toward a more expansive and creative form of sexuality—one that is not defined by how we appear on the outside or what activities we do, but rather by the release and expression of our most authentic Self, accessed through a compassionate and relational process of finding, unblending, and unburdening the parts of ourselves that otherwise limit our access.

As I helped my clients to focus inward and befriend their own sex parts, I noticed that the tenor of our sessions changed. Rather than aligning with the parts of my clients who were pushing for change and meeting the resistance of parts that were opposed, I learned not to take sides and to help my clients to kindly hear the concerns and positive intentions coming from both sides of a power struggle. When I stopped interpreting and hypothesizing, the system would slowly reveal its inner logic and unfold the nested layers of parts that took on roles and burdens in the course of that person's sexual development. Once these parts unblended from Self and felt safe, they disclosed what they had to manage, what outer forces they had to respond to, what beliefs and strategies they had adopted, and who they were trying to protect. They revealed exiles, or what I sometimes call "sex-iles," vulnerable parts often frozen in scenes of confusion, pain, and humiliation, sometimes specifically sexual and sometimes not, but still impacting some aspect of the person's current sexuality.

Through the healing steps of IFS, we were able to retrieve and unburden these parts, relieving pressure on the protective system and allowing for the qualities of Self to come through more consistently. My clients started to smile more, feel more hopeful, and bring more courage and curiosity to their sexual lives. They reported conversing with partners about sex with more ease and humor, that they had surprising moments of pleasure, and that when things didn't go as they might have hoped, they felt more resilient.

I felt a level of confidence and clarity that I had not felt before as a therapist and a welcome sense of energy at a time when I had been starting to weary in my work. I was intrigued by the stories held within each person's system and appreciated that I did not (and indeed could not) know what would bring resolution to a client's dilemmas before the parts were engaged with Self and with each other. I could not have foreseen the resourcefulness, sacrifice and complex relationships among my clients' parts with my former methods, and without having done my own healing work as well.

To learn the IFS model, I had to get to know my own parts first, and I believe that this necessity accounts for much of the model's appeal. Therapists are called to heal, grow, and become more Self-Led themselves as they follow this path—and clients benefit as a result. To help my clients to befriend what I have come to call their internal sexual systems, I had to first befriend my own.

I realized that despite the insights I had gained as a sex therapist and as an IFS therapist, I had not fully integrated this into awareness of my own internal sexual system. My relationship with my parts seemed to end at the bedroom door, and even discovering that was an interesting trailhead for me to explore. Did I have parts that felt shame or embarrassment claiming my own sex parts? Had I bought into the exiling of sexuality that is part of the larger cultures in which I live? Was there a lack of sexual mentorship in my personal and professional life that left a big gap regarding sexuality? Were some of my parts afraid of what I would discover?

I decided to issue a radical welcome to all my parts related to sex and sexuality, meaning that I was feeling open, compassionate, and curious to better know my inner cast of characters, including those with jobs in this area, stories to share, lessons or burdens accrued, and those closely connected to parts of my body. I also invited my parts to share their fears, fantasies, and guilty pleasures with me. And slowly, I started to find my sex parts, and they started to find me.

Sometimes, they showed up first as a body sensation, a memory, an urge, an emotion, or lack thereof. When I noticed something, I made a point of slowing down and allowing it to flesh out further. When a part could sense I was trustworthy and interested, it would let me know more about itself or about my larger story. My fearful and judgmental parts had an easier time allowing this when I let them know that we could witness anything internally without having to act on it in the external world and that no part would be in trouble for what it felt, did, or wanted.

"Really?" asked a few incredulous parts.

"Yes, really!" I reassured them from my calm and confident core.

I met baby parts with a hunger to be cuddled and held. I met adolescent parts with deep longings and insecurities and a few juicy memories. I met an angry old crone demanding that I notice menopausal changes in my body and regroup accordingly. I met a carpenter named Jim who, my system showed me, was the set designer for my fantasies. We laughed, we cried, we cringed, we grieved, we savored. And through this process I grew to feel more spacious, more compassionate, more wondrous, and more electrified. My laugh deepened and my capacity to experience pleasure increased. I more courageously spoke for what I needed and wanted, both in the bedroom and beyond. I became more politically active and through my increased sense of oneness with my own body and the currents running through it, felt a more palpable connection to the earth and to the forces of nature around me.

As I became more able to honor the wishes and boundaries expressed by my physical and psychological sex parts, they not only grew to trust me more, but they also started to collaborate further with each other and to respond more quickly as a group. I could consult with them before making a sexual choice to see if they were all in agreement, a process I came to call Internal Consent. I learned that when I did this effectively, they would unblend further, allowing me to become even more present and embodied. In addition to the 8 Cs already described within the IFS model (Calm, Curiosity, Compassion, Connectedness, Creativity, Clarity, Confidence, Courage), I came to see that in this context Self could also be experienced as Safe, Sensual, Spacious, Sensitive, Steamy and Satisfied. I began to refer to these qualities as The Six Ss of Sexual Self-Energy and discovered many ways that these qualities can serve as parts detectors as well as portals to sexual discovery.

I committed to Behold and Lead my Internal Sexual System (BLISS), and I am still on this journey. Along the way, I have unloaded personal, familial, and collective legacy burdens and become even more passionate about bringing compassion to parts in myself and others that have been exiled in relation to sexuality, and along with them the vitality and life force energy of Self. I have seen that exploring sexuality through the lens of IFS brings many benefits personally, professionally, and collectively. Regardless of whether a person is sexually active or is a therapist who specializes in sexual issues, the process of finding and befriending sex parts, clearing burdens, claiming one's own body, and discerning pathways to joy and pleasure enhances our sense of aliveness and empowers us to manifest our deepest dreams and desires.

I am deeply indebted to Dr. Richard Schwartz and all his collaborators who have brought forth this simple yet profound understanding of who we are and how we can grow and heal based in the idea of multiplicity and the existence of an indestructible Self. Many aspects of the IFS model align extremely well with the exploration of sexuality, and I will elaborate on these in this chapter.

I also see that IFS training alone is sometimes not enough. I see that my additional training in sexuality has prepared me to hold space for a wide range of sexual issues and forms of expression. It has helped me to examine my own sexual values, provide accurate and up to date sexual health information, consider the impact of larger systems on sexual expression and offer a repertoire of behavioral activities for sexual growth. For this reason, I developed an integrative model I call Self-Led Sexuality that brings these perspectives together, and this is what I am sharing with you here. As I have brought this model to clients and colleagues, I have been truly humbled by the level of interest and enthusiasm it has generated. It seems there has been an unmet need in the IFS community and beyond for a new approach to sexuality, one that is contemporary, inclusive, and hopeful, that considers internal and external constraints while also offering a roadmap toward a Self-Led experience of sexuality in whatever form that may take.

ACTIVITY:
MEANINGS OF SEX IN THE INTERNAL SYSTEM

Before moving on to the next section, I invite you to look at the word below for a full minute and to notice what responses arise. These may take the form of thoughts, images, voices, body sensations, emotions, or something else. I suggest that you set a timer for a minute so you can focus without interruption. If that doesn't feel like enough time, you can try 2-3 minutes. Write down anything you might like to remember.

SEX

- What did you notice?
- If some images formed for you, what were they?
- If there were people or body parts, what were their genders, skin colors, body sizes or anatomical features?
- Did you sense your own body responding in any way?
- Did you feel any emotions or attitudes?
- Did you perceive any parts?
- Did you sense being a certain age, or having parts of a few different ages show up?
- Did images or messages from outside of your own direct experience show up such as from mass media, porn or other external sources?
- What was it like for you to do this exercise?
- By inviting you to notice the assumptions and parts that show up for you in relationship to the word "sex," this simple activity can give you a window into your own internal sexual system.

Defining Sex (Avi and Jana's Story)

Pausing to define the words we use is an important step in any sex-related communication, both because the words themselves often hold multiple usages and because we each bring assumptions and emotional responses to these terms which can limit possibilities and obstruct clear communication. People also may use slang, innuendo, or no words at all and expect others to know what they mean. Additionally, the vocabulary around sexuality and gender is rapidly evolving such that a term that seems obvious to one person may represent an utterly unfamiliar concept to someone else. Whether you are a therapist communicating with a client, a parent communicating with your child or teen, or a person in a new or long-term relationship, I recommend taking the time to reflect upon what the words used mean and how they resonate for all parties involved.

This simple inquiry can open meaningful trailheads and is especially useful when working with relationships. Bringing gentle curiosity to how a person learned that meaning or arrived at that emotional response to a word can begin to bring parts to the surface. I'd like you to meet Avi and Jana, who, like every client in this chapter, are a composite of typical clients in my practice. They sought help due to a desire discrepancy in their fifteen-year marriage and wanted to address the feelings of resentment and disconnection that had developed as a result.

At our initial session, we began to discuss the tension they were feeling related to sexual frequency. Avi first defined the word sex as a varied menu of sexual activities. He later used the word as synonymous with penis-in-vagina penetration, stating that he and his wife had not had sex in a month when during that time they had engaged in manual and oral stimulation. This became an opportunity to find and notice some of his parts, including one that felt satisfied by the intimacy and closeness of non-penetrative sex, and another part that craved the physical experience of intercourse. The latter part was closely connected to another one that felt that he deserved intercourse given how hard he worked to support his family. This activated an intellectual part which did not agree with that at all. As these parts relaxed, Avi recognized that a teenage boy part was at times defining sex for him based on beliefs he had acquired from his peers, porn, and the example of his patriarchal father who conveyed indirectly his sense of sexual entitlement.

His wife, Jana, defined sex as penis-in-vagina penetration, even while recognizing that she derived much more pleasure from manual and oral stimulation, which she categorized as "foreplay." She had a part that believed intercourse was "real sex" and her duty as a wife, which she had learned through her religious upbringing and what her mother had told her. She noticed her parts that felt shame and anger when she heard her husband's part say that it was not satisfied with what she had made a significant effort to engage in, and yet another part that wanted to defend herself by explaining the reasons that had limited her availability for intercourse in the last month. As Avi and Jana noticed their parts, they were able to feel more compassion for themselves and each other. They both expressed feeling relief once the parts were named rather than hiding in plain sight, their energetic presence felt but unacknowledged, and they felt curious about what might come next.

I often notice my own parts during conversations like these. Most of my parts hold a very expansive definition of sex that is not defined by specific sexual acts or body parts but instead by a process of sexual relating, free of agenda for any specific outcome but open to what might emerge with presence and permission. I have a teaching part that wants to quickly convey this vision to my clients, and a therapist part that tells it to slow down and let the process unfold. I also have a part that can bristle when it hears a client say something that it perceives as too sexually entitled, or conversely, as not entitled enough. Once I notice my parts, I can take a breath, validate their feelings and positive intentions, and then ask them to soften so that I can bring my full presence to the clients' process.

After exploring my clients' use of some key words, I may share the meanings I bring to offer an alternative possibility. I will often adopt the clients' language once I am clear what it means to them, and closely adhere to the language used by parts during inner work.

DEFINITIONS

Sex is a term that can be used to refer to assigned gender at birth or to the act of penetrative intercourse, or it can be used more broadly to reference any and all erotic acts and processes that occur alone or with partners.

Sexuality is a complex term. This comprehensive definition invites us to consider the many kinds of parts that may have jobs and burdens in relation to the following aspects of sexuality. "Sexuality is *a basic aspect of being human throughout life*, encompasses sex, gender identities and roles, sexual orientation, eroticism, pleasure, intimacy, and reproduction. Sexuality is experienced and expressed in thoughts, fantasies, desires, beliefs, attitudes, values, behaviors, practices, roles, and relationships. While sexuality can include all of these dimensions, *not all of them are always experienced or expressed*." (from World Association for Sexual Health Declaration of Sexual Rights, *emphasis added*)

Sex Parts is a term I use to refer both to the physical anatomy involved in sexual processes as well as the subpersonalities that relate in any way with our sexuality.

The Self-Led Sexuality Model

Self-Led Sexuality is the integrative model I have developed for purposes of individual and collective healing, pleasure, and empowerment. It is grounded in IFS and fortified by the perspectives of Embodied Practices, Education regarding Human Sexuality, A Sexual Justice Lens, and Journeys of Exploration. I will elaborate on each of these in a later section. It offers concepts and processes through which we can find and unblend our sex parts, shed burdens and cultivate an internal collaborative sexual team with Self in the lead. As a result, intimacy with ourselves and others can grow, as can our capacity for joy and fulfillment in both sexual and nonsexual contexts. Whether we are motivated by a specific sexual problem or by a desire to grow and expand sexually, Self-Led Sexuality offers an optimistic and non-pathologizing approach which can yield significant benefits.

Self-Led Sexuality honors our own protective system as well as that of others. It fosters awareness of the nuanced dynamics underlying internal and external consent (and dissent) processes, enabling us to reach meaningful inner agreements and to enact confident outer behaviors that are aligned with our values, preferences, and boundaries. Self-Led Sexuality recognizes the impact of larger systems and power structures that may support or restrict sexual safety, autonomy, and self-expression.

It assumes that in addition to the 8 Cs and the 5 Ps, that embodied Self-Energy has sexual attributes. Given the holographic nature of the internal system in which parts have parts and parts have Self, Self-Led Sexuality assumes that all parts have the potential to have sexual attributes as well, and in a form that makes sense for them. Self-Led Sexuality encourages the understanding of sex as a process of embodied inner and outer relating. It also recognizes the challenges many people face perceiving, relating with and feeling at one with their own bodies, and offers opportunities to increase this capacity.

This approach can help us to relate in more positive ways with our own sexuality. It may help us to feel less self-conscious and more self-curious, less compulsive, and more compassionate, less compliant and more courageous, and less exhausted and more excited. Either alone or with the help of a therapist or guide, we can learn to Behold and Lead our Internal Sexual System (BLISS).

Why Do We Need Self-Led Sexuality?

Perhaps no other aspect of our shared human experience is so fraught with confusing messages, extraordinary expectations, and deep wells of shame as is sexuality. We are born with bodies sensitive to pleasure and pain and genetically programmed to grow into particular shapes, colors, sizes, and reproductive capacities. We are assigned a gender at birth and arrive to the care of our primary caregivers who may hold us with love and acceptance, keep us safe and steward us through our burgeoning sexual development, or instead, leave us alone and unsafe in critical ways and, perhaps, even sexually harm us, violating the boundaries of our bodies and psyches. Our early experiences of safety, attachment, and body acceptance, or lack thereof, set the stage upon which our sexual development unfolds.

We also are born into social groups such as extended families, religious communities, and national cultures that teach us how our bodies should look, behave, and channel their sexual urges and impulses. We may fall neatly within these parameters and experience a sense of belonging and adequacy or fall uncomfortably outside of them, accruing significant burdens as a result. As we mature sexually and emotionally, we may feel attracted to others, engage in sexual exploration, and eventually choose long-term mates. This process will flow easily for some; for others it will be fraught with struggle. We may become parents using our own bodies or alternative methods, which is also a process that will flow naturally for some and be anguishing and out of reach for others. As we grow older, the appearance and sexual functioning of our bodies will change, requiring multiple adjustments, at times with celebration, and at times with sadness and grief.

Sexual burdens and gifts accrue over time and our parts take on roles to maximize our chances for survival and to minimize pain and discomfort. If our sexuality has attracted unwanted attention or put us in harm's way, protectors may fear it and find ways to hide it or avoid what they regard as risky situations.

If our sexuality has helped us to obtain status, safety, or opportunities, some parts might want to capitalize on that to do their jobs and, therefore, have us flaunt our sexuality or use it strategically.

When we discover things that feel good sensually or sexually, protectors assess whether these could enhance or reduce our access to needed emotional and material resources. Parental anger upon discovery of a child masturbating or a partner's disgust when asked to perform a desired sexual act poses a threat to parts that depend on those people for love and connection, maybe even for food and shelter. Manager parts may forbid those pleasures, shaming the parts that enjoyed them. Self-soothing parts, also known as firefighters, may discover that such pleasure offers a brief respite from pain or discomfort or just feels really good and thus learn to return to it repeatedly, willing, to a point, to risk negative consequences. If sufficiently negative consequences ensue, that activity, and the feelings of pleasure associated with it, may become exiled, conflicted, and, possibly, highly erotically charged.

In the current era we face additional challenges. Technology, media, and social networks exert a powerful influence on our sexual systems, impacting how we encounter sexual images, develop sexual expectations, and pursue sexual opportunities. We have front row seats to the explicit exploits of others, setting us up to make comparisons that may reassure us or foster feelings of anxiety and inadequacy. The marketplace then tries to sell us products, pharmaceuticals, cosmetic surgeries, and advice to remedy the latter, luring us to believe that if we could just be thin enough, hard enough, or "perform" like a porn star we could finally find the satisfaction we are supposed to crave.

Additionally, familiar social and sexual scripts can lose relevance as people live longer on average, are more likely to experience divorce, live alone in greater numbers, and have weaker ties to religious and community institutions. An expanding array of sexual orientations, gender identities, and forms of sexual expression such as kink, polyamory, and asexuality are gaining visibility and, in some instances, unprecedented degrees of acceptance and legal protection; in other contexts, the same expressions have become targeted for hate and discrimination.

Given the complexities, our parts have their work cut out for them as they try to help us to navigate this terrain, and even fairly Self-led people may feel challenged at times. So where are we to look for guidance?

A small percentage of people will seek the services of a sex therapist, someone trained in both mental health and sexuality. Though sex therapists vary in their approaches, typically they will conduct an assessment, address medical issues, offer cognitive-behavioral strategies, psychoeducation, and recommend exercises to practice at home. Some clients quickly benefit from these interventions, while others with more complex challenges may not benefit as readily. Finding and working with a sex therapist can be difficult for a variety of reasons including lack of insurance reimbursement, the paucity of well-trained professionals, and client feelings of embarrassment or denial about the issue.

A larger percentage of people will turn for help to therapists who are not specialized in sex therapy for help navigating sexual issues, many of which overlap common therapeutic themes such as attachment needs, self-esteem, body image, identity struggles, forming healthy relationships, and finding life satisfaction. They may name their sexual concerns explicitly or hope that there will be a signal that such topics are welcome. They may not arrive to therapy with a sexual issue in mind, but one may emerge during treatment. They might not recognize the role that sexuality plays in their current situation or how their mental health issue is impacting their sex life without a well-timed prompt from their therapist. Therapy may be their first opportunity to explore sexual thoughts and feelings in a safe and caring context or to unpack complex sexual dynamics before making important life decisions such as beginning or ending a relationship.

How unfortunate it is, then, that so many therapists report not feeling adequately prepared to address sexuality. IFS therapists appear to be no exception. Many have told me that they've never taken a class on sexuality; some have shared working with clients recovering from infidelity, compulsive sexual behavior, or coping with genital pain without ever inviting the client to find their parts in direct relation to these experiences. They acknowledge that they really didn't feel confident to do this, didn't want to intrude, felt nervous, silly, or out of their depth. So, while these concerns make sense and emanate from protective parts with positive intentions, we therapists are often participating, knowingly or not, in the exiling of this important life domain from the consulting room and along with it the parts of the client that are perhaps most in need of healing.

The good news is that the robust nature of IFS offers a clear and effective methodology for working with our therapist parts and increasing access to Self. With the added perspective of Self-Led Sexuality, we can gain comfort navigating our own sexual systems first and, thereby, become more prepared to help our clients to navigate theirs. We can learn when we are out of our depth and may need consultation or to make a referral. We can ensure that we are practicing ethically and maintaining healthy boundaries without becoming rigid, disembodied, shaming, or avoidant. Once our therapist parts relax, those who are skilled with IFS may quickly find that they can help clients to meaningfully address sexual issues. After a half day workshop recently, a participant said that she had been able to immediately show up with more spaciousness for a longstanding client who had a sexual dilemma and facilitate deep and meaningful work.

Five Methods for Cultivating Self-Led Sexuality

While there are a myriad of ways to become more sexually enlightened and fulfilled, I have found the following five methods particularly useful. Of these, I regard IFS as the foundational map and incorporate additional perspectives and methods based on the needs of particular people and systems.

1. IFS

The core assumptions of the IFS model offer a rich conceptual framework for the understanding and exploration of sexuality. Here are just a few examples.

Multiplicity: The understanding of sexuality is deepened and enriched by the recognition of having parts. Suddenly there is an inner logic for the dilemmas that we face, the tensions we feel, and the ways that we behave. We can have contradictory sexual attractions that emerge from different parts of ourselves. We can object to sexual activity based on the concerns of particular parts, even while other parts may want to proceed. Multiplicity can open new possibilities for internal and external relating, allowing us to embrace more of ourselves and others. For therapists, the recognition of multiplicity with regard to sexuality helps us to become curious about our own parts, and those of our clients, and to feel less stuck when our go-to techniques are not working, knowing that is a clue that additional parts may be present. Recognition of multiplicity can enhance common sex therapy techniques such as sensate focus exercises or dilator therapy by inviting clients to discern which parts of themselves are motivated and which parts may object, opening new territory for therapeutic work that can increase receptivity to intervention if all parts can agree.

Example of Sondra: "Some parts of me really want to say yes to hooking up with my ex sometimes because they feel lonely and miss her, and we had great sexual chemistry. But other parts of me don't want to lead her on, and don't want to confuse myself, and remember how raw I felt after we broke up even though I initiated it, and they don't want me to feel that way again."

Self: The belief in IFS that we all have an indestructible Self that can heal, harmonize, and lead the system may be its most powerful medicine, offering hope even to those with heavy sexual burdens. Self can heal parts who have been harmed specifically through sexuality as well as parts that impact our capacity to be present and comfortable sexually. Self can extend compassion even to those parts that have harmed others, offering a path toward forgiveness and restitution. Self can harmonize sex parts that are at odds with each other and help the system to make wise choices and to find creative solutions. As therapists, we are relieved when we know that all of our clients have Self-energy within them even if it is well hidden, and that extending our own Self-energy toward the client's blended parts can facilitate the emergence of the client's own authentic Self.

Example of Jess: "The absolute hardest part of getting sober was remembering how I had used sex to get drugs. I felt overcome with shame, guilt, and regret. I almost didn't tell my therapist, but I remembered how calm and connected he was when I shared other hard things. He remained just as calm and connected when I finally told him what I had done. Soon I was able to unblend from my shame-filled part and felt genuine care and and kindness toward her. Then she showed me how much she hated doing it and how guilty she felt for letting my parents down. Somehow, I knew what to say to her and could see that she hadn't felt she had a choice. She was able to separate from the slimy ball of shame, and together we threw it in the ocean."

Parts take on roles and have positive intentions: Manager, firefighter, and exile roles may all develop in relation to sexuality and, depending upon the amount of burden in the system, may be experienced as helpful, fun, and valued or as extreme, problematic, or highly distressing. Knowing that parts have positive intentions depathologizes sexual problems for client and therapist alike and reduces shame and defensiveness. Respect for the protective system is especially relevant to sexuality where protectors often have big jobs. When we can reassure them that we are not trying to make them stop, but rather, want to offer appreciation and resources so they don't have to work so hard, they often become less extreme and more collaborative.

Example of Pierre: "I felt so frustrated that I often could not get hard with guys I was dating. When the frustrated part stepped back, I discovered a numbing part in my groin that was blocking my sexual feelings. When I asked the numbing part why it needed to do that, it showed me that it did not want me to become like my father who cheated and left me and my mom when I was thirteen. I let the part know that I appreciate how it is trying to protect me from being like Dad and asked what it was afraid would happen if it didn't numb me. It turned out it was protecting a teenager who had to take care of my mom after he left. The teen part felt anger and helplessness and learned that to not be like Dad and be loved and accepted by Mom, he had to shut down his own strong sexual desire. When I was able to retrieve and heal the teen, the numbing part saw it didn't have to work so hard, and it also was more able to look around at my present life. He didn't even know that I only date men now and that I'm super honest in my relationships. He said he would try to ease back. I feel much more relaxed now and don't put as much pressure on myself. I'm not always as hard as I want to be, but I am more of the time and am actually having a lot more fun."

In addition to its benefits for the resolution of sexual difficulties, IFS processes can also support sexual experience in real time, whether alone or with others. Through finding and unblending parts that show up while a sexual experience progresses, we can increase access to Self. We can be with parts in need of attention, helping them to relax. We can use the skills of IFS insight to navigate interior sexual spaces and states of arousal with discernment, choosing where to place our focus, when to allow sensation to take over, and bringing friendly curiosity toward any parts that pull us out of the moment. These might include parts with concerns or burdens but also might include eager parts rushing toward gratification, or fantasizer parts that automatically click into gear.

We can use the 6 Fs (Find, Focus, Flesh Out, Feel Toward, BeFriend, Fears) to better know parts that are reluctant to unblend. The 6 Fs can also help us not only to unblend our own parts but to approach partners in a way that promotes deep intimacy. Whether inside or outside of the bedroom, we can take the time to approach our partners and focus on them, really seeing them and feeling them. We can express our positive feelings toward them, inviting them to share with us anything that would help them to feel known more profoundly. We can demonstrate our trustworthiness for their vulnerability, creating a context for deepening emotional and physical intimacy.

2. Embodied Practices

Embodied practices refer to a wide-ranging menu of activities and approaches that help us to connect more deeply with our bodies. Both cultural conditioning and traumatic experience can contribute to the separation of the body and mind, which is quite relevant to the subjective experience of sexuality. We may be more used to watching our bodies than listening to them, loving them, or being them. I have seen that the internal sexual team is greatly enriched by the recognition of the consciousness of anatomical body parts, or of parts that are closely aligned with them. With patience and persistence, people can learn to dialog directly with any part of their body (or sometimes a representative of it) that is willing. I have helped people to witness the stories of their feet, womb, Fallopian tubes, penis, anus ("Everyone thinks I'm an asshole, but I am actually really sensitive"), and more.

When this Self to body part circuit of connection is achieved, the reunions can be highly emotional and transformational. Often a Self-like thinking part has been making all the sexual decisions without knowing that the body parts have life and awareness of their own and are not merely objects to use and manage. The thinking part may feel shock, relief, wonder, worry about the harm it caused, or resentment of its perceived loss of supremacy in the internal system. A participant in my Internal Consent workshop later told me that the session had really messed her up for a while because she had not realized that her internal team had not included the voice of her body parts. She had been able to work with this and now reported feeling more complete, self-aware, and empowered. In my experience, the body parts are quite forgiving and not emotionally complicated, making clear and simple requests for comfort and health. Of course, there are exceptions, and our more developed subpersonalities can take up residence in parts of the body and be difficult to differentiate until we ask them directly about their role in the system.

The insights of polyvagal theory, developed by Stephen Porges and elaborated by Deb Dana in the book The Polyvagal Theory in Therapy, can also be very helpful when attuning to the body in the context of sexuality. Learning to recognize the state of the autonomic nervous system brings us into closer connection with it as well as with the parts who may have triggered its response. We can gain the trust of our system when we are willing to slow down, assess the safety and comfort of our external situation, and take appropriate self-protective measures such as locking the door or leaving. We can also befriend the part or parts that have triggered the system, getting to know what activated them and seeing what they might need to feel safe and connected. In her book Somatic IFS, Susan McConnell offers many ways for clients and therapists to increase their embodiment by attending to breath, awareness, resonance, movement and touch. These practices as well as other somatic approaches can greatly enhance access to Self in the context of sexuality.

3. Education about Human Sexuality

There are many areas in which education about human sexuality can help to cultivate Self-Led Sexuality. As mentioned above, therapy training programs would do well to close the educational gap for therapists so that more of us could feel confident and prepared. The general public also lacks consistent access to comprehensive sex education, at least in the United States where according to the Sexuality Information and Education Council of the United States (SIECUS) in their July 2022 Sex Ed State Law and Policy Chart, only 29 states and the District of Colombia require sex education, 16 states provide abstinence-only sex education, and 6 states explicitly require instruction that discriminates against LGBTQIA+ people.

Limited access to accurate sexual health information leaves pornography and spotty online sources to fill the gap for many, placing people at higher risk for burdening through misinformation, distorted expectations, and the impact of negative outcomes such as unwanted pregnancy, STIs, and nonconsensual sexual contact. When people lack sexual knowledge, they can get hurt and hurt others.

I have found that some parts in the internal system can be quite knowledgeable about sexuality while other parts in the same system are not, having been siloed in their jobs or frozen in time. I have worked with clients who are professional sex educators who retrieved parts in their systems that knew nothing about sex or carried heavy burdens of shame for having sexual curiosity. In instances like these, the sex education happens between the client's Self and the part, often during the updating or do-over, with my support if needed. I have learned to titrate sexual information to the minimal amount that a part needs to clear its burden, such as learning that a child isn't responsible for an adult's sexual behavior or that the appearance of their genitals is in the normal range. Once the system has unburdened, curious parts may actively seek out and absorb quality sex education resources.

4. Advancing Sexual Justice

Self-Led Sexuality cannot be cultivated without an eye to the outside world. Our parts must feel safe in order to unblend and allow Self to emerge. They are highly attuned to messages of safety or threat from within and without and can easily absorb beliefs from the collective about their value, sexually and otherwise. These may affirm them or, instead, weigh them down with shame and self-loathing, which make it harder for them to feel worthy of love, even from Self.

Obviously, the laws of the land and the social conditions in which we live directly impact the expression of a person's sexuality. If a person is not legally permitted to marry the one they love, to have access to reproductive healthcare, or to walk down the street without being harassed, their health and well-being is jeopardized. Impacts are multiplied when the person holds other identities that additionally marginalize them, such as their race, sexual orientation, gender identity, immigrant status, body size, or abilities. In response, the person's protectors may try to limit their visibility, restrict their sexual activities, or even suggest self-harm as a coping strategy.

Self-led sexual expression can also be impacted by social and economic hardship due to factors such as financial anxiety, working multiple jobs that leave little time for sleep and connection with family, lack of privacy in crowded living spaces, and limited access to the nourishment and healthcare that put us at our sexual best.

Our personal healing is furthered by those who affirm us and advocate for what we need in larger society. As our internal systems heal and we have access to more Self-energy, we may feel more connectedness to others and more courage to step out and speak up to rectify the injustices that we see in the world.

5. Journeys of Exploration

Rather than just thinking about our sexuality, the Self-Led Sexuality model encourages conscious behavioral exploration as a way to surface sex parts, identify sexual trailheads, and enjoy pleasant sensations. Journeys of Exploration begin with ascertaining consent and can include just about anything when approached with an intention of getting to know our internal sexual system better. Simply noticing the rhythm of our breath, visualizing a desired activity, mindfully applying body lotion, or dancing to a favorite sexy song might illuminate parts or just feel enjoyable. Looking at our genitals in the mirror, initiating a courageous conversation about sex with a partner, or engaging in sensual and sexual touch activities are additional examples. Journeys might be guided, solo, or partnered and can range from mild to wild, incorporating varying levels of challenge, explicit sexuality and edgier sexual practices as desired, all within a framework of ongoing parts awareness and consent processes.

Internal Sexual Systems

As we move through the lifespan, our sex parts develop and form a complex system of interactions among themselves. I started to refer to this subset of the larger internal system as the internal sexual system and became curious about its dynamics. I saw that parts have jobs in it and most of these jobs go unnoticed unless something goes wrong. For instance, we may not be aware of parts that manage body functions such as menstruation, personal hygiene, or continence unless there is an embarrassing lapse which might provoke an anxious manager, shaming critic, or humiliated exile.

The parts represented in the internal sexual system might be the same parts that readily show up in other areas of life, like a part that criticizes our sexual performance might be the same part that criticizes how much we ate for dinner or how much money we earn, or a part that feels distant and detached in many situations could show up during sexual activity with the same qualities. Or a part that doesn't show up at other times may activate only when asked to perform an act it finds distasteful or only immediately after orgasm. I developed an exercise to help people to find parts that show up before, during, and after a sexual engagement after recognizing that so many of my clients seemed to encounter quite different parts at those phases. My client Marta discovered she had a flirty protector of a depressed child part who would urgently initiate sexual hook-ups, a dominant part that happily took over during sexual interaction, and then a harsh critic who would show up immediately after, her shaming energy landing upon the depressed child part who would feel even more despairing. When she could recognize this sequence of parts, she was better able to work with this exile so that her protectors could soften and become more collaborative, allowing for a more Self-led sexual experience.

I have also seen that different parts can show up in different sexual contexts, such as when giving versus receiving sexual attention, when alone versus with partners, or when with someone new versus a long-term mate. Given the complex interactions of so many layers of parts, the internal sexual system can be quite complex, and the Self qualities of patience and persistence can be helpful during the befriending process. And just like the larger internal system, the internal sexual system can be burdened, Self-led, or somewhere in between, and the extremeness of the roles parts take on will vary accordingly. Let's take a closer look at common dynamics in burdened and unburdened sexual systems.

ACTIVITY:
IDENTIFYING DYNAMICS IN THE INTERNAL SEXUAL SYSTEM

1. List 10 reasons that a person might choose to engage in sexual activity.
2. List 10 reasons that a person might choose not to engage in sexual activity.
3. Which of these reasons seem likely to be Part-Led?
4. Which of these reasons seem likely to be Self-Led?
5. Do some seem more driven by physiological factors? Explain.
6. Do proactive Managers or reactive Firefighters seem likely to be motivating particular reasons on each list? Explain.
7. What types of vulnerable parts might be present?
8. Did you notice anything about your own parts during this activity? Describe.

Ultimately, we would need to find and ask a part what motivates it, but this quick activity can help you to consider some possible dynamics in a person's internal sexual system.

Burdened Sexual Systems

While few of us get through life without acquiring any sexual burdens, I use the term burdened sexual systems to describe those which have accumulated particularly heavy loads that negatively impact the experience of sexuality over an extended period of time. The burdened parts are often exiled by extreme protectors who try to keep their toxic loads from flooding the system. Manager parts may become highly rigid, controlling, critical, or perfectionistic, and firefighter parts may impulsively binge, distract, dissociate, argue, or shut down. These protectors may turn toward some aspect of sexuality as a resource to do their jobs or may do just about anything to avoid sexuality if it feels too threatening.

The sexual system can become burdened in many ways including but not limited to the following:

1. Sexual violation.
2. Sharing burdens held in the larger internal system that were accrued through nonsexual life experiences but that impact sexuality.
3. Painful or confusing sexual experiences.
4. Shaming responses to sexuality, personally or through observation.
5. Charged moral conflicts and polarizations.
6. Medical trauma or illness.
7. Intergenerational and collective legacy burdens.
8. Oppressive sexual scripts from family, religion, and society.

Some common sexual burdens that exiles may hold include feelings of shame, guilt, and loneliness, believing that pleasure is bad or that they don't deserve it, or that they are unlovable. They may believe that they only exist to serve others, are invisible, or are bad, dirty, or disgusting. Exiles might believe that they are too much or not enough in the eyes of others, or that they are fundamentally broken. They may have inherited legacy burdens from parents and ancestors that impact sexuality such as the belief that sex is sinful, or that a "real" man takes what he wants. Protector parts can hold burdens related to things that they were forced to do to protect the system or feelings of failure for not preventing bad things from happening. These are just a sampling of the heavy loads that burdened parts and systems might carry.

The unburdening protocols of the IFS model work just as well with sexual issues as they do in other areas. When Self can witness burdened parts, their loads can be released, clearing the way for further healing and collaboration of the internal sexual system.

Self-Led Sexual Systems

A Self-Led Sexual System is one where there is ready access to the qualities of Self, and any burdens that are present do not consistently block or prevent desired aspects of sexuality. In a Self-led system, parts are free to take on their natural or preferred roles and can express their own feelings and desires. Self-led sexual managers can serve important functions such as monitoring safety and comfort, ensuring safe sex practices including consent communication, protecting values and commitments, initiating and facilitating sexual activities, and implementing strategies to raise or lower arousal such as fantasy or conscious breathing. When able to trust fully, Self-led sexual managers can let go, say yes, step back, and allow sensation to flow.

Whereas in a burdened system, firefighters may knock the metaphorical door down, Self-led sexual firefighters can be less extreme, ringing the inner doorbell and waiting for permission from Self before doing their jobs. They might engage in sexual activity to self-soothe, distract from physical or emotional pain, meet urgent needs for connection or for the pleasure of sexual gratification. They also can show up with the consent of the system to shut down or prevent sexual feelings quickly, such as feelings that might pose a threat to someone vulnerable.

Self-led young parts, no longer burdened and exiled, can play, be seen and known. They may have their own sexual energy or emotions to express in a sexual scenario, or, instead, prefer to go somewhere else that is safe and comfortable. Self-led young parts may find an age mate in a partner's system with whom they can babytalk or be silly. When our subpersonalities relax and unblend, the physical body in a Self-led sexual system may be able to function in a more harmonious manner, more flowing and fluid, allowing sensations to build and naturally subside without interference. The body's needs, desires, and preferences are noticed, and the arousal cycle can occur in accordance with developmental and biological capacities.

And what about Self? Everyone has a Self, and the Self can and should lead the individual's internal sexual system. The 8 Cs (Curiosity, Confidence, Compassion, Courage, Clarity, Creativity, Calm, Connectedness) and the 5 Ps (Presence, Patience, Persistence, Perspective, Playfulness) have relevance to sexual experience and expression. Self can welcome a variety of parts to bathe in sexual energy, blend, and be fully embodied and vocalized if desired. Self can speak for parts with concerns and is accepting of varied outcomes.

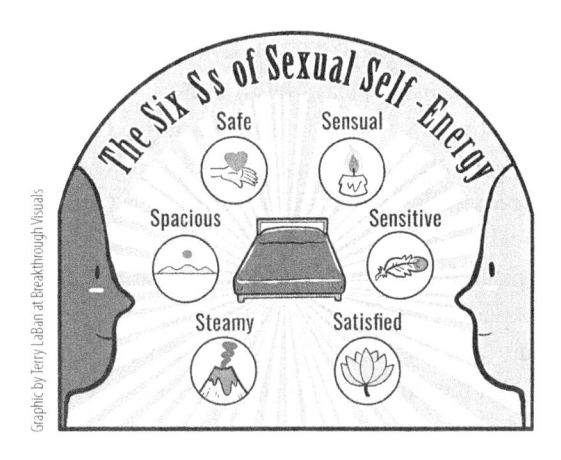

The Six Ss of Sexual Self-Energy

As parts unblend and unburden, constraints to embodied Self-Energy are released. It may be experienced as having the following six qualities.

1. **Safe:** Self-Energy moves toward healing and wholeness, not hurt or harm of oneself or others.
2. **Sensual:** When permitted, Self-Energy flows freely through the body in an enlivening way and welcomes pleasant sensations.
3. **Spacious:** When parts unblend and unburden, Self-Energy can spread throughout and beyond the body, free of constraint or constriction.
4. **Sensitive:** Self-Energy is highly attuned and aware, able to perceive subtle emotional and physical shifts in oneself and others.
5. **Steamy:** Self-Energy can warm the system and support emotional and physical states of arousal.
6. **Satisfied:** Self-Energy can be present to the body's experience without agenda. It does not need a particular outcome to feel complete.

The Six Ss initially occurred to me as I began to teach about IFS and Sexuality. It felt helpful to more easily recognize qualities of Self-Energy that correspond to sexuality, and hopeful to know that these attributes of Self are within us already, accessible as we release constraints. This is different than additive or performative approaches to sexuality and has been very helpful to people who carry burdens of feeling sexually broken. The expression of these qualities might occur in unconventional ways that do not require the functioning of any specific body part.

I found that the Ss could also serve to detect parts that come between us and each of these qualities of Self-Energy. For example, parts not trusting the first S (that Sexual Self-Energy is Safe) might come into focus and open up an area of the system in need of healing. Or parts not allowing the second S, the Sensual aspect of Self-Energy, might carry legacies related to scarcity such as previous generations who suffered hunger passing down values of abstinence and frugality as well as beliefs that sensual pleasure is frivolous or downright dangerous.

As I worked with the Ss as Parts Detectors, I noticed that there seemed to be a sequence from one S to the next and that it tracked with deepening intimacy and eroticism. It seemed that when the system could trust that Self-Energy is Safe, the Sensual qualities of Self-Energy could come into awareness, sometimes felt as soft or warm or pulsating and also as the capacity to more fully savor pleasant sensory experience such as scent or touch. The Self quality of Sensuality could open up Spaciousness as parts relax further, and in that openness Self's Sensitivity might bloom and circulate. Deeper ripples might flow enabling Steaminess to build. The energies of Self embodied can move and dance and play, and passion may rise, a plume of erotic feeling or emotional intensity or deep love, possibly but not necessarily including the arousal of the genitals and climax. And the Self quality of Satisfied reminds us that whatever happens, when Self is at the center, it is enough, that Self was already Satisfied and does not have an agenda for a specific sexual outcome. So, in this sense, the six Ss track along with the progression of entering, experiencing, and exiting a sexual experience.

The Six Ss are relevant to non-sexual contexts as well. They can help us to find and unblend parts, allowing the flow of our life force energy, which might be expressed through deep non-sexual love, art, prayer, athleticism, or other ways. The Six Ss are an extension that I am bringing to the descriptions of Self-Energy as defined in the IFS model, and I am still discovering their applications.

Behold and Lead your Internal Sexual System (BLISS)

By this point, you may feel interest in better knowing your own internal sexual system. There are many ways to begin this inquiry. You might take a moment right now to notice what parts are here as you finish this chapter. I have provided a graphic where you can note these or other parts that show up in relation to a sexual trailhead or trigger (Appendix A).

I have also developed individual and group journeys to BLISS framed by the Six Ss and integrating the five methods for cultivating Self-Led Sexuality. These offer a multitude of ways for people to explore the aspects of their sexual system that most interest them. You can find additional resources in the following section. I am grateful for the honor, challenge, and opportunity of sharing my work with you here and wish you well on your IFS journey.

KEY TAKEAWAYS

- Sexuality is an important aspect of life, and worthy of conscious exploration.
- An ethical IFS therapist can remain within their scope of practice while welcoming exploration of sexual issues, provided that they are aware of their own limitations and know when a referral to a specialist may be needed.
- Parts have roles in the internal sexual system and can be burdened or Self-led.
- Self can not only heal and harmonize the system but also offers qualities of being Safe, Sensual, Spacious, Sensitive, Steamy, and Satisfied.
- You can learn to Behold and Lead your Internal Sexual System (BLISS), a process which invites you on an evolving journey toward healing, pleasure and empowerment.

AUTHOR BIO

Patricia Rich, LCSW, CST-S (she/her) is a Certified IFS Therapist, an IFS Approved Clinical Consultant, and an AASECT Certified Sex Therapist and Supervisor. She fell in love with IFS in 2011, has completed Level 3, and has served as a Program Assistant. She has developed a unique integrative model for helping people to feel more ease, joy and confidence in the realm of sexuality and has originated IFS-informed concepts such as Internal Consent and The Six Ss of Sexual Self-Energy. Patty has presented at the IFS Annual Conference, taught a module for the IFS Institute Online Continuity program and led workshops internationally. She offers training and consultation to professionals and offers opportunities for therapists and insight-oriented folks to Behold and Lead their Internal Sexual Systems (BLISS). She lives in the Philadelphia area where she also has a private practice. You can learn more about her offerings at www.patriciarich.com.

GOING DEEPER

From Patricia Rich

1) Website and Social:
   a. www.patriciarich.com
      i. Individual and Group Coaching Programs
      ii. Clinical Consultation
      iii. Experiential Learning Groups
      iv. Sex Therapy and Supervision
      v. IFS Education and Development
      vi. Free Six Ss of Sexual Self-Energy Graphic: www.patriciarich.com/6sgraphic
   b. Facebook Group: Self-Led Sexuality with Patricia Rich. www.facebook.com/groups/selfledsexualitywithpatriciarich
   c. Instagram: patriciarichconsulting

2) Online Workshops:
   a. Online Continuity Program: *Self-Led Sexuality for Healing, Pleasure and Empowerment* with Patricia Rich and Dr. Richard Schwartz. www.courses.ifs-institute.com/item/selfled-sexuality-ifs-based-model-healing-pleasure-empowerment-65455
   b. Life Architect: *Self-Led Sexuality*: www.lifearchitect.com/self-led-sexuality/

3) Speaking Topics:
   a. Introduction to IFS for Sexuality Professionals.
   b. Self-Led Sexuality for Healing, Pleasure, and Empowerment.
   c. Internal Consent: A Foundation for Safety and Pleasure in the Bedroom and Beyond.
   d. Behold and Lead your Internal Sexual System (BLISS).
   e. Self-Led Sexuality for IFS Professionals.
   f. Behold and Lead your Internal Sexual System (BLISS) Facilitator.

4) Podcast Interviews:
   a. The One Inside. www.theoneinside.libsyn.com/ifs-and-self-led-sexuality-with-patricia-rich
   b. IFS Talks. www.internalfamilysystems.pt/multimedia/webinars/sexuality-through-ifs-lens-patricia-rich

From Other Sources

1) Websites:
   a. American Association for Sexuality Educators, Counselors and Therapists (AASECT). To find professional help or to become certified go to www.aasect.org.
   b. Society for Sex Therapy and Research (SSTAR). www.sstarnet.org
   c. SIECUS: Sex Ed for Social Change. www.siecus.org
   d. World Association for Sexual Health. www.worldsexualhealth.net

2) Books:
   a. Dana, D., & Porges, S. W. (2018). *The polyvagal theory in therapy: Engaging the rhythm of regulation.* W. W. Norton and Company.
   b. Herbine-Blank, T., Kerpelman, D. M., & Sweezy, M. (2016). *Intimacy from the inside out: Courage and compassion in couple therapy.* Routledge.
   c. McConnell, S. (2020). *Somatic Internal Family Systems therapy: Awareness, breath, resonance, movement and touch in practice.* North Atlantic Books.
   d. Rosenberg, L. C. (2013). Welcoming all erotic parts: Our reactions to the sexual and using polarities to enhance erotic excitement. In *Internal Family Systems therapy: New dimensions* (pp. 166-185). Routledge.
   e. Schwartz, R. C. (2013). *Revealing our many selves in the bedroom.* Psychotherapy Networker.
   f. Schwartz, R. C. (2018). *You are the one you've been waiting for.* Trailheads Publication.
   g. Wonder, N. (2013). Treating pornography addiction with IFS. In *Internal Family Systems therapy: New dimensions* (pp. 159-165). Routledge.

522 o ALTOGETHER US

APPENDIX A

Unblending Sex Parts Worksheet

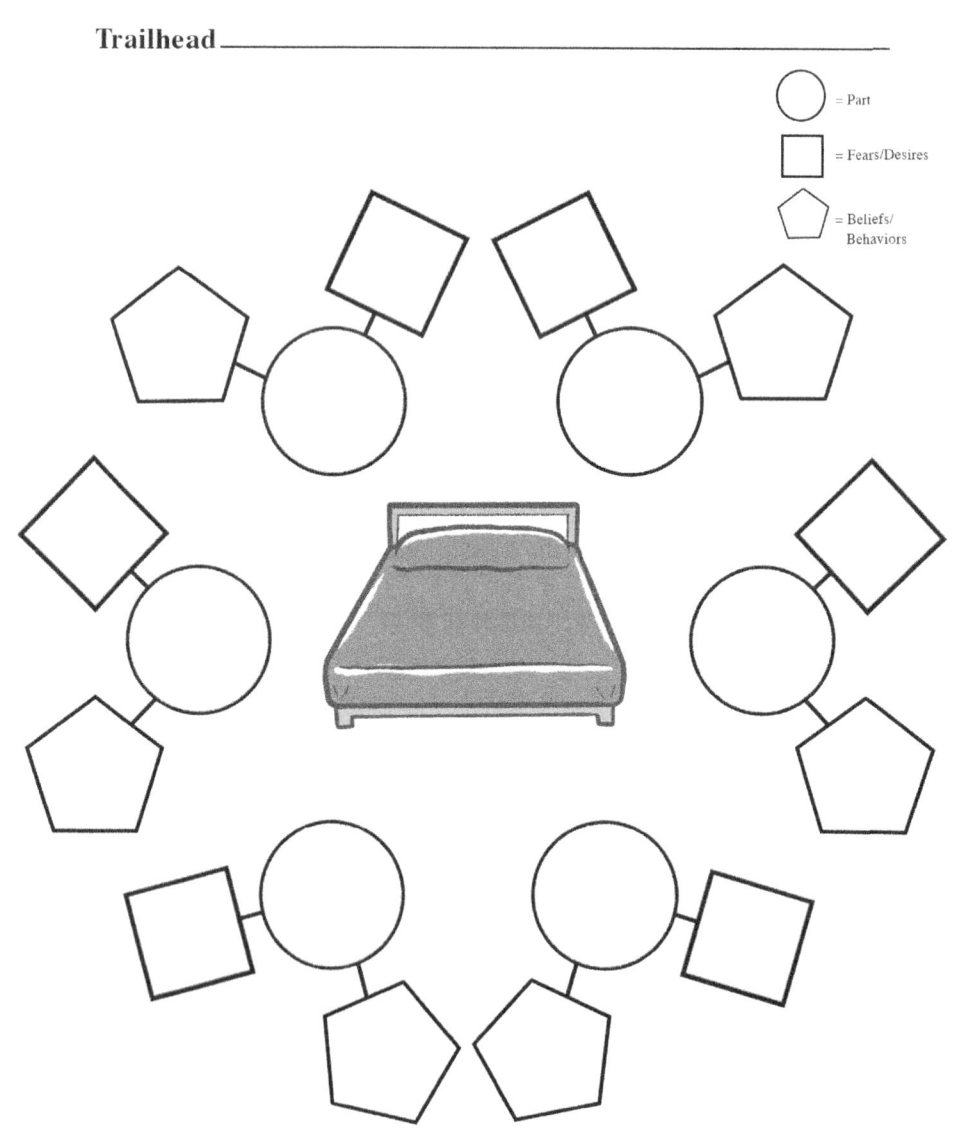

Trailhead _____

◯ = Part

▢ = Fears/Desires

⬠ = Beliefs/Behaviors

©Patricia Rich LCSW, CST
www.patriciarich.com

IFS AND COUPLES

RELEASING SELF-TO-SELF CONNECTION

Mona Barbera, PhD
With contributions by Toni Herbine-Blank, MSN, RN
and Martha Sweezy, PhD

I have had the pleasure and adventure of practicing couples therapy for 27 years, IFS couples therapy for 22 years, and authoring an award-winning book on IFS and couples titled *Bring Yourself to Love: How Couples Can Turn Disconnection into Intimacy*. As an Assistant Trainer with the IFS Institute, I have had the privilege of facilitating Level 1 and 2 trainings, teaching over a thousand clinicians to become skillful in practicing IFS therapy.

My enduring desire has been to help couples get out of disconnected loops, tepid connection, and destructive fighting, and to resolve conflicts as quickly as possible, so that they can love, support, energize, soothe, and support each other in the deep knowing and being known of the path of love. And it has been my experience that IFS is the best way to get there.

IFS couples therapy helps partners access their most potent problem solver: Self-energy. It helps partners befriend and harmonize all their parts, so they can most wisely respond to relationship challenges. IFS helps couples unburden the hurt parts that drive them to defensive and destructive behavior, and unleashes the wisdom, connection, compassion, and creativity they need to go forward as partners in the luminous dance of love.

IFS's revolutionary view of human functioning opens an entirely positive lens for working with couples in conflict.

Core Principles of IFS

Three core principles of the IFS model inform the IFS couples' approach:

1. Self qualities are universal, innate, and indestructible.

The IFS model proposes that everyone has an undamaged Self at their core. As a result, individuals can be loving, skillful, securely attached, and Self-led no matter their personal history. Awareness of this inner healing essence opens great creativity and hope in the transformation of painful cycles of conflict and blame.

Since Self qualities are innate, IFS couples therapy focuses on releasing love, healthy attachment, and problem-solving abilities rather than on building, developing, or teaching them. This applies to everyone, regardless of trauma or attachment injuries. The more IFS couples therapists believe that Self qualities are innate and available, the more effective they will be.

2. Protectors are well-intentioned but ineffective.

Protective parts take on roles to try to help with pain, and they are typically unaware that Self is present, and more effectively able to handle relationship challenges. Burdened protectors are trapped in the past, are stuck repeating ineffective "solutions," and often evoke the opposite response than they desire. For example, if protectors hope that "educating" will help their partners change, they find that partners resist, argue, and feel spoken down to. If they get loud and forceful in hopes of being heard, they find that partners shut down and hear less. If they distance in an attempt to create safety, they wind up feeling overlooked and alone.

There are often multiple protectors in a client's system. One protector may want to get angry, another to be distant and cold, a third to give up. They tend to alternate, leaving the person jumping between different tactics to try and get their needs met but looping and getting nowhere.

3. Exiles trapped in the past drive the behavior of burdened protectors.

The pain of vulnerable parts, called exiles, drives the behavior of burdened protectors. Exiles' pain is so overwhelming that protectors pursue their jobs urgently, trying to prevent the flooding of negative emotions that occurs when exiles become triggered.

An angry protector that escalates and yells may be trying to prevent the triggering of an exile that feels ignored or dismissed. A protector that analyzes and lectures may be trying to prevent the triggering of an exile that feels misunderstood. A numbing protector that shuts down feelings may be trying to prevent a flood of exile emotion from becoming triggered and overwhelming the system.

IFS couples therapists understand that protectors are rarely willing to stop doing their jobs until exiles get help from Self, which is a transformational IFS insight. The unburdening of exiles, when done with permission and safety, is key to releasing protectors from their harmful roles and freeing the couple from hurtful patterns.

Uniqueness of IFS Couples Therapy

IFS offers an empowering, non-pathologizing approach to working with couples, and unique principles guide the way.

Self as Primary Healer. The goal of IFS couples therapy is to release Self-energy in one or both partners so that they can access Self qualities (creativity, confidence, connection, calm, clarity, curiosity, compassion, and courage) and ultimately resolve their problems from a place of Self-leadership. Clients' own Self-energy, rather than the insight of the therapist or any external intervention, is the primary healing force. IFS therapists believe that the skills needed for healthy relating emerge on their own when Self-energy is present.

Systems Are Behind Conflict. The IFS couples therapist has confidence that there is a system of parts that operates behind any relationship difficulty and that Self can form relationships with, and heal, all the parts of the system. Protectors are waiting to be found, understood, and appreciated and exiles are waiting to be known, witnessed, and relieved of their hurt. IFS couples therapy proposes that all the parts in the couple's system have positive intent. Whatever behavior a partner exhibits, no matter how defensive, passive, hopeless, manipulative, or distant, is always understood to be a protector with a positive intent and a story to tell. IFS couples therapists do not ask partners to start or stop behaviors because they know that the industrious protectors driving these behaviors are trying to help, and they need to be witnessed and understood before they can be released from their onerous jobs.

Once partners recognize and have relationships with the protectors and the exiles they protect, they can begin to access Self-energy, speaking for their experience with connection, calm, compassion, and curiosity. Toxic, hypervigilant protector cycles are replaced by the connection, compassion, and creativity of a Self-to-Self relationship.

The Role of the Therapist. The role of the IFS couples therapist is to bring their own Self-energy to the couple, to track the couple's parts as they engage in conflict, and to interrupt conflictual cycles by inviting partners to get to know any activated parts that arise. When enough safety is present, IFS therapists help partners witness and unburden exiles and protectors and to speak *for* their parts (when unblended) rather than speaking *from* them (when blended). The Self of the therapist holds deep compassion for all the client's parts, even when the jobs they are doing are unpleasant, harmful, or even dangerous. The therapist's Self knows that underneath any unproductive behavior lies a positive and good part that has simply gotten stuck in an unhelpful role. Equally importantly, the therapist's Self realizes that the most effective way to help these parts transform is to bring them into relationship with Self's compassion and curiosity.

Since IFS therapists need to bring their own Self-energy to sessions, they must stay aware of their own parts. They are necessarily engaged in their own ongoing parts work, regularly bringing their own healing Self-energy to their parts. Typical therapist parts may want to analyze, teach, find solutions, or judge. Therapists invite these parts to step back so the Self of the therapist can direct the session. Part of the power of Self is that it holds no judgment, doesn't analyze, and trusts that couples can find their own solutions. If judging, fixing, or analyzing parts become triggered, they are understood to be "trailheads" for the therapist's own personal IFS work.

Hence, IFS couples therapists avoid analyzing, advising, or teaching, and instead support and trust the Self of each partner to bring robust, creative, and powerful solutions to the couple's problems. Even if Self-led solutions are the same as what the therapist would have offered, it is more empowering and respectful for them to come from the inner resources of the couple.

Rather than:	IFS Couples Therapists:
Analyze, suggest, educate, coach	Understand, appreciate and validate protectors for the positive intent behind their roles
Offer cognitive insight and guidance	Help clients access the experiential insight and guidance of Self
Foster secure attachment to the therapist	Foster internal secure attachment of Self to parts which will facilitate external secure attachment in the couple

Experiential Solutions. The IFS couples therapist invites the partners to interact with each other experientially, so their problems come alive in the room rather than speaking about their problems from managers' cognitive perspectives. The therapist might suggest that the couple choose one of the problems that brought them to therapy and talk about it, agreeing to let the therapist interrupt when parts emerge.

The IFS therapist invites the couple to interact authentically so that protectors become active, but not so much that protectors inflict damage. When parts are active, the therapist interrupts the couple's cycle of conflict, inviting each partner (usually one at a time) to help their activated parts come into relationship with their inner Self, to be witnessed, appreciated, and eventually unburdened. This trust in the client's Selves is deeply empowering as clients discover that they carry their resources for change and hope within them.

Contraindications to Couples Therapy

As with any couples therapy approach, the initial assessment will determine whether couples therapy is an appropriate intervention. Couples work is usually contraindicated when there is:

- An ongoing affair.
- Active addiction or abuse.
- Lack of time or resources to invest and sustain momentum in therapy.

- Lack of motivation or commitment on the part of one or both partners.
- Unhealed, highly destabilizing trauma.
- Active divorce litigation.

Contracting for the IFS Work

After the assessment, IFS couples sessions begin with a working contract. The IFS therapist is clear that the clients' core Selves hold the answer to their habitual problems, not the therapist. The role of the therapist is to assist clients in detecting and unblending from their parts in order to access the inner Self-energy and wisdom that will allow them to resolve their challenges with clarity, confidence, and connection. Clients agree that the therapist will be a "parts detector" and will pause the interactions when client parts emerge in order to assist with unblending and getting to know the parts and their positively intentioned role in the couple dance.

The Flow of an IFS Couples Session

After assessment and contracting, IFS couples sessions follow a typical flow:

1. **Therapists access their own Self-energy.** The therapist notices if anything is in the way of their Self-energy being present. Are they judging a partner? Do they feel bored and hopeless? Are they tempted to analyze and fix? Are they questioning their competence? If the therapist is feeling anything other than the 8 C qualities of Self, the therapist attends to their own parts, in order to bring their greatest therapeutic resource—Self-energy—into the session.

    That being said, therapists' own parts can function like inner coaches or advisors. Projection, transference, and countertransference become rich resources. Therapists pay attention to which of their own parts are becoming activated to gather non-verbal information below the level of awareness. Parts evoke parts, so when therapists notice their own parts becoming activated within, they recognize it may be a valuable clue to which parts of their clients might have become activated.

2. **Therapists invite, and skillfully interrupt, conflictual pattern enactment in session.** Rather than talking *about* their challenges, couples are invited to allow their protector parts to emerge in real time by beginning to enact their repetitive conflict. When parts become activated, they are more available to work with in the moment. IFS therapists pause interactions when burdened parts emerge and offer help unblending.

    As mentioned, it is important for couples to get into their protective cycles in the session, but not so deeply that they cause damage. The timing of the therapist's "interruption" is therefore critical, and therapists need to be aware if they have parts that wait too long to interrupt protectors or parts that interrupt too quickly before the client's protectors are activated.

Parts that interrupt quickly may be picking up on a partner's desperation for help or perhaps trying to prove the therapist's competence. Parts that wait too long to interrupt may be picking up on fragility, lack of clarity about the problem, or feeling insecure about skillfulness with the IFS model. The IFS therapist's Self will most effectively navigate the energy and the pacing of the interruptions.

3. **The therapist helps partners unblend and get to know protectors.** After being paused, one partner at a time gets to know their activated protectors, understanding and appreciating them. Unblending and witnessing proceed according to the pace and capacity of both partners' systems. Partners have real-time dialogues with their protectors to understand and appreciate their efforts, developing compassion for the difficult roles protective parts have been stuck in. Clients learn what fears are driving their protective parts and gain awareness of the pain of the exiles that drive these protector sequences.

   The therapist often begins after pausing the couple by offering hope ("Would you like it if you could get your point across without criticism?" "Would you like it if he/she did that, and you didn't have to get so angry?" "Would you like it if you could express your concerns but still remain connected?" "What if you could stay present, clear, calm, and grounded even if they keep doing that?"). When the partners accept this invitation, the therapist invites them to unblend from their activated parts in order to bring more Self-energy to the challenging situation.

Sam and Ella:
A Demonstration of Unblending

Sam and Ella (all names in this chapter are changed to protect confidentiality) were in a conversation about how Sam takes care of the finances and becomes irritated when Ella asks for financial information. As the conversation evolved in session, Sam became annoyed and defensive. Since annoyance and defensiveness are not Self qualities, the therapist knew a protective part was present and paused the interaction.

> **Therapist:** "Could I pause you here for just a moment? Sam, I'm wondering if you would you like it if you could remain calm when Ella asks you for financial information?"
>
> **Sam:** "Yeah, I guess I would."
>
> **Therapist:** "Okay then, could you take a minute to notice how you feel right now?"

Sam: "Defensive."

Therapist: "Do you notice that defensiveness anywhere specific in your body? Is it in one place or all over?"

Sam: "It's in my chest."

Therapist: "What's it doing?"

Sam: "It's tight."

Therapist: "How do you feel toward it?"

Sam: "Curious." (evidence of some Self-energy)

Therapist: "Could you take a minute to listen to that defensiveness? Does it have anything to say to you?"

Sam: "It says: 'I need to do the finances by myself, the right way.'"

Therapist: "Can you keep listening? What is it afraid would happen if it didn't take you over and cause you to feel defensive?"

Sam: (with feeling) "It's afraid I'd be a financial failure like my single mother. She did the best she could, but she didn't manage the finances well. Even though she made more money than me, she still ended up poor and couldn't pay the bills. It was embarrassing. When I take care of the finances, and we have enough to pay the bills and save, it's a feeling of success., I'm reassured that I am not like my mother."

Therapist: "So, the defensiveness is trying to help protect you from failure, is that right?"

Sam: "Yeah, I didn't realize that."

Therapist: "Can you send some appreciation to it for how hard it is trying to help?"

Here we see that the therapist helped Sam notice his activated protector, develop awareness of the somatic presentation of the protector (tension in his chest), witness the defensive part with Self-energy (curiosity), and learn that the positive intent of the defensiveness was to help him be successful and avoid being unable to pay the bills like his mother. This awareness allowed the tension to soften and the defensive part to realize Ella was not actually a threat. Sam was able to rejoin the conversation with curiosity and receptiveness.

Many experiential exercises can be helpful in assisting client's unblending as well, one of which follows:

EXPERIENTIAL EXERCISE: UNBLENDING BY MOVING AROUND THE ROOM

This exercise is designed to help couples unblend from, and connect with, parts.

1. Ask the couple to stand in the center of the room in a way that feels good: "Be together like you are when you are really happy together."

2. Ask the couple what might happen to get them out of that place, to lose the flow, connection, or happiness. They might say, "When I tell him that I feel hurt," "When he is controlling," "When she forgets to do stuff for the kids or she is late," or "When she isn't happy with me." Have them select one scenario.

3. Ask one person to say what starts the disconnection, from their point of view. This will be the "active" partner. I might say, "Let's just take it from one person's point of view and see how they experience it, even if you don't agree that's how it happens. We can go with the other point of view another time."

4. The active partner tells the other one what to say to begin the disconnection, including the tone and body posture. The receiving partner does what they are told as much as possible, playing along with the active partner's perception.

5. Ask the active partner to notice how they feel physically, what words they hear in their head, or what they see. (This is the Find and Focus part of the 6 Fs).

6. The active partner chooses a place in the room to feel, think, and speak from one part. They stay there as long as it takes to experience and express this part. (This is the beFriending part of the 6 Fs).

7. To find the next part in the system ask, "When you are done feeling like this, what happens next?" "Do you argue with yourself about this?" or "Does anyone else inside have a different opinion?" The active partner moves to another spot in the room for this second part and gets to know it.

8. Repeat this for as many parts as are present.

9. Ask, "Is there a vulnerability that these parts are protecting?" "What would happen if these parts didn't do what they do?" "What are they afraid would happen if they didn't (explain, argue, give up, judge, drink, threaten to leave)?" "Is there a vulnerable part hidden behind their behavior?" (This is the Fear part of the 6 Fs that reveals the exile).

10. The active partner goes to another location in the room and connects with the identified exile, learning about its experiences and beliefs.

11. The couple comes back together. The receiving partner talks about their experience of watching, and they revisit the original disconnecting situation, perhaps coming up with ways to do it differently.

4. **The therapist continuously assesses whether partners can offer each other connection, compassion, and curiosity.** As partners drop into deeper vulnerability, it's increasingly important that the witnessing partner is present, attentive, and compassionate. In order to offer a safe experience for all parts, the witnessing partner must have a critical mass of Self-energy present. If they do not, the therapist helps the witnessing partner unblend before proceeding with vulnerable exile work (if the witnessing partner cannot access Self, the therapist does not proceed with vulnerable exiles and instead returns to protector work).

5. **One partner at a time has an experiential relationship with an exile.** Often, lasting change requires one or both partners to get to know and unburden their exiles. That's because protectors usually don't give up their jobs until they know Self is able to take care of exiles. Safety, in the form of the witnessing partner's Self-energy, is a critical element for exile work to proceed.

   Most partners are not used to being seen in their most vulnerable states in connection with deeply wounded exiles, as they describe hurtful scenes from the past with raw emotion. They can be shocked that this is possible and that their partners can know them this deeply and still love them. Revealing their deepest shame and wounding and looking into the kind, connected, and compassionate eyes of a life partner can be immensely healing.

   When exiles are triggered in couples therapy, most people believe their partner's behavior is causing the pain. They think the partner's criticism, for example, makes them feel dismissed and unworthy, or the partner's lack of attention makes them feel unimportant or disempowered. When they learn that these circumstances, while not pleasant, are also triggering old feelings held by their exiles, the focus can shift from criticizing the partner to bringing healing to parts. This allows them to effectively address their own pain, while speaking calmly and effectively to their partner about their complaints.

Thomas and Serena: A Conversation to Connect with Exiles

Thomas and Serena had several good connections and touching moments in couples therapy but reverted to distance and criticism at home. It was clear that they needed to connect with their exiles before they could experience more robust change.

Therapist: "Where would you like to start today?"

Serena: "How about with the conflict we had the other night? It doesn't feel resolved."

Thomas: "Yeah, okay. I don't know what you were so upset about, anyway."

Serena: (with strident tone) "I can't trust you. You aren't open with your emotions. I don't feel close to you. When I talked to you about my feelings the other night you just looked blank."

Therapist: "Let me pause you there. Can we try something? Thomas, could you look blank like she thinks you were the other night?"

Serena: "That night he just put his face in his hands and looked down. I felt so alone."

Thomas: "I should do that now?"

Therapist: "Yes, if you could do it the way she thought you did, we'll see what happens with her."
Thomas puts his face in his hands and looks blankly down.

Therapist to Serena: "What's that like for you? What do you do want to do now?"

Serena: (leaning forward, nervous and shaky): "Come on, can you talk to me? What's wrong?"

Therapist: "Okay, let's find a place in the room for the part of you saying, 'Can you talk to me? What's wrong?'"

Serena moves across the room.

Therapist: "Can you listen to the part that reaches out? What does it want you to know?"

Serena: "The part says, 'I have to fix it.'"

Therapist: "'It has to fix it.' Can it tell us more about that?"

Serena: "It's saying if someone doesn't respond well when I ask for something, it makes me take it back and focus on their needs instead. If I take it back, then they won't get mad. It fixes things so people don't get mad (smiling). It says it is creative."

Therapist: "Yes, it is! It sounds like it's creative in trying to avoid people getting mad at you."

Serena: "It seems to be letting me know it's also trying to protect me from feeling bad."

Therapist: "So it's trying to protect a part of you that is feeling bad, is that right?"

Serena: "Yeah"

Therapist: "Thomas, are you able to be compassionate and open for a moment to allow Serena to be with the part that feels so bad?"

Thomas: "Yeah, absolutely. I'm so sorry there's a part that's feeling bad."

Therapist: "Okay, great. Serena, would you be willing to pick a place for the one that feels bad, the one this fixing part is trying to help?"

Serena moves to another spot and collapses.

Therapist: "How is this part that feels so bad doing?"

Serena: "This part that feels bad seems like me as a little girl. Kind of a 'Little Serena.' Little Serena never had a chance. She didn't even play with the other kids. She had no voice."

Therapist: "How is Little Serena responding to you?"

Serena (softly, with tears): "She notices me. She says she can't speak. People get too mad. She knows the fixer tries to help her. She likes the creative stuff."

Therapist: "Let's see how you respond to Little Serena."

Serena to Little Serena: "I'm getting how bad it was for you. Would you like to tell me more?"

Serena continues to witness the exile while the therapist quietly checks to confirm Thomas is present and open.

Therapist to Serena: "Is there anything else you would like to say to Little Serena?"

Serena: "I'm sorry you are hurting, and I'm here for you. You are not alone anymore."

Therapist: "Now that you are with Little Serena, is it okay if we go back to the scene with Thomas holding his head in his hands?"

Serena: "Yes."

Therapist: "I would like to ask the fixer part something directly. When we ask Thomas to hold his head in his hands again, would you be willing to notice that big Serena, in other words, Serena's Self, is taking care of Little Serena, and step back and let her handle this? Could you trust her to do that?"

Serena: "I think so. Fixer saw how I helped Little Serena feel better, and she seems to trust me now—like I can handle whatever happens."

Therapist: "Okay, ready for me to ask Thomas to hold his head and look down again?"

Serena: "Yes."

Thomas: Holds his head, looking down at nothing.

Serena: Silently observes Thomas.

Therapist: "How is that for you?"

Serena: "I feel abandoned."

Therapist: "Okay, let's see what Thomas does."

Thomas (looking up): "I am interested. What did you want to talk about?"

Serena's posture shifts and softens, but still shows skepticism.

Therapist to Serena: "How is it for you to hear that?"

Serena: "I see he is looking at me. I am not sure if I trust it."

Therapist: "How does it feel in your body?"

Serena (standing tall and calm): "Good. Curious."

After helping her exile (Little Serena) connect with her own inner compassionate Self-energy, Serena was able to remain centered and powerful as she observed Thomas. Her skepticism seemed grounded and realistic, not reactive. He became more interested, and she was tentatively receptive.

Serena's fixer part hadn't succeeded in engaging Thomas and even brought up one of his angry protectors. After Serena connected with her exile, she could be present, wisely assessing his openness without needing to fix it. This Self-led stance opened space in Thomas's parts to come toward her more.

GUIDELINES FOR EXILE WORK

- One partner works with exiles while the other witnesses. It is rarely possible to do the deeply attuned process of Self-to-exile relationship with both partners at the same time.
- The witnessing partner needs to be present, compassionate, connected, and kind.
- Always ask protectors for permission to go to exiles.
- The active partner feels, sees, or hears the exile directly. Connection with the exile is experiential. The person talks *with* the exile, not *about* it. Exiles need direct experience with Self.

- The relationship usually starts with the exile not knowing Self and often not initially trusting Self. This is a natural part of building the Self-to-part relationship. We let this happen and avoid telling the exile to trust.

- The exile almost always needs the person to know what happened to them, and what beliefs arose from those events. Allow as much time as needed for the exile to feel fully witnessed.

- Subtle protectors often show up when things get very tender. These protectors are often not as obvious as the ones that come up in the beginning. It's important for the therapist to notice when things change, even if it is an ambiguous feeling. Therapists can ask, "Did something just happen?" Or more directly, "Is another part trying to help?"

- Self-to-exile connection in couples therapy may not need to be as long and thorough as it is in individual therapy, perhaps because of the power of the collective Self-energy in the room. In other cases, Self-to-exile connection may need to happen multiple times with many exiles and many unburdenings. We know it has happened sufficiently when the couple becomes more able to connect to Self-energy outside of session and begins to discover their own Self-led solutions to their problems.

6. **Redo the initial conflict with more Self-energy.** Once protectors and exiles have been witnessed and Self-energy has been accessed, the therapist may bring the couple back to the original conflict for a redo, as was the case with Serena and Thomas. The therapist might observe, "Remember when he asked you to move the salad plate and you got so upset? What would you do or say now if he did that?" or "Now would you like to go back to that incident you were talking about when she was being forceful? What would you do now?"

    Since Self-energy is present, creativity flourishes, and people say and do brilliant things. With Self-energy present, the connection is often deep, light, spacious, humorous, connected, open-hearted, calm, and exciting. The couple can revisit the initial conflict with a clear perspective and find resolution more successfully.

7. **Prepare couples for possible protector snapback after the session.** IFS therapists know that it is critical to gain protector permission to work with exiles before doing the tender work. However, even when permission was given, protector snapback can occur. Protectors are used to doing their jobs, and even if something new and better has happened in the session, they might feel a pull to return to their previous roles. That could look like a fight on the way to the car or a partner feeling numb and shut down for a couple of days. Being prepared with the understanding that protectors might come back makes it less triggering if it happens. Since the therapist

won't be there to help, it's useful to normalize the potential protector activation, and provide couples with unblending tools to help them navigate protector snapback between sessions.

8. **Homework comes out of the work in the session.** It is helpful to ask the couple what was most useful in session and if they would like to commit to doing it at home a few times. For instance, if one partner calmed arguing parts in session, a therapist might suggest, "During the week, notice when your arguing parts emerge. Notice them before, during, or even after they get active. As we did today, notice them with gentleness, acknowledge their positive intentions, and ask them to step aside and let you handle it. Would you like to set a goal of doing this a certain number of times this week? Would it work to mark it on a calendar or paper so you can see how many times you did it?" This experiential homework builds on the new patterns established in session and promotes the growing Self-to-part relationships that will ultimately transform the couple dynamic.

9. **Ongoing Sessions: Momentum, Follow-Up, and Necessary Endings.** Once partners have experienced the power of unblending, developing relationships with protectors and exiles, and experiencing Self-energy it is important to keep the momentum going.

    One way to continue with vitality and focus is to ask the partners to speak to each other in session, instead of to the therapist. The couple might briefly talk about the impact of the last session, or what is important for them today, but it's most important for the partners systems to come alive in the room, and that happens best when they interact directly with each other. It can be helpful to ask them to talk to each other about how the week went, highs and lows, homework, or how they are doing with their original problem.

    The therapist listens for change—has there been a change in the original problem? Do the couples talk about fresh, new experiences? Have protectors come back quickly? If the couple isn't changing, are there other parts in the way? Are there unhealed exiles that need to be addressed to effect change?

    It is important to remember to check back in with the parts that were worked with in the previous session. Parts come to believe they matter when they experience regular connection, and this check in is critical to cementing their new roles and new relationships with Self. When parts are worked with in a session and then subsequently ignored, it often exacerbates their fears of abandonment and makes it harder for them to trust Self. Checking in with parts at the beginning of the next session, even if the work of the following session is orienting around a different topic, is critical to reinforcing the security of the developing Self-to-part relationships.

Sometimes when partners become more Self-led, they gain the clarity and courage to realize they need to separate. This can activate parts of the therapist that want to "help" and think that "help" means keeping the couple together. Therapists may have parts that want to avoid sadness and loss, or parts that fear a couple's separation is indicative of the therapist's "failure." It is natural for these types of parts to be activated, and it presents another "trailhead" for the therapist's personal work. IFS therapists remind their parts that "helping" can mean many things, and it's up to the partners to choose to stay together or leave each other. Witnessing sadness can be a great service. It can be a poignant, inspiring experience to be present with couples when they mourn their relationship. IFS therapists can help clients' parts grieve, move on, feel peace, and know they ended their relationship well.

In summary, IFS couples therapy is a powerful, non-pathologizing tool to help couples find the love they want. By experientially identifying and unblending from protectors and connecting with the exiles that drive them, client's systems open access to Self-led options that can deal with any type of conflict. Effective, connected, compassionate, healthy attachment and communication then naturally occur.

To explore this revolutionary approach, therapists might try first simply believing that clients have an intact Self that knows exactly what to do. The very act of perceiving someone in this way invites new clarity, compassion, and connection.

I wish you well on this journey of Self-to-Self connection. May it bring beauty and transformation to the work!

KEY TAKEAWAYS

The IFS couples' therapist endeavors to:

- Work with their own parts to embody their own Self-energy.
- Trust that Self-energy is the most potent resource.
- Help one or both partners access Self-energy.
- Help partners experientially unblend and relate to protectors.
- Help partners find and heal the exiles behind relationship problems.
- Witness the brilliant solutions of Self-energy.

AUTHOR BIO

Mona Barbera, PhD (she/her) is an Assistant Trainer with the IFS Institute, a psychologist with over 35 years of experience, specializing in couples therapy, couples workshops, and training psychotherapists. She has been quoted in Better Homes and Gardens, Cosmopolitan, and Mens Fitness and has appeared on Fox 25 news, NBC in New York, News 8 in Washington, D.C., Peachtree TV in Atlanta, and KARE 11 in Minneapolis. Her book for couples, *Bring Yourself to Love: How Couples Can Turn Disconnection into Intimacy*, is the winner of the prestigious 2009 Benjamin Franklin Award in psychology/self-help, the Bronze medalist in the 2008 IPPY awards in Relationships and Sexuality, and a finalist in the 2009 Eric Hoffer Awards.

INTIMACY FROM THE INSIDE OUT©
AND COURAGEOUS COMMUNICATION

Excerpt from *Internal Family Systems Couple Therapy Skills Manual: Healing Relationships with Intimacy from the Inside Out*

Reprinted with permission of Toni Herbine-Blank, Martha Sweezy, and PESI publishing

The IFS Institute offers Level 2 trainings in IFS couples work, based on the innovative work of Toni Herbine-Blank, the developer of Intimacy from the Inside Out (IFIO). IFIO features a skill known as Courageous Communication which encourages couples to use IFS tools, such as those discussed in this chapter, to listen and speak skillfully. Toni and her co-author, Martha Sweezy, have graciously offered a brief summary of Courageous Communication, as follows.

COURAGEOUS COMMUNICATION: CHANGE YOUR CONVERSATION TO CHANGE YOUR RELATIONSHIP

Toni Herbine-Blank, MSN, RN and Martha Sweezy, PhD

The Aims of Courageous Communication

- Promote unblending and co-regulation.
- Help the couple move safely from content to process.
- Help the protective system trust that a different way of communicating will bring relief.
- Invite vulnerable parts to be seen and heard.

Courageous Communication: Part 1

Listening Skillfully

- Really listening (listening from Self) when another person describes your impact can be a challenge and takes courage. We invite listeners to be aware that their partner's feedback is not an objective truth and that listening to their partner is an opportunity to learn something about their partner, themselves, and their relationship.
- Breathing deeply while listening helps. If the listener feels reactive, upset, angry, or vulnerable, they may choose to slow the process down and get help.

- It helps to remind clients that a more vulnerable part who has a need lies beneath their partner's reactive behavior. Are the listener's parts willing to relax so they can listen from the Self? Are they available?
- What is the listener hearing? Can they imagine that this feedback will be useful? Are they willing to ask themselves, *What about this rings true and what does not?*
- As they listen, are their parts willing to let them be curious first and speak for their parts with Self-energy after?

Courageous Communication: Part 2

Speaking Skillfully

- In order to speak *for* activated parts *from* our Self, we have to be present and take time to understand our parts.
- This is an opportunity for the speaker to talk about their part's experience with another person. Essentially, they speak about what happens inside when they are relating with the other person. The speaker is not evaluating or criticizing their partner. Nor are they trying to help their partner improve, be more self-aware, or be a better person.
- The speaker should consider their goals before speaking. The way they speak (speaking for their parts) will help them speak skillfully and affect the outcome.
- The speaker should ask if their partner is available to listen before beginning.
- Remind the speaker that they will be speaking about their own experience, not an objective reality.
- Before the speaker speaks, they should check inside to determine if their system is ready to explore vulnerable feelings and needs. If the system is ready, they can speak for a need or a fear. If not, the therapist can help the speaker explore whatever concerns came up.

Helping an Angry Protector Unblend

1. *Validate the anger.* Make eye contact, be compassionate, and be present. Speak to the protector directly: "Given that this is your experience…"
2. *Validate and empathize with the underlying need.* See the exiles beneath the rage. "Your need to be heard makes complete sense…"
3. *Challenge the behavior and name the consequence.* "This kind of communication will not get you what you hope for. Your partner will likely not hear you or be able to respond in the way you want them to."
4. *Offer an alternative that includes your help.* "Will you let me help you speak for your feelings and needs?"

Roadmap for Introducing Courageous Communication

Step 1: Listen, track cycles, and invite the couple to talk about difficult issues in a different way (e.g., "Will you let me help you?").

Step 2: Contract to be their parts detector (e.g., "I am here to help you, so I will slow down or stop the interaction if parts begin to overwhelm.").

Step 3: Invite the couple to negotiate who will speak and who will listen first.

Step 4: Help the listener prepare by noticing parts who might not want to listen. Encourage the listener to breathe and notice their heart. Help the listener unblend and be emotionally available.

Step 5: Coach the speaker to help their parts unblend and be spoken for. Encourage each partner to stay in relationship with their own parts (e.g., "What are you noticing in your body?"). Do not get caught in content or in helping them find solutions. You may need to ask one partner to wait while you help the other unblend and speak for their parts (e.g., "What is this part concerned would happen if it were to unblend and let you speak for it?"). Validate the experience and feelings of the parts of both partners. Confront protectors firmly and kindly.

Step 6: If appropriate, encourage the speaker to move towards speaking for vulnerable feelings or childhood wounding (e.g., "Are these feelings familiar? Is there something happening that reminds you of your childhood?").

Step 7: Help the listener respond from the heart with empathy. No part should be left hanging. Some questions and requests to use with the listener include:

- "Can you reflect the essence of what you just heard?"
- "Does any of this information make sense to you? In what way?"
- "What does your heart say?"

If the listener does not empathize with the speaker, offer empathy yourself. Examples of empathic statements include: "The essence of what I'm hearing is..." and "It makes perfect sense to me that..." It is important to meet the client's self-disclosure with understanding, mirroring, and acknowledgement. Otherwise, a response of deep shame is likely to follow—and perhaps a protective adaptive reaction (Siegal, 2003).

Step 8: Once the speaker has received an empathic response from the listener (or you), ask the listener to pay attention inside.

Step 9: Check back with the speaker. Have they received the response? Has it made an impact? Do the parts who have been spoken for feel understood? Is there anything more to say? The speaker may feel complete and have nothing further to add, or they may feel moved to respond.

Step 10: If there is time, have the listener and speaker switch roles. When switching, remind the couple about the respective jobs of the listener and speaker as needed. When both partners are ready, ask the one who was just listening to speak for their parts.

CONTRIBUTOR BIOS

Toni Herbine-Blank, MSN, RN (she/her) is a Senior Trainer for the IFS institute and the sole developer for the Intimacy from the Inside Out training programs. She runs couple therapy training programs, retreats, and workshops nationally and internationally, and has coauthored the book *Intimacy from the Inside Out: Courage and Compassion in Couple Therapy.*

Martha Sweezy, PhD (she/her) is an assistant professor, part-time, at Harvard Medical School; a program consultant and supervisor at Cambridge Health Alliance; and the former assistant director and director of training for the dialectical behavioral therapy (DBT) program at the Cambridge Health Alliance. She has an online therapy and consultation practice (website: https://marthasweezy.com) and a particular interest in the emotions of shame and guilt. Her most recent book published by Guilford (*Internal Family Systems Therapy for Shame and Guilt,* out August 9, 2023) explores these topics from the perspective of Internal Family Systems therapy. She is also the author of several journal articles on various topics, including IFS; a co-editor and co-author of two books on IFS; and a co-author of five books on various applications of IFS.

GOING DEEPER

From Dr. Mona Barbera

1) Website:
   a. www.monabarbera.com

2) Books:
   a. Barbera, M. (2008). *Bring yourself to love: How couples can turn disconnection into intimacy.* Dos Monos Press.

3) Couples Workshops:
   a. www.monabarbera.com/couples_workshops.html

4) Podcasts:
   a. IFS Talks: Turning Disconnection into Intimacy with Mona Barbera: www.podcasts.apple.com/ca/podcast/turning-disconnection-into-intimacy-with-mona-barbera/id1481000501?i=1000527716936
   b. The One Inside: IFS and Marriage with Mona Barbera: www.theoneinside.libsyn.com/ifs-and-marriage-with-mona-barbera
   c. Safely Embodied with Deirdre Fay. Talking about Affairs with Mona Barbera: www.dfay.com/wp-content/uploads/2013/09/MonaBarbera.mp3
   d. The Therapy Spot with Beth Rogerson. Fighting With Your Sweetie? Mona Barbera Says, Give Them a Gift: www.bethrogerson.com/fighting-mona-barbera/
   e. Moving Past Divorce Interview Series with Terry Gaspard. Episode 1: Bring Yourself to Love: Achieving Vulnerability and Intimacy in Marriage and Remarriage. www.listennotes.com/podcasts/moving-past/episode-1-bring-yourself-to-GsZY5JnuMTp/

From Other Sources

1) Website:
   a. www.toniherbineblank.com (Intimacy from the Inside Out)

2) Books:
   a. Herbine-Blank T., Kerpelman, D., & Sweezy, M. (2015). *Intimacy from the inside out: Courage and compassion in couple therapy.* Routledge.
   b. Herbine-Blank T., Kerpelman, D., & Sweezy, M. (2021). *Intimacy from the inside out: Couple therapy skills manual: Healing relationships with intimacy from the inside out.* PESI.

3) Trainings:
    a. IFS Level 2 training: Intimacy from the Inside Out: www.Ifs-institute.com/trainings/level-2/north-american-trainings
4) Podcast Interviews:
    a. SuperPsyched with Dr. Adam Dorsey: Getting out of your way and getting more love by knowing your parts with Toni Herbine-Blank: www.podcasts.apple.com/us/podcast/superpsyched-with-dr-adam-dorsay/id1512883587?i=1000597458024

IFS AND PARENTING

BECOMING AN IN-SIGHTFUL PARENT

Leslie Petruk, LCMHC-S, NCC, BCC

I know first-hand that skillful parenting is no easy task. As an ADHD mother of three (two daughters with ADHD and a son with special needs), I have had my share of difficult parenting moments. I know that as parents we judge our own failures harshly, and it takes enormous courage to admit that we are struggling. That is why I am passionate about working collaboratively with parents to improve their parenting confidence, relationship with their children, and connection with themselves. As an IFS Lead Trainer and parenting specialist, I have found the strategies I share with you here to be transformational.

In the following chapter, I will discuss the ways in which parents' past experiences impact their parenting style and describe how Internal Family Systems (IFS) helps parents heal their own parts to become less reactive and more connected to themselves and to their children. IFS helps parents unblend, or get space from, their own reactions—or parts—so they can connect with their child from a Self-led place. Self is an ever-present, inner secure attachment resource within every parent and child. When parents access their inner Self-energy and are a compassionate witness for both their own inner parts and their child's, they nurture a strong and secure attachment bond.

My invitation for parents who face challenges with their children is this: *Turn your attention IN-side first. Become curious about your reactions to your child's behavior. As you explore the thoughts, feelings, and sensations that come up IN-side when you interact with your child, you can begin to access your wise inner Self, which is the place from which you will parent most effectively and compassionately.*

I call this process IN-Sight parenting.

In this chapter, we will explore the ways in which working with their own parts helps parents most effectively support their children. We will also discuss the critical IN-Sight parenting skill of repairing a relationship with a child when rupture occurs. All parents will experience ruptures with their children, but ultimately, it is the ability to lovingly repair relational damage that creates safety and trust in the parent/child relationship. Finally, we will explore the critical importance of parental self-care in maintaining a balanced and IN-Sightful approach to parenting.

Trauma and Attachment: How Our Past Shapes Our Parenting

We tend to parent out of our unresolved past experiences. This means that a parent's history and unhealed childhood wounds will likely be activated and replayed with their own children. All the inadequacies, fears, and shame that have been buried will emerge, and, according to Dan Siegel (2014), how parents have made sense of their own childhood narrative will determine how they respond to their children.

Self-energy is the ideal source for secure attachment. When a parent embodies a critical mass of Self-energy, they offer their child a secure attachment figure with which to connect and draw support. This allows the child's system to develop with minimal attachment burdening. However, parents' systems often carry burdens from their own early experiences, and secure attachment becomes impeded when parents burdened parts hijack the parents' system and obscure their access to Self-energy. Burdens directly impact parent's ability to attune to, and make space for, their child's emotions which, in turn, often burdens their child's system. Burdens generationally transmitted in this way are known as "legacy burdens." Similarly, positive relational beliefs and qualities can be generationally transmitted in a process IFS calls "legacy blessings" or "heirlooms."

Because burdened parts are protecting the parent's pain, unresolved trauma in a parent increases the likelihood of a reactive or absent response to their child's needs. For example, a parent with alcoholic and raging parts may raise children with fearful and hypervigilant parts. These children may grow up to become anxious and fearful parents who raise children with hypervigilant parts that believe the world is not safe. Or perhaps a parent with enmeshed and controlling parts may raise children with avoidant parts. These children may grow up to become avoidant parents who do not respond to their own child's cues of distress, leading the child to develop dissociative parts that believe they aren't allowed to have needs or that they don't matter.

Burdens tend to emerge from rupture in relationship. When a child feels rejected, unwanted, abandoned, ignored, shamed, hurt, afraid, or humiliated their parts often become burdened. Burdened parts hold beliefs about themselves such as "I am unlovable," "I am unworthy," or "I don't matter," to name a few. This may lead a child's systems to develop protectors that act out, or display aggression, disrespect, or disinterest. As therapists, we can help parents know that relief is possible, and that by working toward their own parts' healing, they will have more access to Self-energy, thus allowing them to respond to their child's emotional world with more Self-led compassion, curiosity, courage, and connection.

While generational burdening is a reality, it is important to note that this does not mean that parenting struggles are the "fault" of a caregiver or that every parenting challenge is attributable to parents' parts. Parents are raising children in an increasingly complex and mine-filled culture which presents challenges for even the least "burdened" parents and families. IN-Sight parenting simply proposes that, in response to any parenting challenge that originates from any source, parents can respond most effectively from their own Self-energy rather than from parts.

Helping Parents Become More IN-Sightful

"Beneath every behavior there is a feeling. And beneath each feeling is a need. And when we meet the need rather than focus on the behavior, we begin to deal with the cause, not the symptom." —*Ashleigh Warner*

IN-Sight parenting uses IFS principles to encourage Self-led parenting and listen deeply to the messages underlying children's behavior. Thus, the focus in IN-Sight parenting is two-fold: 1) helping parents attend to their own inner landscape of parts that become activated in parenting, so they can 2) bring the clarity, courage, and compassion of Self-energy to their children's feelings and behaviors.

Ann Lamott says it succinctly, "The most profound thing we can offer our children is our own healing."[1] Our children are our best teachers, but they can also be the casualty of our unresolved pain, which is why attending to our own inner healing is a critical part of providing secure attachment to our children. Child psychiatrist, Dan Siegel, contends that it's "not what happened to you but how you made sense of what happened," that predicts your ability to connect with your own child,[2] so the manner in which we have integrated our own childhood experiences directly impacts how available we are to connect with our child and their full range of experiences and emotions. This is no easy task.

Dr. Laura Markham sums it up well, "Reparenting the child within you while also parenting the child in front of you, is one of the most challenging and least acknowledged parts of motherhood."[3]

In light of the fact that most parents come to therapy seeking strategies to change their child's behaviors, focusing on their own inner parts can feel like a counterintuitive approach. I find it helpful to welcome and explore any concerns that parents' protective parts might have about focusing on themselves before they attend to their children's behaviors. When children are struggling, many parents already feel judgement and shame, so it can be vital to be clear that attending to their own inner experience is not about blame, but about hope—hope for their own inner peace so they can most effectively respond to their children's struggles.

True to the IFS model, therapists have the opportunity in these moments to be "hope merchants"—helping clients' protectors see how doing their own internal work can bring their system relief, change their feelings of inadequacy, and improve their relationship with their child. As Dick Schwartz states in *No Bad Parts*, all parts have a positive intention. By honoring all the parts that a parent brings, we help them learn to do the same for themselves which an internal secure attachment. Ultimately, that leads to their child creating an external secure attachment. Holding curiosity, moving at their pace, and honoring all their parts will build the trusting relationship needed for clients to share some of their most vulnerable thoughts, feelings, and experiences related to being a parent.

Little People, Big Emotions

Children often experience big feelings as they learn to live in the world. IN-Sight parenting helps parents explore their own internal reactions to their child's big emotions in order to respond from Self. Burdened parent parts might shame, reject, or capitulate to uncomfortable emotions in their child, while parents' Self can compassionately witness these big emotions and redirect if needed. For example, rather than a parts-led, "Don't cry," or "I'll give you something to cry about," children need to hear a Self-led, "I see you are really sad. Can you tell me about it?" Parents who generally respond to their child in an attuned and Self-regulated manner tend to produce children who respond to life in an attuned and Self-regulated manner. This co-regulating is a secure attachment base that can hold space for all emotions, big and small, with safety, wisdom, and compassion.

Parents are able to welcome the feelings of their child to the degree with which they can welcome their own emotional experiences. I often ask parents, "What is it like for you when your child gets angry?" or "What happens inside you when your child throws a tantrum?" This IN-ward focus typically uncovers core emotional wounds (exiles) in the parent. With some IN-ward exploration, we may learn more about the parent's childhood experience of being shamed for displays of emotion and support the parent in caring for their parts.

Leslie: What is it like for you when your child gets angry?

Mom: I feel scared (exile). I'll let him do anything he wants so he'll quit being angry.

Leslie: That makes sense. Can you ask the scared part of you why it feels so scared?

Mom: When I was little and would get hurt and cry, my dad would rage at me. He'd threaten to hit me if I didn't shut up. It was scary to feel all that anger. I was afraid I'd get hurt. The scared part of me learned to get very small and quiet so that Dad would calm down and nothing bad would happen.

Leslie: That was incredibly resourceful of the scared part to learn to almost disappear. How does this part of you feel when your child gets angry?

Mom: It feels exactly the same as when my dad would get angry. Terrified. It wants to get small and let him do whatever he wants, so he'll stop being angry.

Leslie: Of course, it does. I wonder if that scared part knows how old you are. Can you ask it?

Mom: It thinks I'm four.

Leslie: Can you let it look at you (Self) and see how old you really are? That you are an adult with more ability to help things stay safe now?

Mom: Wow—it's shocked. And so happy to see that I'm all grown up.

Leslie: Would the scared part like it if you (Self) took care of the conflict when your child gets mad, rather than it having to be there?

Mom: Oh yeah—it would like that a lot. It would much rather go play.

Leslie: Perfect—let that little part know it can go play when your child gets angry, and you (Self) will handle the conflict with your own adult compassion and clear-mindedness.

Mom: It's relieved. It likes that!

In this IFS way, helping parents understand the meaning they make (about their child and themselves) of their child's big feelings opens the door to the connection to their own childhood experiences and their own parts that may still be carrying burdens. The IN-Sight Parenting model helps parents care well for their own hurting parts so that they can access Self-energy when their child's parts are hurting. Just as we can't teach our children math if we ourselves haven't learned math, we can't teach our children Self-led emotional intelligence unless we ourselves have Self-led emotional intelligence.

IN-Sight Parenting in Action

IN-Sight parenting, based on the IFS model, invites parents to:

1. Become *curious* about their own reactions,
2. *Connect* compassionately with their own activated parts,
3. *Understand* the meaning they are making of their reaction/child's behavior,
4. *Witness* their activated parts' stories, and
5. Bring *Self-energy* to their own hurting parts, in order to
6. *Respond* to their child from a Self-led place.

The Self-energy of the parent not only brings a calm, clear-minded, and connected response to the situation but also invites the Self-energy of the child to emerge. This mirroring creates both external and internal safety as the parent and child together navigate the challenge at hand.

I'll share from personal experience the power of IN-Sight parenting to transform one of my own parenting dilemmas.

My oldest daughter experienced a hurtful situation with high school friends that was similar to a situation I had experienced at her age. As she shared the experience, I became aware of how activated I was becoming by witnessing her pain. One part of me felt flooded with hurt and another part wanted to intervene to try to fix it. As I noticed my rising emotion and reactivity, I took a breath and a brief time-out, so I could practice the skills of IN-Sight Parenting in order to return to the situation from more Self-energy:

1. I became *curious* about my strong activation and noticed that a wound from my past had been triggered.

2. I *connected* compassionately with the hurt teenager part inside of me, reassuring her that I was there with her and whatever was happening to my daughter wasn't happening to her.

3. I *understood* the meaning this part was making of my daughter's situation was that I was being rejected, unwanted, and excluded.

4. I spent some time *witnessing* my teenage part, letting her show me memories of the pain and shame she had experienced in high school that she was still carrying.

5. With compassionate *Self-energy* I sat with my own inner teenage part in the way that she had needed someone to be with her back then, listening to her pain, and bringing her comfort and care.

6. After taking care of my own hurting part, I was able to *respond* to my daughter's painful experience with Self-energy. Now I could connect with my daughter from a place of open-heartedness, compassion, and curiosity rather than from my own parts' triggered anger, reactivity, and pain. My daughter's experience no longer felt like my experience, and with greater clarity, I could support her in the way she needed. My Self-energy invited her Self-energy forward as she processed the impact of the situation.

MOM   **TEEN DAUGHTER**

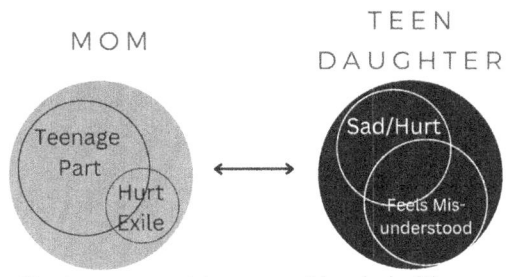

(Diagram: Mom's circle contains "Teenage Part" with "Hurt Exile" overlapping; Teen Daughter's circle contains "Sad/Hurt" with "Feels Misunderstood" overlapping; double-headed arrow between them.)

The teenage part in me was blended with my system and protecting a hurt exile. It could have kept me from being available to hold space for my daughter's parts of feeling sad and misunderstood.

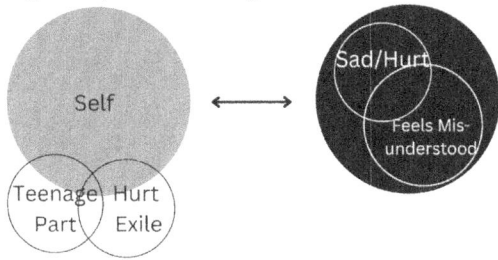

(Diagram: Mom's "Self" circle with smaller "Teenage Part" and "Hurt Exile" below; Teen Daughter's "Sad/Hurt" circle with "Feels Misunderstood"; double-headed arrow between them.)

By connecting with my parts, unblending, befriending them and healing them, I am able to be present and hold space for my daughter's experience.

By taking a few moments to care for my own triggered part, I was able to be present with my daughter and validate her experience without my own historical pain taking over. This created the freedom for my daughter to speak for her own parts' feelings and thoughts, and it communicated confidence that she had the ability to handle the situation.

By bringing more of my Self-energy to the situation, I was able to help my daughter connect to her own Self-energy. I asked, "What does the hurt part of you want you to know?" From a Self-led place, my daughter was able to witness the part of her that felt shame and believed she was not important and didn't have value. My daughter's Self-energy, supported by mine, brought her inner hurt part comfort and reassurance. She ultimately was able to speak for this part to her friend in a very clear and Self-led way.

This ability to care for our own inner systems as parents, so that we can bring Self-energy, rather than judgement, directives, or reactivity, to our children, is one of the primary skills I teach clients. The more we speak with our children from a place of connection and curiosity the more secure our connection to our children and the more effective our interactions become. I use this parts-based lens from the very first session.

The First Few Sessions: Gathering History

When a client seeks my support for parenting challenges, I find it useful to create a genogram in the first session as I gather the client's family history. A genogram is a visual representation of a person's family history, hereditary patterns, relationship dynamics, and medical and mental health histories. Developed by Murray Bowen in the 1970s, it helps both client and therapist identify familial patterns through a psychological and behavioral lens and tracks what in IFS we refer to as "legacy burdens" and "legacy blessings." A sample genogram is shown below:

GRAPH 1
GENOGRAM

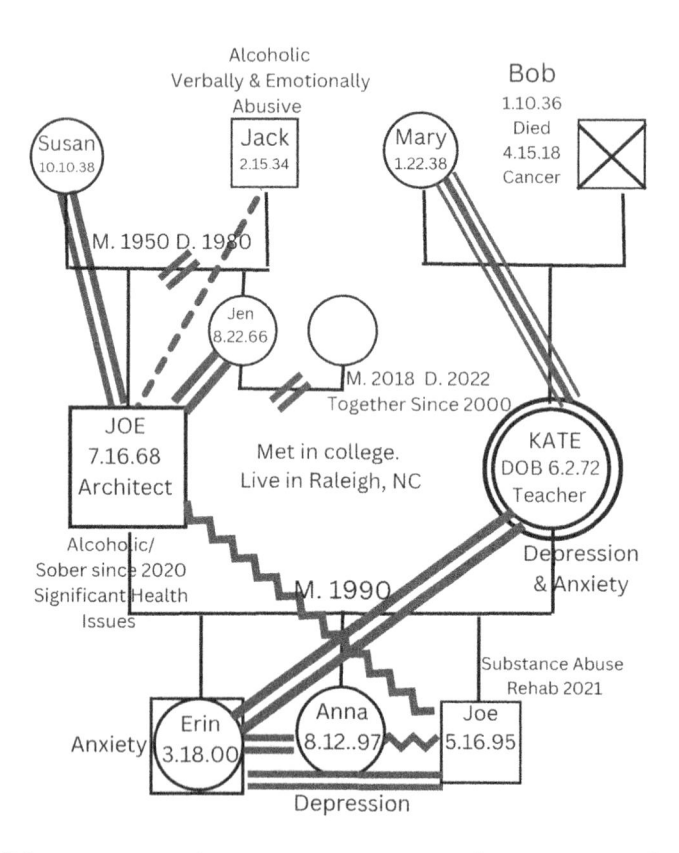

Susan 10.10.38

Jack 2.15.34 — Alcoholic, Verbally & Emotionally Abusive

Mary 1.22.38

Bob 1.10.36 Died 4.15.18 Cancer

M. 1950 D. 1980

Jen 8.22.66

M. 2018 D. 2022
Together Since 2000

JOE 7.16.68 Architect — Met in college. Live in Raleigh, NC

KATE DOB 6.2.72 Teacher

Alcoholic/Sober since 2020
Significant Health Issues

Depression & Anxiety

M. 1990

Erin 3.18.00 — Anxiety

Anna 8.12..97

Joe 5.16.95 — Substance Abuse Rehab 2021

Depression

In addition to constructing a genogram, I invite clients to respond to my IFS Parenting Protcol™ to further identify familiar patterns, extreme parts, burdens, and legacy burdens. The combination of the genogram and Parenting Protocol (see Appendix B) creates a framework within which I can begin to help parents identify their own burdened parts and any familial legacy that they hold. Parents who did not have their own physical or emotional needs met in childhood can feel particularly overwhelmed when faced with the challenges of meeting their own children's physical and emotional needs. Thus, understanding the parent's developmental experiences in the past is key to helping them parent effectively in the present.

Even when their child is older, I like to understand each parent's story of their journey into parenthood. I ask questions such as:

- Were all parts of you in favor of the pregnancy/adoption?
- What parts showed up when you found out you were pregnant/notified the adoption was going through?
- Were you aware of any activated parts when you brought your child home?
- Did/do all parts of you feel supported as a parent?
- Were there other significant events happening in your life during this time?
- What parts of you have shown up around being a parent?
- How did becoming a parent impact your marriage/relationship/partnership? Are there parts around becoming a parent and the impact on your life that need attention?
- For single parents: Are there any parts that need attention related to being a single parent? Do you have support in place? What is it like to be parenting on your own?
- For adoptive parents: What parts were present when you met your baby for the first time? Did/Do you have layers of support around being an adoptive parent?

Finally, it is important to screen for medical, neurological, and pharmacological/substance issues that may be influencing a child's behavior. Not all behavioral or emotional concerns are related exclusively to the inner world of parts, and it is critical to screen appropriately and make any needed referrals.

With this comprehensive assessment as the foundation for our work, we can move forward into our exploration of the present-day concerns for which parents are seeking support.

Transitioning to IN-Sight Parenting: Inviting the YOU-Turn

IN-Sight Parenting focuses on the manner in which parent and child parts react to one another and the impact on attachment that follows those interactions. In order to understand the impact of a child's behaviors and emotions on the parent, we teach parents to do what IFS calls the YOU-turn (Schwartz, 2008). As described above, this means taking the focus temporarily off the behavior of the child and redirecting it to the parent's inner world. We ask parents "When your child does that, what comes up in you?" and explore the meaning that the parent gives to their child's behaviors and emotions.

As parents describe the challenge they are experiencing with their child (e.g., defiance, sullenness, irresponsibility) we track the parts of the parent that emerge. Parents often initially respond to a child's concerning behavior from protector parts such as anger, minimizing, rescuing, or fatigue. We attend to, and befriend, these protective parts to learn what vulnerable exiles within the parent these parts protect. It is ultimately the exiles, or vulnerable young ones within the parents' system of parts, that often drive unhelpful parental responses. It is therefore the exiles healing that has the most ability to transform the parent-child dynamic.

Tender Exiles Within

How then do we identify parents' exiles? Exploring the meaning a parent makes when their child pushes back, expresses big emotions, or doesn't cooperate is a critical step in IN-Sight Parenting and often uncovers important trailheads that lead to parents' exiles.

We might ask "What meaning are you making about your child's behavior?" to which we could discover the parent's belief that the child is "lazy, disrespectful, or irresponsible." A helpful follow up question is, "And if your child is disrespectful/lazy/irresponsible, what does this means about you?" This question often uncovers the beliefs of the parent's vulnerable exiled parts: "It means that I'm a failure," "I'm not enough," or "I'm not loveable." Understanding the core wound (exile) underneath their reactivity (protector) to their child is the cornerstone of IN-Sight Parenting. This helps parents see the connection between their reaction to their child and their own painful childhood experiences. This step often provides "insight" for parents regarding their strong reaction to their child. By identifying the parent's exile parts in this way, we gain awareness about the ways in which the child's behaviors are related to the parent's own wounding as a child. By guiding the parent to compassionately witness the experience of their own inner exiles, parents can effectively "reparent" and unburden the vulnerable ones within themselves through their own Self-energy. This, in turn, allows them to be more available to the vulnerable parts of their child.

When exile parts are unburdened and transformed, protector parts are often ready and eager to take on a new role. Angry parts may become tender, minimizing parts may become curious, distracted parts may become deeply present. In this way, the parts of the parent that engage with the child begin to shift, and the parent-child dynamic begins to change. In this way, IN-Sightful parents develop the capacity to respond to any parenting challenge with calm, clarity, courage, and connection.

Curiosity: A Family Story

IFS describes the qualities of Self with 8 "C" words: curiosity, calm, connected, creative, compassion, clarity, courage, and confidence. In my own parenting, the one I've found most helpful is curiosity. I have a note on my computer that says, "Stay curious!" I confess, I learned the importance of curiosity the hard way.

One of the parenting moments I most regret happened when my oldest daughter was a high school senior. Although it was not my typical practice to check her grades online, I logged on one day during a break at the office to see how she was doing. I was aghast to see four Fs, two Ds and a C by her name! My parts panicked.

A furious, catastrophizing part took me completely over, saying "She will never get into college, will end up homeless, and never be able to support herself!" Despite deep breathing on my drive home and an intention to be calm and curious when I saw my daughter, this part was not about to be contained.

"I can't tell you how upset I am right now!" I exclaimed as I stormed into her room. "I trusted that you were studying only to find out that you are FLUNKING OUT OF SCHOOL! This is your senior year, and you will NEVER get into college with these grades!" As happens with burdened parts in charge, things escalated. "If you think I'm going to support you for the rest of your life, YOU ARE WRONG!"

My daughter burst into tears and tried to defend herself. "Don't start with the tears!" My part interrupted. "I JUST asked you the other day how your grades were, and you told me they were good. You think these grades are GOOD? I am so mad I can't even see straight right now! YOU HAVE BEEN LYING TO ME!"

With that, I stormed off to my room, her tears reverberating in my ears. "Forget Self- energy!" I muttered and threw myself down on my bed.

After a few minutes of deep breathing, I realized I'd been hijacked by my protector parts, and began trying to learn why they had taken me over. After listening to the narrative of my outraged, shocked, and indignant parts, I was able to connect with the more vulnerable exiles they were protecting. My exile parts were feeling powerless to give my daughter the opportunity for college that I knew she wanted and ashamed that I had "failed" her (their perception) as a parent. A strong exile was now also feeling shame that I'd let myself become hijacked and yelled awful things at my daughter. It felt like another person had taken over my body and turned me into an irrational and unfamiliar version of myself. My exiles were deeply triggered. I let them know I was there and reassured them we would figure this out together and that I would make things right with my daughter.

With Self-led remorse, I went back to my daughter's room and apologized. I let her know my behavior was wrong and I was deeply sorry I had hurt her. I asked her to forgive me, and then asked if she could help me understand what was going on with school and how I could better support her with her studies.

With this invitation, the backstory tumbled out. She explained that because she had missed a week of school with the flu, she was still finishing makeup work. Her grades were low because the outstanding assignments were still registered as zeros. In reality, she had As and Bs which would be reflected once she turned in the remaining items.

My inner critic immediately went on the attack, yelling at me: "You are the worst parent on the face of the earth!"

I apologized profusely to my daughter and acknowledged that even if she was failing all her classes, I should never have yelled at her. I spoke for my part that was feeling scared and powerless because I knew she wanted to go to college and thought it wouldn't be possible now. I shared that my angry part was trying to protect my fear, but that its approach was wrong and hurtful, and I assured her I would work with it so that it wouldn't take me over like that in the future. I let her know that I loved her no matter what, and I wanted the very best for her.

I invited her to share what the experience was like for her. She spoke for a part that was scared by my yelling and a part that was hurt that I hadn't asked before jumping to conclusions. I acknowledged those parts made complete sense and asked if there was anything they needed from me to recover from my eruption. I listened until she felt like I deeply understood and validated everything she was thinking and feeling.

Thankfully, she forgave me. And I came away with plenty of trailheads for the next six months of my own therapy.

Parent guilt is no joke. When I called my daughter, who is now 24 and just graduated from college, and asked her permission to share this story, I'm happy to report she only vaguely remembered the incident. That was surprising because to my parts it still feels like a devastating event that I will never forget. Thankfully, I don't hold activation around it anymore, after doing a lot of my own work, but it was certainly a big lesson for me…about the power of staying curious.

P.A.U.S.E and S.H.U.V.—Strategies for Unblending and Connecting

That day at work I had tried diligently to unblend the part of me that was literally shaking (my fear), and the part that was so angry (my fear's protector), but they completely took me over when I went to talk to my daughter. I realized later that my parts were polarized: I had angry, upset parts polarized with parts that were trying to calm me down. But—have you noticed?—telling a person (or a part) to calm down never works.

A better strategy, one that I teach parents when they are activated, is to **P.A.U.S.E.**™ (Appendix A):

P—Be **Present** with your **parts.**

A—**Acknowledge** the **activation** that's happening inside of you.

U—**Unblend**—ask them to give you some space.

S—Connect with your **Self**-energy to gain space in your system.

E—**Extend** compassion to the arising **emotion.**

When our parts feel seen, heard, understood, and valued in this way, they calm down. As parents learn to use this approach with themselves and develop a connection with their inner "children," it translates to more easily connecting with their external children.

One of the greatest challenges of parenting is staying calm, in non-reactive Self-energy. Befriending parts and releasing Self-energy is like a muscle that needs to be worked in order to get stronger. It takes practice! It is an important skill to practice because our Self-energy invites Self-energy in our children and, conversely, our triggered parts evoke their triggered parts. As I demonstrated with my daughter, conflict does not go well when we enter the conversation from triggered parts.

Unblending from activated parts usually requires taking a time out, which may mean asking for support from a friend, family member, or neighbor. It could mean putting Play-Doh in front of the child at the table, while they take some time to settle their system. "Getting space" from triggered parts is the first and most crucial step. It can also be the most difficult step, but as you see from my story, parenting from a blended place can be harmful, so it's essential.

Once some unblending has occurred, clients can explore connecting with their child's parts using the **S.H.U.V.**™ method (see Appendix A).

S—Let the child's part know you **SEE** it and understand it is upset.

H—Let the child's part know you want to **HEAR** what it has to say and then listen.

U—Once you have acknowledged it and listened to it, let it know you **UNDERSTAND** what it has shared, if that is true. If necessary, ask more questions to get a better understanding of the part's experience.

V—**VALIDATE** the parts experience and let your child know you **VALUE** them and their parts and how the parts are trying to help the child feel safe.

Whether dealing with a two-year old, a 20-year-old, or an older child, starting from a place of activation rarely ends well. P.A.U.S.E. and S.H.U.V. would have helped immensely the day I yelled at my daughter. As adults, it is incumbent on us as parents to model regulated behavior and Self-led conflict resolution skills.

Creating Therapeutic Safety

It is important for therapists to validate the very real challenges of parenting. Parents need to know they won't be judged. Their own inner critics have probably already done plenty of that. By the time parents seek professional support, they have often read all the books and tried a variety of strategies without success. The therapeutic alliance is deeply strengthened when we truly believe, and assure parents, that they hold within themselves a deeply wise Self, and all their parts—from those that want the child to 'behave' to those that believe they are 'failing' as a parent—are doing their best to survive with the strategies and burdens they've had to adopt. Our job as therapists is simply to slow things down, guide client's attention inside, and help them connect with their own deep inner resources.

Sandra, Justin, and Andrew

A couple whom I will call Sandra and Justin (all client information has been changed) are parents to a seven-year-old son I'll call Andrew. As we worked together to validate and befriend Justin's protectors, his parts allowed him to access and tend to the young, hurt part inside of him who needed healing. By comforting his own inner exile, Justin was able to relate to his son differently.

> **Sandra:** My husband didn't think we needed counseling. He thinks that I'm just not strict enough with Andrew. But I've tried everything and nothing seems to work!
>
> **Justin:** You let him get away with too much. When I was a kid, I would never have behaved the way he does.
>
> **Therapist:** So, Sandra, it sounds like you are at your wit's end and don't know what to do. Is that right?
>
> **Sandra:** Definitely.
>
> **Therapist:** And Justin, sounds like a part of you believes if Sandra were stricter, then Andrew would be more cooperative. Is that right?
>
> **Justin:** Well, I don't know if that would make him more cooperative, but it might scare him so that he makes better choices. Tough love…that's what I believe in.
>
> **Therapist:** So, I wonder if you ever felt scared as a child, Justin? Is that what made you behave?
>
> **Justin:** Heck yeah, I was terrified of my parents. They would never have put up with things the way we do with Andrew.
>
> **Therapist:** I gather that your upbringing was a lot different than how you are raising your child, and you have some strong feelings about that. What is your relationship like with your parents now?
>
> **Justin:** Oh, we don't have much of a relationship. I hardly speak to them, and we might see them every five years.
>
> **Therapist:** I wonder if you hope for something different with your son. What would you like your relationship with him to be like in the future?

Justin: (Tearfully) I just want to be able to have family time that is enjoyable and to do things without constantly having to battle with Andrew over everything. We've tried spanking, yelling, and grounding. Those were the things my parents did, and it made me behave, but it only seems to make things worse with Andrew.

Therapist: It seems as though there is a part of you that is feeling helpless and uncertain about how to get Andrew to cooperate, and there is also some sadness around that. Is that right?

Justin: (wiping his eyes) Yeah, that's right.

Therapist: And I wonder what it was like for you when you were seven years old? Do you have a sense of what that time was like for you?

Justin: I just tried to be good so that my dad would spend time with me. I wanted his attention, but he was always working, and when he got home, he would be tired and angry. I tried my whole life to get my dad to notice me.

Therapist: Wow, it sounds like seven-year-old you really wanted a connection with dad and worked hard to try to have one but just felt lonely and sad. Is that right?

Justin: (crying) Yeah, that's right.

Therapist: Is it okay for you to feel this sadness?

Justin: (wiping his eyes) Yeah, it's okay.

Therapist: Can you let that seven-year-old part of you know that you really get how sad he is and see how he responds to that?

Justin: Okay, yeah, I see him in my mind's eye. He's in the front yard tossing the football up in the air by himself. He's surprised that I'm there. He's used to being alone.

Therapist: Can you let him know you'd like to understand more about what it's like to be him?

Justin: He just came over and hugged my legs when I told him I was interested in getting to know him.

Therapist: That's great. How are you feeling towards that seven-year-old boy as he hugs your legs?

Justin: I see how sad he is and feel a lot of compassion for him.

Therapist: Can you extend that compassion to him—let him take it in?

Justin: How do I do that?

Therapist: How would you respond to your son if he expressed to you that he was sad and lonely, and he came and hugged your legs?

Justin: Oh, I would rub the top of his head and let him know it was okay.

Therapist: Yeah, so can you do that for your inner seven-year-old?

Justin: (Crying) He just felt so alone…he just wanted his dad to notice him. I didn't realize I had all of this emotion built up inside of me.

Therapist: Sounds like that little seven-year-old has been holding a lot of sadness for a long time and was feeling pretty lonely. See what else he wants to tell you about what it was like for him back then.

Justin: He always felt different from other kids and that his parents didn't care. All they ever did was yell at him and tell him to play on his own. My sister was always having friends over, and they treated her a lot differently. I always thought there was something wrong with me, that I didn't matter to them.

We continued to witness Justin's seven-year-old exile part and eventually unburdened the sadness and loneliness he had been carrying which allowed him to take in qualities of playfulness, connection, and patience. Justin then said, "I wonder if Andrew is being difficult because he's trying to connect with me?" Justin's connection with his own inner wounded seven-year-old created this spontaneous insight into Andrew's behavior.

Justin and Sandra returned the following week reporting that things were much improved with their son. Justin had a conversation with Andrew, apologized for how little time he had been spending with him, and committed to spending more time together doing things Andrew enjoyed. Justin assured Andrew how important their relationship was. Andrew's face lit up and his behavior significantly improved.

Justin and Sandra continued to work with me for nine more months, focusing on the parts that arose in each of them as they worked to improve their relationship with their son. Sandra had grown up with parental domestic violence and had a part that learned to keep everyone happy in order to make her environment "safe." This part became activated when Andrew (or Justin) became upset with her which made setting loving parental boundaries a challenge. As Sandra healed this part's burden, she noticed that Andrew's anxious behaviors dissipated. She had a new sense of self-confidence as a parent and the constant anxiety she had felt for many years lifted. Things with Andrew had become much easier, his teachers reported both academic and social improvements, and she reported her relationship with Justin had improved as well. By connecting with their own inner parts, Justin and Sandra had become IN-Sightful parents to Andrew, and the relationships between all three began to flourish.

Rupture and Repair

In addition to learning how to connect with their children from Self, it is important to teach parents the IN-Sightful art of relationship repair. Conflict is inevitable in any relationship, but the lasting impact of conflict depends on how it is or isn't addressed and repaired. As parents, we will say and do things that we regret, yet it is our ability to acknowledge the impact when we cause hurt that allows for healing. Most parents simply repeat the patterns modeled in their own childhoods, which often are lacking in the skill of repairing a rupture.

I grew up in a family where no one ever apologized. Conflicts just "blew over," although the time required for things to be "okay" again was never clear. As a result, I had a part that became hypervigilant over my parents' moods, particularly after any type of conflict. I also recall going through most of my adolescence constantly asking my friends, "Are you mad at me?" I had a deep fear of being rejected or abandoned if I did something wrong. I had a part that was constantly monitoring the emotions of others to make sure they were okay with me, and I lived in constant fear of people being upset. It wasn't until a college conflict with a friend that I realized apologies were something you could do. It was a painful lesson, and it took a while for me to become comfortable with apologizing. Had I been taught as a child that relationship ruptures are a part of life that can be repaired with a sincere apology, the part that made sure no one got upset with me wouldn't have had to work so hard.

It is important to assess the manner in which conflict was dealt with in clients' childhoods. It is not uncommon for parents who grew up in families where there was a lot of yelling and fighting to either repeat that pattern with their families or go to the opposite extreme and refuse to tolerate or allow disagreements. Parents who grew up with overcontrolling parents who micromanaged their lives may find it "normal" to do the same thing with their own children, or they may swing to the reverse and not have any boundaries with their children. By working with parents' parts that experienced poor or no repair in their own childhoods, we can heal parts and teach the skills for Self-led rupture repair.

An important starting place for healing is often to help parents forgive themselves. We are not "bad" when we make mistakes, simply human, and taking ownership and making reparation allows for reconnection. I will often ask parents, "If your parents walked into this room right now, told you they were truly sorry for the ways in which they hurt you when you were a child, and were able to name the impact they believe it had on you, would that be meaningful to you?" I've never had anyone say no. When done from a place of compassion and sincerity, it's never too late to repair.

Self-Care for Parents

"Many of us were modeled or taught to give until we break—and then refuel so we can keep on giving. But this, we know now, is the roadmap to burnout and resentment. Instead, let's give to ourselves—let's fuel our bodies and souls—so that we can give to others from a place of overflow, not depletion."—*Erica Layne*

In teaching IN-Sight parenting, I often tell clients, "You can't give what ya don't got." If parents are running on fumes and living in a place of overwhelm and self-criticism, they are more likely to be hijacked by parts trying to manage overwhelm, and they are modeling the same for their children. That's why self-care is a critical piece of IN-Sight parenting. This step requires exploring the messages parents received in their families of origin around rest, relaxation, and self-care. In my work with parents, I have found that many hold legacy burdens around taking time for themselves and the belief that you must always be productive. Many grew up in families where self-care was seen as laziness or overindulgence, and their value and self-worth were directly correlated with how hard they worked.

Further complicating the issue, the fast pace of life and expectations, along with ubiquitous technology, now keep us connected to our work 24/7, creating a culture of workaholics. For parents, taking time to rest and recharge allows space for perspective and the ability to be more present with their children. It isn't uncommon for parents to report that after taking a break, they had more patience with their children and their children were more cooperative, ultimately leading to a more positive connection.

Self-compassion is an integral part of self-care. Kristen Neff, a researcher and author on self-compassion, contends that research shows the ability to embrace self-compassion allows for deeper connection with yourself and thus with others.[4] She defines self-compassion as, "accepting yourself unconditionally and welcoming in whatever feelings arise." Her research has shown that the ability to practice self-compassion is linked to less anxiety, stress, and depression, greater coping skills, and improved health.

Research also shows that the biggest block to self-compassion is the fear that it will undermine motivation, however the opposite is actually true. Self-compassion actually fuels motivation and productivity! This awareness illustrates the IFS observation that our protector parts (in this case, inner critics) create the very thing they are trying to protect us from (in this case, loss of motivation). So, loss of motivation is more likely when our protectors become critical and are unable to extend compassion to our parts. The antidote to this internal loop of shaming and blaming is self-compassion. We become more emotionally resilient when we are able to embrace self-compassion. By extending compassion to ourselves, we are acknowledging our humanity and imperfection which allows us to extend the same gift to our children.

As therapists, we must help IN-Sightful parents find ways to take even small breaks to bring joy and rejuvenation into their lives, so they are able to be more fully present with their children and in their own lives. Balanced self-care supports Self-energy which promotes the secure inner and outer attachment that our children need and deserve. Self-care is a necessity, not a luxury.

> "The way we speak to a child matters, for the words travel beyond their ears, settling into the creases of their hearts and the crevices of their self-worth."—*Angela Pruess*

Summing Up

Children are more attuned to parents than we often realize and are exquisitely sensitive to the emotions and behaviors of their parents' parts. While children are skillful intuiters, they are poor interpreters, and they will often draw negative conclusions about themselves when they sense activated parts in their parents. When children feel scared, hurt, shamed, abandoned, or humiliated, they take on negative beliefs about themselves and the world that become burdens. This is how exiles are developed.

Well-meaning parents often struggle to know how to help their children when they express big feelings. If a parent is overwhelmed, they will not have the ability to respond to their child with compassion and understanding. Unresolved hurt from their own childhood creates burdens which can keep parents in a state of overwhelm, unable to parent from Self-energy.

Relief is possible by helping parents gain insight into their own inner system. This not only leads to healing and self-compassion but also to patience and understanding with their children. It is through self-exploration that parents befriend and heal their own inner parts which allows them to parent their children with curiosity, compassion, calm, and confidence.

Repair is always possible and can be addressed whether the rupture occurred 20 minutes, days, or years ago. It is a significant event in the life of a child when a parent acknowledges and apologizes for the hurtful impact they've had, even when it is unintentional. Owning our humanity as parents helps our children own theirs. Just as with modeling the critical art of Self-care, what we *do* as parents is much more impactful than what we say on our journey toward IN-Sightful parenting.

KEY TAKEAWAYS

- By connecting with, and healing, their own internal parts, parents are better able to understand, support, and connect with their children.
- Parents are most able to provide consistent attachment for their child when they have addressed the narrative of their own childhood and healed their own burdened parts.
- The meaning parents make of a child's behavior often leads to parents' parts that need attention and healing.
- Rupture is inevitable; repair is powerful.
- Ongoing self-care is an essential part of IN-Sight Parenting.

AUTHOR BIO

Leslie Petruk, MA, LCMHCS, NCC, BCC (she/her) is a Licensed Clinical Mental Health Counselor and Supervisor, Certified IFS therapist, and IFS Lead Trainer. She began her work as a counselor in 1996 and is currently the Director of The Stone Center for Counseling and Leadership where she focuses on working with parents and providing consultation to therapists working towards IFS Certification and on the intersection of IFS and parenting. As a neurodivergent mother of three adult neurodivergent children (a son with special needs and two daughters with ADHD), Leslie understands the joys and challenges of parenting. Leslie is currently writing a book on IFS and Parenting.

REFERENCES

Bowlby, J. (1988). *A secure base: Parent-child attachment and healthy human development.* Routledge.

Lamott, A. (1993). *Operating instructions: A journal of my son's first year.* Pantheon Books.

Markham, L. (2012). *Peaceful parent, happy kids: How to stop yelling and start connecting.* Penguin Random House.

Neff, K. (2011). *Self-compassion: The proven power of being kind to yourself.* William Morrow Paperbacks.

Neff, K. (2021). *Fierce self-compassion: How women can harness kindness to speak up, claim their power, and thrive.* HarperOne.

Siegel, D., & Hartzell, M. (2014). *Parenting from the inside out.* Jeremy Teacher/Penguin.

Winnicott, D. (1971). *Playing and reality.* Routledge.

Schwartz, R. C. (2008). *You are the one you've been waiting for.* Trailheads Publications.

GOING DEEPER

From Leslie Petruk

1) Website:
   a. www.thestonecenternc.com

2) Social Media:
   a. www.facebook.com/InsightParentingCoach
   b. www.facebook.com/groups/ifswithparentsandchildren

3) Online Courses:
   a. IFS Institute: Parenting with the Internal Family Systems (IFS) Model
      www. courses.ifs-institute.com/speaker/leslie-petruk-957430
   b. Psychotherapy Networker (Both also available through PESI): IFS with Children and Parents: Innovative Interventions that Combine the Strength of IFS with the Power of Play
      www. catalog.psychotherapynetworker.org/speaker/leslie-petruk-167732/18
   c. 2-Day IFS for Children and Adolescents.
      www. catalog.psychotherapynetworker.org/speaker/leslie-petruk-167732/18

4) Podcast Interviews:
   a. The Turning In Podcast:
      i. Episode 14 with Leslie Petruk. www.open.spotify.com/episode/6jiIx4kh0sTGvtQBbK9vTM?si=n3QlMKiDT5i5kIHKXou0NQ&nd=1
   b. The One Inside:
      i. IFS and Parenting with Leslie Petruk.
         www.podtail.com/podcast/the-one-inside/ifs-and-parenting-with-leslie-petruk/
      ii. IFS and Mom Guilt with Leslie Petruk.
         www.theoneinside.libsyn.com/ifs-and-mom-guilt-with-leslie-petruk
         www.youtube.com/watch?v=4WAQUax7DnQ
         www.youtu.be/cefnoTgDR6A
         www.youtu.be/4DpckgwxI38

From Other Sources on IFS and Parenting

1) IFS Parenting Series:
   a. www.ifsca.ca/parenting/

2) Dick Schwartz Video:
   a. www.youtube.com/watch?v=d2q8zbyvSDw

3) Parenting Podcast:
   a. Good Inside with Dr. Becky: www.goodinside.com/podcast/

APPENDIX A

IN-Sight Parenting

1. Identify the need your child is communicating through their behavior, actions and/or words.
2. Notice what happens inside yourself when your child has a big emotion or upsetting behaviors.
3. P.A.U.S.E. and unblend—take a break, or time out, and tend to your parts so you have space inside.
4. Explore the meaning you are making of your child's behavior. What does it mean about your child?
5. Get curious about the beliefs you hold about yourself. If the meaning you made about your child is true, what does it mean about you and your parenting?
6. Connect with Self-energy—once you feel an inner sense of calm and curiosity connect with your own parts first to acknowledge and validate them.
7. Connect with your child using the S.H.U.V. method.
8. Repair with your child when a rupture occurs.
9. Self-care is essential—refill your tank so you aren't running on fumes.

APPENDIX B

IFS Parenting Protocol™

PARENT CHLDHOOD EXPERIENCE

1. What did your caregivers/parents do that you respected and value that you would like to emulate as a parent?

2. What did your caregivers/parents do and/or what qualities did they exhibit that you DON'T want to repeat with your child?

3. What negative beliefs about yourself did you take on as a child that are still present today and get triggered by your child/children?

4. How were feelings dealt with in your family of origin? Were you allowed to be angry, cry, express an opinion that differed from your parents?

5. What were the spoken or unspoken message in your family regarding emotions/feelings and conflict?

6. How was conflict and discipline dealt with in your family growing up?

7. What other unspoken messages did you receive growing up?

8. Is there anything your parents did that you promised yourself you would never do? Is it something you currently struggle with as a parent?

9. List five words to describe the relationship with your primary caregivers/parents:

    1.
    2.
    3.
    4.
    5.

PARENTING EXPERIENCE

10. What intentions do you want to set for your family in regard to how you deal with emotion and conflict?

11. What is your biggest challenge/struggle as a parent?

12. What qualities do you want to exhibit as a parent?

13. What is the most triggering thing your child/ren do/does?

14. When your child misbehaves do you take it personally?
    (Circle One): Yes No Sometimes

15. What happens inside of you when your child experiences strong or big emotion?

16. How do you respond when your child misbehaves?

17. What are your beliefs around disciplining your child/ren?

18. What do you believe about yourself when your child misbehaves (Check All That Apply):

    ☐ I'm a bad parent

    ☐ I'm an inadequate parent

    ☐ My child doesn't like me

    ☐ My child is trying to make my life miserable

    ☐ My child is manipulative

    ☐ My child doesn't love me

    ☐ My child is trying to get back at me

    ☐ My child doesn't appreciate me

    ☐ Other_____

19. What did your parents do that you said you would "never" do to your children?

20. What values/traits/traditions do you <u>want</u> to pass on to your children from your family of origin?

21. What hobbies/activities feel life giving for you?

PARENTING (PARTS) PROTOCOL ASSESSMENT

Name _____

# of Children _____ Ages _____

Please answer the questions with 1 being never and 10 being always thinking about your youngest child.

1. In general, how often would you rate your relationship as being positive with your child?
   1   2   3   4   5   6   7   8   9   10

2. How often would you say you are present and attuned to your child as a parent?
   1   2   3   4   5   6   7   8   9   10

3. How often do you feel triggered by your child?
   1   2   3   4   5   6   7   8   9   10

4. How often do you feel calm when you are parenting?
   1   2   3   4   5   6   7   8   9   10

5. How often do you feel connected when you are parenting?
   1   2   3   4   5   6   7   8   9   10

6. How often do you feel confident as a parent?
   1   2   3   4   5   6   7   8   9   10

7. How often do you feel compassionate towards your child as a parent?
   1   2   3   4   5   6   7   8   9   10

8. How often do you find yourself repeating the positive parenting you received as a child with your children?
   1   2   3   4   5   6   7   8   9   10

9. How often do you find yourself repeating the negative dynamics that you experienced as a child with your child/ren?
   1   2   3   4   5   6   7   8   9   10

10. How often do you feel frustrated as a parent in a typical week?
    1   2   3   4   5   6   7   8   9   10

11. How often do you feel compassionate towards yourself as a parent?
    1   2   3   4   5   6   7   8   9   10

12. How often do you struggle with holding boundaries/limits with your child/ren?
    1   2   3   4   5   6   7   8   9   10

IFS AND ADOPTEES

HEALING PARTS BURDENED BY RELINQUISHMENT TRAUMA

Kathy Mackechney, LCSW

I dedicate this chapter to the adoptee in me who led me here. My heart goes out to her: a young woman seeking therapy to explore how having been adopted as a child impacted her. I see her sitting in the office of her new therapist, talking about what it's been like for her, only to be met with another blank stare. I feel desperation begin to rise in her as she tries harder and starts to tell the professional about what she's read about adoptees. The classic "The Primal Wound" (Verrier, 1997) and "Journey of the Adopted Self" (Lifton, 1994) had made her feel validated and led her to the important discovery: It isn't just me. But none of the therapists she's seen have read these books, and as she finds herself explaining—justifying—her experience to yet another (non-adopted) therapist, she's feeling misunderstood and alone again.

The clock reminds her how many of her precious minutes remain as she pays to help the helper help her. And this is not the first time…

A twenty-something then, I was working as a writer, having gotten my bachelor's degree in journalism, but I wasn't feeling fulfilled. My dissatisfaction, combined with my experiences in therapy, led me to think about making a career change and becoming a therapist myself.

That's when I met Sandy, a psychologist trained in testing. With her help, I realized that, in order to know what I really wanted to do, I had to know who I fully was, which meant finding my birthparents. Sandy introduced me to object relations theory, a psychodynamic model that focuses on the significance of relationships, particularly the mother-child relationship, in the development of the self (little "s" intended). From my IFS perspective now, I believe I was just beginning to understand that it was essential for me to connect with my original, natural, first mother, a.k.a. my birth mother, in order for my parts to be able to trust and connect with me—i.e., my Self.

Nine months later—the incubation period, not coincidentally I believe—I met my birth mom. Two weeks after that, I met my birth father. Two weeks after that, I started grad school. Two years later, I started working as a therapist for adoptees.

What I write on the subject will no doubt continue to evolve, yet I have written here what is in my heart to say on this topic at this point in my journey, and my hope is that it does justice to those it is intended to serve.

First, I propose we begin with an exchange of terms.

Include Relinquished Parts

In order to work effectively with adoptees and adhere to the IFS motto that all parts are welcome, I've found it helpful to substitute the term "relinquishee," or "relinquishee-adoptee," for "adoptee." This starts where many parts' experience started, with relinquishment, or removal, either one being the essential act that was required for someone to get adopted and become an adoptee. Many parts of adoptees feel gratitude for what they received as a result of having been adopted. They may even have gotten trauma- and adoption-informed, compassionate, adoptive parents who helped them heal from the trauma of relinquishment. But adoptees don't tend to seek therapy because of the positive outcomes of their experience. They come for help with, in their words, "adoption issues" or "adoption-related stuff," which tends to be that their mother relinquished them, and the impact of that on parts in their subsequent relationships. The words "adoptee," "adopted," and "adoption" can sublimate the trauma that preceded it and inadvertently exclude the very parts that brought the person to therapy. But the terms "relinquishee" or "relinquishee-adoptee" include parts that may have been overlooked or forgotten, and these terms change the context from the fact that the person was adopted, which sounds positive, to the primary, painful trauma of relinquishment. The vocabulary of relinquishment thus shifts the focus from an adoptive parent-centric perspective of having adopted a child, to an adoptee-centric perspective of having been given up by, or removed from, their mother.

The significance of that is easy to miss with the word "adoptee" and its definitional meaning of "a person who was adopted." But the relinquishment deserves at least equal consideration, if not more, given the profound impact it has, about which Verrier (1997), an adoptive mother and psychologist, wrote this: "It is my belief…that the severing of that connection between the adopted child and his birthmother causes a primal…wound, which affects the adoptee's sense of Self and often manifests in a sense of loss, basic mistrust, anxiety and depression, emotional and/or behavioral problems, and difficulties in relationships with significant others." (p. 21)

It makes sense that someone whose mother relinquished them would have parts that were burdened by that. She is their mother, after all—not the woman who becomes their mother later, through adoption, but the original, first, natural, inherent one: Mother. At least until fairly recently, and sometimes even now, a double standard tends to be applied with respect to her. For everyone who is going to be raised by their biological mom, she is viewed as paramount; it is essential that her child be placed in her arms and on her chest and hear her voice. But as soon as a plan for adoption comes into play, the birth mother is often minimized or dismissed, as though her baby needs her less. Suddenly, people can act as if it's fine for her child to be placed in another woman's arms, as though that child won't notice. Adoptees are not born adoptees. They are born the same as everyone else. Just like all other babies, they grew in their mother's womb and absorbed her experiences and learned her voice and her rhythms and her mannerisms. Just like all other babies, they were intertwined with her. Just like all other babies, they were born to, and of, her, and they arrive looking to, and for, her. But in most cases, unlike all other babies, they didn't find her when they turned their heads expecting her face, or listened expecting her voice, or were touched expecting her skin. They weren't met by her, the only person they knew. They were met by a stranger.

That's how an adoptive mother starts: as a stranger. Babies who become adoptees don't know this person when they first meet her. Even if she is there, ready and waiting at birth, and the *mother* hands her baby to her as the prospective adoptive mother, she is not the mother yet. She may be destined to become Mother—she may even become a wonderful mother—but she doesn't start as Mother. At the beginning, being handed at birth to a stranger is not the way things are supposed to go. It's not how nature works. Self knows this. And Self knows this is trauma. The word "adoptee" buries it; the word "relinquishee" centers it and the parts that become burdened as a result of it.

As if losing one's mother were not traumatic enough, adoptees who were adopted transracially and internationally suffer even greater loss, which adds layers to their trauma and more burdens to their parts. All adoptees experience the "trauma of displacement" (Fields, 2022), because every child who is relinquished, or removed, is displaced from their family and their familial culture of origin. But transracially and internationally adopted people are displaced from not only their family and its culture, but also from their race and country and the cultures of both. The further from home an adoptee is moved, the greater the displacement and, thus, trauma and burdening. A White adoptee born to White parents and adopted by other White parents does not experience the same degree of cultural displacement, and, therefore, trauma and burdening, as a Chinese adoptee born in China and adopted by White parents in the United States. A common part that results is an exile who feels like they don't fit anywhere. For example, an adoptee who was adopted from Korea and is being raised by White adoptive parents in the United States doesn't feel like they fit with Koreans, because they don't have Korean parents who know Korean customs and the Korean language, as other Koreans do, and they don't feel like they fit with their White peers, who also have

White parents, because they're not White. Either way, this part does not feel like it belongs.

One person who was relinquished and adopted, in her own search for the right language for her, landed on the words "a survivor of infant-mother separation." Another described having finally figured out how to tell her story in a way that accurately captured it: Her mother abandoned her at birth, strangers took her home and made her pretend she was theirs, and she never saw her mother again. The person to whom she first told this—in one of those random encounters in a store—remarked, "Oh my God, that's terrible!" which hit the nail on the head and was a stark contrast to the, "You're so lucky!" adoptees often hear and which can trigger parts that feel the opposite. In cases where the permanent separation of a child from the mother did not occur at birth, it happened later, after countless repetitions of turning toward Mother, hoping, assuming, and expecting she would be there this time, and of feeling the intolerable stress of the trauma when she wasn't, and the consequent burdening.

Some adoptees call themselves "adaptees," because they had to adapt in order to survive. A protective part took over and made them adapt to their adopters, as some adoptees call their adoptive parents, to try to fit with them out of fear of being given up again if they didn't.

Unfortunately, many people—even therapists—have a part that doesn't recognize that having been relinquished and adopted is a trauma. One therapist, who is an adoptee herself, works with other therapists and case managers who, when they refer to clients who were adopted, will often say, "They were adopted. I don't know if they have trauma." Yet, if they were adopted, they were relinquished, or removed, from their mother, so they clearly experienced a foundational attachment trauma, which is often held in implicit memory (YouTube, 2010). There's even a Facebook group called "Adoption is trauma." But it can be confusing because it sounds positive: A child got adopted! (Positive is not a given, though. Sometimes the adoption is good news, and sometimes it isn't, depending on the experience of the adoptee, who is the only person who gets to decide.)

When the focus is on the fact that a child got adopted, it begs the question, "How is adoption trauma?" But notice what happens when the question is changed to, "Is relinquishment trauma?" Does any part have to think about whether getting relinquished by one's mom is a trauma? "Relinquishee" centers that. A person who lost a limb is called an amputee, which centers that they lost a limb. There's no question whether that's a trauma. And they aren't called a prosthetic-ee if they get a prosthetic. "Adoptee" centers a dominant narrative that was created by parts of adoption professionals and adoptive parents who centered the adoption over the person who was relinquished or removed and needed to get adopted. That's why remembering from the outset that an adoptee is a relinquishee, relinquishee-adoptee, survivor of mother-child separation, or person who experienced relinquishment and adoption broadens the perspective and welcomes all parts.

While the focus of relinquishment is on the loss of the original mother, it's important to not exclude or minimize the loss of the original father. He often gets overlooked, and some parts feel the loss of him more poignantly.

I am not advocating against all use of the term "adoptee," and for now, I will continue to use it, partly for brevity and, also, because it is the most commonly used term, including by adoptees. But I am advocating for more thoughtfulness about what and who that term centers and what parts it tends to exclude. Throughout the rest of this chapter, I will also use "relinquishee-adoptee" or "person who was relinquished and adopted" or just "relinquishee" as what I believe is a helpful reminder. From a developmental perspective, it only makes sense to start with the relinquishment whereas starting with the adoption is akin to starting a book at Chapter 2. Starting with what happened first helps us start in the right place.

Start with the Parts' Story of Relinquishment and Adoption

When beginning to work with a relinquishee-adoptee, it's useful to start by asking them to tell the story of what they know about the circumstances that led to their relinquishment. Generally, there are parts that are happy to have been asked and given an opportunity to share it. And using the word "relinquishment" is a way the clinician can build rapport with those parts by overtly naming the event that had to happen in order for the person to get adopted. The Self of the therapist can comfortably and confidently inquire about the relinquishment knowing it is not off-limits, because it is an essential piece of the story that probably hasn't been asked about as often as the rest. Parts that may be responsible for bringing the client to therapy notice that someone is asking about their experience, and that helps them relax and feel connected to the clinician, which ultimately helps them feel more connected to the adoptee's Self, which will help them heal. It's similar to asking someone with suicidal thoughts to tell you about them, rather than fearing that asking will make them think about them, as though they didn't. Adoptees are already thinking about having been relinquished.

In doing this, the clinician signals from the beginning that they can talk about adoption-related issues. Many of my clients have talked about the blank looks they've received when they've started talking about adoption-related issues with other therapists, and I want my clients' parts that have been burdened by the trauma of relinquishment to feel understood by me. After asking what they know about what led to the relinquishment, it naturally follows to ask what they know about what led their parents to pursue adoption. These questions could go in intake paperwork but saving them for the first session allows for follow-up questions in the moment and observation of body language, which can come from parts. Plus, these questions build rapport, especially with those parts that wanted help with "adoption issues."

With this in mind, I ask some version of the following. (I won't necessarily ask all of them, depending on the answers I get and the flow of the conversation. Sometimes, I already know from an initial phone consultation or what my client voluntarily wrote in their intake, whether they have searched for their birth mom or birth father and are in contact with them.) As my client responds, I listen with my parts-detector ears for indications of different parts and what they think or feel, which can lead to follow-up questions.

- How do you refer to your birth mom—birth mom, first mom, original mom …? Do different parts of you refer to her in different ways?
- What do you know about what led her to relinquish you? What do some of your parts think and/or feel about that?
- What led your parents to decide to adopt? What do some of your parts think about that?
- When did you decide to search, and what led you to do that? How did different parts feel about that? Were there any parts that didn't want you to do that?
- Tell me about your first contact with your (whatever word they use for birth mom). How was that for your parts?
- Are you in contact with other people in your maternal family? Would any parts like to be? How often do you have contact? How does that amount feel to your parts?
- What do you know about your first/original/birth father? What do different parts think or feel about him?
- Tell me about your first contact with him and how that was for your parts.
- Are you in contact with other people in your paternal family? Would any parts like to be? How often do you have contact? How does that amount feel to your parts?
- How have your adoptive parents responded to you having been in contact with your birth family? How supported by them have your parts felt? (I'm assessing the degree of support the adoptee has felt from their adoptive parents.)
- When you were growing up, how much did your parents talk with you about having been relinquished and adopted? Do different parts wish there had been more or less talk about that?
- Who else was in your family/household growing up? (If they have siblings who were also adopted, I ask if their adopted siblings have had any contact with any members of their birth families.)

- When you were growing up, who, if anyone, did you talk to about having been adopted? Did you know anyone else who was adopted? (If they didn't know anyone else who was adopted, I'll ask what that was like for their parts.)
- What do different parts say overall about having been relinquished and adopted?

If the first session is with a child or adolescent and their parent together, the clinician can ask the child what they know about what led to their relinquishment/removal and adoption and notice if they pause at any point and look to their parent to confirm they got it right or fill in a blank. This can provide an idea of how much the story has been told and discussed, which is important because the ongoing telling of it and discussion help the child's parts incorporate it into their identity. At the same time, the clinician is paying attention to how parents respond if their child says they don't know something. If the parent says something like, "You don't know that? I've told you that," with Self-led curiosity, the clinician can inquire how much the parent has talked about it and if they can tell it again. Then it's important for the clinician to pay attention to how well the child's parts let them take it in and how Self-led the parent seems. Sometimes parents get blended with a part that worries that talking about this will make their child feel badly for having been given up and adopted. The clinician can also notice whether the parent seems blended with a part that has tried to talk about this a lot because the parent heard adoptees of older generations tell them they needed their parents to bring it up. And the clinician can notice whether the child seems blended with a part that's sick of talking about it because their parents have talked about it so much the pendulum has swung in the opposite direction, and they're tired of hearing about the birthparents who gave them up and aren't part of their lives.

If the clinician is meeting with just an adoptive parent, the clinician can ask what the parent knows about what led their child's parents to relinquish them or make an adoption plan, and what led the parent to decide to pursue adoption, including what led them to pursue domestic or international adoption specifically. In cases of the latter, it's helpful to also ask how the parent chose the particular country from which their child came, and then listen for whether they chose international adoption because it decreased or eliminated the chances they would have contact with their child's birthparent(s). If that's the case, it's important to ask what the part that led them to make that decision feared might happen if there were contact. Sometimes a part expresses a fear that it would "confuse" the child, which can be a reason a part gives to protect it, or another part, from feeling threatened by having the original, natural parents in the picture. If there is confusion for relinquished and adopted children whose birthparents are part of their lives, it's likely about why the birthparents didn't feel like they could keep them, and if the birthparents are available to ask, that's often preferable to when they aren't. Generally speaking, any confusion that exists does not come from the child. It comes from an adoptive parent who has a part that feels confused about how to share their child, whether just energetically or tangibly, through some degree of contact with the first parents and make space emotionally/mentally/physically for the presence of those parents in their child's and, therefore, the adoptive parents' life.

The reality is, whether the birthparents are a physical presence in the child's life or not, they occupy mental, emotional, and psychic space inside the child, even if the child doesn't talk about them. Choosing international adoption to decrease the chances of having to deal with birthparents can send a message to the child that there's something wrong with them. Since they came from those parents and are biologically related to them, the child may think that, if their adoptive parents don't want the parents from whom the child came and whose biology runs through their bodies, they must not want them or, at least, significant, immutable parts of them. This can lead to the development of burdened exiles who feel "unwanted."

It's also informative to ask how parents who adopted transracially or internationally have adjusted their lifestyles to try to accommodate their child's culture of origin. In many, if not most, cases, they haven't. They may still live in a predominantly White neighborhood with predominantly White schools, perhaps because it's comfortable, which leaves the adoptee to do all the adapting—hence the term "adaptee." Some adoptive parents intentionally move to an area where they will be the racial minority, so their child doesn't have to be and can have the experience of growing up around other people who look like them—i.e., have racial mirrors.

In asking these things, whether with an adult adoptee or a child who was adopted and their parent, the important message the clinician is communicating to parts that want to talk about adoption issues is, "I recognize that you have these other parents and that you came into your family differently than most people. I know how to talk about that and want to know what that's been like for you, your system, and your parts." Explicit recognition of that is essential in building trust with parts, which is essential in facilitating the Self-to-part connection that's necessary for the internal attachment that will allow parts to relax and heal. Some adoptive parents say they don't think of their adopted child any differently than their biological child. But that is problematic, because the fact is, they are different. It's not bad; it's both good and bad. Mainly, it's just different. And being "adopted-blind" ignores the inherent difficulties that come with having been relinquished and adopted.

Speaking Directly to Parts Can Be Very Helpful

Relinquishee-adoptees can be at a disadvantage developmentally. Their attachment trauma happened early—in many cases, prenatally or at birth—so parts developed burdens at a very early age before they had an opportunity to live life unburdened. Sometimes, they exiled Self and have kept it exiled because they developed a belief that that's what got them relinquished—Self was bad, so their mother didn't want them. Many times, even if Self wasn't exiled, it was blocked, since access to Self begins with healthy attachment and broken attachment bonds negatively impact access parts will allow to Self-energy (L. Petruk, personal communication, October 2, 2022). Subsequently, mirroring becomes very important. Sometimes, an adoptive parent can provide the necessary mirroring to restore, or open, access to Self-energy. But there can be a degree of mirroring that only the biological mother, or another biological family member, can provide, which is lost through relinquishment and impacts parts' ability to trust Self. Add to that the fact that relinquishee-adoptees' experiences are, broadly speaking, not mirrored by society, and parts can develop a belief of not being okay. Thus, it can be extremely helpful for relinquishee-adoptees and their parts to receive mirroring, or compassionate validation and attunement, directly from the therapist—i.e., the therapist's Self. In IFS, this is called direct access because the Self of the therapist talks directly to the clients' parts. This helps build rapport. Just as a part of me relaxed when Sandy nodded knowingly when I told her I needed to search for my birthparents, clients' parts relax when the therapist responds in a way that conveys that what parts say makes sense. Having received understanding and external validation directly from what they view as an expert, parts begin to relax, which opens the door to the relinquishee-adoptee's own Self-energy.

Consider this example from an adoptee I'll call Melissa, who represents a composite of clients:

Melissa described how helpful it was to see different therapists, because they each gave her parts something they needed. The first therapist used Emotionally Focused Therapy and provided the attuned responses Melissa's protective parts needed to be able to begin to relax and trust that it was safe to connect. Once they got what they needed from that therapist, they let Melissa know they wanted one who practiced somatic therapy, which in IFS terms, incorporates the steps of finding and focusing on a part in the body. So, she saw a somatic therapist whose innate warmth and compassion helped Melissa access that within herself, or Self, and deepen her embodied connection to her parts. After that, she heard about IFS. By then, her parts were willing to trust that Melissa could relate to them the same way those therapists had (Schwartz, 2013). Melissa's parts had received the critical mass of understanding that was necessary for them to be able to trust her Self.

Similarly, my clients have often told me they contacted me because they read what I wrote on my website and checked everything on "the list." Here's what resonated with their parts:

- A part of me easily feels rejected or abandoned.
- One part of me wants people close, and another part pushes them away.

- Part of me believes there's something wrong with me.
- Part of me likes to be in control.
- Part of me makes me analyze conversations, second-guess what I say, and worry I've offended someone.
- Part of me feels misunderstood, which leads another part to overexplain—frequently thinking of one more thing it wants to add.
- Part of me feels like it doesn't fit anywhere.
- Part of me reacts strongly to loss.

Having experienced that somebody "gets it," these parts come to my office wanting and needing more of that. They often haven't felt understood, since most people were not adopted, so they haven't been around a lot of other people who've had the same experiences as they have. But a therapist doesn't have to have been relinquished and adopted in order to connect with an adoptee and their parts. There is a lot of readily available information that can help any clinician better understand relinquishee-adoptees' experiences, and the references cited in this chapter offer a few places to start. Perhaps more importantly, therapists can access their inherent ability to understand a relinquishee-adoptee's experiences because Self can easily imagine itself in the relinquishee-adoptee's shoes and then everything their parts think, feel and do makes perfect sense. From there, the compassionate responses adoptees' parts need and deserve, flow. Considering how many decades many adoptees go without compassionate validation, it makes sense that their parts might need to soak up attuned understanding directly from a therapist for a while before they would be able and willing to turn toward the Self of the client.

In suggesting that adoptees might need this type of response from a therapist, though, I don't want to inadvertently contribute to the infantilization of them, as has often occurred. In legislation about an adult adoptee's right to access their birth and adoption records, the adopted person has often been referred to as "the adopted child," as though they never grew up—which can make it easier to deny them, a "child," a right. Language that locks them in perpetual childhood creates a burden. Many adoptees in therapy are adults, and they benefit from direct access by the therapist not because they have less Self than anyone else, but because it's been harder for them to trust Self as a result of how early their parts became burdened and access to Self was blocked. Arriving at this understanding is critical for unburdening to occur.

Be Sensitive to Potential Triggers

Some things that aren't triggering for most people can be for those who were relinquished and adopted. Before getting to that, though, I want to introduce another important term: "biological." It's the word a colleague, who is also an adoptee, Dr. Chaitra Wirta-Leiker, taught me for someone who was raised in their biological family and not adopted: a "biological." In my experience, this usage can help to level the playing field. Historically, there hasn't been a word to designate non-adoptees. They have gotten to be just a woman, a man, a child, a person. They were, and are, the norm. Statistically speaking, that's how it is: Most people are biologicals, having been raised in their biological family, by their biological parents—for better and for worse. Relinquishee-adoptees—and now donor-conceived people—are the ones who are different because, except in cases of intra-family adoptions, they aren't biologically related to their parents. They also are the only group of people who don't have access to their original, and true, birth certificates. So, they're the ones who get the designation because they're different from the norm. As a result of something over which they had no choice—that happened to them and stamped them "adopted"—they are other. And many adoptees' parts feel like it. They live in a world where biologicals' worldview dominates.

The term "biological" equalizes things. There are biologicals, and there are adoptees. (There are also donor-conceived people, who are presented with some of the same challenges from not knowing their donor.) For a therapist who was not relinquished and adopted, this framework can shift their perspective in a way that, again, helps build rapport and trust and, thus, access to Self-energy in the adoptee.

For relinquishee-adoptees, just moving about day to day in a world of biological families can trigger parts. Biologicals' resemblances to one another—in appearances, mannerisms, traits, even inherited conditions—can be fatiguing to relinquishee-adoptees' parts because they are constantly reminded of what they don't have and how they're different. Meanwhile, these parts' experiences often go unseen, which can cause these parts to think the adoptee is invisible—that is, until people are staring at them because they obviously were adopted, based on who they're with. Having a therapist who can imagine the everyday experiences an adoptee might encounter further builds the connection between therapist and client and between Self and parts.

Consider a few scenarios that demonstrate how differences a biological might overlook can trigger parts of a relinquishee-adoptee:

1. **A relinquishee-adoptee who's a successful painter has a showing at a gallery, and one of the guests demonstrates curiosity about the painter's background;** for example, when they started painting and how the interest was nurtured. Not knowing the artist is an adoptee, the guest says, "I bet one of your parents was artistic." The adoptee momentarily freezes. A part makes them flash on the parents they don't know and this very question about which they've wondered a thousand times, while another part weighs whether they want to say, "I don't know. I was adopted," which would risk the response they might hear. Does the adoptee smile and

say a safe, simple, non-revealing, "Yeah" or "No, not really"? A version of this interchange can happen to a biological, too, but it's more likely for an adoptee. A validating therapist can help the adoptee's parts relax by saying something like, "I can only imagine what might have happened inside you when they asked that. Was there a part that made you think about the parents you don't know?" Even if the adoptee says no, the fact that the therapist made an effort to imagine their experience as a relinquishee-adoptee can go a long way in building parts' trust.

2. **A group of friends gets together.** Most of them were not adopted. Everyone is having a lively time, and suddenly, the conversation turns toward talk of traits people inherited. The relinquishee-adoptee in the group falls silent. Part of them makes them wonder what they inherited from their parents, and that makes them wonder who their parents are, if they're even alive, and if they ever wonder about them. Suddenly, they are far away, unable to participate in the conversation. Ultimately, someone pulls out a photo of their mother at the same age they are now to demonstrate how much they look alike, and the adoptee is blended with a part in a downward spiral of pain from not knowing who, if anyone, they resemble. Quietly, they get up and go in another room.

3. **An adoptee is asked about the origin of their last name.** Part of them sighs internally and makes them hesitate before they say, "Scotch-Irish I think. I'm not totally sure. I was adopted." Then the person, having missed the cue that the adoptee's surname doesn't carry the same meaning to them as it often does for a biological, dismissively says, "Well, it's your name," and further triggers that part. On hearing the story, the therapist could express understanding of the miss to help the part feel seen. Then the therapist could ask how much the adoptee's parents (adoptive) have talked about their family heritage and the degree to which they acknowledge that it must be hard for the adoptee to hear about that without knowing their family name or heritage.

4. Here's how **going to the doctor** might come up in a therapist's office and what the therapist could say that might increase connection with an adoptee:

    Client: "Sorry I'm late. I had a doctor's appointment that ran a little over."

    Therapist: "No problem. I'm glad to see you. I know we have a part to follow up with, but your mention of having gone to the doctor makes me curious what that's like for you as an adoptee. I know you don't know your family history, and I wonder what that's been like for you and your parts, maybe especially when you've had to fill out those forms. If you want to, we can explore that sometime."

Client (exhaling): "I really appreciate that. No one has ever asked me about that."

5. **Just a mention of "family" has the potential to trigger parts because the experience of family is complex for relinquishee-adoptees.** It can be helpful if the therapist specifies "birth" or "biological," or "adoptive." That alone can demonstrate respect to parts that care by using language that recognizes there are (at least) two families. This can especially help parts who feel a connection to the birth family. The therapist can ask about both *birth* family and *adoptive* family, and then listen and follow the client's lead, as Dick teaches and so beautifully demonstrates. If a client responds that they refer to their adoptive family as just their family, which is often the case, the therapist would follow suit and drop the qualifying adjective. The therapist wouldn't want a part to feel slighted because, from the part's perspective, the therapist just reduced the adoptee's family to a lesser status by having signified them as the *adoptive* family instead of just family, like biologicals get to do. Note that in situations where the relinquishee-adoptee has ongoing contact with both their birth and adoptive families, the adoptee sometimes drops the identifying qualifiers because they all just feel like family. One can generally tell by context which family the relinquishee-adoptee is referencing. If the therapist has any questions, they can, as we say in IFS, just ask.

   Talk of family can also lead to identifying polarizations between parts who are connected to one family or the other. They may argue about who constitutes the "real" family. Sometimes, the birth mom, her family, and the parts connected to them have been exiled and labeled "not family" by other parts. These parts may fear that acknowledging the birth family as "family" could bring forth overwhelming pain from having been abandoned by that family. Or, these parts may fear that, if the parts connected to the birth family are allowed out, they will take over and jeopardize the adoptive placement, even if the adoptee is an adult. On the other hand, a part can exile the adoptive parents and adoptive family as "not family." In different systems, adoptive family parts or birth family parts can dominate.

   One relinquishee-adoptee described what happened inside her the first time her birth mom called. The first thing the birth mom said was, "Are you my daughter?" The adoptee said she hesitated. One part inside her said yes, for the obvious physical reasons. Another part said no because her birth mom didn't raise her and there was someone else she considered and called mom. Whenever a clinician notices an adoptee hesitating to respond, something like that may have happened, and it can be helpful for the clinician to ask from curiosity, "What just happened?"

6. **Then there is the potential trigger of a relinquishee-adoptee's birthday,** which is often the anniversary of the relinquishment. This presents an opportunity for the therapist to further connect with the client and, potentially, identify and explore a trailhead.

Becoming aware of language and situations that could trigger different parts of someone who was relinquished and adopted increases the chances the therapist won't miss a potential trailhead. If the therapist asks questions that are intended to invite parts that have often been silenced, and then receives responses that indicate those parts don't need attention or won't be allowed by another part to be given it, that's information that can help the therapist meet their client's parts where they are. As always, the therapist follows parts' lead.

Be Mindful of Biological Advantages and Pro-Adoption Parts

Biologicals can take for granted things that adoptees can't, and it can be important to some parts that the therapist demonstrates understanding of this, particularly if the therapist is a biological. For example, biologicals can take for granted that the information on their birth certificate is correct, while adoptees know it's falsified. As a result, there can be parts that carry anger and resentment. The legal system, after all, seals the relinquishee-adoptee's original birth certificate, denies them access to it, and issues them a birth certificate that shows their adoptive parents gave birth to them. One therapist worked with an adoptee who had a part that wanted the therapist to hear their anger that the legal system made them pretend they were born to their adoptive parents. For some parts, this relegates relinquishee-adoptees to less-than status by sending the message that it is preferable to have been born to one's parents than to have been adopted by them. Otherwise, why falsify a legal document and make it appear that their adoptive mother gave birth to them?

When therapists encounter a part that's blended, making the client angry and resentful about the ways relinquishee-adoptees are treated differently, therapists can use direct access, as previously mentioned, to acknowledge the advantages biologicals have and convey understanding to the part of the unfairness of that. Doing so can further build the rapport and trust necessary to open up more access to Self.

Another example is that some parts may carry resentment that biologicals can take for granted that they know who their parents are and what they know about them, including the ugly truths. Relinquishee-adoptees inevitably say they would rather know than not know. Their parts would trade learning something awful about one of their birthparents for not knowing who they are.

Because relinquishee-adoptees cannot *not* be aware of biologicals' advantages, and those advantages carry the potential to create what can feel to parts like an additional power imbalance between therapists who are biologicals and their clients who were adopted, it can be helpful for the therapist to demonstrate awareness of biologicals' advantages. Doing so can help the therapeutic relationship by opening more access to Self. It can also be helpful for the therapist to look for and identify any pro-adoption parts with sentimental feelings about adoption. Although it would also be helpful to check for any anti-adoption parts, it's probably more likely, given the current societal context, that there will be pro-adoption parts that could inadvertently shut down parts of the relinquishee-adoptee. Even a relinquishee-adoptee can have them. To help you identify them, I include here a few quotes from relinquishee-adoptee contributors on a website called Dear-Adoption.com, founded by Reshma McClintock, a transracial, inter-country adoptee from Calcutta, India. Notice any reactions parts may have as you read the following messages from adoptees addressing the adoption itself:

Dear Adoption,
It hurts.

Dear Adoption,
You exhaust me.

Dear Adoption,
Are you proud of me?

Dear Adoption,
Don't use me.

Dear Adoption,
You're so confusing. I'm torn between birth family and adoptive family. To which do I belong? Don't say both.

Dear Adoption,
Your gains are our losses.

Dear Adoption,
I hate that you claim to put fires out but don't acknowledge that everything that was scorched is what actually matters the most to me. I hate you, adoption.

Dear Adoption,
Everything you need to know about adoption can be learned by listening to adopted people.

Dear Adoption,
I strive in spite of you. Not because of you.

Dear Adoption,
In order to be part of the adoptee movement…you must not only listen; you must boldly do your part to elevate our voices.

For any therapist who works with relinquishee-adoptees, it's valuable to notice which parts pop up when you encounter adoptees out in the world. For example, when you see a transracial adoptee with their adoptive parents, is there a part that makes you automatically think that child is lucky to have been adopted by American, usually White, parents? Is there compassion and curiosity about what it's like for parts of them to have been removed from their origins and adopted into another culture?

Lastly, it can be helpful for all therapists who are biologicals to invite forth any of the relinquishee-adoptee's parts that might have concerns or hesitation about seeing a therapist who wasn't adopted. Here's an example of how that could go:

Therapist: "I wasn't relinquished and adopted, so I don't know firsthand what it's like to have grown up having had that experience, and I'm wondering what that's like for your parts."

Client: "Oh that's fine." (possibly spoken from a part who has spent its life taking care of biologicals, such as the adoptive parents)

Therapist: (recognizing the possibility that the client responded from a blended part and inviting other parts forward): "Are there any parts for whom that's not fine and maybe haven't felt comfortable saying so? Would you like to take a minute and ask and then wait for any part that usually hasn't come forward? Maybe check first if there are parts that don't want any parts like that to come forward, and if there are, ask if they would be willing to give space right now."

Such an invitation can be the first step in building trust that will help the person's parts relax and connect. In a perfect world, every adoptee who seeks therapy would get to see a therapist who was adopted, and if the adoptee was adopted transracially from Korea, their therapist would also be a transracial Korean adoptee, and an adoptee of color with White parents would see a therapist who's a Person of Color adoptee with White parents. But therapists do not have to have been relinquished and adopted to be great therapists for people who were. Just like everyone else, what any adoptee needs at a given time depends on which parts are most activated. Sometimes, it's more important for a Black adoptee with White parents to see a Black therapist, whether that therapist was adopted or not. At other times, it's more important for that same adoptee to see a therapist who was adopted. It depends on which parts need attention.

Not All Parts Get Adopted

This came to me one day as I was walking through my house: *Not all parts get adopted*. It ran through my head and instantly resonated, and I knew I had received a capital "T" Truth. It became the title of the next workshop I did at the annual IFS conference and has become an ongoing workshop I offer adoptees, professionals who work with them, and adoptive parents. The feedback I've received is that it inherently makes sense when people hear it. In particular, it resonates with adoptees and the parts of them that didn't get adopted.

What does this mean? Here's what I've uncovered so far:

1. *Not all parts want to get adopted.* Some knew what was coming and were not on board. They didn't want to leave their original mom or family and get adopted by, and into, another one. So, they stayed with her and her family or the birth father's and didn't get relinquished and adopted. They maintained their original, inherent identity that was there at birth; they could be considered parts that are "biologicals."

    Some parts did not want to get adopted for other reasons. For example, one part did not want to get adopted because it already felt abandoned by its first family and didn't want to get adopted and risk abandonment by another one, so it stayed by itself in a protective, isolated limbo with no family. A part also might not get adopted because it froze and couldn't move after the relinquishment, so it got stuck where it was at the time of relinquishment. Author, psychologist, and adoptee B.J. Lifton (1994) describes this when she quotes British psychologist Harry Guntrip's writing that a vital part retreats after being flooded with fear and anxiety (p. 33).

2. *Some parts don't get adopted because parts that were don't want them.* Some parts don't necessarily want to stay behind when the adoption happens but do want to maintain connection to the biological maternal and paternal families. Adopted parts may believe those "biologicals" are responsible for the relinquishment and view them as a threat to fitting in and keeping a spot in the new family. To ensure the security of the adoption and prevent another abandonment, these adopted parts exile those biological parts and don't let them get adopted.

3. *Some parts don't get adopted because the adoptive parents don't want them, for various reasons.* As can be the case with any parent, the adoptive parents may not like certain parts of their child, so they don't accept, or adopt, them. Or certain parts remind the adoptive parents of the biological parents and their child's connection to them, and the adoptive parents feel threatened by that. Or they don't like certain aspects of the biological

parents, and they deny those aspects of their child by not adopting the parts with the same aspects.

Whatever the reason some parts don't get adopted, it can be extremely helpful for an adoptee to connect with them. They can be some of the "juiciest" parts, to use one of Dick's terms, of an adoptee. They don't always carry burdens because they didn't necessarily experience relinquishment and adoption. But they do carry clues to who the relinquishee/adoptee "really" is (i.e., pre-adoption), and can reveal never-before-known characteristics of the relinquishee-adoptee. Many adoptees struggle with identity issues, since they were cut off from the people from whom they came and, with that, some of their biological parts. Until those parts are discovered, there are missing pieces, which Verrier (1997) writes "may result in a feeling that part of oneself has disappeared, leaving the infant with a feeling of incompleteness or lack of wholeness" (p. 38) and "a longing to find the lost Self [sic]" (p. 33). Reconnecting with them is another type of adoption reunion, which occurs between these parts and Self as well as between these parts and the parts that did get adopted. It's a powerful experience. These parts fill in some holes and enrich a relinquishee-adoptee's life with a more fully fleshed-out sense of who they are with all their parts, not just the adopted ones.

Because these biological parts have often been cut off, or exiled, from the very beginning, they don't necessarily present in therapy. But because the healing and integration that's possible once they are contacted can be so profound, it can be helpful for the therapist to seek them out and invite them forward. The therapist can "just ask." Maybe the client is considering searching for their original parents, and one part of them wants to while another part isn't sure. The therapist can ask, "Are there any parts that didn't get adopted that have something to say about it?"

Just naming that there may be parts that didn't get adopted can unveil a whole unexplored and exiled territory, the exploration of which can result in dramatically increased access to Self-energy that can shift the pace of the process. Suddenly, the internal landscape can open up in profound ways as these parts share their innate wisdom and gifts from which the rest of the system has been cut off. In IFS, we know that parts also have Self-energy, and some of these parts that didn't get adopted can be some of the most clear, confident, creative, courageous, connected, calm, compassionate and curious parts of the relinquishee-adoptee, so restoring the connection to them can be a critical piece of healing and transformation. With some of these parts, it is as though they have a direct line to Self.

In order to reduce the risk of backlash, it's important to check first with other parts before exploring unadopted territory. For example, before finding and focusing on parts that didn't get adopted, check with the parts that did and find out if any of them have any fears about connecting with birth parts. The therapist could say, "I'm wondering if there are any parts that didn't get adopted that have something to say about this, and if there are, let's check first if they have concerns about connecting with those parts and inviting them forward." Parts that did get adopted have dedicated their lives to making sure the adoptee is accepted, liked, and wanted, and doesn't get rejected again. Obviously, they don't want anything to jeopardize that. And since they can carry a belief that there was something wrong at birth that led to the relinquishment, why would they want to reconnect with parts that might be responsible for that? It's important to hear what these parts are afraid might happen if the parts that didn't get adopted are found.

Additionally, adopted parts have often formed a large part of the adoptee's identity and often thought they are Self, so they can easily think the therapist or client is trying to get rid of them. These parts need assurance that they will always have a place with the relinquishee-adoptee. They also may worry that a tidal wave of grief will be released if these non-adopted parts are discovered and other parts see how life could have gone if these parts hadn't been exiled and had been able to contribute their gifts all along. For these reasons, taking as much time as these parts need to have their fears heard and addressed is critical. It can be beautiful to witness when parts that didn't get adopted and those that did all come together and are integrated and united in harmony with Self and one another.

Conclusion

Things have come a long way since that 20-something part of me sought therapy all those years ago. In a video that went viral in the adoptee community, adoptees have "flipped the script" and elevated adoptee voices above those of adoptive parents and adoption professionals (YouTube, 2014). And TV shows such as "This Is Us" have led to an increased understanding of the relinquishee-adoptee experience. My goal for this chapter has been to contribute to that understanding using IFS insights and practices.

Remembering an adoptee was a relinquishee first can help a therapist to see them with more clarity. That can help access the confidence to ask for the story of their relinquishment and adoption, in order to connect with the parts that may have brought them to therapy. Implicit direct access can further help parts feel understood, which further calms them so they can, ultimately, relax and trust Self. Awareness of potential triggers for relinquishee-adoptees presents opportunities to identify prospective trailheads, while awareness of biological advantages and pro-adoption parts further increases connection that facilitates healing. Finally, exploring parts that didn't get adopted offers a portal to increased connections that can bring undiscovered riches to the whole system.

All of that would be a good place to start, but more awareness is needed. The narrative that centers adoption as a happy outcome persists. Adoption stories are still told primarily as "adoption" stories, not relinquishment-adoption stories. But "both-and" with all its inherent complexity, is a more helpful approach, and IFS invites a powerfully therapeutic approach for moving toward wholeness. Alongside gratitude of some parts for the experiences and opportunities they had as a result of having been adopted lies enormous grief of other parts from not getting to grow up in their family surrounded by their people. Alongside a feeling of not fitting into either family, birth or adoptive, can be a feeling of fitting into both. Relinquishee-adoptees deserve recognition of their both-and experience and the ambivalence their parts carry. Self sees this.

There is also distance to cover in recognizing adoptees as the marginalized group they are and seeing the parts that developed as a result of that marginalization. The collective Self of all relinquishee-adoptees can envision a day when relinquishee-adoptees are no longer the only group of people denied the right of knowing from whom they came, along with access to their original, true, and accurate birth certificates. The day will come when people scratch their heads in wonder over why relinquishee-adoptees were ever given falsified birth documents. Parts of relinquishee-adoptees can hope for a day when the United States follows Australia's lead and issues an apology to birth mothers/parents and adoptees alike for the systems that forcibly separated them.

But even a formal governmental apology won't heal parts burdened by the trauma of separation from their mother. Only Self can do that, with your skillful help.

KEY TAKEAWAYS

- Include relinquished parts.
- Start with the parts' story of relinquishment and adoption.
- Speaking directly to parts can be very helpful.
- Be sensitive to language and situations that can trigger relinquished & adopted parts.
- Be mindful of biological advantages and pro-adoption parts.
- Not all parts get adopted.

AUTHOR BIO

Kathy Mackechney, LCSW (she/her) is a Certified IFS Therapist and consultant with a private practice in Denver. Kathy specializes in serving adoptees and adoptive parents. Kathy knew she'd found the model for her the first time she heard Dr. Richard Schwartz speak and thought of the 8-year-old adopted girl with whom she'd done inner-child work. Kathy offers a workshop titled "Not All Parts Get Adopted," the title of which came from a part of her after she met extended biological family members. Kathy is in contact with both her maternal and paternal families by birth and relishes the ongoing discovery of what she has in common with them. She also is a stepparent who continues to learn about the overlap between step parenting and adoptive parenting. She is a Buddhist and cyclist who deeply appreciates the natural beauty of the outdoor world and loves reading, writing, skiing, being in the mountains, and doing things with her husband, friends, and family.

REFERENCES

Fields, A. (2022). What does it mean to center marginalized voices? *Anti-Racism Daily*. www.the-ard.com/2022/04/11/what-does-it-mean-to-center-marginalized-voices/

Lifton, B. J. (1994). *Journey of the adopted self: A quest for wholeness.* BasicBooks.

Schwartz, R. C. (2013). *Internal Family Systems therapy: New dimensions.* Routledge.

Schwartz, R. C. (2013). The therapist-client relationship and the transformative power of self. In M. Sweezy & E. L. Ziskind (Eds.), *Internal Family Systems therapy: New dimensions* (pp. 1-23). Routledge.

YouTube. (2014, Nov. 7). *Adoptees "flip the script" on national adoption month.* www.youtube.com

YouTube. (2010). *Adoption and addiction full lecture.* www.youtube.com

Verrier, N. N. (1993). *The primal wound.*

GOING DEEPER

From Kathy Mackechney

1) Website:
   a. www.adopteetherapy.com

2) Workshop:
   a. "Not All Parts Get Adopted." Email kathy@adopteetherapy.com for information.

From Other Sources

1) Websites:
   a. www.adopteetherapy.com
   b. www.aprildinwoodie.com
   c. www.dearadoption.com
   d. www.growbeyondwords.com
   e. www.adoptionmosaic.com
   f. www.theempresshan.wixsite.com
   g. www.adopteesconnect.com
   h. www.adoptionknowledge.org
   i. www.adoptiontruthandtransparency.org

2) Books:
   a. Chung, N. (2018). *All you can ever know*. Catapult.
   b. Clarke, J. I., & Dawson, C. (1998). *Growing up again: Parenting ourselves, parenting our children*. Hazelden.
   c. Easterly, S. (2019). *Searching for mom: A memoir*. Heart Voices.
   d. Eldridge, S. (1999). *Twenty things adopted kids wish their adoptive parents knew*. Dell Publishing.
   e. Heffron, A. (2016). *You don't look adopted*. Anne Heffron.
   f. Lifton, B. J. (1994). *Journey of the adopted self: A quest for wholeness*. BasicBooks.
   g. Lifton, B. J. (1988). *Lost and found: The adoption experience*. Harper Perennial.
   h. Nydam, R. (1999). *Adoptees come of age*. Westminster John Knox Press.
   i. Purvis, K. B., Cross, D. R., & Sunshine, W. L. (2007). *The connected child: For parents who have welcomed children*. McGraw-Hill.
   j. Watson, K. W., & Reitz, M. (1992). *Adoption and the family system*. The Guilford Press.
   k. Ridghaus, & Frank, D. (2018). *Six word adoption memoirs: A picture book*. Mennonite Press Inc.

l. Roszia, S. K., & Maxon, A. D. (2019). *Seven core issues in adoption and permanency: A comprehensive guide to promoting understanding and healing in adoption, foster care, kinship families and third party reproduction.* Jessica Kingsley Publishers.
   m. Soll, J. (2000). *Adoption healing: A path to recovery.* Gateway Press.
   n. Verrier, N. N. (1997). *The primal wound.* Gateway Press.
   o. Verrier, N. N. (2003). *Coming home to self: The adopted child grows up.* Gateway Press.

3) Trainings:
   a. Adoption Mosaic, adoptionmosaic.com/courses
   b. Grow Beyond Words, growbeyondwords.com/events
   c. Paul Sunderland Adoption and Addiction Full Lecture on YouTube

4) Podcasts:
   a. Adoptees On
   b. Born in June, Raised in April
   c. This Adoptee Life (Consider beginning with the interview with Lara Leon (Ep. 12).)

APPENDIX A

Checklist For Working with Adoptees

☐ Am I remembering to reframe them as a relinquishee or relinquishee-adoptee to honor parts that were removed from their biological family?

☐ Did I start by inviting their parts to share their experience of what they know about what led to their relinquishment and adoption?

☐ Am I providing attuned, compassionate validation directly from my core Self-energy?

☐ Am I listening with an ear for things that could be triggering specifically for a relinquishee-adoptee's parts?

☐ (If applicable) Am I examining my own advantages as a biological and identifying and exploring any pro-adoption parts of me?

☐ Have I inquired about exploring parts that didn't get adopted?

IFS AND ANCESTRAL LINEAGE HEALING

RESTORING BELONGING AND RECONNECTION WITH ANCESTRAL WISDOM AND COLLECTIVE SELF-ENERGY

Daphne Fatter, PhD
Reviewer: Daniel Foor, PhD

Both IFS and ancestral lineage healing (ALH) have profoundly changed my life. Integrating these two models has further revealed an unseen world that I am humbly in awe of. I write this chapter from a worldview that suggests life after death, and the notion that developing a direct relationship with one's ancestral guides is possible and beneficial. I propose that integrating IFS and ALH can help clients access more Self-energy and foster ancestral healing, which subsequently can shift the organization of clients' internal system of parts.

I want to acknowledge that the intersection of these two models sits outside of traditional Western medical frameworks. As such, this chapter may elicit a significant shift in perspective that may surprise or even confuse readers from a Western mindset. I want to normalize any disbelief, fear, skepticism, or activation that may emerge as you read this chapter.

Both IFS and ALH are practiced with respect to and inclusion of the client's world view, cultural and spiritual frameworks, and faith and religious identities (if any). To integrate these models, clients ask for consent from their internal parts as needed. In addition, depending on the clients' worldview, clients at the beginning of the ALH process can ask for consent and support from any spiritual resources they may already have a direct connection with (Holy Spirit, God, Yahweh, Allah, the Great Spirit, Olodumare, the Orishas, Buddha, Bodhisattvas, Vishnu, or nature-based beings, to name a few). Clients are not asked to bypass or give up their own cultural and/or spiritual worldview, faith, or identities in order to practice ancestral healing—these are integrated and deeply honored in the integration of these two models.

Given that this approach to ancestral healing may be outside of the realm of familiarity, particularly for Western readers, I encourage you to invite in your own curiosity, befriend parts that may get activated, and ask those parts to consider this integration as a possibility. I invite you to draw your own conclusions honoring your own cultural and spiritual worldviews and identities. There is an open invitation to the reader to journal while reading this chapter to help befriend any parts that may be getting activated throughout the chapter, asking those parts what they need from you, and inviting your system to follow your curiosity.

In this chapter, I will address ways that partnering with ancestral guides for ancestral lineage healing (ALH), based on the work of Daniel Foor, PhD, can be integrated with IFS. Dr. Foor's model of ancestral lineage healing is a structured, intentional process of partnering relationally with one's own ancestral guides and repairing relational ruptures and connection by transforming deceased family members in spirit across time on the lineage to wellness. First, I will explain the assumptions of the ALH lens, the five steps of the ALH method, and provide options with IFS at each ALH step. I then will discuss my clinical experience in integrating ALH with IFS, including proposing ways to partner with ancestral guides for IFS and for unburdening legacy burdens. In addition, I will propose how clients can partner with protective guides to help clients release unattached burdens or when clients have an unwell spirit of the deceased blended with a part.

This integration can offer a theoretical framework for ancestral lineage healing for you or for your IFS clients. After reading this chapter, you can invite in curiosity about how your own parts and/or your client's parts may be connected to their blood lineages. After reading this chapter, you may want to begin the ALH process first by connecting with your own protective guide—any spiritual or other than human resource that you already know and trust (e.g. asking Holy Spirit, God, Buddha, Allah, Vishnu, the Great Spirit, or the Orishas to serve a protective function for you) per this chapter. You are welcome to begin this method of ancestral lineage healing using Dr. Foor's (2017) book along with this chapter for direction to connect with your ancestral guides for your own ancestral lineage healing.

Whether you decide to pursue this practice of ALH or not, this chapter offers ways for IFS therapists and practitioners to create more ease, protection, and discernment in the legacy unburdening process and in working with unattached burdens. In addition, this chapter provides a broad framework for clinicians to work with any spirits that may show up in IFS. Even if you have parts that may feel afraid, skeptical, or uncomfortable, the principles of ALH can assist your work with client's parts and legacy burdens and provide ways to expand a relational sense of family, resilience, and belonging. In addition, the principles of ALH can help clinicians enhance their understanding of common lived experiences, including clients' experiences of grief and bereavement, and assist client and clinician in conceptualizing experiences that may occur for clients in the dying process.

In very practical terms, integrating ALH with IFS can be beneficial when a client:

- Wants to explore cultural identities, belonging, and ways to embody ancestral and cultural gifts.
- Experiences a deep pull to better understand the impact family patterns, ancestral heirlooms, and burdens may have on their parts.
- Discovers parts in IFS that carry burdens that are specifically connected to ancestral and/or collective trauma and/or historical or current systemic oppression.
- Experiences parts with unresolved grief, including grief that may be handed down generationally or through legacy burdens.
- Encounters protectors or exiles that have difficulty trusting Self due to attachment trauma.
- Has unresolved matters with blood relatives who are now deceased including those who passed away abruptly, unexpectedly, prematurely, or in traumatic ways.
- Befriends parts that carry legacy burdens that may not seem to fully resolve in IFS practiced in and of itself.
- Has parts that carry the lived experience of adoption and/or people with adoption histories that feel pulled to explore their blood ancestors whom they may know nothing about.
- Feels pulled in IFS to explore spiritual, transpersonal, or culturally based resources including deepening relationships with other than human guides.
- Wants to make sense of having a deceased loved one or other than human guide, including an ancestral guide, connect with them through dreams, plant medicine journeys, psychotherapy, or during everyday life.
- Has deeply empathic, highly sensitive, or intuitive parts that may sense others energy, or traumas, and/or be burdened by all the sensory input they are receiving from the outside world.
- Experiences parts holding beliefs or burdens due to on-going conflict, estrangement, or cut off relationships with biological family or who have experienced trauma directly from relatives (living or deceased).
- Has deceased relatives blending with their parts in supportive or unsupportive ways.
- Prepares for their own death or the death of a loved one.

Thus, this chapter offers *both* a theoretical roadmap *and* a treatment option for various emergent parts, clinical and transpersonal issues, and drives in clients' systems. That said, as with many other clinical models addressed in this book, guiding a client in the process of ALH requires advanced training and requires a practitioner to have partnered with ancestral guides to repair their own blood lineages in spirit.

So, Who Are the Ancestors?

Ancestors are our deceased blood kin from whom we are descendants. This includes people you may know or have heard stories about, like your deceased extended family, grandparents, and great-grandparents. This also includes family from many generations ago that you may have no narrative or family story about. Even if you don't know your genetic history or are adopted, the ALH model proposes that you have blood ancestors that it is possible to connect with in spirit. I propose that integrating IFS and ALH models provides an opportunity for people to connect with an ancestral guide in spirit which can offer a bi-directional process of healing between your ancestors and you (and your parts).

There are many practices around the world for ancestral healing. I want to acknowledge that the content on the ancestral lineage healing method are used with permission from Daniel Foor, PhD and are from Dr. Foor's foundational book and his courses on ancestral healing which can be found in the Going Deeper section. This method created by Foor is intended for personal and family healing and cultural transformation and is rooted in animism. Animism suggests that living humans are just one part of a much larger web of relationships that all have consciousness, which includes our ancestors.[1] While many cultures practice animism worldwide, the ALH model is not sourced from any specific culture or singular religious tradition.

If You're Feeling Rattled

Just reading this section may rattle your parts. This framework about ancestors or these assumptions about the deceased may activate parts that align with a particular religion or spiritual tradition that is in conflict with these assumptions. That's okay—this approach invites parts' fears and concerns about direct connection with ancestral guides to the forefront. We can invite in curiosity using the 6 Fs from IFS:[2]

- **Find:** Where are you noticing activated parts in and around your body?
- **Focus:** Bring your attention to these parts and let them know that you are right here with them. Remind these parts that they are not being bypassed and we are not trying to get rid of them or their worldview.
- **Flesh out:** How are you experiencing these parts? Can you see, feel, or sense them?

- **Feel Towards:** How do you feel towards these parts? If not, one of the 8 Cs, see if you can invite in more curiosity to find out what these parts wants you to know. Remind them that you are not here to change their beliefs or values.
- **Be-Friend** these parts to find out how old the parts think you are and what these parts are hoping to accomplish. Ask them what they need from you to be willing to read further about these two models, knowing that you are not asking the parts to betray their belief system, or worldview. Are they willing for you to be an inquisitive student as you read?
- **Fears:** What are the fears and concerns of these activated parts? What are they scared would happen if these parts didn't do their job?

It is not uncommon, particularly for Western readers, to have skeptical parts activated when considering the ALH perspective. Befriending skeptical parts can help people find out about the ALH perspective from an inquisitive student standpoint. If you choose to consider the connection between parts and our blood lineages, you are welcome to directly ask any activated parts—"What blood lineage(s) are you connected to?" If you receive an answer, you may learn from your internal system about protective patterns or beliefs potentially passed down intergenerationally.

This approach to ancestral healing, per Dr. Foor, is based on four assumptions about the deceased that align with the worldview of animism:[3]

1. "Consciousness continues after death."
2. "Not all of the dead are equally well," and the dead can change.
3. "The living and the dead can communicate."
4. "The living and the dead can strongly affect one another."

In integrating IFS and ALH models, our parts' gifts, beliefs, and burdens are a microcosm of larger collective patterns within our blood lineages. From an IFS lens, mental health symptoms are due to parts stuck in extreme roles in order to protect the exiles holding unbearable pain.[4] From an ALH perspective, mental health symptoms are not solely due to personal experiences a client has endured but are also connected to a potential backlog of disconnection and burdened deceased (i.e. unwell deceased) in one's own ancestral lineages. Per the ALH lens, the accumulation of energy from the burdened deceased from the multiple sources of collective trauma, cultural harms, and systemic oppressions over time experienced on a given lineage (e.g. impacts of colonialism, racism, genocide, enslavement, land theft and dislocation, poverty, famine, migration, etc.) and lack of conscious intentional connection with ancestral guides contributes to intergenerational and collective patterns in ancestral lineages and contributes to the legacy burdens our parts may carry.

The connection between historical, collective, ancestral, and intergenerational trauma and an individual's current mental health symptoms has been more recently proposed in the field of psychology.[5] In addition, epigenetic literature suggests that the impact of trauma may be passed down through the generations in ways we are still beginning to understand through research (e.g. on pregnant women who witnessed 9/11 World Trade Center attacks in the United States,[6] descendants of Rwandan genocide survivors,[7] descendants of Holocaust survivors,[8] and the development of PTSD[9]). Thus, we can invite in curiosity and consider from various perspectives the multiple potential ways parts may hold, feel, or carry the imprint of our ancestors.

We All Have Ancestral Guides, Just Like We All Have Self

Just like IFS is based on the premise that we have Self that we can connect to, embody, and live from, the ALH model proposes that we also all have well ancestral guides in spirit from somewhere in time on any given blood lineage. In this model, ancestral guides are deceased family members that know how to transform the spirits of the deceased on their given blood lineage to help them become well in spirit and connected with each other in spirit, so that the lineage becomes a fluid collective spirit body of collective Self-energy. Just like our parts can transform, unburden, and shift roles in our internal systems when they are in relationship with Self, in ALH, the spirits of deceased family can transform and shift in the larger ecosystem of ancestors when they connect with a guide. A goal in IFS is to liberate parts such that their natural valuable states can be restored, and their gifts can shine.[10] This aligns with ALH in that we ask the ancestral guide to restore the lineage as a whole to their connected nature so that the gifts of the lineage can move through our parts and our system.

Five Steps of Ancestral Lineage Healing

The first step of ancestral lineage healing is to set a ritual container. The practice of setting a ritual container can be integrated in IFS to help create more safety during legacy unburdening and working with any spirits that may emerge in IFS, as well as in releasing unattached burdens. The ALH model approaches ancestral guides using a specific protocol that honors intention and ritual safety. During each of these five steps, it is important to set a ritual container for this work. It is practiced at the beginning and the end of the session the same way each time until the fifth step of ALH is complete.

The function of ritual protection in this work is two-fold:

1) Energetic hygiene: Like washing your face before bed, we want to release any energetic dirt that we may have inadvertently picked up from the external world.

2) Relational protection and support: This work is relational and having relational support is inherently helpful and can be protective when needed. For example, protective guides can help stand in between us and unwell deceased.

DEFINITIONS

Ritual container: Any intentional practice of creating energetic protection and boundaries in the space around you.

Protective guide: Any supportive spirit guide or being that serves as a protective resource that the client already knows and trusts. This is client-centered based on the client's worldview and lived experience. The client chooses whatever resource that is protective. This may include spiritual figures, deities, angels, animal or nature-based spirits, the elements, or divine love. From a Judeo-Christian tradition, this may include God, Holy Spirit, Yahweh, the Holy Trinity, or specific Saints. From an Islamic tradition, this may include Allah, the Holy Spirit, or calling on guardian angels. From a Buddhist tradition, this may include Buddha, or specific Bodhisattvas. From a Hindu tradition, this may include Vishnu, or specific Hindu Gods or Goddesses. From a Yoruba tradition, this may include Olodumare or specific Orishas. If the client doesn't already have a protective guide or, from a secular perspective, the client, per their choosing, explores their sense of protection by connecting with a sense of love, light, or the natural world such as trees, the ocean, or specific special places in nature where the client feels a sense of being protected. Some people may choose to call on deceased pets as a protective guide.

Unwell deceased: Since the ALH model proposes that not all dead are equally well in spirit, unwell deceased are any deceased who per Dr. Foor's 1-10 wellness scale are within a 1-3 range in being troubled and/or failed to fully make the transition upon death. Using the word "unwell" is not meant to pathologize, disrespect, or judge the deceased or individual deceased family members. Unwell deceased refer to the troubled energetic state of spirits. Based on my clinical experience, I propose that unwell deceased can be thought of as being spirits that are burdened in similar ways that our internal parts carry burdens. In addition, unwell deceased can be spirits who are disconnected from the lineage. Integrating IFS and ALH, I propose that the unwell deceased are very burdened and stuck in a state of being burdened that is potentially impacting parts in the living client and the client's ancestral lineage as a whole.

The way ritual safety is practiced using this ALH method is for the client to call on protective guides or helper spirits they already know and trust (see the call out box for several options). Once the client is in relational connection with their protective guide, the client asks their protective guide to energetically clear their space and then set an energetic boundary around the space within which they sit. This serves as a ritual container, intentionally creating an invisible boundary around their space to shield from negative or unhelpful energy to create a spiritually safe space. In my experience, and per Dr. Foor, when this is practiced over and over again, it creates a rhythm and familiarity for clients' parts which can help further develop critical discernment of what is a part within their internal system and what is not.

Whether or not one proceeds with all five steps of ALH, befriending a protective guide in and of itself is a helpful resource to have for self-care as a therapist. Protective guides can help release vicarious trauma and support energetic hygiene to sustain vitality long-term in the helping role as an IFS therapist or practitioner. In addition, knowing how to support clients to befriend a protective guide is useful to strengthen clients' relational resources and also is particularly helpful to use in releasing blended spirits of the deceased or unattached burdens, which will be discussed later.

Step One: Assessing Blood Lineages

The first step of this approach to ALH is a structured assessment of the client's four primary blood lineages, which are the client's father's father's lineage, father's mother's lineage, mother's mother's lineage and mother's father's lineage. These terms refer specifically to the blood lineages that provided the egg and sperm for ultimately creating the client. During the assessment step, the client identifies how well each of their four main blood lineages are in spirit. Since this may be a new language in discerning the level of wellness of the deceased on a given blood lineage, one helpful method during this step is to use Foor's scale, ranging from 1-10, in which 7-10 is "very well in spirit", 4-7 is "not super well" in spirit, and 1-3 is "unwell or troubled deceased."

While the client may only think of the recently deceased when assessing their blood lineages, it is important that the client assess the health of the lineage as a whole across time. This is not about evaluating individual family members who have passed away—this is noticing the energetic vibrancy of the collective dead over periods of time. Thus, we assess the wellness of three distinct collective areas on the lineage as a whole:

- Ancient ones (2,000 before common era to 300,000 years).
- Middle ones (500-2,000 years ago).
- Recently deceased (Most recently deceased person on the lineage-500 years).

After learning about the wellness of each blood lineage, the client decides which blood lineage to start with. In general, starting with the blood lineage that has the most wellness is a good place to start ancestral healing before working with lineages that need more healing.

Step Two: Befriending and Partnering with an Ancestral Guide

In the ALH method, the second step is to ask for an ancestral guide to make their presence known from a time on the lineage where the ancestors are well in spirit and connected to each other.

Four questions help to discern whether the spirit that shows up is the ancestral guide:

1. Are you a well ancestor on this blood lineage?
2. Are you willing and able to serve as a guide on this lineage with any repair needed?
3. Are you well connected and in good relations with all those elders who came before you?
4. The client is asked to check in their own body and internal system of parts, if they feel good and safe in this ancestor's presence. We proceed only if there is a full "yes."

If the answers to all these questions are "yes," then a process of befriending the guide begins. In the ALH method, the client nurtures the on-going relationship with the guide, just as one would with a respected elder. Whether or not the client decides to complete the full five steps of ALH, connecting with and befriending an ancestral guide can be greatly beneficial for the client's parts, can help provide additional Self-led attachment figures for parts to feel seen by and connected with, and can help the client access more Self-energy.

Honoring Skepticism

It is very common to have a skeptical part emerge in the first step or two of the ALH steps, asking the questions, "Am I making this up?" "Is this real?" Skepticism is a valuable protector that can help keep us from getting in harm's way.

By integrating ALH and IFS, you can:

1. Befriend any skeptical parts, asking its fears and concerns about these steps of ALH.
2. Assure the part that is welcome and, with curiosity, ask the part what lineage is it connected to. Specifically, what lineage does the skepticism come from?
3. Whether or not you complete the 5 steps of ALH, you can ask the ancestral guide on this lineage about the skepticism, any pattern of skepticism on this lineage, what the antidote is for it, and whether it is connected to any gifts or burdens on the lineage.
4. Ask the ancestral guide to directly connect to the skeptical part with Self as a witness. This can provide relational support for the skeptical part from Self and from the ancestral guide.

After befriending the guide and receiving a blessing, the client asks the guide to begin the lineage healing process. This entails asking the guide to specifically encompass the deceased whom are between the guide and the living client in chronological time on the lineage in a healing cocoon, net, or healing space. Once the guide creates a healing cocoon in whatever way that manifests, the guide then begins bringing healing to those in the cocoon, helping any deceased on the lineage who are not yet well in spirit transform to a state of wellness. I propose that from an IFS perspective we can consider this as a collective unburdening process that happens when guides bring healing to those deceased in the cocoon.

A Space for Healing

The use of a healing cocoon is used in ALH by the guides as a "location" where healing occurs. I propose that this can be considered a parallel process to the retrieval step in IFS in that the deceased are in essence moved into a different location (e.g. the healing cocoon) in order to receive healing, similar to how exiled parts are retrieved from traumatic scenes to present day or to a safe space to facilitate being witnessed by Self and be unburdened. The healing cocoon also serves a protective function, so the client does not directly interact with any unwell deceased and any unwell deceased are contained in their own space to receive healing. This acts as another layer of ritual protection and energetic boundary so that the guide is the only one directly interacting with unwell deceased. In my clinical experience in integrating IFS, client's parts may viscerally experience a sense of relief when the unwell deceased are in a healing cocoon.

The guide brings healing to the deceased in the cocoon while the client's Self and their parts witness this process. It is important to note that only the deceased go into the healing cocoon, not the client or anyone who is living. As much as the client's parts may want to help, the client stays in their energetic ritual container while the guide directly interacts with the dead.

Step Three: Healing Among the Older Dead

During this step, the guide brings healing to the older deceased on the ancestral lineage, starting with those that are down lineage that came after the guide in time. During this step, since any unwell dead on the lineage are in a healing container, we ask the guide about the burdens of the lineage and ask for information about what occurred on the lineage as a whole.

In my clinical experience and per Dr. Foor, our ancestral guides have access to the memory networks that include information about our ancestral lineages across time. As ancestral lineage healing occurs, ancestral guides will often share a download of information about "what happened" on the lineage including the expression of gifts as well as legacy burdens. I propose that this can be seen as a parallel process of Self updating our internal parts in IFS. When deceased on our lineages become "ancestralized," they move to a 7-10 in wellness, and are woven in with the collective elders on the lineage. In essence, they become part of collective Self-energy of the ancestral lineage.

Step Four: Healing with the Recently Deceased

Per ALH, the healing process tends to slow down when the guide brings healing to the recently deceased whom typically have more attachment to their life and may be in various states of a transitional process that occurs after death. We, the living, also are more likely to have parts of us connected to or attached to the recently deceased in various ways. Oftentimes, this is a dynamic process when parts get activated, and IFS integration is very therapeutic. This step commonly activates deep grief, sadness, longing, anger, unresolved family conflicts, the impact of collective trauma, and legacy burdens in clients' systems.

Once this step is complete, then everyone deceased on the lineage is well in spirit and connected with each other. We can then ask the guide at the completion of this step to bring a blessing from the lineage to the bones, ashes, and any other remains and belongings of all those deceased on the lineage. This brings the elevated healed energy from the collective lineage to the earth realm in ways that are honoring of the deceased and are tangible for the client.

Step Five: Extending Healed Energy and Blessings to the Living

During this step, we ask the guide to extend the lineage blessings down lineage to the living including the client, each generation of extended family, and future generations. This step often can bring a sense of purpose and increased sense of belonging and can bring an inner re-organization of a client's system to include the ancestors. In integrating an IFS lens, I propose that this is a similar process to inviting in the positive qualities after unburdening an exile. In ALH at this step, all of the client's parts benefit, and positive qualities are sent from the guide to all living family and future generations.

Ways Ancestors Connect with Us: An IFS Perspective

In exploring the intersection of ALH and IFS, it is important to honor three distinct ways our ancestors interact with our internal systems. Per the ALH lens, ancestors can have direct contact with us. Based on my clinical experience, I propose that in addition to direct spirit contact, ancestors relationally connect with our internal systems through our parts' legacy gifts and burdens they carry, as well as through ancestors blending with our parts.

1. Our Ancestors Can Make Direct Contact with Us.

From the ALH perspective, which is consistent with my clinical experience, the deceased, including our blood ancestors, can communicate with the living at any time, even if we do not have any intention to connect and we do not hold a cultural background or spiritual framework for knowing how to connect with them. This is also supported by research on the dying[11] as well as research on people during bereavement when spirit contact with one's ancestors is common.[12]

So, what does this mean for IFS and in everyday life? Just as it is wise to find out who is outside the door of your home before opening the door, similar etiquette is wise to use with spirits wanting to make contact. I suggest that if you or your IFS client have the spirit of a deceased person show up, it is important to not assume that they are well in spirit or can provide help. Per an ALH perspective, it is possible to access a larger web of relational support. The client can call-in protective guides or other spiritual resources that the client already knows as needed. The client can ask protective guides to stand between the client and the deceased showing up if the deceased are not well in spirit. If the client has an ancestral guide on this lineage, the client can ask the guide to surround the deceased in a healing cocoon if they are unwell.

Recently deceased may serve as a relational resource in a way that feels good to the client's internal parts. Yet, from an ALH lens, it is important not to assume that if the recently dead are trying to make contact with the client, that they are well in spirit (i.e., they may not be in a capacity to help). It is also important to not assume that they represent the entirety of lineage just because they are deceased. The client can ask the guide to be a mediator with any unwell recently deceased that may be trying to make contact as needed.

2. Our Ancestors Connect Through Our Parts' Legacy Gifts, Heirlooms, and Legacy Burdens.

According to IFS, legacy burdens are handed down intergenerationally, through child and caregiver interactions and attachment patterns and passed on to us epigenetically from our blood ancestors.[13] They also can be passed down through culture, absorbed from specific group memberships we have, absorbed from the dominant cultures one navigates, and absorbed from the collective.[14] They can manifest in our parts as the ways our parts respond to stress, and protect ourselves, our parts' belief systems, and survival strategies.[15] Per IFS, our parts can also carry legacy burdens for living family and for our ancestors. From my clinical experience integrating IFS and ALH, unwell deceased can impact any of a client's parts, including their managers, firefighters, and exiles through direct spirit contact, legacy burdens, and/or by blending with their parts.

3. Spirits, including the Dead, Can Blend with Our Parts.

According to the ALH lens, this can happen consciously yet oftentimes without us realizing it. This can be a beneficial and positive experience and happen when we are in flow (e.g. during creative expression, through the body in exploring the erotic, movement, or exercise, etc.). Spirits and unhelpful entities (i.e.

what we call unattached burdens in IFS) can also blend with our parts after traumatic experiences, during times of vulnerability or hardship, and/or shortly after a loved one has passed. The unwell deceased can blend with our parts so that they are living through our parts.

Developing Discernment

In integrating IFS and ALH, discernment is developed to help the client better understand:

- What belongs to an internal part?
- What is the relationship between a specific part and one's blood lineages?
- Which blood lineages are connected to the legacy burdens a specific part is holding?
- Is the part blended with any unwell deceased from blood lineages?
- Is the part blended with any unwell deceased that are not from blood lineages?
- Is the part blended with an unattached burden?

It is important to note that our internal systems can be in relationship with deceased that do not belong to our blood lineages. This can include people we knew when they were alive that have passed away, deceased we did not know when they were alive, and unwell deceased that are connected to the land on which we live that hold pain from historical trauma.

In my clinical experience, when unwell deceased blend with a client's parts, they often show up invasively, similar to how exiles show up in IFS. They can also resemble how unattached burdens present themselves. For example, we can invite in curiosity about whether unwell deceased are blending with the client's parts when the client or their parts feel disoriented, confused, overwhelmed, rageful, disproportionately angry, unending grief, despair, insatiable yearning, deep longing, nausea, strong physical pain, strong physical sensations, heaviness, fear, dread, or anticipation in the body that often times do not come with any other information or narrative. In ALH, we ask the client to unblend from those unwell deceased by asking the ancestral guide to move into direct relationship with the unwell deceased to relocate and cocoon them however the guide sees fit. When clients become unblended from unwell deceased in their systems, they can gain more clarity about what parts in their internal systems are more likely to blend with the dead or with unwelcome entities, such as unattached burdens.

Unattached Burdens

It is important to acknowledge that unattached burdens, which are negative entities, can also attach to us in several ways.[16] I want to normalize that. Like catching a cold, it is common for any human being to have an unattached burden at some point in their internal system. Per IFS, if you suspect an unattached burden is present, ask it first if it's a part.[17] In my practice, if it says "no," I then have the client ask it if it is a deceased family member or if it is connected to a blood lineage? If it says "no," then I ask it if is connected to any unwell deceased (e.g., non-blood deceased, lost spirits, ancestors of place, etc.). This question will tease out the unwell deceased from true unattached burdens. (See Appendix for full recommended protocol)

Both Dr. Foor's ALH perspective and what has been written about unattached burdens in IFS propose that unattached burdens can be parasitic in nature and can use fear as a weapon to try to stay in a client's system.[18] Per the ALH perspective, which is consistent with my clinical experience in integrating ALH and IFS, unattached burdens can attach to and blend with the unwell deceased, can be passed down as part of a legacy burden, and can also attach to and blend with a client's internal parts.

In my practice, I take a communal approach and have a general rule to call in relational spiritual support to directly interact with unwell deceased or unattached burdens, rather than having the client attempt to release them. Dr. Foor and Dr. Frank Anderson both propose that some unattached burdens can effectively leave the client's system by directly asking them to leave,[19] or through the unburdening process.[20] When unattached burdens are connected to unwell deceased, I propose to ask the client to call in their ancestral guides and bigger spiritual resources. When bigger unattached burdens are present, it is important for the client to call in bigger relational resources from the spirit realm,[21] such as the client's protective guides, bigger spirits, or deities that they already know and trust.

In my experience, when in the presence of bigger unattached burdens, by design the nervous system, the body, and parts will likely detect potential danger or threat by experiencing fear. In this situation, fear can serve as a form of intelligence,[22] and is not solely from an exile or burdened part. Thus, we want to honor this intelligence by having the client call in relational resources for the client's system. My standard practice is to have the client call in connection with larger spiritual resources to ask them to directly release the unattached burden. My approach contrasts with a common practice in IFS of having Self ask any part to not be afraid, which in my experience could create a relational rupture between Self and the part experiencing fear.

When the client is relationally connected with bigger spiritual resources they already know and trust to directly work with unattached burdens, their nervous system and parts will experience their fear naturally dissipate. This aligns with what we know about Polyvagal theory in that relational resources can cue the client's nervous system to a calm state which overrides any hyperarousal or hypoarousal response.[23] From an IFS lens, the bigger spiritual resources are serving as Self-energy for the client's system. After the client calls in these resources, the client can ask them to directly release the identified unattached burden from their system. Calling in protective guides and bigger spiritual deities to directly work with unattached burdens is effective and also supports a relational communal approach to unattached burdens rather than having the client, a part, or the therapist directly interact with unattached burdens or expect them to extract the unattached burden on their own.

Partnering with Ancestral Guides in IFS

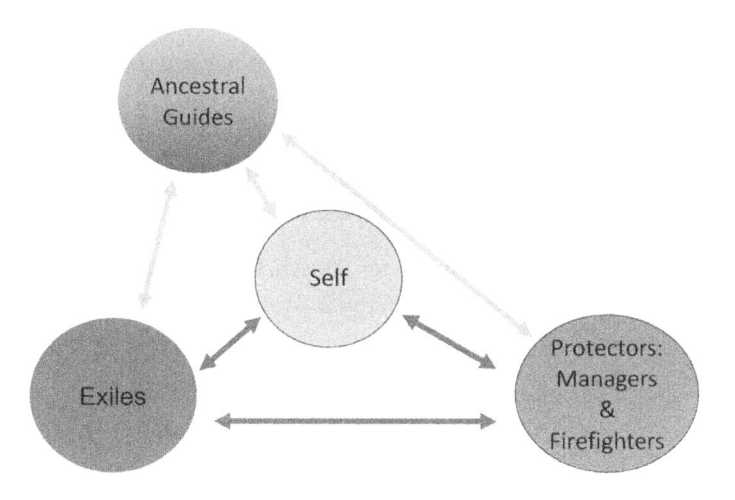

Ancestral guides are sources of collective Self-energy. Ancestral guides can have direct consensual relationships with one's parts as well as a direct consensual relationship with Self.

Partnering with ancestral guides can be used in IFS to:

- Help with unblending: When overwhelmed by a part, ask the guide to connect with the part, and Self.
- Guide the unburdening process of a part either in coordination with Self or from the guide being in direct relationship with a burdened part.
- Serve as an additional relational resource and source of collective Self-energy during the retrieval, witnessing stage, and do-over stages of IFS.
- Help our parts more clearly and intentionally embody heirlooms, gifts, and blessings from our blood lineages. This can provide an inner decolonization and serve as a liberation-informed practice.[24]
- Help us understand how the unwell deceased on the lineage have impacted specific parts.

- Guide the unburdening process of legacy burdens by the guide being in direct relationship with parts holding these legacy burdens.
- Elicit ancestral memory by learning that legacy burdens and ancestral blessings, heirlooms, and gifts are not solely from the remembered dead, but from various points in time along a lineage. This includes the guide providing more information about the impact of larger collective and cultural burdens of one's blood lineages, rather than accessing this information solely from a part.
- Shift our relational orientation to Self, others, and the world, fostering humility and respect towards people with ancestry different than our own.
- Cultivate relational resources that move beyond an individual's system and self-reliance on Self.
- Shift from a lens of individuality towards a felt sense of our belonging to a larger collective eco-system that includes the Earth and spirits, including our blood ancestors.

Whether or not a client completes the ALH steps, if a client has an ancestral guide, the guide can provide Self-energy in systems where the Self of the client is not enough in and of itself to support befriending, witnessing, and unburdening of parts.

Systemic Re-Organization

As clients develop on-going relationships with the ancestral guides from their blood lineages, their internal system begins to re-organize to relationally include the ancestral guides as the face of their collective lineages. Schwartz and Sweezy[25] discuss nested systems, where parts and subparts have a Self. In my experience, we and our parts are the nested systems within the larger ecosystem of our ancestors in spirit.

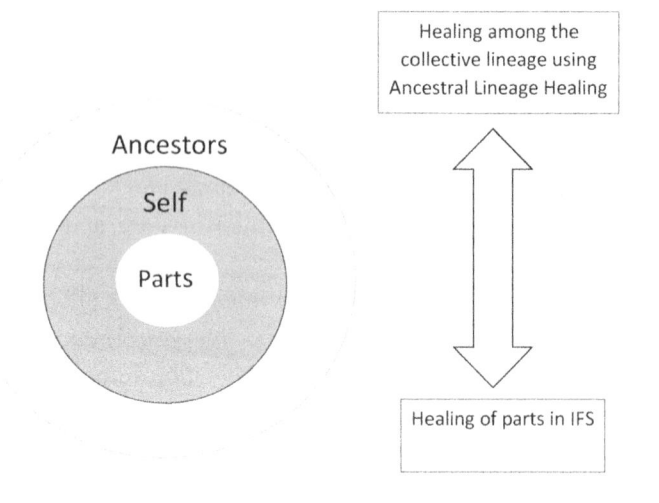

Parallel Process

Just as with our internal parts, these relationships with our ancestral guides are emergent, dynamic, and bi-directional. There is often a parallel process of healing that occurs: As the deceased become well, our parts feel the shifts and the positive impact of the ancestral lineage healing process. Very often internal parts, including those that express themselves somatically, feel, and may mirror, energetic shifts that are happening in the cocoon. As connection becomes restored across the lineage, among the deceased, and between the deceased and the living, our parts receive the healing benefits of this process. As we unburden our parts in IFS, our ancestors fluidly and collectively receive that healing as well.

Just like in IFS, we trust the larger system that includes ancestral guides with how healing needs to unfold and the sequence of the healing process. The result of this re-organization is that legacy burdens that are tied to specific lineages typically emerge in the client's system and unburden more easily. Sometimes a part that holds a legacy burden related to the lineage of focus needs to be befriended by Self first before they trust, or can take in, presence from the ancestral guide. Sometimes parts trust the ancestral guide before being able to repair any relational ruptures with Self. Sometimes parts need to be witnessed by Self and the ancestral guide to release legacy burdens. Sometimes unwell deceased need to be witnessed by the living and the ancient well ones that came before them on the lineage before the unwell deceased are able to be fully received by the lineage as a collective.

The ultimate goal of IFS is to shift towards Self-leadership through attaining balance and harmony within the internal system.[26] In ALH, once a client's four main blood lineages complete the five steps of lineage repair, a shift can happen in which ancestral guides work together with the shared intention of supporting the client. By partnering with ancestral guides, the client has the choice to include the wisdom and perspectives of the guides. In my clinical experience, and per an ALH lens, this does not override the leadership of Self in the internal system, yet it shifts the client's frame of reference to Self being part of a larger ecosystem that includes the ancestors. Thus, Self can work in harmony with ancestral guides, and at the same time, the client can invite in curiosity about the non-dual nature of both being Self-led and being led by the ancestors.

Polarizations: A Microcosm of Opposing Ancestral Protective Strategies

In IFS, polarizations typically occur when there are two parts in extreme roles locked in a power struggle.[27] While there can be many types of pairings of polarized parts,[28] a protector polarized with another protector with opposing protective strategies often protects the same an exile.[29] I have noticed a recurring pattern that the parts that are polarized are connected to different blood lineages.

When this happens and the client has not done ancestral lineage healing, we can be curious about how much the polarization is shaped by unwell deceased moving through the polarized parts.

Based on my clinical experience, this begs the question: how much are we re-enacting ancestral trauma and burdens passed down from our ancestors, particularly in our protective parts and their survival strategies? How is ancestral trauma re-enacted interpersonally with other people's parts? Are ancestral protectors fighting with other ancestral protectors within the internal system intrapersonally and externally interpersonally? Sometimes these can manifest as internal polarized parts embodying complex dynamics that have historic and present-day relevance that is important to acknowledge among the polarized parts (for example, polarized parts connected to ancestors that have been in colonizer and colonized roles, opposing tribes or ancestral lineages with a history of war and conflict, land theft, differing social economic classes, etc.).

Ancestral lineage healing doesn't mean that polarizations within a person's system won't happen, yet when the client has done lineage healing on the two lineages connected to the polarized parts, I invite in the ancestral guides to be present, asking them to work together in the ancestral realm knowing that they are both collectively supporting the living person. I then invite Self and the protective parts to witness this process among the ancestral guides, which often shifts the internal polarization. I propose, which is consistent with the ALH lens, that we can think of this as a 'top-down' or 'up-stream' strategy by working out any conflict between the ancestral guides themselves, which then ripples down the lineage to you and your parts.

In befriending the exile(s) that polarized parts are protecting, we can invite in curiosity and ask the part about any legacy burdens the exile(s) may hold that are connected to more than one ancestral lineage. We also can ask the ancestral guides connected to the polarized parts to move into direct relationship with the exiled parts, asking the guides about any wounding that happened on the lineages contributing to the exile's burdens.

Attachment Patterns and Relational Repair

Ancestral guides are one of many relational options in spirit that the client has access to for Self-led resources to help foster parts' relational repair. In some systems, Self will be enough for parts healing. I have also witnessed that some systems' parts have stronger secure attachments to spirits than to Self. For example, sometimes parts may have a harder time trusting Self and can more easily connect to an ancestral guide as a source of Self-energy.

Attachment wounds, including intergenerational attachment patterns and attachment-oriented legacy burdens, can show up in many ways in the process of connecting with an ancestral guide. Examples include when a client's parts have difficulty befriending a guide, taking in ancestral blessings, trusting the guide's leadership, or receiving love from the guide. In addition, when connecting to a guide, parts can get activated that have concerns about what it means for them to relate to an ancestral guide when there is conflict in the relationship with living family or unresolved conflict with recently deceased family.

The client can ask the guide about the source of attachment patterning and invite in attachments to other than living humans to which the lineage is connected (e.g., animals, deities, elements, specific mountains, or aspects of nature in alignment with the client's worldview). The client can also ask guides about specific ritual practices that may honor and nurture the relationship with the guide and the lineage as a whole. Just as Self can serve as a source of relational repair and healing between parts and Self in IFS, Self and internal parts can receive relational repair and healing from attachment wounds through a secure attachment with an ancestral guide.

Healing Legacy Burdens by Partnering with Ancestral Guides

Our parts carry legacy burdens not solely from the more recent deceased (i.e., any deceased siblings, parents, grandparents, and great-grandparents), but from various points along a lineage. This information can be accessed from the ancestral guide, rather than solely from the burdened part.

While there are many effective ways in IFS to unburden parts holding legacy burdens, partnering with ancestral guides offers two options that can be used together. This is a "both/and" approach in that you are unburdening the part in your internal system, and you also ask the guide to turn towards the deceased to heal any deceased connected to the legacy burden, fulfilling a deeper layer of healing among the dead on the lineage. Doing both of these systemic approaches offers 'outward to inward' healing (from a collective repaired ancestral lineage to guide to parts) and 'inward to outward' healing (from parts to guide to collective repaired lineage). This bi-directional healing moves backwards and forwards across the lineage that includes you and your parts. After these steps are completed, we then ask the guide to bring healing to living family members connected to the legacy burden. (See Appendix for full recommended protocol.)

As in IFS, we follow the sequence of healing that needs to occur to release the legacy burden. In my clinical experience, sometimes parts carrying the legacy burden need the leadership of the ancestral guide in addition to Self. Sometimes the whole internal system benefits from a system-wide update with information about the legacy burden directly from the ancestral guide.

Ideally, legacy burdens are best addressed among parts after the five steps of ancestral healing have been completed. If unwell deceased on the lineage are connected to a given legacy burden, the ancestral guide is the only one working with unwell dead (i.e., you and your parts are not putting forth any effort to make something happen). This helps avoid any role confusion for parts in your internal system and ensures ritual safety when working with the dead.

Common Obstacles During Unburdening Legacy Burdens

1. Connecting with the dead without an ancestral guide. A common practice in IFS is to 'send the burden back' through the lineage without an ancestral guide and without a repaired lineage.[30] Yet, while this may elicit healing in some systems, per Dr. Foor's ALH perspective, this approach presents a level of risk. After all, "sending the burden back" is typically practiced without any protective layers of a ritual container or intentional energetic boundaries around the client's space and doesn't include additional, intentional protective spiritual support (e.g. protective guide). From an ALH perspective, to proceed without an ancestral guide reinforces an individualistic/self-reliant relational patterning that requires that the client or the client's parts do all the work in healing the whole ancestral lineage. This can put the client or the client's part carrying the legacy burden in the relational position to heal the lineage. In addition, the 'sending the burden back' method typically involves asking each ancestor to send their burden back to the end of the generational line, which relates to the lineage as individual members, rather than a collective whole.[31] By contrast, when partnering with an ancestral guide, the guide heals the collective lineage and directly interacts with the deceased, rather than the client or their parts.

2. Loyalty. Another common obstacle in releasing a legacy burden is the client's system being concerned about loyalty to family, loyal to their cultural group, fear of loss of identity, or loss of connection with family or cultural or ethnic group membership.[32] In my clinical experience, partnering with ancestral guides to release legacy burdens helps the client and the burdened part know they don't have to carry this legacy burden to belong. The burdened part can connect with the ancestral guide directly which provides collective Self-energy from the collective ancestral lineage itself, helping the part experience that no matter what, they are communally connected to and belong to the ancestral lineage. This can release aspects of loyalty that may be embedded in the part's burden.

3. Concern for hurting deceased or living family members. Another common obstacle in releasing legacy burdens is the fear that by releasing the legacy burden, it will somehow harm living family and/or hurt the deceased.[33] By completing the ALH process, the client's deceased family are well in spirit and connected to the collective lineage, which the client and the burdened part can witness and experience through the on-going relationship with the ancestral guide. If there is a particular family member or group of family (living or deceased) that the client is concerned will have to carry the burden if they release it,[34] then the ancestral guide (in addition to Self) can directly respond to these concerns. In addition, the client can ask the ancestral guide to extend healing to family members (living and deceased) that the client may be concerned about, which the client's part and client's system can witness.

4. **Assumptions regarding deceased spirits that show up or may be invited in during legacy unburdening.** Sometimes in IFS, a deceased family member in spirit spontaneously shows up or is intentionally invited to witness the burdened part. As previously stated, it is important to take the time to pause and discern the wellness of who you are connecting with before looking to them as a resource. Sometimes our parts drive us to connect to any ancestor that shows up, especially the recently deceased.

Cultural and Collective Legacy Burdens

Cultural and collective legacy burdens will vary depending on the client's ancestry, histories of oppression, and social location/positionality across lineages, including past and present relationship to dominate cultures over time, intersectionality of multiple identities the client and their parts embody, as well as the current state and history of the land on which the client resides. Given that many cultural and collective legacy burdens are on-going in present day, the client can ask the ancestral guide for an antidote to this collective burden on the lineage as well as specific insight, support, and blessings for inner vibrancy in navigating present-day obstacles, hardship, or challenges. The client can access information from the ancestral guide about these collective legacy burdens. In my clinical experience, the ancestral guide may start a process of cocooning those deceased particularly impacted by the collective burden. Even though the guide may approach the healing process of cultural and collective burdens similarly, if not the same as it was when the guide completed the steps of ALH, the guide is bringing healing and antidote to a specific cultural wound or burden. While the antidote cannot control or change external systemic conditions, the antidote may lead to the client further accessing strengths, navigational strategies, and heirlooms from the lineage that can foster resilience.

Paradigm Shift Towards Being Part of a Collective

The more we do our own ancestral healing, the more we are connected to being part of the larger system of our ancestors. In my personal and clinical experience, integrating ALH and IFS can lead to a paradigm shift from reliance on Self to a relational positionality of interdependence, receptivity, and being part of collective. I propose that this is a transpersonal shift away from solely approaching one's internal system through an individual lens and toward relating to one's individual system and internal parts as part of a nested system within a larger relational web that includes the ancestors. This also can shift one's relationship to land, bodies of water, and other beings in nature. This can heighten one's embodied experience of living within an ecosystem on planet Earth with responsibilities to honor the wellness of shared humanity, the planet, and the planet's resources.

Cultural and Collective Repair

As a client's sense of belonging strengthens through this integration of ALH and IFS, the client's system has more capacity and agency to accept the responsibilities that come with being a descendent of their ancestors. Per Dr. Foor, this process can "right-size" us as the living in a way that is steadily generative of humility. It also inherently brings into client's awareness their relational position within the ancestral lineage to receive the mentorship from their ancestral guides in their respective down-lineage position. In my personal and clinical experience, this can challenge our sense of individuality and help us gain clarity and perspective of our collective responsibilities towards larger systemic change and cultural repair in the world.

The evolving relationship with ancestral guides includes an on-going accountability to them. By that I mean that ancestral guides can help provide direction in how to honor the gifts of the lineage to serve the greater good of global humanity, including contributing to larger cultural repair and social justice. Misusing the relationship with ancestral guides for only feeling good, or living in isolation disconnected from everyday life while escaping into just relating with the ancestors—would be a form of spiritual bypassing. Spiritual bypassing occurs when one uses spiritual practices to avoid or circumvent unresolved wounds and developmental tasks.[35]

Being authentically in relationship with our ancestral guides requires humility, respectful reverence, deep listening, and on-going cultivation. This means navigating relationships with ancestral guides while being an active participant in the living world, including tending to present-day suffering. It also includes asking our guides which ancestral gifts can help us navigate current worldwide stressors, atrocities, and injustices. In addition, this includes an examination of the relationship of one's ancestors with larger cultural burdens, while engaging in opportunities for collective healing and communal repair in the world.

Dr. Frank Anderson[36] proposes that love heals trauma through connection between Self and parts. I propose that when the connection between Self and one's ancestral guides is restored, love and the sense of belonging also heals parts. When ancestral guides bring healing and connection to lineages, parts can more easily embody ancestral gifts, which brings relational and cultural repair both personally and collectively.

KEY TAKEAWAYS

- Consider the ALH perspective that parts may be connected to one's blood lineages, and thus one's ancestors.
- ALH and IFS can be integrated to support a client accessing Self energy by connecting with external relational resources that provide collective Self-energy.
- Cultivating relationships with protective guides and ancestral guides can, in and of themselves, provide support for client's systems, including navigating working with unwell deceased and unattached burdens.
- Completing the five ALH steps can re-organize a client's internal system of parts to support the embodiment of ancestral gifts and heirlooms.

AUTHOR BIO

Daphne Fatter, PhD (she/her) is a licensed psychologist, certified Internal Family Systems (IFS) therapist, and Approved Clinical IFS Consultant. She is a certified ancestral healing practitioner, per Dr. Daniel Foor's method of ancestral lineage healing. Dr. Fatter guides groups and workshops for therapists on ancestral lineage healing and IFS worldwide. She practices from an anti-racist, queer-inclusive, and culturally mindful framework in her private practice in Dallas, Texas, on the unceded lands of the Comanche, Wichita, Caddo, and Kickapoo peoples.

REVIEWER BIO

Daniel Foor, PhD (he/him) is a licensed psychotherapist, doctor of psychology, and the author of *Ancestral Medicine: Rituals for Personal and Family Healing*. He is an initiate in the Òrìṣà tradition of Yoruba-speaking West Africa and has learned from teachers of Mahayana Buddhism, Islamic Sufism, and the older ways of his English and German ancestors. Daniel is passionate about training aspiring leaders and change makers in the intersections of cultural healing, animist ethics, and applied ritual arts. He lives with his wife and two daughters near Granada, Spain in the foothills of the Sierra Nevada Mountains.

GOING DEEPER

From Daphne Fatter, PhD

On IFS and Ancestral Healing

1) Website:
   a. www.daphnefatterphd.com

2) Trainings:
   a. Ancestral Lineage Healing Groups and consultation groups in integrating working with ancestral guides with IFS.
   b. IFS consultation.

3) Podcast Interviews:
   a. IFS Talks: https://podcasts.apple.com/ca/podcast/how-ancestral-medicine-informs-ifs-legacy-burdens-work/id1481000501?i=1000526889560

On Other Topics

1) Trainings:

For continuing education credit and professional development (live and on demand): See www.daphnefatterphd.com for upcoming trainings or to schedule an online training.

   a. Integrating Traumatic Memories: Conceptualization and Clinical Considerations in Evidence-based Approaches to Trauma Processing.
   b. Utilizing Phase-Oriented Treatment and Adjunctive Interventions to Regulate Arousal in Trauma Treatment.
   c. An Introduction to Internal Family Systems Therapy.
   d. Using Internal Family Systems for Therapist Self-Care.
   e. Using Internal Family Systems Therapy in Trauma Treatment.
   f. Internal Family Systems Therapy: Why it Works and How to Know If It's a Good Fit
   g. White Race Socialization and White Therapists: Treatment Considerations Surrounding Racial Traumas among BIPOC clients.
   h. A Self-Inquiry into Race Socialization and Internalized Whiteness for White Therapists Treating Racial Trauma.
   i. Befriending White Parts that get Activated by Race and Racism.
   j. Trauma-Informed Stabilization Tools.

2) Podcast Interviews:
   a. The One Inside: www.theoneinside.libsyn.com/ifs-and-hope-for-racist-parts-with-daphne-fatter

3) Other:
   a. Anti-racist groups for white-identified people focused on white race socialization and befriending parts activated by race and racism.

From Daniel Foor, PhD

On Ancestral Healing

1) Website:
   a. www.ancestralmedicine.org
2) Books:
   a. Foor, D. (2017). *Ancestral medicine: Rituals for personal and family healing.* Bear and Company.
3) Trainings and Courses:
   a. Ancestral Lineage Practitioner Training
   b. Ancestral lineage healing online course
4) Podcast Interviews:
   a. www.ancestralmedicine.org/podcasts

On Other Topics

1) Online Courses:

Dr. Foor and Ancestral Medicine offers live and on-demand online courses found at: www.ancestralmedicine.org on the following topics:
   a. Practical Animism
   b. Animist Psychology
   c. Initiations: A Life of Ritual
   d. The Opening Earth
   e. Foundations of Ritual
   f. Care for the Dead and Dying
   g. Inhabiting the Times

Other Sources

On IFS and Legacy Burdens

1) Books:
   a. Sinko, A. (2017). Legacy burdens. In M. Sweezy & E. L. Ziskind (Eds.), *IFS: innovations and elaborations in Internal Family Systems Therapy* (p.p. 164-178). Taylor and Francis.
   b. Anderson, F. G. (2021). Roadblocks to healing. In F. G. Anderson (2021), *Transcending trauma: Healing complex PTSD with Internal Family Systems therapy.* PESI Publishing and Media.

   c. Schwartz, R. C., & Sweezy, M. (2020). *Internal Family Systems therapy* (2nd ed.). The Guilford Press.

Other Sources

On On Animism and Ancestral Medicine

1) Website:
    a. Ancestral Medicine Practitioner Network of trained ALH Practitioners: www.ancestralmedicine.org/practitioner-directory
2) Books:
    a. Harvey, G. (2005). *Animism: Respecting the living world.* Hurst and Co. for more information about animism.
    b. Bojuwoye, O. (2013). Integrating principles underlying ancestral spirits belief in counseling and psychotherapy. *IFE Psychologia: An International Journal,* 21(1), 74–89.
    c. Cadena, M. de la, & Blaser, M. (2018). *A world of many worlds.* Duke University Press for more information about animism.

APPENDIX A

Steps to Partner with an Ancestral Guide for Legacy Unburdening

1. First, ask a protective guide that you already know and trust (e.g. Holy Spirit, Allah, Buddha, the Great Spirit, the Orishas, or nature-based beings) to set a ritual container by clearing one's energetic space and creating an energetic boundary with the unseen world.
2. Then call on an ancestral guide (see earlier steps for befriending an ancestral guide). Ask the ancestral guide:
   - Where did the legacy burden come from?
   - What events or circumstances contributed to the legacy burden?
   - Where in the lineage is it tied to?
   - What impact did it have through the lineage?
   - How did it get handed down?
   - Ask the guide any other questions you (i.e., Self) or your parts want to know.
3. Ask the guide: What is the antidote for this legacy burden?
4. Ask the guide to turn to the deceased on the lineage and bring the antidote to those among the deceased who were impacted by this burden. Sometimes a collective group or individuals will need to be cocooned again to receive healing from the guide. This healing may take some time. Remember that the ancestral guide is doing the work of continuing to repair the lineage from that specific legacy burden rather than the client having any interaction with the deceased connected to this legacy burden.
5. Ask the guide to bring this antidote to the burdened part(s). Ask the guide how to release/unburden this legacy burden from any parts in client's system carrying it.
6. Oftentimes, after the burdened part receives an "update" from the information about the legacy burden over the course of time in the lineage from the ancestral guide:
   - The guide moves into direct relationship with the burdened part.
   - The guide can serve to help witness alongside Self if the part needs to share its experience carrying the legacy burden.
   - The guide may directly facilitate the unburdening of the part.
   - Unburdening can happen directly between the exile holding a legacy burden and ancestral guide with Self as the witness. This can happen spontaneously, or we can ask the guide for direct connection between burdened part(s) and the guide with Self as the witness.
   - Trust the sequence of how this unfolds following the leadership of the ancestral guide. Sometimes really old legacy burdens show up

solely somatically. Sometimes the deceased that have been re-co-cooned need to collectively unburden before the target part in one's internal system can unburden.

7. Once parts carrying the legacy burden have been unburdened and the deceased have also received healing from this legacy burden on the lineage, ask the ancestral guide to bring the antidote to any other living family that also may carry it or were impacted by the legacy burden. This is done energetically through the guide, not through the client or their parts. Thus, the client is a witness during this step.

Is it an Unattached Burden or the Spirit of the Unwell Deceased?

Per IFS, if you suspect an unattached burden is present:

1. In the befriending process, have the client ask it first if it's a part.[37]
2. Per my practice, if it says "no," then have the client ask it if it is connected to a blood lineage? If it says "yes," then have the client ask which blood lineage it is connected to and if it's a legacy burden or a deceased relative. In my clinical experience, this question teases out if it's a part holding a legacy burden or a spirit.
3. If it says "no," then have the client ask it if it is connected to any unwell deceased (e.g., non-blood deceased loved ones, lost spirits, or ancestors of place, etc.). In my clinical experience, this question will tease out the unwell deceased from true unattached burdens.
4. If it is an unattached burden or any deceased (blood relations or otherwise), I take a communal approach and have a general rule to ask the client to call in relational spiritual support to directly interact with unwell deceased or unattached burdens, rather than having the client attempt to extract/release them. Also, ask the client if there are any parts that have fears and concerns about the unattached burden or deceased being released. (This may reveal an exile(s) that the UB or deceased are attached to; use IFS interventions to attend to the exile(s) as needed.)
5. Some unattached burdens can effectively leave the client's system by the client directly asking them to leave,[38] or through the IFS unburdening process.[39]
6. Ask the client to call in their protective guides and any bigger spiritual resources (e.g. Holy Spirit, Allah, Buddha, Great Spirit, the Orishas, or nature-based beings, etc.). Once the protective guides and/or bigger spiritual beings are present, ask them to directly release the identified unattached burden from the client's system. If the entity is actually an unwell deceased spirit, ask the protective guides and/or spiritual beings to help unblend this spirit from the client's system and help the spirit receive

their own healing, being relocated away from the client and directly connecting with the protective guides or bigger spiritual beings for support. Trust the leadership of these guides—in my clinical experience, they know what to do and just need to be asked.
7. When bigger unattached burdens are present, it is important for the client to call in bigger spiritual beings and ask for them to release the unattached burden from the client's system. Sometimes, additional IFS support of further befriending the specific part that the unattached burden and/or unwell deceased are attached to is needed before the unattached burden or the spirit of the unwell deceased will release from the part.

IFS AND THE ENNEAGRAM

CONNECTING TO PARTS USING THE ENNEAGRAM MAP

Joan R. Ryan, JD
and Tammy Sollenberger, MA, LCMHC

The collaboration and friendship that led to the following piece began with a phone call in 2019. Tammy had been producing her popular IFS Podcast, "The One Inside" and had recently learned about the Enneagram system of nine personality types. After spending time back home at Thanksgiving, she realized the system helped her to understand her own role and others in her family. She was intrigued and looked for an experienced Enneagram professional to interview. She found Joan from an IFS email list, reached out to her, and from that first conversation a partnership was born.

Tammy's passion for IFS matched well with Joan's passion for the Enneagram. Joan was an established Enneagram expert and teacher and had been working with the material for 25 years. Yet she had often been frustrated that the Enneagram seemed to lack a method that could help individuals in their own growth. Fortunately, she was also IFS level one trained, fascinated by the possibilities of combining the systems, and looking to connect IFS methods to Enneagram practice.

We both agreed that growth and change, regardless of system or model, needed to come from inside the learner to be effective and sustainable.

From that came…synergy!

Our first podcast together led to a series of discussions. Joan interviewed Tammy to help her explore her Enneagram type through the narrative lens (i.e., through facilitated self-observation), and our discussions ranged widely. Ultimately, we landed on a hypothesis and moved forward together to test it out. Fast forward a couple of years, when we presented a workshop on Exploring the Enneagram and IFS at the 2021 IFS Annual Conference, and since then, we have led several multi-session IFS and Enneagram courses along with a series of podcast episodes to further the study. We are currently working together to pilot test a course in how to use IFS method in enneagram typing interviews to help new students find their type and further explore their inner family.

Our interweaving of the Enneagram with IFS theory and techniques is based on a hypothesis.

"Each Enneagram type pattern will appear, in each individual, as a constellation of parts, many of which will be similar in persons of that type, but with some different parts generated by the uniqueness of each individual and their experiences. In effect, these parts are holding the type structure together."

We have found that individuals tend to be comprised of the parts that hold their Enneagram type together. These same parts are protecting vulnerable exiles that are similar from person to person within a type group. When we help the client to unblend and to begin to unburden these specific parts, the "pins" that hold the Enneagram type pattern in place tend to loosen. This allows space for both Self-energy and the positive attributes hidden in the type structures to shine through. Self draws from the positive attributes of all the types, so the more Self-energy we have, the more access we have to the positive qualities of each type.

This chapter is the story of our ongoing exploration.

Interweaving the two models has helped us bring detailed focus and awareness to our internal landscape. Both models encourage curious inquiry towards our personality traits, limitations and gifts, and our inner family. Recognizing the pattern of Enneagram types can provide us with a parts map to be used for deeper self-discovery and insight. By contrast, IFS inquiry can help us to recognize the automatic, unconscious, habitual patterns of our Enneagram type and allow us to make Self-led choices about actions and interactions.

Protector parts utilize the structure of the Enneagram type to keep exiles locked away, out of conscious awareness. Here are two examples.

1. Joan is an Enneagram Type 9, which is characterized by a laid-back attitude, a reliance on gut instinct and a more relaxed view of goals and timelines. Her approach to a project is almost the direct opposite of Tammy, an Enneagram Type 3 who is very task-oriented, with a talent for seeing the most efficient route to a goal. The parts that support Tammy's Type 3 will encourage her to ignore emotional reactions, her own and those of others, in an effort to get things done. This manager part believes that efficient accomplishment is the best way to protect an exile who feels unworthy.

2. The parts that drive Joan's Type 9, in contrast, are more tuned to the feelings, comfort, and potential upsets of other people than they are to progress towards the goal. Joan is likely to have a manager part who uses accommodating others as a strategy to protect an exile desperate to fit in. As it prioritizes avoiding conflict, this manager will likely work hard to convince Joan that her own opinion and preferences do not matter. In both examples the manager is protecting the exiles from being triggered. Because they share a type, other Type 9s are likely

to have similar parts to Joan's, and other Type 3s will likely have similar parts to Tammy's.

Combining this detailed knowledge of the Enneagram with IFS allows each of us to look for the parts that are controlling our actions and reactions and to unblend and unburden them where possible, thereby relaxing the restrictions of the type. In this way, we can make space for more Self-energy, positive growth, and often smoother relationships.

Our purpose is to help you map the parts that are holding your type together and learn how they may interact inside your system. We hope to give you more awareness in IFS terms of how your Enneagram type might be in control by operating with and through some specific parts. This awareness can lead to befriending, witnessing, and unburdening your exiles. When you can see the automatic patterns of thoughts and feelings in action, you can make different choices leading to growth and change.

If you are reading this book and you know a lot about IFS but little about the Enneagram, you probably have two questions: "What's my Enneagram Type? And how can I use the Enneagram with my IFS clients?" If you are reading this book and you know about the Enneagram and IFS, your first question might be, "How do I integrate Enneagram insights with IFS therapy and practice?" If you are reading this book with only a little knowledge of both systems, we hope you will enjoy learning about both and how they complement each other. Whatever your entry point, we encourage you to be open and curious, and to join our ongoing exploration.

What is the Enneagram?

The Enneagram is a map of nine distinct yet limited lenses through which individuals see the world. These lenses are unconscious and habitual but can be made visible, and we can work to expand our views. The Enneagram diagram[1] is a nine-pointed, star-like figure surrounded by a circle. Each point on the star delineates a type numbered 1 to 9. While the types are different, they are all equally valid ways to see the world.

Each type describes a pattern of thinking, feeling, and experiencing and highlights some positive capacities embedded in the pattern. The types describe qualities, attributes, and potential barriers that the individual is likely to encounter in life. Types on either side of the core type around the circle are called "wings." The types at the other end of the diagram lines are called "connected points." (More on the impact of this later).

Each Enneagram type defines patterns that are normally outside conscious awareness but when brought to light can explain the individual's habits of thinking, feeling, and experiencing the world. These habits are in most cases limiting. Bringing them to awareness can allow an individual a broader view of current reality, moment to moment.

The Enneagram Diagram[*]

Mediator 9
Protector 8
1 *Perfectionist*
Epicure 7
2 *Giver*
Loyal Skeptic 6
3 *Performer*
Observer 5
4 *Romantic*

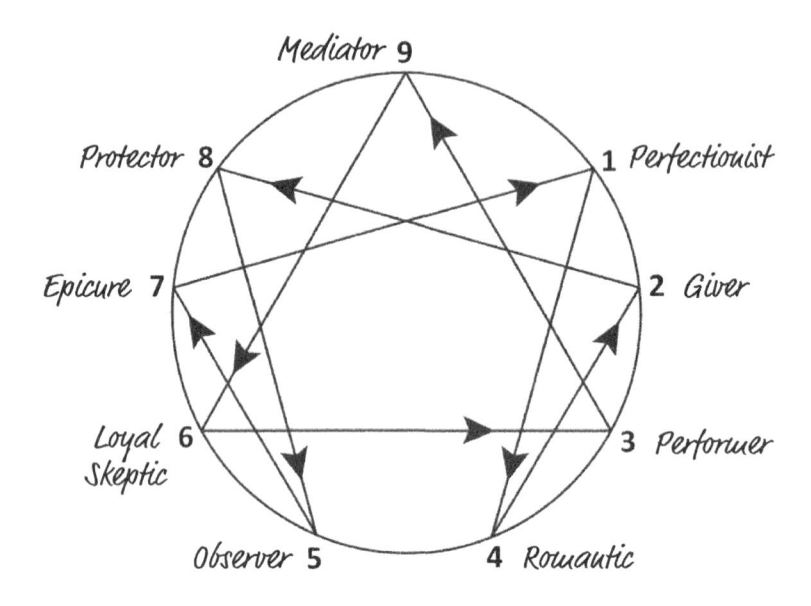

Focus of Attention

Each Enneagram type has a defined primary focus of attention. This is a sector of input that is highlighted by the type from all the information coming toward the individual at any given moment. We believe that a person of that type will have managers and firefighters that serve to keep the focus on these distinct issues as a means of shielding the exiles in that individual, and that the exiles will have similar wounds from person to person within that type group.

Having a specific focus of attention doesn't mean that other input is ignored, just that some is given more space, focus, or weight as part of the strategies of the protectors. Knowing one's type can be a map to find these parts and exiles. Knowing the parts and exiles can lead us to the primary type of the individual.

The idea of parts limiting our attention makes sense in terms of what we know about how parts protect. If a manager part keeps our attention on one thing, ignoring other stimuli in our environment, it can keep the exiled part from being triggered. And, when the exile is triggered, a firefighter part turns our attention to that one thing as a way to calm down the exile.

Take a Type 3: Their focus of attention is on what needs to get done in order to be successful. This will be the role of many protective parts in the system which will either keep exiles from being activated or help the system when an exile is activated.

---

[*] The Enneagram Diagram as shown has been in common usage across Enneagram schools since the 1970s. For more specific information see, Palmer, Helen. *The Enneagram*. Harper: San Francisco, 1988.

Another way to say this is that *our attention is naturally, habitually, and unconsciously noticing and magnifying a certain sector of reality at any given time.* Each type will place a different emphasis on information in the environment. Knowing where the attention goes by unconscious habit is very important information. In fact, when two people are in the same space and subject to the same input, the Enneagram can tell them where their views will be similar and where they will differ and why. This is helpful in working on communication issues. The areas where the attention focuses are listed in the chart below.

While you explore the insights of the Enneagram, see if you recognize one or more of these primary areas of attentional focus. Then see if you can find the parts keeping your focus of attention on the listed concerns. What exiles might they be protecting? Why do the parts believe this information is so important to keeping you safe? What is the part afraid would happen if it did not keep your attention focused in this way?

Note here that different authors have used different identifying words for the types. We have used the labels from Joan's Narrative Enneagram orientation. Here are the types with their primary focus of attention.

Type	Focus of Attention
1. Perfectionist	Errors and mistakes
2. Giver	Needs of others
3. Performer	Tasks, goals
4. Romantic	What is missing
5. Observer	Gathering knowledge
6. Loyal Skeptic	What can go wrong
7. Epicure	Options and planning
8. Protector	Power and control
9. Mediator	Other's agendas

Childhood Survival Strategies

One way to look at the Enneagram types is as survival strategies that were necessary at earlier times in our lives. As we grow and change, these strategies tend to get "stuck" or narrowed in limiting ways. They are very similar to the strategies that our parts use; often parts continue to use strategies that made sense in the past but may not make sense in the present. In IFS, these strategies are known as a part's burdens. As you review this information, see what parts and exiles these strategies might include for you. We have made some suggestions, but feel free to add from your own experience.

Childhood Survival Strategies by Type

Type	Typical parts strategies and beliefs
Type 1	Child tries to create order to avoid or buffer perceived chaos. Protector strategy: judging right and wrong. Exile belief: *I'm bad.*
Type 2	Child perceives it is their job to caretake needs in family or environment. Protector strategy: focus on other's needs at the expense of their own. Exile belief: *I'm not wanted/needed.*
Type 3	Child only feels recognized and seen for achievements. Protector strategy: work hard for approval and recognition. Exile belief: *I'm not worthy.*
Type 4	Child feels abandoned (real or perceived). Protector strategy: attention-seeking (positive or negative). Exile belief: *I'll be abandoned.*
Type 5	Child experiences environment as either very intrusive or very emotionally cold. Protector strategy: Gather knowledge. Exile belief: *I'm not connected.*
Type 6	Child often experienced an unreliable and/or inconsistent authority figure. Protector strategy: Prepare against possible harm. Exile belief: *I'm helpless.*
Type 7	Child often experienced painful situations when very young. Protector strategy: Imagine wonderful future options. Exile belief: *I'm not loved.*
Type 8	Child perceives that the adults aren't taking charge, leading to chaos/danger. Protector strategy: take control and take action. Exile belief: *I'm defenseless.*
Type 9	Child feels overlooked. Protector strategy: stay quiet, small, make no demands. Exile belief: *I'm unimportant.*

These brief examples show how our internal systems (protectors and exiled parts) are formed around burdened beliefs. The beliefs are held by exiled parts, and protective parts will take on jobs in alliance or in defense of the beliefs.

Parts take on coping skills or jobs for us when we are younger. In many cases, a part's roles operate as survival strategies that are very similar to the strategies of each Enneagram type. Which is why, when you understand your type structure, you get a clearer map of the relationships between your parts.

Note that we do not find a direct correlation of a specific part to a specific type. In fact, some parts may appear in different ways in several types, and usually for different reasons.

Centers of Intelligence

Another way to approach the Enneagram is to understand that there are three groups of three types ("triads") clustered around one of the centers of intelligence in the body: the mind, the heart, and the body sensations; or "thought," "emotional intelligence," and "bodily instinct." We all have all three but usually rely on one more than the others.

The three types in each triad have many characteristics in common. Sometimes it is easier to find your triad as a step towards finding your type.

In these brief descriptions of each triad, you will notice that the three types in each triad are identified by a "fuel" or "driver." These are universal emotions or energies (anger, fear, and grief) that we all have at different times. What is meant by fuel in this context is one particular emotion plays a larger part in the structure of the type.

In IFS terms, unblending from feeling parts will be more difficult for heart types. Unblending from intellectual parts will be more difficult for head types. Unblending from bodily sensation parts will be more difficult for body types.

The way a client responds to the basic questions in the IFS protocol will be impacted by their primary center of intelligence. For example, if we ask, "Where do you notice this part in or around your body?" a feeling type is likely to answer with a feeling, a head type with a thought, and a body type with a sensation.

If a client appears blank when asked, "How do you feel towards a part?" we may have a body- or head-centered type. On the other hand, if a client has a hard time with, "Where do you find it in your body?" we may have a heart- or head-centered type. If a client has trouble describing a part, we may have a heart type. These are, of course, generalizations, but our intention is to demonstrate some of the ways we can screen for parts and/or type.

The heart, or emotionally sensitive types, are Types 2, 3 and 4. The key parts we expect to find here are concerned with image, connection, and feelings. The underlying fuel or burden which we would expect to find in their exiles is grief.

The head, or mentally centered types, are Types 5, 6, and 7; they lead with their minds. They share high reliance on mental skills, analysis, and logic. The key parts we expect to find here are concerned with preparedness, predictability, and certainty. The underlying fuel or burden which we would expect to find in their exiles is fear.

The body centered types include Types 8, 9 and 1; they lead with their gut or bodily instincts. The key parts we expect to find here are concerned with control, belonging, and being heard. The underlying fuel or burden which we would expect to find in exiles here is anger.

This information may fast track an understanding of the major players in an internal family system. The key parts are the protectors, and the drivers are the exiles. Remember that the driver emotion is not necessarily expressed more often; rather, it is the emotion that is key to the structure of the type.

Finding Enneagram Type

Most people new to the Enneagram are very curious about what their own core type might be. Determining this can be easy for some, very difficult for others. A variety of tests which may help are available, but be aware that most tests have very limited reliability. Much is dependent on one's skills at self-observation. Still, the tests can help you to become familiar with the patterns and characteristics of the different types.

Knowing IFS and being familiar with or learning about parts will yield good clues to type. Knowing type will yield good clues to parts. In the following section, we walk through key information about each type. Working with IFS protocols in the internal world, we want to be curious and begin to map protectors and exiles. Interweaving enneagram information with these maps can bring detail and clarity to our exploration. This creates opportunities to see patterns in type and in the inner family. Certain parts must be present in an individual of a specific type as these parts hold the type together.

The information from your individual map of type and parts can be used as a guide to deepen your exploration of your inner world. The enneagram tells us which protectors and exiles are most likely to be present according to type.

We have provided worksheets on which you can map type characteristics to protectors and exiles.

Descriptions of Enneagram Types

(Adapted from previously unpublished material
from Joan R. Ryan, copyrighted 2022)

Type One: The Perfectionist (Gut Triad)

Focus of attention: correctness and error.
Preoccupation: quality, improvement, responsibility.
Likely strategies of parts: ethics, conscientiousness, detailed, improvement, severe inner critic.
May appear: judgmental, irritable, resentful.
Likely exiles: *I am bad or I am unworthy.*

Type Two: The Giver (Heart Triad)

Focus of attention: needs of others.
Preoccupation: relationships, needs, helping, giving advice.
Likely strategies of parts: nurturing, pleasing, empathy, avoiding own needs.
May appear: self-sufficient, attention seeking, pushy, manipulative.
Likely exiles: *I am loved only when I am helpful.*

Type Three: The Performer (Heart Triad)

Focus of attention: tasks, goals, accomplishments.
Preoccupation: recognition for efforts, accolades, and rewards.
Likely strategies of parts: goal focus, efficiency, success, recognition.
May appear: driven, impatient, unemotional.
Likely exiles: *I am loved only for my accomplishments.*

Type Four: The Romantic (Heart Triad)

Focus of attention: what is missing, lacking or unavailable.
Preoccupation: connection, authenticity, creativity, uniqueness.
Likely strategies of parts: fine sense of aesthetics, depth, empathy, emotional sensitivity.
May appear: overly emotional, dramatic, self-absorbed, dissatisfied.
Likely exiles: *I have been abandoned, and it's my fault. I am fatally flawed.*

Type Five: The Observer (Head Triad)

Focus of attention: seeks increasing levels of knowledge and information.
Preoccupation: observing, privacy, monitoring time, and energy.
Likely strategies of parts: reserved, detached, emotional control, self-sufficient.

May appear: aloof, uncaring, detached, withholding.
Likely exiles: *I'm not wanted by, or connected with, others.*

Type Six: The Loyal Skeptic (Head Triad)

Focus of Attention: what can go wrong.
Preoccupation: doubting, questioning, preparation, worst case scenario thinking.
Likely strategies of parts: troubleshooting, preparing, logical analysis, dutiful.
May appear: defensive, argumentative, contrary, fearful or domineering.
Likely exiles: *I am helpless and defenseless.*

Type Seven: The Epicure (Head Triad)

Focus of attention: planning for positive possibilities.
Preoccupation: positive options, adventures, avoiding limits and pain, planning.
Likely strategies of parts: visioning, strategizing, seeing interconnections, optimism.
May appear: self-absorbed, distracted, uncommitted, uncaring.
Likely exiles: *I'm not loved. Limitations are painful.*

Type Eight: The Protector (Gut Triad)

Focus of attention: power, control, fairness.
Preoccupation: justice, taking charge, protecting others.
Likely strategies of protectors: protective, leadership, direct, energetic.
May appear: blunt, bullying, excessive, domineering, angry.
Likely exiles: *I am vulnerable and powerless.*

Type Nine: The Mediator (Gut Triad)

Focus of attention: other people and their agendas.
Preoccupation: seeing the validity in all points of view, mediating conflict, harmony.
Likely strategies of protectors: seeing all sides, supportive, empathetic; seeing big picture.
May appear: indecisive, lost, placating, insecure.
Likely exiles: *I am unimportant and unacceptable.*

Connected Types

The Enneagram types are interconnected or interwoven on the diagram in significant ways. Notice what types reach across to other types according to the lines on the diagram. These lines are referred to as the connected points. When you find your core type you can locate your connected types by following the lines on the diagram, i.e., 9 is connected to 3, and 6 or 7 is connected to 1 and 5. In the Enneagram literature, these connections are sometimes labeled as the "stress or action" types and the "heart or security" types, but that level of detail is beyond the scope of this chapter.

Connections between types can make the process of finding core type difficult as sometimes the strength of these connections vary between individuals. As you are exploring this material, if you see yourself in two types, notice whether they are connected by a line on the Enneagram diagram. If so, it is worthwhile to look for the parts and exiles in each of those types to see if one is stronger in you than the other.

You may find that parts of your connected types react to the parts in your type. For example, the parts found in Type 5 may have strong opinions and reactions to the parts in Type 8. The connected trio of parts illustrate where polarization of parts can be seen inside the Enneagram system. For example, parts in Type 3's drive for success can be overwhelming for the parts in Type 6, and the parts in Type 9 can shut it all down to give rest and relief.

It is helpful to bring curiosity to how the parts inside the connected points relate and react to one another. Harmony and healing come when the parts in a type, who are only looking and reacting to one another, come into connection and relationship with each other and with Self.

A Note about Wings

The types on either side of the core type around the Enneagram circle are called "wings." The effect that they have on the core type can best be described as a "flavoring." In IFS terms, the wing types may carry some managers that impact the behavior of the parts that are supporting the structure of the core type.

For example, a Type 4 with a stronger 5 wing may have some 5-like parts that cause a more reserved stance in certain settings. The 4 doesn't become a Type 5 but can take on some 5 characteristics. Similarly, a Type 4 with a stronger 3 wing will likely have parts that are more focused on tasks, goals and accolades. Both wings are present in all individuals, but one is normally much easier to see and work with than the other. In fact, the less dominant wing can actually be hidden or internalized. Parts in the Wing type may react against some characteristics of the core Type in a critical manner.

Internal polarizations can occur with wings too. Type 9 conflict avoidant parts may bristle at Type 8 assertiveness parts. Type 2 helping parts may struggle with the productive focus of the Type 3. Type 7 parts may want to focus on fun and feel frustrated with the hesitancy and fear of the Type 6 parts. Type 1 who works hard to avoid mistakes and errors may be irritated at Type 2's intense focus on meeting the needs of another rather than on getting it all right.

Note: Some Enneagram authors treat the dominant wing as the sole influence on the core type and actually identify individuals by their wing, ex. Type 2/wing 1 as distinct from Type 2/wing 3. We find this to be too limited and encourage our students to seek out both wings as vehicles for self-understanding.

Critical Parts and Type

We believe that all of us, no matter what our Enneagram type, have one category of part in common: the inner critic. The critics may sound and feel differently in each type, yet they are the easiest to identify in any person or any type, and they are among the first parts we tend to work with in IFS.

In fact, identifying how your critics show up in your own system is another way to help you find your type. We all have parts that are critical of our type, and parts that are critical within our type.

When we notice a part that is critical of our Enneagram type, the key is to recognize that it's a part and, as such, is not all of who we are. Similarly, we want to recognize that the type is not all of who we are. When first discovering your type, you are likely to find a critic who does not like the description of the type or of its structure. Sometimes this happens when you notice a similarity in a type description to someone you know who you do not really want to emulate. And sometimes the type description does not match with your favorite perception of yourself.

Critical parts inside each type will look, sound, and feel differently from person to person. In Type 3, for example, critical parts will typically interfere with a desire to slow down. To these critic parts, slowing down will almost always feel dangerous. This is because they believe that slowing down will allow emotions to surface, and they fear that if emotions surface, they will overwhelm the system.

The Enneagram map tells us that these critics are almost certainly protecting vulnerable exiles. We find a similar mapping in all Enneagram types where protective parts shield the exiles to avoid flooding. Another way to say this is that protector parts utilize the structure of the type to keep exiles locked away, out of conscious awareness.

We suggest you start with getting to know the critics that are specific to your core type. As you read these examples, what do you notice about your internal reactions? Is one critic more familiar to you than the others? Do you notice parts who are uncomfortable? Take this in small steps—one part at a time—to help you create sustainable change.

What Critical Parts Might Say Within Type

Type 1 – *You are not doing it right. You're not good enough. Work harder and don't mess up.*

Type 2 – *You are not helpful enough. You're not as important as others. Don't have needs or ask for help.*

Type 3 – *You are not accomplished enough. You're not enough. You must achieve more (work, money, awards).*

Type 4 – *You are not unique or special. You don't matter. You need to make an impression—any impression is better than being overlooked.*

Type 5 – *You should be invisible. You aren't secure or connected. You don't have enough information, time, or energy.*

Type 6 – *You are unprepared and there are dangers looming. You're not safe. You'd better anticipate the worst.*

Type 7 – *You should not allow any limitations. You don't have what you really want. You must maintain freedom.*

Type 8 – *You can never let them see you sweat. You're not strong enough. You have to protect.*

Type 9 – *You can't handle conflict. You're not ok if others aren't ok. You have to make peace.*

An exercise like this is an example of how IFS technique and the Enneagram complement each other. It gives language that says, "Here's how you can work with that." When we identify the parts that are holding the structure together, we can befriend, unblend, and unburden them.

Enneagram and IFS in Daily Life: A Children's Birthday Party

Enneagram types show up in our daily life and in our relationships through our parts. We know it is beneficial to understand that other people operate from their parts. It is also helpful to understand that other people see the world through the filter of their Type.

Imagine how you would think, feel, and act during a children's birthday party. This helps illustrate how we all experience life from our Enneagram type and how our parts collude with type to protect exiles. Placing yourself at the party illustrates how we might expect each type to handle, plan, and be in this scenario. Be aware of what parts might be involved and motivated in relation to an Enneagram type.

Type 1 is setting the rules or organizing the gift opening, writing down each person's name and gift so thank you cards can be sent in a timely matter. Looking deeper, with an IFS perspective, we expect to find managers who want to ensure they make no mistakes to protect their exiles who fear being found irresponsible.

Type 2 is the helper, urging everyone to eat more cake, comforting the shy kid in the corner. Looking deeper, we expect to find managers who want to be as visibly helpful as possible in order to protect their exiles who fear exclusion or rejection.

Type 3 is the super-efficient doer making sure it's all moving along efficiently. Looking deeper, we expect to find managers who want to create efficiency and recognition in order to protect exiles who fear failure.

Type 4 is the decorator with the creative flare making it all very unique and special. Looking deeper, we expect to find managers who want to be creative and different in order to protect their exiles who fear the shame of being ordinary.

Type 5 is the person studying the books on the shelves or sitting with kids in the quiet corner. Looking deeper, we expect to find managers who want to monitor time and energy expended in order to protect their exiles who fear being exhausted and empty.

Type 6 is the person making sure the kids are all safe as well as having a good time. Looking deeper, we expect to find managers who want to be prepared for any dangers in order to protect their exiles who fear being left defenseless.

Type 7 is the fun person causing all kinds of trouble by daring the kids to jump off the sofa. Looking deeper, we expect to find managers who want to create maximum fun and distraction in order to protect their exiles who fear pain or emotional upset.

Type 8 is the super protective, super loud, super opinionated grandfather. Looking deeper, we expect to find managers who want to control the party in order to protect their exiles who fear showing any vulnerability.

Type 9 is the person running around trying to make sure everybody is comfortable. Looking deeper, we expect to find managers who want to keep everyone happy and harmonious in order to protect their exiles who fear conflict.

We hope this example has given you a lot to work with as you explore Enneagram type in your own life. This is a gift that the Enneagram gives to IFS. Examples give us a great entry way to parts. Once you become aware of your parts as they are connected to your Enneagram type, you as your authentic Self can build relationships with, unblend, and unburden these parts leading to significant healing.

Essence Qualities of Type and C Qualities of Self

Enneagram theory teaches that embedded in each type structure, often covered up by the limited habitual patterns of thought, feelings and sensations, are essence or positive qualities. Each type has a positive emotional quality that can shine through when the parts are unburdened and the type is relaxed. Similar to Self-energy, the essence states of our own type can give us access to the essence states of the other types.

Essence Qualities Mapped by the Enneagram[2]

Type	Higher Emotional Quality
1	serenity
2	humility
3	veracity
4	equanimity (balance)
5	nonattachment
6	courage
7	sobriety (constancy)
8	innocence
9	right action

The higher qualities of the Enneagram types are access points to the qualities of Self-energy. Both systems require that we make space so that we are not blended with our parts and the parts that hold the structure of our type in place. I am not my type, and I am not my parts.

The One Inside

Most of the chapter up until this point has been focused on identifying parts found in type and differentiating between types as a way to connect more fully to the internal world. What has been missing is "Who is the one connecting?", "Who is the one noticing?" and "Who is the one being aware?"

The authentic Self, the higher Self, or simply the Self is the one inside—the one who emerges as we unblend and unburden our parts and as our type relaxes. When we can show parts that might be stuck in type our curiosity, send them compassion, and open our hearts to them, we create relationships with them. Note that in Enneagram work, Helen Palmer identifies an "inner observer" which has many of the qualities of IFS Self, but we are not yet ready to say that these are the same.

The limited focus of attention of each type is a protective strategy that parts utilize early in development. By focusing on certain stimuli, behaviors, emotions, and/or sensations, other parts are kept from taking in information that could be unsafe, harmful, or dangerous. Self can hear and be a witness to parts and their stories about how this was helpful and beneficial in the past. Self can update parts so that parts learn that Self is here now and this limitation of focus is not as necessary as it was in the past.

Strategies for survival in childhood are other examples of parts being stuck in the past and using coping skills that helped then but may not be helpful now. Self can ask these parts what they are afraid would happen if they did not do this, and this will lead to core fears and beliefs of exiles in the system. In turn this will help the parts which support the type to relax.

In the centers of intelligence parts have learned to take in and receive the world primarily through the body, the mind, or the heart. This is another way that parts have of limiting our perception of the world. Self can let parts know it is not dangerous to widen, expand, and have more spaciousness in order to fully experience the world through each center. Each type will always have a preference, but with Self in the driver's seat, there can be more ability to receive in the entire body, mind, and heart.

Befriending the inner critic is a good starting point for the system to experience a Self-to-part relationship. As Self sends curiosity and compassion to the critics, parts will begin to let Self know the reasons, concerns, and story behind their important roles. As other parts step back from their own reactions and responses to the critic part(s), Self can be more present and available to each critic part. Once a relationship is built between Self and the critic parts, working within the system to get to know the parts inside type becomes a bit easier.

Thinking back to the parts that show up in each type at the children's birthday, it is interesting to consider who shows up, and why. Self can anticipate this, hear from the parts who have concerns about the experience, and negotiate with parts so they can let Self be there a bit more fully. Self can let parts know this is a good time to practice saying to them, "Let me be here."

"Let me be here," is a message from all the parts in type. It reminds parts of Self's leadership in the system. It reminds parts of the now and the present. It soothes and comforts hard working managers, activated firefighters, and vulnerable exiles. Self says to them all, "I am here with you now."

Per an IFS perspective, Self can be identified by "C" qualities of calm, connectedness, creativity, confidence, courage, compassion, curious, and clear minded. There is not, however, a particular C quality of Self that matches any particular type. Certain types may have an easier or a harder time accessing certain C qualities. In both systems, reaching for these qualities is not effective. You cannot reach for Self-energy or the essence quality of type. Rather, we make space for them to emerge by relaxing back, asking for space from parts, and loosening the hold or pin of type.

Here are suggestions of types that may find easier access to some of the C qualities of Self-energy. (Note: These are not the only types with this access.)

Type	C Qualities That May Lead to a Doorway to Self
1, 5, 9	Calm
2, 9	Connected
1, 3, 5	Clarity
6, 8	Courage
4, 7	Creative
2, 4	Compassionate
3, 7, 8	Confident
4, 6, 7	Curious

Regardless of your type, keep monitoring the feeling state of the type and of your C quality experiences. If there is Self-energy present, there is likely to be more space for the essence Enneagram quality. If the type's Enneagram essence qualities are present, there will be more access to Self.

The goal of the two systems is the same: more harmony and healing. Using both systems together we can get to know how our type shows up in our lives and befriend the parts who protect and need protecting. This happens on a continuum of parts receding and type relaxing. What emerges is your true essence, who you have been all along.

The Enneagram Is About How We See the World

IFS is not just a parts model, and Enneagram is not just a personality typing system.

The difference between the Enneagram and other personality systems is that the Enneagram is not about behavior; it is about how we see the world and what concerns are the most important. Yet it also allows for growth and change within the type. In IFS terms, our inner systems and burdened parts are created and developed around concerns which are largely driven by our exiles. Our protective parts work hard to keep the fears and concerns from happening and keep our exiles, who hold the fears, from flooding us. Both systems provide a way of understanding, exploring, and getting to know your inner world.

Both systems can be seen and used as spiritual tools that show us the way to live our best lives. They show us the filters we have been looking through while also showing us that everyone is not looking through the same filters. They show us that our parts react to others' parts (often in predictable ways) and this causes tension, miscommunication, and turmoil in our relationships. They show us that we are capable of living out of a calm, centered place where we can show up with our unique gifts and perspectives. They show us that we can grow and heal in our inner and outer worlds.

Interweaving the Enneagram with IFS is a way to get to know those parts who make up your type more deeply. When you begin to get to know your parts, you begin to feel the pins of your type loosen. Parts unblend, type loosens, which opens the doorway to more Self-energy. More Self-energy helps you create a world inside of you and around you that you desire—an inner and outer world full of compassion towards yourself and others, calmness as you deal with all the hard things of life, and confidence that no matter what is happening, you are here and present for your parts.

That is the hope and goal of the Enneagram and IFS—a hope for healing your inner world so that your outer world can be one of peace, harmony, and fulfillment.

KEY TAKEAWAYS

- All nine Enneagram types are different, but equally valid, lenses through which to see and experience the world.
- Knowledge of type provides a map to find protective parts and exiles. IFS protocols for identifying parts (and unblending and unburdening) facilitate loosening the limitations of one's Enneagram type and allow positive attributes, or Self-energy, to shine through.
- Finding your type helps you map your parts, and mapping your parts helps you find your type.
- Unblending from type and from parts can lead to unburdening and greater access to Self-energy (integration).
- Our parts use the primary focus of attention of the type to protect our exiles.
- Part's survival strategies in childhood vary from type to type but are similar within type and are protecting similar exiles.
- Three centers of intelligence help us understand the drivers in our Internal Family System.
- Your authentic Self has been there all along inside your type. Self-energy supports the essence qualities of the type, and the essence qualities of your type support Self-Energy.

AUTHOR BIOS

Joan R. Ryan, J.D. (she/her) is a Senior Leadership Coach, IFS Practitioner, Certified Enneagram Teacher (and a "recovering" lawyer). Based in Boston, she started her Enneagram journey in 1992 and has worked with it internationally ever since. She was certified to teach the Enneagram in the Narrative Tradition in 1996. When she found IFS in 2011, she recognized theory and technique to make best use of the Enneagram for herself, her students and her clients. She co-created a podcast series with Tammy Sollenberger in 2022 that is illustrative of the work described in this chapter.

Tammy Sollenberger, MA, LCMHC (she/her) is a Certified IFS Therapist and Approved IFS Clinical Consultant with a private practice in Dover, NH. She fell in love with the Enneagram when it helped her understand herself and her family during the holidays. She produces and hosts an IFS podcast and is the author of the book, *The One Inside: Thirty Days to Your Authentic Self.* (PureCarbon Publishing, 2022)

GOING DEEPER

From Joan R. Ryan and Tammy Sollenberger

1) Trainings and Workshops:
   a. Introduction to IFS and the Enneagram course twice a year www.tammysollenberger.com and www.creativecollaborations.net
   b. Workshops, webinars, and conferences on the Enneagram and/or IFS: Tammysollenberger.com or JoanRRyan@gmail.com for details and information.
2) Podcasts:
   a. The One Inside: An Internal Family Systems Podcast: www.tammysollenberger.com/podcast/. Introduction to IFS and the Enneagram on episode 71. Six-part series on episodes 108-113.

From Joan R. Ryan

1) Website: Website: www.creativecollaborations.net:
   a. Workshops:
      i. Enneagram workshops with IFS techniques
      ii. Enneagram Typing Using IFS Protocols
   b. Typing interviews for locating primary type or deepening knowledge of type
   c. Enneagram Cards: "Help Me Find My Enneagram Type"
2) Connect:
   a. email: JoanRRyan@gmail.com
   b. Facebook: Enneagram Learning with Joan Ryan

From Tammy Sollenberger

1) Website: www.tammysollenberger.com
   a. Workshops
      i. Exploring the Enneagram through the Lens of IFS
   b. Consultation for IFS certification or for mental health professionals interested in exploring their own system.
2) Books:
   a. Sollenberger, T. (2022). *The one inside: Thirty days to your authentic self.* Pure Carbon Publishing.

From Other Sources
1) Books:
    a. Daniels, D., & Price, V. (2009). *The essential Enneagram* (2nd ed.). Harper One.
    b. Palmer, H. (1998). *The Enneagram.* Harper Collins.
    c. Palmer, H. (1994). *The Enneagram in love and work.* Harper Collins.

APPENDIX A

Key Beliefs Embedded in Each Type

Type 1: Life is an opportunity to improve, to be right, be better, be responsible. To survive and thrive I need to always work towards the ideal result.

Type 2: Life is an opportunity to help, to be of service, be significant, be connected. To survive and thrive I need to be useful to others.

Type 3: Life is an opportunity to achieve, be efficient, be the solution, be accomplished. To survive and thrive I need to be successful.

Type 4: Life is an opportunity to feel deeply, be special, be unique, be significant. To survive and thrive I need to distinguish myself from the ordinary.

Type 5: Life is an opportunity to study and learn, to be objective, be precise, be independent. To survive and thrive, I need to protect my time and energy.

Type 6: Life is an opportunity to debate, to be logical, be certain, be safe. To survive and thrive, I need to be prepared for anything that might happen.

Type 7: Life is an opportunity to play, to be fun, be adventurous, be clever, be interesting. To survive and thrive I need freedom to experience all that life has to offer without limitation.

Type 8: Life is an opportunity to be in charge, to be big, be powerful, be protective. To survive and thrive I need to be strong, decisive and in control.

Type 9: Life is an opportunity to calm, to be comfortable and peaceful. To survive and thrive I need to keep the peace and blend in.

©Joan R. Ryan 2017

ENDNOTES

SECTION ONE: ORIGINS AND ACCESS

Chapter 1

1. NREPP is a national repository of evidence-based programs and practices, which is maintained by the United States Government's Substance Abuse and Mental Health Services Administration (SAMHSA).
2. Participants who had rheumatoid arthritis had a 16-session course of IFS therapy. It reduced their depression and anxiety and also significantly improved their rheumatoid arthritis as compared to a control group.
3. For a more complete, routinely updated list of IFS publications, see Research and Bibliography at the IFS Institute website (www.ifs-institute.com/resources/research).

Chapter 2

1. Not to be confused with Karen Horney's three interpersonal trends (Horney, 1945).
2. www.ifs-institute.com/trainings
3. www.foundationifs.org/resources/ifs-leadership-fellows
4. Cece Sykes, Level 2 IFS training: *Compassion for Addictive Processes.*
5. Cece Sykes, Level 2 IFS training: *Compassion for Addictive Processes.*
6. Cece Sykes, Level 2 IFS training: *Compassion for Addictive Processes.*
7. Cece Sykes is also credited for the past, present and future focus of exiles, firefighters and managers.
8. Cece Sykes, Level 2 IFS training: *Compassion for Addictive Processes.*
9. A term introduced by psychotherapist and Buddhist teacher John Welwood in the 1980s.

SECTION TWO: MODEL INTEGRATION

Chapter 4

1. Shapiro, F. (2018). *Eye movement desensitization and reprocessing: Basic principles, protocols, and procedures* (3rd ed.). The Guilford Press, and Shapiro, F. (2007). EMDR, adaptive information processing, and case conceptualization. *Journal of EMDR Practice and Research*, 1(2): 68-87. DOI: www.dx.doi.org/10.1891/1933- 3196.1.2.68.
2. Shapiro, F. (2018). *Eye movement desensitization and reprocessing: Basic principles, protocols, and procedures* (3rd ed.). The Guilford Press.
3. Schwartz, R. C. (2021). *No bad parts: Healing trauma and restoring wholeness with the Internal Family Systems model.* Sounds True.
4. Ecker, B., Ticic, R., & Hulley, L. (2012). *Unlocking the emotional brain: Eliminating symptoms at their roots using memory reconsolidation.* Routledge.
5. Shapiro, F. (2018). *Eye movement desensitization and reprocessing: Basic principles, protocols, and procedures* (3rd ed.). The Guilford Press.
6. Schwartz, R. C. (2021). *No bad parts: Healing trauma and restoring wholeness with the Internal Family Systems model.* Sounds True.
7. Contributed by Dr. Daphne Fatter, PhD and Dr. Kendhal Hart, PsyD.
8. O'Shea Brown, G. (2020). Internal Family Systems informed eye movement desensitization and reprocessing an integrative technique for treatment of Complex Posttraumatic Stress Disorder. *International Body Psychotherapy Journal*, 19 (2), 112-122. Also, Krauze, P., & Gomez, A. (2013).

EMDR therapy and the use of Internal Family Systems strategies with children. In C. Forgash & M. Copeley (Eds.), *Healing the heart of trauma and dissociation with EMDR and ego state therapy* (pp. 295-311). Springer Publishing Company. Plus, Twombly, J., & Schwartz, R. C. (2008). The integration of the Internal Family Systems model and EMDR. In C. Forgash & M. Copeley (Eds.), *Healing the heart of trauma and dissociation with EMDR and ego state therapy* (pp. 295-311). Springer Publishing Company.

9   Contributed by Dr. Daphne Fatter, PhD. and Dr. Kendhal Hart, PsyD.
10 Contributed by Dr. Daphne Fatter, PhD. and Dr. Kendhal Hart, PsyD.
11 Schwartz, R. C. (2021). *No bad parts: Healing trauma and restoring wholeness with the Internal Family Systems model.* Sounds True.
12 Schwartz, R. C. (2021). *No bad parts: Healing trauma and restoring wholeness with the Internal Family Systems model.* Sounds True.
13 Contributed by Dr. Daphne Fatter, PhD. and Dr. Kendhal Hart, PsyD.
14 Shapiro, F. (2018). *Eye movement desensitization and reprocessing: Basic principles, protocols, and procedures* (3rd ed.). The Guilford Press.
15 Shapiro, F. (2018). *Eye movement desensitization and reprocessing: Basic principles, protocols, and procedures* (3rd ed.) The Guilford Press.
16 Shapiro, F. (2018). *Eye movement desensitization and reprocessing: Basic principles, protocols, and procedures* (3rd ed.) The Guilford Press.
17 Jarero, I. N., & Artigas, L. (Dec. 2022 in Press). The EMDR therapy butterfly hug method for self-administer bilateral stimulation. In EMDR protocols for prolonged adverse experiences. Also, Artigas, L., & Jarero, I. N. (2010). The butterfly hug. In Luber, M. (Ed.), *Eye movement desensitization and reprocessing (EMDR) scripted protocols: Special populations* (pp. 1-8). Springer Publications.
18 See Parnell, L. (2008). *Tapping in: A step-by-step guide to activating your healing resources through bilateral stimulation.* Sounds True, for review.
19 Jarero, I. N., & Artigas, L. (Dec. 2022 in Press). The EMDR therapy butterfly hug method for self-administer bilateral stimulation. In EMDR protocols for prolonged adverse experiences. Also, Artigas, L., & Jarero, I. N. (2010). The butterfly hug. In Luber, M. (Ed.), *Eye movement desensitization and reprocessing (EMDR) scripted protocols: Special populations* (pp. 1-8). Springer Publications.
20 Schwartz, R. C., & Sweezy, M. (2020). *Internal Family Systems* (2nd ed.). The Guilford Press.
21 Contributed by Dr. Daphne Fatter, PhD and Dr. Kendhal Hart, PsyD.
22 O'Shea Brown, G. (2020). Internal Family Systems informed eye movement desensitization and reprocessing an integrative technique for treatment of Complex Posttraumatic Stress Disorder. International Body Psychotherapy Journal, 19 (2), 112-122. Also, Twombly, J., & Schwartz, R. C. (2008). The integration of the Internal Family Systems model and EMDR. In C. Forgash & M. Copeley (Eds.), *Healing the heart of trauma and dissociation with EMDR and ego state therapy* (pp. 295-311). Springer Publishing Company.
23 Twombly, J., & Schwartz, R. C. (2008). The integration of the Internal Family Systems model and EMDR. In C. Forgash & M. Copeley (Eds.), *Healing the heart of trauma and dissociation with EMDR and ego state therapy* (pp. 295-311). Springer Publishing Company.
24 Schwartz, R. C., & Sweezy, M. (2020). *Internal Family Systems* (2nd ed.). The Guilford Press. Also, Twombly, J., & Schwartz, R. (2008). The integration of the Internal Family Systems model and EMDR. In C. Forgash & M. Copeley (Eds.), *Healing the heart of trauma and dissociation with EMDR and ego state therapy* (pp. 295-311). Springer Publishing Company.
25 Schwartz, R. C., & Sweezy, M. (2020). *Internal Family Systems* (2nd ed.). The Guilford Press. Also, Twombly, J., & Schwartz, R. C. (2008). The integration of the Internal Family Systems model and EMDR. In C. Forgash & M. Copeley (Eds.), *Healing the heart of trauma and dissociation with EMDR and ego state therapy* (pp. 295-311). Springer Publishing Company.
26 Contributed by Dr Daphne Fatter, PhD and Dr. Kendhal Hart, PsyD.

27 Twombly, J., & Schwartz, R. C. (2008). The integration of the Internal Family Systems model and EMDR. In C. Forgash & M. Copeley (Eds.), *Healing the heart of trauma and dissociation with EMDR and ego state therapy* (pp. 295-311). Springer Publishing Company.
28 Contributed by Dr. Kendhal Hart, PsyD.
29 Kluft, R. P. (1988). Playing for time: temporizing techniques in the treatment of multiple personality disorder. *American Journal of Clinical Hypnosis*, 32, 90-98. Also, Shapiro, R. (Ed.). (2005). *EMDR solutions: Pathways to healing*. Norton and Norton Company.
30 Contributed by Dr. Daphne Fatter, PhD and Dr. Kendhal Hart, PsyD.
31 Schwartz, R. C., & Sweezy, M. (2020). *Internal Family Systems therapy* (2nd ed.). The Guilford Press.
32 Schwartz, R. C., & Sweezy, M. (2020). *Internal Family Systems therapy* (2nd ed.). The Guilford Press.
33 Contributed by Dr. Kendhal Hart, PsyD.
34 Twombly, J., & Schwartz, R. C. (2008). The integration of the Internal Family Systems model and EMDR. In C. Forgash & M. Copeley (Eds.), *Healing the heart of trauma and dissociation with EMDR and ego state therapy* (pp. 295-311). Springer Publishing Company.
35 O'Shea Brown, G. (2020). Internal Family Systems informed eye movement desensitization and reprocessing an integrative technique for treatment of Complex Posttraumatic Stress Disorder. *International Body Psychotherapy Journal*, 19 (2), 112-122. Also, Twombly, J., & Schwartz, R. C. (2008). The integration of the internal Family Systems model and EMDR. In C. Forgash & M. Copeley (Eds.), *Healing the heart of trauma and dissociation with EMDR and ego state therapy* (pp. 295-311). Springer Publishing Company.
36 Contributed by Dr. Daphne Fatter, PhD and Dr. Kendhal Hart, PsyD.
37 Parnell, L. (2013). *Attachment-focused EMDR: Healing relational trauma*. Norton and Company.
38 Contributed by Dr. Daphne Fatter, PhD and Dr. Kendhal Hart, PsyD
39 Schwartz, R. C. (2021). *No bad parts: Healing trauma and restoring wholeness with the Internal Family Systems model*. Sounds True.
40 See Robinson, N. S. (2023). Legacy attuned EMDR therapy: Toward a coherent narrative and resilience. In Nickerson, M. (Ed.), *Cultural competence and healing culturally based trauma with EMDR therapy: Innovative strategies and protocols* (pp. 383-391). Springer Publishing Company; second edition for review.
41 Shapiro, F. (2018). *Eye movement desensitization and reprocessing: Basic principles, protocols, and procedures* (3rd ed.). The Guilford Press.
42 Contributed by Dr. Kendhal Hart, PsyD.
43 Contributed by Dr. Kendhal Hart, PsyD.
44 Contributed by Dr. Daphne Fatter, PhD and Dr. Kendhal Hart, PsyD.
45 Twombly, J., & Schwartz, R. C. (2008). The integration of the Internal Family Systems model and EMDR. In C. Forgash & M. Copeley (Eds.), *Healing the Heart of Trauma and Dissociation with EMDR and Ego State Therapy* (pp. 295-311). Springer Publishing Company.
46 Contributed by Dr. Kendhal Hart, PsyD.
47 Contributed by Dr. Kendhal Hart, PsyD.
48 Contributed by Dr. Daphne Fatter, PhD and Dr. Kendhal Hart, PsyD.
49 Contributed by Dr. Daphne Fatter, PhD and Dr. Kendhal Hart, PsyD.
50 Contributed by Dr. Kendhal Hart, PsyD.
51 Contributed by Dr. Daphne Fatter, PhD and Dr. Kendhal Hart, PsyD.
52 Contributed by Dr. Kendhal Hart, PsyD.
53 Contributed by Dr. Kendhal Hart, PsyD.
54 Shapiro, F. (2018). *Eye movement desensitization and reprocessing: Basic principles, protocols, and procedures* (3rd ed.) The Guilford Press.
55 Shapiro, F. (2018). *Eye movement desensitization and reprocessing: Basic principles, protocols, and procedures* (3rd ed.) The Guilford Press.

56 Shapiro, F. (2018). *Eye movement desensitization and reprocessing: Basic principles, protocols, and procedures* (3rd ed.) The Guilford Press.
57 Shapiro, F. (2018). *Eye movement desensitization and reprocessing: Basic principles, protocols, and procedures* (3rd ed.) The Guilford Press.
58 Contributed by Dr. Daphne Fatter, PhD and Dr. Kendhal Hart, PsyD.
59 Shapiro, F. (2018). *Eye movement desensitization and reprocessing: Basic principles, protocols, and procedures* (3rd ed.) The Guilford Press.
60 Shapiro, F. (2018). *Eye movement desensitization and reprocessing: Basic principles, protocols, and procedures* (3rd ed.) The Guilford Press.
61 Shapiro, F. (2018). *Eye movement desensitization and reprocessing: Basic principles, protocols, and procedures* (3rd ed.) The Guilford Press.
62 Contributed by Dr. Daphne Fatter, PhD and Dr. Kendhal Hart, PsyD.
63 Shapiro, F. (2018). *Eye movement desensitization and reprocessing: Basic principles, protocols, and procedures* (3rd ed.) The Guilford Press.
64 Contributed by Dr. Daphne Fatter, PhD and Dr. Kendhal Hart, PsyD.
65 Contributed by Dr. Kendhal Hart, PsyD.
66 Contributed by Dr. Daphne Fatter, PhD and Dr. Kendhal Hart, PsyD.
67 Shapiro, F. (2018). *Eye movement desensitization and reprocessing: Basic principles, protocols, and procedures* (3rd ed.) The Guilford Press.
68 Contributed by Dr. Kendhal Hart, PsyD.
69 O'Shea Brown, Gillian. (2020). Internal Family Systems informed eye movement desensitization and reprocessing an integrative technique for treatment of Complex Posttraumatic Stress Disorder. *International Body Psychotherapy Journal*, 19 (2), 112-122.
70 Contributed by Dr. Kendhal Hart, PsyD.
71 Shapiro, F. (2018). *Eye movement desensitization and reprocessing: Basic principles, protocols, and procedures* (3rd ed.) The Guilford Press.
72 Twombly, J., & Schwartz, R. C. (2008). The integration of the Internal Family Systems model and EMDR. In C. Forgash & M. Copeley (Eds.), *Healing the heart of trauma and dissociation with EMDR and ego state therapy* (pp. 295-311). Springer Publishing Company.
73 Contributed by Dr. Daphne Fatter, PhD and Dr. Kendhal Hart, PsyD.
74 Contributed by Dr. Kendhal Hart, PsyD.
75 Contributed by Dr. Daphne Fatter, PhD and Dr. Kendhal Hart, PsyD.

Chapter 6

1 Mitchell, R. R., & Friedman, H.S. (1994). *Sandplay: Past, present and future.* Routledge.
2 Lowenfeld, M. (1979). *The world technique.* George Allen and Unwin.
3 Kalff, D. (1980). *Sandplay: A psychotherapeutic approach to the psyche*, Sign Press. Also, Lowenfeld, M. (1979). *The world technique.* George Allen and Unwin.
4 Weinrib (1983). *Images of the self: The sandplay therapy process.* Sign Press.
5 Lowenfeld, M. (1939). The world pictures of children: A method of recording and studying them. *British Journal of Medical Psychology*, 18, 65-101.
6 Lowenfeld, M. (1979). *The world technique.* George Allen and Unwin.
7 Anderson, V. (1979). Origin of the world. In M. Lowenfeld, *The world technique* (pp. 277-281). George Allen and Unwin.
8 Bowyer, R. (1970). *The Lowenfeld world technique.* Pergamon Press.
9 Homeyer, L., & Sweeney, D. (2023). *Sandtray therapy: a practical manual* (4th ed.). Routledge.
10 Landreth, G. L. (1991). *Play therapy: The art of the relationship.* Brunner/Mazel.
11 Homeyer, L. E., & Lyles, J. (2021). *Advanced sandtray therapy: Digging deeper into clinical practice.* Routledge.
12 Kalff, D. (1980). *Sandplay: A psychotherapeutic approach to the psyche.* Sign Press.

13 Buhler, C. (1951a). The world test, a projective technique. *Journal of Child Psychiatry*, 2(1), 4-23. Buhler, C. (1951b). The world test: Manual of directions. *Journal of Child Psychiatry*, 2(1), 69-81.
14 Petruk, L. (1996). *Creating a world in the sand: A pilot study of normative data for employing the sandtray as a diagnostic tool with children* [Unpublished master's thesis, Texas State Univsetity, SanMarcos].

SECTION THREE: INTERSECTIONALITY

Section Three Introduction

1 Crenshaw, K. (1989). Demarginalizing the intersection of race and sex: A black feminist critique of antidiscrimination doctrine, feminist theory and antiracist politics. *University of Chicago Legal Forum*, 1989(1), 8.
2 www.whitesupremacyculture.info
3 Jones, K., & Okun, T. (2001). *Dismantling racism: A workbook for social change groups*. ChangeWork.

Chapter 8

1 www.zippia.com/mental-health-therapist-jobs/demographics
2 www.nami.org/Your-Journey/Identity-and-Cultural-Dimensions/Black-African-American
3 www.pewresearch.org/social-trends/fact-sheet/facts-about-the-us-black-population

Chapter 10

1 www.pewresearch.org/fact-tank/2021/04/29/key-facts-about-asian-americans/
2 The discussion here focuses on clients who have Asian-White backgrounds. I want to acknowledge that multiracial clients may not have any White heritage (e.g. Asian-Black, Asian-Latinx) in which case their experiences are even more nuanced. Practitioners need to be aware of how all aspects of their clients' racial identity impact their lived experience.
3 www.census.gov/newsroom/blogs/random-samplings/2014/04/about-half-of-internationally-adopted-children-were-born-in-asia.html#:~:text=About%20half%20(51%20percent)%20of,(25%20percent)%20in%20Europe.
4 www.asian-nation.org/adopted.shtml#sthash.rSoWkMsM.dpbs
5 www.asian-nation.org/adopted.shtml#sthash.rSoWkMsM.dpbs
6 www.latimes.com/business/story/2021-04-16/asian-adoptees-and-their-experiences
7 For more on how IFS can be integrated with ancestral healing work, please see Dr. Daphne Fatter's chapter in this book on this topic.
8 www.npr.org/sections/codeswitch/2017/04/19/524571669/model-minority-myth-again-used-as-a-racial-wedge-between-asians-and-blacks
9 www.pewresearch.org/social-trends/2018/07/12/income-inequality-in-the-u-s-is-rising-most-rapidly-among-asians/
10 www.thepractice.law.harvard.edu/article/the-model-minority-myth/
11 www.washingtonpost.com/graphics/2018/world/too-many-men/
12 www.pewresearch.org/religion/2022/08/23/indias-sex-ratio-at-birth-begins-to-normalize/#:~:text=From%20a%20large%20imbalance%20of,%2C%20conducted%20from%202019%2D21.
13 www.endcorporalpunishment.org/asia-and-the-pacific/
14 www.psychologytoday.com/sg/blog/minority-report/201406/asian-shame-and-honor
15 www.archives.gov/milestone-documents/chinese-exclusion-act
16 www.theatlantic.com/ideas/archive/2021/04/california-klans-anti-asian-crusade/618513/
17 www.npca.org/articles/2860-from-the-gold-rush-to-the-covid-pandemic-a-history-of-anti-asian-violence?gclid=Cj0KCQjwtvqVBhCVARIsAFUxcRtTdaEY9NB6Tjg3XAfx9V33dhNXwl8xFTnCFtrzNrfQ4sLC_pNFfUcaAj67EALw_wcB

18 www.noplaceproject.com/theproject
19 www.noplaceproject.com/rock-springs1
20 www.census.gov/quickfacts/bellevuecitywashington
21 www.bellevuewa.gov/sites/default/files/media/pdf_document/bnoa-presentation-4-5-18-demographics.pdf
22 www.noplaceproject.com/newcastle
23 www.washingtonpost.com/history/2021/03/18/history-anti-asian-violence-racism/
24 www.newyorker.com/news/daily-comment/the-forgotten-history-of-the-purging-of-chinese-from-america
25 www.theconversation.com/asian-guys-stereotyped-and-excluded-in-online-dating-130855
26 www.huffpost.com/entry/asian-hate-crimes-2021-covid_n_602c00e8c5b6c95056f3dd41
27 www.today.com/tmrw/what-bamboo-ceiling-here-s-what-asian-americans-want-you-t212014
28 www.pewresearch.org/fact-tank/2021/04/21/one-third-of-asian-americans-fear-threats-physical-attacks-and-most-say-violence-against-them-is-rising/
29 www.getabstract.com/en/summary/subtle-acts-of-exclusion/38312#:~:text=Summary-,%E2%80%9CSubtle%20acts%20of%20exclusion%E2%80%9D%20(SAEs)%20are%20words%20or,or%20may%20not%20be%20present.
30 www.globalnews.ca/news/7891698/sexuality-asian-women-community/
31 www.fairgirls.org/asian-american-womens-vulnerabilities-to-exploitation-rooted-in-stereotypes-and-racism/
32 www.cnn.com/style/article/andrew-kung-asian-american-men/index.html
33 www.washingtonpost.com/world/2022/06/15/tokyo-same-sex-japan-lgbtq/
34 www.pewresearch.org/religion/fact-sheet/gay-marriage-around-the-world/
35 www.fairgirls.org/asian-american-womens-vulnerabilities-to-exploitation-rooted-in-stereotypes-and-racism/
36 www.encyclopedia.com/history/encyclopedias-almanacs-transcripts-and-maps/religion-western-presence-east-asia

Chapter 11

1 Kluckhohn, C., & Kelly, W.H. (1945). The concept of culture. In R. Linton (Ed.). *The science of man in the world crisis* (pp. 78-105). Columbia University Press.
2 Swift, J. K., Callahan, J. L., Tompkins, K. A., Connor, D. R., & Dunn, R. (2015). A delay-discounting measure of preference for racial/ethnic matching in psychotherapy. *Psychotherapy*, 52(3), 315–320. www.doi.org/10.1037/pst0000019
3 Petersen, P., (2008). *Culture-centered counseling* [DVD]. Retrieved from www.apa.org/pubs/videos/4310778?tab=4
4 Riemersma, J., (2020). *Altogether you: Experiencing personal and spiritual transformation through Internal Family Systems therapy*. Pivotal Press.
5 Hays, P. A. (2022). *Addressing cultural complexities in practice: Assessment, diagnosis, and therapy* (4th ed.) American Psychological Association.
6 Tervalon, M., & Murray-Garcia, J. (1998). Cultural humility versus cultural competence: A critical distinction in defining physician training outcomes in multicultural education. *Journal of Health Care for the Poor and Underserved*, 9, 117-125.
7 Schwartz, R. C., & Sweezy, M. (2020). *Internal Family Systems therapy* (2nd ed.), (pp. 156-157). The Guilford Press.
8 Pew Research Center. (2012, April 4). *V. Politics, values and religion*. Retrieved February 2023, from www.pewresearch.org/hispanic/2012/04/04/v-politics-values-and-religion/
9 Santiago-Rivera, A. L., & Altarriba, J. (2002). The role of language in therapy with the Spanish-English bilingual client. *Professional Psychology: Research and Practice*, 33(1), (pp. 30–38).

10 Foster, R. P. (1998). The clinician's cultural countertransference: The psychodynamics of culturally competent practice. *Clinical Social Work Journal*, 26(3), 253–270. https://doi.org/10.1023/a:1022867910329

Chapter 12

1 Kort, J. (2018). *LGBTQ clients in therapy: Clinical issues and treatment strategies*. W.W. Norton and Company.
2 Obergefell v. Hodges. (n.d.). Oyez. Retrieved March 15, 2023, from https://www.oyez.org/cases/2014/14-556
3 Carter, D. (2004). *Stonewall: the riots that sparked the gay revolution*. St. Martin's Press.
4 American Psychiatric Association. (1952). *Diagnostic and statistical manual of mental disorders* (1st ed.). American Psychiatric Association.
5 American Psychiatric Association. (2022). *Diagnostic and statistical manual of mental disorders* (5th ed., text rev.). https://doi.org/10.1176/appi.books.9780890425787
6 https://www.science.org/doi/10.1126/science.aat7693
7 https://www.scientificanerican.com/article/massive-study-finds-no-single-genetic-cause-of-same-sexual-behavior/
8 Anderson, F. G. (2021). *Transcending trauma: Healing complex PTSD with Internal Family Systems therapy*. PESI Publishing.
9 Kort, J. (2018). *LGBTQ Clients in therapy: Clinical issues and treatment strategies*. W.W. Norton and Company.
10 Anderson, F. G. (2021). *Transcending trauma: Healing complex PTSD with Internal Family Systems therapy*. PESI Publishing.
11 Anderson, F. G. (2021). *Transcending trauma: Healing complex PTSD with Internal Family Systems therapy*. PESI Publishing.
12 The Trevor Project. (2020). *National survey on LGBTQ youth mental health 2020*. Retrieved from https://www.thetrevorproject.org/survey-2020/
13 Cass, V. C. (1979). Homosexual identity formation: A theoretical model. *Journal of Homosexuality*, 4(3), 219-235.
14 Kort, J. (2018). *LGBTQ clients in therapy: Clinical issues and treatment strategies*. W.W. Norton and Company.

Chapter 13

1 James, S. E., Herman, J. L., Rankin, S., Keisling, M., Mottet, L., & Anafi, M. (2016). *The report of the 2015 U.S. Transgender survey*. National Center for Transgender Equality. Retrieved from: www.ustranssurvey.org/
2 James, S. E., Herman, J. L., Rankin, S., Keisling, M., Mottet, L., & Anafi, M. (2016). *The report of the 2015 U.S. Transgender survey*. National Center for Transgender Equality. Retrieved from: www.ustranssurvey.org/

SECTION FOUR: EMERGING TRENDS

Chapter 15

1 www.ncbi.nlm.nih.gov/pmc/articles/PMC3917651
2 www.doi.org/10.37602/IJSSMR.2020.3417
3 www.doi.org/10.37602/IJSSMR.2020.3417

Chapter 16

1 McConnell, S. (2020). *Somatic Internal Family Systems therapy*. North Atlantic Books.
2 McConnell, S. (2020). *Somatic Internal Family Systems therapy*. North Atlantic Books.
3 Galeano, E. (1993). Window on the body. In E. Galeano (1993), *Walking words*. Norton.
4 www.hrc.org/resources/stances-of-faiths-on-lgbt-issues-southern-baptist-convention

Chapter 17

1 The conference table concept was originated by Michi Rose, PhD, an early collaborator with Richard Schwartz.
2 Images of sitting in front of a kitchen table, campfire, open room, etc., are all useful.

Chapter 18

1 Based on current lifetime prevalence, incidence and mortality data, it was estimated that 28.8 million Americans alive in 2018-19 will have an ED at some point during their life—either in the past, present or future. As 21.0 million people have had an ED during their life (past and present), 7.8 million Americans alive in 2018-19 will develop an ED in the future. Of these new cases in the future, approximately 1.9 million will occur in children and adolescents before they are 20 years old. Deloitte Access Economics. (2020, June). *The social and economic cost of eating disorders in the United States of America: A report for the strategic training initiative for the prevention of eating disorders and the academy for eating disorders*. Available at: www.hsph.harvard.edu/striped/report-economic-costs-of-eating-disorders/.
2 According to a Report by the Strategic Training Initiative for the Prevention of Eating Disorders, Academy for Eating Disorders, and Deloitte Access Economics there are an estimated 10,200 deaths directly resulting from an eating disorder yearly, or one death every 52 minutes in the U.S. Deloitte Access Economics. (2020, June). *The social and economic cost of eating disorders in the United States of America: A report for the strategic training initiative for the prevention of eating disorders and the academy for eating disorders*. Available at: www.hsph.harvard.edu/striped/report-economic-costs-of-eating-disorders/.
3 Marques, L., Alegria, M., Becker, A. E., Chen, C., Fang, A., Chosak, A., & Diniz, J. B. (2011). Comparative prevalence, correlates of impairment, and service utilization for eating disorders across U.S. ethnic groups: Implications for reducing ethnic disparities in health care access for eating disorders. The International Journal of Eating Disorders, 44(5), 412–420. www.doi.org/10.1002/eat.20787. Also, Becker, A. E., Franko, D. L., Speck, A., & Herzog, D. B. (2003). Ethnicity and differential access to care for eating disorder symptoms. International Journal of Eating Disorders, 33(2), 205-212. www.doi:10.1002/eat.10129. Plus, Wade, T. D., Keski-Rahkonen A., & Hudson J. (2011). Epidemiology of eating disorders. In M. Tsuang & M. Tohen (Eds.), *Textbook in psychiatric epidemiology* (3rd ed.) (pp. 343-360). Wiley.
4 National Eating Disorders Association. (2018, February 21). Eating disorders in LGBTQ+ populations. Retrieved February 22, 2021, from www.nationaleatingdisorders.org/learn/general-information/lgbtq. Also, Muhlheim, L., PsyD, CEDS. (2020, June 20). Eating disorders in transgender people. Retrieved February 22, 2021, from www.verywellmind.com/eating-disorders-in-transgender-people-4582520. Plus, Duffy, M. E., Henkel, K. E., & Earnshaw, V. A. (2016). Transgender clients' experiences of eating disorder treatment. Journal of LGBT Issues in Counseling, 10(3), 136-149. www.doi.org/10.1080/15538605.2016.1177806
5 Men represent 25 percent of those with anorexia nervosa and 25 percent of those with bulimia nervosa and 36 percent of those with Binge Eating Disorder. Hudson, J., Hiripi, E., Pope, H., & Kessler, R. (2007). The prevalence and correlates of eating disorders in the national comorbidity survey replication. *Biological Psychiatry*, 61, 348–358. Also, various studies suggest that risk of mortality for males with ED is higher than it is for females. Raevuoni, A., Keski-Rahkonen, A., & Hoek, H. (2014). A review of eating disorders in males. *Current Opinions on Psychiatry*, 27-6, 426-430. Plus, subclinical eating disordered behaviors (including binge eating, purging, laxative abuse and fasting for weight loss) are nearly as common among males as they are among females. Mitchison, D., Hay, P., Slewa-Younan, S., & Mond, J. (2014). The changing demographic profile of eating disorder behaviors in the community. *BMC Public Health*, 14(1). www.doi:10.1186/1471-2458-14-943 www.nationaleatingdisorders.org/statistics-research-eating-disorders
6 Zhao, Y., & Encinosa, W. (2011, September). *Update on hospitalizations for eating disorders, 1999 to 2009. HCUP statistical brief #120*. Agency for Healthcare Research and Quality. www

.hcup-us.ahrq.gov/reports/statbriefs/sb120.pdf. Also, Mitchison, D., Hay, P., Slewa-Younan, S., & Mond, J. (2014). *The changing demographic profile of eating disorder behaviors in the community*. BMC Public Health, 14(1). www.doi:10.1186/1471-2458-14-943

7 People of all shapes and sizes can have anorexia nervosa, bulimia nervosa, binge eating disorder, or Other Specified Feeding or Eating Disorder (OSFED), including atypical anorexia. In fact, less than six percent of people with eating disorders are medically diagnosed as "underweight" according to the BMI. Flament, M. F., Henderson, K., Buchholz, A., Obeid, N., Nguyen, H. N., Birmingham, M., & Goldfield, G. (2015). Weight status and DSM-5 diagnoses of eating disorders in adolescents from the community. Journal of the American Academy of Child and Adolescent Psychiatry, 54(5), 403–411.e2. www.doi.org/10.1016/j.jaac.2015.01.020.

8 Schwartz, R. C. (2023) *Introduction to Internal Family Systems*. Sounds True.

9 American Psychiatric Association. (2013). Diagnostic and statistical manual of mental disorders (5th ed.). www.doi.org/10.1176/appi.books.9780890425596

10 Knoll, J. (2019, June 14). Opinion | Smash the wellness industry. *The New York Times*. www.nytimes.com/2019/06/08/opinion/sunday/women-dieting-wellness.html

11 Social media, books, diet lifestyle coaches, food plans, magazines, television shows, cosmetic surgery create the culture, driven by capitalism. The global wellness market is worth $4.4 trillion as of 2022 and the U.S. wellness industry is valued at $1.2 trillion. Personal care and beauty is the largest sector of the global wellness industry at a value of $955 billion. The global health eating, nutrition, and weight loss sector is worth $946 billion. www.zippia.com/advice/health-and-wellness-industry-statistics/

12 www.custommarketinsights.com/press-releases/us-weight-loss-market-size/

13 National Academies of Sciences, Engineering, and Medicine, Health and Medicine Division, Board on Population Health and Public Health Practice, Committee on Community-Based Solutions to Promote Health Equity in the United States, Baciu, A., Negussie, Y., Geller, A., & Weinstein, J. N. (Eds.). (2017). Communities in action: Pathways to health equity. National Academies Press. Available from: www.ncbi.nlm.nih.gov/books/NBK425845/

14 According to Sabrina Strings author of Fearing the Black Body: The Racial Origins of Fat Phobia. "My research showed that anti-fat attitudes originated not with medical findings, but with Enlightenment-era belief that overfeeding and fatness were evidence of 'savagery' and racial inferiority." Strings S. (2019). *Fearing the black body: The racial origins of fat phobia*. New York University Press. Retrieved April 14, 2023, from www.degruyter.com/isbn/9781479891788.

15 Research shows that they spend less time with larger people on office visits, provide them with less medical information, and often hold biased, stigmatizing views of fat people, including that they are non-compliant or undisciplined. Alberga, A. S., Edache, I. Y., Forhan, M., & Russell-Mayhew, S. (2019). Weight bias and health care utilization: A scoping review. Primary Health Care Research and Development, 20. www.doi.org/10.1017/s1463423619000227

16 Schwartz, R. C. (2021). *No bad parts. Healing trauma and restoring wholeness with the Internal Family Systems model*. Sounds True.

17 van Hoeken, D., & Hoek, H. W. (2020). Review of the burden of eating disorders: mortality, disability, costs, quality of life, and family burden. Current Opinion in Psychiatry, 33(6), 521–527. www.doi.org/10.1097/YCO.0000000000000641

18 Strohacker, K., Carpenter, K. C., & McFarlin, B. K. (2009). Consequences of weight cycling: An increase in disease risk? International Journal of Exercise Science, 2(3), 191–201.

19 van der Kolk B. A. (1997). The psychobiology of posttraumatic stress disorder. The Journal of Clinical Psychiatry, 58 Suppl 9, 16–24.

20 McConnell, S. (2020). *Somatic Internal Family Systems therapy: Awareness, breath, resonance, movement, and touch in practice*. North Atlantic Books.

Chapter 19

1. Burris, C. (2022). *Creating healing circles: Using the Internal Family Systems model in racilitating groups.* B. C. Allen Publishing.
2. Burris, C. (2022). *Creating healing circles: Using the Internal Family Systems model in racilitating groups.* B. C. Allen Publishing.
3. Note that the permission to use this example was granted from the participant, and their name has been changed for privacy.
4. In the group setting, the availability of participants who can help sculpt, illustrate, and externalize a compressed and burdened system is extremely valuable.

SECTION FIVE: RELATIONSHIPS

Chapter 22

1. Lamott, A. (1993). *Operating instructions: A journal of my son's first year.* Pantheon Books.
2. Siegel, D., & Hartzell, M. (2014). *Parenting from the inside out.* Jeremy Teacher/Penguin.
3. Markham, L. (2012). *Peaceful parent, happy kids: How to stop yelling and start connecting.* Penguin Random House.
4. Neff, K. (2011). *Self-compassion: The proven power of being kind to yourself.* William Morrow Paperbacks, and Neff, K. (2021). *Fierce self-compassion: How women can harness kindness to speak up, claim their power, and thrive.* HarperOne.

Chapter 24

1. Harvey, G. (2005). *Animism: Respecting the living world.* Hurst and Co., and de la Cadena, M., & Blaser, M. (2018). *A world of many worlds.* Duke University Press. Retrieved August 25, 2022 from www.doi.org/10.1215/9781478004318.
2. Adapted from: Anderson, F. G., Sweezy, M., & Schwartz, R. C. (2017). *Internal Family Systems skills training manual: Trauma-informed treatment for anxiety, depression, PTSD and substance abuse.* PESI Publishing and Media.
3. Harvey, G. (2005). *Animism: Respecting the living world.* Hurst and Co., for more information about animism, and see de la Cadena, M., & Blaser, M. (2018). *A world of many worlds.* Duke University Press., for more information about animism. Retrieved August 25, 2022 from www.doi.org/10.1215/9781478004318.
4. Schwartz, R. C. (1995), *Internal Family Systems therapy.* Guildford Press. Also, Schwartz, R. C., & Sweezy, M. (2020). *Internal Family Systems therapy* (2nd ed.). The Guilford Press, and Schwartz, R. C. (2021). *No bad parts: Healing trauma and restoring wholeness with the internal family systems model.* Sounds True.
5. DeGruy, J. (2017). *Post traumatic slave syndrome: America's legacy of enduring injury and healing.* Uptone Press. Also, Hübl, T., & Avritt, J. J. (2020). *Healing collectivetrauma: A process for integrating our intergenerational and cultural wounds.* Tantor Audio, plus Menakem, R. (2017). *My grandmother's hands: racialized trauma and the pathway to mending our hearts and bodies.* Central Recovery Press, and Menakem, R. (2022). *The quaking of America: An embodied guide to navigating our nation's upheaval and racial reckoning.* Central Recovery Press.
6. Yehuda, R., Mulherin, S. E., Brand, S. R., Seckl, J., Marcus, S. M., & Berkowitz, G. S. (2005). Transgenerational effects of Posttraumatic Stress Disorder in babies of mothers exposed to the World Trade Center attacks during pregnancy, *The Journal of Clinical Endocrinology and Metabolism,* 90(7), 4115–4118. www.doi.org/10.1210/jc.2005-0550
7. Perroud, N., Rutembesa, E., Paoloni-Giacobino, A., Mutabaruka, J., Mutesa, L., Stenz, L., ... Karege, F. (2014). The Tutsi genocide and transgenerational transmission of maternal stress: epigenetics and biology of the HPA axis. *World J Biol Psychiatry,* 15, 334–345. www.doi.org/10.3109/15622975.2013.866693, and Vukojevic, V., Kolassa, I. T., Fastenrath, M., Gschwind, L., Spalek, K., Milnik, A., Heck, A., Vogler, C., Wilker, S., Demougin, P., Peter, F., Atucha, E., Stetak, A., Roozendaal, B., Elbert, T., Papassotiropoulos, A., & de Quervain, D. J. (2014). Epigenetic modification of the glucocorticoid receptor gene is linked to traumatic memory and

post-traumatic stress disorder risk in genocide survivors. *The Journal of Neuroscience : The Official Journal of the Society for Neuroscience*, 34(31), 10274–10284. www.doi.org/10.1523/

8   Yehuda, R., Daskalakis, N. P., Bierer, L. M., Bader, H. N., Klengel, T., Holsboer, F., & Binder, E. B. (2016). Holocaust exposure induced intergenerational effects on FKBP5 methylation. *Biological Psychiatry*, 80(5), 372–380. www.doi.org/10.1016/j.biopsych.2015.08.005

9   Zannas, A. S., Provençal, N., & Binder, E. B. (2015). Epigenetics of posttraumatic stress disorder: current evidence, challenges, and future directions. *Biological Psychiatry*, 78, 327–335. www.doi.org/10.1016/j.biopsych.2015.04.003

10 Schwartz, R. C. (1995), *Internal Family Systems therapy*. Guildford Press. Also, Schwartz, R. C., & Sweezy, M. (2020). *Internal Family Systems therapy* (2nd ed.). The Guilford Press, and Schwartz, R. C. (2021). *No bad parts: Healing trauma and restoring wholeness with the internal family systems model*. Sounds True.

11 Dam, A. K. (2016). Significance of end-of-life dreams and visions experienced by the terminally ill in rural and urban india. *Indian Journal of Palliative Care*, 22(2), 130–134. www.doi.org/10.4103/0973-1075.179600. Also, Kerr, C. W., Donnelly, J. P., Wright, S. T., Kuszczak, S. M., Banas, A., Grant, P. C., & Luczkiewicz, D. L. (2014). End-of-life dreams and visions: a longitudinal study of hospice patients' experiences. *Journal of Palliative Medicine*, 17(3), 296–303. www.doi.org/10.1089/jpm.2013.0371. Also, Levy, K., Grant, P. C., Depner, R. M., Byrwa, D. J., Luczkiewicz, D. L., & Kerr, C. W. (2020). End-of-life dreams and visions and posttraumatic growth: A comparison study. *Journal of Palliative Medicine*, 23(3), 319–324. www.doi.org/10.1089/jpm.2019.0269

12 Streit-Horn, J. (2011). *A systematic review of research on after-death communication* (ADC) [Doctoral dissertation, University of North Texas].

13 Anderson, F. G., Sweezy, M., & Schwartz, R. C. (2017). *Internal Family Systems Skills training manual: Trauma-informed treatment for anxiety, depression, PTSD and substance abuse*. PESI Publishing and Media. Also, Anderson, F. G. (2021). *Transcending trauma: healing complex PTSD with Internal Family Systems therapy*. PESI Publishing and Media, plus Schwartz, R. C. (1995), *Internal Family Systems therapy*. Guildford Press. Also Schwartz, R. C., & Sweezy, M. (2020). *Internal Family Systems therapy* (2nd ed.). The Guilford Press, plus Schwartz, R. C. (2021). *No bad parts: Healing trauma and restoring wholeness with the internal family systems model*. Sounds True. Also, Sinko, A. (2017). Legacy burdens. In M. Sweezy & E. L. Ziskind (Eds.), *IFS: Innovations and elaborations in Internal Family Systems therapy*. (pp. 164-178) Taylor and Francis.

14 Anderson, F. G., Sweezy, M., & Schwartz, R. C. (2017). *Internal Family Systems skills training manual: Trauma-informed treatment for anxiety, depression, PTSD and substance abuse*. PESI Publishing and Media. Also, Anderson, F. G. (2021). *Transcending trauma: healing complex PTSD with Internal Family Systems therapy*. PESI Publishing and Media, plus Schwartz, R. C. (1995), *Internal Family Systems therapy*. Guildford Press. Also, Schwartz, R. C., & Sweezy, M. (2020). *Internal Family Systems therapy* (2nd ed.). The Guilford Press, plus Schwartz, R. C. (2021). *No bad parts: Healing trauma and restoring wholeness with the internal family systems model*. Sounds True, and Sinko, A. (2017). Legacy burdens. In M. Sweezy& E. L. Ziskind (Eds.), *IFS: Innovations and elaborations in Internal Family Systems therapy*. (pp. 164-178). Taylor and Francis.

15 Anderson, F. G., Sweezy, M., & Schwartz, R. C. (2017). *Internal Family Systems skills training manual: Trauma-informed treatment for anxiety, depression, PTSD and substance abuse*. PESI Publishing and Media. Also, Anderson, F. G. (2021). *Transcending trauma: healing complex PTSD with Internal Family Systems therapy*. PESI Publishing and Media, plus Schwartz, R. C. (1995), *Internal Family Systems therapy*. Guildford Press. Also, Schwartz, R. C., & Sweezy, M. (2020). *Internal Family Systems therapy* (2nd ed.). The Guilford Press, plus Schwartz, R. C. (2021). *No bad parts: Healing trauma and restoring wholeness with the internal family systems model*. Sounds True, and Sinko, A. (2017). Legacy burdens. In M. Sweezy& E. L. Ziskind (Eds.), *IFS: Innovations and elaborations in Internal Family Systems therapy*. (pp. 164-178). Taylor and Francis.

16 Anderson, F. G. (2021). *Transcending trauma: healing complex PTSD with Internal Family Systems therapy.* PESI Publishing and Media.
17 Anderson, F. G. (2021). *Transcending trauma: healing complex PTSD with Internal Family Systems therapy.* PESI Publishing and Media.
18 Anderson, F. G. (2021). *Transcending trauma: healing complex PTSD with Internal Family Systems therapy.* PESI Publishing and Media. Also, Foor, D. (2017). *Ancestral medicine: rituals for personal and family healing.* Bear and Company.
19 Anderson, F. G. (2021). *Transcending trauma: healing complex PTSD with Internal Family Systems therapy.* PESI Publishing and Media. Also, Foor, D. (2017). *Ancestral medicine: rituals for personal and family healing.* Bear and Company, and Foor, D. (n.d.) *Ancestral lineage healing: Practice for personal and cultural transformation* [online course].
20 Anderson, F. G. (2021). *Transcending trauma: healing complex PTSD with Internal Family Systems therapy.* PESI Publishing and Media.
21 Anderson, F. G. (2021). *Transcending trauma: healing complex PTSD with Internal Family Systems therapy.* PESI Publishing and Media. Also, Foor, D. (2017). *Ancestral medicine: rituals for personal and family healing.* Bear and Company.
22 de Becker, G. (2000). *The gift of fear.* Bloomsbury Publishing PLC.
23 Dana, D. (2018). *The polyvagal theory in therapy: Engaging the rhythm of regulation.* W. W. Norton. Also, Porges, S. W. (1995). Orienting in a defensive world: Mammalian modifications of our evolutionary heritage. A polyvagal theory. *Psychophysiology*, 32(4), 301-318, and Porges, S. W. (2018). Why polyvagal theory was welcomed by therapists. In S. W. Porges & D. Dana (Eds.), *Clinical applications of the polyvagal theory: The emergence of polyvagal-informed therapies.* W.W. Norton and Company.
24 See Comas-Díaz, L., & Torres Rivera, E. (2020). (Eds.) *Liberation psychology: Theory, method, practice, and social justice.* American Psychological Association, for review.
25 Schwartz, R. C., & Sweezy, M. (2020). *Internal Family Systems therapy* (2nd ed.). The Guilford Press.
26 Schwartz, R. C. (1995), *Internal Family Systems therapy.* The Guildford Press. Also, Schwartz, R. C., & Sweezy, M. (2020). *Internal Family Systems therapy* (2nd ed.). The Guilford Press, plus Schwartz, R. C. (2021). *No bad parts: Healing trauma and restoring wholeness with the internal family systems model.* Sounds True.
27 Anderson, F. G., Sweezy, M., & Schwartz, R. C. (2017). *Internal Family Systems skills training manual: Trauma-informed treatment for anxiety, depression, PTSD and substance abuse.* PESI Publishing and Media. Also, Anderson, F. G. (2021). *Transcending trauma: healing complex PTSD with Internal Family Systems therapy.* PESI Publishing and Media, plus Schwartz, R. C. (1995), *Internal Family Systems therapy.* The Guildford Press. Also, Schwartz, R. C., & Sweezy, M. (2020). *Internal Family Systems therapy* (2nd ed.). The Guilford Press, plus Schwartz, R. C. (2021). *No bad parts: Healing trauma and restoring wholeness with the internal family systems model.* Sounds True.
28 Schwartz, R. C., & Sweezy, M. (2020). *Internal Family Systems therapy* (2nd ed.). The Guilford Press.
29 Anderson, F. G., Sweezy, M., & Schwartz, R. C. (2017). *Internal Family Systems skills training manual: Trauma-informed treatment for anxiety, depression, PTSD and substance abuse.* PESI Publishing and Media. Also, Anderson, F. G. (2021). *Transcending trauma: healing complex PTSD with Internal Family Systems therapy.* PESI Publishing and Media, plus Schwartz, R. C. (1995), *Internal Family Systems therapy.* The Guildford Press. Also, Schwartz, R. C., & Sweezy, M. (2020). *Internal Family Systems therapy* (2nd ed.). The Guilford Press, plus Schwartz, R. C. (2021). *No bad parts: Healing trauma and restoring wholeness with the internal family systems model.* Sounds True.
30 Sinko, A. (2017). Legacy burdens. In M. Sweezy & E. L. Ziskind (Eds.), *IFS: Innovations and elaborations in Internal Family Systems therapy* (pp. 164-178). Taylor and Francis.

31 Sinko, A. (2017). Legacy burdens. In M. Sweezy & E. L. Ziskind (Eds.), *IFS: Innovations and elaborations in Internal Family Systems therapy* (pp. 164-178). Taylor and Francis.
32 Schwartz, R. C., & Sweezy, M. (2020). *Internal Family Systems therapy* (2nd ed.). The Guilford Press. Also, Sinko, A. (2017). Legacy burdens. In M. Sweezy & E. L. Ziskind (Eds.), *IFS: Innovations and elaborations in Internal Family Systems therapy* (pp. 164-178). Taylor and Francis.
33 Schwartz, R. C., & Sweezy, M. (2020). *Internal Family Systems therapy* (2nd ed.). The Guilford Press.
34 Schwartz, R. C., & Sweezy, M. (2020). *Internal Family Systems therapy* (2nd ed.). The Guilford Press.
35 Welwood, J. (1984). Principles of inner work: Psychological and spiritual. *Journal of Transpersonal Psychology*, 16(1), 63–73.
36 Anderson, F. G. (2021). *Transcending trauma: healing complex PTSD with Internal Family Systems therapy*. PESI Publishing and Media.
37 Anderson, F. G. (2021). *Transcending trauma: healing complex PTSD with Internal Family Systems therapy*. PESI Publishing and Media.
38 Anderson, F. G. (2021). *Transcending trauma: healing complex PTSD with Internal Family Systems therapy*. PESI Publishing and Media. Also, Foor, D. (2017). *Ancestral medicine: rituals for personal and family healing*. Bear and Company, plus Foor, D. (n.d.) *Animist psychology* [online course].
39 Anderson, F. G. (2021). *Transcending trauma: healing complex PTSD with Internal Family Systems therapy*. PESI Publishing and Media.

Chapter 25

1 The Enneagram Diagram as shown has been in common usage across Enneagram schools since the 1970s. For more specific information see, Palmer, H. (1988). *The enneagram*. Harper.
2 Palmer, H. (1995). *The pocket enneagram*. HarperOne.

Made in United States
North Haven, CT
13 July 2024

54725685R10370